CH'ÊN SHOU-YI was born in Canton, China, and received his A.B. from Lingnan University in that city in 1920. He was Fellow in Comparative Literature at the University of Chicago in 1926–27 and received his Ph.D. there in 1928. He settled in the United States in 1937, first as Research Professor of Chinese History at the University of Hawaii, then as Chairman of the Department and Professor of Oriental Studies at Pomona College.

CHINESE LITERATURE

A Historical Introduction

CH'ÊN SHOU-YI
PROFESSOR OF CHINESE CULTURE
POMONA COLLEGE

THE RONALD PRESS COMPANY · NEW YORK

Library of Congress Catalog Card Number: 61–9426

PRINTED IN THE UNITED STATES OF AMERICA

To the memory of my parents

Ch'ên Ch'ing-T'ao

and

Ch'ên Hsü Yün-Ying

Foreword

Iᴛ ɪs welcome news to all students of the Far East that an important
gap in the field of Chinese literature has now been filled, and in a
competent, scholarly and worthy manner, in Professor Ch'ên's book.
A history of Chinese literature, of the forms and creative urges in
prose and poetry, has been lacking; to my knowledge, not even an
elementary outline of Chinese literary periods and developments
exists. Professor Herbert A. Giles' *History of Chinese Literature*,
written about half a century ago, was a misnomer; it was a series of
attempted essays on certain Chinese works, and was not even an
outline covering the successive periods. There have been translations of different poets, studies of certain interesting aspects, and
compilations of much-needed reference material. But a comprehensive outline of the story of Chinese literature has been conspicuous
by its absence.

What we have here is not merely a brief skeleton of the facts; it is
most gratifying to find that it is a full, comprehensive, and ambitious
work which embodies the results of the author's lifetime of studies
and insights in this field. I understand it took him eight or nine years
of spare labor. Writing such a literary history is assuredly a difficult
task; it involves evaluations and personal judgments at every step.
This is not the journeyman-like compilation of facts that are "safe"
by common agreement; it shows in every chapter the author's direct
convictions and judgments. It is eminently readable and discursive,
like a good evening's discussion among intelligent, educated friends,
and always makes the reader ask for more.

I find particular delight in the discovery that Professor Ch'ên was
able to rise above the narrow, sectarian view of the "Ch'ing philologists" of the last three centuries. The philologists were concerned
with upholding the purity of the Han School; they had their curious
idea of "orthodoxy" and "apostolic succession" (*shih-ch'êng*), which
presumed that there could be only one correct text of the classics
and made no allowance for variant texts (witness the dozens of
variant texts of Marco Polo's *Travels*, for example). Their exegesis

was excellent, but their higher criticism was unscientific and inadequate. What made this school of prevalent philology vicious and dangerous is that they denounced variants, not as variants, but as forgeries, and started a fashion for crying "forgery" on totally inadequate evidence, a fashion which is carried on to the present day. It was as if all England accepted as final the theory that "Bacon was Shakespeare" just because of a doubt. The merest suggestion of a "doubt," perhaps based on some later interpolation, is enough to condemn an important work as "forgery" without further ado, until now this tendency has reached ludicrous extremes. I understand that Professor Ch'ên is a great grandson of the great Ch'ing scholar, Ch'ên Lanfu, who already rose above such sectarianism. In this book, Professor Ch'ên mentions that the vigorous fight against the new texts which came to light in the first centuries was because of the vested interests of the occupants of the fourteen chairs of the classics of the Han Dynasty, with high emoluments attached to them.

I think this is a great project worthily carried out. Chinese scholars have been remiss in communicating the enormous mass of material and making it available in English. I am glad to see this book written. There should be, not one, but several histories of Chinese thought, so that the intelligent student can have a slightly more intimate knowledge of Chinese philosophy outside Confucius and Laotse. (Professor Fung Yulan's *History of Chinese Philosophy*, translated into English, suffers from the above-mentioned limitations of "Ch'ing scholarship.") There are many fine points expressed in this book about this or that class of composition with which a scholar may disagree; but I know that the author is able and qualified to defend his views. His opinions are worth listening to. For a long time, this will remain the authoritative work on the history of Chinese literature available in English.

LIN YUTANG

Preface

Recent years have seen a remarkable surge of interest in things Oriental, not the least in Chinese poetry and prose. But this interest has been frustrated by a lack of an up-to-date, comprehensive survey of the field. This volume provides for Western readers the material necessary to appreciate the literature of China.

Presented in chronological order, here is the entire range of Chinese literature, from the earliest truly historical period to the end of the Chinese Empire in 1911 and the effects of Western influence in the 1920's and 1930's. Literary trends, of course, have been discussed, but I have tried to devote enough space to the lives and works of particular writers so that my readers will see these men as individuals interesting in their own right and not merely as steps in a historical progression.

I have tried conscientiously to make use of the most recent scholarship. It is, after all, over half a century since Professor Herbert A. Giles wrote what he characterized as "the first attempt made in any language . . . to produce a history of Chinese literature." Since then, almost every aspect of the subject has been treated by numerous scholars in China, Japan, and the Western world; yet, as specialists will, these scholars have addressed themselves to other scholars. I have tried to give enough detail to enable the reader to put into perspective the major authors and literary trends, but I have attempted to avoid tedious controversies and unnecessary critical apparatus.

Many translated examples are given of the Chinese poetry and prose of each period in order to bring out the full flavor of the Chinese literary achievement. Many of the translations are my own; where I have used the translations of others, these are gratefully acknowledged in the text.

No man's view is broad enough to enable him to sketch out, unassisted, the dimensions of the great Chinese literary tradition. I have culled the work of many literary historians and various translators. Among literary historians, I owe a special debt of gratitude to Dr. Hu Shih, whose erudition has contributed heavily to the whole book; and among translators, I am most grateful to Mr. Arthur Waley, who, through his many excellent translations and sound interpretations, has probably done more than any other single individual to stimulate Western interest in, and to deepen Western understanding of, the literature of China and Japan.

My thanks are due to Dr. David H. Stevens, formerly of the University of Chicago, for suggesting the project; to Professor Jeremy Ingalls of Rockford College and to my brother, Professor Shau Wing Chan of Stanford University, for reading several of the early chapters with helpful comments; to Mrs. Philomene Harrison for generously and patiently assisting me throughout the writing of the book and for typing the manuscript; and to the Rockefeller Foundation for giving financial assistance which enabled me to give up teaching for over a year in order to get the writing started. My thanks are due also to the John Simon Guggenheim Memorial Foundation for a fellowship which enabled me to read some of the Tunhuang manuscripts in the Bibliothèque Nationale and the British Museum. I am grateful to Dr. Lin Yutang for his kind Foreword and to my wife, Helen Lei Ch'ên, for her constant encouragement and patient assistance.

CH'ÊN SHOU-YI

Claremont, California
  July, 1961

Acknowledgments

Thanks are due to the following for permission to reprint copyright material:

George Allen & Unwin, Ltd.: For Songs 15, 22, 32, 45, 46, 63, 86, 87, 98, 99, 129, 131, 139, 238, 246, and 278, and adaptations from Songs 259 and 276, from *The Book of Songs* by Arthur Waley. Copyright 1937 by George Allen & Unwin, Ltd. For the poems "Song of the Orphan," "Fighting South of the Castle," "Song of Lo Fu," "The Ruins of Lo-Yang," "A Peacock Flew," "Poem by T'ao Chih," "The Old Man with the Broken Arm," and "The Herd Boy" from *Chinese Poems* by Arthur Waley. Copyright 1946 by George Allen & Unwin, Ltd. For the poem "You Have Done Well" from *The Life and Times of Po Chü-i* by Arthur Waley. Copyright 1949 by George Allen & Unwin, Ltd. For passages from pages 1, 2, 3, and 52 of *Monkey* by Wu Cheng-ên, translated by Arthur Waley. Copyright 1943 by George Allen & Unwin, Ltd.

The Bodley Head, Ltd.: For passages from pages xiv–xv, 350–51, and 454 of *Chin P'ing Mei*, translated by Bernard Miall and Franz Kuhn. The Bollingen Foundation, Inc.: For the translation from Lu Chi on pages 98–99 of *The Art of Letters* by E. R. Hughes. Bollingen Series XXIX, copyright by the Bollingen Foundation, Inc.

E. J. Brill, Publisher: For selections from the poem "The Lament of the Lady of Ch'in" by Wei Chuang, translated by Lionel Giles, from *T'oung Pao* XXIV, (1926–27), pages 337–49.

The John Day Company, Inc.: For the poems "How Rare the Moon" and "After a Drink at Night," and for passages from pages 164 and 230–31 of *The Gay Genius* by Lin Yutang. Copyright 1947 by the John Day Company. For a passage from page 314 of *The Importance of Living* by Lin Yutang. For passages from pages 1, 2, 3, and 52 of *Monkey* by Wu Chêng-ên, translated by Arthur Waley. Copyright 1943 by the John Day Company.

Harvard University Press: For the poems "Twenty-two Rhymes to H. E. Wei Tsi," "Pretty Women," "To Tease Professor Cheng Ch'ien," "The Autumn Gale Tears off my Thatched Roof," "A Recruiting Officer at Shih Hao," "I Recall," and "Eight Immortals of the Wine Cup," and selections from the poem "The Trip North," from *Tu Fu: China's Greatest Poet* by William Hung. Copyright 1952 by the President and Fellows of Harvard College.

Dr. Hu Shih: For his numerous translations from Chinese poetry and prose.

Alfred A. Knopf, Inc.: For the poems "Song of the Orphan," "Fighting South of the Castle," "The Ruins of Lo-Yang," "Poem by Tao Ch'ih," "The Old Man with the Broken Arm," and "The Herd Boy" from *Translations from the Chinese* by Arthur Waley. Copyright 1941 by Alfred A. Knopf, Inc. For the poems "A Song of the Yen Country" and "The Inlaid Harp" from *The Jade Mountain* by Witter Bynner. Copyright 1935 by Alfred A. Knopf.

Mrs. Grace M. Lyon: For the poems "Lines at a Farewell Feast to Shu Yün Held in the Hsieh T'iao Memorial Hall" and "To the City of Chinling" by Li Po, translated by the late Dr. David Willard Lyon.

The Macmillan Company: For the poem "You Have Done Well" from *The Life and Times of Po Chü-i* by Arthur Waley. Copyright 1949 by The Macmillan Company.

Dr. John C. H. Wu: For his numerous translations of Chinese poems.

Contents

CHINESE LITERATURE

A Historical Introduction

Key to Pronunciation

Most spelling of Chinese names follows the Wade-Giles Romanization System. The spelling of a few common place names conforms to usage adopted by the Chinese Postal System. For example, Chungking (Wade-Giles spelling would be Ch'ung-ch'ing).

Consonants (initials)

Note the sign of aspiration (') used after certain consonants and consonant combinations.

ch, as "j" in "jam."

ch' as "ch" in "church."

hs as English "s" in "see" followed immediately by "h" in "he," but for practical purposes it may be pronounced as "sh" in "shield."

j as "r" in American English, e.g., "run," but without any lip motion.

k as "k" in "sky."

k' as "k" in "keen."

p as "p" in "spy."

p' as "p" in "power."

sz (ss) as "s" in "see" and "z" in "zeal."

t as "t" in "stem."

t' as "t" in "tale."

ts as "ds" in "seeds."

ts' as "ts" in "seats."

tz and tz' are used only before the vowel "ŭ" (see list below), and are pronounced like "ts" and "ts'," respectively.

g, r, and z, are never used initially, while b, d, q, v, and x are never used at all. Other consonants not mentioned here have their English values.

Vowels (finals)

a as "a" in "father."

ai as "ai" in "aisle."

e as "e" in "met."

ê as "u" (but longer) in "us."

ei as "ei" in "deign."

erh as "er" in "herb."

i as "i" in "machine."

iao as "e" and "ow" in "the owl."

ie(h) as the final and initial "e's" in "he edits."

ih (only after ch, ch', j, and sh) is like a vocalized "r." The way to pronounce "shih," for example, is to say "sh" and then immediately say the vocalized "r."

iu as "eu" in "feud."

o after the gutturals k, k', and h, as a separate syllable in itself is like "e," but after other consonants it is like "uo."

ou as "ou" in "soul."

u as "u" in "rule."

ŭ (ǔ) is used only after sz [ss], tz, and tz' to show the buzzing quality of the initial. The way to pronounce "tzu," for example, is to say "tz" and then immediately vocalize it by keeping the tip of the tongue at the back of the teeth with lips open and retracted.

ü as "ü" in German "grün" or "u" in French "menu."

ua as "o" and "a" in "to arm."

uei (ui) as "way."

uo as "o" and "a" in "to awe."

CHAPTER 1

The Earliest Records

A LITTLE over fifty years ago, at the turn of the nineteenth and twentieth centuries, the great majority of Chinese students of literature would have traced the earliest development of China's literary tradition back to the middle of the third millennium before Christ. They would have accepted an extensive array of supposedly early prose and poetry which, upon critical examination, was oftentimes but a projection of the imaginative minds of later ages into the remote past. When Herbert A. Giles, Professor of Chinese at the University of Cambridge, wrote in 1901 the first systematic history of Chinese literature to be published "in any language, including Chinese," he decided boldly but wisely to brush aside China's high antiquity with a very brief summary, and begin his narrative with Confucius. Writing at about the same time, Professor Wilhelm Grube of Berlin, whose *Geschichte der Chinesischen Literatur* was published in 1902, approached the subject with the same cautiousness, and, venturing into what he called pre-Confucian literature, dared to tread warily only as far back as Kuan Chung who had died in 645 B.C., scarcely more than a century before the birth of the Chinese sage in 551 B.C. These, and other scholars of kindred mind, knew enough to realize that, to put it mildly, few literary documents before Confucius were even approximately datable.

Benefiting from the critical scholarship of the last several decades, and especially from the fruits of archaeological excavations, we have access today to thousands of original written records actually produced between 1400 B.C. and 1100 B.C. If these records, incised on bones and tortoise shells, like the records on bronzes of that period, have preserved for us no soul-stirring literary gems from antiquity, they have at least confronted us with a valuable body of authentic specimens from an early phase in the development of China's written language. The discovery of these records, an intriguing tale in itself, deserves at least a brief review.

The inscribed bones and tortoise shells were first discovered, quite accidentally, in 1899, slightly over two miles northwest of the walled

3

city of the district seat of Anyang in Honan Province on the North China plains. There stood the insignificant, sleepy little village of Hsiaotun with the Huan River skirting quietly northeast of it. According to historic records, however, this village had not always been insignificant, for, according to Ssŭ-ma Ch'ien (145-after 86 B.C.), "the Herodotus of China," it was the location where the famous General Hsiang Yü (323-202 B.C.) met one of his subordinates in 207 B.C. in order to converge their troops for a concerted attack on their adversaries. Under another name, probably erroneously given, the village had been noted in the prefecture or county gazetteer as the area of the wastes of an ancient city, and was also described in an illustrated guide to archaeological objects, *K'ao Ku T'u* (1092), as a locale where antique vessels had often been brought to light.

Nonetheless, nothing consequential had happened here until 1900, when bones and shells from this area found their way finally to Peking, the imperial capital. Previously, cotton planters had dug up bits of bones and shells from time to time while working in the fields, and had sold them to apothecaries as "dragon bones"—something of a panacea, and especially efficacious in curing rheumatism. But more than a thousand pieces of these bones were brought to the old cultural center in the spring of 1900 by two dealers. Immediately the interest of many antiquarians, Chinese and foreign, was aroused. Among Chinese collectors, the most notable was Liu E, who, by 1902, had assembled as many as five thousand pieces for his private collection. Thenceforth, as attractive prices were offered for these peculiar finds bearing inscriptions in Chinese characters over three thousand years old, the supply was increased as a result of more feverish digging by local farmers. Counterfeits—often consisting of genuine old bones with newly forged inscriptions—also found credulous buyers, especially when they were inserted in groups of authentic pieces.

These curious finds were gradually sent abroad to form collections in foreign countries—in Britain and the United States, in France and Germany, in Russia and Japan. Despite the avidity of the buyers and collectors, the origin of these artifacts remained a secret until 1903. From that time on, however, the Huan riverbanks near Anyang were frequented by antiquarians, Chinese and foreign, and the annual yield of archaeological bones and shells was increased. In 1914 alone as many as fifty thousand pieces were unearthed. The famine of 1920 and the failure of crops in 1928 resulting from civil war, lured farmers away from their agricultural labor to look for more bones and shells for a livelihood.

It was this type of unscientific and often destructive digging which aroused the attention of the newly organized Academia Sinica and sent it to the field to undertake systematic excavations. Between 1928 and 1937, when the work was interrupted by the Sino-Japanese War, there were no less than fifteen excavations under the auspices of the Academia Sinica.

These excavations, though sadly cut short by international disruptions, have completely revolutionized our concept of early Chinese culture and society. The artifacts brought to light were so numerous and divergent in nature that even a brief summary cannot be attempted here. Of the inscribed records alone, the Academia Sinica has unearthed no fewer than twenty-three thousand bone and shell examples and over three hundred tortoise shells of unusually large size.

These shells and bones, often referred to as "oracle bones," contain the records of divinations performed at the royal capital in China over three thousand years ago. When direction was needed from the deities or the departed spirits of ancestors for the solution of a wide range of problems—selection of a date for the performing of a sacrificial ceremony to an ancestor, what kind of animals were to be sacrificed and how many of them; how soon it would rain or snow; whether the harvest would be plentiful; whether it would be propitious to launch a campaign, go on a hunting trip or cross a river—an elaborate religious service would be solemnized and the deities or spirits invoked. During the service, the officiating priest would use a piece of bone previously prepared, usually a scapula bone of cattle, and apply a heated stylus to a hole half-bored through the underside of the bone, causing it to crack. The cracks thus produced, called *chao* in technical language, were then interpreted by the priest. To assure full responsibility for accuracy of interpretation, the date and the theme of the oracle consultation were later written on the bone with a fine writing brush; the characters were then incised to insure permanence, and the incisions colored in red or black to increase legibility. Sometimes the fulfillment of the oracle was also noted on the bone. In cases of grave questions, tortoise shells—usually the nether portions only—were used instead of bones.

At this point, we should make two observations on these curious oracle bones and shells. First, significant as the inscriptions are, their value is archaeological and historical rather than literary. Among the thousands of these records, there is yet to be found a single poem, a single story or anything that arouses our esthetic or emotional response. All the entries are factual and brief. Second, though these records are by far the most important specimens of ancient Chinese writing, they are not the only ones we have. For two thousand years ancient bronzes, some of which date back to the era of the oracle bones, have continually been brought to light and have engaged the attention of scholars. These bronzes often bear inscriptions in ancient Chinese characters the forms of which in the main agree with those found on the bones and tortoise shells.

These two classes of early inscriptions, then, converge to focus our attention on a basic fact in China's literary history, namely, that the written aspect of the Chinese language, with all its uniqueness, had already taken shape by 1400 B.C. and had been in use for some time. Chinese script was no longer in a primitive stage, for it had a vocabulary of approximately three thousand characters, which have been classified and tabulated in recent years, and approximately half of which have been deciphered and identified with their modern forms. If it is reasonable to assume that there are many other written records still buried underground and that many words (characters) in actual use at that time had failed to find their way into inscriptions, it seems possible that by 1400 B.C. there might have been as many as five thousand characters in the written language of China.

Before we pause briefly to examine the salient characteristics of this ancient system of writing, and the archaic spoken language of which these characters were but the written symbols, it is appropriate to call attention to a problem of China's early literary history which probably will never be solved. Faced as we are with these numerous bits of writing in which a sizable vocabulary was used, and with other artifacts excavated from the same site, including artistic bronzes as well as exquisite ivory figurines, tokens of a high level of social refinement, it seems probable that contemporary with these objects, and with the buildings which we now see only in ruins, there must have been beautiful songs sung, touching prayers said, and interesting stories told. Might these not have been committed to writing on some material more perishable than bones, shells, and bronzes and therefore irrevocably lost to posterity? Admiring the artistry of the inscriptions on these bones and noting the great certainty and delicacy of the incised lines, along with the freshness of the red ink so skillfully painted into the grooves with fine writing brushes, we can feel almost sure that a total absence of literary activities in those days would be difficult to fit into the picture. And yet, unless the spades of the archaeologists yield us new finds of an unexpected kind, we must continue to bear the tantalizing silence of the millenniums that separate us from the creative youth of ancient Anyang.

Further speculations being idle and likely to provoke resentment from the scholarly-minded, let us return to the more tangible though prosaic subject of the literary tool.

As the peculiar character of this early language was to exert an unmistakable influence upon the development of Chinese literature —especially on prosody and the evolution of literary genres—it is appropriate that we take note of a few of its fundamental traits.

Beginning with the written aspect of the Chinese language, we should note that first of all Chinese writing was, as it still is, ideogrammic rather than phonographic. In other words the units of the Chinese script, commonly referred to as "characters," instead of spelling out the sounds of words which they represent, seek to convey their meanings by means of picture writing. Thus, when the character for *tortoise, fish, sheep, swine,* or *cattle* was written in 1400 B.C. it took one of several conventionalized forms as shown in Figure 1. It will be seen that the Chinese script appeals to the eye rather than to the ear, and that the written word in Chinese is more detached from pronunciation than in any of the Indo-European languages. Thus, in a European language the spelling of a word changes usually with the change of its pronunciation, whereas in Chinese, the character remains the same, making it possible for the latter to serve as a common symbol to several people who may each speak a different dialect, as well as to people separated by centuries during which time the spoken language may have undergone multiple changes in pronunciation.

As the Chinese written language is nonphonographic, so is it nonalphabetic. When a new word is invented, the task involved in the creation of a character is to represent the object, the idea, the action, the relationship, or whatever the content of the new word happens to be, and not the recording of its sound by means of an assemblage of letters in an alphabet. To one accustomed to a written language like English, the question at once arises: how can pictograms like these suffice beyond the elementary stage of saying "tortoise" and "fish," "sheep" and "cattle"? And if new words are needed, how are the characters "coined"? As Professor Bernhard Karlgren of Sweden has pointed out, "this pure picture writing, which is not a unique invention of the Chinese, but which has its parallels in various other ancient languages, could not suffice for very long."

Despite the absence of a formalized alphabet, the solution that naturally suggested itself to the early Chinese was the combination of two or more of these simple pictograms to form a new graph (see Figure 2). Thus *sty* was compounded from enclosure and pig, and *corral* from fence and cow. Similarly, *to burn* was made up of

Tortoise   Swine

Fish   Cattle

Sheep

FIG. 1. Chinese pictograms of about 1400 B.C.

Enclosure   + Pig   = Sty

Fence   + Cow   = Corral

Trees   or grass + Fire   = To burn

Dog   + Mouth   = To bark

Rain   + Two hands   = Snow

Man   + Man   = Follow

Man   + Man   = Together

Tree   + Tree   = Forest

Skein   + Skein   = Silk

FIG. 2. Pictograms combined to form new characters.

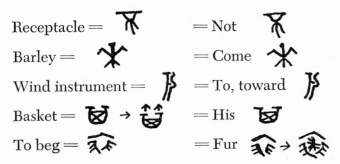

Receptacle =   = Not

Barley =   = Come

Wind instrument =   = To, toward

Basket =   →   = His

To beg =   = Fur   →

FIG. 3. Borrowed graphs.

High   + Meat   = Grease

FIG. 4. Phono-ideograms.

trees or grass and fire; *to bark,* of dog and mouth; and *snow,* of rain and two hands, i.e., that kind of rain which could be picked up by hand. Or sometimes the same graph was written in duplicate to form a new character: *follow* consisting of two men, one following the other; *together* consisting of two men standing in a row; *forest* consisting of two pictures of a tree, suggesting the plurality of trees; and *silk* consisting of two skeins.

Most of these early elemental characters had no indication of pronunciation, but it is not to be inferred too readily that phonetic considerations did not play an important role in the forming of new characters or that the ancient Chinese were not in search of economy in their use of language. This economy, or laziness, expressed itself for a time in "borrowing" instead of inventing a graph. In other words, the practice was followed of using one graph, not for its pictorial or ideogrammic value but for its sound, to indicate a word pronounced like the graph but having a different meaning. The practice is analogous to writing "to" for "two" in English. In ancient Chinese, as in modern English, there were homonyms, words that sounded identical but had different meanings, such as *to, two,* and *too;* and *right, write, rite,* and *wright.* Homonyms were understandably more numerous in Chinese, as Chinese characters were all monosyllabic—one syllable for each character—and without the advantage of polysyllabic combinations.

If the phenomenon of "loan" words sounds perplexing, we shall make it clear with a few examples (see Figure 3). The idea of negation was one not too easy to represent in a graph, but it happened that the ancient Chinese word for *not* sounded like the word for a flower receptacle, and so the lazy way suggested itself of using the graph for *receptacle* to stand for the word *not.* This was adopted by the small reading and writing public, for few would misread the sentence "I don't know him" for "I receptacle know him," as the English sentence "I don't no him" probably would convey the desired meaning despite the substitution of one homonym, *no* for the other, *know.* Similarly, the word *come* is hard to represent in a graph and so the graph for its homonym in oral archaic Chinese, *barley,* was borrowed as the written symbol for *come,* and people were satisfied, because the sentence written in characters, "Here I come," was almost never misinterpreted to mean "Here I barley." Again, the idea of "to" or "toward" was abstract and hard to denote, and so the graph for its homonym, a wind instrument made of bamboo or sometimes of crockery, became the borrowed form for the preposition. For the same reason, a graph meaning "basket" was borrowed for the pronominal adjective "his"; and the graph for "fur," borrowed for its homonym meaning "to beg," or "to solicit," or "to look for."

Such loans as these, however, were good and clever only if the originals were rarely used and if ambiguity could be ruled out by the context. If they were made in large numbers and without discrimination, the result would necessarily be hopeless uncertainty and endless confusion. Even such a phrase as "looking for his fur in his basket" might be baffling enough, and so this procedure was early modified in favor of a new method of character creation.

The method of combining two or more extant graphs to form a new one was utilized again but with some modification. Instead of drawing upon each of the component graphs for meaning in forming the new symbol (such as combining trees and fire to suggest *burn*), the new formula utilized a homonym in current use as a pronunciation indicator and one or more component graphs to suggest the general meaning. The word for *grease* or *fat* (lard), for example, was an exact homonym of the word for *high* whose graph was a picture of a tower or tall building (See Figure 4). If the loaning principle had been followed, the pictogram of the tower would have meant sometimes "high," sometimes "grease," to be determined by context. But this would create unusual confusion since both *high* and *grease* were words of daily use. So, instead of the lazier solution of using one form of the "tower" pictogram as a loan symbol for *grease* or *lard,* and instead of the more strenuous attempt to picture a pan of grease or a lump of lard, a compromise was reached by utilizing the symbol and adding onto it another graph meaning meat, the picture of a cut of meat, to indicate it was the word *kâu* related to meat and not the word *kâu* meaning "high."

This method of piecing old characters together to form new ones, registering sound by one component part (the phonetic) and suggesting meaning by another (the signific), was already in use in the age of the oracle bones and tortoise shells and came to be the chief formula for creating new characters in the Chinese language in subsequent centuries. It is no exaggeration to say that seven characters out of ten in current use are of this category—phono-ideograms.

Efforts at greater refinement and simplicity were made all the time, of course, and local variations were necessarily numerous, but no drastic deviations were observable to upset the tradition already established in the fourteenth century before Christ. We can not speak with any certainty about the development of the script prior to this period. It makes good sense to assume, however, that an extensive number of graphs, running up to the thousands, could not have been accumulated in a short period, and that the conventionalization of written symbols, removing them gradually from the primitive picture-writing stage—a trait already well developed at the time of the bronze and bone inscriptions—could only have been the result of a long process of slow evolution.

If the Chinese script has had a long history, the beginnings of the spoken Chinese tongue go back even further into antiquity. In fact, linguistic researches of the last few decades have attempted to steer the time machine backwards not only to look at proto-Chinese itself —the most ancient stage of the language—but also to discover the parent stock from which proto-Chinese was descended. This sounds extremely ambitious, but thanks to the solid contributions of comparative philology and historical phonology, the hypotheses advanced seem to rest on fairly sound foundations. The scroll unrolled thus far is, to be sure, as yet far from being complete, interrupted, as it is, by gaps here and beclouded with uncertainties there. And yet it is profoundly true that, by and large, the student of Chinese in the middle of the twentieth century knows more of how Confucius spoke around 500 B.C. than did many preceding generations of scholars.

Related to Tibetan, and in a less intimate way also to Thai and Burmese as well as to a number of dialects in central and southeastern Asia, Chinese is, by virtue of the large number of its modern speakers and the bulk and quality of its literary records, decidedly the most important member of the Sinitic (or Sino-Tibetan) family of languages. Regarding the parent language from which these languages and dialects have descended, very little is as yet known, except that it was spoken sometime in the remote past before Chinese and Tibetan had acquired sufficient characteristics of their own to become separate languages. It has been suggested hypothetically, that this parting of the ways probably took place during the third millennium before Christ.

For our present purpose, we need to concern ourselves only with a later phase of the development of the language, namely, archaic Chinese. Though it sounds antique, archaic Chinese is not too remote to be of interest to the modern student, for it has many features which have been preserved in the living language spoken and especially written by Chinese of the twentieth century. Before we go any further, it may be well for us to note specifically what archaic Chinese is. To give a brief answer to a complicated question, archaic Chinese is the label given to that period of the Chinese linguistic development the reconstruction of which has been made on the basis of Chinese literary documents produced between 1000 B.C. and 700 B.C. As there are no evidences of abrupt changes in the language either immediately before or after these dates, it is also extended to cover the age of the oracle bones on the one hand, and the language of Confucius, Mencius, and their contemporaries, down to about 200 B.C. on the other.

One basic fact of which we are certain regarding archaic Chinese in its sound aspect is that all the written graphs, almost without exception, were monosyllabic and isolating. In other words, archaic Chinese was a language in which nearly all the roots of the words were monosyllabic, and inflectional changes were not only reduced to the minimum, but also usually indicated by other ways than the addition of one or more syllables. In case such an addition was deemed imperative, the added syllable was treated as a separate word rather than the ending of the word to which it was affixed. A few simple illustrations will make these points clear. In English, such words as *summer, winter, flower,* and *beauty* are two-syllable units which cannot be split or shortened. In archaic Chinese they are all monosyllabic: *hia, tuong, hua,* and *mjwi* respectively. Moreover, each of the four English words may be prolonged by one syllable to serve different functions: *summery, winterer, flowering,* and *beautiful,* etc. In archaic Chinese, the four stem-words would remain intact. A change from one part of speech to another would be indicated by the position of the word with reference to the context. The continuous process implied by *flowering* and the idea of the agent in *winterer* would each be indicated by an additional but separate character.

This preponderant monosyllabism of archaic Chinese could not help but produce an embarrassing result—the large numbers of homonyms, that is, words having the same pronunciation but different meanings. Moreover, with the simplification of pronunciation, the number of homonyms increased. Many syllables that had been distinguishable at an earlier period merged into identical sounds. Though this process was not accelerated until after the third century before Christ, there are suggestions that it was already in operation during the archaic period.

To keep the situation under control, two remedies were employed. One was to vary the length of the syllable to differentiate between the meanings of a pair of homonyms. Thus the verb *to invade* in its active voice was pronounced quickly *bjiwat,* but in its passive voice, *to be invaded,* was prolonged, *bjiwāt,* although in both cases it was pronounced as one syllable. Fortunately, this remedy was early discovered to be of no great assistance, since the comparative length of a syllable was something hard to standardize; confusion arose when a sound meant by a leisurely speaker to be short seemed long to an impatient listener.

The second remedy consisted in a variation of the tone or pitch of the syllable to designate the differences in meaning. The syllable *kam,* for example, pronounced in an even pitch or tone, meant "sweet"; but when pronounced in an uneven or slightly slurring tone, would mean "brave" or "to dare to." *Mian* might mean "cotton" in one tone, and "face" in another. Similarly, *ma* would mean "horse" in one tone, and "hemp" in another. The usage may sound distressingly confusing but the tone in archaic Chinese was much less complicated than in medieval Chinese or modern Cantonese. There were more initial and final sounds and a greater number of vowel combinations, making possible a more extensive syllabary. In other words, there were more combinations of sounds to use in making up single-syllable units, and therefore fewer homonyms.

Although we do not know exactly how many tones there were in standard archaic Chinese, we know that intonation was an inherent and vital part of the pronunciation of each spoken word. In other words, intonation was already assuming a linguistic function entirely different from its counterpart in any of the languages of the Indo-European group. In English, for example, the existence of tones is just as easily discernible as in Chinese; but the variation of intonation in saying a word, such as "good" in a question, and "good" in a reassuring answer, does not change the meaning of the word or necessitate two distinct symbols as it often does in Chinese. Or, to approach the situation from a slightly different angle, whereas a word in English may be spoken at various pitches to suit the context, a Chinese word is in general affixed permanently to a given tone, and so its tone is a vital part of its correct pronunciation.

To the best of our knowledge at present, there were three, or possibly four, tones in archaic Chinese. This observation is based on our study of the rhyme schemes of early songs and poems. Words ending in *k, p,* and *t* formed a tone-group by themselves and the remaining words were intoned on two (or three) levels. End rhymes in Chinese poetry written between 1000 B.C. and 700 B.C. showed not only correspondence in terminal sounds, as usual, but also identity in tone, or in a tonal group which might include minor gradations. Thus we are led to assume that even before 1000 B.C. the Chinese language had acquired tonality as a fundamental feature and that the literary compositions, when read aloud, made a direct musical appeal to the ear, just as the written graphs made an esthetic appeal to the eye.

The fixing of a well-defined tone for each monosyllabic word in Chinese, archaic and modern, may give the erroneous impression that the language sounds stilted and unnatural. If intonation is so strictly regulated, a Westerner is inclined to ask: how can an exclamatory sentence, for instance, be spoken or a question asked in such a way as to be clearly distinguishable from a declarative statement? The ancient Chinese succeeded in showing this distinction by the use of a class of words which had no meaning of their own but which had specific functions in a phrase or sentence not unlike those performed by interjections and punctuation marks in English. These "final particles," pronounced in rising or falling tones, as the case might be, not only helped clarify sentence types but rendered more vivid the emotional utterances in poetry.

Another grammatical characteristic of the Chinese language resulting from the monosyllabic and isolating nature of Chinese words is the extreme dimness of the lines of demarcation between the so-called parts of speech. The word for "summer" in Chinese may serve as both a noun and an adjective very much in the same way as the English word "summer" in "summer school" may be made to serve an adjectival function. Most of the so-called "content words" or *shih-tzŭ* in Chinese can be used as nouns, verbs, adjectives, or adverbs without change in pronunciation or appearance, the part of speech to which they belong being clearly determinable from the word sequence. Whenever a distinction is deemed highly desirable —for example, the conversion of an adjective into an adverb—it can be achieved with the help of an added particle. Even instances of this kind are extremely rare in Chinese writings. The fluidity created by words acting as different parts of speech gives rise to a literary subtlety which defies transference to a different language, and creates difficulties for even the most competent translators.

To summarize, then, we have seen that (1) when the first songs and documents were recorded around 1000 B.C., the Chinese language was already an effective tool. (2) It was a language made up of monosyllabic, isolating sounds pronounced in carefully differentiated tones, relatively free of flexions, recorded in individual conventionalized graphs slightly reminiscent of earlier picture writing. (3) This language was destined not only to continue as a literary medium for the Chinese people for three thousand years to come, but also to perform a similar service for their neighbors in Korea, Japan, and Vietnam.

CHAPTER 2

The Book of Songs

THE first great monument of ancient Chinese imaginative literature is the *Shih Ching* (also *Shih King*) or the *Book of Songs*, which contains the words of 305 songs of various types composed and sung between about 1000 B.C. and 700 B.C. While these Chinese contemporaries of the Homeric rhapsodists and Hesiod were busy weaving their simple patterns of literary beauty, the land and people of China were going through some fundamental changes.

The Shang-Yin Dynasty (1766-1122 B.C.*), celebrated for its exquisite bronzes, for its bone and bronze inscriptions, and for the urban civilization of its great capital city, had now fallen. The Shang-Yin people, inhabitants of the coastal areas and alluvial plains of what we call North China today, had been subjugated by their cousins from the west, the Chous, erstwhile roving mountaineers who had now mastered the technique of agriculture, and who were hard-working and sensible, though definitely more rustic.

The new conqueror's lack of refinement, however, was not to continue for long, for as soon as the Chou Dynasty was established (1122 B.C.) an attempt was made to absorb the culture as well as to consolidate the territory of the vanquished. The cultural assimilation was accelerated during the regency of the Duke of Chou (1115-1105 B.C.), who was well versed in letters as well as the arts of war and administration, and to whom many a classic was accredited by later ages. As a result of his influence, the old tradition was so warmly approved and persistently followed that the dynastic trait of the Chou house came to be known as *wên*, or artistic refinement.

Probably the most important asset appropriated by the new dynasty from the cultural bequests of the Shang-Yin people was the written language. This was easily accomplished as the conquerors presumably spoke the same tongue as that of the conquered. As the

---

* It has recently been established on ample evidence by Professor Tung Tso-pin that the Shang-Yin dynasty fell in 1111 B.C., and that the year 1122 B.C. merely marked the coronation of King Wu of the new Chou Dynasty.

15

geographic extent of the Chou Kingdom was greatly enlarged with the annexation of the eastern regions, numerous feudal states were established to keep the people in subordination, to protect the royal domains and capitals, and to reward the services of kinsmen and supporters of the new dynasty. The chieftains of outlying zones, too strong and too far away from the centers of military power to be subdued, were enfeoffed in a similar manner, though their fealty was rather nominal than actual. These new feudal courts, counted by tens if not by hundreds, thus became centers for the transplanting of courtly refinement and propagation of the use of the written language.

The torchbearers in the new movement for literacy and enlightenment were survivors of the *ancien régime*—members of the priesthood who had worked with oracle bones, and members of the vanquished nobility now completely dispossessed of their feudal holdings. Impoverished and dispersed by the conquerors, they were forced to seek their livelihood by becoming expert practitioners of the arts of peace: writing, reckoning, music, and above all, rituals, upon which so much of the well-being of the individual and community was believed to depend. Despite their bitter experience in relocation, they found ready employment in the new centers of culture to serve the new nobility and even the commoners. Their role in the intellectual development of the formative era of the Chou Dynasty was not unlike that of the educated Greeks in Rome after the Roman conquest about the middle of the second century before Christ. In their various capacities as priests and diviners, chroniclers and librarians, teachers and secretaries, scribes and acolytes, experts on rituals, and storytellers, they were, in the true sense of the word, the forerunners of the philosophers and littérateurs of the age of Confucius and Mencius.

The composite Chou culture and political overlordship maintained itself with relative stability until 771 B.C., when King Yu, twelfth in the Chou house, was killed by the "Dog Barbarians" (Ch'üan Jung), and the capital—known as Kaoching, Chungchou, or Ch'angan (near present-day Sian)—was sacked. In the following year (770 B.C.) King P'ing, abandoning the old capital, established his court in the eastern co-capital of Loyang where the seat of the royal government was to remain, in gradually depreciating power and waning prestige, until the formal end of the dynasty in 249 B.C.

Although few of the songs in the *Shih Ching* can be accurately dated, the bulk of them came into being, as we have noted, approximately between 1000 and 700 B.C., i.e., from the early reigns of the Chou Dynasty to within a few decades after the removal of the capital. As to exactly when and how these three-hundred-odd songs were first collected and arranged, we have no verifiable information. According to one early tradition, most of them were collected by royal agents sent out to the various feudal areas during the second month of each year for the benefit of the government. By listening to the collected songs, the king and his ministers could learn of the happiness and bitterness of the people without traveling abroad. According to another early tradition, first recorded by the great historian, Ssŭ-ma Ch'ien (145-after 86 B.C.), there had been collected in the manner described above more than three thousand songs at the time of Confucius. The Chinese sage, eliminating the duplications and those that had no special bearing on the art of living and the standard of righteousness, selected for his "definitive" edition only 311 of these songs, six of which were represented by mere title and name of tune alone without text.

The *Shih Ching* has come down to us practically intact, despite the many periods of turmoil in Chinese history during which a great number of literary works were lost or destroyed. The theory of Confucius' editorship immediately put around the collection a halo, and elevated it to the dignity and sanctity of a "classic," thus ensuring its preservation to a remarkable degree.

The dignity and sanctity of a classic, however, gave rise to certain disadvantages. In conformity with established Confucian standards, each song in the *Shih Ching* was forced by commentators to imply a moral; and, in order to justify the moralistic interpretation, many songs were linked artificially to historical events in pre-Confucian times and attributed to historical personages on doubtful grounds. As conflicting schools of interpretation grew up, they only increased the confusion regarding the authorship and the original meaning of the songs. The immense accretion of exegetical literature on the *Shih Ching*, therefore, is of little assistance except to the specialists, and the symbolism insisted upon by the commentators need not be discussed here.

If Confucius did not actually edit the *Shih Ching*, he did refer to the *Three Hundred Songs* on more than one occasion, thus suggesting by implication the probability that the number had been widely sanctioned by expert acclaim during and even before his time. These songs were classified into sections or books, and the classification was retained in later "authorized" editions as follows:

(1) *Fêng* or popular songs, subdivided geographically into fifteen sections, totaling 160 songs.

(2) *Ya* or courtly songs, subdivided into two sections on the basis of musical accompaniments, totaling 111 songs.

(3) *Sung* or sacrificial and temple songs, subdivided into three sections on the basis of geographical origin, totaling forty songs.

The *sung* division, the least important in literary merit and the smallest in bulk, consists mainly of songs sung to the accompaniment of music and group dancing on the occasion of the king's or feudal lord's ancestral worship and commemoration of the heroic feats of his ancestors. The first group, known as the Chou *sung*, were probably the earliest specimens of Chinese poetry we have, dating back to the period between the eleventh century and the eighth century before Christ. Besides the typical sacrificial and commemorative dance songs, there are a number of songs on miscellaneous subjects—moral exhortation, agricultural life, etc.—sung for the entertainment of the royal household and their guests.

At this distance, it is impossible to determine the authorship of these songs, although many plausible conjectures have been suggested on the strength of internal evidence. The truth of the matter is that the writers of these early Chou songs, though their political position might have been significant, were novices in literary art. Even if there had been remnants of earlier poetry, these obviously had not been utilized as models. The early Chou bards could not make up their minds, for one thing, as to the distinctive feature of verse. A few songs, probably the oldest in the whole *Shih Ching*, had no rhymes at all. A little later, end-rhymes were introduced, but only awkwardly and irregularly with no obvious pattern of interspersion and recurrence. Finally the rhyming scheme became regular and sufficiently varied to avoid monotony. Thus was founded one of the basic conventions in Chinese versification, a convention which China shares with most other nations, namely, the end-rhyme, with all its variations and ramifications.

Another general feature of the songs in the *Shih Ching* that took definite shape in this subsection of the anthology is the four-character (or four-syllable, since each character was monosyllabic) line. There are variations in the line length from one to eight words as exacting readers have often pointed out, but these exceptions are so few that they cannot invalidate the over-all observation that the typical *Shih Ching* line is a four-syllable line.

The other two groups of the *sung* division are the Lu *sung* and Shang *sung*, both of which are similar to the Chou *sung* in general theme but were current in the capitals of the feudal states of Lu and Sung, respectively, and compiled after the catastrophe of 771 B.C. when Kaoching fell to the barbarian invaders. Lu, the native state of Confucius, had been enfeoffed to the descendants of the great pioneer of art and letters, the Duke of Chou, and had been noted for its preservation of orthodox western Chou culture. In fact after the Chou royal court had moved eastward to the co-capital, Loyang, to continue the dynastic span in reduced prestige and splendor, it was frequently said that all the orthodox culture of the dynasty was to be found in Lu. Such a claim was not unwarranted, though difficult to substantiate, since the loss of literary records, musical instruments, and sacred vessels and vestments as well as other types of cultural treasures as a result of the fall of the capital must have been immense.

If the feudal state of Lu was an important cultural area as the home of the most respected collateral branch of the Chou royal house, the state of Sung was significant as the appanage of the Shang royal domain, which, despite the Chou conquest of 1122 B.C. and the pacification campaigns of subsequent years, continued to hold the respect and interest of their military conquerors who had become in large degree their cultural converts. Thus for centuries the musicians continued to sing of the grandeur of their ancient kings in conformity with the universal standard of filial piety, and when these dance-songs were compiled, any trace of subversiveness that the wording might suggest had completely lost its original meaning.

It is not difficult for us to understand, then, that of all the feudal *sung* songs, those of the feudal states of Lu and Sung were alone preserved in the anthology.

The second division, known as *ya*, is divided into two separate sections, the greater *ya* and the lesser *ya*. The Chinese word *ya*, usually meaning "elegant" or "refined," has a special musical application in this usage. With the irrevocable destruction of the *Book of Music* along with musical scores in the third century before Christ, we are unable to determine its exact nature, though we know that in the *ya* songs, the dancing accompaniment no longer played the major role, as it did in the *sung* songs.

The greater *ya* contains thirty-one songs, of which the most common themes are felicitations and eulogies, offerings to gods and ancestors, and dining and drinking. While these songs have in their substance a good deal in common with the *sung* songs of a slightly earlier age, they evidence a superior literary artistry. They exhibit more variety and consistency in rhyming pattern. They indicate a mechanical obviousness in transition from stanza to stanza, often repeating the last line of a foregoing stanza for the first line of the ensuing stanza. They have more lines to the song, and are more successful in developing the themes in a sustained manner.

The lesser *ya* poems, treating of the same themes and sung to a similar type of music, were composed at a later age, many of them after the removal of the Chou capital in 771 B.C. One striking difference between the two groups lies in the superiority of the later poets —lively description, minute observation, and increasing artistic self-mastery and restraint. Another novel feature of the lesser *ya* songs is the first trace of lyricism, a note almost entirely absent in the earlier songs in the *sung* and the greater *ya* sections.

In a poem dealing with the Chou campaigns in the northwest against the Hsien-yün barbarians *circa* 800 B.C., for example, the warriors were represented as singing:

> We plucked the bracken, plucked the bracken
> While the young shoots were springing up.
> Oh to go back, go back!
> The year is ending.
> We have no house, no home
> Because of the Hsien-yün
> We cannot rest or bide
> Because of the Hsien-yün.

After repeating these sentiments in two stanzas similarly worded and describing the chariots and teams of their lord in command, the song ends with the following strain:

> Long ago, when we started,
> The willows spread their shade.
> Now that we turn back
> The snowflakes fly.
> The march before us is long,
> We are thirsty and hungry,
> Our hearts are stricken with sorrow,
> But no one listens to our plaint.
>
> (*Song 167*, Arthur Waley's translation No. 131 *)

Another group of songs that deserves mention before we leave the two *ya* sections of the *Shih Ching* are a number of odes which retell the chief legends and events from the obscure beginnings of the Chou Dynasty. One Chinese literary historian, Lu K'an-ju, has selected ten such odes and suggested that, when rearranged in their proper order, they approximate ten fragments of a Chou national epic.

This series of songs covers a traditional chronological span of no less than fourteen centuries and records the high lights of the

---

* In this and subsequent references to the *Shih Ching*, the traditional song number is given first. Where Arthur Waley's translation is used, the second figure refers to the number scheme in his *Book of Songs* (London, 1937).

legendary and recorded history of the Chou people. It begins with an account of Hou Chi, purported founder of the Chou house, by telling how his mother, by treading God's toe print, had her barrenness removed.

> Indeed she had fulfilled her months,
> And her first-born came like a lamb
> With no bursting or rending,
> With no hurt or harm.
> To make manifest His magic power
> God on high gave her ease.
> So blessed were her sacrifice and prayer
> That easily she bore her child.
>
> Indeed, they put it in a narrow lane;
> But oxen and sheep tenderly cherished it.
> Indeed, they put it in a far-off wood;
> But it chanced that woodcutters came to this wood.
> Indeed, they put it on the cold ice;
> But the birds covered it with their wings.
> The birds at last went away,
> And Hou Chi began to wail.
>
> Truly far and wide
> His voice was very loud.
> Then sure enough he began to crawl;
> Well he straddled, well he reared,
> To reach food for his mouth.

> (Song 245, Waley's translation No. 238)

Then in other songs of the series, we hear of other illustrious forebears of the dynasty; of Kung Liu, Hou Chi's great-grandson, who led his tribesmen to Pin where he established growing agricultural communities to which other tribes were soon attracted (Song 250); of Tan Fu (ten generations removed from Kung Liu), who led another migration and revived the vigor of his people (Song 237); of King Wên, Tan Fu's grandson, who, on account of his virtues and talents, laid the foundation of the royal dynasty, although he himself was never crowned king (Song 241); and of his son King Wu, who finally received the mandate of heaven to take over the kingship from the Shang-Yin Dynasty:

> The armies of Yin and Shang—
> Their catapults were like the trees of a forest.
> They marshalled their forces at Mu-yeh:
> A target set up for us
> "God on high is watching you;
> Let no treachery be in your hearts."

The field of Mu-yeh spread far,
The war chariots gleamed,
The team of white-bellies was tough,
The captain was Shang-fu.
Like an eagle, he uprose.
Ah, that King Wu
Swiftly fell upon Great Shang,
Who before daybreak begged for a truce.

(*Song 236*, Waley's translation No. 246)

After the establishment of the dynasty and the lapse of three reigns, the Chou kingdom began to lose its vigor and vigilance, and under later kings, had to launch various "punitive" campaigns against the border tribes: against the Hsien-yün under King Li, 878-828 B.C. (Song 168); against the Ching barbarians to the south in 782 B.C., (Song 178); against the Huai barbarians in the southeast (Song 262); against the Hsien-yün a second time (Song 263), all under King Hsüan, 827-782 B.C. The following lines are typical of these campaign songs.

Majestic, terrible,
Very splendid, a Son of Heaven,
Our King quietly set to work,
Not idling nor loitering.
The Hsü was mightily shaken;
Startled as by an earthquake was the land of Hsü.
As at a roll of thunder, as by a clap of thunder
The land of Hsü was startled, and quaked.

The King's hosts swept along
As though flying, as though winged,
Like the river, like the Han,
Steady as a mountain,
Flowing onward like a stream,
Rank on rank, in serried order,
Immeasurable, unassailable;
Mightily they marched through the land of Hsü.

(*Song 263*, Waley's translation No. 139)

If we detect any measure of epical potentialities in the substance and manner of these songs, their brevity alone will rule them out as components of an epic, for the whole assemblage of these ten songs contains fewer than six hundred lines, numbering fewer than twenty-five hundred words. Wisely has Arthur Waley labeled them merely "dynastic legends."

Ancient India had its *Mahabhārata* and ancient Greece its *Iliad* and *Odyssey;* many similar creations were to be found throughout Europe. China did not even have a literary epic; she could not boast of a Virgil or a Milton. For a while she had the distinguished company of Iran; but around A.D. 1000, when Firdausi (Abul Qasim Mansur), the Persian Homer, broke the silence with his *Shah-Nameh* or *Epic of Kings,* China was left alone; it is the only outstanding nation with a literary attainment completely devoid of an epical tradition.

This is a literary anomaly that has brought forth many attempts at explanation. Has there really been no epic in China, or was it lost in the preliterate age? Is it true that as China's ideal human type is the sage and not the hero, she is not interested in the epical narration of heroic feats? To these questions there is, unfortunately, no positive answer.

Whatever had caused the apparent absence of the epical tradition at the time of the *Shih Ching,* there was no evidence that the lack was keenly felt by the literary segments of the Chinese people. No attempt was made to fill the gap, as no native literary epic of the *Aeneid* type was to engage the creative talents of Chinese poets. They and their audiences seemed contented with shorter compositions, mainly those with a lyrical turn.

We shall now return to the *Shih Ching,* especially to its first section of *fêng.* The Chinese word *fêng*—a word of common usage—means "wind." In its derived meaning, it also can be translated as "customs" and "airs"—things that are current, like the wind itself. The *fêng* section in the *Shih Ching* consists of songs *par excellence.* Of these we have 160 pieces preserved for us, arranged in fifteen groups (or thirteen, according to a theory advanced by a recent scholar, Wang Kuo-wei) related to their geographical origin. The great majority of these songs were written by unknown authors and their words had been freely tampered with by various singers who felt justified in making improvements of one kind or another. Thus, it should not be too hastily inferred that these so-called folk songs were the primitive voice of untutored commoners or the random attempts at song-making by men and women in the street.

Many of the songs, of course, retained their original simplicity. Let us take, for example, the following:

> Thick grows the plantain;
> Here we go plucking it,
> Thick grows the plantain;
> Here we go gathering it.

Thick grows the plantain;
Here we hold it between the fingers,
Thick grows the plantain;
Here we are with handfuls of it.

Thick grows the plantain;
Here we have our aprons full of it.
Thick grows the plantain;
Now apronfuls are tucked in at our belts.

(Song 8, Waley's translation No. 99)

If the repetitiousness of such a song sounds sometimes monotonous or dull to the modern reader, he should remember that the words were sung to music and that the recurrence of words and phrases was no more conducive to monotony than the repetitious gestures involved in plantain picking. Plantain was valued by expectant mothers in ancient China, who were taught to believe that it would ensure easy delivery, and the light-hearted rhythm of the song made the task of picking plantain an easy one.

In a similar vein was the following song sung by a bride-to-be while gathering the white aster in preparation for a ceremony at the bridegroom's ancestral hall, where her marriage was to be solemnized as an event of the whole clan:

Where do we gather the white aster?
By the pool, on the islets.
Wherefore do we use it?
At the rituals of prince and lord.

Where do we gather the white aster?
Down in the ravine.
Wherefore do we use it?
In the ancestral hall of prince and lord.

.　　.　　.　　.　　.　　.　　.

(Song 13, adapted from Waley's translation No. 98)

Equally dependent on music for their full artistic effect and equally delightful in verbal repetitions are many of the love songs of the various feudal areas.

A moon rising white
Is the beauty of my lovely one.
Ah, the tenderness, the grace!
Heart's pain consumes me.

A moon rising bright
Is the fairness of my lovely one.
Ah, the gentle softness!
Heart's pain wounds me.

A moon rising in splendor
Is the beauty of my lovely one.
Ah, the delicate yielding!
Heart's pain torments me.

(*Song 143*, Waley's translation No. 32)

Replete as most of these songs of the *fêng* section are with the freshness of popular airs, they also frequently reveal a considerable degree of verbal refinement and studied artistry, especially in the use of imagery. The beauty of Chuang Chiang, whose marriage in 757 B.C. was celebrated in folk songs as well as in feudal court, was described in one song thus:

A splendid woman and upstanding;
Brocade she wore, over an unlined coat,
Daughter of the Lord of Ch'i;

   .   .   .   .

Hands white as rush-down
Skin like lard,
Neck long and white as the tree-grub,
Teeth like melon seeds,
Lovely head, beautiful brows,
Oh the sweet smile dimpling,
The lovely eyes so black and white.

   .   .   .   .   .   .

(*Song 57*, Waley's translation No. 86)

For the second stanza, we would approach the original more closely if we imagined we were reading the words in four-syllable lines. Expanding the original to more than twice the number of words, James Legge has given us the following translation:

Like blades of white grass were her fingers fine;
    Her skin like purest ointment hard congealed;
Her neck like larvae on the tree which shine
    So long and white. Her opening lips revealed
    Her even teeth, behind their screen concealed,
Like melon seeds. Her front cicada-square
    Displayed her eyebrows curved upon its field,
Like horns of silkworm moth; and dimples rare,
    With dark and lucid eyes, showed face beyond compare.

A song like the foregoing, so laconic, so carefully worded, and so obviously occasioned by a state event linking various princely families in a marriage alliance, was most probably composed and sung by minstrels at the feudal courts before it found its way to the common people. Songs of this type, originating from the feudal courts, are numerous in this section of the *Shih Ching,* and in fact in the whole anthology. Now that these feudal courts were increasingly conscious of the dignity and value of refinement, it was only natural that the best versifiers and singers were to be found there. It was therefore likely that even songs of popular origin, after they were "collected" by official agents, were also edited, if not rewritten, by these "literati" of the feudal period to conform with the current standards of language purity and prosodic correctness.

As a result, there are relatively few localisms in the anthology, although local color is readily detectable. This does not necessarily prove that there was a standard language, a kind of *koine,* used by all song-makers of the time. The number of songs now preserved in the *Shih Ching* is too small to serve as a basis for such a hypothesis. Attention should rather be called to the fact that the ordinary language of the people was, as it always is, capable of refined and artistic usage. It should also be borne in mind that only the best of the songs were able to traverse feudal boundary lines to become the common property of all song lovers of the various feudal states and to find their way to inclusion in the immortal anthology.

This mutual sharing of the best of the poetic language among the different states explains the occurrence of the same figures of speech in widely divergent areas. The emotional likening of a single day during which a loved one was missed, to the length of three months (or even three years), for example, was expressed in a song sung in the Royal Domain:

> Oh, he is plucking cloth-creeper,
> For a single day I have not seen him;
> It seems like three months!
>
> Oh, he is plucking southernwood,
> For a single day I have not seen him;
> It seems like three autumns!
>
> Oh, he is plucking mugwort,
> For a single day I have not seen him;
> It seems like three years!
>
> (*Song 72,* Waley's translation No. 45)

The same sense of a long day was projected in a similar song in the state of Chêng:

> Oh, you with the blue collar,
> On and on I think of you.
> Even though I do not go to you,
> You might surely send me news!

Oh, you with the blue collar
Always and ever I long for you.
Even though I do not go to you,
You might surely sometimes come?

Here by the wall gate
I pace to and fro.
One day when I do not see you
Is like three months.

(Song 91, Waley's translation No. 46)

While the English renderings are differently worded, the two lines involved in this comparison are identical in the Chinese original, which merely reads, word for word:

One day not see
Like three months, oh!

And yet the general absence of unintelligible provincialisms in the songs should not be misinterpreted to mean a self-conscious sophistication on the part of the song-makers. On the contrary, the main difference between these early songs and the writings of later Chinese poets lies in the childlike forthrightness and earnest simplicity of the <i>Shih Ching.</i> The following narrative poem is representative of the artless presentation of the woes of a forsaken wife:

You came as an innocent fellow,
Bringing cloth to trade for silk.
But you did not come to trade for silk,
You came to propose to me.
I escorted you across the Ch'i
As far as T'un Hill
"It is not I who have delayed you,
You have no good match-maker.
Please don't be angry,
Let's set our date sometime in the autumn."

I climbed up the steep wall
To gaze toward Fukuan;
But failing to see Fukuan
I shed floods of tears.
And later I saw Fukuan
And I laughed and I talked.
You had consulted the divination sticks and turtle
And there was no bad omen.
You came with your carriage
And moved me and my belongings.

Before the mulberry tree sheds its leaves
They are glossy and soft.
Oh you doves,
Do not eat the [intoxicating] berries!
Oh you maidens,
Do not indulge in pleasure with men!
When a man indulges himself in pleasure,
He will be excused,
But when a maiden so indulges herself,
She will not be excused.

Now the mulberry leaves have fallen,
They are yellow and withered.
Since I came to you,
For three years I have eaten poverty.
The Ch'i River flowed in rising torrents,
Wetting the carriage and its curtains.
The woman has committed no fault;
The man has changed his ways,
The man has debased himself,
Now changeable and fickle.

For three years I was your wife,
I hardly rested in my chamber.
I got up early and went to bed late;
An idle morning I never had.
Then came your unsparing words.
And later your explosive roughness.
My brothers would not know of this,
Audibly they would laugh!
As I thought about it all when alone,
I had only myself to bemourn.

"Together you and I will grow old."
Now that oath makes me grieved!
The Ch'i has its banks
The swamp has its bounds,
In our looped-haired days,
How gaily we talked and laughed!
How solemnly we pledged our troth!
Now you would not recall.
As you would not ever recall,
This shall be the end of it all!

(*Song 58*)

For generations the *fêng* section of the *Shih Ching* has been ad-mired for its many love and courtship songs which are imbued with the same natural beauty and unrestrained simplicity. In a way, they are even more representative than the narrative songs, of the general spirit and forms of early Chinese poetry. The following is a courtship song probably sung at a festival participated in by boys and girls lined up as opposite teams:

> Drumming and dancing in the valley,
> How light-hearted was that tall man!
> Subtler than any of them at capping stories,
> And he swore he would never forget me.
>
> Drumming and dancing along the bank,
> How high-spirited was that tall man!
> Subtler than any at capping songs,
> And he swore he would never fail me.
>
> Drumming and dancing on the high ground,
> How gay was that tall man!
> Subtler than any at capping whistled tunes,
> And he swore his love would never end.
>
> (*Song 56,* Waley's translation No. 15)

The following sounds almost like a universal love song:

> Of fair girls the loveliest
> Was to meet me at the corner of the Wall.
> But she hides and will not show herself;
> I scratch my head, pace up and down.
>
> Of fair girls the prettiest
> Gave me a red flute.
> The flush of that flute,
> Is pleasure at the girl's beauty.
>
> She has been in the pastures and brought for me rush-wool,
> Very beautiful and rare.
> It is not you that are beautiful;
> But you were given by a lovely girl.
>
> (*Song 42,* Waley's translation No. 22)

Besides its many delightful love songs and impressive tableaux of the rural scenery and country life, the *Shih Ching* also contains many important social documents which are at the same time excellent folk poems. The compilation of the anthology took place, it must be recalled, during a period of cultural change and social upheaval, and it is only natural that the voices of protest, the wails of despair, and the lamentations over what could not be helped were faithfully recorded in the popular airs.

Dissatisfaction with misrule and cursing of the powers that were, were frequent themes. "Big Rats" is a good example:

> Big Rats, Big Rats,
> Don't eat my millet!
> Three years I have spent with you
> None of you cared to look after me.
> Now I shall leave you
> To go to the happy land.
> Happy land, happy land!
> There I shall find my abode.
>
> Big Rats, Big Rats,
> Don't eat my wheat!
> Three years I have spent with you
> None would be good to me.
> Resolutely I shall leave you
> To go to the happy country
> Happy country, happy country!
> There I shall get my due.
>
> Big Rats, Big Rats,
> Don't eat my cereal-sprouts!
> Three years I have spent with you
> None would reward me
> Resolutely I shall leave you
> To go to the happy state,
> Happy state, happy state
> Where none will wail and groan.

(*Song 113,* adapted from Waley's translation No. 276)

Many songs refer to the great lords with considerable sarcasm, like the following stanza:

> Kam, Kam, the tan tree is being cut
> And laid on the river bank.
> Oh how the waters are flowing, clear and rippling!
> Neither sowing nor reaping,
> How did one get three hundred stack-yards of cereals?
> Neither chasing nor hunting,
> How did one see your hall adorned with hanging badgers?
> Oh, those gentlemen!
> They never eat the bread of idleness!

(*Song 112,* adapted from Waley's translation No. 259)

The futility of protests and sarcasm easily gave rise to fatalism:

> I go out at the North Gate
> With my heart full of sorrow.
> Straitened am I and poor,
> And who cares for my distress?
> So be it!
> Heaven has done it:
> Wherefore should I complain?
>
> (*Song 40*, Hu Shih's translation)

And pessimism would occasionally take an epicurean turn and transform itself into a spirit of decadence.

> Mountains have their thorn-elms
> And swamps their white elms.
> You have fine robes;
> But you don't wear them.
>
> You have carriages and horses;
> But you don't drive and ride them.
> The moment you are dead,
> Others will enjoy them!
>
> (*Song 115*, adapted from Hu Shih's translation)

It was these 305 poems—once actually songs sung to the accompaniment of music, sometimes elaborate and sometimes simple—that make up this collection which have been regarded for over two thousand years as the highest models of poetic composition.

There is no question that the collection is an important and valuable monument, capable of exerting an immense influence upon the poetry of subsequent ages. This influence, however, was not the kind that should be normally expected, for the poems were generally exalted simply as lessons in moral edification.

Its purely literary influence was felt in three ways. In the first place, the four-syllable-line poem was to persist as a cherished form, especially in religious and didactic poetry. It was only in the hands of a few exceptional talents that the *Shih Ching* form was successfully employed in lyrical pieces. It is conceivable that the evenness of the four-word line would easily produce a stilted rhythm, comparable to steady 4/4 time in music. This situation is especially noticeable in the case of poems to be recited without the advantage of musical accompaniment and the rhythmical movements of the dance.

Second, the *Shih Ching's* technique of artistic and emotional restraint—the esthetic counterpart of kindliness and reciprocity in the moral realm—was an ideal long cherished, if not often practiced, by later poets. This so-called perennial "lesson of the classic of poetry" was most often summed up in four words: mellowness and softness; empathy and readiness to forgive. In other words, "good poetry was never intemperate, flamboyant, excessive, or exhaustive."

In the third place, the *Book of Songs* continued for centuries to set a pattern for what might be regarded as orthodox poetic diction and imagery. From 136 B.C., when doctoral chairs were founded by the Empire for authoritive interpretation of the Five [Confucian] Classics, down to literally yesterday, nearly all versifiers—and in fact all students with three years of schooling—were taught to commit to memory all the 305 songs. It was no wonder, therefore, that the words and phrases of these ancient songs became permanent assets in the vocabulary of the learned and that echoes of the *Shih Ching* reverberated in Chinese poetry and even in prose for over two thousand years.

CHAPTER 3

The Confucian Analects
and the Book of Lao-tzŭ

THE *Book of Songs,* as we have seen, contains many omens of the decline of the Chou house after the reign of the third king, so that the so-called Age of the Poets was really an era of rapid social and cultural change and disintegration.

The constant wars of conquest and annexation did not take place only among the full-fledged feudal states, nor was China in those days peopled by the Chinese alone. In the North China plains were numberless non-Chinese tribal units living in rather close juxtaposition with the Chinese communities. Racial and cultural differences, in these instances, increased mutual dislike and suspicion, and intensified the struggle for power and dominance. As a result, by a slow process, these non-Chinese elements in the Central States were finally absorbed and culturally assimilated.

The various non-Chinese and semi-Chinese states bordering on China were destined, however, to play a more fortunate role. Situated on the periphery of the Chinese cultural orbit, they had little need to worry about threats coming from the rear and could therefore afford to focus their attention on the Central States (sometimes referred to in English as the Middle Kingdom) and await their opportunities to enter the arena to bid for power. Besides encroaching upon the lesser Chinese states, they could increase their prestige and overcome racial enmity by denying their non-Chinese origin and claiming descent from one legendary Chinese king or another. They vied with the Central States not only in building up military and economic power but also in diffusing China's cultural usages and traditions, and, above all, by gradually adopting the Chinese language, both spoken and written.

To add further confusion to the Chou world, and to accelerate the decline of the dynasty, the Hsien-yün people (later on known as Hsiung-Nu, and usually identified as Huns), who had harassed the Chinese from time to time for centuries, were more daring and destructive in their periodic raids. In 771 B.C. they climaxed their devastative invasions with the sack of the Chou capital and the murder of King Yu, thus ending the following year the span of the Western Chou Period. The capital was moved eastward to Loyang by the murdered king's son and successor, and the Eastern Chou Period began.

Chinese society was shaken to its very foundations, for, accompanying these political crises, the rise and fall of feudal states, social changes were also rapid and numerous. The loss of life, property, and social station became something of daily occurrence. Men's minds were so upset and their souls so stirred that ancient religious teachings ceased to give consolation and to explain away the causes of the evils and tragedies of life. In the sorrowful strains of many a singer it was evident that people began to be skeptical about even the basic kindness and righteousness of heaven. One poet gave vent to his skepticism thus:

> I look up to great Heaven,
> But it shows no kindness.
> It has long disquieted us,
> And now great calamities befall us.
>
> The people are now in peril,
> In vain they look to Heaven;
> All is dark and dumb.
> Let its determination be fixed
> And there is none whom it will not overcome.
> There is the great God—
> Does he hate anyone?

While such complaining was going on, some poets began to sense the meaninglessness of life. One of them sang:

> When I was young,
> Peacefully did time pass.
> But since my youthful days,
> All these evils have befallen me.
> I would I might sleep, and never wake again.

And another lamented:

> Ah! Had I known it would be thus with me,
> I had better not have been born.

This mood of utter despair oftentimes was expressed in the form of a question:

> Oh Thou distant and azure Heaven!
> When shall all this end?

(Hu Shih's translation)

Was this the rhetorical question of a disillusioned poet, or the persistent query of a budding philosopher? Frankly, we do not know, as such a line of demarcation is hard to draw. We do know, however, that soon after the political catastrophe of 771 B.C. philosophical schools began to rise in China, and that all the early philosophers were to deal with the problems of their age. In a sense, China's adversity was the generator of its philosophy.

This "adversity" may be described in a summary manner as the complete disintegration of the feudal social structure, with all its taboos and regulations, its religious and political dogmas, its insistence on the necessity of a hierarchic society and the basic principle of subordination in human relationships. In a word, this adversity was the sum total of myriad changes making up the greatest social debacle that China had gone through since the dawn of history. This sudden breakdown of the conventional pattern created confusion and chaos of course, but at the same time it was, in its more healthy aspects, also a liberation.

Our primary concern here, however, is not to trace the development of philosophical schools or to analyze the theories of the different philosophical systems arising from the disintegration of feudal society, but rather to place the writings of these philosophers in their proper perspective in the development of Chinese literature. We are to study the manner rather than the matter of the writings of the philosophers, and their influence upon Chinese letters rather than upon the evolution of ideas. This distinction between letters and philosophy in ancient China, however, should not be pursued too far, for as in early society everywhere, the literate man in China was also a general practitioner of the arts of peace, and, in many instances, he was the poet and musician, physician and astronomer, philosopher and magician, and historian and civil service expert all rolled into one.

The intellectual phase of this liberative process was to crystallize into what might be called the first stage of Chinese philosophy. Among the people who were unconventional enough to question the validity of traditions and accepted beliefs, there were a few who had rethought with thoroughness the problems of the meanings of life and the universe. These men came to be known as "philosophers," and among them, two were especially remembered by posterity: Lao-tzŭ and Confucius.

Of Lao-tzŭ's life, much has been written but little is known. According to his first biographer, Ssŭ-ma Ch'ien, who lived four centuries later, he was born in the south, possibly in the semi-Chinese state of Ch'u, bore the family name of Li, and was for a time the keeper of the Royal Archives in the Eastern Chou capital. It is also recorded that sometime between 518 and 511 B.C., Confucius met his senior contemporary. Lao-tzŭ was born about 570 B.C., but of his death there is no reliable record.

This paucity of details provided ample room for the speculation and imagination of later writers, especially hagiographers, in their attempts to embellish the life of the early philosopher with the supernatural and the miraculous. More important, this paucity of data has aroused the suspicion of modern critics as to the historicity of Lao-tzŭ, and the date and authenticity of the book bearing his name. Many scholars of our day are of the opinion that the philosopher Lao-tzŭ was not born until the fourth century before Christ, that the book attributed to him was not written until a century later, and that consequently there might have been no connection between the man and the book. While these contentions contain many points extremely interesting even to the literary historians, they are and will remain mere hypotheses until further discoveries of important ancient documents furnish us with a new basis for revaluation, and they do not warrant a revision of the chronological sequence we have been using.

As Keeper of the Royal Archives, Lao-tzŭ was easily the most learned man of his age, well versed in both the niceties of past and current rituals and the lore of history. It was probably this saturation in formal learning that had led him to go beyond data and minutiae in search of basic values and meanings, and finally to a revolt against and repudiation of the traditional and cultural heritage with all its ramifications. He rejected the teachings of ancient religion about a just and knowing heaven and substituted for it the nonanthropomorphic concept of a naturalistic universe. He deplored the ideals of good, positive, even sage government and glorified the type of political ordering which approached anarchy by practicing nondoing. He denounced the arts, including music, as well as the degenerative effect of learning and knowledge, and advocated the desirability of returning to the nameless simplicity of nature. He spoke against even the cardinal virtues treasured for generations, such as benevolence and righteousness, filial piety, and kindheartedness, as signs of a corrupt age in which distinctions and contrasts had become sharp and clear. On the positive side, he upheld Tao as the nonpersonal and yet universal and everlasting principle, the prime factor of being and nonbeing, accomplishing everything by doing nothing. In ethics, he taught as the *summum bonum:* nonknowledge, nondesire, nonaction, nonstriving; in a word, identification with nature.

This sketchy summary—sketchy because the main topic of our inquiry here is not philosophy—is based on the *Book of Lao-tzŭ*, popularly known in subsequent times as *Tao Tê Ching* or the *Canon of the Way and of Virtue* (a title translated by Arthur Waley as *The Way and Its Power*). When, how, and by whom this book was written and later on transmitted, we do not know. We do know, however, one central fact, and that is, Lao-tzŭ himself did not write it, despite the often repeated legend that he did it against his own volition when he wanted badly to leave China, and the chief guard of the Western Pass would not let him go unless he wrote a book for the guard's edification.

Lao-tzŭ probably did not write any book. On the other hand, we are not justified in dissociating the *Book of Lao-tzŭ* completely from the philosopher simply on the ground that the latter did not write it with his own hand, or in dismissing the significance of the book by labeling it a forthright literary forgery. In studying Chinese literature of this period, we must adapt our concepts of authorship and authenticity to the peculiar circumstances under which books came to be made. Private ownership of a literary composition was something unheard of, and exclusive identification of a person as an actual author of a document or a poem was proffered and accepted only in the loose sense that he had been responsible for originating the idea rather than for the actual labor of literary creation.

Thus the *Book of Lao-tzŭ*, like all similar literary output of that age, began as a random collection of the philosopher's memorable sayings made by some of his immediate followers. These followers, as they met together from time to time, would compare notes with one another, and, as a result, the total collection of sayings grew gradually in number of entries. While this process of occasional "redaction" was at work, nothing ensued in the nature of a "definitive" edition until a much later date, often a few generations, if not centuries, after the passing of the master. As the making of records and copies was both cumbersome and expensive, economy exerted a notable influence upon the formation of literary style. Thus, in recording events and summarizing discussions, succinctness and clarity were always aimed at. This was necessarily the case, for, though considerably simpler than inscribing on bronze, writing was ordinarily done with brushes dipped in lacquer on sizable boards and bamboo slips especially prepared, and binding meant the stringing of these "pages" together with leather straps. Hence, detailed narratives and lengthy expositions were out of the question. Recordings of a brilliant philosophical discourse would take the form of a few disconnected aphorisms, often completely isolated from the context. And, as punctuation was not used, verse form with end-rhymes was sometimes used to avoid misunderstanding through mispunctuation, as well as to aid memorizing and oral transmission.

This loose stringing together of isolated sentences and paragraphs and the long period during which they were circulated as "floating literature" invited interpolations. In most instances, however, there was little, if any, conscious tampering with the text as we understand the term today, or any intentional forgery on anyone's part. An explanatory passage thrown in by a reverent expositor, a restatement by a disciple to insure greater clarity, an occasional remark by way of reaction to the master's cryptic words: these, when recorded, would by mistake find their way into the records and be confused with the original sayings. Inasmuch as they were echoes of, and elucidations on, the same basic ideas held in common by the school, they were not exactly spurious. To sum up, the authorship of the *Book of Lao-tzŭ* belonged to the philosopher Lao-tzŭ with the assistance of his disciples and their own followers, with the latter doing and continuing the writing for generations.

Despite the many uncertainties concerning the history of the text, the possibilities of interpolations, the textual corruptions, and the interference of later editors in devising book and chapter divisions, the significance of the *Book of Lao-tzŭ* is almost as great in the development of Chinese literature as it is in the evolution of ideas. For generations, the five thousand words of this little book continued to exert their influence on thinkers, literary men, and artists alike. While it is idle to extol its literary merits as though they could be extracted in pure forms, unalloyed with philosophical wisdom, it is possible to underscore certain ways in which the book has appealed to people in search of good literature.

In the first place, the sayings of Lao-tzŭ have won acclaim for their originality and their challenging fortitude. Whether or not the reader is in agreement with the ideas, he must admire the honesty and courage with which the ideas were expressed. When the arts were attacked, for example, there was no holding back:

> The five colours blind the eye.
> The five tones deafen the ear.
> The five flavors cloy the palate.
> Racing and hunting madden the mind.
> Rare goods tempt men to do wrong.

> (Chapter 12, John C. H. Wu's translation)

It was a direct result of this unique vision and fearless honesty rather than of a mere fondness for rhetorical effect that there were the numerous seeming paradoxes in his pages:

> The greatest perfection seems imperfect,
> And yet its use is inexhaustible.
> The greatest fullness seems empty,
> And yet its use is endless.
>
> The greatest straightness looks like curve.
> The greatest skill seems like clumsiness.
> The greatest eloquence sounds like stuttering.
>
> (Chapter 45, John C. H. Wu's translation)

> When the Great Tao was abandoned,
> There appeared Sympathy and Duty.
> When intelligence and wit arose,
> There appeared great hypocrites.
> When the six relations lost their harmony,
> There appeared filial piety and paternal kindness.
> When darkness and disorder began to reign in a kingdom,
> There appeared the loyalists.
>
> (Chapter 18, John C. H. Wu's translation)

The second characteristic of the *Book of Lao-tzŭ* which appeals to the Chinese litterateurs of later ages is its simplicity, or, to use a metaphor from the book itself, that state which resembles an uncarved block of wood. This seeming unconcern with literary craftsmanship is largely due to the almost childlike wonderment felt in the philosopher as he succeeded in his unique manner in probing into the mystery of the Great Way. Like many other major prophets in the history of ideas, he was often so overpowered by the magnitude of his ideas that he did not have a vocabulary adequate to express them. The result was a seeming clumsiness, an earnest groping for words and phrases, an open-minded experiment with modes of expression. Unmistakable was his hesitancy in using even the very term *Tao:*

> There was Something undefined and yet complete in itself,
> Born before the Heaven-and-Earth.
> Silent and boundless,
> Independent and changeless,
> Moving through immensity tirelessly,
> It may be regarded as the Mother of the world.
> I do not know its name;
> I style it "Tao."
> And, in absence of a better word, call it "The Great."
>
> (Chapter 25, John C. H. Wu's translation)

In order further to suggest what Tao—the Way—was like, the philosopher thought of something abstract and yet conprehensible: *Wu*, or nonbeing:

> Thirty spokes share the same hub.
> Where there is "nothing,"
> Lies the usability of the carriage.
> Fashion clay into a vessel.
> Where there is "nothing,"
> Lies the usability of the vessel.
>
> Cut out door and windows to make a house.
> Where there is "nothing,"
> Lies the usability of the house.
> Thus it is, while it is advantageous to have something there,
> It is useful to have "nothing" there.
>
> (Chapter 11)

Not yet fully sure of the aptness of the analogy, the author would try to elucidate the attributes of the Tao by likening it now to a valley and now to water. This lack of certainty and artistry, however, is apparent rather than real. The five-thousand-word treatise in its first recorded form was the result of a long process of recasting and tempering, the residue of considered distillation. If there are obscure passages defying commentators and translators, like so many pieces of unsplittable rock, those same passages were once clear reminders of mystical deliberations which the initiate would patiently explain to the novices.

In the third place, the *Book of Lao-tzŭ* is an important monument in Chinese literature because, besides being a philosophical classic, it is also a book of poetry. As poetry, it was committed to memory. As poetry, it has the unique feature among early Chinese writings of containing no proper noun, biographical or geographical, real or imaginary. As poetry, it more often communicates its messages by suggestions and implications than by exposition:

> Of old those who knew the art of commanding an army,
> Were subtle and flexible, profound and comprehensive,
> Their minds are too deep to be fathomed.
>
> Because they are unfathomable,
> One can only describe them vaguely by their appearance.
> Hesitant like one wading a stream in winter;
> Timid like one afraid of his neighbors on all sides;
> Cautious and courteous like a guest;
> Yielding like ice on the point of melting;
> Blank like an uncarved block;

Hollow like a cave;
Confused like a muddy pool;
And yet who else could quietly and gradually evolve
    from the muddy to the clear?
Who else could slowly but steadily move from the inert
    to the living?

(Chapter 15, John C. H. Wu's translation)

Likewise his picture of Utopia:

Let there be a small country with a tiny population
Where tools multiplying man's power tenfold and hundredfold
    would not be used;
Where the people would not take death lightly and migrate far.
Though there were carriages and vessels, none would ride them.
Though there were armor and weapons there would be no occasion
    to display them.
People would again tie knots on strings and use them.
People would enjoy their food,
Beautify their clothing,
Feel comfortable in their homes,
And happy in their customs.
People could see their neighboring countries
And hear each other's cocks crowing and dogs barking,
But would not, even till the end of their lives, visit back and forth.

(Chapter 80)

It is not difficult to appreciate that this poetic appeal to the simple and natural modes of life captured the imagination of men during each period of storm and stress in the long annals of the Chinese people.

Among the contemporaries of Lao-tzŭ, the greatest man indisputably was K'ung Ch'iu, whose honorific name, K'ung Fu-tzŭ in Chinese, has been Latinized in the Western world since the sixteenth century as Confucius (551-479 B.C.). Like Lao-tzŭ, he was a member of the small learned profession, the *ju,* and steeped in the cultural heritage of the past, especially in the technical details of *li,* the sum total of the ancient art of living. Like Lao-tzŭ, he was roused by the myriad changes taking place in that age, and made a sincere effort to think the basic problems through. Like Lao-tzŭ, he won a following to the way of life he had proposed, and, although he had not written a single line himself, had his sayings recorded and passed on as precious gifts to posterity. Again like Lao-tzŭ, though his teachings had been dressed up and enlarged upon endlessly, his original doctrines were so coherent, as a whole, that even after a lapse of more than two millenniums, it is still possible to place him in his proper historical perspective—even though scholarly criticism has not yet found the last word to say in sifting fact from fiction.

But, between the two great teachers there are also striking dissimilarities. If they have both exerted an incalculable influence upon the development of the artistic, literary, and philosophical patterns in China down to the middle of the twentieth century, they have stood for different, if not diametrically opposite, sets of ideals and aspirations. Lao-tzŭ was a rebel against China's ancient traditions, standing on the extreme left; his younger contemporary, Confucius (by nature something of a conservative, or a transmitter instead of an originator, as he himself had modestly put it), was more interested in searching for new implications and applications of old fundamental principles, and in discovering fresh meanings and directions for established usages. Thus, while a strict conformist to accepted religious rituals, he placed new emphasis upon their meanings rather than upon their minute details, and boldly stated that it was more urgent for man to learn to serve his fellow men than to serve the spirits, as it was more urgent for him to know about this life than the life hereafter. Similarly in politics, while deploring the political confusion of his age, he believed it not only possible but also immediately practical to restore order and good government through the rectification of names (through a serious semantic approach) and through men in all stations living in conformity with the ideals called for.

This positivism of his was expressed in favor of refinement and education. Unlike Lao-tzŭ, who had condemned all desire for progress, Confucius believed in the perfectibility of man through a tireless effort to raise himself above the plane of mere biological impulse and barbarity. Thus he firmly believed in education which should eventually erase not only existing class barriers, but also the differences separating barbarians from the refined members of the Central States.

It should be remembered that Confucius was no mere armchair philosopher. Scion of an old Shang-Yin aristocratic family in the state of Lu, the state representing cultural orthodoxy *par excellence,* he was not only a member of the *ju* group consisting of the practitioners of the arts of peace, but, reduced to relative poverty when young, also adept in menial tasks of various kinds. It was this general acquaintance with people of divergent backgrounds which gave his wisdom a comprehensive mellowness and urged him on to an active participation in political and social reform. Circumstances, however, were against him, and his public career both at home and abroad ended in comparative failure. His extensive travels to many of the Central States, on the other hand, gave him firsthand knowledge of the larger cultural circle outside of his native state and eventually raised him above the profession of which he had been a member.

Despite his many-sided gifts, and despite the mystical purposefulness read into his life by his followers and hagiographers of later ages, Confucius was above all an educator. Even during his travels in search of a public career to give effect to his political and social ideals, he never tired of discoursing with his disciples on the meaning of life and its many problems. According to one early tradition, as many as three thousand pupils had sat at his feet at one time or another, and among these, seventy-two were especially distinguished. Before this time, formal education was an inherent part of high social station in feudal society. The Chinese sage seems to have been the first one to disregard any social qualifications among his pupils and to accept a commoner who could offer only a few pieces of bacon by way of tuition just as readily as young aristocrats who could afford to pay much more.

With his following drawn from many social levels, backgrounds, and temperaments, the discussions were anything but dull, especially toward the end of the master's life. When he had become weary of politics and retired to his native district to devote himself to teaching on the Apricot Terrace, the gist of these informal discussions and conversations, as well as the sayings of the master himself, were carefully recorded. But as recording was still a complicated and expensive process, the notes taken were brief and concise, and often lifted out of their general context. These assembled notes were finally edited to form the *Lun Yü,* referred to in English as the *Analects.*

The *Analects* consists of twenty books or chapters, compiled and arranged without any obvious plan, possibly by more than one hand, as is suggested by a few duplications. Moreover, the many references to Confucius' disciples in honorific terms tend to indicate that some of the writing was not done until the generation of the disciples' followers, or roughly around 400 B.C. As the writing was not done continuously on one occasion, and as it was undertaken by more than one man, the style of the book is not uniform, although linguistically, it was written in the refined language as it had been used in the state of Lu. As a rule, the recorded material took the form of a dialogue. Whenever the questions addressed to the sage were of no special significance, or the occasions provoking his comments were occurrences well known to the listeners, these would be omitted, much to the bewilderment of later readers. A comment like "for a man to sacrifice to a spirit which does not belong to him is flattery," recorded without reference to the circumstances under which it was made, often makes us wonder what the full implication was. There were, on the other hand, many examples of fuller recording such as the following:

> Duke Ling of [the state of] Wei asked Confucius about tactics. Confucius replied, "I have heard all about sacrificial vessels, but I have not learned military matters." On this, he took his departure the next day.
>
> When he was in Ch'ên, their provisions were exhausted, and his followers became so ill [of hunger] that they were unable to rise. Tzŭ-lu, with evident dissatisfaction, asked, "Has the superior man likewise to endure want?" The Master said, "The superior man may indeed have to endure want, but the mean man, when he is in want, gives way to unbridled license."

(Legge's translation)

The last two statements, we should realize, could have been recorded without the advantage of the fuller context, like so many other entries in the book, which appear now like concise monologue jottings, but which in reality were the animated and memorable sayings made by the master in lively conversations. Not realizing the effect the scarcity of writing materials had upon the style of early writings, the occasional "imitators" of the *Analects* in later ages seem to have wasted their efforts in an unwarranted direction.

Generally speaking, there is a uniformity of style in the *Analects*. It can even be argued that this style was expressive of the personality of the Chinese sage himself by assuming that his sayings had been recorded verbatim. And yet the literary importance of the *Analects* is probably to be found in Confucius' critical comments on the *Book of Songs* and in the record of his observations on music and poetry in general. In his educational creed, music and poetry (especially that of the *Book of Songs*) played a vital role. He was fond of singing. He could discuss music as an expert. When he heard the musical masterpiece "Shao" while sojourning in the neighboring state of Ch'i, he was so overwhelmed by that esthetic experience that for three months he was unable to distinguish the taste of the meat he ate.

Although he was aware of the practical values of the study of poetry such as the enlargement of one's vocabulary and the refinement of one's speech habits as might befit the training of a diplomat, he was no mere utilitarian. Although he stressed the edifying function of poetry, he was no mere didactician. Addressing a number of disciples one day, he said, "Little ones, why do you not apply yourselves to the study of poetry? Poetry is capable of arousing your emotions, sharpening your powers of observation, making you sociable, and regulating your feelings of resentment." Here by poetry, Confucius meant chiefly the *Book of Songs,* which he read and appreciated as literature. There was a song known in his day but now excluded from the collection which ran:

> The flowers of the aspen-blossom,
> They flutter and they turn!
> How can it be I don't think of you?
> But your house is so far away!

On this the master's comment was, "It is just the want of thought. How can it be too far away for thought?"

The omission of this song from the *Book of Songs,* according to some exegetical writers on the Confucius classics, was due to Confucius' discernment in considering it bad poetry. As we have pointed out in a previous chapter, the controversy as to whether the sage had edited the *Book of Songs* is a complicated one which cannot be settled easily. On the other hand, there should not be any question about his great fondness for the anthology or about his great care in setting right the musical scores accompanying the more stately songs in the collection, for in his own words according to Legge's translation, "I returned from Wei to Lu, and then the music was reformed, and the pieces in the Royal Songs [*Ya*] and Praise Songs [*Sung*] all found their proper places." In this work the master should have achieved outstanding success, for he was a devoted student of music and could play at least two musical instruments.

These bits of information on the Confucian attitude toward and handling of music and poetry are perhaps of even greater significance to the literary historian than the twenty chapters of the *Analects* themselves, which are, in comparison with the *Book of Lao-tzŭ,* much more prosaic and disjointed. Still, because of special circumstances, to be made clear in later chapters, the so-called Confucian classics were to exercise an influence on Chinese literature entirely incommensurate with their inherent merits, because they were to be recognized as units of the literary orthodoxy.

In this connection, let us consider one other "classic" which for ages was regarded as having been edited by Confucius' own hand, the *Spring and Autumn Annals,* known in Chinese as the *Ch'un Ch'iu.* In the light of Confucius' saying that he was rather a transmitter than a creator, and Mencius' comment that insubordinate ministers and rebellious sons trembled with fear when Confucius "wrote" the *Spring and Autumn* annals, it is possible that the sage had something to do with the annals, though the exact nature of his editing cannot now be precisely determined.

The historical significance of the *Ch'un Ch'iu* has been great, for the whole period of Chinese history from 722 to 481 B.C. has derived its name from this book of *Annals*, and all subsequent writings of a similar arrangement are said to be continuations of this historiographical tradition. Likewise, the doctrinal significance of the work has been great. For centuries it has been accepted by scholars in China as a "canon" in which the basis of Confucius' moral evaluation of political events and public personages has been outlined, and in which the Confucian principle of the "rectification of names" has been fully exemplified. As a matter of fact, however, the *Ch'un Ch'iu* was only one of at least three such annals kept by the feudal courts of that time, with but minor variations in style and content, excepting for greater details in recording events happening in the state in which the entries were made and preserved. The acquirement of pre-eminence by the *Ch'un Ch'iu* was probably due to multiple circumstances.

First, the rival annals of the two other feudal states were lost at an early date. Second, its place of origin was the feudal state of Lu, the center of cultural refinement and learning and Confucius' own birthplace. Third, Mencius, coming 150 years after Confucius, and the great expositor of the Confucian school, attached great importance to the book, as we have noted. Fourth, three separate "commentaries" were written on it to give greater details of the events and to elucidate the meaning of the recording.

Leaving the commentaries to a later chapter and examining the *Ch'un Ch'iu* itself as pure literature, we find it interesting only as a historical landmark, as the first full-length example of recording, in the most concise manner, the gist of happenings from year to year. Entries for the year 722 B.C., the first year covered by the *Annals*, follow:

Duke Yin

1. [It was his] first year, the spring, the king's first month.
2. In the third month, the duke and Yi-fu of Ch'u made a covenant in Mieh.
3. In summer in the fifth month, the Earl of Chêng overcame Tuan in Yen.
4. In autumn, in the seventh month, the king [by] Heaven's [grace] sent the [sub-] administrator Hsüan with a present of [two] carriages and their horses for the funerals of Duke Hui and [his wife] Chung Tzŭ.
5. In the ninth month, [the duke] and an officer of Sung made a covenant in Su.
6. In winter, in the twelfth month, the Earl of Ts'ai came [to Lu].
7. Kung-tzŭ Yi-ssŭ died.

Disjointed sentences like these run through the whole of the *Ch'un Ch'iu* classic, reminding the reader of headings of the modern daily newspaper rather than serious historical writing. In fact, an unconventional Chinese scholar-statesman of the eleventh century actually referred to this classic disparagingly as "shredded fragments of a court gazette." Though this low estimate of the literary value of the work was not entirely incorrect, the critic had failed to note the historical circumstances which had called for such cryptic entries. In the period of the annals, literary style was conditioned by the scarcity and high cost of writing materials, and brevity was not only a virtue but also a necessity. Even more so than in the case of the sayings in the Confucian *Analects*, these *Ch'un Ch'iu* records of events were entered without the luxury of contexts.

However subjectively the merits and demerits of this curious work might have been assessed by later critics, the *Ch'un Ch'iu* was destined to exert an immense influence upon later writers. Aside from the purported ethical meanings of its contents, it obviously came to be accepted as the norm for compiling official annals for individual states. Once this technique was accepted as standard, it had the tendency of being followed blindly by official historians and imitated as a matter of course without reference to changes in material and social environment. In other words, despite noticeable progress in prose development, and despite the increasing facility in obtaining writing materials, the concise recording of events, irrespective of context, and the deliberate refusal to incorporate details of causal relationships in the composition of a connected narrative continued to be the prevailing style for many writers.

CHAPTER 4

The Ch'u Elegies

THE general formula of regional rivalry in culture and politics in ancient China was one of opposition between east and west. Beginning with the dawn of China's recorded history and lasting for almost two thousand years, this east-west opposition gradually gave way to another regional competition—that between north and south —which according to many students, has left an impression on art and literature, religion, and philosophy down to our own day.

The southward expansion of China from the Yellow River area into the regions of the Yangtze may be traced at least as far back as the ninth century before Christ. Lying south of the two royal domains of Kaoching and Loyang, there was the feudal territory of Nan (literally "south") and beyond that the nebulous state of Ch'u where the people and culture contained many non-Chinese elements, although most of its leaders were descended from immigrants from the Shang-Yin areas.

The Nan territory, at first created as a sort of buffer area between the Middle Kingdom and the habitats of non-Chinese groups further to the south, became not only the region to which Chou culture was transplanted, but also the sanctuary into which many dynastic records and national treasurers of the Chou house were dispatched at the time of the alien invasion of the Western metropolis, Kaoching, in 771 B.C.

It was in this area, the southern fringe of the Middle Kingdom, that local poetry sung to the accompaniment of music was developed to new heights during the ninth and eighth centuries before Christ. Not only were the two sections devoted to Nan (one consisting of songs originating from the royal domain there and the other of those originating from feudal states) assigned priority when the anthology *Shih Ching* was compiled, but Confucius himself, the literary critic, attached special importance to those southern songs. He remarked that "the man who has not studied the Chou-nan and Chao-nan [sections of the *Book of Songs*] is one who stands with his face right against a wall."

The attractiveness of these southern songs in the *Shih Ching* may have been due to several possible factors. One of these, about which we know little, was its elegant music, soft in tune and slow in tempo. A clear-cut comparison is impossible since the musical scores for the songs, as we have noted before, were lost long ago. Another factor was the reflection of the standards of refinement in the songs. The third factor is the fact that, considered purely as literature, the Nan songs exhibited almost without exception a considerable amount of artistic restraint and emotional self-control. This is noticeable in the love songs. To many Chinese critics the Nan song that is exceptional is the following:

> In the wilds there is a dead doe;
> With white rushes we cover her.
> There was a lady longing for the spring;
> A fair knight seduced her.
>
> In the wood there is a clump of oaks
> And in the wilds a dead deer
> With white rushes well-bound;
> There was a lady fair as jade.
>
> "Heigh, not so hasty, not so rough
> Heigh, do not touch my handkerchief.
> Take care, or the dog will bark."
>
> (*Song 23*, Waley's translation No. 63)

Aside from the above quoted, all other love songs show a noticeable measure of restraint; for example, the famous first song of the Chou Nan group:

> "Fair, fair" cry the ospreys
> On the island in the river.
> Lovely is this noble lady,
> Fit bride for our lord.
>
> In patches grows the water mallow;
> To left and right one must seek it.
> Shy was this noble lady;
> Day and night he sought her.
>
> Sought her and could not get her;
> Day and night he grieved.
> Long thoughts, oh long unhappy thoughts,
> Now on his back, now tossing on to his side.
>
> In patches grows the water mallow;
> To left and right one must gather it.
> Shy is this noble lady;
> With great zithern and little we hearten her.

In patches grows the water mallow;
To left and right one must choose it.
Shy is this noble lady;
With songs and drums we will gladden her.

(*Song 1*, Waley's translation No. 87)

In about 700 B.C. the Nan area, including both the royal domain and the feudal states, were conquered and absorbed by the rapidly expanding state of Ch'u, situated on the middle reaches of the Yangtze, at the confluence of the Han River, from which the name of the present-day city of Hankow is derived. In comparison with the lands watered by the Yellow River and its tributaries, Ch'u had a much milder climate, a more luxuriant vegetation, and a much more varied and picturesque landscape. Its human scene, likewise, had characteristics of its own. Relatively free from the catastrophes of flood and drought, blessed with a fertile soil stretching far into the south and east, and by a relatively sparse population, the people of Ch'u enjoyed a degree of economic security unknown to the inhabitants of the northern climes. Moreover, on account of its geographic situation it had little fear of being invaded. In fact its role for centuries had been that of the territorial expansionist rather than the victim. This feeling of security, political and economic, ensured the Ch'u people a life of relaxation and leisureliness, in striking contrast to the tension and seriousness felt by the people of the Middle Kingdom.

This difference in temperament and attitude was clearly reflected in its literature, and especially in its mythology. The founder of the Ch'u royal house was not the hard-toiling god of agriculture of the Chou clan, but the hovering, dazzling, ethereal god of fire. The river deity of the southerners' imagination was not a genius of hydraulic engineering controlling and bringing to an end the Great Deluge, but a young pretty maiden with charming glances and enchanting smiles, though never a sinister siren like Lorelei. In Ch'u mythology, one looks in vain for a counterpart to the Chou god of metal and punishment, possessed of a human face, tiger paws, white fur all over the body and battle ax in hand, but finds a god or goddess of fate, attired in lotus leaves, girded with an orchid belt, sheltered under a canopy of peacock plumes, and flanked by banners of kingfisher feathers. To these gods and goddesses were offered as sacrifice, not the whole roasts of beef or pork, mutton or venison, but clusters of varieties of orchids, cassia wine, and pepper broth. The celebrants at religious services were not hoary and learned recorder-priests, but gaily-attired and nimble religious danseuses called *Wu*.

In one particular respect, however, the Ch'u people were drawn toward the cultural orbit of the Middle Kingdom with which they were finally to be completely identified. The Ch'u speech, of which we know but little on account of the imperfect records, seemed to be a dialect (if not a separate spoken tongue) far removed from the standard Chinese of the north. As late as the fourth century before Christ even the educated leaders of the Ch'u people were still noted for their provincial pronunciation, and often contemptuously described as "shrike-tongued" barbarians. It should not be inferred, however, that when it came to writing, a different system had ever been used or attempted, for we have a bronze bell cast by the Ch'u people during the reign of the Chou king, Hsüan (827-782 B.C.), which bears a lengthy inscription in characters in complete conformity with the style current at Kaoching, the Chou capital. This tends to show that the same written medium had long been in use in the state of Ch'u and that literary models of the north had been followed by the southerners.

Probably much older than their use of Chinese characters was their tradition of song and poetry. Despite their proximity to the Nan area, the Ch'u bards did not seem to have been greatly influenced by the style of the *Shih Ching*, which by comparison was conservative and frigid. For the circumstances were that the northern models were imitated for a while and then abandoned to give room to the revival of early Ch'u rhythmic patterns.

The earliest specimen of song that showed an unmistakable Ch'u flavor and rhythm was a curious bit of translation. In the middle of the sixth century before Christ, so the record goes, a Ch'u nobleman, brother of the king, was enjoying himself on his pleasure barge sailing in midstream. Enchanted by the beautiful music being played, an oarswoman from the state of Yüeh (east of Ch'u) broke out in a native Yüeh song consisting of thirty-one syllables which were totally unintelligible to the party. Whereupon the nobleman asked for an interpreter who gave this translation.

> What an evening this is,
> To sail down the river past the Isle!
> What a day this has been
> To be with the Prince on the same barge!
> Bashful and enchanted,
> I am not even ashamed of my own immodesty.
> The unending bittersweet of knowing you, Oh Prince.
> Oh, how my heart glows unceasingly!
> Hills have trees and trees have branches,
> But you know not, Oh Prince, how much I love you.

A little later, when Confucius was traveling on a highway, an unconventional man from Ch'u passed the sage, singing:

> O phoenix! O phoenix!
> How thy virtue has declined!
> What is gone warrants no reproof:
> What is coming may yet be mended!

The first group of Ch'u songs after these miscellaneous strains was the *Chiu Ko* (*Nine Songs*), actually consisting of eleven pieces, the *nine* being used in a figurative rather than a mathematical sense, to mean "many." They were current and recorded in about the fifth century before Christ when, after the extensive use of iron in warfare and agriculture, the Ch'u state felt proud of its new military and economic ascendancy. These songs, sometimes attributed to Ch'ü Yüan on rather insufficient grounds, were popular religious songs sung to various local deities such as the mountain spirit, the goddesses of the river Hsiang, and nameless national martyrs.

In prosody and in spirit, these songs set the pattern of the Ch'u poetry, sometimes described in English as the Ch'u elegies. The songs, as well as the lines of which they are composed, are irregular in length. Each line freely works out its own rhythm, sometimes almost as freely as prose, and is punctuated in the middle by an emotional syllable (called by grammarians a particle), *yiei,* which in this particular case plays the definite role of the caesura. The rhyming scheme is freely changed even within a single poem, although as a rule end-rhymes are used as in the *Shih Ching,* with "even" tones and "deflected" tones clearly differentiated. (Words intonated at the highest and lowest pitches of the musical scale, subsequently labeled "even" tones, are regarded as forming one cluster for end-rhyming purposes and are kept separate from those of intermediate pitches, or "inflected" tones. Although when spelled out in letters of a Western alphabet the two clusters look rhymable, they are segregated in Chinese usage.) The general rhythmic effect of the elegies was to suggest a slow-moving, languishing incantation, noticeably different from the crisp regularity of northern poetry.

The décor and substance of the *Chiu Ko* also reveal a different geographical and cultural background. The myths and legends, the flora and fauna, the gods and goddesses, all suggested a southern fragrance.

The rise and continuation of this ancient poetry of the south as a literary type, the *Ch'u tzŭ,* was made possible by a single creative genius who gave it special distinction and permanence. In fact, Ch'ü Yüan (343?-290? B.C.) was the first distinguished man of letters in

China's long annals. To be sure, there had been many writers before his time, but these had written mainly as philosophers or historians, and it was Ch'ü Yüan who broke through the long twilight of anonymous or collective authorship to become China's first poet.

Like many of his contemporaries, Ch'ü Yüan lived an eventful life details of which were only very imperfectly recorded. In fact, so many inconsistencies and discrepancies crept into his first biography, written well over a century after his death, that some modern critics have doubted even his historicity. While legendary accretions are many, a few facts in the life of Ch'ü Yüan seem to be clearly separable from fiction.

The poet was born about 343 B.C., of aristocratic parents in one of the prominent families related to the royal house of Ch'u—probably a collateral branch. Like other male members of the aristocracy Ch'ü Yüan was given a nobleman's education, including the formal learning of the Middle Kingdom which the Ch'u state was rapidly absorbing. In 319 B.C., upon the completion of his schooling, he was appointed Left Counselor, a position second in importance only to that of prime minister. He had held the office for five years and discharged his duties well both at home and abroad when he was dismissed due to the sabotage of unscrupulous political rivals. What was a political loss to the state of Ch'u proved a permanent asset to Chinese literature, for it was probably in that year, 319 B.C., that the disappointed statesman turned poet and wrote his masterpiece, "Li Sao," a title usually translated "Fallen into Sorrow."

Though out of office, he continued to watch closely over the foreign policy of his native state. The "international" situation in China in those days was relatively simple. The Chou Dynasty was continuing its shadowy existence only in name with its royal domains and power diminished beyond recognition. Of the so-called "warring states" there were only seven, and of these seven, only three were seriously to be reckoned with: (1) Ch'i, on the seacoast in the east; (2) Ch'u, spreading itself along the Yangtze in the south; and (3) Ch'in, expanding in territory, power, and wealth in the northwest.

Ch'in's rise to power had been spectacular, especially from 359 B.C. on, with the rapid introduction of a series of reform measures. In the other six contending states, statesmen and diplomats were racking their brains as to what to do about the rapidly rising power of Ch'in. Among them there grew up two schools of international strategy, one advocating the formula of "collective security," insisting on a general alliance of the six states against Ch'in; and the other advocating an appeasement policy in order to share a few crumbs of war booty either in the form of loot or territorial aggrandizement. For Ch'u, the dilemma was neatly reduced to a choice between allying itself with Ch'i against Ch'in and the reversal of such a policy. As neither prospective ally was to be fully trusted, each path seemed thorny and the two camps of political opinion gave rise to painful dissension and a constant change of policy which in the end weakened and wrecked the Ch'u state.

By temperament and training, Ch'ü Yüan had early associated himself with the anti-Ch'in party and became its most eloquent and vehement spokesman, thus making many enemies at home and in Ch'in, the tiger-and-wolf state. These enemies persuaded the Ch'u king to send him into exile in 313 B.C. to clear the deck for pro-Ch'in negotiations.

Complex politico-military events followed in rapid succession, and finally, on the fall of a "vertical" anti-Ch'in alliance, Ch'ü Yüan tasted again the bitterness of exile. From this he was destined never again to return home. For several years (296-290? B.C.) he roamed from place to place writing poems, of which the exact number has not been determined. According to a long-cherished tradition, he eventually drowned himself in the Milo River.

This brief review will throw some light on the immediate environment of the first known poet of China, from which he learned the uncertainty and variability of life. More than any of his contemporaries he was a bundle of contradictions, and failed to resolve the resulting emotional conflicts within him. A warm lover of life—of the here and now—he also detested its sordidness; endowed with a piercing intellect and cool analytical, philosophical faculties, he also had an intense emotional fire; unwilling to lose himself in identity with his worldly associates, he lacked the power and authority to hold them in check. Though these conflicts led him to self-destruction, they also made him a great poet.

The exact amount of Ch'ü Yüan's literary bequest to posterity is a controversy that has continued for almost two thousand years. The first bibliography mentioning his poetry (the *Han Dynasty History* or *Han Shu,* completed in A.D. 82) ascribed twenty-five pieces to him without enumerating their titles. From that time on, pronouncements as to authenticity have varied from age to age and no two critics have reached complete agreement.

The one poem with which Ch'ü Yüan has been accredited even by the most skeptical is, as has been noted before, "Li Sao" or "Fallen into Sorrow" (also merely "Sorrow"), the longest of the whole group. Though short as compared with many ancient poems of other nations, it exceeds in length all other pieces written in China up to that time.

The poem opens with a factual recital of the poet's ancestry and parentage, his date of birth and "christening," and his intense efforts to cultivate himself morally, intellectually, and esthetically. The poet then depicts his emotional response to the rapid lapse of time, the fleeting passage of sun and moon, and the alternation of spring and autumn, hence his desire to achieve merit and distinction before the onslaught of old age. Upholding the examples of three legendary sacred personages and showing the practicality of the ways of the sage-emperors Yao and Shun, he tries to lead King Huai to the royal road of enlightened government. The king, however, is surrounded by seekers of office and pleasure, and "branches at midway." In disappointment, the poet continues to sing:

> With lotus leaves I made my garment
> And hibiscus flowers my lower garment.
> What matters if there is no recognition,
> If my sentiments are truly fragrant.
>
> .   .   .   .   .
>
> Men delight in many different things,
> But for me, delight lies in this pursuit.
> I would not change even if dismembered,
> Never will my resolve be recanted.

Opposing this uncompromising resolution comes the imploring and scolding Nü-Hsü, a feminine character about whom we know little, though it has been suggested she might be the poet's elder sister. With great sympathetic understanding and considerable patience she warns him that his intransigence may lead directly to his destruction. Her eloquent entreaty ends the first half of the poem.

The second portion is a touching narration of his imaginary travels—imaginary because the travels he has planned to undertake have probably been canceled on account of Nü-Hsü's exhortations. In fantasy he travels south to address himself to the semihistorical Emperor Shun, reviewing the chief events and personalities since the earthly existence of the latter and dwelling finally upon his own bitter experiences. Then he leaves Ts'ang-wu, the legendary burial place of Shun, in an attempt to reach the abode of the Supreme Deity, going through a number of important mythological landmarks and enjoying the company and assistance of such personages as the Sun, the Moon, the Wind, the Phoenix, the Thunder Master, the Cloud, and the Rainbow.

Refused admission by the guardian of the heavenly gates, Ch'ü Yüan rambles on to other locales in search of an understanding goddess or of a perfect woman like those recorded in myths and legendary history. Such a being, however, he is not destined to find. Completely despairing a second time, he seeks the wise guidance of expert diviners. By them he is encouraged to remain firm in his search and to move on. This he does, and he traverses noted areas like the K'unlun Mountains, the nearby Heavenly Ford, Floating Sands, and the Scarlet Waters. From this elevated area, he begins to achieve great heights. But,

> Ascending toward the dazzling brilliance of Heaven
> We chanced to glance down at the land we had left below
> My driver began to grieve, my horse remembered home,
> They stopped, looked back and would go on no more.

In lamentation, the poem closes:

> Alas, all is over!
> Since there is no one left who knows me now,
> Why should I pine for the royal city that I knew?
> Since no one there now knows what good kingship is,
> I shall follow P'eng Hsien to his abode.

Thus the poet makes up his mind to join the company of P'eng Hsien, who, about a thousand years before that, had drowned himself after counseling in vain with his king.

Besides this long poem, a few others have been attributed to Ch'ü Yüan on fairly reasonable though not indubitable grounds. One, "In Praise of the Orange," reveals a less mature technique and a regularity of verse form—four character lines, rhyming in couplets—reminiscent of the verse scheme in the *Shih Ching*. Written in highly symbolic language, it praises the virtues of the orange which the poet himself was desirous of emulating: a lovable external form and a respectable inner quality, worthy both as friend and as mentor.

Similar in regularity of the line, but different in content and treatment is "T'ien Wên," or "Questions Addressed to Heaven," a philosophical poem continually firing in rapid succession some two hundred questions with no answers supplied. These questions may be divided into three distinct classes: (1) those concerning the beginnings of the universe and the whys and wherefores of various natural phenomena; (2) those about historical events and some thirty noted personages of the past, esteemed sage-emperors as well as corrupt rulers and murderers; and (3) those concerning myths and legends, such as the size of the serpent that had swallowed a whole elephant, how the sun god diffused his light, or why the moon should harbor a rabbit in its belly. The striking feature of the poem is its apparent lack of organization and arrangement. The questions follow no apparent plan but seem to be all jumbled up. Even the questions on history follow no chronological order. For this reason, the poem has been regarded as having more psychological and folkloric than literary value. And some critics have denied its having been written by the author of "Li Sao."

A group of the so-called last lyrical compositions by Ch'ü Yüan, a medley under the general title of *Chiu Chang (Nine Poems)* assembled by his first editor, Wang Yi (also spelled Wang I), in A.D. 125, are of the same melancholy tone of "Li Sao" but all considerably shorter. Of these later elegies, two at least deserve special mention. One is "Drawing Thoughts" ("Ch'ou Ssŭ"), supposedly written in 305 B.C. when the poet was in his second exile. According to the editor, he was sorrowing over the doom which seemed to be approaching his native state and he could not bear to forget some of its centers of culture, like the great city of Ying.

> The way home is long and grows daily less familiar.
> How I wish I could say what I feel.
> I weep as I look up longingly to the Northern Hills
> I sigh as I look down at this southern river.
> I had looked forward to midsummer's short nights,
> Why do they now seem a whole year long?
> Long is the way to the city of Ying
> To which my soul wanders nine times each night.
> No longer sure whether winding or straight the road,
> And looking to the south for guidance from the moon,
> My soul seeks out the straightest way
> But only wanders in and out unceasingly.

The other poem, the last attributed to the poet by his first biographer, is "Hugging Sand in the Bosom" ("Huai Sha"), his resolution at self-destruction. It is short, choppy in rhythm, and forthright in spirit.

> Safe in packs the city dogs bark
> At anything they do not know.
> To hate the great, distrust the good,
> Of course, is only right.
>
> With a strong heart and ready mind
> What have I to fear?
> Since I know there is no escape from death,
> Let me not cling to a foolish love of life.

It was after the completion of this poem that Ch'ü Yüan ended his life. While his first biography, on which the foregoing presentation has been based, contains many discrepancies and is largely a mixture of fiction and fact, the influence of China's first major poet was doubtless immense, immediate, and long enduring. The supposed day of his tragic death, most probably also an early folk holiday among the southerners in ancient China, has come to be celebrated as a folk festival. It is popularly known as the Dragon Boat Festival, and is held on the fifth day of the fifth month in the lunar calendar. His eminence in folklore was due largely to his great success as a major pioneer in southern literature.

After Ch'ü Yüan's death, a sizable body of southern poetry grew up gradually and the name *Ch'u Tzŭ* ("poetry of Ch'u") was soon to denote a newly established literary genre. While these elegiac pieces varied considerably in their rhythmic pattern, meter, length, and literary skill, they had certain common characteristics. They all tried to conform to the doleful, languorous tune of "Li Sao," often even making verbal borrowings. They all tried to adhere to what were regarded as Ch'u idioms, and made constant references to Ch'u flora and fauna, customs, and costumes. They all had come from admirers of Ch'ü Yüan, who by this time had become a "Homeric" figure, so to speak, of the southern literary tradition, to whom quite a few pieces had been ascribed. While many such ascriptions stood on faulty grounds, the "apocryphal" poems were not forgeries in the sense that they were intended purposely to mislead our judgments. Many of them, such as "In Praise of the Orange" or "Questions Addressed to Heaven," were mere poetic offerings placed on the altar of the poet by his followers.

In certain specific cases, the errors of attribution are obvious. "The Diviner" ("Pu Chü") and "The Fisherman" ("Yü Fu"), for example, both begin with the clause, "after Ch'ü Yüan was exiled," and both refer to him in the third person, presenting him in conversation with the consultant. Another example of an early imitation wrongly assigned to Ch'ü Yüan is "Distant Travels" ("Yüan Yu"), in which verbal borrowings from the "Li Sao" are impressively numerous. Its theme, however, is the nonchalant abandonment of the mean and troubled world of men, and the search for absolute tranquility to be found in nondoing or nonaction, a theme clearly reminiscent of the teachings of the Taoism of Lao-tzŭ instead of the positive, nonescapist philosophy of Confucianism permeating the life and writings of the Ch'u poet.

This elegiac tradition became such a strong current of the literary development of the south that even folk incantations had the good fortune to be rewritten by the poets. The summoning of the wandering soul of a person seriously ill and delirious, an ancient popular superstition with survivals in many parts of present-day China, was performed with incantations such as had been embodied in a curious poem of uncertain authorship, "Summoning of the Soul" ("Chao Hun").

This poem, sometimes attributed to Sung Yü (third century before Christ), best known among the early continuers of the Ch'u school of poetry, was addressed to the wandering soul which was in danger of leaving the body permanently. The incantation consists of two parts: (1) a detailed description of the dangers and monstrosities in distant areas in all four—in fact, six—directions, and (2) an elaboration of the different facets of the good life available in the state of Ch'u.

The poem begins with a question addressed to the soul as to why it has left the body. Then, the summons:

> Come home, O Soul!
> Tarry not in the East,
> Where huge giants measuring a thousand cubits
> Prowl around for human souls;
> Where ten suns rise in rotation,
> Melting rocks and corroding metals.
> To this, the giants are wont;
> But should you venture there, Soul,
> You would be no more.
> O come home, you cannot live there.

Similar threats abounding in the other areas, including both heaven and hell, the soul is exhorted not to roam any more.

> Come home, O Soul!
> You must not descend to the gloomy nether world
> Where Hadean guards twist their bodies ninefold,
> And have sharp, menacing horns.
> With thick-set trunks and fingers dripping with blood,
> They pursue humans with lightning speed.
> With three eyes, tiger heads,
> And bodies resembling those of buffaloes,
> They all relish human beings.
> Come home, lest you plunge into catastrophe!

The second part, the more positive phase of the summons, presents all the attractiveness of living in Ch'u: its magnificent buildings with their comfortable, luxurious subdivisions; its beautiful, enchanting maidens; its delectable and varied foods and drinks; its charming dances and intriguing games; all of which are described in minute detail as appeals to the wandering soul to return home.

More elaborate and more self-conscious in its artistry is the "Great Summons," probably later in composition date but of equally uncertain authorship. From the fact that Ch'u is repeatedly mentioned in contrast to other geographical areas, it seems likely that the author had developed a concept of the far-flung empire. In other words, by the time of the composition of the "Great Summons," Ch'u poetry had ceased to be regional in character, having become a distinctive and inherent part of the cultural heritage of the entire Chinese people. This elegiac form was destined not only to survive the extinction of the state of Ch'u, but also to perpetuate its imprint on the minds of Chinese poets down to our own day. It is interesting and significant to recall that when Chinese translations were made of Lord Byron's "Isles of Greece," two of the four translators—Liang Ch'i-ch'ao and Hu Shih—saw fit to transfuse the essence of the English romantic poem into the rhythmic and tonal patterns of Ch'u elegies.

CHAPTER 5

The Confucian Classics

AMONG the peoples of Asia, the Chinese seem to have been the most historical-minded. Their fondness for historical records and interest in their preservation became manifest at an early date, as we have seen, in the inscriptions on bone, shell, and bronze. Besides these, there may have been longer records of events and discourses dating back to the Shang-Yin dynasty, which for one reason or another failed to be preserved. One plausible factor accounting for their poor preservation is the probable use of fragile materials. But of this we are uncertain, as none of the early characters deciphered thus far point clearly to any documents other than those incised on bone and shell.

The earliest collection of historical fragments known to us is the *Shu Ching* or the *Classic of Documents*, referred to in early times simply as *Shu*, or as *Shang Shu*. The transmission of this early collection was attended with many vicissitudes in later ages. It would be out of place in this general survey to go into its various forgeries in any detail. According to tradition, the collection, as "edited" by Confucius, comprised a hundred "chapters," or separate documents. Of these, only fifty-eight are said to have been handed down to us; and out of these fifty-eight, at least thirty are of questionable authorship. The remaining twenty-eight chapters (sometimes counted as twenty-nine) as transmitted by Fu Shêng (270?-175 B.C.) in their new definitive form have been accepted by critical scholars as essentially authentic.

Disregarding the apocryphal documents as belonging more properly to the history of Chinese classical scholarship than to that of literature, let us see what these authentic chapters of the *Shu Ching* are like.

They are disconnected, individual official papers of diverse kinds —minutes of deliberations at the royal council, memorials to the throne, records of political beliefs and policies, orations, charges to feudal lords, notes on geographic divisions with observations on their produce, quality of soil, and special attributes. These fragments naturally do not make up a continuous history of early China, but they are nonetheless important as they constitute the most ancient collection of Chinese prose writings.

The *Book of Documents* in its present "edition," which has been accepted as one of two major versions for over two thousand years, contains four sections of unequal bulk and is composed of documents purported to have been handed down from four historical periods: (1) *Yü Shu*, 2255-2205 B.C.; (2) *Hsia Shu*, 2205-1766 B.C.; (3) *Shang Shu*, 1766-1122 B.C.; and (4) *Chou Shu*, 1122-628 B.C. Thus, these documents stretch over a period of seventeen centuries, although they leave many large gaps. For the legendary dynasty of Hsia, for example, the documents stop with the year 2195 B.C., leaving a complete dearth of information for over four centuries, from 2195 B.C. to the supposed fall of the dynasty in 1766 B.C. Similarly, of the thirty-one kings of the Shang-Yin Dynasty the *Shu Ching* documents touch on the reigns of only four. The same thing is true even of the "literary" Chou dynasty, during which official historical documents were doubtless produced in greater abundance.

Although these records are fragmentary, and we know little of the circumstances under which they were collected and transmitted, their significance should not be underestimated. From the time of Confucius down to our own days, the *Shu Ching*, as one of the major Confucian classics, has exerted an uninterrupted influence upon the literary style and taste of the Chinese people. In the days of the empire (roughly from the beginning of the second century before Christ to the end of the nineteenth century), all candidates in the state examinations had to familiarize themselves with this classic. Throughout the centuries, all important state papers echoed and re-echoed its phraseology. Even after the establishment of the Republic in 1912, the wording of one version of the national anthem was a mosaic reflection of the literary gems in the *Shu Ching*.

This vast influence was due, no doubt, to its didactic content and unquestioned antiquity so highly valued and adroitly utilized by the Confucianist state; yet these qualities alone would not entirely account for the veneration accorded the book by many generations. Examined from the purely literary standpoint, these ancient documents have inherent merits.

One outstanding trait of the classic that has appealed to the Chinese literati is its concise style, its laconic brevity. The fourth document, "Kan Shih," for example, is an oration supposed to have been delivered by King Ch'i of the Hsia dynasty in 2195 B.C. to his hosts before they took battle against one of the feudal lords. James Legge's translation of the first paragraph reads:

There was a great battle at Kan. (Previous to it,) the King called together the six nobles (the leaders of his six hosts), and said, "Ah! all Ye who are engaged in my six hosts, I have a solemn announcement to make to you."

Instead of the thirty-five words in the English version, discounting the ones in parentheses, there are only nineteen in the Chinese original:

Greatly battled at Kan. Then summoned six ministers. King said, "Oh people of six services I solemnly tell you."

This compactness or economy of words is, of course, partly due to the very nature of the Chinese language itself and is not to be interpreted as a feature of the *Shu Ching* alone; it is, however, more readily observable here than in most other ancient Chinese writings.

The *Shu Ching* documents were primarily produced for practical, political purposes and preserved as archival materials, and yet they were written with a great deal of rhetorical effectiveness and literary charm. In the tenth document, "Mu Shih," we have an oration made by King Wu, first king of the Chou Dynasty, when he was about to mobilize his armies and those of his allies into battle against the last ruler of the Shang Kingdom in 1111 B.C. Preceding his address there is an introductory note:

The time was the grey dawn of the day Chia-tzŭ [first in the sixty-day cycle]. On that morning, the King came to the open country of Mu, in the borders of Shang, and addressed his army. In his left hand he carried a battle-axe, yellow with gold, and in his right he held a white ensign, which he waved, saying, "Far are ye come, ye men of the western regions,—ah, ye hereditary rulers of my friendly states; ye managers of affairs—lift up your lances, join your shields, raise your spears, I have a [solemn] speech to make."

In his address, he first called attention to the corruption and dereliction of the Shang king in listening to the advice of his evil consort; but he strengthened his charges by quoting an ancient adage:

The ancients have said, "The hen does not announce the morning. The crowing of the hen in the morning indicates the subversion of the family." Now Shou, the King of Shang, follows only the words of his wife. In his blindness he has neglected the sacrifices which he ought to offer, and makes no response (for the favors that he has received . . .).

Then he proceeded to say that in leading the expedition, he was "simply executing respectfully the punishment appointed by Heaven." His appeal to the officers and men was to fight energetically to the bitter end, urging them to be "like tigers and panthers, like bears and grizzly bears." These expressions, especially the former, were to become stock phrases in proclamations of a similar nature for many centuries to follow.

The great esteem with which this book has been held in China for so many centuries, aside from the contents of the documents, is obviously due to its charming and elegant style. A pertinent question to raise at this point is that of authorship. Each document, as it was presented in the early collected "edition" is prefaced by a short note indicating the circumstances under which the document was written as well as its authorship. These notes, while interesting, are not to be taken literally. The kings and lords to whom the documents were ascribed were more likely the personages in whose name the drafting was done and approved. The actual writers were the grand secretaries of the different courts of the various periods, who were probably the most literate members of their times. From the perpetuation of certain rhetorical devices and even of diction, we are tempted to infer that these writers formed a hereditary caste, passing the technique on from father to son or from master to pupil. They were also the custodians of the archives, authorities on court ceremonies, and celebrants at religious services and civil celebrations.

As of their authorship, we must speak with considerable cautiousness and tentativeness of the dates of composition of the different documents of the *Shu Ching*. The dates of the purported earliest document and the latest one, as we have noted before, are supposed to be more than seventeen centuries apart; but a careful reader would find little evidence of sufficient change in literary style and diction to warrant that contention. Aside from the somewhat elusive arguments from style, a certain amount of internal evidence points to the hypothesis that all the documents were written or rewritten sometime between 1100 B.C. and 600 B.C., during the so-called Western Chou Period. The first piece, entitled "Yao Tien," for example, contains in its existing version the statement that "a round year consists of three hundred sixty and six days, and by utilizing the intercalary month the four seasons are adjusted and the year completed." The intercalary month was a device to adjust the four seasons in a lunar calendar which synchronizes the full moon with the middle of the month. It was a technique that did not hark back to the twenty-third century before Christ, however, for in the bone and shell inscriptions there is not a single reference to any intercalary month. Instead, the thirteenth month of a year has been mentioned. It has been demonstrated by modern critical scholarship that the document in its present form—possibly a rewriting of an earlier version, although how much earlier we cannot surmise—was committed to writing between the years 776 B.C. and 600 B.C., or approximately fifteen centuries after the recorded events had supposedly taken place.

This same hypothesis seems applicable to the second and third sections of the book recording events and discourses in 2205-1766 B.C., and 1766-1122 B.C. respectively. In other words, hardly any documents in the whole collection of the four sections were written before the founding of the literary Chou Dynasty in 1122 B.C.

Thus our understanding and appreciation of the *Shu Ching* is as yet very limited, the host of commentaries of the last two thousand years notwithstanding. One erudite scholar of our period observed twenty-five years ago that he dared not claim to understand fully the meaning of more than 30 per cent of the *Book of Documents* and the *Book of Songs*. Though by nature a modest man, he was probably not exaggerating his own uncertainties. And since that statement was made, scholarship has certainly not yet substantially improved the situation, although progress is being made from day to day.

This "obscurity" of the *Shu Ching* is no doubt due in large measure to its archaic language, in the main the highly polished court language used in the western Chou capital, Chungchou, not unmixed, however, with current localisms and popular idioms. It is not until these special phrases, binomes, and trinomes are more thoroughly unraveled that the documents can be better comprehended. (A binome in Chinese philology is an unbreakable compound of two syllables transcribed with two characters. A trinome is a similar phenomenon involving three characters. The compounds often have meanings different from the same characters not in combination.) Progress in this regard, however, is bound to be slow, as handicaps are many. For one thing, other contemporary documents which may be used for comparative study are so few, there being only the *Book of Songs* and the bronze inscriptions.

We shall now turn to the bronze inscriptions. Chou bronzes, like their predecessors, are more than literary monuments, for they are also significant objects of art. Here, of course, we are concerned only with the inscriptions. In Shang-Yin times, inscriptions were usually factual and brief—containing, as a rule, only the owner's name and honorific title, the use of the vessel, and a short stereotyped exhortation to the effect that sons and grandsons should treasure it as they used it. In extreme instances, the inscription would consist of only one or two characters. With the establishment of the Chou Dynasty, however, inscriptions became much longer and more florid, although the art of bronze casting itself soon declined.

Of all the Chou inscriptions extant, the best known, the most often discussed, and the most lengthy is that found on the Mao Kung Ting, or Lord Mao's tripodial vessel. It contains thirty-two rows or vertical lines totaling 491 characters. The vessel, though undated in the inscription, was most probably cast in the reign of King Hsüan (827-782 B.C.), and thus was contemporaneous with the latest documents of the *Shu Ching* and may be regarded as the culmination of the long tradition of bronze inscriptions.

According to the inscriptions, all in prose, the nobleman at whose order the vessel had been cast and inscribed was Lord Mao, as yet unidentified on account of the scarcity of contemporary records, but unquestionably a distinguished royal vassal of that time. The occasion for the casting was his reception of important orders and honors from King Hsüan, who had counted on his loyal servants to revive the glory and grandeur of the Chou Dynasty. The elegant text of the inscription, without punctuation or paragraph divisions, may be broken up into six sections and summarized as follows: (1) Addressing Lord Mao as "sire Yin," the king reviews the early splendor of the Chou house, made possible by the co-operation of the king and his ministers and the harmony between men and heaven. Then he bemoans the degeneracy and disorders of his own era and resolves to double his efforts to restore peace and prosperity. (2) The king proclaims his investiture of Lord Mao and expresses his expectation of the latter's services in assisting him in external as well as in internal affairs; participating in governmental duties great and small; to "magnify your wisdom in assisting me who am neither mediocre nor stupid." (3) The king further elaborates upon the significance of the investiture, traces the misrule of past reigns to the unconditional submission of ministers to the monarch, and orders that thenceforth all royal decrees be issued only on Lord Mao's concurrence and that the latter announce to the court that decrees without his countersignature be withheld. (4) The king re-enforces his resolve by being more specific in his advice against the penning up of popular feelings and muzzling of public opinion, against heavy taxation and exploitation of widows and orphans, and against drunken revelries among officials. (5) The king specifies Lord Mao's duties and functions and enumerates the various items of personal adornments in gold and jade, chariots and horses, banners and standards, vessels and weapons bestowed by way of insignia accompanying the investiture. (6) Lord Mao does homage to the Son of Heaven for his bounty, orders that the vessel be cast to commemorate the occasion, and to "pass on to sons and grandsons forever to treasure it as they use it."

The text of this inscription is a major landmark in China's literary history in a number of ways. Almost completely a monologue, it is the most important example of this structure recorded in its original form and transmitted to us without the interference of editor or copyist. Second, it shows that toward the end of the ninth century before Christ, literary prose had developed sufficient conciseness and clarity to express rather complex thoughts and emotions. The obscurity of certain passages is due to the inability of the modern reader to decipher accurately a few key characters, and not to the clumsiness of the original document itself. Third, its unquestioned authenticity serves us as a reliable standard for the comparative study of early documents believed to have emerged from this general era.

Our singling out of the Mao vessel does not imply, however, that other bronze inscriptions are not worthy of our attention. On the contrary, there are many pieces which are equally interesting, especially some written in rhyme.

Of this latter class, no fewer than seventy-two texts have been rediscovered and deciphered. Like the ones in prose, these inscriptions in rhyme were engraved on all sorts of bronze vessels: bells, gongs, cooking and serving utensils, pots, trays, and basins. For illustration, we shall examine in translation the text of one inscription on a basin-like vessel known as *p'an*. (*R* in brackets indicates rhyming line.) It was cast for a nobleman of the ninth century before Christ, the young Prince Pai of the feudal state of Kuo, situated on the borderland between present-day Shensi and Honan. Accepting the verdict of modern scholarship in attributing the vessel to the reign of King Hsüan of the Chou Dynasty, we identify the date of the inscription with the year 816 B.C.

> In the reign year ten and two,
> The young Prince of Kuo made a precious p'an.
> Prince Pai the most glorious,
> Exerting his prowess on Barbarians
> Had busied himself in four directions [R]
> He chastised the Hsien-yün
> On the northern bank of Lo. [R]
> He beheaded five hundred,
> Captured fifty,
> Thereby winning the day. [R]
> Mighty, mighty Prince Pai
> Then presented his booty to the King. [R]

> The King, full proud of Pai's loyalty,
> Betook himself to the Chou Temple,
> And offered sacrifices. [R]
> The King said, "Uncle Pai,
> Thou art indeed brave and brilliant." [R]
> The King bestowed on him a riding horse
> Wherewith he would support His Majesty; [R]
> Bestowed on him a bow
> With a crimson arrow in its middle; [R]
> Bestowed on him a halberd
> Wherewith to subjugate barbarian regions. [R]
> Sons and grandsons,
> A milliard years and ever more. [R]

This inscription, like all the others in rhyme, was not exactly what may be considered poetry. Factuality is still its dominant trait. The remarkable thing about it is that its language is already sufficiently refined to be worthy of any creative poet. Moreover, the rhyming scheme is already faultless and comparable to that used by the immortal though anonymous poets of the age whose creations have been preserved in the *Book of Songs*. In other words, the times were ripe for the emergence of real poetry.

Transmitted with the *Book of Songs* and the *Book of Documents* for the last two millenniums to make up the traditional Five Classics or Five Canons (*Wu Ching*) of Confucianism are (1) the *Book of Changes* (*Yi Ching*), (2) the *Spring and Autumn* (*Ch'un Ch'iu*), and (3) the *Book of Rites*. These should be mentioned briefly for, although they are not works of literature in the strict sense, they have exerted an immense influence on Chinese writers for over two thousand years as integral parts of the "Pentateuch," so to speak, of China, presented vital problems in Chinese scholarship, and furnished the bases of many classical allusions frequently used in folklore as well as in more formal writings.

The *Book of Changes*, originally referred to merely as *Yi* or *Chou Yi*, is a manual of divination which went through diverse stages of accretion in the pre-Christian centuries before its text was standardized with the establishment of professorial chairs in the respective classics at the imperial universities. For this reason, its authorship has been a complex riddle in itself, involving the names of such revered "sages" as the prehistoric Fu Hsi, King Wên of the Chou Dynasty, Confucius himself, and a few others in between.

What concerns us most immediately was why the book was so popular in ancient times and how it was used in its most elementary form. The sixty-four compounds or hexagrams it contains were summaries of possible situations involved in human life. Thus, when *water* was stacked up on *fire* it meant defeat and the reversal would naturally mean triumph or victory. Similar meanings were attributed to the other hexagrams. A person facing perplexity could seek supernatural guidance by resorting to consultation of the tortoise-shell oracle described in a previous chapter, but some obvious drawbacks were that the operation was expensive as it would involve the staging of an elaborate ceremony, and that the cracks on the tortoise shell caused by the heat of the iron spit had to be interpreted by experts whose advice to the consultant was not always clear-cut or convincing. Now, by using a bundle of milfoil sticks and grasping at random from the bundle anyone could conduct his own divination. Without our going into technical details, the odd and even numbers would automatically translate themselves into continuous and broken lines. Repeating the performance six times, the consultant would build his own hexagram from the bottom up. The operation, in fact, was so simple that, as one modern Western reader of the *Yi* has suggested, not even milfoils or other grain stalks are necessary. Throwing a common coin six times would build a hexagram just as accurately and effectively. As soon as the hexagram had been obtained, the consultant would seek his appropriate answer from the early edition of the *Yi* with its sixty-four *kua* (hexagrams) for guidance in charting his course of action.

According to traditional scholarship, Confucius found the *Book of Changes* in its simplest form with short chapters containing (1) a proposition or judgment on each *kua* or hexagram, and (2) six separate propositions or judgments on each of the six lines of the *kua*. The *kua* judgment was usually an observation on the character or quality of the *kua*, which was determined by the quality of its component trigrams. The line judgment, also known as the *hsiao-*judgment, would state the quality of the line which was determined by its continuity or brokenness and by its positional relation to the other lines of the *kua* or hexagram.

What we have just described was the elementary stage in the development of the sacred book, supposed to have been formulated by Fu Hsi and interpreted by King Wên. Many early users of the manual, especially when they faced critical decisions, were not completely satisfied with the short answers given without explanation. Hence, the manual was destined to grow.

In its present form the *Book of Changes* contains the "Ten Wings" or "Ten Appendices" traditionally attributed to Confucius. With these new accretions the popular fortune-telling manual was to become a book of wisdom. The "Ten Wings" or "Ten Appendices" consist of the following:

1. Two sections devoted to explanatory notes on the sixty-four *kua* judgments.

2. Sixty-four explanations of the "ideas" or abstract meanings of the *kua*.

3. Three hundred eighty-four explanatory notes on the 384 *hsiao* or line judgments.

4. "Appended Remarks" on the book as a whole, remarks so numerous that they occupy two appendices.

5. Remarks on the first two *kua*. By way of example to illustrate how the charting of a course of action was a matter of ethics and philosophy.

6. Remarks on some other selected *kua*.

7. An essay on the order of the sixty-four *kua*.

8. "Miscellaneous Remarks."

Modern scholarship has found it impossible to attribute all these appendices to Confucius. It is even possible that Confucius had no share at all in the writing of the book. Nonetheless, in the early traditions of the Confucian school, the book was held in high esteem and many of the sayings in the "Appended Remarks" and "Miscellaneous Remarks" were prefaced with the introductory phrase: "The master said." Even if Confucius had not been responsible for those sayings and even if the story that Confucius had consulted the book so often as to have broken three times the leather straps used in binding the bamboo or wooden "pages" is of late origin, the classic as a whole undoubtedly reflects an attempt made by the early Confucian school to purify the popular manual by substituting philosophical rationalization for early folk superstition. In spite of the survival of early elements of folk belief and in spite of later interpolations by non-Confucian editors, the basic recommendations for the charting of action to seek security and avoid disaster rested squarely on logic and ethics. If the *Book of Songs* has preserved itself through its appeal to the literary appreciation of the people, the *Book of Changes* has saved itself from destruction by being a guide to practical living. In the Burning of Books Decree in 213 B.C., books of divination, alongside those on medicine and agriculture, were not banned. It is possible that even the dictatorial regime realized the difficulty of proscribing a manual which was found literally in every household.

Another Confucian canon is the *Ch'un Ch'iu* or *Spring and Autumn*. We have noted that in its original form it contained brief entries making up the annals of the feudal state of Lu for 242 years from 722 to 481 B.C. Also, that in entering the chief events of each year the author exhibited an uncompromising rigidity by calling a spade a spade. Not only was it considered proper to strip all feudal dignitaries of the titles they claimed, but also to register a king by his personal name when his acts were unkingly. In addition, some of the titles seemed to have been carefully considered before inclusion, thus resulting often in abnormal syntax. One entry that is often cited as an illustrative example is the following: "Stones fell in Sung, five" instead of "Five stones fell in Sung." According to later commentators, the accepted word order was the most logical. First, the stones falling should take precedence because it constituted the major anomaly—that of meteoric stones landing on the surface of the earth. Second, the locale of the incident should follow immediately. It was not until people had rushed to the site and done their counting that the exact number of stones that had fallen was discovered.

Not all entries, however, were as amusing. In fact, the *Spring and Autumn* was such an extremely meager work that it certainly would have been completely lost if it had not been for the three major commentaries, all claiming to have been handed down from the latter part of the fifth century before Christ, which buttressed it by expanding the brief titles either into fuller narratives or essays expounding the meaning of the wording of each entry or by reference to personalities and events. In fact, it is only in its grafted form to these major commentaries that the work has been preserved. In other words, instead of having the original *Spring and Autumn* as a separate book by itself, we have the book fragmented into chapter headings in the three commentaries. Each entry is reproduced verbatim preceding each expanded commentary.

From the literary standpoint, the most influential commentary is the one by Tso, sometimes identified with a younger contemporary and possibly a disciple of Confucius. In this commentary, the chronicles of various feudal states were utilized to expand the narration to full length, making it, therefore, similar to a news story as compared with the headline or a chapter of the Bible compared with the heading. Although the Tso Commentary is now proved to be the oldest and fullest of the three, yet it was not rediscovered until the end of the Former Han Dynasty at the beginning of the Christian Era. It is in the Tso Commentary that many of the fascinating episodes in the 242 years were recaptured and narrated in a masterful style with major emphasis on characterization and unfolding of plots worthy of the greatest storytellers in world literature.

The other two commentaries, namely, the Kung-yang Commentary by Kung-yang Kao and the Ku-liang Commentary by Ku-liang Chi, represented the accumulation of oral teachings within two schools of commentators upon the original sketchy classic of the *Spring and Autumn*—two schools which had magnified the why and wherefore of the wording and word order in each entry. These exegetical attempts seemed from very early times to have stressed the mystical and occult connotations which Confucius was supposed to have had in mind. Extremists in the Kung-yang school even advocated that the ancient sage had transmitted prophetic messages to posterity and that all the happenings of subsequent times including the establishment of the Han Dynasty had been anticipated in the original entries. To the entry "The First Year of the Duke Yin Summer Fifth Month the Count of Chêng Overpowered Tuan at Yen," Kung-yang had the following to offer in his commentary:

> What is meant by overpowering? It means killing him. If it is mere killing, why say overpower? It is done to magnify the badness of the Count of Chêng. Why magnify the badness of the Count of Chêng? The mother wanted to pass on the patrimony to him, the Count himself killed him. Who was Tuan? He was the younger brother of the Count of Chêng. Why was the term younger brother not introduced? Because he was regarded as though he had been the chief of state.

We can see that not much light was thrown by the commentator on that line. Let us next examine the Ku-liang Commentary:

> Why "overpower"? It meant capacity. What capacity? Capacity to kill. Why not say "kill"? Because it was seen that Tuan had his numerous following and Tuan was the younger brother of the Count of Chêng. How do we know he was such a younger brother? Because the victim was killed by a nobleman. Since he was a nobleman, we know he was the younger brother of the count. Although Tuan was such a younger brother yet no mention is made of the relationship because he was a feudal prince, yet no reference is made to a feudal prince because it was intended that he should be degraded. Tuan certainly had lost his way of being a younger brother. Thus, Tuan was degraded and the Count of Chêng was exposed in full. Why expose the Count of Chêng in full? To show that the Count had continuously calculated and plotted to consummate this act of killing. "At Yen" indicates distance. It is tantamount to saying "Taking him from the bosom of his mother and killing him." This is exposure in full. Under these circumstances, then, what should the Count of Chêng have done? He should have been slow in his pursuit and let the culprit escape, then he would have fulfilled the way of being kind to a king.

Although this explanatory commentary is even wordier than the one offered by Kung-yang, scarcely any more light is shed. Neither commentator was interested in reviving the full episode captioned by the entry. And now for comparison here is the Tso Commentary:

At first, Lord Wu of Chêng had taken his wife from Shên who was known as Lady Chiang who gave birth to Lord Chuang and young Prince Tuan. Lord Chuang was born when his mother was asleep. Lady Chiang was scared, named him Sleep Born and disliked him. She was fond of Prince Tuan and wanted to make him heir apparent. But on consulting her husband, Lord Wu, the Lord did not agree. After Lord Chuang had ascended the throne, she asked for her younger son the town of Chi as a special grant. The Lord said, "Chi is a precarious town where [former] lord Kuo died a tragic death. He can have any other town you might command." The town of Ching was then requested and granted, wherefrom the younger brother derived the title of the Grand Uncle of the Fortified City of Ching. Ts'ai Chung said, "When a fortified city has a wall of more than a hundred crenelations, it will be a source of trouble to the state . . . now that Ching is in excess of regulations you will face trouble in the future." The Lord replied, "Lady Chiang wants it, how can I avoid trouble?" The reply was, "When will lady Chiang be satisfied? It is better to plan for it when it is early so that nothing will ramify, because ramification is hard to stop. Even ramified weeds are hard to kill, how much more so would be the favorite younger brother of a ruler." The Lord said, "The accumulation of unrighteousness will be suicidal. You will please wait and see." In a little while the Grand Uncle ordered his western and northern suburban areas to deflect their loyalties to himself. Prince Lü counseled, "No state can stand deflection. What is your majesty going to do? If you want to turn everything over to Grand Uncle, your servant will ask to serve him. If you don't, you must get rid of him so as not to sow the seeds of disloyalty among people." The Lord said, "There is no need. He will catch himself." Thereupon the Grand Uncle enclosed the two suburban areas as his own to the extent of Linyen. Tzu Fêng [Prince Lü] said, "He is going to do it. Added power will win the masses." The Lord said, "In justice it can not be hidden. Additional power means collapse." The Grand Uncle assembled his men and resources and organized his armor and weapons and readied his war chariots in preparation for an attack of the Chêng capital. The Grand Lady was going to open the gates. As soon as the Lord heard of the appointed time, he said, "This is it." He commanded Tzu Fêng to lead a force of two hundred chariots for launching a punitive expedition against Ching. The people of Ching rebelled against the Grand Uncle and the latter fled to Yen. The Lord attacked Yen himself. In the fifth month on the day Hsin Ch'ou, the Grand Uncle took flight to Kung wherefore it was written [in the *Spring and Autumn*] "the Count of Chêng overpowered Tuan at Yen." Tuan was unbrotherly, so he is not called a younger brother. The two were like two chiefs of state, therefore, the word overpowered was used. The Count of Chêng was so titled in derogation to indicate that he had failed to teach the younger brother. The flight is not mentioned to underscore its difficulty. Then Lady Chiang was removed to the town of Ying with an oath, "We shall not see each other unless and until we are in the Yellow Springs."

With such amplifications, the *Ch'un Ch'iu* gained value as a full exemplification of the Confucian theory of the "rectification of names," thanks to the efforts of Tso Ch'iu-ming.

This theory had two separate aspects: linguistic precision and accuracy in moral judgment. In Confucius' day the word *ku*, which had originally been the name of an angular-shaped wine container, was being loosely used for all decanters irrespective of shape. Such usages provoked Confucius and in this instance prompted him to say, "Now people apply the name *ku* indiscriminately to containers even when they are no longer angular." And he asked repeatedly for emphasis, "Are they still *ku*?"

On the other hand, moral judgment is discernible in this instance: The Chinese graph *chêng*, which means "government," was originally a graph meaning "erect" or "just." When despotic rulers and corrupt officials called their activities "*chêng*," Confucius considered it a mockery of the term. He explained his theory to Duke Ching of the Ch'i State when approached for advice on government by saying, "There is government when the king is king, the minister is minister, the father is father and the son is son." That everyone has a share in social responsibility, should know his duties and faithfully perform them, is another way to summarize this portion of his theory.

The Canon of Li or *Li Ching* was the most imperfectly preserved of the five Confucian canons even before the burning of the books in 213 B.C. Although the upholders of the traditions of the Confucian school have long insisted that toward the end of his life the sage had given a definitive redaction to documentary materials that were to be known in early Han times as the *Canon of Li* and the *Canon of Music*, it was also early admitted that even in his lifetime the documents were already in a very imperfect state. Deliberate destruction of these *Li* documents, it was noted, was begun by those feudal rulers who, in their eagerness for the seizure of power, found it convenient to scrap the specifications which had been laid down as standards of propriety.

What Confucius was accredited with "having edited" was further impaired after the proscription and burning of the books in 213 B.C. When the ban was lifted in 191 B.C. a scholar from Lu, the birthplace of Confucius, by the name of Kao-t'ang Shêng transmitted seventeen chapters bearing the title of *Shih Li* or *Li for Scholars*. These fragments were considered remnants of the Confucian *Li Ching* or *Canon of Li* and apparently became the major text when a doctoral chair on that classic was founded by Emperor Wu in 136 B.C. Meanwhile, in about 150 B.C., Prince Kung of Lu (Liu Yü, died 128 B.C.) accidentally discovered in the demolished walls of the home of Confucius fifty-six chapters of the *Li Ching* besides 131 chapters of notes supposedly committed to writing by the pupils of Confucius' disciples. Thus thirty more chapters of the *Li Ching* had come to light. These later found their way into the collection of a princely bibliophile, Prince Hsien of Hochien, who in turn presented them to the imperial court. For some unknown reason, these new finds were soon lost to posterity and only the seventeen chapters which had been current constituted the *Canon of Li*.

These remnants, obviously only a small portion of the *Canon of Rites*, if one had actually existed in definitive form, consisted of a series of minute directions for the scholar-knight (*shih*) to follow on such occasions as capping (attainment of adulthood), marriage, reception of guests, ceremonious drinking parties at which selected scholars were presented to the feudal court, and funeral and mourning rites.

Besides these, there had been an accumulation of notes or records on rites from the fourth century B.C. on, complementary to but distinct from the so-called classic or canon. According to most entries these notes totaled 131 pieces, all of which, according to Han tradition, represented records made by the followers of the pupils of Confucius as they heard oral traditions transmitted to them. Among the thirteen schools of Li experts the most prominent were headed by two members of the Tai family, Tai Tê and his nephew Tai Shêng, both fifth-generation pupils of the first principal expositor and authority, Kao-t'ang Shêng. Tai Tê, being more conservative in nature, transmitted eighty-five chapters, and his nephew selected forty-nine chapters for perpetuation. Although the two collections had a good deal in common, it was the latter collection that was destined to be elevated later on to the dignity of a Li classic bearing the title *Li Chi* (*Li Ki* according to James Legge). Both Tai Tê and Tai Shêng were made Doctors of the Li Classic during the reign of Emperor Hsüan (73-49 B.C.) and both taught in their respective doctoral chairs on the so-called *Classic of Seventeen Chapters* but they hardly realized that in due course, the compilation of the nephew was to supersede the original fragmentary classic in school curriculums.

Students of the Confucian School from Han times down stopped using the term *Li Ching*, for the original seventeen chapters were soon designated by a different title, namely *I Li*, and soon there was to enter into current bibliography a third work usually accepted as forming a component member of the San Li composite or the trilogy on Li. This last-mentioned work, usually bearing the title of *Chou Li*, was actually a description of the constitution of the Chou dynastic government. In fact, its original title was *Chou Kuan* or *Offices of Chou,* having practically nothing to do with rites. It was composed of six neatly organized sections each dealing with a major component part of the Chou dynastic government: the Office of Heaven, or the Prime Ministry; the Office of Earth, or the Office of Education and Social Welfare; the Office of Spring, or Office of Rites and Ceremonies and Protocol; the Office of Summer, or the Department of Defense and Security; the Office of Autumn, or the Department of Justice and Punishment; and the Office of Winter, or the Department of Public Works and Economic Production. In its present form, the last chapter is missing and replaced by a curious document entitled *K'ao Kung Chi* or *A Record of Researches on Manufacture.*

These three works, then, composed the so-called three Classics of Rites: The *I Li* of seventeen chapters, the *Li Chi* of forty-nine chapters, and the *Chou Li* of six sections. In theory they received equal veneration as the components of the nine classical works of the T'ang Dynasty and of the thirteen classics from Sung times (A.D. 760-1279) to the present day. But in fact, both the *I Li* and *Chou Li* are studied only by experts whereas the *Li Chi* or *Record of Rites* has engaged the universal attention of students who go beyond the *Analects, The Book of Mencius, The Book of Documents,* and the *Book of Songs.* The reason for this is quite apparent. The *I Li* had, ever since its recovery in Han times, impressed even specialists as being extremely difficult to understand and rather conducive to boredom. The *Chou Li,* with its detailed descriptions of the functions of offices and personnel of all branches and sub-branches of the dynastic government, is always rewarding to students in constitutional law and government; the whole design, however, was so neatly organized and contains so many elements of later statecraft that even the most credulous doubt its authorship by the Duke of Chou. Moreover, its descriptions are so abundantly contradicted by other records that at best it was only an idealization of what the Chou dynastic government would have been if the Duke of Chou had had his way in building a utopian kingdom. For the average reader its contents present very little of interest.

Outstanding in the trilogy, especially from the standpoint of literature, is the *Li Chi* or the *Record of Rites.* The forty-nine chapters vary not only in length and in contents, but also in their process of accretion. With their nuclei taking definite form during the age of the warring states and continuing well into early Han times, many of the chapters remind the reader of philosophical works of the late Chou Period. Although the forty-nine chapters do not constitute so many organized essays, except for the chapters on music and on the seasons and months of the year,—most of them being paragraphs strung together—a scheme of classification according to contents is obvious. In many of the chapters, anecdotes are retold to throw light on the art and problems of living. The following represents Confucius as a severe critic of repressive government:

When Confucius was passing through the foothills of T'ai Mountain there was a woman weeping bitterly at a grave. The Master sat up in respect when he heard her and sent Tzŭ Lu to ask her saying: "Your weeping seems to suggest extreme sorrow." "Yes," she replied, "Father-in-law was killed by a tiger some time ago and then I lost my husband the same way and now my son is also killed." "Why don't you go away from this area?" the Master himself asked. And she said, "There is no repressive government here." And the Master said, "Note this, young men. Repressive government is worse than tigers."

Here is another anecdote revealing the personality of the master:

The dog kept by Chung-ni [Confucius] having died, he ordered Tzŭ Kung to bury it saying, "I have heard that a worn-out curtain should not be thrown away but may be used to bury a horse in; and that a worn-out umbrella should not be thrown away but may be used to bury a dog in. I am poor and have no umbrella. In putting the dog into the grave, you can use my mat; and do not let his head be buried in the earth."

Especially touching are some of the isolated accounts based on oral traditions of the little anecdotes in the life of Confucius. For example, the following record of how Confucius approached the end of his life:

Confucius rose early [one day] and with his hands behind him and trailing his staff, paced leisurely near the door singing:

> The T'ai Mountain, will it not crumble;
> The strong beam, is it not breaking;
> The wise man, is he not withering away like a plant?

Having thus sung, he went in and sat opposite the door. Tzŭ Kung had heard him and asked, "If the T'ai Mountain crumbles, to what shall I look up? If the strong beam breaks, on what shall I lean? If the wise man withers, whom shall I imitate? The Master, I am afraid, is going to be ill." He then hastened into the house. The Master said, "Tz'ŭ, why do you come so late? In the Hsia Dynasty the body [of the deceased] was dressed and coffined at the top of the steps on the east, so that it was where the deceased used to go up [as master of the house]. The people of Yin performed the same ceremony between the two pillars, so that the steps for the ghost were on one side of the corpse and those for the guests on the other. The people of Chou perform it at the top of the western steps, treating the deceased as if he were a guest. I am a man [descended from a house] of Yin, and last night I dreamed that I was sitting with the offerings to the dead by my side between the two pillars. Enlightened kings have not arisen and who under Heaven is able to take me as his master? I understand I am about to die." With this, he took to his bed and was ill for seven days and died.

The above quotation from the chapter entitled "T'an Kung"—possibly the most interesting in the book—may be supplemented by another excerpt from the chapter "Li Yün."

Once Confucius was present as a guest at the Cha sacrifice [a thanks-giving service offered at the end of the year] and when it was over, he went out for a stroll on the terrace over the Gate of Proclamations, feeling sad and sighed. What made him sigh was the State of Lu. Yen Yen was by his side and said, "What has a Superior Man to sigh about?" Confucius replied, "The prevalence of the Great Way and the flowering of the three dynasties, I was not born early enough to see, but in them resides my purpose and ambition.

"When the Great Way prevails, the world is a common state. Officers are elected according to their wisdom and ability, mutual confidence and harmonious relations are cultivated, so the people regard not only their own parents as parents and not only their own children as children. The young are able to employ their talents; the juniors are free to grow; the helpless widows, the lonely orphans, the crippled and the deformed are well provided for. Men have their occupations and women their homes. While not to be wasted, wealth is kept not necessarily as personal property; while not to be penned up in idleness, energy is exerted not necessarily for personal profit. Thus scheming and intrigue cease to exist; banditry and violence do not arise. As a result, outer gates always remain wide open. This is the age of the Great Commonwealth."

Besides enriching the Confucian tradition, the *Li Chi* further exerted its influence upon the school population of China for close to two thousand years through two of its chapters which have been extracted from the book to form separate units for the education of the young. These two chapters are "The Great Learning," attributed to Confucius, and "The Doctrine of the Mean," attributed to Confucius' grandson, K'ung Chi, better known by his courtesy name, Tzŭ Ssŭ, purportedly the teacher of the teacher of Mencius. These two titles, usually bound together to serve as a primer, make up the four books of Confucianism together with the *Analects* and the *Book of Mencius,* the basic unit of all Chinese schools since the middle of the twelfth century. It is little wonder that the *Li Chi* not only has become the most popular among the three Li classics but also has had its stories and phraseology echoed and re-echoed in subsequent literature.

Around 90 B.C. there existed in China two sets of Confucian classics, classified according to the script in which they were written; these represented not only two editions but also two schools of interpretation. One school was that of the state doctors founded on oral transmission and recorded in current Han script, known as the school of the modern script. The other was based on early written records and circulated among the people and known as the ancient script. At first sight the difference between the two schools seemed to be one of language rather than editions. All writings committed before the beginning of the Han Dynasty were recorded in what was then called the ancient script and those reconstructed or re-copied in Han times were done in modern script. These two scripts were comparable in a sense to German books printed in German script and those printed in Roman script. One was easily convertible into the other without arousing much antagonism. The situation in Han scholarship, however, was not as simple as this. In the newly discovered books, now called ancient because they were in ancient script, there were not only variant readings of sentences and para-graphs but also new chapters heretofore unseen, and new books heretofore unrecognized by the state. The question immediately arose which ones were classics worthy of the name. Such a problem in the context of the free inquiry of modern scholarship would not have arisen at all. Each scholar would enjoy perfect freedom in choosing his own field of specialization and presenting his own views of interpretation. In Han times, however, the scholarly climate was entirely different. Classical studies were the concern of imperial government and were linked to the dignity of state recognition. The problems of the completeness of a classic and the problem of its authenticity were naturally great issues. Moreover, the doctoral chairs of the imperial state carried with them not only coveted honor but also attractive stipends of four hundred to six hundred bushels of grain yearly. Furthermore, involved in this controversy between specialists on classics recognized by the state and specialists on those circulated among the people were the problems not only of his-torical authenticity but also political interpretation having a direct bearing on governmental policies and educational trends.

In the Han Dynasty this controversy centered around the estab-lishment of doctoral chairs. When the doctoral chairs were es-tablished in 124 B.C. they were all chairs of the modern script. When the ancient-script classics emerged they engaged, for a time, the attention of scholars in their private capacity. As some scholars be-came expert in the new classics they sought state recognition, but their petitions for the founding of new doctoral chairs were all blocked consistently by the occupants of existing chairs, who all belonged to the modern-script school. Thence arose the real con-troversy. During the reign of Emperor Hsüan (73-49 B.C.) a conven-tion was summoned by imperial decree in 51 B.C. to assemble the most reputable scholars at one of the imperial libraries, the famous Stone Conduit Hall, to thrash out the differences of the Five Classics. Several new chairs were founded but none were captured by the ancient scriptists. During the reign of Emperor Ch'êng (32-7 B.C.) it was proposed to establish chairs on three ancient-script classics in the imperial archives, namely, the *I Li,* the *Shu Ching* and the Tso Commentary of the *Spring and Autumn annals.* But the proposal was voted down. Toward the end of the Western Han Dynasty, during the reign of Emperor Ai (6-1 B.C.) the imperial librarian, Liu Hsin, recommending the founding of four doctoral chairs on the ancient script, was ordered by the emperor to sit in conference with the state doctors, but those worthies managed to circumvent discussion on purely technical grounds.

Enraged at the situation, Liu Hsin wrote a famous letter in which he bitterly accused the state doctors of "holding on to what is fragmentary and of being jealous of others in possession of what is authentic," in spite of the fact that his own learned father, Liu Hsiang, was one of the state doctors. In retaliation the learned doctors countercharged Liu Hsin with attempts to wreck the established standards. When the last Han emperor came to the throne in the first year of the Christian Era, the dynastic glory of the Western Han was almost in complete eclipse and Emperor P'ing (reigned A.D. 1-5) was only a puppet of the Prime Minister, Wang Mang, who was to usurp the throne and found a new dynasty (A.D. 9-22). It happened that Wang Mang, as distinctly different from all other usurpers in Chinese history, had interested himself as a young man in classics of the ancient script. In fact, he based his claims to imperial succession upon the theories which he had extracted from the old classics. When he was prime minister to Emperor P'ing, he had braved all opposition to establish four chairs for classics of the old script. When he ascended the throne himself he increased the number of doctoral chairs and elevated the positions of neglected classics, upon the advice largely of Liu Hsin.

The triumph of the ancient-script school, however, was short-lived. When the brief Hsin Dynasty was overthrown and the Han dynastic rule was re-established by Emperor Kuang Wu (reigned A.D. 25-57) the old doctoral chairs were restored. Besides the fourteen traditional chairs, two were set up for the Fei version of the *Book of Changes* and for the Tso Commentary on the *Spring and Autumn annals,* but these were soon terminated on account of persistent opposition from the state doctors of the modern school. Emperor Chang (reigned A.D. 76-88), a great lover of the ancient script *Shu Ching* and of the Tso Commentary, summoned scholars of the empire to discuss these works in the White Tiger Hall. Although no doctoral chairs were established, four lectureships were set up to take care of four ancient-script classics. During the reign of Emperor Ling (reigned A.D. 166-188) the eminent scholar, Lu Chi, petitioned for the establishment of doctoral chairs for the *Chou Li,* the Tso

Commentary, and for the Mao Ch'ang version of the *Book of Songs,* all in ancient script, but the petition was rejected. To sum up, except for the short period during Wang Mang's usurpation, all the state-recognized classics were those in modern script monopolized by fourteen state doctors.

Nevertheless, classics of the ancient script were rising steadily not only in following but also in dignity. At the end of the dynastic span there arose a great scholar who combined the traditions of both schools but confirmed the authenticity of all the ancient-script classics. This great paragon of learning was Chêng Hsüan (A.D. 127-200), a scholar so universally revered by the common people that even the most fearsome organized bandits of the age—the Yellow Head-bands—not only piously stayed away from his home district but also bowed low to him when they met him accidentally in his travels.

Somewhat later, the heated controversy drew to a colorless close when, during the mass migration and flight of the imperial court in A.D. 317, all the major texts of the modern script were lost. After the period of political division, the ancient-script classics became state sponsored in the T'ang Dynasty.

Although the controversy between the modern scriptists and the ancient scriptists was mainly one between the state-sponsored scholars and the nonsponsored scholars, in thought content the progress of the controversy bore out the major stages of intellectual development in the Han Empire. The earliest classicists, who were exclusively modern scriptists (as classics in the ancient scripts were then nonexistent), were appointees of the state and were therefore intimately connected with the imperial dynasty, rubber-stamping the major state policies by declaring them in conformity with the teachings of the sage. Even a few independent minds who tried to make Confucianism into a living intellectual and political force were circumscribed in their critical activities. Then Tung Chung-shu developed his somewhat supernatural theories of the interpretation of astronomical anomalies and natural freaks, intending to curb political despotism by intimidating the monarchs with the powers of heaven. Once this trend was started, however, supernaturalism was so expanded that some members of the Confucian school decided to deify Confucius by enlarging upon his supernatural powers, including that of prophesying unto untold generations.

This gave rise to the emergence of a class of apocryphal books known as *Wei Shu* to supplement the *Ching Shu,* the original classics. Thenceforward, each of the five classics had a *wei* attached to it by way of appendix to bring out all its meanings not self-evident in the text of the *ching.* The word *wei* literally means the woof of a web as contrasted with *ching*, the warp. Into the context of these *wei* appendices were read all the occult elements of folk beliefs, including some of the stupidest divinations. The impact upon politics was that with this mystification of the matter-of-fact original texts of the *ching*, Han Confucianism evolved in time the divine right of kings.

It was against this supernatural interpretation that scholars of the ancient-script school protested. As these were not holders of government positions they taught the importance of knowledge for its own sake rather than as a means to hierarchal advancement. They looked upon the classics as historic records rather than mystical prophecies. They emphasized the law of nature to discredit supernatural interpretation and they promoted the square facing of moral challenges to replace emphasis on abnormalities.

The Tso Commentary is now conclusively demonstrated to have been a piece of talented and clear chronicling instead of a forgery by Liu Hsin to help Wang Mang in his usurpation, as was stated in the nineteenth and early twentieth centuries in China by followers of the modern-script school. All the three Li books were later compilations which had not been worked on by Confucius. That the *Li Chi* was a Han compilation had always been admitted. The *Chou Li*, instead of being the handiwork of the Duke of Chou, was most probably a projection of the mind of a group of political utopianists in the Warring States period, and the *I Li* was not what Confucius had taught his own disciples, but the salvaging of a number of etiquette manuals which had been handed down privately among members of the Confucian school. In other words, with the original *Li Ching* lost, these three purported classics filled the gap psychologically, if not documentarily, for two thousand years.

CHAPTER 6

Three Late Chou Philosophers

Aᴛᴇʀ the death of Confucius in 479 B.C., Chinese society and culture underwent more rapid and drastic changes than ever before, and these changes were clearly reflected in the writings of the so-called Warring States period (403-221 B.C.)

The very nature of interstate warfare was no longer what it had been during the period of the *Spring and Autumn annals*. Though the standing army of the most powerful state in the earlier period could not have exceeded a hundred thousand men, at least four of the seven Warring States claimed over a million men each, fully armed. Though "national defense" had once meant primarily the protection of the capital and a few key cities, all walled, now the fortification of all frontiers became a necessity, calling for the erection of "great walls" to safeguard strategic areas. And though in the Spring and Autumn Era the main objective in warfare had been the taking of loot and prisoners rather than the inflicting of a crushing defeat on the enemy and occupying his territory, now the glories of a military victory consisted in territorial aggrandizement and the complete destruction of the enemy. As rewards were meted out to warriors on the basis of the number of foes they had slain, the war reports boasted of beheading a hundred thousand or two hundred thousand, or burying four hundred thousand alive, or massacring a whole beleaguered city. This awful destructiveness was made possible not only by the highly specialized men directing military operations but also by more efficient weapons of war now made of iron instead of copper and bronze as in the old feudal days.

The displacement of copper by iron in the casting of implements also had telling effects on the peaceful realm of human activities, noticeably in industrial and agricultural production. For the first time in Chinese history, enterprises yielding large private fortunes independent of land holdings appeared on the economic scene. Merchant princes dealing in grains, silk, lacquer, salt, iron, livestock, etc., began to rival the feudal lords in riches and in influence. Increased production had been aided by the use of slaves. There was also hired labor available in the various cities, which had grown immensely in population and also in unemployment. Cities with ten thousand families were no longer exceptional. Though there were no detailed census figures, one coastal city (Lintzǔ) had seventy thousand families about 330 B.C., with "carriage wheels scraping one another, human shoulders rubbing one against another." And near the end of this period, the city of Loyang, the one-time eastern capital of the Chou kingdom, centrally located in the North China plains, had more than a hundred thousand families. And the Chinese family typical of these two areas was considerably larger than that of present-day America with its average of 3.5 human souls.

The seven states had become kingdoms. Ch'in in the west, Ch'i in the east, and Ch'u in the south, had emerged as the three most powerful entities and, as we have noted, Ch'in came to be the most feared as "the country of tigers and wolves." The foremost problem was how to deal with its rising power and growing ambition. By 221 B.C. this state had gobbled up all six of its rivals and established an empire.

The impact of these rapid and far-reaching changes on the human mind was immense. Covering the many shifts of emphasis and attempts at revaluation, the most striking intellectual phenomenon was the decline of the sense of dynastic loyalty and traditional patriotism. The symbol of kingship had suddenly lost its meaning. Devotion to the state of one's own birth gradually diminished; by and large, feudal patriotism was on the wane. Dispossessed members of the nobility of a vanquished state had to make the best out of tragic disillusionment in new lands far away from home. Wandering scholars were as a rule hard pressed by circumstance to make their grand tours from state to state in search of sincere patronage. Keen minds, now further sharpened by extensive travel and increased intellectual intercourse, saw the shallowness of local variations in human conduct, and grasping firmly the basic sameness of men, preached universal doctrines applicable "everywhere under heaven." The concept of *T'ien Hsia,* the whole world, or literally "all under heaven," loomed large. Some consciously and others unconsciously were paving the way intellectually for the formation of an empire.

All these turbulent streams of change and revolt, appearingly somewhat far-fetched, left their indelible imprint on literature, especially with regard to content. Moreover, the rivalry of philosophical systems and the opposition between points of view provided ample room for discussions and argumentation. Meanwhile, the ease with which state barriers might be crossed, resulting from the rapid improvement in transportation and the construction of military highways, made it possible for the dissenters from orthodoxy to seek sanctuary in a neighboring state. In fact, it is no exaggeration to say that as a rule, a doctrine persecuted in one state would be warmly welcomed in an adjacent territory, a situation that had many analogous examples in the evolution of ideas outside of China itself.

This relative freedom of thought and expression, heretofore unheard of in feudal China, together with the rapid advancement in the procurability of writing materials, had a profound influence upon Chinese literary style, and especially prose style. For one thing, the records of discourses and events became more lengthy, narratives were written with fuller details and characterization, and conversations and adages were recorded in context, making the individual sayings much more comprehensible by placing them in logical sequence. In addition, the anecdotes, stories, and parables thrown into a conversation or a discussion to enliven it were no longer omitted. Though the age still could lay no claim to the existence of *belles lettres* as was understood by later generations, its writings came closer to our definition of literature.

To illustrate the more elaborate recordings of sayings and conversation at the beginning of the Warring States Era, a striking contrast may be seen between the Confucian *Analects* redacted about 400 (?) B.C. and the *Book of Mencius,* edited about 125 years later, consisting of fourteen chapters, recording the sayings and dialogues of Mêng K'o, the greatest expositor of the teachings of Confucius.

Mêng K'o (372-289 B.C. [one school of computation suggests 390-305 B.C.]), better known by his latinized appellation in the Western world, was born in the tiny feudal state of Tsou not far away from the state of Lu, Confucius' birthplace, a little over a hundred years after the death of the great sage. Like Confucius, he lost his father in his early years, but more fortunate than Confucius, he grew up under the loving care of a virtuous mother who, according to a popular tradition, took the trouble to move three times in search of proper environment for the bringing up of her young son. When he grew up, he sat at the feet of a disciple of K'ung Chi (492-431 B.C.), grandson of Confucius. Like his great predecessor, he roamed from state to state trying to find a sovereign who would accept his program for the realization of the Wang Tao or the Kingly Way, relying on human-heartedness and righteousness rather than military might for the building up of a great society. He tarried for a while in the states of Ch'i and Wei, but discovering that the monarchs were more interested in immediate gains and benefits, he returned home and resumed the work of a philosopher-teacher. With a handful of disciples, he discussed in an orthodox Confucian manner a variety of subjects ranging from the innate goodness of human nature to the meaning of contemporary events.

But the age in which Mencius lived was even more disconcerting than the last years of the Spring and Autumn era. Confucius had met with little theoretical disagreement among his contemporaries save a few recluses who thought the sage was a futile busybody. Mencius, living in an age of more marked intellectual discord, came into contact with numerous exponents of rival systems of thought. There were two schools of thought which he detested especially, the hedonistic school of Yang Chu (395-335 B.C.) and the altruistic school of Mo Ti (480?-390? B.C.). It was speaking against these two schools which gave him the reputation of being disputative.

The disciple Kung Tu said to Mencius, "Master, the people outside our school all speak of you as being fond of disputing. I venture to ask whether it be so." Mencius replied, "Indeed I am not fond of disputing, but I am compelled to do it. A long time has elapsed since this world received its being, and there has been an alternation along its history now a period of good order, and now a period of confusion. . . .

"When sage kings cease to rise, and the princes of the states give the reins to their lusts, unemployed scholars indulge in unreasonable discussions. The words of Yang Chu and Mo Ti fill the world. . . .

"I also wish to rectify men's hearts and to put an end to these perverse doctrines, to oppose their one-sided actions, and banish their licentious expressions; and thus to carry on the work of the three sages. Do I do so because I am fond of disputing? I am compelled to do it.

"Whoever is able to oppose Yang and Mo is a disciple of the sages."

(Legge's translation, III, B, 9)

This ambition on the part of Mencius to "imitate" Confucius, his devotion to the sayings of the sage-kings in opposition to that of the warrior-kings, his conviction of the goodness of man's nature, his emphasis on the importance of the people in politics, and his critical attitude toward utilitarianism all involved him in many controversial discussions and made him an effective defender of the school of Confucius.

For this work he was well prepared. Being a major expositor of the Confucian school, Mencius obtained his basic literary training from the classical books of songs and documents, both of which he frequently quoted. He also showed familiarity with the *Spring and Autumn Annals* and originated the theory of Confucius having not only edited but actually written the work.

As a keen reader never losing sight of common sense in higher criticism, however, Mencius rose above the literal acceptance of every iota in the ancient texts. In interpreting the *Book of Songs,* he advised against "stubbornness" (VI, B, 3). Suggesting what freedom from stubbornness might be, he elaborated the proper way to interpret the songs by saying:

> Those who discourse on the poems should not allow single words to do injustice to a stanza, or a single stanza to do injustice to the general expression [of the whole poem]. Use your imagination to meet the general idea expressed. That is the way to apprehend it.
>
> (V, A, 4)

This same view was expressed by Mencius with regard to the *Book of Documents;* he warned his pupils that it would be better to be without the documents than to lend unconditional credence to each one of them (VII, B, 3). The occasion which had elicited such an emphatic statement was his discussion of a chapter in the *Book of Documents* recording King Wu's subjugation of the last of the Shang-Yin kings, Shou Hsin, in the year 1122 B.C. In that document there was a statement to the effect that so much blood had been shed that it had floated the pestles out of the mortars. Explaining his refusal to take that statement at its face value, he said:

> Men of human-heartedness have no enemies under heaven. When the most human-hearted man [King Wu] launched a punitive expedition against the least human-hearted [King Shou Hsin], how could it be that blood flowed until it floated the pestles out of the mortars?
>
> (VII, B, 3)

Thus a careful and understanding reader of the "classics" recommended if not edited by Confucius, Mencius continued the tradition of the Confucian school by teaching and encouraging inquiry among the pupils whom he readily accepted irrespective of social station. These sayings of Mencius, which most probably he did not commit to writing himself, were collected to form the book now bearing his name.

Compared with the *Analects,* the *Book of Mencius* is longer, containing 34,685 words, whereas the former numbers only 12,700. It also reveals more careful collecting and editing. Many entries are grouped together in the same chapter on the basis of subject matter or of locale. And all entries contain sayings of Mencius, in monologue form or in conversation. Moreover, the recording is much more extensive, making the book as a whole much more understandable without the aid of commentaries. In the *Analects,* for example, when Confucius was discussing human nature, only eight words were recorded, which in Legge's translation read: The Master said, "By nature, men are nearly alike; by practice, they get to be wide apart." (XVII, 2.)

This, probably an extreme but by no means exceptional case, was recorded without context. To Confucius' immediate disciples, for whom the notes were collected, the notation of the topical sentence would have seemed sufficient, and the oral transmissions of the participants in a given dialogue would supply the narration of events and circumstances leading up to the key sayings. But with such brief adages lifted out of context, it should be no surprise to us that to even expert commentators of the Former Han Dynasty, not too far removed from the age of Confucius, the *Analects* presented many puzzling problems.

When Mencius expounded on the goodness of human nature, the record was much fuller in detail. One of the dialogues follows:

The philosopher Kao said, "Man's nature is like water whirling round in a corner. Open a passage for it to the east, and it will flow to the east; open a passage for it to the west, and it will flow west. Man's nature is indifferent to good and evil, just as the water is indifferent to the east and west."

Mencius replied, "Water indeed will flow indifferently to the east or west, but will it flow indifferently up or down? The tendency of man's nature to good is like the tendency of water to flow downwards. There are none but have this tendency to good, just as all water flows downwards.

"Now by striking water and causing it to leap up, you may make it go over your forehead, and by damming and leading it, you may force it up a hill:— but are such movements according to the nature of water? It is the force applied which causes them. When men are made to do what is not good, their nature is dealt with in this way."

(Legge's translation, VI, Pt. 1, 2)

This more elaborate recording of discourse, besides being a reflection of the improved facilities in the physical aspects of writing, which were potent factors in molding the literary style of his age, was also an expression of Mencius' personality as a speaker and writer. As was pointed out by Chao Ch'i (A.D. 110?-201), his earliest commentator, he was especially fond of using parables and allegories. It was not uncommon for Mencius, instead of answering a question in a prosaic manner, to tell a story. To show that the means by which riches and honor, gains and advancement were attained were often dishonorable and shameful even in the eyes of common men and women, he told a spirited story.

In the state of Ch'i there was a man who had a wife and a concubine living with him in the same house. Whenever the husband went out, he would always come home after feasting and drinking to his satiation. And when his wife asked him about the people with whom he had dined and wined, they were all rich and distinguished people.

The wife said to the concubine, "When our good man goes out, he always comes home well filled with meats and wine; and when I ask him about his eating and drinking companions [he tells me] they are all rich and distinguished people. And yet no prominent man has ever come here. I shall spy out where our husband goes."

Rising early [one morning] she deviously followed him wherever he went. Throughout the whole city, there was no one who would stand or talk with him. Finally he went to those who were offering sacrifice among the tombs outside of the eastern city wall, and begged for what was left over. Not being satisfied, he looked around and went to another party. This was the way he fed himself to satiation!

The wife returned and told the concubine, saying, "A husband is what one looks up to for one's whole life. Now he is like that!" Whereupon she reviled her husband with the concubine, and they wept together in the central hall.

Meanwhile, the husband, knowing nothing of all this, came in with great self-complacency, putting on airs to his wife and concubine.

(IV, B, 33)

Mencius seemed to take delight not only in the telling of anecdotes from history, legend, and imagination to illustrate and advance his argument, but also in the use of picturesque language to make his expressions concrete and memorable. To suggest utter impossibility, he would say "leaping over the North Sea with T'ai Mountain held in one's arm pit"; and to describe futility, he would say, "like climbing up a tree in search of fish." Though the Book of Mencius was written primarily for a philosophical purpose, its influence on Chinese literature was immense, especially after A.D. 1177 when it was made one of the Four Books of Confucianism, and continued to be learned by rote in all the schools in China until the second decade of the twentieth century.

The philosophers whom Mencius denounced most bitterly were Yang Chu and Mo Ti, whose words, according to his charges, had "filled the whole world." This statement was obviously an exaggeration with reference to Yang Chu, at any rate, for there was no mention of that name at all by any other Chinese writer in Mencius' age, let alone writings ascribed to him. The first summary of Yang Chu's teaching in a chapter incorporated in a larger work attributed to Lieh-Tzŭ (Lieh Yü-k'ou, flourished 600 B.C.) was not noted until 14 B.C. and the present text of the Lieh-Tzŭ was probably not compiled until after A.D. 317.

Mo Ti, however, was not only an authentic historical person, founder of an important school of philosophy (in fact, the founder of a religion), but also the purported author of a book which was a milestone in the development of prose literature. The teachings of this unique philosopher were to fall into such complete desuetude that we have but very scanty knowledge of his life. In fact, the very dates of his birth and death have been topics of controversy, although most critics agree that he flourished in the fourth century before Christ, between Confucius and Mencius.

He was born shortly after the death of Confucius, in the state of Lu, of parents tracing their ancestry to the state of Sung. Thus by descent and nurture, Mo Ti had intimately associated himself with the traditional culture of the Shang-Yin group as well as with its enriched and modified form, now considered typical Chou culture, as it had been advanced in the state of Lu. He had early acquainted himself with the classical books of the time such as the *Book of Documents* and the *Book of Songs*. He had also studied the teachings of Confucius, which were winning a great following in the Central States. His life spanning the end of the Spring and Autumn Era and the beginning of the Warring States period, he keenly felt the inadequacy of the Confucian school and boldly launched a revolt against it. A pragmatist in temperament and philosophy, he was also a man of action. He lived a busy life in serving his fellow men, teaching, studying, preaching against aggressive warfare, inventing defensive weapons and war machines, and traveling long distances to discourage warmongers. According to an early tradition, he never sat down long enough during his waking hours to warm a seat.

A number of facets of his teachings may be briefly summarized as reactions against Confucianism. To oppose the Confucianist scepticism with regard to the spiritual order, he taught the reality of ghosts. To discredit the Confucianist practice of elaborate burials and long mourning periods, he advocated the reverse. In disapproval of the Confucianist emphasis on music and ritualism, he decried the futility of music. And, to counteract the Confucianist belief in the ordering of human lives by heaven, he preached his doctrine of anti-fatalism. But he was much more than a mere adversary of an influential school, for he had his own system and his own gospel. His fundamental tenet was a firm belief in a knowing and loving *T'ien* (heaven). The extension of this ideal in the ethical realm was universal love, and its application in politics called for universality of standard, for the elevation of the virtuous, and for thrift so that benefit might result for all human beings. It followed as a logical and ethical necessity that all aggressive warfare was a total evil to be unconditionally condemned.

Mo Ti, then, was primarily a religious teacher, the greatest that China has ever given to the world. At the same time, he lived his own preachments. In order to stop offensive war and to bolster up defensive measures for would-be victims of aggression, he became one of the most distinguished strategists of his age as well as a remarkable military engineer. In order to defend his tenets against the attacks of rival schools of philosophy, he developed the most elaborate system of logical method in ancient China.

For reasons not fully understood, the teachings of Mo Ti underwent an almost total eclipse for over two thousand years and his *Book,* preserved by happy accident, as it were, did not enjoy a careful transmission from age to age, so that ten chapters were completely lost and eight are missing except for their titles. The remaining fifty-three chapters, then, constitute what we have now in the *Book of Motzŭ.* These fall into five groups dealing respectively with (1) apocryphal comments, (2) records of the master, (3) basic teachings, (4) military organization, and (5) strategy. These groups of chapters are uneven in value, dissimilar in style, and divergent in authorship. Like the Confucian *Analects* and the *Book of Mencius,* it may really be regarded as a collection of the writings of Mo Ti's school.

To the student of Chinese literary history, the chapters in Groups 2 and 4 are of special importance, because they give us more information about the words and deeds of the master of this school, and because, if the style is the man, they are more directly imprinted with Mo Ti's personality. Of course, as in the case of Mencius, we have no evidence as to whether Mo Ti himself had a hand in the writing of any of these chapters; or if they were the records of his disciples, whether the record was faithfully made and shown to the master himself. This is why, when we study China's early philosophical writings, we do not feel justified in dismissing the possibility of composite authorship.

While the *Book of Motzŭ* is full of literary merits of many types, the really unique feature is to be found in the essays in Group 2, especially the synoptic chapters. These latter are essays on some cardinal teachings of the school, such as the elevation of the virtuous, universal love, intelligence of heaven, antifatalism, and condemnation of aggressive war. The treatment of each one of these topics in three or two essays similar in structure, content, and phraseology is perhaps due to the fact that the same speech by Mo Ti was recorded and elaborated upon by different pupils or groups of pupils. The simplicity of style, clarity of exposition, depth of conviction, and directness of appeal with which these essays so impress us lead us to believe that the originals were actually delivered as sermons rather than written as essays. Let us read, for example, from the first of the three synoptic chapters (or essays) on condemnation of war:

Here is a man who enters his neighbor's orchard and steals some peaches and plums therefrom. When this is known, he is condemned by the public, and, when caught, will be fined by the government. Wherefore? Because he has injured his neighbor to profit himself.

And if he steals from his neighbor a dog, a pig, or a chicken, he commits a wrong greater than the stealing of peaches and plums. Why? Because he has done a greater injury to another man; and the greater the injury he does, the greater is the wrong, and the severer shall be his punishment.

And if he steals his neighbor's horse or cow, he commits a wrong still greater than stealing a dog, a pig, or a chicken. Why? Because he does a greater injury to another; and the more he injures another, the greater is the wrong, and the severer shall be his punishment.

And if he goes as far as to waylay an innocent man, take away his fur coat and cloak, and stab him with his sword, then his crime is still greater than that of stealing a horse, or a cow. Why? Because he has done thereby a still greater injury. And the greater the injury a man does to another, the greater is his crime, and the severer shall be his punishment.

In all these cases, the gentlemen of the world agree to condemn this man and declare, "He is wrong!"

Now here is the greatest of all crimes—the invasion of one nation by another. But the gentlemen of the world not only refuse to condemn it, but even praise it, and declare, "It is right!"

Shall we say that these gentlemen know the distinction between right and wrong?

Killing one man constitutes a crime and is punishable by death. Applying the same principle, the killing of ten men makes the crime ten times greater and ten times as punishable; similarly the killing of a hundred men increases the crime a hundredfold, and makes it that many times as punishable.

All this the gentlemen of the world unanimously condemn and pronounce to be wrong.

But when they come to judge the greatest of all wrongs—the invasion of one state by another—(which is a hundred thousand times more criminal than the killing of one innocent man), they cannot see that they should condemn it. On the contrary, they praise it and call it "right." *Indeed, they do not know it is wrong.* Therefore they have recorded their judgment on it to be transmitted to posterity. If they know it was wrong, how could we explain their recording such false judgments for posterity?

Here is a man who sees a few black things and calls them black, but who, after seeing many black things, calls them white. We must all say that this man does not know the distinction between black and white.

Here is another man, who tastes a few bitter things and calls them bitter, but who, having tasted many bitter things, calls them sweet. We must all say that this man knows not the distinction between bitter and sweet.

Here is a world which condemns a petty wrong and praises the greatest of all wrongs—the attack of one nation upon another—and calls it right. Can we say that the world knows the distinction between right and wrong?

(Chapter XVII, Hu Shih's translation)

In the same simple, flowing style, but from slightly different angles, offensive war was condemned in two other essays (Chapters XVIII and XIX), one proving the futility of even military victory, and the other showing warfare to render no service to heaven on high, to the spirits in the middle, and to the people below.

Among the later philosophers of the Chou period, none was to wield greater influence on posterity in art and letters than Chuang Chou, generally known by his honorific appellation, Chuang-tzŭ (365?-290? B.C.). A native of the feudal state of Sung, whose princes were descendants of the vanquished Shang-Yin Dynasty and whose territory, though much reduced, still comprised the center of the old cultural orbit, Chuang-tzŭ grew up in the rich traditions of learning and refinement. But as he did not seek a public career and seldom talked about himself, we know little about his life.

The closest approximation to a public office that he ever held was a minor clerkship in his native district of Mêng. This experience gave him no satisfaction, for later on in life, according to early tradition, when he was approached by an emissary from the king of the powerful Ch'u State to consider its premiership, he spoke to the dignitary in the following way:

"I have heard," said Chuang-tzŭ, "in your king's possession is a sacred tortoise, dead these three thousand years, but still lying in the king's treasure chest. Now, were the tortoise to have his choice, would he die so as to leave his bones as relics to be treasured by men, or would he rather live and wag his tail in a mud pool?" "He would rather live and wag his tail in the mud pool," said the messenger. Whereupon Chuang-tzŭ dismissed him, saying, "Please be gone. I want to wag my tail in the mud pool."

This episode symbolizes both the spirit of Chuang-tzŭ as thinker and writer, and his search for the "ideal man." This ideal man is one in whom the contrasts of life and death, longevity and short life span, success and failure, gain and loss, yes and no, praise and blame, are blurred; by whom all the desires of the human world and distractions of joy and sorrow, pleasure and anger are transcended; with whom heaven and earth and the myriad things animate and inanimate are one, and in whom the ego and nonego are merged. He is a completely free person.

At the time of Chuang-tzŭ, the Chinese language was going through some noticeable changes. The divergence of dialects among feudal areas was creating a serious problem in cultural unity and administrative efficiency. As soon as the empire was unified in 221

B.C. a solution to this problem would be sought. As the standardization of the numerous dialects into a language to be spoken throughout the length and breadth of the empire would obviously be impossible, a more practicable way out would be resorted to—the adoption of a uniform code of writing, more or less detached from the spoken dialects, as a common literary medium. This was to be based on the standard writings of the preunification centuries in regard to both vocabulary and syntax. In later ages this style of writing, which consciously deviated from the living tongue to conform with the established models, was to be known as *ku-wên* or ancient style, ancient in the sense that it was crystallized into a general pattern before the writings of the period of Mencius, Mo Ti, and Chuang-tzŭ as well as their predecessors.

As has been mentioned before, the recording of events or ideas had expanded from the extremely compact and isolated entries typical of the *Analects* to include descriptive amplifications. An illustration contrasting an entry from the *Analects* and its amplification in the *Book of Chuang-tzŭ* may highlight the progress that had been made from the single-sentence unit to the group of paragraphs.

In the *Analects* (Section IX) we read: "[It is when] the year becomes cold that we know how the pine and the cypress are the last to lose their leaves." This laconic remark of Confucius' was given in fuller context in Section XXVIII of *Chuang-tzŭ* as follows:

Confucius was destitute in the Ch'ên and Ts'ai area. For seven days he ate no cooked food, his bramble broth contained no rice at all. His face looked extremely tired and yet he was playing his lute and singing in his room. Yen Hui was trimming some herbs while Tzŭ Lu and Tzŭ Kung gossiped with each other saying, "Our Master was twice banished from [his native State of] Lu, forced to leave Wei, threatened with the lopping of the tree in Sung,* reduced to penury in Shang and Chou, and now besieged and harassed in Ch'ên and Ts'ai. It would be no crime to kill him, nor misdemeanor to insult him. And yet he has kept up with his singing and playing of the lute. Can a Superior Man be so devoid of a sense of honor?"

To this Yen Hui had no reply. He went in and told it to Confucius. Confucius pushed the lute aside, heaved an audible sigh, and said, "Yu (Tzŭ Lu) and Tzŭ (Tzŭ Kung) are petty people. Summon them and I shall speak to them." As Tzŭ Lu and Tzŭ Kung entered the room the former said: "Circumstances like this may be described as dire destitution!" "What were you saying?" asked Confucius. "A Superior Man is successful when he is successful in *Tao;* and he is destitute when he is destitute in *Tao.* Now I harbor the *Tao* of human-heartedness and righteousness in my heart and yet squarely face the bitter trials in this confused and chaotic world. What destitution can this be to me? When I look within myself, there is no destitution in *Tao,* and when

---

* When Confucius was in Sung, he practiced the classic rituals with his disciples under a big tree. Huan T'ui wished to kill the sage by lopping down the tree.

I face an ordeal, I do not lose my virtue. It is only as the cold weather arrives and as rain and snow fall that I know the pine and cypress are exuberant. My adversities in Ch'ên and Ts'ai will only do me good."

Decisively Confucius returned the lute to his side and sang to its accompaniment. Cheerfully Tzŭ Lu held the ceremonial staff and danced.

Appraising Chuang Chou and contrasting him with other thinkers of the age of philosophers, the author of the "T'ien Hsia Pien," epilogue of the Book of Chuang-tzŭ, had this to say:

In paradoxical language, in bold words, and with subtle profundity, he gave free play to his imagination and thought, without following any particular school or committing himself to any particular line. He looked at the world as so heavily laden and muddy that it was impossible to speak to it seriously. He realized that the world would regard roundabout language as aimlessly irrelevant, accept arguments ad verecundiam as genuine truth, and consider parables as signs of breadth of vision. Therefore he lived in a world of Heaven and Earth and the Spirit, and refused to be bound by the things in the universe. He made no distinction between right and wrong, so that he lived in peace with the common crowd. Although his writings are inimitable and unique, they seem circuitous and innocuous. Although his utterances are irregular and formless, they are unconventional and readable. His substantiality is without end. Above he roams in company of the creator and below he consorts with those who are beyond the pale of life and death and transcend the level of beginning and end.

(Based on Hu Shih's translation)

Tributes paid to Chuang Chou as a writer are many. The most remarkable feature of these countless observations is that many of them have come from writers who were bitterly opposed to the philosopher's system of thought, but who admire his literary style, only vaguely realizing that his literary charm and his philosophy and acumen are really inseparable. Other critics say that all altercations with Chuang Chou on philosophical grounds are superfluous. They hold that he was serious when he appeared to be frivolous, and when he was not serious, he would tell jokes and stories. It has been suggested that he was devoid of a point of view so that it would be futile to pin him down on anything; that he had no succinct standards of right and wrong, so that his relativism amounted to an evasive absence of logical consistency.

While assertions like the foregoing are stimulating, they are not altogether fair to Chuang Chou, whose philosophy, no matter how subtle externally, does emanate from a central theme—"holding the middle of the huan in response to the infinite [problems of life]." The word huan in ancient Chinese had the general connotation of roundness, expressing its related concepts in cognate graphs meaning the firmament, a ring, a circle, a circular area, a compass with which a circle might be drawn. Hence, to most commentators, Chuang Chou met the problems of life and the universe by posing himself, as it were, at the center of a circle and allowing the circumference to expand and contract as it would. This interpretation, while it gives the philosopher a position of enduring consistency, delimits its flexibility. Actually, by the middle of the *huan*, Chuang Chou meant the center of the circumference, or the drawn circle, for elsewhere in the book the *huan* was described as having neither a beginning nor an end.

CHAPTER 7

Ch'in Literature

In the intense struggle for power among the feudal lords during the fourth and third centuries before Christ, the final prize, in the form of the first unified empire in Chinese history, was carried away by the state of Ch'in, which, according to some scholars, accounts for the origin of the name "China."

The details of the origin of the Ch'in people are hidden in obscurity. The ruling house was first formally infeudated in 897 B.C., as a reward for its faithful service in horse-raising for the Chou king. In 827 B.C. the Lord of Ch'in distinguished himself by launching successful campaigns against the "Western barbarians" and Huns. It was not until 770 B.C., however, when the royal house of the Chou Dynasty moved eastward to Loyang, that the state of Ch'in was officially recognized as a member acceptable to the Central States. Moreover, in return for the bodyguards supplied him in his eastward flight from the invaded old capital, the Chou king graciously promised Ch'in the privilege of occupying the western royal domain and adjacent territories if it had the power to oust the invaders. Once this was done, the state of Ch'in seemed to have whetted its appetite for further eastward expansion—in other words, for further movement into the orbit of orthodox Chinese civilization.

But cultural change is always a slow, if not a painful, process. As was usually true of border tribes, Ch'in culture long remained heterogeneous, absorbing various elements from divergent groups with which it came into contact. As late as the middle of the fourth century before Christ, when Prince Hsiao decided to make an attempt to revolutionize the old Ch'in ways, the peculiar custom was still prevalent among the common people of crowding into one bedroom all the members of a sizable family, possibly the survival of the usage of the tent unit in their nomadic days. At the same time, their typical abode was the log cabin as compared with the brick or pounded-mud houses of the Central States. Their music consisted of rhythmic sounds made with earthen jars and vessels, simple stringed instruments, slapping of thighs, and long doleful singing.

In short, their mode of living continued for centuries to be characterized by crudity and fierceness, daring and quick temper, hardly touched by the refinement of the rituals and music of the so-called Central States.

The princely house and the aristocracy in Ch'in, possibly less non-Chinese in descent than the commoners, were more aware of the attractions of Chou cultural refinement. At court and among government agencies, the Chinese written language had been long in use, although the formation of the written characters and their pronunciation were necessarily subject to many local variations. The Ch'in diviners, astrologers, priests, and recorders were familiar with the historical documentary style as well as the general principles of versification and courtly music. As we shall see in greater detail later, a Ch'in document and ten Ch'in poems deserved their inclusion in the collections of the *Shu Ching* and the *Shih Ching* respectively.

We should not hastily infer, however, that aside from the importation of the rules and tools of writing and of the standards and usages of courtly manners and superficial refinements there was any significant indication of acceptance by the Ch'in people of the religious tenets, ethical standards, and philosophical concepts generally current in the central and eastern portions of ancient China. The three ways of life as taught by Confucius, Lao-tzŭ, and Mo-tzŭ (Mo Ti) did not seem to reach the state of Ch'in in their purity at all. With the improvement of communication and transportation and the ever widening itineraries of the wandering scholars, it was almost impossible to keep new ideas out, especially as the Ch'in state policy wavered between the welcoming and banning of visitors. But, wandering scholars or no wandering scholars, the Ch'in State knew what it desired—all the means available to advance her position to military supremacy and economic leadership. These became not only the acid tests which "alien ideologies" had to pass but also the filter which would change their nature and colors.

With statism thus consciously and unconsciously glorified, the value of law seemed more demonstrable than that of ethics or of religion. It was, therefore, no coincidence that practicality was underscored in all the philosophical systems that found their way into Ch'in, and that the Legalist school had its fruition, if not inception, in this northwesterly border state. Though in disagreement with all earlier schools of philosophy, the Legalist school culled freely from their writings, utilizing such of their ideas as fitted into the new pattern. The idea of the unity of the world, and the accompanying idea of the universality of standards popularized by philosophers from Confucius down, for example, were fully capitalized and given a practical and political interpretation. Legalism was developed by experts from the Central States, but it was in Ch'in, the state of cultural heterodoxy, that it gained an earnest hearing and underwent a full flowering.

The military supremacy of Ch'in was an indisputable fact when Crown Prince Chêng ascended the throne in 246 B.C. in his thirteenth year. At the same time the formula of collective security among the six powers against Ch'in had been completely broken up, making it possible for Ch'in to embark on its own program of liquidating its rivals one at a time. In the brief duration of nine years, 230-221 B.C., the six kingdoms were ruthlessly crushed, and Prince Chêng declared himself "Shih Huang Ti"—which can be roughly translated as "first emperor of the Augustus type."

In order to facilitate thought control and to insure the submissive acceptance of imperial orders, the First Emperor, acting upon the advice of his prime minister, issued orders and meted out penalties that were entirely contrary to all established traditions. In the fateful year 213 B.C., for instance, came the decree of the Burning of the Books, which meant all histories except those kept by the imperial historian, all literature and books privately owned except those on medicine, divination, and horticulture. At the same time, all group discussions of the proscribed writings were declared criminal offenses against the state. In the following year, as though to display the teeth of the law, the government inflicted the death penalty upon some four hundred and sixty nonconformist scholars. They were buried alive in trenches at the imperial capital, Hsien yang, where the remnants of the old ruling houses of the six vanquished kingdoms and ten thousand of the wealthiest families in the empire had been uprooted from their homes and relocated under close official surveillance. Meanwhile, to fill the intellectual gap left open by the proscription of books and discussions, the imperial dynasty promoted belief in magic and superstitions on one hand, and, on the other, ordered all prospective seekers of education to go to government clerks for instruction and guidance.

The Ch'in Empire was so short-lived (221-206 B.C.) that its political and cultural potentialities were hardly realized at all. Yet, despite the endless condemnation of later historians, Ch'in contributions to subsequent dynasties were immense, especially in law and imperial administration.

As to what literature the Ch'in people had before they were drawn close to the cultural orbit of the Central States in that last quarter of the ninth century before Christ, we have no information. The earliest collection of Ch'in poetry extant is included in the *Shih*

Ching, in a special section traditionally entitled "Ch'in Fêng" or "Ch'in Airs," containing the words of ten songs. These songs show no appreciable variation from the songs of other states. The language is refined, the prosody is regular, and the general composition shows artistic self-restraint. In these respects they evidence the successful absorption of Chou refinement at the Ch'in court during the two centuries following the formal infeudation. In other words, these songs should be regarded more properly as examples of Ch'in composition in the style of the Central States than as expressions of the temperaments and emotional traits of the Ch'in people themselves. The ten songs, however, are not inferior poetry. Take, for example, the following courtship song:

> Thick grow the rush leaves;
> Their white dew turns to frost.
> He whom I love
> Must be somewhere along this stream.
> I went up the stream to look for him,
> But the way was difficult and long.
> I went down the stream to look for him,
> And there is mid-water
> Sure enough, it's he!
>
> Close grow the rush leaves,
> Their white dew not yet dry.
> He whom I love
> Is at the water's side.
> Up stream I sought him,
> But the way was difficult and steep.
> Down stream I sought him,
> And away in mid-water
> There on the ledge, that's he!
>
> Very fresh are the rush leaves;
> The white dew still falls.
> He whom I love,
> Is at the water's edge.
> Up stream I followed him;
> But the way was hard and long.
> Down stream I followed him,
> And away in mid-water
> There on the shoal is he!

(*Song 129,* Arthur Waley's translation No. 34)

From this example we can readily see that in the use of imagery there is no characteristic that was peculiarly Ch'in, and if we resort to the original, we shall find that the verse form and rhyming scheme in this poem also conform to the general pattern of songs sung in other areas. But, while it is mainly true that the ten Ch'in songs are more revealing of the acceptance by the Ch'in people of the art of song-making current in the Central States than of local literary style, the point should not be pushed too far. As popular songs of a well-defined area, their themes and contents were apt to reflect local customs and mores. The old Shang-Yin usage in which a king was followed to the grave by his dearest survivors, a practice which had disappeared almost completely in the Central States, seemed to have lingered on in this border region. A song lamenting the tragic death of three brothers in the interment of Duke Mu in the year 621 B.C. contains a note of the people's protest to Heaven:

> "Kio" sings the oriole
> As it lights on the thorn brush.
> Who went with Duke Mu to the grave?
> Yen-hsi of the clan Tzŭ-chü.
> Now this Yen-hsi
> Was the pick of all men;
> But as he drew near the tomb-hole
> His limbs shook with dread.
> That blue one, Heaven,
> Takes all our good men.
> Could we but ransom him
> There are a hundred would give their lives.

> (*Song 131*, Arthur Waley's translation No. 278)

With the wording slightly varied and the rhymes in the opening hexastich changed to accommodate the names of the two other brothers, the stanza is repeated twice to complete the song.

We should point out here that during the third quarter of the seventh century before Christ, when Prince Mu was on the Ch'in feudal throne (669-621 B.C.), and when the assimilation of the formalities of the orthodox culture was undergoing a process of acceleration, conformity had been sought in prose documentary style as well as in prosody and song-making. Besides the ten songs in the *Shih Ching*, early Ch'in literature in prose was preserved in the *Shu Ching* or the *Book of Documents*. The last document, "Ch'in Shih" or the "Oath of Ch'in," was supposed to have been proclaimed by none other than Prince Mu himself, although the exact historical context of the piece is uncertain as there are two schools of commentators linking the piece to two different events. Like other documents of this type in the *Shu Ching*, the "Ch'in Shih" purports to have been a speech solemnly delivered by the duke to his warriors after they had lost a battle. Instead of blaming his men and officers for the defeat, he held himself responsible for the disaster and publicly acknowledged his failure to listen to his wise counselors.

As a literary composition, the speech exhibits few deviations from the current Chou documentary style in either language or mannerism. It begins with the same interjection commonly used to call the attention of the crowd to the message that was to follow. It is decorated with refined phrases we find in similar documents and contains no expressions that we can identify as localisms and provincialisms. If the duke did not speak in the polished court language of those days on that special occasion, his recorders certainly represented him as doing so, or the recorded speech was so carefully revised in process of transmission that it finally lost all trace of the characteristics of the frontier dialect. In the thought pattern, however, there was a significant tendency toward absolutism when the duke virtually identified himself with the state, proclaiming "the state's peril comes from the One Man; the state's prosperity and devotion likewise is the One Man's success."

As the bronze inscriptions agreed in style and spirit with the transmitted early Chou literature of the songs and documents, so Ch'in inscriptions were in line with the fragments in verse and prose preserved in the classics. While the practice was adopted from the older cultural areas, of inscription on bronze, one innovation seemed to have originated in this frontier country—the perpetuation of records inscribed on stone.

Among the early specimens we have of China's stone inscriptions are the series of ten hunting songs inscribed on boulders more generally known by the misnomer of "stone drums." These granite boulders are of irregular form and size varying from one and a half feet to nearly three feet in height and averaging seven feet in horizontal circumference. They all taper from flat bases to rounded tops, reminding us of short truncated pillars rather than drums. The inscription, engraved in perpendicular lines in accordance with general usage, is on one side of the circumference of each "drum." Many a tourist who has seen them neatly arranged in two rows in the old Imperial College in Peiping, will recall that the inscriptions were gradually disappearing because of the ravages of time. In fact, the inscription on the eighth "drum" had completely disappeared a century ago, and only the one on the first boulder approached complete legibility.

On the date and authenticity of these inscribed boulders, a great deal has been written since their rediscovery in A.D. 818. There seems to be increasing evidence now that these commemorative stones once thought to have been inscribed and set up in Ch'in during the reign of Duke Mu (659-621 B.C.), actually date from the reign of Duke Ling around 400 B.C. when the high tide of the Sinicization of the border state had been made possible, as we have seen, by its expansion eastward centuries earlier to include the area of the old royal capital abandoned by the Chou king. The style of the inscribed characters, upon comparison with those found on bronzes of that age, bears a striking resemblance to the Chou script, on one hand, and to Ch'in metal inscriptions on the other.

Of more immediate concern to us are the contents of the inscriptions themselves—ten songs reminiscent of the ones in the *Shih Ching,* one on each "drum." The song on the first "drum" follows:

> Firm are our chariots
> And well trimmed our horses.
> Good are our chariots
> And strong are our horses.
> Here goes our lord a-hunting—
> Hunting and frolicking—
> Here roam the hinds and stags—
> Objects of our lord's pursuit.
> Of the many horn-bows in his possession,
> One bow he holds full stretched.
> We pursue the large stags
> And they come briskly galloping.
> And they come in droves,
> We meet them and await them.
> The hinds and stags are now wary.
> And they come [in larger numbers]
> We give chase to the largest ones
> As they come haltingly
> He shoots the strongest and fattest.

The other nine songs, though equally spirited to then contemporary ears, are no longer exciting to us twenty-five centuries later. One fact, however, stands out significantly—and that is, that the language and phraseology in these songs are almost indistinguishable from those in the *Shih Ching.* In fact, in the first and ninth songs in the series, there are actual verbal borrowings from the *Book of Songs.* This should leave no doubt in our minds that in poetry as well as in other features of refinement, the Ch'in folk of the fifth and fourth centuries before Christ were hearty imitators of the established patterns of the Chou court and of the feudal Central States.

This avidity in adopting the literary usages of the Central States, however, should not be lightly passed over as an ordinary phenomenon of border tribe acculturation, for it was to be an effective step toward the epoch-making work of empire building itself. Moreover, latecomers like the Ch'in people were recipients of this literary heritage; they succeeded in making unique contributions of their own which set the patterns for later ages, although strictly speaking, these contributions did not fall into the realm of creative artistic writing.

Although numerous literary works of the Central States must have found their way into Ch'in, not many of these were favored by the Ch'in court. Most of the wandering scholars visiting the frontier area were more interested in selling their own ideas than in glorifying the doctrines of schools well established in the east. This was true even in the case of Hsün Tzŭ.

Hsün Tzŭ, or Master Hsün, whose full name was Hsün K'uang (325?-245? B.C.), achieved eminence among thinkers of the Warring States period as a major expositor of the Confucian doctrines, splitting honors with his predecessor, Mencius. Born at a later age and in an area farther away from the sea, in the state of Chao whose rulers claimed common ancestry with those of Ch'in, Hsün Tzŭ was no mere echo of the sage, but developed new theories of his own. Opposed to Mencius, the advocate of the goodness of human nature, he taught that human nature was inherently bad and that all goodness in man was the result of postnatal efforts and conscious cultivation. Hence nurture and education were of utmost importance in subduing the beast in man and turning him into a civilized being.

Besides being a prose writer of great clarity and logical directness, Hsün Tzŭ was also dexterous in versification whenever he attempted it. The few pieces in rhyme that are found in the *Book of Hsün Tzŭ* are more reminiscent of the terseness and regularity of the *Shih Ching* than of the romantic freedom and exuberance of Ch'ü Yüan, although they bear the name of *fu,* a name mainly used for the writings of imitators of the southern poet. Occasionally in his essays, however, we find Hsün K'uang singing in the more irregular meter.

> You glorify Nature and meditate on her:
> Why not domesticate her and regulate her?
>
> You obey Nature and sing her praise:
> Why not control her course and use it?
>
> You look on the seasons with reverence and await them:
> Why not unfold your own ability and transform them?

You meditate on what makes a thing a thing:
Why not so order things that you may not waste them?

You vainly seek the course of things:
Why not appropriate and enjoy what they produce?

Therefore, I say: To neglect man and speculate about nature
Is to misunderstand the facts of the universe.

(Chapter XVII, Hu Shih's translation)

Obviously Hsün Tzǔ was regarded by most of his contemporaries as a follower of Confucius, for despite the novel notes he had sounded there was nothing in the thirty-two chapters of his book that contradicted or radically deviated from the teachings of the sage. And yet, by dint of his emphasis on the natural "badness" of human nature, on the corrective value of discipline in rituals and music and on the preferability of latter-day enlightened despots to ancient kings as models for good rulers, Hsün Tzǔ was the first Confucianist to approach the stand taken by a relatively new school which was to exert an immense influence on the kingdom of Ch'in—namely, the school of the Legalists.

While Hsün Tzǔ himself was not enough of an innovator to be identified with the new school, or to have exerted a direct influence upon the rising kingdom of Ch'in where the Legalists found the most unswerving patronage, two of his pupils played vital roles in shaping its destiny.

Han Fei (280?-233 B.C.), the more brilliant of the two as a writer, was of princely descent in the kingdom of Han, immediate neighbor of Ch'in on the east, and smallest in area among the seven Warring Kingdoms. Fond of the study of law and statecraft but handicapped in speech, he devoted himself to writing, especially to memorializing his king regarding state policies. These letters to the king, however, failed to win their author any position of responsibility, although the Han kingdom was being continually reduced in size and power. Han Fei then began to write in greater earnest such essays of distinction as "Solitary Vexation" and "The Five Vermin" (Chapters 11 and 49 in the *Book of Han Fei*).

Soon after this, the kingdom of Han was attacked. At first little happened, but as the attack became more unrelenting, Han felt the crisis and despatched Han Fei as special envoy to Ch'in, where he failed in his mission and committed suicide in prison.

The current edition of the *Book of Han Fei* comprises fifty-five essays, some of which, like essays in other philosophers' books, were doubtless by other hands. An advocate of the undependability of history and human nature, a spokesman for the supremacy of law, and a student of statecraft and administration, Han Fei expressed forthright belittlement of the art of letters. And yet in the eight or ten essays which have been established as authentically his, he proves himself a rare master of ancient Chinese prose style, clear, forceful, incisive, and provocative. In his essay on the "Distinguished Schools of Thought" (No. 50), for example, he points out that the Confucian school split itself up into eight sects after the death of the Master and the Mohist school into three after the death of its founder, all claiming to be orthodox followers of Confucius and Mo Ti respectively though differing among themselves as to what to accept and reject from the masters' original teachings. And yet,

Since Confucius and Mo Ti could not be resurrected, whom could we rely on to decide [the authenticity of] the learning of the later generations?

Furthermore:

Both Confucius and Mo Ti mentioned [the illustrious examples of] Yao and Shun and yet differed from each other on points of acceptance and rejection while both claimed to have represented Yao and Shun faithfully. Now that Yao and Shun could not come to life again, whom could we rely on to determine the truthfulness of Confucius and Mo Ti? The Yin-Chou period was over seven hundred years [before our time] and the Yü-Hsia period [preceding that] over two thousand years, during all of which time it was impossible to form a true picture against which the representations [of Yao and Shun] by Confucius and Mo Ti might be checked. And now we want to ascertain the ways of Yao and Shun of three millennia ago, is it not well nigh impossible to be sure [of anything]? To be sure of anything, without corroborating evidence is stupidity. To base an argument on anything of which one cannot be sure is perjury. Therefore he who bases his arguments forthright on [the authority of] the ancient sage-kings and is dogmatically sure of Yao and Shun is either stupid or perjurious.   (XC)

The other pupil of Hsün Tzŭ who was active in Ch'in and who, according to an early tradition, gave Han Fei the poison for suicide, was Li Ssŭ. But before we discuss this peculiar scholar-statesman, let us turn our attention to his benefactor, Lü Pu-wei, who sponsored Li Ssŭ's entry into the powerful border state.

Lü Pu-wei (290?-235 B.C.) was a notable figure in early Chinese literary history in his own right, for he was the producer of the first loosely organized "book" in China.

We have discussed in a previous chapter how philosophical prose gradually developed from the brief and laconic recordings of sayings and dialogues to the well-knit essay and the coherent group of essays. The emergence of a full-length book had to wait for the rise of a comprehensive empire-mind.

The man who supplied this was Lü Pu-wei, a wealthy merchant in the populous city of Yangti, erstwhile capital of the kingdom of Han (400-375 B.C.). He succeeded in amassing a huge fortune by buying up consumer goods when they were cheap and selling them when their prices were high. His wealth he used to great advantage in cultivating the friendship of a Ch'in prince who was in Han as a hostage. At his suggestion and with his financial assistance and active participation, the prince followed an intricate plan of diplomacy and bribery to obtain the status of heir-apparent to the Ch'in throne. As the latter succeeded to the kingship in 249 B.C. a beautiful dancer formerly in the Lü household, whom he had married, was declared queen. Three years later her son, Chêng, who was to shake the Sinitic world in more ways than one, became the Ch'in king at the age of thirteen. By both monarchs, Lü was made prime minister.

Lü Pu-wei was no stranger in the kingdom of Ch'in when he went there with the former prince in hostage in 249 B.C., for he had been there before as an interstate merchant and participant in subtle political intrigue. This time, however, he was powerful in political influence although whether or not he had personal designs on the Ch'in throne is a problem that cannot be solved. Following the general trend among feudal grandees of the age to expand their corps of retainers, or "guests on the payroll," Lü attracted as many as three thousand talented scholars to his household whom he supported with the income from his extensive estate at Loyang of one hundred thousand families. Before his political career ended with his removal from office in 237 B.C., and banishment to present-day Szechuan two years later (which he averted by taking a deadly poison), he had already accomplished a new literary experiment, the compilation of the *Lü-Shih Ch'un Ch'iu,* or *The Spring and Autumn of the House of Lü.*

Compiled in 240 B.C. as a work of collective authorship under Lü's direction, this book comprises 160 essays totaling 173,054 words organized into twenty-six sections which are, in turn, grouped into three parts.

Into the mechanical structure of this book was poured the learning of diverse schools of the Sinitic world, from the Confucian classics and the writings of the philosophers as well as the folklore of the time. The contents are eclectic but the literary style is fairly uniform. Just as its contents purported to be comprehensive of the vast empire that was in process of formation, its conscious strivings for pure rhetorical effect were portentous of the making of a universal literary language. Moreover, its neat arrangement of materials set a pattern for later generations in the writing of a full-fledged book.

Li Ssŭ (280?-208 B.C.) was the most distinguished of Lü Pu-wei's scholar-guests. Before his arrival in Ch'in in 247 B.C., he had served as a government clerk in his native state of Ch'u, and, inspired by an ambition to rise high in officialdom, had sat at the feet of the philosopher Hsün Tzŭ to study the ways of kings and emperors. Under the patronage of Lü Pu-wei, his talents began to bear fruit. He memorialized the Ch'in throne on the timeliness of unification by military conquest and diplomatic intrigue and was immediately rewarded with the enviable position of guest-minister. In 237 B.C., he even succeeded in bringing about the retraction of a Ch'in decree to banish all alien sojourners which would have included himself among those to be expelled. He witnessed the tragic death of his host in 235 B.C., and the suicide of his school friend, Han Fei, two years later, but transitoriness of fortune and fame in the human world failed to dampen his vaulting ambition. On the contrary, he took delight in his steady rise in the Ch'in official hierarchy, being supreme justice at the triumphant unification of the Ch'in Empire in 221 B.C. and finally prime minister eight years later. Many of the innovations in law and administration of the empire were his handi-work and many of the inspection tours of the First Emperor were made in his company. His assent to the palace intrigues following the sudden death of the First Emperor finally embroiled him in further conspiracies and brought about his execution in the awful form of being cut in two at the loins.

His busy political career did not entirely interfere with his literary activities. In fact many of his literary productions were inherent parts of his political life. As a writer, Li Ssŭ was greatly indebted to Hsün Tzŭ and Han Fei for style and contents although he never came close to being their equal. Yet, as he was the chief architect and participant in empire building, he left unique and indelible imprints on the history of early Chinese literature. He had at least confirmed and typified, even if he did not originate, the Ch'in usage of memorializing the throne in writing—a practice that became the popular vogue in subsequent dynasties, oftentimes with memorials running to book length. These memorials may be regarded as essays, argumentative and expository, written for the perusal of one person, the emperor, the prince, or the feudal lord to whom it was submitted. The usage was not unknown outside of Ch'in, especially during the Warring States Era, but it was in Ch'in that it took on a definite pattern and became something like a frozen literary genre, with Li Ssŭ's memorial against the banishment of alien guests and Han Fei's memorial in favor of the preservation of the state of Han as superb examples.

Li Ssŭ's memorial presents in eloquent and lucid prose a lesson from Ch'in history: that the rise of the border state to power was the result of the full utilization of such foreign talents as had been available. Then it argues from contemporary trends to prove that Ch'in did not discriminate against the products of other states for the increase of its own wealth and luxuries, nor against the cultural assets of other areas for the improvement of its refinement.

"Now when it comes to the selection of talents," the memorial goes on,

the standard is reversed. No question is asked as to whether it is right or wrong; no consideration is given as to whether it is straight or crooked. He who is not a native of Ch'in must go. He who is a guest must be banished. This means an emphasis on beauties and enjoyment of jades and pearls and a disregard for people. This is not the way to dominate the world within the Four Seas, or to subjugate the rival princes. Your servant has heard it said that when a land is vast, its grains are plentiful; when a country is great, its people are numerous; when weapons are strong, the troops are brave. Therefore, as Mount T'ai does not belittle the tiny sods, it has succeeded in attaining its great size; and as the Yellow River and the Sea do not reject puny streams of water, they have succeeded in achieving their depth; as the [model] kings did not disregard the diverse little people, they succeeded in radiating their royal virtues. And so, no land was regarded as out-of-the-way, and no person as alien. With the four seasons exuding bounty and the gods and the heavenly host conferring blessings, the Five Emperors and the Three Kings [of antiquity] were for this reason absolutely peerless.

Now [it is proposed] to give up men, supplying them to enemy states, and to reject the guests, building up the rival princes, causing the scholars of the wider world to shy away from facing west, and to tie up their legs against entry into Ch'in—which is tantamount to arming invaders with weapons and sending bandits food supplies.

Many are the things not produced in Ch'in which are yet valuable, and many are the scholars not natives of Ch'in, who are yet willing to become loyal subjects. But now [it is proposed] to banish the guests to aid the enemies, and to increase the population for the benefit of rivals, weakening the country from within, and planting grievances among the various foreign princes. Though efforts are made to keep the country free of danger, it cannot be done.

Li Ssŭ won the argument and the result was not unexpected.

The second notable contribution made by Li Ssŭ to the literary trends of his time was the innovation of a special verse form, the panegyric. On the many inspection tours made by Shih Huang Ti, the First Emperor, huge stone tablets were inscribed to commemorate the occasions. These inscriptions for the most part came from Li Ssŭ's hand. The new genre of panegyrics consisted of four-word (i.e., four-syllable) lines with every third one rhyming. Though monotonous in its contents, the tune played was not too irksome to imperial ears, as is evidenced by its repetition on many an innocent stone. The following, inscribed at Chihfu (Chefoo) in 218 B.C. may be taken as a typical example:

In the twenty-ninth year [of this Reign]
[His] Imperial Majesty [makes a] spring trip
To inspect the distant regions.

Arriving at the seacoast
He subsequently ascends Chihfu [and]
Brilliantly faces the morning sun.

Surveying the distant and the beautiful.
His accompanying ministers all call to mind
[That] the Primal Way is the most evident.

[When] the Holy Law was just proclaimed,
[It] illumined and pacified the land
And punished violence beyond [its confines].

[Its] military prowess radiated unopposed,
Shook the four extremities of the world
[And] captured and destroyed the Six Kings.

[It] extended and unified [all areas] under Heaven
Ending [all] harms [and all] ills
[And] lay idle for good [all] war weapons.

[With this] Bright Virtue, his Majesty
Rules over the Universe,
Seeing and hearing tirelessly.

[He] creates and establishes the great Principles,
Improves designs and perfects implements,
All embodying the ideal pattern.

Officeholders obey his orders
Each knowing what to do
With neither doubt nor suspicion.

The black heads [i.e., the people] are transformed,
Enjoying one standard, near and far,—
Since creation without peer.

[With] cardinal functions thus fixed,
Posterity [shall] follow the great work
[And] forever benefit from the sage rule.

[We] diverse ministers admiring His Virtue,
Prayerfully extol His Holy Majesty
[And] petition to inscribe [this at] Chihfu.

Besides patterning the memorial and innovating the panegyric, Li Ssŭ also took an active part in language standardization and educational regimentation as well as thought control.

In language reform, the more difficult task of unifying the spoken tongue was never attempted, for the multiplicity of local dialects and the slow absorption of non-Sinitic groups scattered over the empire would have rendered the task impossible. Since the written script had much less to do with actual pronunciation than in the case of an alphabetic, phonetic language, uniformity was sought instead in the structure of the graphs throughout the empire. Besides this, syntactical usages were also made to conform to the Ch'in empire norm, so that to all literate persons of the empire any written document would have a uniform meaning.

Li Ssŭ's share in this literary phase of the work of empire building was also notable. He played a leading role in revising the word books, and in bringing them up to date.

Although these three Ch'in vocabulary compilations are now lost, they seemed to have set the pattern for similar manuals for many centuries to come. For economy, each graph was used only once in the text, and to facilitate memorizations, the words were arranged in lines of equal lengths with end-rhymes. They were used not only as primers and lexicons, but also as penmanship models. The Chinese script was thus not only standardized, but also perpetuated as a common literary medium for a far-flung empire, even to be shared by a number of contiguous regions in eastern Asia.

CHAPTER 8

The Fu

A NEWLY evolved literary form which dominated four centuries of the Han dynasty (206 B.C.-A.D. 220) which followed the Ch'in (221-206 B.C.) was the *fu*. This fairly flexible genre reflected the changing tastes of its patrons from generation to generation not only in subject matter but also in mood and form. In the beginning it had been used during an era of social and political transition to convey sharp but veiled criticism of conditions. During the solidification of the new Han Dynasty it had acquired literary elements and dropped some of its useful purpose. As peaceful conditions encouraged the growth of cultural centers at the various princely courts, refinement increased. Then, after the middle of the second century before Christ, in accordance with the tastes of newly elegant, leisurely courtly circles, the *fu* severed all connection with reality and became glorification pieces, sophisticated and intricate but sadly lacking in spontaneity, creativeness, or depth.

Regarded by critics and anthologists of later ages sometimes as verse, and sometimes as closer to prose, this literary type is so elusive that a short summary of its evolution is warranted.

The significative component of the *fu* graph is the pictogram of a sea shell, symbolic of economic value. Originally, the word stood for local tributes-in-kind, as well as for their payment, collection, and exhibition. Whether on the submission of such tributes there were chantings of the names, attributes, and uses of the different articles, we do not know; but we do know that when the word *fu* was used in reference to literary activities from the eighth century before Christ on, it functioned almost exclusively as a transitive verb meaning to recite or to chant. Ministers of the state, we learn, were expected to recite adequate verses when they ascended a scenic mountain, and diplomats to quote passages from the *Book of Songs* to suit special occasions. The words of a song might be sung to music, or elaborately chanted. In the latter case, the process was known as *fu*.

The earliest use of the word *fu* as the name for a type of literary composition occurred in the *Hsün Tzŭ Book.* A chapter entitled "Fu" contains five unique pieces in rhyme on "Li" or the art of living, on "Wisdom," on "Clouds," on "Silk worms," and on "Needles." Each piece begins with a statement of the subject phrased in the form of a query, without mentioning it by name, chiefly in four-syllable lines resembling those found in the *Book of Songs.* In response to this request for identification comes the answer, which further elaborates on the subject but refrains from identifying it explicitly until the very end. The second section of each piece takes a more irregular line pattern, at times faintly suggestive of the minor pieces of the Ch'u elegies. These early speciments of *fu* were, in a way, logogriphs and conundrums in verse, usually admired for their rhetorical cleverness as well as for their didactic allegory. These five rhymed pieces were labeled *fu,* for instead of being sung, they were only to be chanted. Hence the tradition was early established that *fu* pieces were not accompanied by musical scores.

At the time these five *fu* pieces were written, toward the end of the fourth century before Christ, few new songs were being composed of the four-syllable line variety. The music and the songs of the southern regions were beginning to win popularity even among the northerners. And when verses were to be chanted without the advantages of musical accompaniment, the monotony of the regular four-syllable lines would be all too obvious. Hsün Tzŭ, who had sojourned in Ch'u about 255 B.C. and was acquainted with Ch'u poetry, probably had this in mind when he varied his rhythmic pattern in the latter half of each of his five *fu* pieces and purposely introduced irregular lines for contrast.

Though the name *fu* as first used by Hsün Tzŭ was retained for over two thousand years, the new literary type inherited little of the form and technique of the five pieces we have just mentioned. The *fu* in Han times was rather an offshoot of the Ch'u elegiac tradition. In fact, in the eyes of Han writers and bibliographers, the elegies of Ch'ü Yüan as well as the rhymed pieces in the *Book of Hsün Tzŭ* were summarily grouped together under the general name of *fu.*

As a forerunner of the *fu* composers of later times, Hsün Tzŭ was much less influential than Ch'ü Yüan. And yet the towering figure of the latter as a literary genius cast such a long and intense shadow that the individuality and stature of his many followers were blurred. Among his followers, only Sung Yü (290?-222? B.C.) was fortunate enough to retain a little of his identity and a few traces of his literary works. His popularity as the most gifted continuator of the Ch'ü Yüan school of writing and the eagerness of the southerners to greet new voices combined to turn him into a sort of Homeric figure so that many *fu* of anonymous authorship were attributed to him. And as these attributions grew in number with the lapse of time, anecdotes were told of his life which probably had no historical foundation at all, but were mere embroideries upon the meager narrative elements in pieces which Sung Yü himslf had never written.

Spanning the several decades of a stormy century for his native state of Ch'u, Sung Yü seems to have led an uneventful life, the greatest personal disappointment to him being the loss of a minor clerical job in the government. As to his literary works, of the fourteen *fu* ascribed to him, we are not sure of the authenticity of a single piece. Perplexing as the situation is, we cannot deny, on the other hand, that he was an important milestone in the early development of the *fu* style, for in literary history, a long-accepted attribution often weighs more than a long-obscured or forgotten fact.

Aside from the intrinsic beauty of the Ch'u elegies, the tragic debacle of the Ch'u State in 223 B.C., which was intensely lamented, might have been instrumental in popularizing the folk songs of the southerners. Thus, after the rise of the Ch'in Empire, among the vanquished people, folk rhymes attributed to an old man arose symbolizing the hope of the eventual overthrow of tyranny:

> Though Ch'u might have but three families [left];
> It will be none but Ch'u that spells the doom of Ch'in.

It did not take long to see this bit of folk prophecy fulfilled. In 209 B.C., hardly a year after the passing of the first Ch'in emperor, three separate uprisings broke out in the southerly regions, all capitalizing in one way or another on the memory of the Ch'u State. Then the fire of rebellion rapidly spread to other areas despite the full mobilization of the imperial troops, and soon all the vanquished states were resurrected one after another. In 207 B.C. the second emperor was forced by his eunuch-premier to take his own life and was succeeded by a nephew who, after sitting for forty-six days on the precarious throne, had to surrender the empire to Liu Pang, a Ch'u general commanding the first detachment of insurgents to arrive at the imperial capital.

In 202 B.C., four years after the extermination of the Ch'in Dynasty, when Liu Pang was fighting the last rival contender for the imperial throne, Hsiang Yü (232-202 B.C.) of Ch'u, the Han hosts were ordered to sing in Ch'u style so as to confuse the enemy's judgment under cover of night. The order was carried out so well that Hsiang exclaimed, "How can there be so many Ch'u men!" It is evident that the southern style of singing was well known to Han soldiers. When Hsiang soon faced crushing defeat, he burst out in elegiacs in his own native style to his favorite Lady Yü and his pet piebald horse, Chui:

> Though my prowess may root up mountains, hieh,
> And my vigor overshadow the world,
> When times are adverse, hieh, Chui will not go.
> Now that Chui goes not, what can be done.
> Oh Yü, oh Yü, what else is there for me to do for you!

It should not be forgotten that Liu Pang, victor among contenders for the imperial throne and founder of the Han Dynasty, was himself a native of the Fêng-P'ei area, an eastern extension of the former state of Ch'u, and therefore had been familiar with folk songs in the Ch'u tradition in his boyhood. What was more natural, then, for him than to burst forth in Ch'u song when he made his triumphant return to his home town after declaring himself emperor? Thus at a banquet to which he had invited his own townspeople, old and young, he played for them on the simple folk-lute as he sang with one hundred twenty boys he had personally trained:

> While the great wind rises, hieh, the clouds fly and scatter.
> With augustness over all within the seas, hieh, I return home!
> Where can I find valiant soldiers, hieh, to guard the four corners
> [of my realm]?

This prevalence of the Ch'u type of song-making was an important contributing factor to the rise of the new literary type, but these pieces that we have just noted were not yet fully developed specimens of the *fu* itself. The promotion of the new genre had to wait for the conscious patronage of another emperor.

Such an emperor came to the throne in 140 B.C. This lad of sixteen, known in China's annals as Wu Ti, or Emperor Wu, was to reign over the far-flung empire for fifty-four years (140-87 B.C.), re-enforcing the foundations of the imperial dynasty and extending its frontiers in all directions, especially toward Central Asia. Besides being an epoch-making soldier and administrator, he was also a conscientious patron of learning and letters.

After the death of its founder, Liu Pang, the Han Empire saw the reign of three succeeding rulers, who, for different reasons, were all indifferent to the promotion of belles-lettres. One of these, Emperor Ching (reigned 156-141 B.C.) was said to have positively no taste for the *fu*. Although the new genre failed to receive active encouragement at the imperial court, it seemed to have fared better at some of the feudal courts of the princely states where patronage was generous and readily available. It was, therefore, at these minor centers of learning and refinement away from the capital of the empire that we find the chief writers of the *fu* before the accession of the epoch-making Emperor Wu in 140 B.C.

To these princely courts people of talent were often sent when they had fallen into disfavor at the imperial court but were not criminal enough to incur the penalty of regular exile. It was in the gloomy days of such semi-exile that Chia Yi (200-168 B.C.) wrote his *fu* pieces, as well as his fifty-eight memorable essays. A native of Loyang, Chia Yi rose to distinction as a literary man when he was only seventeen. Four years later, Emperor Wên summoned him to the capital and gave him rapid promotion in the administrative hierarchy. By this time he had already written a considerable number of political pieces in prose, which we shall mention in another chapter. Jealousy among court circles, unfortunately, cut short his career, and led to his appointment as grand tutor to the Prince of Ch'angsha. After four unhappy years spent at the southern fringe of the orbit of Chinese civilization, he was recalled to the capital in 174 B.C. and given an audience by Emperor Wên, who asked him questions about the fundamentals of gods and spirits which kept him talking until past midnight. Despite the emperor's admiration for his extensive learning, he was again appointed grand tutor, this time to Prince Huai of Liang. In 169 B.C. his prince-pupil died heirless from a fall while horseback riding. Chia Yi, mourning the untimely death of the prince as a result of his own dereliction as tutor, followed his prince to the grave in his thirty-second year.

While his sojourn to the southern region of Ch'angsha dampened his *joie de vivre*, it brought him to the land of Ch'ü Yüan, whose misfortunes in life he could not fail to liken to his own. Thus when he crossed the River Hsiang in 179 B.C. he addressed an elegy directly to the Ch'u poet. The piece "Tiao Ch'ü Yüan," in close imitation of the prosodic style of Ch'ü Yüan's "Fallen in Sorrow," is the first *fu* of the Han Dynasty of whose date and authorship we are perfectly certain. Although the word *fu* is not in its title, no question has ever been raised that it was a *fu*, which fact indicates that in that first period of its development, the *fu* was indistinguishable from *ch'u tz'ŭ* or the Ch'u elegies except that it was written later and that it might or might not be by a Ch'u hand. In fact the term *fu* was so elastic that to bibliographers in the Han Dynasty the writings of Ch'ü Yüan himself came under its general classification.

Another *fu* written by Chia Yi at the feudal court of the principality of Liang was entitled "The Owl" (*Fu Niao*) in which he combined the northern style of Hsün Tzŭ and the southern cadence of

Ch'ü Yüan. This he did by linking two four-syllable units with the exclamatory *hieh* in the middle.* The occasion was the arrival of an owl in his house, an evil omen according to southern folklore, foreboding the early death of the master of the house. To dispel his pent-up melancholy in the humid atmosphere of southern China, he sought consolation in the teachings of Chuang Chou.

Besides the princely court at Ch'angsha, there were other centers of culture and literary activity, in which the production of *fu* was given special patronage. Among these, two are particularly worthy of mention: the court of Prince An of Huainan, and that of Prince Wu of the principality of Liang, recreated in 173 B.C.

We shall discuss Liu An (179?-122 B.C.), the famous prince of Huainan, in a later chapter in connection with the evolution of philosophical prose. We shall now simply point out that like so many others of the Han Dynasty, he showed more than a passing interest in the *fu*, although his main cultural pursuit lay in other domains. He made a special effort to attract the leading writers of his age to his court, and these wrote a total of forty-four *fu* pieces; the Prince himself was even more prolific, with eighty-two on record. Although all except one or two of these are now lost, there is no doubt that the prince was a master in the art of versification in the Ch'u style and as such had won recognition at the imperial court itself.

It was at the princely court of Liang under Prince Hsiao, however, that the writing of *fu* engaged the exclusive attention of a sizable coterie of aspiring writers. Although by and large, the peripatetic peddling of political ideas and diplomatic strategies of the fourth century before Christ was now a thing of the past, writers and advisers at a princely court did not hesitate to leave one principality for another for personal safety when the prince refused to listen to their counsel.

It was under such circumstances that in about 155 B.C. a whole group of writers left the principality of Wu in the southeast to seek more intelligent patronage and greater personal security at the court of Liang, to which Prince Hsiao had been transferred to revive the state of his half-brother killed in the riding accident. Receiving many favors from the imperial court, as the youngest son of the empress dowager, he built luxurious parks and pleasure houses which provided an ideal environment for the creation and enjoyment of a type of literature removed from the political and economic problems of the age. In more than one way it was at the Liang court that the salient features of the new literary type were given definite shape.

---

* In some early transcriptions the word *hieh* was sometimes omitted. The modern pronunciation of the graph is "hsi."

The most distinguished *fu* writer at Liang was Mei Shêng (before 200-140 B.C.) who shared honors with Chia Yi as the master of the new technique in its formative period, i.e., before 140 B.C. While Chia Yi adhered to the intensely individual lyricism of Ch'ü Yüan, singing almost exclusively to himself, and thus continuing, instead of departing from, the tradition of Ch'u elegy, Mei Shêng was the first one to blaze new trails in *fu* writing in early Han times.

Mei Shêng's reputation as a *fu* writer had been well established even before he went to Liang, for while in Ch'u (circa 180 B.C.) he had written *Ch'i Fa* (*Seven Stimuli or Suggestions*), a seven-part composition preceded by a prologue. The plan is a simple one. The prologue introduces the crown prince of Ch'u who was ill, and his guest from Wu who, wanting to find out the cause of his ailment, proposed to seek its cure in apt verbal stimuli instead of ordinary medication. One after another and without haste, the guest from Wu tried to wean the prince away from his illness by elaborating upon the doleful beauty of the music of the lute, the enticing flavor of foods and drinks prepared by culinary experts, the attractiveness of chariots and horses driven by great horsemen, the joy of luxurious banqueting with women preceded by extensive travel to picturesque spots and enlivened by popular melodies, and the delight of hunting for game in ideal environs and with strong bows and sharp arrows. To all these stimuli the prince was yet unable to respond, but sunniness was visible in his countenance and the tide of his health was beginning to turn.

Seeing that the prince was pleased, the guest produced his sixth stimulus—the wonderful grandeur of midautumn at the bend of the Kuangling River on a full-moon night. Even to this the prince pleaded illness and inability to respond. Then the guest presented his seventh stimulus—his proposal to recommend to the prince people of talent and wisdom who would discuss the meaning and the mystery of the universe and the right and wrong of myriad things. Thereupon the prince, supporting himself on the low table, rose to his feet and exclaimed, "Great it is to hear the words of eloquent and sage people!" He began to perspire and presently his illness left him.

In more ways than one, the *Ch'i Fa* set the pattern of *fu* in Han times in its basic characteristics, in spite of the fact that it was not labeled a *fu* in its title and in the eyes of many a later critic was not classified as such. It is extravagant in its elaboration, lavish in its diction, far-fetched in its imageries, and yet attractive in the general impression it created in the minds of its patrons and admirers.

Besides writing a *fu* on the T'u Yüan, the pleasure garden of the prince, Mei Shêng also took part in a contest set by the latter in which the *fu* was used as a gauge of literary talent. To the seven participants were assigned seven different topics, the willows, wine, the low table, the stork, the gentle deer, the moon, and the folding screen. Among the contestants, Han An-kuo failed to complete his composition on the low table and Chou Yang, who must have finished his assignment on wine early, wrote on the low table for the former. Both the giver and receiver of aid were subjected to the not unpleasant penalty of the loser's drink of three pints of wine, while to each of the five successful contestants rewards were made of five scrolls of silk.

Mei Shêng's *fu* on the willows, like the other pieces completed in the contest, is light and meager in its contents. Instead of delineating the beauty and virtue of the willow, he paints with preciosity a brief word picture of the environs of the tree and proceeds to describe the prince's party in the pleasure garden and how the poet himself is insignificant in this company. Of particular interest are the following transitional lines:

> Our Prince, with dignified magnificence
> Presides over and amuses himself with the talented ones.
> And I, his petty servant, seeing and hearing nil
> In their midst, submit these words.

Unlike his contemporary, Chia Yi, who took the new genre in all seriousness, Mei Shêng seemed to have sensed a touch of the formality and frivolity with which the *fu* was soon to be imbued. Following the footsteps of Ch'ü Yüan, Chia Yi sang alone to himself, and his *fu* were elegies. Writing mainly for an audience with a prince as patron, Mei Shêng's *fu* naturally became panegyrics. The difference between their approaches and techniques epitomizes the transition from the *tz'ŭ* of Ch'u (Ch'u elegies) to the typical *fu* of Han times.

Although with the advantages of a clearer perspective and a wider range of materials for comparison we no longer rate these full-fledged *fu* pieces as having great literary merit, yet in the eyes of contemporaries they represented, particularly in the case of Mei Shêng, great specimens of literary excellence. They had departed from the riddles in rhyme of Hsün Tzŭ by being more melodious and rhythmic, less didactic, and therefore more interesting. Moreover, they expressed in peculiar ways the spirit of the newly stabilized empire and gave satisfaction to the self-glorification urge of the emperors and princes.

The greatest patron of the *fu*, as we have mentioned, was Emperor Wu, the dynamic and ambitious monarch whose influence was profoundly felt in many facets of Chinese history. Since he himself was an ardent admirer and creditable writer of poetry in the southern tradition, it was not surprising that soon after his coronation he sent for Mei Shêng, the senior *fu* writer of the empire, to proceed to the imperial capital in an especially made chariot with fine rush tires around the wheels to ensure traveling comfort. Unable to avail himself of these imperial honors, Mei Shêng died in the very year he was summoned (140 B.C.), at the age of over sixty.

Emperor Wu's interest in the budding literary genre remained unabated. Two clansmen of his, both participants and patrons of *fu* writing, came to his court from their feudal principalities to pay him homage—the prince of Huainan, Liu An, in 139 B.C.; and the prince of Chungshan, Liu Shêng, in the following year. Meanwhile, through the mediation of the chief superintendent of imperial hounds, he had come to notice the literary talents of a *fu* writer who was probably the most thorough representative of the *fu* in Han times and who continued to be held up as a model by his followers.

Ssŭ-ma Hsiang-ju (179-118? B.C.), who was a great admirer of the knight errant Lin Hsiang-ju (flourished 281-271 B.C.) and had named himself after the latter, was a colorful character. A native of Ch'êngtu, in present-day Szechuan province, but in his time very much on the frontier of China's cultural orbit, he had trained himself in book learning as well as fencing and had secured a position at court as imperial bodyguard to Emperor Ching (reigned 156-140 B.C.). Though Little Doggie (as his parents had nicknamed him) was unhappy in this position, he had the pleasant experience of meeting many of the literary figures of his generation who had traveled to Ch'angan in the retinue of the feudal princes on their occasional tours to render homage to the Son of Heaven. Though he knew the emperor had shown no interest in *fu* writings, he himself had been fascinated by the coterie of *fu* writers from Liang under the leadership of Mei Shêng. Ssŭ-ma Hsiang-ju soon left the imperial city to relocate at the princely court of Liang.

During his sojourn in Liang he wrote his first *fu*, the "Tzŭ Hsü Fu" or "Master Nil" in 145 B.C. Master Nil, imaginary ambassador from the principality of Ch'u, after he had been entertained in an all-day hunting trip by the prince of Ch'i, called upon Mr. Never-was, a native of Ch'i, in whose house a third imaginary character, Lord Nonexistent, happened also to be visiting. Answering his host's queries about the experiences of the day, Master Nil boasted he had derived the greatest delight from his successful attempt to impress the Ch'i prince with the thrilling experience of hunting in Ch'u. In reporting to his two friends the word picture he had painted earlier in the day of the least of the seven marshes in the principality of Ch'u, Master Nil burgeoned forth in rhyme:

> Its mountains—
>> Wind and twine,
>> Slant and converge,
>> Tower and erupt,
>> Sharpen and taper,
>> Impend and overhang,
>> Jut and vary,
>> Hide and eclipse
>> The sun and moon:
>> Interlock and overlap,
>> Threatening the blue clouds above,
>> Meander and wander,
>> Touching the rivers below.
>
> Its soil—
>> Is red and green,
>> Brown and off-white,
>> Crystal white and ocher yellow,
>> Leaden and bluish,
>> Golden and silvery.
>> The diverse colors sparkle and flow
>> Brilliantly, radiant like
>> The scales of the dragon.
>
> Its stones—
>> Are agate and mica,
>> Beryl and granite,
>> Chiamlak * and onyx,
>> Marbles white
>> And red and blue.

In a similar vein, Master Nil elaborated upon the four quarters of the principality of Ch'u before introducing a verbal tableau of how the prince would exert himself during the hunting expedition and seek relaxation in dining and wining, and in the company of beautiful women afterward. To his claim that Ch'i was probably no equal, the Ch'i prince had made no reply. On hearing this boastful summary of the happenings of the day, Mr. Never-was made his rebuttal and drew his moral. Besides surpassing Ch'u in its grandeur

*A semi-precious stone of less value than jade.

and in its ability to "swallow eight or nine [lakes the size of Lake] Yünmêng into its belly without feeling the slightest discomfort," Ch'i would never play up its large parks and frolicking sports on account of its subordination to the empire.

> Moreover, you are being a guest and our prince
> saw fit not to retort.
> Why say then, he had no answer!

Thus ends the "Tzŭ Hsü Fu" which was destined to give its author assurance of considerable imperial recognition and lasting literary fame. But these were not to come to him immediately. Forced to seek a livelihood after the death of his patron, the prince of Liang, in 154 B.C., he returned to his native home and lived on the generosity of a friend who had become mayor of Link'ung but who still did not command his respect. Through the introduction of the mayor, he made the acquaintance of a millionaire, Cho Wang-sun, and seduced with lute music his newly widowed daughter, Cho Wên-chün, who eloped with him to find nothing besides four empty walls in his home in Ch'êngtu. He returned to Link'ung with his wife in desperation and sold his carriage and other little belongings to buy a saloon. One day, while he was wearing shorts and cleaning up and Wen-chün was sitting at the counter as hostess and barmaid, his fortune began to turn. His millionaire father-in-law relented and gave them money and slaves. He went back to Ch'êngtu with his wife, bought himself horses and farms, and lived in style as a rich man.

Meanwhile he had entrusted a copy of the "Tzŭ Hsü Fu" to his friend and fellow townsman, Yang Tê-yi, who, as superintendent of imperial hounds, was close to the emperor in his majesty's lighter moods. It was no coincidence then, that the composition was finally read by the emperor and won his admiration. "How I wish," he exclaimed, "this man were alive today!" Whereupon the identity of the author was revealed, Ssŭ-ma Hsiang-ju was immediately summoned to court and his ambition of writing for the emperor was fulfilled. In his first audience with the emperor he spoke slightingly of the "Tzŭ Hsü Fu," as it had been written on the affairs of mere feudal princes. Now he begged permission to write one on the imperial hunt.

The result was "Shang Lin Fu" or the "Supreme Park," which was really a continuation of the "Tzŭ Hsü," now probably revised to fit into the new companion piece to form a harmonious whole. While the "Tzŭ Hsü" features Master Nil and Mr. Never-was as engaged in a verbal tilt, each glorifying his native principality, the "Shang Lin" presents Lord Nonexistent as spokesman for the united empire. The empire, far superior to any of its constituent units in its size, scenery, flora and fauna, architecture, and wealth, boasts also of the truly majestic hunt and sumptuous post-hunting banquets and entertainment and, above all, a sage-emperor who, philosophizing upon the splendor and excitement of the occasion, calls a halt to it all and returns to the pursuit of virtue, refinement, and benevolent government.

"In comparison with this," exhorts Lord Nonexistent in prose again, "are not the affairs of Ch'i and Ch'u lamentable? In a total area of a thousand square *li,* the hunting park occupies nine hundred. . . . Your servant fears it is the common people who will bear the burden!" Whereupon the other two gentlemen's expressions change, and they admit their stupidity and thank Lord Nonexistent for his words of wisdom.

The success of this *fu* was immediate. Ssŭ-ma Hsiang-ju was given a post at court and appointed in 130 B.C. chief of a diplomatic delegation to the southwestern border tribes to correct the harsh measures of an earlier mission. While he was passing through Link'ung with his entourage and receiving salutations from local dignitaries, he so impressed his father-in-law that his wife was reinstated in the millionaire's affections and given her due share of the family fortune. Thenceforth to the end of his life, he lived in comfort and continued as the master of the *fu* par excellence.

Of the twenty-nine *fu* that Ssŭ-ma Hsiang-ju was recorded to have written, only six are extant. Aside from the ones just mentioned, two others deserve notice. One is "Mei-jên Fu" ("The Beauty") which is an elaborate verbal picture of the charms of a beautiful woman waiting for her lover—an early example of the great length to which a writer could go in delineating the sensual as well as the emotional aspects of a beautiful woman. Another piece by which the author is remembered is "Ch'ang Mên Fu" (literally, "Long Doors"), written at the request of Empress Ch'ên, the alienated consort of Emperor Wu, who offered the writer a hundred thousand Chinese cash for a composition that might win back the favors of her emperor husband. It was a presentation of the loneliness and yearning of Empress Ch'ên in Ch'ang-mên Palace in which she had been living in isolation. The writer showed remarkable ability in placing himself in the emotional state of the empress, and Emperor Wu, according to one tradition, was so profoundly moved that he decided to restore the empress to her former status. In commenting upon this piece, a later *fu* writer, Yang Hsiung (53 B.C. to A.D. 18), remarked: "It is not of this world. Could it be the product of something other than a human hand?"

A rival to Ssŭ-ma Hsiang-ju in *fu* writing, Yang Hsiung (53 B.C.– A.D. 18) was also a native of Ch'êngtu in Szechuan Province. To us he is instructive in pointing out the hollowness of a literary type even in its heyday, when that type is far removed from the life and feelings of the common people. His *fu* compositions were all done in his youth, which he regretted profoundly in his maturer years by comparing that obtuse art to the carving of little worms—something that a real man would not do. Apparently he was aware of the fact himself that his *fu* compositions were slavish imitations of his predecessors. His great works were a compilation of variant dialect expressions systematically arranged (*Fang Yen*) and a dictionary of synonyms. These he probably had utilized in his *fu* in which an extensive vocabulary parading synonyms and cognate words had already become a requirement in padding rhetoric to ensure a glamorous façade. Deviating further from the beaten literary path of the dynasty, he did attempt two compositions in prose for greater literary and philosophical permanence: an imitation of the *Book of Changes* entitled *T'ai Hsüan* and an imitation of the Confucian *Analects* entitled *Fa Yen*. These, it is true, were also frankly imitative. Nonetheless, they were free from the frivolities and trivialities of the typical *fu*. Yet when these were shown by Yang to his classicist friend, Liu Hsin, the latter remarked, "You are overexerting yourself in vain. . . . I'm afraid posterity might use these as covers for condiment jars." No contemporary suggested that Yang Hsiung's *fu* compositions might be subjected to similar abuse.

But no matter how feelingly Yang Hsiung tried to belittle *fu* as literature, the literary type had not only come to stay but also to monopolize the creative activities of all major writers as the literary type of the empire. Its massive production alone was impressive. The bibliographical section of the *Han Shu* or *Dynastic History of Han* lists twenty writers of descriptive *fu* with 361 titles; twenty-one lyrical *fu* writers with 274 titles; twenty-five narrative *fu* writers with 136 titles; and twelve humorous *fu* writers with 233 pieces. Although numerous *fu* writers had tried their hands at more than one type, the very fact that a total of 1004 *fu* compositions were recorded as worthy of mention unmistakably indicates the preponderance and popularity of the type continuously for nearly four hundred years.

The deepening of the convention provoked sporadic revolts from time to time, as would be expected. A mild defier of the *fu* tradition was Wang Pao of the first century before Christ, who wrote a story in *fu* style by utilizing the vulgate language of the people. It describes the imposition of certain rigid regulations of conduct and service by a tricky housewife on a bonded slave boy and tells how the latter cleverly succeeded in by-passing the letter of each regulation in the bond contract. Finally he was outwitted by Wang Pao, who gave a new twist to the interpretation of each stipulation. At the end, the slave boy humbly submitted himself to all the requirements called for. This unique piece so exaggerated the technique of elaboration as currently employed in *fu* writing that it underscores some of the ludicrous elements in grandiloquent rhetoric.

Besides writers who were quick to see humor in formalized rhetoric, students who were eager for real scholarly attainments, like Yang Hsiung, were also aware of the emptiness of the literary gymnastics involved in *fu* composition. Another outstanding intellectual who had no use whatsoever for *fu* compositions was the Confucian classicist, Lu Chi (died A.D. 192; not to be confused with the great *fu* writer and literary critic of A.D. 261-303). The classicist, Lu, was not only a pupil of the great scholar, Ma Yung (A.D. 79-166), but was also a lodger at Ma's home. Irony would have it that Ma Yung was not only a classical authority of his time but also a nephew of an empress and a great master of *fu* composition who had trained his own troupe of beautiful dancers and women singers to do the chanting. It is recorded that the pupil had developed such deep-seated aversion for *fu* compositions that he would not even turn his head around to look at the beautiful girls while they were studying the composition texts. He would not submit himself to the regimentation of taste.

This tyranny of literary convention perpetuated the *fu* tradition for another two centuries after Yang Hsiung, keeping it in high official esteem throughout the Eastern or Later Han Dynasty. Meanwhile, however, there was an outstanding wit, Tung-fang Shuo (circa 161 B.C. to circa 86 B.C.) who, conforming to the rules of *fu* composition, was daring enough to turn the prevailing literary genre into a vehicle for fun-making. Of his twenty compositions, the titles are all recorded but the texts of only three have been preserved. In all these three we see clearly a distinctive feature—the evidence of his individual personality rising above the conventional formula of composition and rhetoric.

With the shifting of the imperial capital from Ch'angan to Loyang in A.D. 25, inaugurating the Eastern Han Dynasty, which lasted until A.D. 220, the *fu* persisted as the dominant literary type, casting its spell over all the major writings of the period. While it is impractical to discuss or even to mention all the *fu* writers, two of them deserve at least cursory review. One of these is Pan Ku (A.D. 32-92) who, as a distinguished historian-soldier and member of an illustrious family, will be treated more fully elsewhere. As a littérateur he immortalized himself as the author of two compositions on the two imperial capitals. Modeled after the "Tsŭ Hsü Fu," these companion pieces were eulogies of the two capital cities of Ch'angan and Loyang—elaborately and boastfully presented from the vantage point of two spokesmen. The political implication of these compositions was obvious—to justify the change of the imperial capital, with the representative from Ch'angan being completely overpowered by the spokesman for Loyang.

If a historian like Pan Ku submitted himself to this prevailing mode of literary gymnastics and acrobatics, the great mathematician and astronomer Chang Hêng (A.D. 78-139) did no better. This constructor of astronomical and meteorological instruments spent ten years writing similar artificial pieces on the two capitals entitled "The Liang Ching Fu." The only evidence of the scientific bent of Chang's mind is that he did not permit himself to describe the two capitals on the basis of hearsay or booklore.

At the end of the Han Dynasty there arose a great poet trying out a new verse form with new meter. Ts'ao Chih (A.D. 192-232) effectively extended the life span of the *fu* by drastically changing its nature. Instead of devoting himself to description and elaboration, he reintroduced lyricism into the *fu*. This experiment of pouring new wine into an old bottle changed both wine and bottle. At any rate, the *fu* as a Han dynastic literary genre had spent its full force by A.D. 220 and the retention of the name in later ages as the label of shorter and more lyrical compositions should be discussed separately.

CHAPTER 9

Han Literature Exclusive of the Fu

Wʜɪʟᴇ the polite literary form of the *fu* was being cultivated and developed through its various stages, other pursuits more worthy of the name of literature were also being undertaken that were more mindful of the taste and creativity of the common people.

Early experts on the *Book of Songs* were both literary critics and musicians. By the end of the Spring and Autumn Era (about 400 B.C.) a trend toward specialization had already started so that musicians neglected the study of the texts and scholars ignored the musical scores. Since most of the musicians then were blind men and therefore least fit to survive the destruction of widespread warfare, it is easily understandable that by 206 B.C., at the time of the founding of the Han Empire, only twenty-six songs had their musical scores preserved. Of these, eight were soon to disappear; at the end of the Han Dynasty (circa A.D. 220) only four were left; and by A.D. 318, as the result of mass migrations, all ancient music was lost beyond repair.

Ancient Chinese prosody previous to the second century before Christ had followed two patterns: the northern, or Yellow River, pattern of the four-character line taking shape during the period 1000 to 700 B.C., if not earlier, and fully reflected in the majority of the poems in the *Book of Songs;* and the southern, or Yangtze Delta, pattern of the long and irregular line broken by an auxiliary syllable in the middle functioning as a caesura, a pattern coming to full flowering during the fifth and fourth centuries before Christ, perpetuated in the poetry of the Ch'u school, and utilized by most of the *fu* writers.

At the beginning of the second century before Christ, a new verse form with five-syllable lines grew up to supplement the irregularity of the southern and the heavyness of the northern pattern when read aloud without the advantage of musical accompaniment. This new form came to be known as *Han shih,* i.e., Han poetry, and con-

127

tinued to be the dominant feature of versification down to the end of the sixth century. The problem in Chinese literary history is when and how this new verse pattern came into existence.

The traditional assertion that this new verse form based on the five-syllable line had its birth at the beginning of the Han Dynasty in 206 B.C. is no longer seriously accepted. In fact, even medieval critics in China had expressed considerable doubt as to whether Mei Shêng (219-140 B.C.), Li Ling (died 74 B.C.), or Su Wu (140?-70 B.C.) could have been the real inventors of the full-fledged five-word-line poems attributed to them. Modern students have taken pains to amass evidence to show that the verse form could not have been originated in the minds of a few poetic geniuses, but had long been popular in folk songs and had wielded immense influence before being adopted by the leading poets.

These popular songs, composed predominantly of five-syllable lines, have been categorically classified and labeled as *yüeh fu* and have been regarded as a literary genre by themselves. Actually, *yüeh fu*, meaning literally "Music Bureau," was an official agency of the imperial government going back at least to the Ch'in Dynasty and representing a continuation of an even earlier tradition of government envoys whose mission was to collect popular songs sung by the common people to express their hopes and fears, their joys and disappointments. These, together with their musical scores, were considered invaluable as records of popular reaction to the royal as well as the feudal governments. This tradition was probably discontinued during the disorderly times of the warring states and when a music bureau was established during the Ch'in Empire which continued in the early years of the Han Empire, its officials had to satisfy themselves with preserving rather than collecting. As long as quietism was followed as the guiding principle of the imperial court, any activity that might disturb the rest which the people craved would be curtailed. For fully eighty years the Han Music Bureau simply continued its existence in dormancy.

In 125 B.C., however, the ambitious and active Emperor Wu wakened to a new need. In one of his decrees issued in that year, he lamented the disuse into which the cultivation of music and the art of living had fallen as a result of the tyranny and disturbances created by the Ch'in Dynasty, and ordered the restoration of the Music Bureau to full vigor. The new activities of the bureau were so productive and impressive that even contemporaries were misled into thinking that the institution was an entirely new enterprise. Besides preserving what was already in its archives—words of popular songs sung in the empire—the bureau now went out in all directions in its search for new unrecorded songs, with major emphasis on preservation of their accompanying music. Of particular significance was the concern of the bureau with outlying frontier regions, especially those in the north and in the west, areas contiguous to the so-called western regions inhabited by non-Chinese peoples.

Many of the frontier songs thus collected express beautifully the mind and heart of the common people. They dealt with such crises in their humble lives as participation in warfare. A good example is the following:

Fighting South of the Castle

(Anonymous; *circa* 124 B.C.)

> They fought south of the Castle,
> They died north of the wall.
> They died in the moors and were not buried.
> Their flesh was the food of crows.
> "Tell the crows we are not afraid;
> We have died in the moors and cannot be buried.
> Crows, how can our bodies escape you?"
> The Waters flowed deep
> And the rushes in the pool were dark.
> The riders fought and were slain:
> Their horses wander neighing.
> By the bridge there was a house.
> Was it south, was it north?
> The harvest was never gathered.
> How can we give you your offerings?
> You served your Prince faithfully,
> Though all in vain.
> I think of you, faithful soldiers;
> Your service shall not be forgotten.
> For in the morning you went out to battle
> And at night you did not return.

(Arthur Waley's translation)

Although the folk songs were to exert their unmistakable influence upon the poets in due course, their influence at the imperial court and at the minor centers of literary activities was not to be felt immediately. In fact, when the Music Bureau was first established, Emperor Wu was primarily eager to see new religious songs created for the dynasty, and appointed well-known writers such as Ssŭ-ma Hsiang-ju to undertake the writing of the sacrificial songs. The wording of some of the nineteen songs thus composed which have been preserved reveal an archaic stateliness that seemed to be commensurate with imperial dignity. Likewise, the subject matter cele-brated in these sacrificial songs concerned important events of the imperial state. In the tenth piece, entitled "Heavenly Horses," for example, the event celebrated was the military victory in 101 B.C. over the Central Asian state of Ferghana and the beheading of the king of Ferghana by General Li Kuang-li. Other songs in the group were written in memory of such events as the rediscovery of an antique vessel in 113 B.C., the appearance of a white unicorn in 122 B.C., and the appearance of a crimson swan in 94 B.C. Dignified as these subject matters were and formal and stilted as the wording had to be, the music adopted was anything but classical, for the Dynastic History (*Han Shu*) had this to say:

> At this time Prince Hsien of Hochien submitted to the imperial court col-lections of classical music which he had compiled. . . . These, however, were not frequently made use of by his imperial majesty. What was frequently utilized for the emperor's personal entertainment and for religious services to the supreme deity and to the imperial ancestors was not classical music. . . . Both the musical talents of the imperial palaces and the experts in the Music Bureau outside of the Forbidden City [Imperial Palaces] applied undignified popular music at the imperial court.

According to the *Shih Chi*, "Li Yen-nien was superb as a singer and changed the rendering into new tunes."

It should be added that many of the popular songs with "undigni-fied" musical accompaniments collected by the Music Bureau were written in divergent forms of prosody with lines varying from three to seven words to the line, and often resulted in poems composed of lines of varying lengths. A good illustration of this deviation from the five-syllable line is the "Song of the Orphan."

> To be an orphan,
> To be fated to be an orphan,
> How bitter is this lot!
> When my father and mother were alive
> I used to ride in a carriage
> With four fine horses.
>   But when they both died,
>   My brother and my sister-in-law
>   Sent me out to be a merchant.
> In the south I travelled to the "Nine Rivers"
> And in the east as far as Ch'i and Lu.
> At the end of the year when I came home
> I dared not tell them what I had suffered—
> Of the lice and vermin in my head,
> Of the dust in my face and eyes.
> My brother told me to get ready the dinner,

My sister-in-law told me to see after the horses.
I was always going up into the hall
And running down again to the parlour.
My tears fell like rain.
In the morning they sent me to draw water,
I didn't get back till night-fall,
My hands were all sore
And I had no shoes.
I walked the cold earth
Treading on thorns and brambles.
As I stopped to pull out the thorns,
How bitter my heart was!
My tears fell and fell
And I went on sobbing and sobbing.
In winter I have no great-coat;
Nor in summer thin clothes.
It is no pleasure to be alive.
I had rather quickly leave the earth
And go beneath the Yellow Springs.
The April winds blow
And the grass is growing green.
In the third month—silkworms and mulberries,
In the sixth month—the melon-harvest.
I went out with the melon-cart
And just as I was coming home
The melon-cart turned over.
The people who came to help me were few,
But the people who ate the melons were many.
"At least leave me the stalks
To take home as proof.
My brother and sister-in-law are harsh,
And will be certain to call me to account."
When I got home, how they shouted and scolded!
I want to write a letter and send it
To my mother and father under the earth,
And tell them I can't go on any longer
Living with my brother and sister-in-law.
At fifteen I went with the army,
At fourscore I came home.
On the way I met a man from the village,
I asked him who there was at home.
"That over there is your house,
All covered over with trees and bushes."
Rabbits had run in at the dog-hole,
Pheasants flew down from the beams of the roof.
In the courtyard was growing some wild grain;
And by the well, some wild mallows.

I'll boil the grain and make porridge,
I'll pluck the mallows and make soup.
Soup and porridge are both cooked,
But there is no one to eat them with.
I went out and looked towards the east,
While tears fell and wetted my clothes.

(Arthur Waley's translation)

These popular songs of irregular meter, numerous as they were, were just as much, if not more, favored by the people as the ones composed of five-syllable lines. In this connection, we must not forget that Chinese songs and poems, besides being sung, could also be chanted, and that singing was usually accompanied by dancing as in other nations. When no musical instruments were available, chanting would naturally be resorted to, particularly when chanting was accompanied by a dance. In this respect the advantages of the five-word line with its metric regularity were obvious. Thus, many *yüeh fu* poems follow the five-syllable-line pattern.

The importance of the collection of these popular songs cannot be overemphasized. In the first place, the songs of the people were to enjoy the privilege of being committed to writing, a good morale-building procedure. In the second place, the recording of popular songs made them readily available to professional poets, providing a bridge between popular and polite literature. In the third place, after the men of letters had been impressed with the attractiveness of these popular songs, they would improve upon their original wording in conformity with the musical scores. This kind of work often gave the established poets new sources of literary inspiration, inducing them to write in imitation of the popular songs and making their masterpieces more in keeping with the tastes of the common people.

The first Han poet to benefit from this trend was the distinguished historian Pan Ku (A.D. 32-92) who, primarily interested in history, utilized the new verse form in dramatizing and evaluating major events and personalities in history. His efforts show considerable naïveté and experimentalism in using the new verse form. Similarly, the great scientist-astronomer, Chang Hêng who, like Pan Ku, dallied in *fu* composition, also tried his hand in utilizing the new verse form. But, again, Chang's imitations of popular poetry were mediocre in quality.

By A.D. 200, however, the five-syllable-line poem had attained full maturity. The distinguishing note was a new wealth of lyricism injected into the contents. It was about this time that nineteen poems of the *yüeh fu* type of unsurpassed beauty became widely known. Many of these were erroneously attributed to various poets. Recent critics and historians have agreed that these nineteen old songs were probably written by more than one hand and emended by various other hands. Their common feature was their unanimity and their naturalness, indicative of popular and composite authorship. Despite the tampering of professional poets, these nineteen poems have occasionally retained the beauty of rusticity and the lyricism of the common people, thus rightly being considered major milestones in the evolution of Chinese poetry.

A further development of this new verse form is to be seen in its utilization in narrative poetry. In the earlier development of the *yüeh fu,* narration had been attempted, as in the "Song of the Orphan," and all earlier narrative poems had been written in irregular meter. With the emergence of the regular new five-syllable-line form, longer folk songs of anonymous authorship began to spread such as "The Mulberry," also known as "The Song of Lo-fu":

> The sun has risen on the eastern brim of the world,
> Shines into the high chambers of the house of Ch'in.
> In the house of Ch'in is a lovely lady dwelling,
> That calls herself the Lady Lo-fu.
> This lady loves her silk-worms and mulberry-trees;
> She's plucking leaves at the southern corner of the walls.
> With blue thread are the joints of her basket bound;
> Of cassia-boughs are the loops of her basket made.
> Her soft hair hangs in loose plaits;
> The pearl at her ear shines like a dazzling moon.
> Of yellow damask is made her skirt beneath;
> Of purple damask is made her coat above.
> The passer-by who looks on Lo-fu
> Drops his luggage and twirls his beard and moustache.
> The young men when they see Lo-fu
> Doff their caps and tie their filets on their brows.
> The labouring ploughman thinks no more of his plough,
> The hind in the field thinks no more of his hoe.
> When they come home there is temper on both sides:
> "You sat all day looking at Lo-fu!"
> The Lord Prefect drives his coach from the south;
> His five horses suddenly slow their pace.
> He's sent his officer: "Quickly bring me word
> Of what house may this lovely lady be?"
> "In the house of Ch'in the fair lady dwells;
> She calls herself the Lady Lo-fu."
> "Oh tell me, officer, tell me how old she may be!"
> "A score of years she has not yet filled:

To fifteen she has added somewhat more."
The Lord Prefect sends to Lo-fu:
"Tell me, lady, will you ride by me or no?"
She stands before him, she gives him answer straight:
"My Lord Prefect has not ready wits.
Has he not guessed that just as he has a wife
So I too have my husband dear?
Yonder to eastward a band of horse is riding,
More than a thousand, and my love is at their head."
"By what sign shall I your husband know?"
"His white horse is followed by a black colt,
With blue thread is tied the horse's tail;
With yellow gold is bridled that horse's head.
At his waist he wears a windlass-hilted sword
You could not buy for many pounds of gold.
At fifteen they made him the Prefect's clerk;
At twenty they made him a Captain of the Guard.
At thirty he sat at the Emperor's Council Board,
At forty they gave him a city for his very own—
A wholesome man, fair, white and fine;
Very hairy, with a beard that is thick and long.
Proudly and proudly he walks to his palace gate;
Stately, stately he strides through his palace hall.
In that great hall thousands of followers sit,
Yet none but names him the finest man of them all."

(Arthur Waley's translation)

A longer narrative poem in the new meter was written by a major
Han poetess, Ts'ai Yen (flourished A.D. 206), daughter of the famous
writer, Ts'ai Yung (died A.D. 190). While living with her father after
the death of her husband, she was captured by Hunnish horsemen in
A.D. 194 or 195 and became the consort of a South Hsiung-nu chieftain. She lived at his court for twelve years and gave birth to two
sons. She was later redeemed and returned to China to be remarried
to Tung Chih. After her return to China she reflected upon the tragic
life she had lived and summarized the chief events of her life in two
poetical compositions, one in the style of Ch'u poetry of irregular
meter and the other in the newly-perfected verse form of the five
syllable line.

Song of Distress

Version I

Calamity befell me with the reduction of family fortune.
My clan was fallen and I was left alone.
As a prisoner of war I went through the Western Pass.
Going through many trials, I went into the barbarians.

The mountain peaks faded away and the road stretched endless,
As I turned eastward to look back I could only sigh with grief.
I should have slept after nightfall but could not,
I should have eaten when hungry but I had no appetite.
With tears unceasing my eyes were never dry.
With little resolution I could not die.
Though alive I cherished neither form nor spirit.

Oh, that region, it is far, far from the sun,
Where the spirit of Yin crystallized and where snow fell in summer,
Where the desert blocks all directions with its blinding dust,
Where even in spring the trees and grass showed no green,
Where humans eat the prey of birds and fowl,
Where the languages were wrangling and the land looked obscure.

.   .   .   .

My family sent for me, now I should return.
Facing the long road I had to abandon my children.
My children lost their voices crying as they called me mother.
I stopped up my ears, I could not suffer hearing them.
They held on and ran after me as I parted alone.
I turned to look at them with my broken heart.
I went through death before I was alive again.

Song of Distress

Version II

[The first section describes the descent of the barbarians upon the helpless dwellers of the Middle Kingdom.]

They slaughtered all and spared none,
Leaving dead bodies in confused juxtapositions.
From the sides of their horses dangled men's skulls.
Behind their horses were cartloads of women.
Going unopposed they marched westward through the Pass,
Where the roads were narrow, winding and precarious.
A backward glance revealed a misty expanse
Causing the heart to sink and the internal organs to rot.
Captives were counted in myriads
But they were not allowed to assemble, not even among kinsmen
Who wanted to talk but dared not.
A mere slip in compliance,
The command would be "The surrender-slaves will die.
You will perish by the sword. Your lives we shall not spare."
Their lives were no longer precious,
But none could stand the insult,
Nor the corporal punishment,
Which was rained like poison without cease.

In daylight they marched in tears,
At night they sat together with moans.
They could neither end their own lives,
Nor find aught to live for.
When had they offended against heaven that they should meet with this dire
    fate?

.   .   .   .

*[After giving up hope of seeing home again, she is surprised by messengers
sent to redeem her. She is not happy, however, for she cannot take her children
with her.]*

The little ones were sewn to my heart,
How could I leave them with no hope for reunion?
To be separated in life and death I could not say farewell.
My sons came forth to embrace my neck
And asked, "Where is Mother going?
People say once Mother is gone,
She will never come back again
You have been so kind to us,
How can you now be unkind?
We have not grown up to manhood,
How can you leave us behind?"
As I faced this I felt my five internals sink
Then I felt I was losing my senses.
I wept as I caressed them,
As I hesitated on point of departure.

And then there were people of my own generation
Who had come to bid me farewell.
Envying my unique chance of returning home,
They wailed with voices husky and shrill.
The horses stood still in perplexity,
The carriages stopped rolling on their wheels.
The lookers-on all sighed and sobbed;
The passers-by did likewise.
Suppressing my emotions, I took my leave,
And for days and days I was on the road.
Long, long winded the thousand miles,
Giving me no assurance of a reunion.
Each time I thought of my own children,
My heart was dashed to pieces.
On arriving home, I found no kinsman left—
Neither of my husband's family or of my own—
City and suburbs were now hills and forests,
Courts and gardens were grown with thorns and mugworts.
White bones which could not be identified

Lay hither and yon all exposed.
Walking out, I could hear no human sound,
Only the howl of jackals and wolves.
Silently I face my own shadow
With distress reducing my heart to a pulp.
I climbed the hills and gazed afar,
And I felt as though my soul had suddenly left me—
As though my life would have ended there—
If it had not been for the persuasion of standers-by.
Though against my will I am living again,
What is there now for me to live for?
I am trusting my fate to my new man,
And exhausting my efforts to still myself.
Wandering and drifting may have debased me,
And I fear I may be abandoned again.
How long, oh, how long can one live?
I will harbor my sorrow until life's end!

Throughout the ages critics have disagreed among themselves about the authenticity of the two poems. Some consider the one in regular meter authentic while others have regarded it as an elaboration by later hands of the true original which was in irregular meter in accordance with the true elegy style. It is quite possible, as a third group of critics have pointed out, that the poetess was so completely overwhelmed by her emotions that she felt compelled to express herself in both verse forms. At any rate, the poem in regular meter composed after A.D. 208, as was also its companion piece, was one of the longest narrative poems of the Han Dynasty with its 108 lines.

A contemporary narrative poem of anonymous authorship reflecting the technique of popular songs is "Southeastward Flies the Peacock," a great narrative poem of 353 lines. According to its short preface, it was written in commemoration of the tragic death of the wife of a petty clerk, Hsiao Chung-ch'ing. This greatest masterpiece of folk poetry in Han times begins with two lines that appear to have little to do with the main text:

A peacock flew, far off to the southeast;
Flew for a mile, then always dallied in its flight.

These two lines, consisting of only five syllables each in the Chinese original, were probably an indicator of either the tune to which the song was set or of the rhythm in which the incantation should be presented. Following this was a forthright presentation of how the clerk's young wife had found it almost impossible to please her mother-in-law.

> At cock-crow I went to the loom to weave;
> Night after night I toiled and got no rest.
> In three days I would finish five bits,
> And yet I would be chided for being slow.
> It is not I who weave too slowly
> I have found it hard to be a wife in your house.
> It is not in my power to do the tasks I am set;
> There is no use for me to stay on here.
> Go then quickly, speak to the lady, my mistress,
> And while there is time let me go back to my home.

In his attempt to plead his wife's cause, the clerk incurred the further displeasure of his mother. Instead of listening to her son she insisted that the young woman was unworthy of him and that after the divorce he could seek the hand of the daughter of one of their neighbors. Whereupon the clerk knelt down and further pleaded:

> "Bowing before you, Mother, I make my plea.
> If now you send her away
> I will live single all the days of my life."
> And when his mother heard him
> She banged the bed, flying into a great rage.
> "Little Son," she said, "are you not afraid?
> Dare you answer me in such a wife's praise?
> By this you have forfeited all my love and kindness;
> Do not dream that I will let you work your will."

Unable to resolve the difficulty, the young couple felt completely helpless, and the heroine, Lan-chih, begged permission to go. At dawn she rose and prepared ceremoniously for her departure. After offering her apologies to the old lady she made her farewell to her young sister-in-law:

> From her little sister it was worse work to part;
> Her tears fell like a string of small pearls;
> "When new-wed I first came to your home,
> You had just learned to lean on the bed and walk.
>   Today, when I am driven away,
> Little Sister, you have grown as tall as I.
> Work for Mother, cherish her with all your heart,
> Strive to serve and help her as best you may.
> Those seventh days and last days but one [holidays]
> Do not forget what nice romps we had!"

Then touchingly, husband and wife parted. On her arrival back home,

> She enters the gate, she mounts her father's hall,
> Languidly moves with no greeting in her face.
> "Child," cries her mother, and loud she claps her hands,
> "We little thought to see you home so soon.
> For at thirteen I taught you to weave silk,
> At fourteen you could cut clothes.
> At fifteen you played on the small lute,
> At sixteen you knew the customs and rites.
> At seventeen I sent you to be a bride,
> And fully thought that nothing had gone amiss.
> What is your fault, what wrongs have you done
> That uninvited you now come back to your home?"

In slightly over ten days the magistrate of the county sent a matchmaker to inquire of the maiden's availability for his third son who was graceful and handsome and gifted with talents and eloquence. Upon Lan-chih's resolute resistance the offer was tactfully declined. Soon afterward came a similar offer from the governor of the circuit. Although the mother respected the oath her daughter had made to the young clerk never to marry again, Lan-chih's elder brother was completely enchanted by the prospects of such a highly desirable marriage alliance. Since her brother was head of the family and had her completely at his mercy, she knew her fate. After a date had been selected as the most auspicious for the wedding, elaborate preparations were made by the governor's household. It was in the midst of this gorgeous display of official pomp and luxury that the tragedy was to begin. To her mother's query why she was so unmoved and listless on the eve of her wedding day,

> She did not answer, she did not make a sound;
> With her handkerchief she covered her face and wept,
> Her tears flowed as water pours from a jar.
> She shifts her stool that is bright with crystal beads
> And close to the front window she sets it down.
> With her left hand she wields ruler and knife;
> In her right hand she holds the silk gauze.
> In the morning she finishes her lined, broidered gown;
> By evening she has finished her thin gauze robe.
> The day was over, and she, in the gathering gloom
> With sorrowful heart walked sobbing to the gate.

Meanwhile her husband, Chung-ch'ing, had heard of the tragic complication:

> When the clerk her husband heard of what had passed
> He asked for leave to return for a little while.
> He had still to ride two leagues or three
> When his horse neighed, raising a doleful moan.
> The young wife knew the horse's neigh;
> She slipped on her shoes and set out to meet him.
> Woefully they looked on each other from afar,
> When each saw it was his dear one that had come.
> She raised her hand, she struck the horse's saddle,
> Wailing and sobbing as though her heart would break.
> "Since you left me—" she said,
> "Things happened to one that cannot be foreseen—
> It is true that I have not done as I wished to do;
> But I do not think that you fully understand."

Failing still to understand her, the clerk said in reply:

> "Well done!" he cried, "Well done to have climbed so high!
> The great rock that is so firm and square
> Was strong enough to last a thousand years.
> The river reed that once was thought so tough
> Was a frail thing that broke between dawn and dusk.
> From glory to glory will my fine lady stride,
> While I go down to the Yellow Springs alone."
> Then answered the young wife and to the clerk she said:
> "What do you mean, why do you speak to me so?
> It was the same with both; each of us was forced;
> You were, and so was I too.
> In the land of death you shall not be alone;
> Do not fail me in what today you have said."
> They held hands, they parted and went their ways,
> He to his house and she back to hers.
> That live men can make a death-parting
> Is sorrowful more than words can tell;
> To know they are leaving the world and all it holds,
> Doing a thing that can never be undone.

After this the consummation of the tragedy moved rapidly. On the night of Lan-chih's wedding, she drowned herself, and Chung-ch'ing, her husband, hanged himself on a tree.

> The two families buried them in the same grave,
> Buried them together on the side of the Hua Shan.
> To east and west they planted cypress and pine,
> To left and right they sowed the wu-t'ung.

The trees prospered; they roofed the tomb with shade,
Bough with bough, leaf with leaf entwined;
And on the boughs are two flying birds
Who named themselves Birds of True Love.
They lift their heads and face to face they sing
Every night till the fifth watch is done.
The passing traveler stays his foot to hear,
The widowed wife rises and walks her room.

This tale is a warning for the men of the afterworld;
May they learn its moral and hold it safe in their hearts.

(Based on Waley's translation)

The evolution of prose during the four centuries of the Han dynastic span was equally lively and commensurate with the spirit of the new empire. In the realm of the literature of thought, the unification of China effected a change from political argumentation to the quieter form of political memorials. These memorials, actually lengthy dissertations on specific ideas, had been used by both Li Ssŭ and Han Fei at the end of the Warring States period. With the foundation of the new dynasty, political and economic theories that were to be aired to the empire at large began again to take the form of memorials submitted to the crown. The first man to distinguish himself by reaffirming this tradition was Lu Chia, who tried to sell his political ideas to Emperor Kao, founder of the Han Dynasty. Also, during the reign of Emperor Wên (reigned 179-157 B.C.) Chia Shan repeatedly memorialized the throne. His "Chih Yen," a dissertation of over two-thousand words, was an excellent example of his persuasive power. It is no wonder that he has been mistakenly singled out as the first champion of this literary form. Following him were a host of writers presenting essays to the crown in the form of memorials. Among these the most distinguished was Chia Yi (200-168 B.C.), who, besides writing *fu* poetry in the style of Ch'ü Yüan, as we have noted before, and authoring an essay in three parts entitled "Kuo Ch'in Lun," in which the faults of the Ch'in Dynasty were thoroughly ferreted out and analyzed, also submitted a memorial discussing the political trends of his age in a long essay form of about six-thousand characters. These writers, despite the vigor of their lucid prose style, were chiefly remembered for their originality of ideas rather than for their literary ability.

More deserving of attention are the writers on philosophy of whom Prince Huainan (died 122 B.C.), at once patron of *fu* literature and promoter of the new eclectic Taoism of the Han Dynasty, was one. As a promoter of Taoism, Prince Huainan climaxed a long continuous development. Before Han times the school of Lao-tzǔ had not attracted an extensive following. With the establishment of the Han Dynasty, when quietism was fervently desired by the rulers as well as the governed, the teachings of the Taoist school, now bearing the hyphenated title of Huang-Lao (that is, Huang-Ti, the Yellow Emperor, and Lao-tzǔ), had become a distinguished school and subtly but persistently vied with Confucianism for supremacy. General Chang Liang, who studied Taoism, "being willing to abandon the affairs of the human world and tread in the footsteps of the philosopher of the red pines" had already established its high status. His contemporary, the Prime Minister Ts'ao Ts'an, was ready to practice as a major program of the government the policy: "Value quietism and the people will pacify themselves." The excellent record of peaceful government during the reign of the Emperor Wên was concrete evidence of the effect of Taoism on administration. Empress Tou, consort of Emperor Wên, was most fond of "the sayings of Huang-Ti and Lao-tzǔ." Consequently her son, Emperor Ching, and her various nephews of the Tou family, could not help but study *Lao-tzǔ*, and highly "valued its teachings." The culminator of this tradition, Prince Huainan, was a grandson of the founder of the dynasty. His father, accused of treason during the reign of Emperor Wên, and sentenced to exile as a reduced penalty from execution, had died of fasting on the road. Harboring his grievance against the imperial court and influenced by his own counselors who frequently reminded him of the family tragedy, he felt constantly attracted to staging a rebellion. Being a follower and a chief advocate of eclectic Taoism, however, the prince failed to develop a resolute will power for action. The upshot of this inherent conflict in his personality was the exposure of his plans before they had matured, which led directly to his suicide in 122 B.C.

Among the literary works attributed to this famous Prince An of Huainan is the composite compendium known as *Huainan–Tzǔ*, a work continuing the tradition of *The Spring and Autumn of Lü Pu-Wei*. This book of the prince of Huainan derives its strength not from originality of thought but from the systematic arrangement of the varying and conflicting interpretations of Taoist teachings into a harmonious whole. This systematic correlation of parts with varying subdivisions paved the way for the composition of organic treatises of comprehensive scope. The prose style of the collaborative authorship, based on the contributions of over a thousand litterateurs under his patronage, is remarkable for its fluency, clarity, and stylistic harmony. The uninformed reader would suspect that this monolithic monument was the product of a single hand.

Competing with the followers of Taoism, the Confucianists of the early Han Dynasty also worked hard to seek distinction—including distinction in literature. Their signal victory in competing with the Taoists did not come to pass until Emperor Wu had inherited the throne. The five state doctors responsible for the orthodox interpretation of the five Confucian classics were first appointed in 136 B.C. Later on in the same year, following the recommendation of Tung Chung-shu (flourished 156-117 B.C.), Emperor Wu adopted the policy of suspending the study of the Hundred Schools to give priority to the six Confucian classics, thus elevating the status of Confucianism almost to that of a state religion. This state-approved Confucianism, however, represented in reality a new melting pot. Behind a Confucian façade there were huge admixtures of various forms of folk beliefs as well as elements from the Taoist-Legalist and even the Mohist schools. This blurring of the barriers between schools of thought and currents of literary style were probably unavoidable accompaniments of the erasure of former geographical frontiers in a now unified empire.

The writings of the Confucianists were voluminous, particularly in the form of commentaries on the Confucian classics. One commentator surpassed all previous examples of verbosity by writing a commentary of over thirty-thousand words in exegetical explanation of the first four characters in the *Book of History* or *Shu Ching*. Other Confucianists did little better on account of the limited scope of their learning and their preoccupation with moralistic and mystical considerations. The various schools of commentators on the *Book of Songs* or the *Shih Ching*, for example, felt tempted to use the three hundred odes as moral lessons for the imperial court and for scholars. In a word, Han Confucianists had certain common characteristics. They tried to derive learning not from life but from books, and they used writing not as a healthy substitute for speaking, but wrote for writing's sake. Their literary productions, as a result, were impressive for their verbosity and their thought was largely characterized by their bookishness.

Among the prose writers the most distinguished were unquestionably the historians. The greatest literary figure of the Han Dynasty was a historian. By virtue of the manner and substance of his masterpiece, he not only set a pattern for the main branch of China's historical literature for centuries to come, but also established the tradition of intimate relationship between literature and history. If it had not been for the wonderful records which he left to posterity, many of the data which we have now on early Chinese literature would have been unavailable.

Ssŭ-ma Ch'ien (145-86? B.C.) was the scion of a reputable old family and son of a far-sighted royal astrologer-recorder. The father, Ssŭ-ma T'an, an expert in astrology, divination and the Taoist doctrines of Lao-tzŭ, had much to contribute to his son's literary career. It should not be thought, however, as has erroneously been done so often, that the young man had merely trod in his father's footsteps when he took up the writing of the epoch-making work *Shih Chi* or *Records of the Historian*. In his own words in the last chapter of his monumental work, which was an autobiography, Ssŭ-ma Ch'ien

read the Classics in archaic script at the age of ten. At twenty he traveled southward to the Yangtze and Huai River deltas, climbing the mountain of Kueichi, exploring Yü Yüeh, admiring the Chiu Yi ranges of mountains, sailing on the Yüan and Hsiang tributaries of the Yangtze and northward floating on the rivers of Wên and Ssŭ which flow into the Yellow River, studying in the former capital cities of Ch'i and Lu, to study the long-lasting influence of Confucius, practicing the ancient rituals of archery at the birthplace of Mencius at Tsou and Yi, suffering poverty in the site of ancient cities of P'i, Hsieh, and P'êng-ch'êng, and, finally, traversing the old feudal states of Liang and Ch'u to return home

which was Ch'angan. Later on in the autobiography he also mentions that he had served on the diplomatic mission westward to areas south of Szechuan, touching the southernmost city of Kunming. When he returned from this mission in 104 B.C. he had enough time to see his father, who was dying of disappointment as an imperial historian barred from participation in the major celebration of the imperial court—a great blow to his pride. He was appointed three years later as successor to his father, in which official capacity he had access to all the books and documents that were in the imperial archives.

After eighteen years of preparation and compilation, as well as actual writing, this monumental work in history covering the major events and personalities of approximately three thousand years before his time was completed in 91 B.C. as a complex but well-organized masterpiece of 130 chapters in half a million characters. It was the first general history of its kind to be published in China and possibly in the whole world; it set a pattern in the organization and presentation of historical materials that was respectfully adhered to with only minor modifications by subsequent writers of the so-called dynastic histories for over two thousand years; and it was a great storehouse in which many documents of antiquity pertaining to religion, philosophy, folklore, politics, and other human activities in China were preserved intact. In addition the *Shih Chi* has its own epoch-making significance in literary history which concerns more than the historian.

First, it founded the tradition and confirmed the prevailing trend of the intimate relationship between history and literature. The professional historian in ancient China, important though his role seemed to be, was assigned a place scarcely more dignified than that of the fortuneteller, astrologer, religious acolyte, and court jester. In fact, according to Ssŭ-ma Ch'ien's own admission, the historian was expected to have the gifts and training of all these. Despite these limitations placed upon the profession of the historian, Ssŭ-ma Ch'ien had even surpassed his great predecessor, Tso-ch'iu Ming, in soaring above the lowly plane of factual chronicling into literary creation.

Second, too free to be hampered by the shackles of imitation of the classical style, the great historian boldly deviated from convention in utilizing the living speech of his own days especially in recording the dialogues and sayings of his biographical subjects, representing them as actually speaking in the living language of the people as befitted the divergent types of historical characters. Even when he was making direct use of classical documents such as the *Shu Ching* he would revitalize his quotations by paraphrase instead of verbatim citations from the original source.

Third, his approach to historical materials was characterized by the wholeness of interest in human affairs and distinguished personalities of a major poet rather than that of an academic historian. In this regard this vastness of his canvas in depicting human variations and eccentricities was clearly unequaled by the works of any of his followers in the field of history writing. In addition to preserving the records of emperors and sages, administrators and generals, poets and philosophers, reformers and rebels, dreamers and scholars, he made a special point of perpetuating the memory of assassins and adventurers, crooks and wits, speculators and criminals, eunuchs and courtesans. Many of his biographies still palpitate with color and life today; he wanted to recreate antiquity convincingly, and he succeeded.

Let us see in the following excerpts how he presented the biography of Shu-sun T'ung, a prominent Confucianist of the early Han Dynasty.

Shu-sun T'ung was a native of the district of Hsieh, not far away from the birthplace of Confucius. After serving the Second Emperor of the Ch'in dynasty, then the temporary Emperor of Ch'in, then Hsiang Yü who had claimed the title of King of Ch'u, he finally defected to the future founder of the Han Dynasty, Liu Pang, who was then assuming the title of the King of Han.

The King of Han was pleased that Shu-sun T'ung had surrendered to him with his pupils and other scholars numbering over one hundred. T'ung, however, had little to tell the king except the stories of the various bandits and men of physical prowess. His pupils all secretly complained about him among themselves, saying, "We have served our master several years and have by sheer luck followed him in surrendering to Han. Now, why is it that instead of presenting us to the king, he should be talking about the artful and cunning all the time?"

On overhearing this, Shu-sun T'ung said to them: "The King of Han is presently engaged in great battles in his struggle for empire. Can any of you take part in military combat? Now you understand why I have been telling him by way of prelude about fighting men who could slay the commanders and capture the flags of the enemy. Please just wait, I have not forgotten about you."

Three years later the new empire had been founded and the King of Han had declared himself emperor; but as the meticulous court etiquettes of the Ch'in dynasty had been dispensed with, the emperor saw the need to put a stop to the reckless drinking, the brawling and yelling, and the hacking of the pillars of the audience hall with swords by his former associates and comrades-in-arms. Shu-sun T'ung then proposed that new court etiquettes should be formulated and enforced.

The emperor said, "You may try, but make them simple, and especially easy for me to follow." Whereupon Shu-sun T'ung recommended the summoning of over thirty scholars from Lu. There were two scholars in Lu who were unwilling to leave. They said [to Shu-sun T'ung], "You have served almost ten different masters and have invariably won favors and honors from them by forthright flattery. Now the world has just regained its peace. The dead are not yet buried and the wounded have not yet arisen [from their sick bed], and now you want to promote music and rituals. The rise of music and rituals is impossible without the accumulation of enlightened and virtuous rule for a hundred years. We cannot bear to do what you do; and what you do does not conform with [the teachings of] antiquity. Please go! Don't smear us with your own mud!" Shu-sun T'ung smiled and answered, "You are indeed petty scholars, incognizant of the changes of the times!"

After considerable work with his staff, including rehearsals in the suburb for over a month, he invited the emperor to see the whole procedure for approval. The emperor said, "I can do it," and ordered his ministers to take part in the rehearsals. On New Year's day in the seventh year of the Han Dynasty (200 B.C.), in commemoration of the completion of the Ch'ang Lo Palace:

The ceremonies began at dawn. The grand marshal ushered all to enter the court gate in accordance with precedence. In the court square were arrayed cavalrymen and infantrymen for the protection of the palace, with their banners unfurled. Below the palace building, the tier of steps was flanked by commanders of the palace guards on both sides. On the steps were several hundred dignitaries. The meritorious ministers [who had taken major parts in empire building], the various [classes of] feudal lords, the different generals and other military officers formed a line according to ranks on the west, facing east; civil officers from the prime minister down formed their line on the east, facing west. The Office of the Imperial Receptionists had nine ushers of different ranks in position to relay orders seriatim downward and upward.

Then the emperor made his appearance.

The various officers attended to their duties and relayed the order to attention. All the ranks of feudal lords and princes down to the civil officials drawing annual salaries of six hundred bushels of rice were conducted in order to perform their homage. And all from the ranks of lords and princes down were without exception tremblingly reverent.

After the ceremony was over, regulation drinks were served. Those who were seated in the palace building all prostrated [themselves] with their heads bent low, and drank to the health of his majesty in the order of their ranks. After nine rounds had been served, the grand marshal announced drinking was now terminated. Meanwhile officers of the censorate were on duty, ready to lead those away who might have violated court etiquette. During the whole morning while wine was served, not a single person dared to be noisy or indecorous.

Whereupon the emperor said, "I have not realized until today how glorious and elevated it is to be emperor!"

The first distinguished follower of Ssŭ-ma Ch'ien was Pan Ku (A.D. 32-92). Member of an outstanding Han family, he was the son of Pan Piao, distinguished writer and historian. In A.D. 58, four years after the death of his father, Pan Ku made known to Prince Ts'ang of Tungp'ing, in a memorial, that he had decided to continue his father's work in the writing of history. This led to his imprisonment in A.D. 62 for the violation of a dynastic ruling by tampering with dynastic history in his private capacity as a citizen. As a result of the intercession of his younger brother, Pan Ch'ao, the distinguished general, he was acquitted and appointed imperial historian in the same year. Sixteen years later the *Han Shu* or the *History of the Han Dynasty*, now more generally referred to as the *History of the Former Han Dynasty*, was completed—a work of eight hundred thousand words recording the major events and personalities of about two hundred years. With this work largely completed, Pan Ku was eager to take part in the political and military activities of his age, leaving the work of minor revisions and additions to his distinguished younger sister, Pan Chao (A.D. 52?-125), herself a scholar-poet of such great distinction that such classicists of established fame as Ma Yung humbly approached her as pupils in the reading of the newly redacted work. Meanwhile, Pan Ku, on the staff of General Tou Hsien, fought against and defeated the northern Hsiung-Nu in two extensive campaigns. In A.D. 92 he died in prison for guilt of association with the now fallen Tou family.

Pan Ku's place in Chinese literary history rests on this work of his more than on the two *fu* compositions on the two capitals which we have previously mentioned. Following the pattern of *Shih Chi,* the *Han Shu* could claim no originality, comprising as its predecessor did four major divisions: (a) imperial biographies serving as the basic chronological framework besides presenting the respective emperors as living personalities around whom the major events of the empire had revolved; (b) charts and diagrams of events, genealogies, personnel of the chief administrative offices and the like, incorporated for clarity as well as for economy; (c) institutional dissertations presenting selected facets of historical development and evolution in topical form, such as court etiquette, music, economy, navigation, army organization, etc; and (d) biographies of distinguished men and women other than emperors. Compared to the *Shih Chi,* the new dynastic history was much more than a slavish imitation. It had a more definite and shorter chronological coverage and therefore a fuller and more systematic treatment. Moreover, confined as it was to treatment of a later age, it had many more well-preserved documents and original sources to draw from. Although utilizing a more cautious and considered prose style, it had not deviated too far from the naturalness and freedom of the living speech of the people. Again, like his great predecessor, the author of the *Han Shu* took special pains to dramatize the chief episodes and leading personalities in history so that despite his great concern with authenticity and accuracy, many portions—particularly the biographies—have the charm of fiction.

In this connection, brief mention should be made of another historian of note, Hsün Yüeh (A.D. 148-209), author of *Han Chi.* In response to the orders of Emperor Hsien (reigned A.D. 190-220), who had been troubled by the length of Pan Ku's work, Hsün Yüeh abbreviated and digested the contents of the *Han Shu* into annal form in imitation of the Tso-ch'iu Ming style in recording the events of the *Spring and Autumn Classics,* thus confirming and continuing the annal form of historical writing, in which verbal economy and moralistic reflections are the chief characteristics. Much less distinguished as literature, the *Han Chi* served as an impetus to its writer for the composition of five philosophical essays reflecting on the lessons of history and current politics under the general title of *Shên Chien.*

As philosophical writings of the Han Dynasty were as a whole of only secondary importance from the standpoint of literary excellence, the essays of one unconventional writer stand out in great merit by comparison—the various collections of essays by Wang Ch'ung (27–circa 100 A.D.). Born in humble circumstances, grandson of "a mere merchant," he later distinguished himself as a university student at the imperial capital, pupil of no less eminent a man than Pan Piao. After his return to his native district in Kueichi, in present-day Chekiang Province, he taught school and served as chief assistant to a provincial governor for a time, spending most of his later years after voluntary retirement in writing and meditation on diverse topics from refreshingly new angles.

On account of his unconventionality, strangely enough, most of Wang Ch'ung's writings have not been preserved. The greatest loss to posterity was probably a collection of twelve essays entitled *Chi-su Chieh-yi* or "Satires Against Prevailing Conventions and Concepts" in which the vernacular instead of the literary style was boldly used. Also lost were a book on politics entitled *Chêng Wu* and another work on the preservation of life consisting of sixteen chapters entitled *Yang Shêng Shu.* Our estimate of Wang Ch'ung must then rest on the incomplete data of his only work which has survived, namely, his *Lun Hêng* of eighty-five essays in which all are extant except one. In his autobiographical chapter of the *Lun Hêng* he announced:

Lun Hêng means the levelness of discourse. With tongue and mouth the function should be revealing of what is intended to be expressed, with a brush the preoccupation should be the full revelation of what is intended to be written. In the elegant writing of really high scholars there is none which is not understandable and there is none of which the message is not clearly seen. In reading their books one feels illuminated like blind people with their eyesight restored and the deaf regaining their auditory powers. . . . Writing is like speaking. Some seems shallow but clearly revealing, others seem deep, discursive and elegant; which ones are more successfully eloquent? As spoken words are for the purpose of communicating ideas and as spoken words are perishable, we commit them to writing. The written sentence and the spoken word should serve the same purpose, wherefore should one aim at leaving something for people to guess at? . . . People of late ages did not realize that with the lapse of generations and instead of calling stylistic variations linguistic changes, as they should be called, labeled them grandeur of literary talent. When simple writings are read the verdict was lack of skill instead of clarity. When the first Ch'in emperor read the book of *Han Fei* he exclaimed, "Oh, how I regret I am not a contemporary of the writer!" Han Fei's writing was easily understandable, therefore his themes are provocative of thought. If they [Han Fei's writings] had been profound and elegant and had necessitated a teacher to make their study possible, they should have been thrown on the floor. What need was there of an exclamation?

This probably was the most emphatic indictment of the literary trends of his age. Like his writings, Wang Ch'ung's personality was lucid, frank, and uninhibited. Unlike his contemporaries, he did not mind inviting adverse criticism of his contemporaries and posterity by describing his father's life as the old sire had lived it, not entirely free from occasional meannesses and other temperamental short-comings. He seemed to believe in the glory of the imperfect.

Passages like the following would not fail to charm any forthright reader:

Wang Ch'ung is a native of Shangyü in Kueichi circuit. . . . His great-grandfather, Yung, habitually gave reign to his passions with the result that there were few whom he had not offended. During bad years he would par-ticipate in batteries and killings on the highways, making numerous enemies. It happened that the world was growing in disorder and confusion and for fear of capture by unfriendly elements his father, Hsin, moved the family with all its belongings to seek safety in Kueichi where he settled in the district of Ch'ient'ang and became a merchant. He had two sons. The elder one was named Mêng and the younger one Sung, the father of Ch'ung. The passionate and tempestuous personalities of the ancestors once inherited by Mêng and Sung became all the more excessive. Hence, in Ch'ient'ang, Mêng and Sung bullied others with their prowess and foolhardiness. Finally they entered into such a feud with the powerful family of Ting Po that they moved their families to Shangyü. In the third year of the reign of Chien Wu, Ch'ung was born. In his association with playmates as a young boy, Ch'ung was not fond of silly games or rough-housing. Each time his companions were busy at their fond sports of catching birds, grasping cicadas, or gambling, Ch'ung would not join in. Sung considered him odd and unusual. When he was taught the first lessons of reading and penmanship in his sixth year, he was respectful, well-behaved, kind, and obedient. Besides attending to all the minute details of etiquette, he was dignified and independent, having the attitudes of an adult. He was never flogged by his father or scolded by his mother nor even criticized by his neighbors.

In his eighth year he was sent out to a school where there were over a hundred school boys, all of whom were reprimanded for misbehavior and whipped for their poor schoolwork. In their midst, Ch'ung's studies improved daily and his behavior was faultless. When the small manual had been finished he requested his teacher to give him lessons on the *Analects* and the *Book of Documents* from which he read a thousand words daily. When the classics were understood and his character training had been accomplished he thanked his teacher and went into specialized studies by himself, eliciting admiration from the people each time he undertook writing. The books that he had read increased in number daily. While his talents were of a high caliber, he did not compose carelessly; and while his eloquence was acknowledged he was not fond of talking. Unless he had found the right party he would remain quiet all day. Each time he spoke up he would sound in the beginning as though his arguments were at odds with those of other people but when he had finished his say they would agree with him. The same is true when he committed his thoughts to writing. The same is true in his conduct of himself and in his service to his superiors. . . . He frequently mentions the good qualities of others and seldom said anything about their shortcomings. He made a special point of recommending those who were unknown and of absolving from error those who were already advanced to office. . . . He would not clear himself when he was misunderstood and felt no disappointment when his position was not advanced. He was so poor that he did not have a mou of land [one-fifth of an acre] to support himself and yet he lived in perfect contentment as though he were a prince or duke. He was so lowly that he had no official rank which would yield him even the meager sinecure of one bushel of rice and yet he was happy as though he had the income of ten thousand measures. He was not elated when he was appointed to office and never downhearted when he had lost his job. His desires were never uncurbed when his circumstances were favorable and his attitudes were never lax when he was faced with poverty and adversity. He had a wanton love for the reading of ancient literature and he felt sweetly rewarded when he heard unusual words. He was much discontented with popular books and prevailing theories. He would live alone in isolation and quietude in order to examine into truth and falsehood.

Wang Ch'ung's influence was not widely felt but the new trend he started might account for the simple and clear prose style that was used in philosophical writings of the second and third centuries of the Christian era in China.

A great contemporary of Wang Ch'ung's whose contributions to Chinese literary history were embodied in a somewhat nonliterary form was Hsü Shên (A.D. 55?-149) compiler of the first methodical dictionary of the unique and almost unmanageable Chinese written language. Being nonalphabetic in their written forms, the Chinese scripts presented unequaled technical difficulties to lexicographers. By the second century of the Christian era, the number of Chinese scripts or characters had already exceeded the ten thousand mark. As literacy gradually expanded among the common people and as writings of various types increased in number and diversity, some attempts had to be made for the compilation of general works of reference akin to the nature of dictionaries. Some of these took the form of books of synonyms, such as the *Erh Ya,* traditionally attributed to the Duke of Chou, but which was actually a work of gradual accumulation reaching a definitive form during the early decades of the second century before Christ. Others were books of synonyms paying special emphasis to the equating of dialect forms current in the various areas of the empire. Still others were lengthy compositions with no single character used twice in the text, with sentences uniformly containing a given number of characters each, usually four, and divided into sections with end-rhymes in alternate lines to facilitate memorization and to guarantee ready reference. The purpose of these were to teach a large number of individual characters with the least pain to teacher and student and to serve as a reminder to those who could think of the pronunciation of a character that was to be used but who had forgotten how the character in question was constructed. Although none of these were dictionaries in the proper sense of the word, they had effectively filled the gaps created by the total absence of a real dictionary.

Hsü Shên's attempts were truly epoch-making in that they were effectively made in ferreting out certain basic units from among the component parts of the written characters and singled out 540 of them, more or less arbitrarily, as radicals. These numerous radicals were then utilized as pegs on which characters having the same radical as their component parts were hung together to form a compartment or *pu*. The next problem that he had to face was the arrangement of these radicals into a sequence that would make some semblance of sense. In this regard the compiler could not help being a child of his own age. The order in which the radicals were arranged was forced to yield a metaphysical meaning, beginning with the radical meaning "one" and ending with the character *hai* which was the twelfth stem used in the Chinese time cycle, representing the last process in the creation of the cosmos. Within each compartment the number of entries would vary from a few to several hundred. These entries were arranged not according to complexity by counting the number of strokes added to the radical, as was the practice in later dictionaries, but were entered in accordance with their meanings; thus characters representing livestock of different colors would be grouped together, and characters representing different types of precious stones resembling jade would be put together. It is not surprising that even the initiated often had to spend time in locating a character, but all people appreciated the *Hsuo Wên* as a boon, for any dictionary was better than none. Besides its antiquary value for having listed all out-of-the-way characters, some of which had already been falling out of normal usage even in the compiler's own time (such as those for a two-year-old horse, two-year-old cow, or four-year-old goat), the standard reference work had also a direct effect on the writers of literature by serving as a constant reminder to them of the great and growing riches of the Chinese language in its recorded form.

CHAPTER 10

Wei and Tsin

IT HAS long been observed by historians of Chinese literature that political and literary developments in China did not wax and wane in parallel, although there was considerable interaction between the two. Political disintegration which gave rise to social disorder and personal insecurity did not necessarily lead to accompanying chaos in the realm of creative and critical literature. This phenomenon is well illustrated by the striking discrepancy between literature and politics immediately following the disintegration of the Han Empire. After four hundred years of political unification under its first great empire, China was to undergo a painful process of territorial and administrative division in the early part of the third century of the Christian era, thus starting and confirming a cycle of integration and break-up which was to become a popular theme harped upon by the narrators of historical romances for many centuries to come.

In A.D. 221 the united Han Empire, after a rapid succession of short-lived reigns by young emperors dominated by powerful ministers, was subverted by a powerful house which set itself up in the north as the Wei Dynasty. A collateral branch of the Han imperial house, refusing to submit to the usurpers, proclaimed itself a continuation of Han rule in present-day Szechuan Province in the southwest, becoming known as the Shu. A third regime rose in the southeast, establishing itself as the kingdom of Wu. This triangular split-up of China which lasted slightly over half a century, generally known as the Three Kingdoms Period, was ended by "voluntary" abdication in favor of a powerful house in the north which succeeded in liquidating the two southern regimes of Shu and Wu to build up the new Tsin Empire. The trends of division, however, were to run their course. The restive non-Chinese tribes in the north created new political and social problems and permitted less than four decades to lapse between the elimination of its rivals by the Tsin house in A.D. 280 and the flight of the Tsin imperial court southward to Nanking in 318. From that point on, China was to be split into two halves for over two and a half centuries with alien dynasties dominating in the north and native dynasties cherishing what purported to be cultural and political orthodoxy in the south—the period of the Southern and Northern Dynasties.

During this long period of political division and social transformation, Chinese literature was to undergo a series of meaningful changes, although at the beginning of this period there did not seem to have been striking disruptions in literary trends. A whole group of prominent writers bridged the gap of dynastic change between the Han and the Wei. The same vehicles in literary form continued to be cultivated and utilized. Even the themes developed by the major writers seemed to have remained substantially the same. Underneath the veneer of the smooth continuity, however, there was a subtle realization, especially among poets, that the function of literature was more than the fulfillment of an ethical and social mission. This mission inherited from the past and frequently expressed in didacticism, satirization, or glorification of the authorities, was unmistakably broadened and enriched by the new creed that literature should serve to express the full feelings and aspirations of the individual. In other words, literature felt that it had come of age and this "self"-consciousness liberated it from its secondary role as chambermaid to ethical idealism and political utopianism. For the first time Chinese literature refused to be subservient to external direction and social or political delimitations.

To understand this sudden and significant change we must take note of the change in cultural climate at the beginning of the third century. The most impressive manifestation of the incoming of a new age was the decline of the influence of Han Confucianism. The causes of this decline were the inability of Confucianism to retain the devoted following of a new generation whose basic faith had been shaken, and its failure to compete with new currents of thought stimulated by sudden changes in the social and political environment. To recall how Confucianism was given a new coloring and subjected to accretions of heterodox interpretations, we should note that when Emperor Wu of the Former Han Dynasty decided to uphold Confucianism as the state cult it was converted into a synthetic school in which elements of the occult, particularly those advocated by the Yin-Yang school, completely obscured the original positivism of the Chinese sage. During the high tide of superstition in the Han Empire, even the *Book of Songs* was read as a virtual manual of fortunetelling. This tendency of reading mystical meanings into the ancient lyrics was to persist in spite of the objections repeatedly raised by such clearheaded critics as Chang Hêng and Wang Ch'ung.

The objections were entirely ineffective except among a negligible few because the mystical scholasticism of the age hiding itself beneath the mask of classical Confucianism had served the ambitions of monarchs and of scholars equally well. As the historian Pan Ku had openly pointed out, the flowering of this type of pseudo-Confucianism was largely due to the fact that it was the shortest cut to officialdom and its ample rewards. During this period of the distortion of Confucianism, even the dynastic glorification of ethical ideals led to comical and sometimes shameful results of hypocrisy and artificiality. The two ideals of *hsiao* (filiality) and *lien* (incorruptibility) were healthy ones in and of themselves but when they were heralded by the dynasty as yardsticks for election to office and promotion in the hierarchy, they led to absurdities. People would run away into hiding after the death of a father so as to leave the patrimony to their brothers or virtually fight for the most dilapidated huts in the estate of the deceased so as to distinguish themselves as filial and incorruptible.

It was not at all surprising under these circumstances that when the dynasty-subverter Ts'ao Ts'ao (A.D. 155-220) arose to power as prime minister at the end of the tottering Han Dynasty, he completely disregarded all the old yardsticks of ethical standards and elevated to high positions people of special talents. This, in actuality, was a revival of legalism reminiscent of the political philosophy of the Ch'in Empire. The step was taken by Ts'ao Ts'ao, who has been unfairly criticized by posterity because he saw clearly that a revision of values was demanded by the age. Legalism, on the other hand, failed to give satisfaction in a disorderly age even to Ts'ao Ts'ao's son, Ts'ao P'i (A.D. 186-226), who, as the first emperor of the Wei Dynasty, was eager to revive the Taoistic laissez-faire administration of the early Han Dynasty. Ts'ao P'i, known as Emperor Wên of the Wei Dynasty, in his many rescripts decreeing disarmament and reduction of penalties and taxation, and prohibiting the search for vengeance, revealed himself as a great admirer of Taoism. Moreover, in the capacity of a gifted poet himself, he frequently felt the transitoriness of human life and devoted himself to singing as a Taoist poet. This new note sounded in literature by a monarch went far to discredit Confucianism as a school of cultural orthodoxy.

In the second place, the era under review was one of extreme political confusion and social insecurity. The imperial court of this time was characterized by struggles for supremacy between eunuchs and external relatives, by confusion in strategy for dealing with insurrections in the provinces, by dynastic subversion of powerful ministers, and by the continual threat of barbarian invasions. These political disorders were accompanied by destructive warfare, widespread famine, and uncontrollable pestilence. In this period of the abandonment of farms, sharp reduction in population, and large-scale migrations, there was a need felt by commoners and intellectuals alike for a new faith and a new philosophy. Moreover, the chaos of the age had made the lives of scholars and writers especially insecure. The tragic deaths of many prominent literary figures of the age, victims of party strife or of guilt by association, were frightening to the literate elements of the population. As a result, many scholars sought refuge in reclusive living, harboring themselves in caves or in huts built in treetops, while others purposely feigned madness or sought satisfaction in Taoist and Buddhist discourses, all shunning the tedium of public life.

In the third place, the escapism inherent in Taoism rose to fill the philosophical vacuum. The naturalism of Lao-tzǔ and Chuang-tzǔ advocating that things were so because they were so and that all changes had come about undirected seemed to give greater satisfaction than the Confucian insistence upon the close relationship between a universal deity and man. The growth of this adherence to Taoist naturalism led eventually to a very peculiar phenomenon, that of reinterpreting the Confucian classics, especially the Confucian *Analects,* in accordance with Taoist principles. The Confucian *Book of Changes,* or *I Ching,* had become required reading of the age. This fusion between Confucianism and Taoism paved the way for the eventual integration of Buddhism into the genuinely Chinese intellectual scene. What had been regarded as cultural orthodoxy in Han times was now entirely scrapped. Followers of the Buddha, who had been discriminated against among scholars at the end of the Han Dynasty, now began to come to the fore. Nearly all the major writers of the period of political division were to be either converted to the alien faith in whole or in part or desirous of the friendship of eminent Buddhists. Although the influence of Buddhism on Chinese literature did not come to a full flowering until the T'ang Dynasty, the liberalizing effect of the Buddhist faith was already felt.

All these trends led to an abandonment of conventions. Unconventionality was the hallmark of all the leading intellectuals and poets, as can be seen from the following extracts from a collection of anecdotes illustrative of the intellectual life of the age:

> During the mourning period of the death of his mother, Juan Chi was in the company of Prince Wên of Tsin and meat and drinks were being served. The chief of the civilian officers, Ho Tsêng, who was also present, said, "Your Highness has just adopted the policy of ruling the country with the basic

principle of filial piety. And now Juan Chi, who is deep in mourning, is prominently showing himself at your banquet drinking wine and eating meat. It seems to me fitting that he should be banished to beyond the seas so as to set a good example for the kingdom." The Prince replied, "Why is it that you cannot share with me my anxiety over Juan Chi's failing health? Moreover, according to the standards of the mourning rites, it is always permissible to drink wine and eat meat when one is ill from undernourishment." Meanwhile, Juan Chi stopped from neither drinking nor eating, holding his composure as though nothing had happened.

. . . .

Liu Ling, being ill from a thirst for wine, begged his wife for wine. After throwing away the wine and smashing the wine services, his wife pleaded with him in tears, "You have been drinking excessively and violating all the ways of healthful living. Now you must quit resolutely." To this, Ling replied, "Very well, since I cannot work up enough will power to quit drinking, the only way out is to invoke the gods and spirits before whom I will make a vow to end the habit. Please get the wine and meats ready." The wife said, "Your order is respectfully taken." Whereupon she arranged wine and meats on the altar in front of the gods and requested Ling to take his oath. Ling knelt down and prayed:

> Heaven has given birth to me, Liu Ling
> Who has acquired fame in drinking
> A gallon at one sitting,
> And half of that again to sober up.
> As for the wife's words
> It is best we don't listen.

At that point he drew his wine and ate his meat, getting drunk as a rock in a little while.

. . . .

Liu Tao-chên was fond of fishing in grass-grown lagoons in the days of his youth. He was so good in singing and whistling that those who listened to him would tarry long. There was an elderly woman who knew him to be an exceptional man and who was extremely fond of his singing and whistling. She roasted a whole pork to entertain him. Tao-chên ate up the best portions of the pork without thanking her. Seeing that he was not satisfied yet, she served him another whole pork. Of this he ate one half and returned the other half. Later on he became a commissioner in the ministry of civil affairs and the woman's son was a minor clerk in the same ministry. All of a sudden, the young man was promoted several ranks for no special reason that he knew. He asked his mother, who told him what had happened, whereupon a whole beef and quantities of wine were presented to Tao-chên who said, "Please forget it. I don't need any reward."

. . . .

Chang Chi-ying had no regard for conventions and was nicknamed by his contemporaries, the Foot Soldier from East River. A certain man said to him, "You may be able to defy all established rules to please yourself for a while, but are you not doing something to insure yourself a good name after death?"

He answered, "To me, post-mortem fame is not as good as an immediate flask of wine."

. . . .

Wang Tzŭ-yu was staying temporarily in a friend's empty house and he ordered bamboos to be planted. He was asked why he should take all the trouble, knowing he was not going to stay long. Wang hummed and whistled for a while, then he pointed directly to a bamboo and said, "How is it possible to live even one day without this gentleman's company?"

. . . .

Wang Tzŭ-yu was living in Shanyin. There was a heavy snow one night when he woke up. He pushed aside all the curtains and ordered drink to be brought to him. He looked in all four directions and saw everything silvery white. Then he arose from his seat and paced the floor reciting Tso Ssŭ's poem on the hermit. Suddenly he thought of Tai An-tao who was in the county of Yen. Without hesitation, he engaged a small boat, starting in the night toward Yen. It was not until he had spent two nights in the boat that he arrived there. He walked up to the door, then without going further he turned around to go home. He was asked why he should do that and said, "I started coming because I was inspired by an interest. Now that that interest has worn out, why is it necessary for me to see Tai?

Between the two extremes of adherence to orthodoxy, on the one hand, and forthright cynicism, on the other, the huge majority of the intelligentsia were possessed of two common characteristics. One was t'ung which means literally "go through" or "see through," and the other was t'uo which means "unwrapped," "to outgrow" or "to take off." With t'uo, noninhibition, writers undertook to express their emotions and sentiments, whether of a happy or sorrowful kind, with no reservation. With t'ung, or transparency, writers tended to delight in the exposition of mystical doctrines in logical expositions. Both of these tendencies being liberative in nature tended to swing literary endeavors into channels that might be described as romantic.

This unannounced declaration of independence by literature of ethical and religious limitation substituted individualism for didacticism and developed out of the former into pure estheticism of the southern dynasties at a later period. The bridge which spanned the Han Confucianist literary theorists and the southern dynasties' glorification of the beautiful was, therefore, the Wei-Tsin period. Among critics of the Wei-Tsin era, Ts'ao P'i, or Emperor Wên of the Wei Dynasty, was the first to advocate literature for its own sake. In a famous essay entitled "Tien Lun" in which he discussed the meaning of literature, he wrote:

The art of letters is a great undertaking in the building of a state, a glorious achievement that is immortal. Life and honors, however, are limited by time, and glories and happiness are confined to one person. Both of these necessarily reach their point of termination sooner or later and are, therefore, unlike the everlastingness of literature. Consequently the writers of old dedicated themselves to ink and paper and revealed themselves on pages and in volumes. Relying neither on the phraseology of good historians nor on their rise to power through promotion, they succeeded in perpetuating their names to posterity.

Building on this pronouncement of the divergence between literary attainment and political achievements, a later writer, Lu Chi (A.D. 261-303), wrote his famous essay on letters in the *fu* style. On account of the obscurity and circuitousness of language inherent in the *fu* style, his ideas would seem vague upon a cursory first reading. Nonetheless, his central thoughts can be clearly discerned after a sustained analysis. In the first place, he tried to give equal emphasis to the content and the form of literature. Without disagreeing with the Han critics upon the importance of matter in literature, he stressed the equal significance of manner. "Reason supported substance to erect the trunk and rhetoric multiplied the branches to consummate the fruits and flowers." In the second place, he gave equal stress to imagination and emotion. Without true emotions, he pointed out, all lyrical expressions would resemble the moaning sounds of an invalid. The delineation of emotions should not be factual if the results desired were to be artistic, and the tempering process to elevate fact into art and poetry is provided by the exercise of writers' imagination. In the third place, he championed a new note in creative literature by advocating the futility of imitation. It is imitation that kills individuality. Most clearly he stated his advice:

> Although it might be something long cherished in my mind
> My fear still is that it might have been expressed.
> If there is a suspicion of plagiarism
> It must be abandoned, no matter how dearly loved.

If his suggestion had been taken seriously by his followers, a good deal of the repetitiousness and slavishness in Chinese literature would have been avoided.

Another writer on literature was a man better known for his Taoist lore than for his literary criticism, Ko Hung (A.D. 254-334), author of the philosophical treatise, *Pao P'u Tzŭ*. Counteracting the overemphasis laid by Confucianists on the moral integrity of the writer at the expense of his literary technique, Ko Hung pointed out that the two were of equal importance in a literary career, one being three feet and the other a yard. Going even beyond this, he pointed out that whereas virtuous living might be cultivated with deliberate and conscious effort, literary attainment had to rely on natural gift and, therefore, was more difficult of realization even than ethical integrity. Again, counteracting a traditional concept advocated by late Han Confucianists to the effect that all human institutions had degenerated with the lapse of time so that excellence and antiquity were virtually synonymous, Ko Hung boldly advocated, as a good follower of Chuang-tzŭ, his theory of literary evolution. According to his estimation:

> Scholars of antiquity were neither ghosts nor gods. Although the forms and shapes of their inventions were developed in a remote age, their spirits were all written out in black and white. Their feelings are still revealed in their words and their intentions are clearly discernible.

With this major premise established, that the ancients were neither ghosts nor divinities but just common mortals like contemporary men, he went on in the same essay to demolish the age-old superstition that the writings of the ancients, just because they were hard to understand, were not necessarily superior and might even possibly be inferior to later writings.

> Ancient writings are mostly obscure, not necessarily because the ancients purposely wanted to make them hard to understand. Possibly it was only the result of linguistic changes resulting from lapse of time or dialect divergence owing to difference in locale. Many of them have been neglected while others have been deranged and thus, owing to long oblivion, their texts became imperfect on account of missing pages or other forms of derangement. For this reason they appeared as though they were deep and unfathomable.

Moreover:

> Life in high antiquity was simple and unadorned but now nothing exists without decoration and embellishments. Changes in the way of the world resulting from the lapse of time are only matters of the course of nature.

As though his meaning might yet be missed, he pressed his point further without mincing his words:

> The Book of Documents (Shu Ching) is a collection of political papers but it is not comparable in clarity and ornate beauty to the rescripts, military reports and memorials of recent ages. The Book of Songs (Shih Ching) transmitted to us by the Mao school is an anthology of beautiful and colorful poetry but cannot compare in the range of variety and expansiveness to such fu as "The Imperial Forest," "Imperial Hunting" and the "Two Capitals" and "Three Capitals. . . ." Our attitude regarding what the ancients wrote as divine and what the moderns have written as cheap, our appreciation of what is remote and our depreciation of what is near, are due to habits of long standing. For this reason a new sword would have its price raised by a counterfeit inscription

and a ragged page would increase its value through a forged colophon. For the same reason, an ancient book, though its substance is crude, will be regarded by scholars of this mundane world as having fallen down from Heaven and a new piece of writing, although its substance is gold and jade, will be equated by the ordinary people with pieces of broken tiles.

This new atmosphere which gradually permeated the literary world during the transition period between the Han and T'ang Empires was to manifest itself with varying features and shifting centers of emphasis from generation to generation and, later on, with local geographical variations.

The first age to feel the impact of the new spirit was a short one under Emperor Hsien, the last Han emperor. This age within his reign was known by the reign-period name Chien An ("Reconstruction-Tranquillity"), and extended from A.D. 196-220. This period, although it lay at the end of the Han dynastic span, did not connote any degeneracy or lack of vigor which one would associate with the fall of an empire. On the contrary, it was a period in literary development which opened up many new vistas in both prose and poetry. During the reign of Chien An conscious attempts were made to set up a new discipline for the fostering of new verse forms. Poems consisting purely of five-syllable or seven-syllable lines with rhythmic vitality and regularity were to replace the stately but lifeless four-syllable-line verse form used in sacrificial and court singing that was slavishly imitative of the prevailing pattern in the *Book of Songs*. In folk poetry the irregular verse form composed of lines of varying length—a verse form that seemed to follow no rules at all but only the impulse of the singer and the nature of the subject matter—also yielded ground rapidly to the new convention. In addition, the age saw a remarkable rapprochement between the writings of the literary class and the spontaneous songs of the populace. This latter trend was especially noticeable in the way that folk poetry, with its popular themes and lively ryhthm, exerted a clear influence upon the major poets, who now entitled their poetical compositions in the style of folk songs. In this conscious imitation of folk literature the stark realism of folk poetry was intimately adhered to. The major poets of the age had not adopted the escapist attitude of their followers and still kept their eyes wide open to the tragedies that were rapidly befalling the common people.

On the other hand, continued exposure to the increased sufferings of mankind had begun to disturb the optimism of even the major poets. An outstanding example of this creeping pessimism can be revealed in this excerpt from a poem entitled "Short Song" written

by a man who was the real power behind Emperor Hsien's throne.
Ts'ao Ts'ao (A.D. 155-220):

> Here is wine, let us sing;
> For man's life is short,
> Like the morning dew,
> Its best days gone by.
> But though we would rejoice,
> Sorrows are hard to forget,
> What will make us forget them?
> Wine, and only wine.

(Translation by Herbert A. Giles)

This "Short Song" is indicative of the transitional stage not only because of its constant references to such sentiments as the similarity between human life and the morning dew and the unseverability of the stream of sorrow but also because of the verse form used, that of the four-syllable line of the *Shih Ching* type, which this politician-poet could use with surpassing dexterity.

Among the so-called seven masters of the Chien An Period the most distinguished were Wang Ch'an (A.D. 177-217) and Liu Chêng (died 217). Wang, a member of the advisory staff of Ts'ao Ts'ao, was noted for his erudition and for the meticulous care with which his lines of poetry were polished and repolished. This preoccupation with diction, in which every single character would be weighed and considered with reference to its phonetic fitness and its potential imagery, was definitely a departure from the spontaneous lines of Han poetry, and paved the way for the extreme ornateness of the poetry of the southern dynasties that was soon to follow. Such lines as:

> The curved lagoon unfurled its clear waves
> And the aligned trees spread their red glories.

were certainly a far cry from the lines of the folk songs or even of the nineteen anonymous poems.

Liu Chêng was rated highly by all his contemporaries and immediate followers, but we are unable to reconstruct the basis of his literary reputation on the fifteen poems which have been preserved. Surpassing both Liu and Wang was Ts'ao Ts'ao's second son, Ts'ao Chih (A.D. 192-232), better known as Ch'ên Ssŭ-wang, or Prince Ssŭ of Ch'ên. His rise to literary eminence was not an especially easy one, because both his father and his elder brother, Emperor Wên of the Wei Dynasty, were poets of great reputation. In his twelfth year he won the admiration of his father by having written a *fu* on the Bronze Bird Terrace. Soon afterward, according to an unverified tradition, he fell in love with Lady Chên, a woman ten years older than himself, who became the consort of his elder brother, Emperor Wên. These circumstances, coupled with the political jealousies of his elder brother after the latter's ascension to the imperial throne, rendered his life in exile extremely difficult. His poem, generally known as "The Seven Pace Poem," was an illustration of his point. He had been summoned from his feudal state of Ch'ên to the imperial capital and ordered to write a poem while taking seven paces in the imperial audience hall. He realized it was a political trap to which he responded with the following:

> A fine dish of beans had been placed in the pot
> With a view to a good mess of pottage all hot.
> The beanstalks, aflame, a fierce heat were begetting,
> The beans in the pot were all fuming and fretting.
> Yet the beans and the stalks were not born to be foes;
> Oh, why should these hurry to finish off those?

> (Herbert A. Giles' translation)

The cruel treatment accorded by his elder brother was later on counteracted by the mildness of his nephew when the latter had ascended the throne. As he was making a last attempt to contribute to the newly built empire, he died at the age of forty.

If anyone had contributed substantially to the five-syllable-line poetry of the Chien An Period, no one could rival Ts'ao Chih in demonstrating that the new verse form could be utilized in all types of poetical expression from extended narration to the most ethereal type of lyricism.

The Ruins of Loyang

> I climb to the ridge of the Pei-mang Hills
> And look down on the city of Loyang.
> In Loyang how still it is!
> Palaces and houses all burnt to ashes.
> Walls and fences all broken and gaping,
> Thorns and brambles shooting up to the sky.
> I do not see the old old-men;
> I only see the new young men.
> I turn aside, for the straight road is lost;
> The fields are overgrown and will never be ploughed again.
> I have been away such a long time
> That I do not know which path is which.

How sad and ugly the empty moors are!
A thousand miles without the smoke of a chimney.
I think of our life together all those years;
My heart is tied with sorrow and I cannot speak.

(Arthur Waley's translation)

The short-lived Wei Dynasty ended in A.D. 265 after a dramatic enactment of an abdication ceremony, in pretty much the same manner in which the dynasty had been founded. On nine different occasions the abdicating emperor entreated the aspirant to accept the Mandate of Heaven. It was only on the ninth occasion that the recipient of the mandate "yielded to the pressure of popular request." Such an odious repetition of history in the course of a half-century proved excessive to the sensitive feelings of the populace. While the first performance might be shocking, its repetition was irksome. It was this bit of dynastic hypocrisy that drove the principal thinkers and writers of this period into Taoism as an escape. All the noted scholars tried to minimize the importance of the world of actuality. Among them the most noted seven formed themselves into a coterie, spending their time in bamboo groves instead of palace buildings, thus earning for themselves the nickname of the Seven Worthies of the Bamboo Groves. Contrasted with the Seven Masters of Chien An, the Seven Worthies had no use for the company of emperors and aristocrats, seeking their consolation in their little world of wine drinking and poetry writing in a naturalistic environment. Even those who had made temporary sorties into political life did not give up their basic philosophy. In creative literature, realism gave way to symbolism and lyricism acquired a mystical accretion.

Of the Seven Worthies, two stand out clearly with their literary legacies better preserved. The gifted Juan Chi (A.D. 210-263), a native of present-day Kaifêng in Honan Province, acquired fame for his unconventionality. Seeing that many of the serious-minded scholars had been mercilessly slaughtered by unreasonable monarchs, he joined others in giving up hope for political reforms and social betterment. It should be pointed out that his decadence was actually a psychological smoke screen put up for self-preservation. His continual drunkenness for sixty days was a means of noncommitment when he had been approached by the usurper, Ssŭ-ma Chao, for a marriage alliance between the two clans featuring his son, Ssŭ-ma Yen. Noted for his ability to indicate his approval and disapproval of his contemporaries by rolling his eyeballs in two separate ways (revealing more of the pupils symbolized approval and revealing more of the white indicated condemnation), he succeeded in saving himself political recriminations and punishment by the tactful avoidance of words. Whenever, as a poet, he could not sustain himself in silence, he would resort to allegory. Thus, in one essay, he compared the universe to the limited space around the seat of a pair of pants and individual human beings to fleas and lice in them. Again, in his enumeration of the most substantial contributors to human civilization, he singled out the inventor of wine for unconditional praise. It is against this background that his eighty-two poems, summarily entitled *Yung Huai* or *Singing of What I Feel*, should be read. These, which should be considered eighty-two separate compositions on so many different occasions, do not form a harmonious unit. Each one was inspired by a separate theme and individually couched in a mystifying language with *double-entendre*.

Like many of his contemporaries, Juan Chi was badly bemused by the sudden and extensive reversal of moral standards and human values in an age of turbulent dynastic changes brought about by scheming, intrigue, and subversion; but unlike them he was able to steer through the stormy era in which many men of letters were incriminated and liquidated on extremely doubtful grounds. Having seen two dynastic collapses and having been forced by circumstance to bear with the principal actors on the political stage, he accepted official posts and honors that had come his way with neither relish nor remorse. As it were, his sense of complete detachment and release from the accepted standards of political loyalty was a manifestation of his philosophy of survival. On one hand, he sought refuge in drinking, and on the other, he did not consider a nominal post in the government as a burden on his personal freedom or as a compromise that would tarnish his personality. In consequence, he showed no hesitation in applying for a secretaryship in the infantry division of the imperial army simply because he had heard that the chef at headquarters was an expert in rice wine brewing and that he had stored up a reserve of over a thousand gallons. On account of a special gift he was able to maintain a high degree of cautiousness if not complete sobriety at drinking parties and was, therefore, free from personal involvements in political intrigues and factional strife. Although he moved frequently in the company of political opportunists practically unscathed, he was aware of the danger to which he was being continually exposed. This feeling is clearly discernible in his thirty-second lyric:

A day and then an evening,
An evening and another morning,
My complexion is no longer normal,
And my spirits are grinding themselves away.
In my heart there are fire and boiling water
And changes are continually beckoning me.
The myriad things know of no end
But wisdom and discretion are bitterly lacking.
I fear that in a few fleeting moments
My souls will be wafted away by the wind.
I have trod on thin ice all these years
But who knows that my inner being is badly scorched?

It is no wonder that two centuries later one of the leading critics, Liu Hsieh, noted that Juan's meanings were remote and deeply hidden.

In his prose writings he maintained the necessity, as he did in his poetry, of outgrowing the shackling standards of traditional confucianism. Besides developing his own misanthropic views by comparing human beings to fleas and lice, he was an advocate of a subtle form of anarchism. He believed that "without kings the multiple objects would take care of themselves and without ministers the myriad affairs would be automatically tidied up." Furthermore, he believed that "without honor and nobility, the underprivileged would not feel discontented and without abundance and riches the impoverished would not struggle. If each person feels contentment in himself, there would be no desperate searches for anything."

In both his poetry and his prose writings, Juan had distinguished himself by a clearly personalized style. In the handling of themes, the proffering of ideas, and the employment of rhetorical niceties, he stood out prominently as an individual, whereas all the other great poets of his age, distinguished as they were by their technique, seem to impress the modern reader as so many members of a well-knit school sharing a common pool of literary technique and refined cultural traditions.

Other poets worthy of mention follow. Hsi K'ang (A.D. 223-262) took special delight in writing philosophical poems to underscore the teachings of Taoism. In his prose writings he successfully intermingled his serious thoughts with touches of light humor. Being the chief advocate of the virtues of indolence, he frequently made fun of himself by describing his own eccentricities in complete disregard of the minimum standards of cleanliness and attention to worldly affairs. In one of his letters to a friend, Shan T'ao (A.D. 205-283), he proudly announced that he "constantly condemned

King T'ang and King Wu and belittled the Duke of Chou and Confucius" without realizing that such a statement could be interpreted as a *lèse-majesté* against the Tsin Dynasty. The new emperor actually took offense and, under pretext of Hsi K'ang's involvement in a plot against the state, sentenced him to capital punishment. P'an O (A.D. 247-300) had the good fortune of avoiding involvement in the vicissitudes of dynastic change and of rising steadily in the official hierarchy in the Tsin Empire to the magistracy of the city of Ch'angan. In spite of his dexterity in avoiding disasters in his official career, he finally had to face capital punishment for his share in a palace intrigue. His writings are shot through with a deep note of tragic melancholy. His *fu* compositions describe the emotions suggested by such a theme as widowhood. He was also noted for lyrical compositions written in artistic epistolary prose addressed to the spirits of the deceased. His most remembered contribution is a new type of lyrical poetry written in memory of his wife, giving rise to a unique category known in Chinese as *tao wang* or "lamenting the death of a wife."

Lu Chi (A.D. 261-303) was the first important writer in the kingdom of Wu, one of the three kingdoms set up after the disintegration of the Later Han Empire in A.D. 220. Born in the coastal area in the southern half of China and fourth son of the Wu commander-in-chief, Lu K'ang, he was the first important representative of the southward extension of Chinese civilization. Being devoted to the traditional ideals of loyalty, he declined to go into public service for ten years after the subjugation of Wu by the Tsin Empire which succeeded in reunifying China for a short period. In those days, before the overrunning of North China by the remnants of the Hunnish race and their allied tribes, the main seats of cultural orthodoxy were still the old capitals of Ch'angan and Loyang. As Ch'angan had been ravaged and sacked more than once, it had yielded its priority to the eastern capital. To meet and pass the supreme test for scholars and writers to attain enduring fame, Lu Chi and his younger brother, Lu Yün, decided to proceed to Loyang. Their reception by the literary coteries at the imperial capital was of a most cordial and obliging kind. Lu Chi was immediately appointed president of the national university, from which post he rose steadily in the imperial officialdom, and was later on made a member of the nobility. On account of involvement in various political plots he was eventually exiled and later on executed.

As a child of his age he wrote a considerable volume of poetry mainly imitative in style and, therefore, not entirely free from artificiality. Nonetheless, his individuality stands out in spite of the fact that he was necessarily limited by the patterns set by his predecessors. More important than his poems was a *fu* which he composed in the spirit of a critical essay. Entitled "Wên Fu" or a "Fu on Letters," this important document on literary criticism presented certain basic keys for the guidance of writers to achieve high standards. Instead of expressing his thoughts and feelings on the meaning and excellences of literature, he chose to write in the highly schematic *fu* prose of parallel structure. He was a great master of the *fu* style as well as an original thinker on the intricate problems of literature. However, there are passages in the "Wên Fu" which are vague and require analysis and probings before they are understandable.

Another writer of distinction in the Wei-Tsin period was Tso Ssŭ (flourished A.D. 265-305). He may be regarded as the last master and the culmination of the *fu* tradition of the old Han school. His attainment in this literary type was so high that later *fu* writers had to discover new techniques and try new experiments, with the result that elaboration was replaced by lyricism, and long structures replaced by brief compositions. This new trend in *fu* writing, which really warranted a new designation, will be discussed later. What Tso Ssŭ accomplished in this field can be seen in his trilogy of *The Three Capitals,* in which he presented in graphic word pictures, projected against the historic backdrop of consecutive tableaus, the capitals of the Three Kingdoms. On the three monumental members of the trilogy the author had spent fully ten years during which he continually rewrote and revised, changing rhyme schemes and improving diction all the time. When it was released, the trilogy attracted so much attention and so many copies were made that the price of paper in Loyang was said to have risen sharply. At least one reason for the popularity of the work and for the demand for individual copies was the fact that the trilogy was so rich in string after string of glamorous phrases and colorful synonyms that it could serve as a most effective manual for young aspiring *fu* writers. This peculiar literary reference work, although lacking emotional appeal, was compiled with great devotion and painstaking labor. As the author confesses in his own preface, it was a tour de force as a digest of historical and geographical literature:

> As I have admired the two *fu* on the capitals [by Chang Hêng] I have decided to treat similarly of the three capitals. For this work maps were consulted as regards the mountains and rivers, cities and fortified towns; local gazeteers were studied as regards the flora and fauna of each region. Folk songs and folk dances revealing local customs are appropriately appended and outstanding personalities are recorded in strict keeping with old traditions.

His excessive preoccupation with embroidering a matter-of-fact theme with rhetorical embellishments was no indication that he was lacking in literary originality. As soon as he steered away from *fu* writing he could be so unconventional as to use the vernacular in his five-syllable-line poems.

In the company of the foregoing writers was a host of outstanding craftsmen in rhetoric and other phases of literary technique. Perfectly trained in the art of versification in all its intricacies, they are pleasant to read but they are not outstanding in the main current of Chinese literature.

Now the imperial court of the Tsin Dynasty was rapidly approaching catastrophe and its flight to Nanking in A.D. 318. Among writers who witnessed this disaster was Liu K'un (A.D. 271-318). Eventually to face decapitation himself, he saw the social confusion and the mounting of human suffering on the eve of the barbarian migrations. Thus, singing of the old metropolitan area of Fufêng, he rose high above the level of songs of geographical lore.

> A rainbow at morning was bridging the sky,
> And fragrant a stream full of lilies hard by,
> When lo! I beheld a young maid of fifteen,
> Who stood, sweetly smiling, behind the canteen.
>
> She outshone the flowers which blossomed around;
> Men grudged that her shadow should fall on the ground;
> So peerless her beauty and youth,—in a trice
> I found I had paid for my wine double price!
>
> (Herbert A. Giles' translation)

A poet of similar vein, Kuo P'u (A.D. 276-324) has been remembered by posterity mainly as a learned commentator. His works of erudition included commentaries on the classical *Book of Synonyms, Erh Ya,* an accumulative work variously attributed to ancient authors from the Duke of Chou down; on the *Fang Yen* of Yang Hsiung, an interesting work in which dialect variants of nouns, adjectives, and verbs had been grouped together; and on the *Shan Hai Ching,* or *The Mountain and Sea Classic,* a peerless treasury of early myths, legends, and folktales in far-off regions which had delighted the imagination of curious readers. Even surpassing these in interest and curiosity is Kuo's commentary on the *Mu T'ien-tzŭ Chuan* or the *Biography of the Son of Heaven, Mu.* This biography had been newly rediscovered in an ancient tomb among other rare items all written on bamboo slips. As it was not written in the style of the normal biography but covered details of the purported travels of

King Mu (who flourished in 900 B.C.) to regions outside of China such as the Kunlun Mountains and the land of the Western King Mother (Hsi Wang Mu), a new commentary was not only welcomed but also needed by readers in search of romantic literature.

Though tireless as a compiler of commentary notes, the fact that he was a philosophical thinker of the Taoist school was enough guarantee that Kuo P'u was no learned dunce. As a poet he wrote a series of poems collectively entitled *Traveling Immortal* (*Yu Hsien Shih*). In these he depicted imaginary travels occasionally based upon actual experience, in which he would take time off to elaborate upon philosophical concepts. Instead of relying on abstractions he, as an outstanding poet, would suggest his logical arguments by clothing them in concrete images. To indicate his personal optimism in spite of the dismal changes and disruptions which surrounded him, he simply wrote, for example:

> May I ask of the many ants,
> How can you tell the age of tortoises and cranes?

In these two short lines he suggested the ultimate prevalence of order and harmony after temporary confusion and disorder.

The great literary giant after the disorders of the dynastic flight and the loss of the northern half of China to alien groups was T'ao Ch'ien, also known by his alternate name, T'ao Yüan-ming (A.D. 365-427). Born in the district of Hsinyang in present-day Kiangsi Province, he was a southerner and the scion of a great official family. His great-grandfather was the famous Duke of Ch'angsha, T'ao K'an (A.D. 257-332), a meritorious official known for his superior personal integrity among court ministers of the early Tsin Dynasty. Among the many anecdotes told of this remarkable ancestor of the poet, one narrates with detail how he would remove for daily exercise a hundred pieces of heavy tile from the courtyard to his studio and back. It was not the official distinction attained nor the habits of diligence cultivated by his ancestor that the poet admired most but rather the readiness with which the Duke decided to resign from all his official honors. Of his own father he said, in a poem intended for his own sons to read, "He lodged himself temporarily on rising clouds and rose above anger and satisfaction," which was another way of suggesting that he had thought lightly of the position once held as a county magistrate. His "external" grandfather (mother's father) of whom the poet wrote a biography, was described as a person "who did not conform casually or speak haughtily, never revealing extreme delight or anger, never losing his balance despite his fondness for heavy drinking, and when fully satisfied, happily disassociating himself from his immediate environment, acting as though there were no one nearby."

Exercising a formative influence upon his personality was the sudden change of the political scene in his lifetime. Whatever stability had been attained in the early period of the Tsin Dynasty now yielded ground to a whole series of factional strifes among manipulators of dynastic power. Moral integrity was practically a lost trait at the imperial court and the acceptance of bribery was the usual phenomenon of the day. Outside of the metropolitan area, garrison commanders in the different provinces vied with one another in building up their military power and in disregarding the orders of the central government. When T'ao Ch'ien was thirty there was a usurpation of the throne by a feudal prince who had brought political disorder to a boiling point. Thanks to the efforts of a garrison commander, Liu Yü, the usurper was liquidated and peace and order were restored. Under his command the Tsin armies were even able to recover a good deal of the territory lost to the barbarian tribes. Unfortunately Liu was too eager for the role of emperor. Instead of pushing his military campaigns with full might he abandoned the fruits of his reconquest and waited for his own subversion of the Tsin Empire in A.D. 421.

According to his own account, the poet sought his livelihood by joining the civil service to support his aging mother and his impoverished family. For three years he was a consultant in the garrison army where he had met Liu Yü as a colleague. Later on he served as the magistrate of P'êngtsê County for slightly over a year. The cause of his resignation was his unwillingness to put on his official belt when reporting to his superior. To celebrate that occasion, he wrote his famous "Kuei Ch'ü Lai Tz'ŭ" or "Homeward Bound." He was then only thirty-three but he was already tired of the bothersome nature of the various ties of officialdom. Thenceforth he declined resolutely all summonses to return to public life. According to a tradition which is probably ill founded, he discontinued to use the reign year of the new Sung Dynasty * in dating his compositions to express his loyalty to his own Tsin Dynasty. It is more likely that his refusal to return to public life was an expression of his escapism from the torrid and turbulent politics of his days rather than personal devotion to any specific imperial dynasty.

T'ao's philosophy was an interesting and harmonious combination

* This dynasty which extended from 420 to 478 and which ruled the southern half of China was founded by Liu Yü. Hence it is sometimes referred to as the Liu-Sung dynasty to avoid confusion with the Sung Dynasty Proper, so to speak, founded by Chao K'uang-yin in 960, and conquered by Kublai Khan in 1279.

of elements from Confucianism, Taoism, and Buddhism that appealed to him. As a follower of Confucianism, he regulated his life with strict ethical discipline. On the other hand, he followed in the footsteps of philosophical Taoism in outgrowing the rigid formularies upheld by the orthodox Confucian school. Moreover, in the year that T'ao Ch'ien had made up his mind to forsake official life, a distinguished Buddhist, Hui Yüan, had built up his following in a monastery situated at Tunglin, only about seven miles from T'ao's village. It was only natural that an exchange of visits between the poet and the Buddhist was extremely frequent, as is borne out by T'ao's own writings.

As a poet, T'ao Ch'ien tried to behave and sing as a member of the masses. It is recorded in his biography in the *Dynastic History* that after his return home he never paid visits to the noble and the great, being fond only of short trips to farmhouses and the scenic areas of Lu Shan, the resort mountains which have kept their beauty and fame to this day. This avoidance of contacts with officialdom was due to his fondness of nature, a delight derived from his freedom from shackles. As a result, his poetry is only a natural expression of the life he sought to live involving no extraneous efforts and, therefore, engendering no artificiality. To him, even the titles of his groups of poems were of no great moment and could therefore be selected at random. A poem entitled "Drinking" might have nothing to do with drinking at all, such as the following:

> I build my house in the world of man
> And yet I don't feel the noise of carriages and horses.
> "May I ask how you manage to do it?"
> When your heart is remote, your abode is reclusive.
> As I pick chrysanthemums at the eastern hedge relaxedly,
> I see the southern mountains from afar.
> The mountain air is good both day and night
> And the flying birds keep my company.
> In this there is a real meaning,
> Wishing to express it one had already forgotten the power of speech.

Even his so-called "poems imitative of ancient style" were not imitations in spite of the title.

> Setting sun and a cloudless sky—
> The spring breeze is fanning up a subtle warmth.
> The beautiful ladies, delighting in the clear night,
> Drink and sing merrily till dawn.
> After the songs are ended—a deep sigh
> Over a thought profoundly stirring:

The moon brightly shining amidst the clouds
And the flower radiantly blooming in the foliage,
These are indeed beautiful for a while
But for how long will they endure?

His return to nature is frequently fully expressed in his wine-drinking poems like the following:

In the quiet of the morning I heard a knock at my door;
I threw on my clothes and opened it myself.
I asked who it was who had come so early to see me;
He said he was a peasant, coming with good intent.
He brought with him a full flagon of wine,
Believing my household had fallen on evil days.
"You live in rags under a thatched roof
And seem to have no desire for a better lot.
The rest of mankind have all the same ambitions;
You, too, must learn to wallow in their mire."
"Old man, I am impressed by what you say,
But my soul is not fashioned like other men's.
To drive in their rut I might perhaps learn;
To be untrue to myself could only lead to muddle.
Let us drink and enjoy together the wine you have brought;
For my course is set and cannot now be altered."

(Arthur Waley's translation)

His adherence to what he called a set course, a course of being natural and of following the ways of nature, was something that gave him full satisfaction both as man and as poet. To the onlooker, however, this matter of going against the way of the world might appear toilsome as it did even to a Taoist friend of his, T'an Tao-chi (died A.D. 436), who remarked to him, "Why should you give yourself bitterness like this?" The question must have struck his ear like a riddle, for there was no evidence in his writings that he had given himself any bitterness. The following are the two poems he wrote in justification of his house moving:

I have wanted to live in the southern village
Not for the good luck of the house.
I have heard that there are many simple-hearted people
And I would love to spend my days with them.
Having cherished this for years, today I am engaged in moving.
An old house need not be large,
Barely enough to accommodate mats and couches.
To me, neighbors will constantly come
For conversation and reminiscence,
Rare writings are appreciated together,
And doubtful points are cleared by mutual efforts.

Some old friends who think well of me
Came to me with a kettle of wine.
Sitting on a mat under the pine tree,
We were soon drunk after a few cups.
Talking and drinking at random,
We were unmindful of rules of seniority,
I no longer felt even the reality of self,
Much less the value of things.
I was enchanted by this lingering experience,
Indeed, there is a deep meaning in wine drinking.

This attitude of his was charmingly described in his will written in his deathbed to his sons—more of a lyrical family letter than a legal document:

When I was young I learned to play the lute and to practice calligraphy. Occasionally I am especially fond of leisure and quiet. I would open my book and feel I was getting something so that in my happiness I would forget to eat. [At other times] I would see trees clasping their branches to yield shade and I would hear birds of the season changing their notes in singing whereupon I would feel profoundly happy. I used to say frequently that during the fifth and sixth months, lying down under the northern window and meeting transitory drafts of a cool breeze would make me call myself a person of high antiquity.

A fuller picture of his ideal society was the picture he drew in prose of the *Plum Blossom Fountain* or *T'ao-hua Yüan*.

In the reign of T'ai Yüan of the Tsin Dynasty, there was a professional fisherman of Wuling who walked along a creek and had forgotten the distance he had covered. All of a sudden he was confronted with a forest of plum blossom trees. On both sides of the stream for a distance of several hundred paces there was no other tree. The grass underneath was beautiful and fresh and the fallen petals were profuse and beautiful. Wondering at this, the fisherman again resumed his walk, wanting to get to the limit of this forest. Outside of the fringe of the forest there was the fountain of the creek by which there was a mountain. In the mountain-side there was a little opening through which light seemed to be seen. He then left his boat and went through the opening which was so narrow that it would admit only a single person. After walking several tens of paces the vista began to open up brightly. The land was expansive and flat and the houses and huts neatly arranged. There were good farms, beautiful ponds, bamboos and mulberry trees. Communication was facilitated by pathways of different widths and the crowing of roosters and the barking of dogs were easily heard between communities. The style of clothing worn by men and women going about and doing farm work were all like people outside. Old people and youngsters felt naturally happy and satisfied. As they saw the fisherman they were greatly surprised and asked him where he was from and when he had answered their questions in full he was invited to go home where wine was prepared and chickens were cooked and served.

Other people in the village having heard of this man all came to visit with their questions. These people said that their progenitors, fleeing from the confusion of the Ch'in Dynasty, had come with their wives, children and fellow townsmen to this exclusive place and had never left it again. That's why they had been isolated from the outside world. Asking what dynasty was reigning they knew nothing of the Han, leave alone the Wei and the Tsin. The fisherman told them one item after another and they responded with sighs to what they heard. Other people also invited him to visit their homes by turn and they all treated him to wine and dinner. After a stay of several days he took his leave whereupon the people urged him not to tell outsiders about his visit. After coming out he found his boat and retraced his directions, leaving marks here and there. When he arrived at the county seat he reported thus and so to the prefect. The prefect immediately dispatched people to follow him in search of the marks he had left, but in the search they were confused and unable to retrack the course. Liu Tzŭ-chi was a scholar of extremely high quality who, having heard of this, happily decided to go himself in search. Before he left he died of an illness. Thereafter, there was none who asked about the place.

From the foregoing any reader is easily convinced that T'ao Ch'ien, in the cultural makeup of his personality, was more deeply indebted to Taoism than to Confucianism. On the other hand, he displayed no violent reactions to traditional Confucianism as was true of so many of his contemporaries. While to many the artificialities and misinterpretations of late Han Confucianism seemed to be mere shackles imposed upon the spontaneity of life, T'ao succeeded in transcending and by-passing these later accretions to rediscover for himself the simple ethical teachings of the master such as the cultivation of the esthetic sense for spiritual enrichment and concern with the well-being of one's own family and immediate group of friends. Thus he was able to blend harmoniously the teachings of two ancient conflicting schools into an eclectic philosophy of life based on an extremely healthy type of naturalism. In this new synthesis the heritage of Taoism was naturally predominant. In the biography of his maternal grandfather, Mêng Chia, he made the latter also an advocate of the natural. When the statesman-general Huan Wên wondered why it was that in listening to the musical performances of sing-song girls, silk (stringed instruments) seemed to be inferior to bamboo (wind instruments) and, in turn, bamboo seemed to be inferior to flesh (voice), Mêng's reply was that it was so because these different types varied in their approach to nature. Again when he was about to leave the city for the farm he wrote in one of his poems:

> Having long lived in cages and behind fences,
> Now I succeed in returning to nature.

In describing his own temperament in his famous and unique composition of the *fu* type entitled, "Homeward Bound," he wrote:

My temperament is as it is (naturally conforms to nature) and does not lend itself to forced efforts and imposed guidance. While hunger and cold are intimately felt, going against my nature will give me even more pain.

This philosophy of life was applied without any conscious effort to his creative writings, which were, after all, incidental parts of his life as a whole. Both his poetry and his prose may therefore be regarded as a natural overflow of his personality and no attempts were made to make them beautiful. Later poets who made deliberate efforts to write in the style of T'ao seem to have missed the most vital point in his message.

To T'ao the love of nature was synonymous with the love of freedom. In consequence, what he would deplore most was "to enslave one's spirit by one's body" and yet his exaltations of man's spirit involved no asceticism, no mortification of the flesh.

I once traveled far and wide
Until I reached the shores of the Eastern Sea.
The roads were winding and long,
Winds and waves impeded my progress.
What had induced me to undertake those travels?
I seemed to have been driven by hunger.
I made every effort to fill my belly,
But a little was more than enough.
Fearing that I had miscalculated
I rested my carriage and returned to leisurely living.

The first poet to realize the wisdom of a late Chou philosopher, Sung Chien (360? B.C.-290? B.C.) who said, "Men's desires are few but they all imagine them to be more than they are," he summarized his appreciation in two lines in one of his drinking poems:

One nourishes his body as though it were worth a thousand gold pieces,
But on facing death his treasures were found to be vanishing.

According to a recent critic and scholar, Liang Ch'i-ch'ao, these two lines were a condensation of seven thousand scrolls of the Buddhist Tripitaka. To his many Buddhist friends such as Hui Yüan, T'ao probably was not too close to nirvana, as T'ao's views were still largely subjective and tied down by considerations of the self, though it might be that this was a "natural" self. The poet himself, however, felt that such an ordering of his life was sufficiently satisfying. This feeling he depicted in a charming prose piece entitled "A Biography of Mr. Five Willows" which, according to the best authorities was a fairly accurate self-portraiture—that of a man who derived full enjoyment from drinking and the writing of poetry; a man who spent his whole life in oblivion of gains and losses. When he had to face his own "transformation" he undertook, with neither grief nor flurry, the writing of three poems and one essay to serve as dirges and obituary lamentations. These pieces, unlike compositions of a similar type written by people for amusement while they were enjoying excellent health, were actually parting messages left by the poet on his deathbed.

We will now consider the forms of the unsullied discourse and prose literature. We have seen how the orthodox scholasticism of Han Confucianism, as it was gathering momentum and rallying universal following, was challenged and smashed by Wang Ch'ung. Thenceforth all advocacy of the pre-eminence of one Confucian classic at the expense of other classics and all controversies regarding the urgency of establishing official professorial chairs at the state university were to subside for centuries. As a result, Confucianist masters who were contemporary with Wang Ch'ung manifested a deviation from narrow specialism and comprehended the whole range of the Confucian canon. Scholars like Ma Yung and Chêng Hsüan were not only experts in exegetical researches but also learned men of diverse interests. This widening of the horizon of Confucian scholarship was the beginning of a tendency to seek real contributions to living in the ancient texts.

The culmination of this trend was reached when scholarly interest and philosophical searches exceeded the bounds of Confucianism. We have noted that rise in the Han official hierarchy was largely based on what was termed "Ch'ing Yi," which literally means "pure criticism" or "objective opinion." In other words, whether a man was worthy of appointment or promotion was determined by the consensus or majority of objective estimates concerning him made by the prevailing opinion of the scholarly world. To make the system workable, a number of standards were set up, such as filial piety and incorruptibility in money matters. Once such standards were agreed on, questionable efforts were made by seekers of official honors and emoluments to attain those objectives. The net result was despicable hypocrisy and farcical artificiality.

The daily routine of the intelligentsia in China was rapidly undergoing a change. Instead of plying their Confucian texts with devoted and undivided attention and instead of undertaking collation of texts in teams of two seated in opposite directions as though they were prosecutor and attorney of the defense, the noted scholars would sit in relaxation around a low table each holding in his hand a fly whisk and detachedly engage in philosophical conversation. These day-long sessions would sometimes address themselves to fine analyses of logic and philosophy and sometimes to the evaluation of personalities immediate and remote. Often these casual and cursory comments, usually detached from current events and politics, would be recorded, and were read with such avidity among younger scholars that many copies were made by hand.

In due course the fad became so intense that participants, deeply absorbed, would forget their regular meals, which had been reheated and served several times. The pattern followed consisted in a complete disregard of conventional etiquette and the complete ignoring of the urgent affairs of everyday living. A short-cut to fame as mapped out by one of the participants in satire was, "to have leisure all the time, to drink wine until it hurts, and to read the Li-Sao— no need for special gifts." In spite of a very important protest launched by a thoughtful scholar of the Tsin Dynasty, P'ei Kuei (A.D. 267-300), in an essay of his entitled "The Importance of Positivity," the trend went ahead unchecked. According to some later critics, this complete lack of concern with the burning issues of the age and this indulgence in conversation and discussion devoted to abstract philosophical theories unsullied by political and worldly concerns led directly to the disintegration of the Western Tsin Dynasty and its southward flight in A.D. 318 before the southward onslaught of the barbarian tribes.

To blame a dynastic collapse on this indulgence in philosophical speculation exclusively might be an exaggeration. At any rate, in the realm of literature the apparently negative activities of the intelligentsia had at least ushered a draft of fresh air into the stuffy atmosphere of late Han formalism. The new emphasis placed on argumentation, which was a reversal of the attitude of unconditional subservience to masters and authorities, did a good deal to improve the quality of prose writing. A new precedent was made in which writers were expected to expound both sides of a debate. For example, one of the masters of the unsullied-discourse school, Ho Yen, had written an essay to advocate his belief that a sage was entirely free from the sway of emotions such as pleasure and anger, grief, and enjoyment. As soon as this essay was made public, his literary opponents retaliated with essays advocating exactly the reverse.

Another theme that was extremely popular in this type of literary give-and-take and philosophical advocacy and refutation was the importance and finality of nonentity (Wu). Other controversies were grouped around such topics as whether the love of learning comes about naturally, whether a lodging might inherently be lucky or unlucky, and whether sounds by their very nature connoted happiness or sorrow. While some of the topics seemed even to contemporaries to be trivial, and while the development of argumentation appeared more like gymnastics and acrobatics in reasoning than real creative thinking, the movement as a whole was not unfruitful in bringing about a lucidity in statements, in increasing attention to logical reasoning, and in encouraging the taking of a definite stand and advancing uncompromising arguments in support of that stand.

These participants in the unsullied-discourse movement, keenly as they appreciated the value of individuality and refusal of compromise, had a number of characteristics in common. With almost no exceptions they boldly and purposely entertained extreme views. Extremism in this regard usually took the form of nonconformity. This trait in literature led to an enrichment of content in prose writings, at least with regard to the clarity of attitudes and a deliberate attempt to avoid platitudes. In the second place, they were all serious-minded students of philosophical Taoism in a liberal manner, by which is meant they were not hesitant in culling wisdom from all conceivable sources. In the third place, most of them were so eager to assure themselves of the availability of leisure that except for verse writing, in which they showed an especial aptitude, they were not especially productive in literature. Avoiding regularity and hard work as they all did, they seemed to derive greater pleasure and stimulation from unconventional living such as leaving their long hair undressed, wearing as little clothing as permitted by weather, and taking part in protracted private drinking parties in their studios. A story was told of how, after the dynastic removal to the south, a number of the living wits of the age were holding an exclusive club meeting one day. An escapee from North China of similar philosophical persuasion called on the group but was refused admittance by the gatekeeper. To insure his admission, the caller unbraided his hair, took off his outer garments and crawled through the dog hole. As he was taking a look at the assembled company he emitted peculiar sounds to simulate barking, whereupon his identity was established and he was immediately admitted to complete the roll call of the Eight Unconventionals.

No matter how piously these unconventional intellectuals steered away from practical problems, they often wandered away from their sacred grounds of impracticability, as the line was hard to draw between what was purely unsullied and inconsequential and what was utilitarian and applicable. Thus one of the outstanding experts on the *Book of Changes* and the *Book of Lao-tzŭ*, Juan Hsiu (flourished circa A.D. 300), had chosen to write an essay on the nonexistence of ghosts. He must have thought that the subject matter was definitely a purely speculative one, but when he argued by saying, "Now those who have seen ghosts all claim the latter to be wearing the same clothing they had been wont to wear while alive. Granting people after their death continue to live as spirits, how can they argue that garments also have spirits?" he was heading unawares toward the dispersal of popular superstitions and social and religious reforms.

While the undaunted fighters against tradition and formalism were making their retreats from the realities of political and social facts, the northern frontiers of the Tsin Empire were astir with standing threats from the barbarian tribes who were making rapid encroachments upon China. The harsh realities of imperial defense and national security began to force a modicum of common sense and minimum alertness to even the most unconcerned. Thus, an unsullied speculator, Chiang T'ung (died A.D. 310), had suddenly awakened to the seriousness of the frontier situation and boldly wrote a political essay, "Hsi Jung Lun" or "On the Urgency of Resettling the Barbarians." His recommendation was, in brief, a plan to give financial assistance to the non-Chinese elements in the border towns so that they could return to the lands of their origin. Workable as his proposal might sound, the situation was already too far gone. The whole political situation was to undergo a drastic change and together with it the prospects of medieval Chinese literature.

CHAPTER 11

Medieval Literature

MEDIEVAL Chinese literature, instead of coinciding with the periodization of political history, extends from the southward flight of the Tsin imperial court in 318 to the opening of China to the outside world again after the disruption of the Mongolian Empire around 1521. Contrasted with the ancient age, the medieval period in Chinese literature was largely characterized by the cultural cross-fertilization between China and India. Almost uninterruptedly for twelve centuries cultural borrowings and adaptations from India were actively maintained, sometimes overtly and at other times less openly. As the result, many new literary types were born, such as the transfiguration pieces, long and short plays, and, above all, sustained fiction either in pure prose or in a commingling of prose and verse. Similarly, the motifs and themes of Indian literature were gradually naturalized. It is difficult to imagine what monotony might have dominated the Chinese literary scene if there had been no cultural borrowings from the land of Buddhism.

Nor should we allow ourselves to be misled by the mere label "medieval" which, in European history, has always suggested a long hibernation and recovery, if not quite complete darkness. Whereas Europe, and especially western Europe, between the fall of Rome and the fall of Constantinople looked gloomy most of the time, China's middle age was characterized by fine weather in the main. To be sure, there were people's migrations, political divisions, and religious controversies and disputes, situations reminding us of their European counterparts in the Middle Ages. In Chinese literature, however, medievalism is synonymous with progress and brilliance.

This long period of twelve hundred years may be more easily grasped by its three subdivisions.

The first subdivision extends from the establishment of the Southern Tsin Dynasty in Nanking in 318 to the early reigns of the T'ang Dynasty prior to the reign of T'ien Pao (742-755). During this time traditional poetry and prose still dominated the scene but within these two literary types and thought patterns, the motifs and even the diction and phraseology were already bearing the imprints of

181

Buddhism and Indian culture. The foreshadow of prose fiction was already discernible but the economy and discipline exercised by Chinese cultural traditions were still exerting a restraining influence upon scope and length. Short stories of the French *contes* type were still the preferred length. In poetry, the seven-syllable line was already competing with the earlier five-syllable line for ascendency.

The second subdivision extends from 742 to the end of the Northern Sung Dynasty, 1127, the year which saw the southward transference of the Sung capital from K'aifêng to Hangchou. During these centuries the influence of Buddhism and Indian culture took more overt forms than the supplying of themes, motifs, and phrases. Indianization was pervading the whole of Chinese literature. One unique type of Indian literature in which prose and verse were alternately used had been naturalized in China for the recounting of stories of the life of the Buddha. As the originals, even in translation, were too literary or too alien to audiences which were composed partly of illiterates, they were revised, sometimes quite radically, to suit Chinese tastes and manners. These "revised versions," known in Chinese as *pien wên* (not to be confused with *p'ien wên* or "balanced prose") grew steadily in popularity. This interspersal of prose narrative with occasional songs or hymns was to leave an indelible impression upon Chinese prose fiction of subsequent ages. Moreover, in the trail of Indianism pouring into China, there had been introduced numerous types of songs from Central Asia and from various border regions in China adjacent to those parts, in which the musical scores as well as the wording had been profoundly influenced by India. This type of singing, at first adopted by and influencing folk songs, was to influence the workmanship of polished writers of poetry. The product was an irregular type of poetry known as *tz'ŭ*, intended to be sung to musical accompaniment; it was to become the most lively type of poetry during the Sung period. In prose literature there arose a revolutionary movement known as the Classical Prose Movement whose activities were to demolish the pedestal of *p'ien wên*, the kind of schematic parallel-structure prose which, despite its rhythmic cadences were extremely pleasant to the ear, was after all only a poor instrument for the expression of emotions and the presentation of logical arguments. The freeing of prose from the frozen mold of schematic parallelism contributed directly to the formation of a new literary type—that of the charming prose romances.

The third subdivision includes the centuries between the relocation of the Southern Sung courts at Hangchow in 1227 to the end of the reign of Chêng Tê of the Ming dynasty in 1521. During this time, although all previous modes of poetry continued as living ve-hicles for poets, singing became more spontaneous and closer to the life of the common people. The irregular type of poetry known as *tz'u*, which had been continually refined in the hands of highly ed-ucated poets, had drifted away from the manners of folk songs. Re-placing the *tz'u* there arose a new type of lyrical poetry intended to be sung to musical accompaniment known as *san ch'ü*, which means literally "occasional lyrics." In the new lyrics, the influence of Indian literature was even more obvious and more vigorous. The so-called traditional literati of China had already unconditionally assimilated much of Indian thought into their philosophical systems. Indian storytelling, which had confined itself to the spacious courts in front of temples and monasteries and had been monopolized exclusively by Buddhist monks and novices, had become a cultural asset of China's populace. When committed to writing, these narratives, all utilizing the language of the common people, were to take diver-sified forms ranging from the shorter pieces known as *tz'ŭ hua* (admixtures of plain narration and spirited singing) to historical romances of enormous length known as *chiang shih* or "narrated history." The uniquely Indian type of transfiguration pieces, con-tinually influenced, on one hand, religious and semireligious nar-ratives interspersed with songs known as *pao chüan* or "precious scrolls," and on the other, a newly evolved type of Chinese poetry known as the *chu kung tiao* or "series of songs in different musical keys."

The anomaly in Chinese literary history of the absence of dramatic literature was also corrected by the writing of plays possibly in imitation of dramas from India. At first popular only in a limited lo-cality on the southeast China coast, namely, the county of Wênchow, its spread to other areas was immediate and rapid. In North China, stimulated by local traditions of skits and the shadow play and uti-lizing the artistic singing encouraged by the rise of *chu kung tiao*, the imitation of Indian counterparts evolved itself into the typical northern Chinese play known as *tsa chü*. It was in this maturity of full flowering of old and new literary forms that the literature of medieval China greeted the final drop of the curtain.

These rapid changes in literary development were at least in part called forth by the whole series of political and social upheavals occurring in the Chinese Empire. During the twelve centuries under survey, the Chinese people were periodically plunged into abysmal disorder and suffering, making the gloom of political failures and military reverses stand out all the more in contrast to the brilliance reflected in Chinese art and letters. For at least eight hundred years

China was threatened by invasion and domination by the northern tribes; and at least for four hundred years the northern half of China was completely enslaved by alien dynasties. In the midst of the latter there was a whole century during which China was completely inundated in the dictatorial dominance of the militarized Mongol nomads, and their first cousins, the so-called Golden (Kin or Chin) and the Khitan (Liao) Tatars.

This tragedy of foreign domination was, of course, first begun by the so-called invasion of the Five Barbarian Tribes. It was after the fall of Changan in 316, and the murder of the Tsin Emperor, Ming, in 317, that the Chinese people had gradually begun to nourish a kind of endurance and bravery for survival under an alien administration. After disunion and confusion had run their course for over two centuries, a native Chinese dynasty founded by Yang Chien, the Sui, unified North China in 581 and annexed the native Chinese southern regime in 589. Then this transitional dynasty was replaced in 618 by the glorious T'ang Dynasty.

The four centuries of political division and gloom saw the tremendous expansion of the influence of Buddhism. Emperors and commoners alike sought from this great religion consolation and freedom from suffering. The translation projects which flourished both in north and south, the rapid adoption of alien music and Indianized incantation as well as the popularization of Buddhist stories, were in part a literary response to this great spiritual need.

With the recovery of peace and order made secure by the T'ang Empire, and especially since 626 under the leadership of Emperor T'ai Tshung (reigned 627-649), himself a member of a prominent clan which had combined the subtlety and refinement of China and the bravery and vigor of the western regions in its blood, reunited China now had regained its full confidence. Militarily, the T'ang Empire was strong and administratively it was well regulated and orderly. Thus situated, it felt that it could well afford to reactivate its cultural relations with the West. In consequence, Indian and Central Asian cultures, in their material as well as spiritual and intellectual aspects, were extensively imported into China. The importation of songs and music as well as dramatics and dances was particularly noticeable. This peace and quiet was rudely disrupted by the rebellion in 755 of a non-Chinese military commander, An Lu-shan, which was an almost inevitable result of the badly co ordinated dynastic program with regard to the handling of non Chinese elements in the imperial army. This disruption smashed to pieces the dreams of the vast T'ang Empire. Romantic utopianism yielded ground to a critical realism symbolized by the poetry of Tu

Fu and Po Chü-i. Despite the quenching of the rebellion, the foundations of the T'ang Empire had been shaken to the core and the cohesion of the imperial administration could not be restored. From the middle of the eighth century on, the continuation of the T'ang Empire was merely formal, as the local military commanders had become war lords of the worst type dominating their own spheres of influence, refusing to honor the orders of the central government, and leaving the common people to fend for themselves in their dire distress. The literary manifestations of this social and political retrogression was the search for an escapist type of literature which glorified imaginary folk heroes of the Robin Hood type, who would take law into their own hands and redress the wrongs done to the little people as they saw fit.

Meanwhile the Khitan Tatars were making their military expansion felt on the northern border, and after the fall of the T'ang Dynasty in 907 China was to go through the rapid change of five dynasties, each averaging scarcely more than a decade. These so-called Five Dynasties, despite their claim to imperial dignity, gained political control only of one part of China, with ten kingdoms claiming political autonomies of their own with varying lengths of span for their respective kingdoms. While this was going on the Khitan tribe had achieved so much military strength and harbored so great a political ambition, that the Sung Dynasty, which had reunified China in 960, did not dare "to shoot a single arrow" in the direction of the Khitans. In 1125 the Sung Empire, in an attempt to solve the problem of Khitan menace, concluded an offensive alliance with a newly risen tribe of the Chin or Golden Tatars. The defeat of the Khitans, however, only paved the way for the extermination of the Sung regime at K'aifêng by its former ally in 1127.

To return to the point in political history where our last chapter ended, it will be remembered that the Tsin Dynasty had fallen. In 386 the House of Topa of the Hsien Pi Tribe had succeeded in establishing its hegemony in founding the Northern Wei Dynasty and some semblance of peace and order began to prevail again in the north, in opposition to the succession of five short-lived dynasties in the south. This period is generally referred to as the period of the Southern and Northern Dynasties. This period of opposition between north and south lasted more than two centuries and if to this we add its immediate predecessor, the age of the so-called Sixteen Kingdoms of the five alien tribes and the period of the Three Kingdoms, we have a political disunion of close to four hundred years. The preservation of the Southeast intact through all this upheaval was no less than a cultural miracle.

Equally impressive was the gradual conversion of the conquering tribes in the north to Chinese culture. In order to impress their conquered subjects in China and to establish their cultural orthodoxy deserving of the unconditional respect of the conquered, the dynastic court saw fit not only to ban the use of their mother tongue and their clothing style, to encourage the adoption of Chinese surnames and the picking of Chinese wives, but also to found schools in strict conformity to Chinese classical traditions, to revive and rectify Chinese music and rituals, and to adopt Chinese court etiquette. Toward the end of the Topa Dynasty another step was taken. On the recommendation of an outstanding Chinese conservative, Su Ch'o, the details of the Confucian classic, *Chou Li*, or the *Rites of the Chou Dynasty*, were actively followed and all government papers were written in the style of the *Book of Documents*, making the Topa Dynasty even more antiquely Chinese than the south. The cultural conversion and assimilation of the northern alien tribes was already an accomplished fact.

The most distinguished feature of this period of political division was the rise to pre-eminence of the folk literature of the two halves of a now divided China. In the south there had been an unnoticed development of a vernacular literature in the former kingdom of Wu. The leading theme of this southern or Wu folk literature was the composition and singing of love songs. As contrasted to the south, a new theme was also being gradually built up in the north, a theme glorifying the heroism of the warrior. Unfortunately, few of the northern folk songs were committed to writing as a result of the overemphasis placed by the northern monarchs on classical traditions. Nonetheless, the glorification of the warrior can be clearly seen in the few remnants we have of the northern folk songs. For example, the "Lela Song" originally translated from Hsien Pi but now preserved in Chinese translation:

> Lelak River, below the Gloom Mountains
> The firmament is like a tent sheltering the wilderness.
> Blue is the sky and vast the land,
> The wind blows, the grass bows, and cows and sheep appear.

Again, the spirit of the north is clearly seen in the following:

> The Song of the Langya King
>
> The five-foot sword I have just bought
> Is hanging from the middle beam.
> I fondle it time and again daily
> With more devotion than I would a maiden of fifteen.

And in this song, written to the tune of "Breaking of the Willow Branch":

> Looking at Mêng Tsin River from afar
> And seeing willow branches dancing in luxuriance.
> I am a barbarian youth
> Unable to sing the songs of Han.
>
> A strong lad needs a fast horse,
> A fast horse needs a strong lad.
> Galloping in the yellow dust
> The real champion will emerge.

Even in the delineation of pain, heroism was still undiminished by languorous sorrow.

The Lungt'ou Song

> Water is running from Lungt'ou
> Flowing and skirting the foothill.
> The limitless wilderness is all around me!
>
> I left Hsinch'êng in the morning
> And now I am sleeping at Lungt'ou by night,
> It is so cold I cannot talk
> And my tongue rolls itself into my throat.
>
> Water flows from Lungt'ou
> Flowing with a choking sound.
> As I look at the Ch'in River
> My heart is dashed to pieces.

Contrasted with the north, dominated by non-Chinese tribal governments and generally devastated by continual warfare, the southern half of China, especially the portions close to the seacoast, presented a different cultural and literary picture. Located in an area reminiscent of the luxuriant vegetation of the ancient Ch'u kingdom, and characterized by a more mystical landscape which was to give rise to the southern school of Chinese painting, the inhabitants cherished the limited security under the Southern Dynasties which, despite changes in personnel resulting from several palace revolutions, were able to keep traditional Chinese culture intact. Out of this milieu of delicacy and softness there arose among the people popular songs composed of five-syllable lines and attributed to a young woman by the name of Tzŭ Yeh. These folk songs, which were numbered by the hundreds, naturally could not have been compositions by a single hand; the most that she could have done was to start a new vogue. As was popularly sung in one of them,

> Among hundreds of people's songs
> The Tzŭ Yeh are the most lovable.
> Their sentiments are real,
> Their cadence is clear,
> As though they had evolved
> Out of nature itself.

This comment brings out the outstanding features not only of the southern folk songs, but also of the whole body of romantic literature in the southern half of the now enlarged China. Like the *tzŭ yeh* songs the southern folk songs were collected in groups, possibly according to their origin. Some interesting samples from the different groups are the following:

I

> Let us break a willow branch.
> In the garden forest a hundred birds are singing,
> Chirping the name of my lover unceasingly.

II

> Vines on the pine tree,
> I wish you were a floating cloud
> Passing by me from time to time.

In these folk songs we find unlimited freedom in varying the verse form in poetry. Not only were three-syllable lines inserted to vary the music of the poems, but also considerable liberty was taken to lengthen or shorten the stanza. Contrary to the traditionally preferred four-line group, which especially pleased the Chinese taste for symmetry and regularity, there emerged three-line poems in impressive numbers such as the following from the *Hua Shan Chi* folk poems:

> What can I do!
> Among numberless people in the world
> I persistently think of just you.
>
> .   .   .   .
>
> Seeing you off on the Lao Lao beach
> I wonder at the fullness of the Yangtze.
> It is my tears that have made it so.

That brevity in itself is not to be belittled is seen in the following, also from the same group:

> I dare not promise you forthright.
> Last night I overheard the family council
> Disapproving of you and me.

The economy with which a tragedy was summarized in fifteen words in the Chinese original may be more evident in the following word-for-word rendering:

> Not dare just promise you
> Night heard my family say
> Not hold you and me.

These folk songs in both north and south had a subtle but unmistakable effect in changing the trends of polite literature produced by the literary leaders of the age. Orthodox literature, however, was slow in benefiting from the vitality and simplicity of the voices of the common people. The formalism and love of dignity during the long life of the Han Dynasty as exemplified in the *fu* had produced an indelible impress on all literary compositions. Even the prose writers who should have been the most straightforward and matter-of-fact had fallen under the spell of the magic wand of the *fu*. As a result there arose a peculiar literary phenomenon which blurred almost completely the line of demarcation between prose and poetry, and which had practically no parallel in the literary history of other parts of the world. This unique phenomenon was later on given the name of *p'ien wên* or "balanced prose" (not to be confused with *pien wên,* the Buddhist narrative poems), when the regulations were further perfected and rigidity further imposed. The basic pattern was the creation of two sentences or clauses in parallel form with characters in one strictly matching the corresponding characters in the other. In addition to this symmetry in structure there was gradually developed an added feature which was the antithesis of tone: a low-toned character in one column was to be counterbalanced by a character of high tone in the other.

In China this fondness for literary parallelism went back into early classical times, as could be illustrated with passages from the classics of the Confucian school as well as writings of the philosophers. Psychologically there were numerous factors in traditional Chinese culture which would favor this trait. In the first place, there was a fondness for symmetry in design, from the fashioning of ornamental trinkets to architecture. Second, there had arisen early in

Chinese thought a preoccupation with the meaning of apparently opposite but fundamentally supplementary elements such as day and night, sun and moon, fire and water, heaven and earth. This later was developed into folk belief and even into a philosophical school known as the Yin-Yang School and was universally reflected in the discourses of nearly all the philosophical systems, Confucian and Taoist included. Third, in a more strictly literary realm, this emphasis on symmetry was further enhanced by the monosyllabic nature and uniform size of the written Chinese characters, making Chinese writing ideally adaptable to this peculiar usage. Among the late Chou philosophers who had made use of this literary device effectively the following from the *Book of Hsün Tzŭ* may be cited as an illustration:

> Shên (spirit) is never greater than when it evolves with Tao (the Way); bliss is never more enduring than when it avoids catastrophe. I have spent my days thinking, but have not done as well as learning for a short while; I have tipped my toes gazing, but have not seen as far as from an elevation. When one ascends a height and waves, his arms are not any longer but they are seen farther; when one turns in the direction of the wind and shouts, his voice is not any louder but it is more clearly heard. He who utilizes vehicles and horses does not improve his legs but does travel a thousand miles; he who depends on boats and oars is not necessarily an expert swimmer but does traverse the Kiang and Ho Rivers. A superior man is not one differently born, but one who is good in his wherewithals.

It is this careful balancing of the sentence structure of two columns in literary architectonics and the accumulating of dazzling and euphonic nouns, verbs, and adjectives in the *fu* style which had turned the new prose style into something almost unrecognizable as prose. This style pervaded the whole realm of literary composition —argumentative as well as narrative prose, lyrical as well as narrative poetry, even the descriptions of landscape beauty in either prose or verse.

To give a supreme example, when the literary giant of the Tsin Dynasty, Lu Chi (died 303), wrote his essay on letters, he embodied it in the *fu* form instead of doing it in clear and easily understandable prose. Suggesting the process of literary creation he wrote:

> What joy there was in all this, the joy which sages
> and worthies have coveted.
> He was taxing Non-Being to produce Being, calling to
> the Silence, importunate for an answer:
> He was engrossing the great spaces within a span of
> silk, belching forth torrents [of language]
> from the inch-space of the heart.

> Words were expanding the theme, the more as it proceeded:
> thought was bringing it under his hand, as it became
> the more profound.
> He was scattering a fragrance of delicious hanging-
> clusters, putting forth a profusion of green-budding
> twigs.
> A laughing wind was flying by and whirling up a solid
> shape, a mass of shining cloud was arising in the
> garden of letters.
>
> (E. R. Hughes's translation)

This, especially in the Chinese, is extremely pleasing to the ear of the listener and easy on the speech organ of the reader. The only trouble is that neither reader nor listener is sure of what the writer has meant. In those days, however, nobody questioned the value and validity of the style, because it was in the established pattern. Argumentative and expository writings were often expressed in the form of the *fu,* or in the case of the slightly more sensible writers, in preponderantly balanced-prose style which actually straddled the paths of prose and poetry, as did Ko Hung in his Taoist philosophical treatise, *Pao P'u Tzŭ,* Liu Hsieh (flourished 530) in his famous critical essays in *Wên Hsin Tiao Lung,* and Chung Jung (flourished 504) in his essay on poetic criticism *Shih P'in.* These shackles, though difficult to surmount, did not prevent the rise of truly great literary talents. Many of the major poets of this period kept at least one ear cocked to the spontaneous music and unfettered sentiments of the little people.

Pao Chao (died 466), for example, was able at least partly to bypass the literary conventions of his age. In one of his poems he said:

> Sitting at table, I cannot eat.
> I draw my sword, hit the column and sigh,
> "How long is the span of man's life on earth,
> How can one fold his wings and walk about?"
> Let me resign from my office,
> And seek my rest at home.
> I bade farewell to my parents in the morning,
> At evening I am still by their side.
> I play with my child in front of the couch,
> I watch my wife weaving at the loom.
> Sages have been destitute even since antiquity—
> Who are we to try remaining unbent?

Pao was criticized by his contemporaries as being precarious and vulgar. This was tantamount to saying that he was neither willing to conform to established usage nor timid in employing the language of the common people, as is illustrated in the poem quoted above, written when he was nineteen. New impositions, however, were forthcoming. One was the use of literary allusions. Instead of describing a scene or narrating an event in plain language, the writer would ransack ancient and contemporary literature for stories and situations akin to the one in question. This led to the use of one or two key words in summarizing a whole situation or an event with the result that one who was unfamiliar with the source of the literary allusion would find it utterly impossible to guess at the real meaning from the surface meaning of the key words themselves. While the possible virtue of such a practice was economy, the usual outcome was utter obscurity. No wonder that the poetic critic Chung Jung lamented that most of the writings in the middle of the fifth century were no more than mere patchwork of borrowings from previous writers. Even more deadening was the imposition of phonological regulations. This was not entirely unexpected. Ever since the earliest times the Chinese language had been characterized by a small syllabary ensuing in a large number of homonyms and the variation of tones in pronunciation to minimize misunderstanding and ambiguity.

During the age of the *Book of Songs* at least three tones were already in existence. In other words, a syllable could be pronounced in any one of three pitches to yield three different meanings, as represented by three entirely different characters. Thus *fang* in its highest pitch would mean "direction," in its lowest pitch would mean "chamber," and in the middle pitch would mean "set free." As the spoken language grew in vocabulary, and written graphs were multiplied in writing to catch up with the parallel growth of the language in the spoken word, homonyms were naturally increased as a result and the range of intonation was necessarily expanded to avoid confusion. This process was greatly encouraged and accelerated by influences from India and Central Asia. With the introduction of Buddhism from the first century before Christ onward, the niceties of tonal variation in Buddhist recitals and incantations were adhered to by Chinese converts. The mispronunciation or wrong toning of a single syllable might render a whole religious service ineffective, and Chinese Buddhist monks found it an essential part of their training to study Indian phonology as well as music intensively.

By the middle of the fifth century of the Christian era there had grown up eight tonal variations possible in the pronunciation of any given syllable, technically grouped into four levels. As a result, endless bans and taboos were meted out for the guidance of writers concerning the sequence in which the syllables should be arranged. One of these taboos was technically termed "the flat top," in which it was clearly stated that in a couplet of ten syllables, the first and sixth syllables should not be on the same tonal level. Again, there was the taboo known as "the crane knee," which specified that the fifth and fifteenth syllables in a quatrain of twenty syllables should not be on the same tonal level. Still another taboo was labeled "the grand assonance," which specified that in a couplet none of the first nine syllables should rhyme with the tenth. These minute regulations, naturally, would result in the stifling of all literary attempts.

The chief exponent and great summarizer of these regulations, Shên Yüeh (441-513), realized the stultifying effects of such legislation. And so, not completely blinded by his environment, he recommended three other principles for literary composition. One: easiness in seeing subject matter. Two: easiness in recognizing characters. Three: easiness in reading, both silent and aloud. By easiness in seeing subject matter, he might have meant the use of those classical allusions which were self-evident and needed no further explanation; and by ease in reading he might have referred to his own theories of phonology. However, if these three standards were advocated even by a chief exponent of literary conventionalism it was evident that conservatism was close to having run its whole course.

The folk literature which had been in process of accumulation for nearly five hundred years, especially folk and popular songs, was now due to produce far-reaching results. In the first place, nearly all the emperors of the Liang Dynasty (502-554) wrote *yüeh fu* or songs to be set to music. Emperor Wu was apparently indebted to the romantic literature of the southern coastal regions when he wrote the following in imitation of the songs of Tzŭ Yeh:

> Fragrance from the steps enter my bosom,
> Flowers in the garden brighten my eyes.
> Once the heart of spring opens up like this,
> Emotions will respond without limit.

or the following:

> My Love Will Hear

> Lovely, lovely is the maiden in the golden tower
> With a heart like lotus in the jade pond.
> With what shall I reward the thoughts of my lover?
> I wish together we shall tour Brahma's heavens.

Similarly his son, Emperor Wên of the Liang Dynasty, was profoundly influenced by popular literature as is evident in the following:

Spring River

Travelers are bent only on their roads,
Struggling to be ferried across.
Who knows people on the bank
Are wiping tears and waving in vain?

South of the River

On treetops amidst branches spring has returned.
Willow twigs are sweeping the ground and plum blossoms
    flying.
Fresh breezes refresh people and sunshine illumines
    their garments,
Light illumines gowns and the sun will set. Let's spend
    our golden pieces
For our beloved guests.

The close attention paid to folk literature sensitized the minds of professional writers to the sentiments, aspirations, and language of the common people. The leading anthologies of the period reflected this trend clearly by alloting increasing space to the inclusion of popular songs. In the second place, without apology, the acknowledged poets of the age wrote in frank imitation of the themes and meter of folk literature. At the culmination of this tendency stood the romantic last emperor of the Ch'ên Dynasty (resigned 583-589). According to authentic historic records, he would give huge parties to his guests and court ladies and encourage them to write "new poetry" in response. He would select the most attractive of these compositions to be set to music and sung by hundreds of beautiful court women in rotation. As intelligibility should be the principal feature of poems sung to music without advantage of the printed page, these preferred compositions would naturally bear great resemblance to the songs of the people.

When China was reunited in 589, the vigor of popular literature was to be fully felt again. This is not to say, however, that folk literature had dominated the whole Chinese literary arena, for the highly polished glamour of the writings of the professional poets had continued to be the pride of the age among courtly circles and the aristocracy of the succeeding periods. Nonetheless, that type of literature which had relied for its excellence upon the slavish following of formalities and upon perfunctory imitation of standard models, had lost its following.

While the artificial and imitative literature of the Southern and Northern Dynasties was at its zenith of glory, there were already present in China certain disruptive elements which deliberately refused to be embodied in the formalized literary forms of the age. These disruptive elements were the translated writings of Buddhism. This alien but extremely attractive cult from India had pressed its way into China both by sea and by the overland routes. In the face of this gloriously rich and complex imported religion, the traditional cult which had been characterized by simplicity and practicality had made an extremely poor show. For centuries the whole Chinese world from emperors to peasants was swept off its feet by this new religion. The result was no less than a total conquest of the Chinese people by Buddhism. For its propagation by Indian and Central Asian monks, as well as for the acceptance or rejection of this new faith by the Chinese, translation had become an urgent need. Once translation was started, the process became never-ending; one sacred book would necessitate the parallel translation of many others. When an Indian monk wagged his head in rhythm as he began re- citing from the sacred Buddhist texts, he would not stop until he had completed ten or twenty thousand Gathas. Once he began writing, he would not stop until tens of scrolls were used up. These Indian sages seemed to be unlimited by space or time. When worlds were described they came in three thousands and superthousands. When heaven was described it came in layers of more than thirty-three. And when the inferno was depicted, it revealed itself in ten depths, eighteen depths, and more. Everything was limitless and inex- haustible. It is easily understandable, therefore, that once the trans- lation enterprise was started, it continued for over a thousand years and that with the lapse of the thousand years, the horizon of the translators seemed to be even further removed. No reliable statistics have been preserved to indicate the exact number of translations undertaken and completed. Counting the ones that are extant, in- cluding the commentaries and exegetical treatises written by Chi- nese monks, we have over three thousand titles in over fifteen thousand books or scrolls.

Such a vast undertaking was naturally beyond the scope of a few selected traditional and imitative literati. It was also beyond the compass of the vague and unprecise style of the prevailing balanced prose of the age. Thus Chinese literature was given a chance to look into endless new vistas and there resulted the creation of new lit- erary types to accommodate the endlessly varied new materials. The new materials and new vistas thus available need no further ex- planation; but why was a new literary genre needed? In the first place, the new substance refused to be supported by old and out-moded scaffoldings. Second, the masters of translation for a long time were non-Chinese, people who had not been brought up in the indigenous literary traditions of China. Third, the prospective readers for whom these translations were made were preponderantly actual or prospective converts in China's masses. Fourth, religious scriptures had as their foremost objective the transmission of truth, for which accuracy was of much greater importance than florid literary adornment. The emphasis was, therefore, upon readiness in understanding and not on literary elegance. Consequently the early masters in translation continued to reinforce among themselves the basic principles of "no adornment, no obscurity, no deviation" from the original.

The exact date of the beginning of translation of Buddhist litera-ture from Indic and Central Asian languages is controversial and has not been completely settled. According to tradition, the Buddhist sutra of forty-two sections and therefore known in Chinese as the "Forty-Two-Chapter Canon" was translated during the reign of Emperor Ming of the Later Han Dynasty (58-75) by Kâśyapa Mâtanga of Central Asia, and other writings from Buddhism were translated by his fellow missionary, Chu-fa-lan. The record of the search for Buddhist doctrines by Emperor Ming in 67 was nothing more than a chronological landmark invented by the faithful and is to be regarded as a pious legend rather than as a historical fact. The introduction of Buddhism into China took place at a much earlier date. Hence in his rescript to Prince Ying of Ch'u, the same emperor had already used three words of sanskrit origin—po-t'o, yu-p'o-sai, and suang-mên—proving that at that time Buddhist expressions were already clearly understood, possibly proving also that there had al-ready existed a small body of Buddhist literature.

It should be pointed out here, however, that technically speaking, the "Forty-Two-Chapter Sutra" was not a translation, as there had been no original from which it was translated, but rather a compila-tion in which was presented a digest of the most important docu-ments. For this reason, it was not listed in any of the early Buddhist bibliographies, and hence its exact age of composition is not easy to determine. We can only say generally that during the first century of the Christian era there had been in circulation in China a small amount of Buddhist literature.

Among the Buddhist translators of the second century, An Shih-kao, a Parthian of princely descent, was the most outstanding. His translations were esteemed in the *Kao Sêng Chuan,* or *Biographies of Eminent Monks,* as "setting forth the doctrines clearly and discerningly, using the Chinese language justly and accurately, eloquent without being ornate, simple without being rustic, inducing all readers to develop an untiring interest." An Shih-kao's literary activities extended from 148 to 170. Besides him there were at least five other eminent Buddhists who were engaged in translation activities, all distinguished for their clarity and simplicity. During the following century translations from Buddhist literature were even more noticeable in both quantity and quality. During the first half of the third century literary activities among Buddhists were carried on mostly in southern China with two great centers at present-day Nanking and Wuchang. Chih Ch'ien alone was responsible for as many as forty-nine separate translations. The care with which Buddhist literature was translated is clearly indicated in the unsigned preface to one version of the *Dhammapada Sutra*, conjointly translated by two monks from India, Wei Ch'i-nan (Vighna?) and Chu Lü-yen, as the Fa Chü Ching:

... When Wei Ch'i-nan, from India, first arrived in Wuchang in the third year of the reign of Huang-wu [224] I received from him the reading of this five-hundred-Gatha edition and requested him to collaborate with his colleague, Chu Chiang-yen, to undertake a translation. Although the latter was well versed in the languages of India, he was not fully informed of the usages in Chinese. And so, in his interpretation, sometimes I got mere transliterations from the Sanskrit and at other times I got paraphrases all of which sounded substantial but straight. I at first was dissatisfied with the apparent lack of elegance. Wei Ch'i-nan said to me, "The Buddha said we should follow his meaning without adornment, accept its truth without decoration. Those who transmit the sutras should make them easy to understand and lose none of their meanings. This is to be considered good work." All present said, "Lao-tzu once said beautiful words are not true and true words are not beautiful...." Now that we are engaged in translating from the Indic languages, we should aim directly at faithfulness. Hence, as each Gatha was received from the translator verbally, its original meaning was recorded down without decoration. When that which was translated was not clearly understood, that section would be left out untranslated. Therefore, there were numerous omissions. But though what is presented here may appear laconic and simple in language, it is deep and extensive in meaning and implications.

By the end of the third century there emerged in North China a great Buddhist translator, Dharmaraksha of Tunhuang, who was better known by his Chinese name of Fa-hu. Descended from natives of Yüeh Chih, in Central Asia, Dharmaraksha's family had lived for generations in Tunhuang. Converted to Buddhism when young, he later followed his masters to different parts of Central Asia and had acquired numerous Central Asian languages when he returned with numerous sutras to Tunhuang. According to the *Biographies of Eminent Monks*, he had collected 165 sutras and he spent long years in copying and translating them. Assisted by two Chinese converts, Nieh Ch'eng-yüan and his son, Nieh Tao-chên, Dharmaraksha's translations, all characterized by forthright faithfulness and simplicity of language, gave a new dignity to Buddhist literature.

Although the fourth century saw great disorder and warfare spread over the northern half of China, translation activities of Buddhist literature went on uninterrupted. It was not until the turn of the century, however, that Kumârajiva emerged to help Buddhist literature attain full maturity. Born in Kucha of Indian parents, he demonstrated remarkable powers of memory when young and had traveled extensively in the various Central Asian kingdoms in search of training in Buddhism. Brought back to China in 383 by a northern general, Lü Kuang, as a captive from Kucha, Kumârajiva resided in the frontier city of Liangchou for eighteen years, where he mastered Chinese in both the spoken and written aspects. In 402 he was brought to Ch'angan by the war lord Yao Hsing, who honored him as state mentor and urged him to undertake the translation of Buddhist classics. The result was the Chinese renderings of over three hundred scrolls comprising some of the basic sutras in Mahâyâna Buddhism. According to the *Biographies of Eminent Monks,* Kumârajiva was equally at home in Chinese and in Sanskrit. Despite his unusual equipment for the work of translation, he was so conscientious in his assignment that despite his high attainments he was not entirely satisfied with the fruits of his labors. He was quoted as saying, "In India the native customs rated literary compositions extremely high. Their poetical compositions are written with a view to being set to music. . . . When these are converted into Chinese, however, the startling beauty of the original is lost. Although the gist is retained, the attractiveness of the original is screened off. This is comparable to chewing rice to feed others. Not only the original flavor is lost, but also those receiving will feel irked."

This low evaluation of his own work was indicative of the high standard which he had set up for translation. His literary influence was immense. Among the numerous translations by Kumârajiva, the most important from the standpoint of Buddhist doctrines was the *Mahāprajñāpāramitā Sūtra.* Those most widely circulated and most influential on literature were the *Diamond Sūtra,* the *Lotus Sūtra,* and the *Vimalakirti Sūtra,* a Buddhist book of fiction overflowing with literary interest. A Buddhist layman was ill, according to the story, and the Buddha asked his disciples to call on the sick man with the Buddha's greetings. Ten of the most outstanding disciples had declined one after another, on the pretext that the patient was so excessively wicked they did not want to turn themselves into fools. The Buddha then requested three bodhisattvas to undertake the difficult task. But similarly, they all backed off. Finally, there was only left Manjusri, who boldly accepted the Buddha's instructions. What was recorded in the sutra was the verbal contest between the two, which reads at times like a novel and at other times as a drama. The contest has been utilized by poets and storytellers as well as by painters of murals in monasteries and temples, in all parts of the vast Chinese Empire. The most significant evolution in the realm of letters of this unusual translation is its elaboration into a great narrative epic by subsequent popular songwriters.

Although the *Lotus Sūtra* was not a book of fiction, it had its own literary charm, especially the fables in it which have received repetition and adaptation in Chinese literature.

Indian literature had a special type in which prose and verse were peculiarly blended. After narration in prose, the same substance would be repeated and highlighted in verse. This verse part was called *Gatha*. Gathas served a valuable function in India as its early literature was nearly all verbally transmitted. Verse form, therefore, was a great aid to memory. When this genre was introduced into China, however, it produced numerous unexpected consequences. Besides aiding immensely in the spread of Buddhism among the Chinese populace, it was to produce a permanent impress on Chinese narrative literature, especially prose fiction. Whenever an exciting scene or a touching emotional experience was described, these would be rehearsed in verse to deepen the impressions on the reader's mind.

When Kumârajiva was about to die, in 409, he bade farewell to his disciple monks, saying, "I have usurped the function of translator in spite of my limited gift and training. Among the three-hundred-odd scrolls from my pen, only one title was not abbreviated...."

His use of abbreviation was to elicit endless criticism against Kumârajiva as a translator, but it is in this very fault of which he had accused himself that his Chinese readers had found his principal virtue. Unlike the Chinese, Indian writers seemed to be extremely fond of repetitiousness and elaborateness. And in order to adapt Indian literature to Chinese taste through translation, abbreviation was probably a necessity and a sign of discretion.

Besides abbreviation, Kumârajiva had also shown good taste in so changing the original in his translation that once the rendering was completed it would read as Chinese. He also deviated from the established standards of previous translators by crossing the barriers freely between prose and verse. What was originally in prose would end up in his translation in summary as Gathas. And what was in Gatha form might be translated into simple prose. Moreover, he would take liberties in substituting for obscure biographical and geographical terms names that were already well known among Chinese readers.

Despite Kumârajiva's distinguished attainments, the high tide of translation from Buddhist literature was not reached until the fifth century. The greatest translation organization was in Ch'angan and the participants often numbered by the hundreds. According to one of the principal participants, Sêng Chao:

> Monk Shih produced the newly arrived sutras at Ta-shih Monastery. . . . Monk Dhyana taught Zen doctrines at Wa Kuan Monastery to his disciples to the number of several hundred. . . . Monk Tripitaka produced books of law at the Middle Monastery, all intact from cover to cover, as though they had been newly written. Monk Bhivasa produced at Shih Yang the Sanskrit edition of the *Shari Pupitama*. . . . My humble self was delighted in sharing in this conjugation of good luck and in taking part on this wonderful occasion. Although I did not take part in the original redaction of the Tripitaka in India, what is there any more to regret?

Another important center was established at Ho Hsi in the northwest where the Buddhist monk, Tamajama (died 433), was also an extremely careful and devoted translator. He insisted that one of his assistants spend three years learning Chinese before the latter should be permitted to take part in translating Buddhist sacred texts. His great contribution was the translation of the *Buddhacharita,* written by the great Buddhist poet Asvaghosha. This great epic of the Buddha's life was translated by Tamajama into Chinese in five-syllable blank verse, consisting of twenty-eight divisions totaling 9,300 lines in 46,000 words, indisputably the longest poem in existence in the Chinese language. Comparable to this is another long poem on the Buddha's life translated by Monk Pao-yün, who was even more experimental in the use of Chinese verse form. Writing also in blank verse, Pao-yün would vary his meter by adopting the four-syllable lines in certain stanzas and seven-syllable lines in other stanzas to avoid monotony.

Chinese literature before this influx of Indian masterpieces had been on the whole lacking in imagination. Even Ch'ü Yüan and Chuang-tzŭ, one dreaming of an extended flight to the high heavens and the other magnifying a bird with wings comparable to enormous clouds, were mere dwarfs beside the giants of Indian literary imaginativeness. The long narrative poems like "Southeastward Flies the Peacock" had done well in the realistic telling of events but were totally lacking in supernatural imagination. In this regard the imaginative literature of the Indian people served a truly liberating function in the enrichment of Chinese letters.

These translation activities were not limited to north China alone. Nanking and Lushan had also become important centers of Buddhist translation activity. Among Buddhist scriptures translated in the south, three sutras were probably the ones of greatest influence: The *Nirvana Sutra*, the *Avtamsaka* (*Hua Yen*) *Sūtra* and the *Lānkāvatāra* (*Ling Chia*) *Sūtra*.

The *Hua Yen Sutra* may be considered a textbook in imagination, hence a kind of textbook in saying things contrary to fact. According to its instructions, anything in the cosmos could be split into tens: ten kinds of circumstances, ten kinds of understanding, ten kinds of tolerance, etc. If one were daring enough and tireless enough one could always discover ten possibilities and move on to other tens of categories to no end. This technique, although not always attractive, lent itself easily to being utilized. Toward the end of the *Hua Yen Sutra*, over one-fourth of the book was devoted to the narration of the experiences of the boy, Shan Tsai, in search of the secrets of Buddhism. After going through one city to another and seeing one great monk after another, what the youngster had gone through was developed into a long novel of the picaresque romance type without organization or essential plots, by the author's merely knitting together a whole series of unrelated incidents. Nonetheless, the influence of this literary and imaginative technique upon subsequent novels was immense.

At this point it should be pointed out that despite this high tide in the translation and propagation of Buddhist literature in the fourth and fifth centuries, the influence was not felt by Chinese literature until after 500. It is true, Buddhist expressions and alien proper names appeared in ever increasing numbers in poems and essays, but the mere use of an expression for adornment was not a sign of profound organic literary influence.

The surprising phenomenon which evidenced the slowness of the direct impact of Buddhist literature on Chinese literary men is the fact that from 300 to 500 Chinese literature betrayed no foreign influence on its form and style. Moreover, the writings of the Buddhist monks of that age aside from translations all followed conscientiously the prevailing "balanced," or *p'ien wen* form. The three great anthologies of Buddhist writings of this time—the *Hung Ming Chi*, *Kao Sêng Chuan* (*Biographies of Eminent Monks*), and *Hsü Kao Sêng Chuan* (*More Biographies of Eminent Monks*)—were concrete evidences. The first was a collection of essays in defense of Buddhism and the other two were collections of biographies—subject matter into which the artificiality of the prevailing prose style would hardly fit. Nonetheless, not a single one of the Buddhist writers who had been exposed to the relative freedom of Indian style had ever thought of deviating from the ruts of Chinese literary form when he was called upon to do writings of his own. In this age, therefore, we saw only the Sinicization of Buddhist writers instead of the Indianization of Chinese men of letters.

From 400 on, Chinese followers of the Buddha had learned and practiced the intricate Indian technique of declamation and incantation in connection with the reading of the translated literature. In other words, Buddhist literature, with all its novelties, was widely disseminated among the common people. This technique of reading music and rhythm into the printed or written page, even if the printed page were mere prose, was a technique unheard-of in pre-Buddhist China. Once introduced into China from Central Asia, it was picked up avidly by all, first in the recitation of Buddhist texts and later on in all sorts of reading aloud. Chanting which identified the village school all over China was until recently traceable to this important influence from India.

Especially interesting is this fifth-century record of a Buddhist religious service:

Then the preacher emotionally held up the incense burner and rhythmically enunciated his eloquent sermon with endless variations to suit the subject matter. Discoursing on transitoriness, he caused souls and bodies to tremble and shiver; describing the Hadian regions, he caused the flowing of tears and the rising of fears; to prove the karma of the past he presented bygone deeds as though they were being lived visibly again. Explaining the inevitability of causality, he demonstrated the future fruitions as if they had already occurred. Speaking of happiness, he filled his hearers with overflowing ecstacies, and in delineating sorrow and sadness, he elicited dripping tears and profound sorrow. Thereupon the whole audience had their hearts swayed and their emotions sharpened. They prostrated themselves on the mats, literally crushing their heads to express their grief, each one snapping their fingers and each one murmuring the name of Buddha.

Since the populace by far outnumbered royalty and aristocrats, these "heavenly tones" incantation techniques from India were more heartily embraced by the common people than the rhythm of the stilted prose of p'ien wên. What was more interesting, there arose in the different parts of China local schools of incantation, which is another way of saying that local improvisations were readily permitted. These non-Buddhist as well as Buddhist pieces written for incantation became extremely popular. In order to make these incantations attractive and understandable, the language used as a whole closely approached the spoken tongue of the people, although not a few of even the Buddhist writers deliberately followed the practice of professional prose writers in decorating their compositions with classical allusions and literary archaisms. As a whole, however, intelligibility was maintained as the basic standard, particularly in the case of narrative incantations by itinerant Buddhist monks to solicit alms-giving and larger donations. According to an early seventh-century record, there was a kind of Buddhist religious service commonly called "fallen blossoms." In these, Buddhist laymen freely participated. To enlarge the sources of alms-giving, they would assist in singing and acting to enlist financial support for the erection of monasteries and pagodas. The celebrant would vary his words in accordance with the divergent alms-givers, rhyming his sentences, continuing the recitation without stop, and avoiding repetitiousness of words and ideas. In response, men and women spectators would watch intensely and then splash money about them like so many raindrops. Some would even cut off their long hair and sell it for donations.

CHAPTER 12

The Age of Disunion

W E have noted that from 318 to 589, China was neatly split into two halves, with the center of Chinese cultural activities relocated in the Yangtze Valley and the north dominated by non-Chinese tribes. Thanks to the peculiarity and clumsiness of the nonalphabetic nature of the written language, it could be used by the conquerors in only one way—by forthright adoption. The conquering tribes were devoid of any writing system of their own. It had never occurred to them to develop one as it was to occur to their centuries-later followers who benefited from observing their failure. Since most, if not all, of their subjects were Chinese and since they had to make their wishes known to these subjects in writing, what was more natural than for these alien conquerors to follow the route of least resistance by capitalizing upon the literary vehicle of the conquered? For a time they looked upon the adoption of the Chinese written language as a sheer political expediency—possibly even as a necessary evil. So, partly aware of the attendant dangers, they cautiously decreed against the adoption of Chinese usages and customs. Thus the conquerors made a point of refusing to acquire proficiency in writing, relying principally upon their Chinese secretaries and learning enough Chinese themselves to check on the accuracy of the secretarial staff. While this was perfect in theory, it was impractical in actual practice for no one was certain where the line should be drawn beyond which their education in Chinese was to make no further advance. The result was that as time passed the conquerors were more and more tempted to wield the Chinese writing brush themselves.

With the consolidation of the multiple barbarian states in the north into a few opposing regimes, this tendency toward rapid Sinicization was all the more noticeable and remarkable. The well-being and military strength of a newly established kingdom would have to depend in large measure upon the loyalty of the Chinese subjects, and the promotion of this loyalty would have to depend on insight into Chinese psychology. Moreover, the continual existence of the Southern Dynasties in the Yangtze Valley where Chinese cultural orthodoxy was upheld posed a permanent challenge. The northern regimes naturally felt compelled to impress their subjects with their maintenance not only of standards of refinement but also of cultural orthodoxy.

The very personification of such a political and cultural policy was Emperor Hsiao Wên of the Northern Wei kingdom. In the year 493 he issued a series of decrees to suppress the use of the Topa language even among his own kinsmen, who should thenceforward speak and write only Chinese. In the same gesture he ruled that all polysyllabic clan names of the conquering tribes should be dropped and standard Chinese family names adopted. Non-Chinese attires were tabooed and intermarriages greatly encouraged. New schools were organized in which only Chinese subjects were taught. In less than one century the Topa was to disappear completely from the scene, becoming undistinguishable from any other Chinese.

We have noted before that the translation of Buddhist literature and the collection of Buddhist anecdotes were first sponsored in the northern regimes and that these literary labors were the distinctive contributions of the Northern Dynasties to the enrichment of Chinese literature. Besides these attainments what was their literary record?

Ever since the flight of the Tsin imperial court from Ch'angan to Nanking in 318 there had been more political and economic disorder in the north than in the south. The exodus of the powerful families southward left the northern half of China greatly impoverished. Among the so-called barbarian kingdoms there were incessant disputes and continual warfare. And every so often there would be attempts made by the Southern Dynasties to recapture the north by force of arms. Reunification for a time even looked unattractive on account of the devastation which had befallen the north where internecine warfare kept on raging for a long time. It was not until 440 that the northern kingdoms were all liquidated and there were really for the first time two neat empires standing in apposition. In less than a century, however, in the year 535, the north again was split in two, until 577. It is easily understandable, therefore, that aside from the production or translation of religious literature in monastic centers far removed from the cities, the atmosphere of continued disturbance was not conducive to the cultivation of literary pursuits.

As soon as the northern conquerors were saturated in the traditions of Chinese literature the literary currents from the south began to rush northward. Practically speaking, therefore, the promotion of literature in the north was in a very peculiar sense the precursor of the political unification that was to come later.

Although many of the distinguished writers in the north were actually southerners who had preferred to distinguish themselves in the north and therefore were hardly distinguishable from their confreres in the Yangtze Valley, the cultural trends in the north continued to maintain characteristics of their own. In the first place, classical studies on the Confucian canon were maintained at a much higher level in the barbarian north than in the decadent south. This was at least partly due to the efforts of the alien dynasties to substantiate their claim of cultural orthodoxy. Also it was partly due to the fact that asceticism and austerity warranted in the north were not too comparable with the laissez-faire attitudes elicited by the study of the Taoist classics and of leisurely and nonpractical salon conversations in the south. Hence, many of the great commentators on the Confucian classics were scholars of the northern region. In the second place, experts on political institutions and educational systems, in close conformity with what they had been in classical China, were also Chinese residents in the northern kingdoms. Contrasted with the Confucian commentators, this line of scholarship may be loosely identified as historical research, a type of work that the mellow landscape and leisurely living of the south did not inspire in particular. The many names included in the literary biography section in the *Pei Shih* or *History of the Northern Dynasties* are numerous but when they are compared to corresponding names flourishing in the south, the fair-minded critic has to concede that for the most part these northern littérateurs were second-rate imitators of the southern masters.

The first northern writer of distinction, Yen Chih-t'ui (529-591), known for his erudition, was a member of a prominent Shantung family who had escaped to the south. He was captured and brought to the Chou Kingdom in the northwest and later escaped to Ch'i in the northeast. In this instance it is difficult to say whether he was a southerner or northerner except that he lived for years in the north. He lived long enough to see north and south unified, so probably he would consider himself a child of both regions. Although he tried his hand at poetry and belles-lettres, he is mainly remembered for a collection of essays known as the *Chia Hsün* or *Family Instruction*. The twenty chapters of this book cover a wide range of subjects such as literature, the teaching of children, and the nurture of life and life ideals, as well as the various arts and crafts. In these various essays, written in beautifully simple language, the author would at times communicate his personal reactions to various problems of the day or delineate current phases of social life or narrate anecdotes and assess the merits of personalities. Written more or less in the form of familiar essays, these chapters appeal to the reader on account of their intimacy and great sincerity, making the reader feel that he is sitting in the company of this veteran soldier of life. An entry like the following in the chapter on the instruction of children connotes a feeling of deep pathos at the limited and subservient attitude of the father:

An official member of the northern Ch'i court once said to me, "I have a boy already seventeen years of age. He knows a little of writing and the classical commentaries. He is being given lessons in the Hsien Pi language [Topa] and the playing of the p'i p'a [a kind of Topa guitar]—just enough to understand the basic principles—for with these talents he should be able to serve the noble lords to gain favors. That seems to be important also." On hearing that, I lowered my head without venturing an answer.

The following entry in the essay on belles-lettres reveals his cautiousness in his social dealings.

The literary custom in the Yangtze area is to invite criticism from others. Knowing where one's weaknesses lie one can readily correct them. . . . In areas near Shantung the established practice is to refrain from making unfavorable remarks. When I first went to Loyang I did not offend people with this and have regretted it to this day. I hope you young people will not come out lightly with critical remarks.

While most Chinese writers of the north kept an eye diligently on literary trends in the south, real northerners occasionally were able to maintain the forthrightness of northern society. An outstanding example was Topa Hsieh (or Yuan Hsieh; flourished 508) who, in response to an imperial order to sing of a mountain pine, wrote the following:

> I asked the pine trees,
> "Pine trees, how many winters have you gone through?
> Are the mountains and rivers what they once were?
> Are the winds and clouds the same as of yore?"

Topa Hsieh's own son, Topa Tzǔ-yu, later on known as Emperor Hsiao Chuang (507-530), was also a poet maintaining Topa simplicity. After his coronation, when he was about to be killed by a rebel at the age of twenty-three, he wrote a four-line poem:

> With no power left, the end of life is in sight!
> Laden with endless sorrow, long, long spreads the path of death.
> With sadness I left the capital,
> Now with a grieving heart I enter the realm of the dead.

In this connection it is fitting that we take note of two southern literary masters kidnapped in 552-554 by the Northern Chou Empire. They were Yü Hsin and Wang Pao.

Wang Pao (513?-577), who became a prisoner of war in 554, had already distinguished himself before this catastrophe. The striking feature of the latter half of his literary career is its sudden change of style after his relocation. The impact of personal vicissitudes and of the changes subsequent to his military defeat and surrender so completely changed his literary style that floridity gave way to deep feelings and mechanical rhetoric was replaced by an inner beauty that grew out of the tragedy of life. The occasional poems he wrote on crossing the Yellow River might well illustrate this change of style:

> The autumn wind is blowing down the leaves
> Reminding us of waves on the Tungt'ing Lake.
> The Ch'ang Sierra dominates the northern county
> And pavilions gird the Yellow River as it winds.
> Only sorrow responds to alien music
> As frontier melodies break the traveler's heart.
> Accompanied by my warhorse in the eventide
> I have lost my way in the vales of the northern mountains.

Like Wang Pao, Yü Hsin (512-581) began to acquire a completely changed literary personality after his abduction in 552. In his many poems he expressed in metaphorical language his tragedy of having to serve the court of an enemy nation against his own wishes. Thus he would say:

> Even in summer heat the flowers are unspirited
> And in windy weather the water would ripple in unevenness.

or:

> In how many days would the barbarian dust subside,
> And how soon again will shine the moon of the Han Empire?

Lines like these are sharp contrasts to the flowery poems he had written in the days of his southern residence. His great masterpiece, however, is his long and touching *fu* entitled "Lamenting the Southern Area." In this *fu* he not only summed up the chief stages of his personal wanderings but also the series of devastations perpetrated by the northern conquerors upon Chinese civilization and the Chinese people.

Besides numerous writers of northern origin who wrote traditional poetry and essays, there were two writers in the northern regimes who deserve special mention. Both were authors of full-fledged utilitarian historical books. One was Yang Hsien-chih of Peiping (flourished 530-550). His *Loyang Chia-lan Chi* or *Record of Buddhist Temples in Loyang,* written between 547 and 549, was a magnificent record of contemporary changes. Although the subject matter was a detailed and artistic description of Buddhist temples established in the capital city of Loyang, it reflects the rise and fall of the Northern Wei Dynasty. Into the great mosaic work making up the treatise, we find various anecdotes of the tragic and heroic—remnants of alien barbarians committing atrocities in this ancient capital and during the same time offering fervent prayers and sitting in penitent meditation. The fluidity of the style of a great prose master permeates all five sections of the book. In Book 5 we find an abbreviated version of the itinerary records of the eminent Chinese monk, Sung Yün, in his westward travels in search of Buddhist sacred books—a record not only invaluable in the history of Buddhism, but also in that of historic relations between Chinese Central Asia and Northern India. In the preface, he announced what he intended to record:

In the fifth year of the reign of Wu Ting [547] while on an official mission, I had the opportunity of revisiting Loyang. The city walls were torn down and the palace buildings dilapidated. The religious edifices were in ruins and the temples and pagodas had been reduced to ashes. Walls and ramparts were covered with wild growths and the narrow lanes of the city were blocked by thorny bushes. Wild beasts were lurking behind deserted steps and mountain birds were nesting on garden trees. Street urchins and cowherds were wandering in the main boulevards and farmers were planting cereals right in front of palace entrances. The whole situation reminded one of the barrenness of the wastes of Shang-Yin and the desertion of the Chou capital after the Hunnish sack! In the cities and suburbs of the imperial capital there had once been over one thousand monasteries. Today there is only solitude and silence. The sound of bells is hardly heard. For fear that posterity would not hear of this, I now leave this record.

The other distinguished writer was Li Tao-yüan (flourished 526), a contemporary of Yang, who wrote a detailed commentary on an anonymous classic known as *Shui Ching* or *Water Classic.* Although the author entitled his work *A Commentary,* it was in large part a book of creative writing based largely on careful historical and documentary researches. In other words, he had deliberately broken loose from the strait-jacketed formulary followed by commentators on the Confucian classics which had prevailed for five-hundred years. Where the original text of the *Water Classic* had a simple unadorned statement describing the course of a certain river, the commentator would exhaust all his sources of information concerning the area watered by the said river, telling the folk tales current in the area, preserving all legends and myths, and presenting the notable personalities who had lived and died there. As a result, what he had written by way of commentary was somewhat reminiscent of the best of travel literature in the world. He delighted in detailed description of the scenery as well as taking pride in retelling some of the most attractive of the narratives. The following is an excerpt from his description of one section of the Yangtze River:

From the Three Gorges down for seven hundred *li* both banks are flanked with uninterrupted mountain ranges without a single break. These double and triple layers of mountains hide the blue heavens and shade off the sun. It is only at high noon and midnight that one may peek at the moon or the sun. At the time of summer high tide the rushing currents are such that sailing in either direction would be extremely precarious. In case of the emergency of a posthaste royal order, it would not be rare for one to leave the White Deity City [a town in Szechuan] and to arrive at Chiangling County at dusk, having covered one thousand, three hundred *li* [about 400 miles], hardly less speedily than riding with the wind. In spring and winter, however, there are white foamy currents flowing quietly into the depth of the blue water reflecting everything on the two banks in clear outline upside down. On the tops of the mountains there are plentiful pines and firs looking down on the waterfalls resembling hung fountains spraying their foam to make the area clear and luxuriant and full of interest. After each rainy season and on a frosty morning, when the forests are cold and the streams serene, we often hear the long scream of monkeys, weird and melancholy as they are echoed and re-echoed through the empty valley, dying out only after a prolonged process. Hence, the fishermen of the area frequently sing:

> Long, long is the waterway through the Three Gorges of Patung.
> Monkeys scream three times and you are tearful.

It is in similar vein that the forty chapters on all major and minor waterways in China were elaborately described by the commentator. In the original *Water Classic* are described 137 rivers. But in the commentary, which did so much to popularize the original classic, these waters were traced in detail to 1,252 tributaries and it is a remarkable feat of authorship that none of the minor tributaries were carelessly glossed over.

The merits of the *Water Classic's Commentary* that appeal to people looking for literary interest lie principally in the commentator's attempts to deviate from scientific exposition and pause for descriptions of natural scenery. Thus, in delineating one of the tributaries of the Fên River, noted for the quality of its water in wine-making, the commentator, Li Tao-yüan, recorded what he saw of the Chiang River:

The Chiang River has its source east of the Chiang Mountain. Cool springs gush forward vigorously, flowing northward with their exuberant torrents, and then taking the form of a hanging waterfall dashing down toward the ravine over a hundred feet below. The bluish cliffs are like spots of ink and the white swirling waters spread out like bleached cloth—a most wonderful sight.

Similarly, tracing one of the sources of the Yellow River as it flows northward from Khotan, receiving many riverlets flowing southward, and then turns east into a little lake situated thirteen hundred Chinese miles west of the strategic pass of Yü-men or Jade Gate, the commentator pauses at the little lake:

[The lake]is four hundred *li* around. Its water is quiet and clear, drying up neither in winter nor in summer. In its middle, undercurrents whirl in circles and flow at lightning speed. Directly above them birds fly vigorously in the clouds and tumble one and all into the deep waves.

At the lower reaches of the rivulet Hsü, which flows into the Yi River, famous for the heroic farewell party given in honor of the swordsman, Ching K'o, who had volunteered to go into the state of Ch'in during the Warring States period and at which many touching farewell songs were sung, the commentator almost felt obliged to convey to his readers the scenery which had been observed:

The streamlets are winding and the springs are clear. The mountains rise high and the forests are dense. The misty particles of the atmosphere are gently spread around by soft breezes, providing a pleasant abode for men's rest from their emotional strain. Recluses are still making use of the old building today and enjoying themselves in the woods.

At times the commentator would explain the folklore origin of the mountains. In the following terms he explained why a mountain had been named the Mountain of the Mourning Birds or Tiaoniao Shan:

Here the birds gather by the hundreds and the thousands, six times a year. They seem to chirp grievously. Local folk tales say the phoenix died on this mountain and the multitude of birds have come here periodically to mourn its death.

Even more interesting are his interjections of long-cherished folk tales into the commentary. These, it is to be noticed, were included for one good reason or another and were, therefore, not artificial attempts at padding. In the region of the River Tuan in the southwestern border area of China proper, where a bamboo king was worshiped, there had been current this story:

Formerly there was a girl bathing at the bank of the river. She noticed there was a bamboo stem with three large nodes flowing between her feet. She pushed it away but it would not go. She heard it utter a sound, brought the stem home, and slit it open. She found an infant boy inside who [when he grew up] became the chieftain of the Pu barbarians, adopting the word *chu* meaning "bamboo" as his family name. The bamboo stem which had been slit open and thrown away grew into a grove—now the bamboo grove near the Temple of the Bamboo King. The king had joined other men one day in resting up on a huge rock where he gave order to have some broth made. His retainers told him that no water was available. Whereupon the king chopped open a rock with his sword and water began to flow out—now the Bamboo King's stream. Later on [General] T'ang Mêng opened up the Changk'o region and beheaded the Bamboo King, making the border tribes extremely restive. As they realized the Bamboo King had not been born of common mortals they petitioned for the building of a temple in his memory. The emperor made the three sons [of the Bamboo King] noblemen. After their death they were also enshrined in the temple to share their father's honors.

Likewise, a mountain called the Eight Grand Old Men on the River Fei seemed to the commentator to warrant an explanation. On the bank of the Fei River there had been a royal prince living in seclusion in search of a diet that would ensure his physical immortality:

Suddenly eight grand old men all wearing long white beards and eyebrows came to his door and asked for an interview. The doorman said to them, "My prince is interested in physical immortality. Now you gentlemen are obviously incapable of stopping your own aging. I don't dare to announce your arrival." Whereupon all eight men transformed themselves into blooming youths. The prince on receiving them was extremely courteous.

The eight gentlemen were all versed in the transformation of base metals to gold and in compounding pills of immortality. Moreover they could walk in and out of compact objects. They then accompanied An [the Prince of Huainan, author of the philosophical text] to the top of a mountain where, after burying the gold in the ground, they all ascended to heaven in plain daylight. The remnant of the drug left in the vessel was lapped up by the chickens and dogs which later on also ascended into heaven. At the place of ascension all the footprints were dented into the rocks preserving the footprints of men and beasts. This is how the mountain came to be known as the Eight Grand Old Men.

When I went up there, the footprints of men and beasts had already vanished but a temple and the images were still there.

We have seen that with the fall of the Later Han Dynasty in 221 the unified control propaganda of a cultural orthodoxy was replaced by free interplay of new trends of thought most of which failed to conform to the Confucian pattern. The hemmed-in intellectual atmosphere was dispersed by a revival of interest in non-Confucian philosophies which seemed like an exhilarating adventure. This partly accounts for the rapid appreciation of Buddhism and a renewed interest in the philosophies of Lao-tzŭ and Chuang-tzŭ. And although the Northern Dynasties soon retrogressed to formalism and orthodoxy, these elements did not survive the great exodus and establishment of the Southern Dynasties.

In the south, the shedding of conventions led to an awakening of the self in both thought and letters. In the realm of thought the quest was for a way of life that would give the greatest satisfaction to the individual, and in the realm of letters the search was mainly for enjoyment and self-realization rather than for support of supposedly unchanging ethical and metaphysical truths. Hence, the function of writing was no longer that of a vehicle for the conveyance and transmission of Tao or The Way. Poetry was to be read for delight rather than for edification and rhetoric was to be studied to enhance the esthetic effect of writings in verse as well as in prose. It is this increasing realization that literature was valuable as an end in itself rather than a means to an end that elevated the status of belles-lettres for the first time in the history of Chinese literature. This childlike rapture of the discovery that prose writings were not necessarily utilitarian led the writers and the critics to redefine what was to belong to the proper province of literary as contrasted with nonliterary prose, for the notion had suggested itself that not all prose was literature.

The line of demarcation which was discovered and followed for two-hundred years was one principally based on mechanism. This mechanism was *yün* or consonance. That which was endowed with consonance was regarded as *wên,* a Chinese word which might mean "writings at large" but had come to have a special significance in this period meaning "literary prose." Writing in which consonance was not stressed was labeled *pi* (the writing brush), applied or utilitarian prose such as official documents from receipts to lengthy proclamations. According to this definition, all poetry was akin to and might be, in fact, included in *wên.*

This definition was rather confusing than enlightening as a definition went. In literary effect, however, it had peculiar repercussions. We can see at once that the demarcation was just as arbitrary as the one usually drawn between the so-called fine arts and applied arts. Consonance, as defined in those days, included more than the pleasant arrangements of words according to their sounds. It involved all those elements in rhetoric and lyrical feelings that would distinguish a piece of writing. These being the beliefs among writers, the technique of *wên* was elevated to an art whereas that involved in *pi* was only comparable to a craft. As all writers would naturally aspire to be artists instead of craftsmen, attempts were deliberately made to clothe utilitarian writings in the finery of lyrical prose. In other words, the hair-splitting care with which the categorization was made had resulted in so much labor lost. The new phenomenon was often amusing when matter-of-fact prose compositions were made superfluously ornate.

On the other hand, however, it was in this period that a graceful and esthetic prose style was born. Lyrical prose had begun to make its appearance when the Han Empire was disintegrating. The personal letters written by the poets of the age were characterized by many unmistakable lyrical strains which, in a peculiar way, had made them what we might call poetic prose. After the migration of the leading families in 318 to the Yangtze Valley, the natural beauty of their new habitat aroused in them a feeling of the poetic quality of their environment. Moreover, the territorial loss of the northern half of China and the vicissitudes of the migration and the relocation were so full of nostalgic melancholy that even memorials to the southern courts were naturally overflowing with emotionalism. It is easily understandable that in these circumstances, as far as content went, the distinction between prose and poetry was indeed tenuous. One outstanding writer who illustrated this peculiar literary trend was Wang Hsi-chih (321–379), who is equally remembered for his calligraphy and his short prose writings. It was he who continued to confirm a peculiar tradition in Chinese epistolary style in which attempts were made to make even business correspondence less bland than necessary. Whether it was a note to accompany a small gift, or a card in acknowledgment of receipt of a longer letter, the few lines flowing from the writing brush of the calligrapher conveyed expressions of the personality of the writer in such a manner that the receiver would be reluctant to throw it away. Enhanced by this fine calligraphy, these short letters and notes were treasured by contemporaries and posterity beyond their utilitarian value.

Hsi-chih makes a bow in addressing you: The other day I was greatly intoxicated so that I cannot recall taking leave of you. I felt released on arriving home, and realizing we are now separated, I feel that my regrets are beyond words. Meeting and parting are normal orders in life. I don't want to dwell on these further, and only wish that you will treasure and care for yourself above all so that we shall meet again. So I am sending you this letter in anticipation of further news from you after you have crossed the river. As I face the stationary my emotions are ceasing to flow.

Or,

I am presenting to you three hundred oranges. The frost has not fallen yet. I cannot get more.

Better known is his preface to a collection of poems written by his literary coterie on a spring day at his famous orchid pavilion, Lan T'ing, in which vessels of wine were passed to his guests in trays floating down gently on the surface of a winding creek. In this preface he not only recorded the pleasantries of the gathering but also his speculations on the transiency of life and the fleeting passage of the ages so that future generations would regard the present as those who were living that day looked upon the events of the past.

This short lyrical piece in prose, made famous by its own merit and by the merit of the calligraphy of its composer, became the most widely circulated piece of medieval Chinese prose. Its wide diffusion was due partly to the charming quality of the lyrical prose but also partly to the graceful calligraphy, which was soon inscribed on a stone tablet. In fact, it was the calligraphy exemplified in the writing of this piece which was to start a fad in artistic handwriting. Rubbings or squeezes from the original inscription were soon, in turn, used as master sheets for the duplication of the inscribed tablet at new locales. This process went on, giving rise to a ramification of a whole family tree of secondary and tertiary ramifications, so that these replicas numbered over five hundred and were located in virtually all parts of the Chinese empire.

Coming later than Wang was T'ao Ch'ien. Just as Wang's reputation as a prose writer was eclipsed by his attainment in calligraphy, so T'ao's merit was completely overshadowed by his poetry. Though his prose writings were short and few, they stand out clearly as important monuments not only revealing the inner personal life of the poet but also as important landmarks in the development in artistic prose. Unlike his contemporaries who had to rely on rhetorical devices to lend coloring to their prose writings, T'ao's prose pieces were nearly all unadorned autobiographical pieces. His "Biography of Mr. Five Willows" was a charming self-portrait that every grade school child in old China could recite by rote. Mr. Five Willows has come from Nobody-Knows-Where. Nor does anyone know what his real full name is. At the side of his house there are five willow trees and so they are used as his alias. He is a man of composed habits and few words, with little interest in honors or wealth. He is fond of reading but doesn't seek to exhaust the meaning of what he has read. Whenever he feels an unusual meeting of the minds he is so enraptured that he forgets about his meals. He is fond of drinking rice wine but since he is poor, he frequently cannot afford it. Knowing these circumstances of his, his friends and relatives invite him to parties where rice wine is amply provided. Each time he responds to such an invitation he drinks to satisfaction. With satisfaction he goes home without feeling sorrow at bidding farewell. The walls that surround him are unadorned, hardly keeping him protected from sun and wind. He wears a short jacket with a few holes and patches. His rice bucket and his soup bowl are frequently empty. He feels nonetheless unperturbed. He often writes to amuse himself and occasionally to express his feelings. He is unimpressed by gains and losses and thus he finishes the span of his life.

This philosophy of life he projects onto a larger canvas to form his utopia—the "Peach-Blossom Spring." In this utopian piece it was rather his interest to delineate the satisfying way of life than to win followers for his political philosophy. In fact, he was never interested in elaborating his political creed. He was rather more interested in sharing with his readers the extremely simple message of how he was contented with the little that he had in life. In this natural presentation of the simple life without glorifying it is to be found T'ao's greatness as a man and as a poet. This simplicity of style was not artificially cultivated or purposefully exhibited to his readers. The same tone was maintained when he was writing to his own sons. In describing his life in an ordinary family letter he wrote:

When I opened a book and felt I had something I would be so happy that I would forget to eat. Whenever I saw the trees casting shadows, one upon another, and the birds of the season change their tunes as they sang, I would also feel exhilarated. As I often lay beneath the northern window on an early summer day I would call myself a pre-Fu-Hsi man with the coming of an occasional and temporary cool breeze.

Although T'ao's reputation was immense, his influence upon subsequent prose writers seems to have been little. His followers greatly admired and profoundly respected him but at the same time they realized that his literary style, like his very personality, would defy conscious imitation.

After T'ao, lyrical prose took the form mainly of epistolary writing, giving to this genre a touch of the feeling of the familiar essay. Most of the writers to distinguish themselves in prose were better known as poets. Nonetheless, their enrichment of the prose tradition should not be minimized although their writings in prose fell short of being masterpieces. As a result, the art of letter writing received such undue attention and conscious cultivation that it became an art sharing the limelight with, if not challenging the legitimacy of, poetry. Peculiar instances were even recorded of political dignitaries asking epistolary experts to write letters home to their wives by proxy. Apparently the feeling was that sending a nicely worded letter home was comparable to sending a piece of embroidery. This tendency of turning personal letters into familiar essays and little prose poems tended to blur the distinction between prose and verse on which so much had been written. Now that the consensus agreed to accept poetry as inherently superior to prose, what was more natural than for the most ambitious writers to dedicate themselves to the cultivation of poetry? Under these circumstances those writers who are not born poets would find it difficult to take second place in the literary realm.

Among the many writers who were gifted in prose but who, nonetheless, wanted to distinguish themselves in poetry as well, the most interesting writer was Jên Fang (460-508). Voluminous in his prose writings, devoted largely to biography and geography, he was considered an equal to Shên Yüeh with Shên surpassing him in poetry but definitely behind him in prose. Not quite satisfied with this dictum, he tried desperately hard to be Shên's equal in poetry, too, without being able to reverse the judgment of the leading critics. Nonetheless, he seemed to be more aware of the distinction between prose and poetry than any of his contemporaries. While he was capable of writing lyrical prose or poetic prose of the highest order in order to keep in pace with the poet, he could write also the most matter-of-fact type of prose in which clarity was his foremost objective. Among his preserved writings there is a peculiar memorial of indictment against an official, Liu Chêng. In this memorial he did something which was extremely unconventional. In the preamble in which he introduced the case he followed the pattern set by his contemporaries of an extremely elegant and highly polished prose. But when he came to the presentation of the actual narrative of how the indicted man, Liu Chêng, had been ungenerous to his widowed sister-in-law after the decease of his own father which called for a settlement of the family estate, all the petty plottings and sordid maneuvers against the poor widow would naturally have lost all their poignancy and human interest if the narrative had been translated into the highly formalized documentary legal style. Instead of following the trend of his time in making simple country people speak in highly polished court language, often adorned with quotations from the Confucian classics or the *Book of Lao-tzŭ,* Jên boldly introduced the original complaint submitted by the widow with all the slang and liberties of expression of everyday folk language. This has become a jewel of vernacular literature preserved intact from the fifth century.

It has been observed that prose literature of the so-called Six Dynasties was more successful in lyrical expression than in exposition and argumentation. This critique is justifiable only in a limited way. The illusion that prose writers were not interested in exposition and argumentation was largely due to the fact that most prose writers were poets by their own preference. And most of the prose pieces included in anthologies were selected mainly for their lyrical appeal. The Six Dynasties Period was not only an age of rapid development in poetry but also an age in which religious controversies and sectarian apologetics had attracted the attention of the new converts to Buddhism and Taoism. The body of translated Buddhist literature was to produce a far-reaching influence upon the native creative literature of China. Also, aside from translations and commentaries upon translations, religious controversial literature occupied a paramount position in the prose literature of the Six Dynasties. Buddhism, it should be borne in mind, had already taken root in China. While the Han Dynasty represented the age of absorption of Buddhist doctrines, the Six Dynasties was the age during which the indigenous thought of China and the imported alien faith were engaged in a series of controversies. These decisive literary battles left in the history of Chinese thought and literature brilliant relics by the defenders of Buddhism. By and large, it could be stated that the defenders of Buddhism had made a much more effective show than their opponents. There did not seem to be any systematic co-ordination among the attackers of the new faith. They sometimes would take the position of traditional Confucianists and at other times lean heavily for armament upon the new philosophical Taoism. At other times they would resort to making capital of a narrow nationalism to discredit the gospel of the Buddha. In spite of this disparity between the two camps, their controversial engagements were brilliant performances in prose literature. In a way, the excitement produced was unmatched by similar controversies of later ages.

The controversy began in 435 with the publication of a peculiar essay entitled "On Black and White." This essay, written by a Buddhist monk, Hui Lin, was dedicated to a theory that the traditional religion of China, as expounded by the Confucian school, and the Gospel of the Buddha were sound in their own respective ways and should be given a chance to exist side by side. This discussion was worked out in dialogue form between Mr. White Learning, representing Confucianism, and the preacher of the way of Black Learning, as an exponent of Buddhism. This position taken by a Buddhist monk immediately provoked adverse criticism from many a follower of Buddhism. Hui Lin was accused by some of being a religious fifth columnist who had entered Buddhist monkhood in order to destroy the Buddhist doctrine. By others he was regarded as the most level-headed discussant of the rival faiths. Among the latter group there was a prominent leader of Confucianism, Ho Ch'êng-t'ien (370-447) who, greatly impressed by a Buddhist monk who had written in praise of Confucianism, decided to give publicity to the essay by having duplicate copies made to be sent to all the prominent leaders at court and in the scholarly world. The repercussions were that nearly all converts to Buddhism who could wield a writing brush actively took part in the controversy to denounce monk Hui Lin. Among these defenders of the alien faith, most prominent and most eloquent was Tsung Ping (375-443), who wrote several long letters to Ho in defense of the Buddhist doctrines. Now that Ho was involved in the controversy, he gave up his neutralist position as disseminator of the controversial literature and took up the position of defender of China's national faith.

Later on the Black and White Controversy gave birth to a new topic of discussion introduced by an essay written by Ku Huan (420-483), entitled "Yi Hsia Lun" or "The Discussion of Chinese and Barbarians." In this the author recounted a Taoist legend to the effect that Lao-tzŭ, after he had arrived in India had, during an afternoon nap of Queen Māya, entered her body through her mouth to be reborn later on as Sākyamuni. With this as his major premise, the main body of the essay confirmed his judgment that Taoism was Buddhism and Buddhism was Taoism. But since the lands of diffusion were different, rituals were differently developed. With the publication of this essay, refutations were numerous from the pens of the laity as well as the clergy. Without going through the details of the argument it must be stated that the attackers of Buddhism again had failed to hit the target. Instead of being retarded by the controversy, the cause of Buddhism was actually served and advanced.

But the greatest controversy was one that was more purely doctrinal, in which emotional elements such as barbarianism could not find a logical place. The new theme around which the debate was organized was whether the soul was destructible. The author of the essay which touched off the great controversial explosion was Fan Chên (flourished 505). Although the date of composition of Fan's essay on the destructibility of the soul is unknown, it was in the early years of the sixth century that the controversy arose; a controversy in which Emperor Wu of the Liang Dynasty entered in person heartily. This problem concerned the core of the doctrine of Buddhism which in its teachings to the laity had taken for granted that the soul of man was indestructible. If the human soul is destructible then all the teachings of Buddhism in China would fall to pieces. This is why this third controversy was much more important than its two predecessors. It is to be noted also that this essay was published at a time when Buddhism in the Southern Dynasties had reached its zenith, claiming a loyal following from emperor and princes down to common men and women. It is, therefore, a feat of intellectual bravery that Fan Chên advanced his theory of the destructibility of the soul.

Someone asked me, "You say the soul is destructible. How do you know it is destructible?" My answer is, Soul is the same as Body and Body is the same as Soul. Therefore, when the body is wholly present then the soul is present. And when the body decays, the soul perishes. . . . The soul in its relation to the body is the same as sharpness in relation to the knife and the body in its relation to the soul is exactly the same as the knife in relation to sharpness. The name of sharpness is not identical with knife and the name of knife is not identical with sharpness. And yet without sharpness there can be no knife and without knife there can be no sharpness. I have never heard that without a knife sharpness could exist. And how does it follow that there can be a soul without a body?

Then he goes on to point out that the Buddhist church and the monastic order were spelling ruin to Chinese civilization and society. The falsehoods of Buddhism, he declared, were difficult to combat because of the subtlety with which the theories were advanced. With such a thrust at the heart of Buddhism it is easily understandable why, in addition to many replies volunteered by the leading Buddhist authors of the age, the imperial dynasty saw fit to promote, almost officially, statements to discredit the original essay. Shên Yüeh alone had written three fairly lengthy pieces in refutation of the anti-Buddhist essay. And the emperor himself gave Fan Chên what we might call an extended verbal spanking. A kind of gentlemanly tolerance was maintained, however, and Fan Chên wound up the debate without incurring the loss of his life. These controversies, taking on new facets and acquiring new emphases from time to time, grew in number if not in intensity until the collapse of the Liang Dynasty in the middle of the sixth century, when Buddhist influence kept steadily mounting as never before and when the imperial court had grown in its religious zeal to such a degree as to silence the arguments of all skeptics.

The Six Dynasties also produced philosophical works of a more placid nature. One is *P'ao P' Tzǔ* written by Ko Hung (A.D. 254-334), a Taoist who had been well versed in Confucian lore and who had distinguished himself in younger days as a brilliant military commander. Claimed by popular Taoism as one of the pillars of the medieval Taoist tradition, the many-sided Ko Hung was more than a Taoist expositor. There was no question that he was seriously interested in Taoist alchemy, for his motive in seeking the magistracy in Koujung county was entirely motivated by the soil of that district, and in the so-called inner chapters of his philosophical treatise he went to great lengths in explaining alchemical formulas and theories. It should be pointed out that instead of having written one book,

Ko Hung was actually the author of two separate works erroneously put together and separately labeled "inner chapters" and "outer" chapters. In the former he elucidated the different facets of medieval Taoism as he saw them, while in the latter he expounded such doctrines as "The Importance of Learning and Education," "The Ways of Kings," and "The Incorruptibility of Ministers," which were more akin to Confucian orthodoxy. It has been suggested that his possession of a dual personality was so marked and indisputable that he could seek entree into the company of medieval alchemists just as easily as the spiritual fraternity of the Duke of Chou and Confucius.

Another work that reflects the spirit of the age was a philosophical work titled *Chin Lou Tzŭ* or the *Master of the Golden Tower*, written by Emperor Yüan (508-554) of the Liang Dynasty. It consists of fourteen chapters, including an autobiography in which the author rambles freely from high antiquity to abnormalities of his own age. More in the nature of a well arranged book of anecdotes than a philosophical work presenting a special way of life, this work was a storehouse of medieval booklore and early legends.

In this particular regard the *Chin Lou Tzŭ* was one of the works ushering in a new trend of reference book compilation known in Chinese as *lei shu* in which anecdotes and allusions were arranged in accordance with a preconceived scheme ranging from astronomical and meteorological phenomena through the divisions of the earth with their diverse mineral content and vegetation to the multiple diversities of the affairs of man and human relationships. In due course reference books of this kind were to expand in volume and in exhaustiveness and these were to fulfill the function of comprehensive and classified vocabularies which the long *fu* of the Eastern Han Dynasty had tried so earnestly but so uninterestingly to fulfill.

As we have pointed out before, the *fu* as a literary type underwent a subtle transition when the Han Dynasty was interrupted in the middle of its span by the usurpation of Wang Mang. Although superficially both the technique and mechanism of *fu* composition seemed to have remained unchanged, the spirit of the times made its imprint visible in the finished products that were to follow the interregnum. The long descriptive *fu* written by Pan Ku and Chang Hêng, in which they described and eulogized in relative terms the imperial capitals, had followed strictly the tradition of the Western Han *fu* pieces on the imperial parks. In originality of treatment the *fu* composed in Eastern Han times might even be inferior to those of the Western Han. In both cases impressiveness was built up by a peculiar cumulative process, that is, by the use of endless minutiae in description and enumeration. Within the sameness of pattern, however, there was a major difference in the attitude of the composers toward their compositions. Whereas the Western Han *fu* writers considered themselves primarily as high-class court jesters and royal entertainers, their objective in writing was almost invariably the pleasing of the monarch or the feudal prince whether or not they had written in response to overt royal or princely orders. These writers were not only devoid of personal dignity and pride but even oblivious of the traditional sense of loyalty. A deplorable instance was to be found in Yang Hsiung, a highly respected *fu* writer of the Western Han Period who allowed himself to become one of the staunch supporters of the Wang Mang usurpation. It is readily understandable that the Eastern Han *fu* writers took this moral lesson very much to heart and deliberately refused to make their *fu* occasional poems for the entertainment of their patrons, thus giving distinguishable personality to their compositions.

This gain in the dignity of the *fu* writers, however, was offset by another trend. As the Western Han writers had their monarchs in mind all of the time, they tried in devious ways to impress their patrons with morals they had to impart. The result often was an approximation to poetry insofar as the matter of expression was not forthright. Behind their lengthy narratives and their repetitive description, there was often a political message veiled in rhetorical artistry. With the refusal of *fu* writers of the Eastern Han Period to please or instruct their royal patrons, the elaboration technique became an end in itself—an artificial array and enumeration of attributes, products, flora, and fauna which resembled catalogues. No wonder many of the *fu* of this type were written over a period of eight or ten years before they were satisfactorily completed. These compositions were avidly copied and studied during the period principally because they satisfied a need—the need for word lists and classified vocabularies.

Fu composition of this orthodox kind naturally could not continue for long. Nor was there much room left for new ventures; for, even if one word list is more exhaustive than another, it could lay no claim to being better literature if literature it ever was. Once it was appreciated by creative writers that the end of a dead alley had been reached, they decided to put new wine into the old bottle. Abandoning description, they now used the *fu* as a literary device for lyricism. Instead of cataloguing nouns and adjectives ad infinitum, they reduced the length of the *fu*. The dialogue form which was frequently utilized for the elaboration of a theme or the narration of a story was permanently shelved. Instead, a deliberate attempt was made to return to the lyricism of the *ch'u tzu* types. Moreover, to vary the rhetorical device, the technique of *p'ien wên* or balanced prose was utilized for new embellishments. During the Six Dynasties this new type of *fu* composition, shorter, more direct, and definitely more lyrical, continued to spring up and replace the Han *fu* permanently.

To illustrate the rise of this new technique in composition two writers may be cited. Chiang Yen (444-505), whose literary career was at its maturity during the Liang Dynasty, was best remembered in his capacity as poet for his *fu* composition "Pieh Fu" or "On Departure." Instead of telling one touching story dealing with the pathos of departure, he succeeded in creating a mood by explaining that "although departure was of one type in human experience, the incidents of departures are varied endlessly." Following an introductory paragraph describing the varying moods of departure as dictated by divergent circumstances, he described in lyrical terms a number of typical classes of departure recorded in Chinese history and literature: the departure of national heroes who voluntarily took on the missions of assassin, fully realizing that life itself might end with the failure of the mission; the departure of the soldier for the distant front, bidding farewell to brothers and parents; the departure of an exile into foreign lands taking a last glance at the homestead before undertaking the almost unending journey; the departure between lovers anticipating the recollection of many pleasant hours spent together and anticipating long days of woe in summer and long nights of frozen feelings in winter; and even the departure of the Taoist who is ready to attain immortality taking his leave of the human world for a short sojourn to the world of the immortals for a mere millennium. What Chiang attempted to do was to suggest in a few master strokes the diverse emotions called for by parting. Instead of reciting cumulative instances of departure as recorded, he ended this little *fu* with the self-effacing remark that even the greatest geniuses of the world, past and present, were unequal to the task of dealing with the topic of parting conclusively and extensively. This was tantamount to a confession that the task which he had imposed upon himself was only one of suggestive delineation.

The tradition of the new *fu* reached its culmination in Yü Hsin (513-581). A prominent official in South China under the Liang Dynasty, Yü Hsin was sent as a southern diplomat to the capital of the non-Chinese regime of Western Wei in Ch'angan which was captured by the Northern Chou in 557. Here he was detained and forced against his own wish to serve the Northern Dynasty until his death. As a *fu* writer he excelled in and made permanent two leading trends. One of these, which was to exert an immense influence upon subsequent times, was a combination of the antithetical structure of *p'ien wên,* or balanced prose, and the end-rhyme of the traditional *fu.* Hence a new name was given to this type of composition, namely, *p'ien fu* or balanced *fu.* Since this kind of composition submitted itself to two sets of regulations, one of balanced structure and the other of the end-rhyme, it was also known by the name of *lü fu* or regulation *fu.*

With regulation and discipline as its chief feature, other regimentary features were added in later times, such as the specification of rhyming schemes in accordance with a given line of well-known poetry. This added feature, unknown in other literary traditions in world literature, would make sense only in a language preponderantly monosyllabic. When two lines of poetry consisting of eight graphs were specified as governing the rhyming scheme of the regulation *fu,* the requirements were to be met by dividing the composition in question into eight parts or cantos in which the end-rhymes of the consecutive cantos would correspond to the rhymes called for by the eight graphs of the specified lines of poetry. The following example will illustrate the requirements of the regulation *fu.* The title is from the twenty-fifth chapter of the *Book of Lao-tzŭ:* "There is a being wondrous and complete." The specified rhyming scheme is indicated in two lines from a commentary on Lao-tzŭ meaning "The phenomenon of the great void was born before the beginning of heaven and earth." In Chinese these eight characters read:

> Hsü hsiang shêng tsai
> Tien ti chih shih.

The end-rhymes in Section 1, then, were suggested by the first character of the quotation, *hsü,* and are *mu, chu, tsu,* and *hsü.* In Section 2 the end-rhymes responded to the second character of the quotation, *hsiang;* and they were the given character *hsiang,* a homonym *hsiang, wang,* and *yang.* The third character of the quotation, *shêng,* called for *mêng, shêng,* and *chêng.* The fourth character, *Tsai,* was responded to by *kai, hai, tsai, kai.* The remaining four sections can be tabulated as follows:

> 5. Tien: hsien, chien, chien, tien.
> 6. Ti: lei, ti, chi, chi.
> 7. Chih: chih, yih, shih.
> 8. Shih: chih, shih, chih.

This type of regulation *fu,* which first became popular during the later half of the ninth century when the T'ang Dynasty was on its decline, was later adopted as a literary type to constitute a portion of the government-sponsored competitive examinations. The rigidity of the requirements made the type an effective yardstick in measuring the literary attainments of the candidates. Although it was not as mechanical as some of the so-called "objective tests" in contemporary education it did provide an easy device for the examiners to rate literary excellence, for all that one had to do was to see how the key words of the set quotation were effectively cemented to the rest of the lines in their functions as rhymes. Many a *fu* of this type was naturally little more than an exhibition of rhetorical acrobatics and for this reason the type as a whole was never seriously regarded by the literary critics as genuinely creative writing.

The technique of merging the parallel structure of *p'ien wên* and the use of end-rhymes in the creation of a new *fu* type was successfully carried out by Yü Hsin toward the end of his life. His great masterpiece was a long *fu* in which he lamented the weakening of the Southern Dynasties. The various glories and honors bestowed on him by the northern regime after he had been detained in the north as an emissary from the south had apparently done little to reduce his yearning for his native state. The culmination of this feeling of tragic homesickness was brought out in full in this *fu.* Beginning with a statement of his ancestry and family background, he gave a summary of his public career and his observation of the political turmoil to which he was himself an eyewitness in the two divided parts of China. Then, bravely, he went on to criticize the traitorous blunders made by the southern political and military leaders, at times even accusing the Western Wei Kingdom in the north in which he was held in hostage. Finally he came out with a bold statement to the effect that in spite of all the gracious attempts which had been made by his host country to humor and honor him, his heart still yearned for a return to his native country.

Both in the prelude and in the main body of this long *fu,* entitled "Ai Chiang Nan" or "Lamenting the Southern Region," all assertions were made in the form of classical allusions, which partly explains why a superb *fu* like this has not been translated into any Western language. To his contemporaries, however, the numerous classical allusions were not a hindrance to understanding but rather a method of literary economy in which the apt turn of a phrase would suggest either a historical parallel or a mood which had been reflected in the literary masterpieces of previous generations.

His gift as a *fu* writer had already been manifest in his younger days when he was immersed in the literary tradition of the south, where the *fu* form had been changed in nature to serve a lyrical instead of an elaborative purpose. The scope as well as the physical length of the *fu* had already been reduced in a *fu* of his on the theme of spring, for example. Instead of cataloguing all the birds and flowers connotative of spring as a Han writer would have done, he sketched, in a few delicate but meaningful strokes, the spirit and mood inherent in the return of the season. But it was not until after he had left home to be detained permanently in the northern regions that Yü Hsin became the outstanding master of the short *fu* technique and gave to it his lasting personal stamp. In his "K'u Shu Fu" or "The Fu on the Withered Tree," for example, he merely suggested a word picture of the subject matter in question and then laid stress on lyricizing the mood suggested by a withered tree.

> As opportune moments never arrive,
> My detention and tarrying have no end. . . .
> Sunken in a dilapidated lane,
> And buried behind a thorny gate,
> It not only laments its sad fate,
> But also deplores the approach of decline and decay.

Then, in substance, he quoted the famous words of the soldier-poet Huan Wên:

> Formerly—when the willows were planted,
> Tenderly, endearingly they stand south of the Han River.
> Now they are dropping their leaves and withering,
> Standing lone and sad near the water.
> If even trees are like this,
> Could it be more bearable for men?

Again, in the lyrical *fu* "Shang Hsin" or "The Broken Heart," his principal theme was the expression of sorrow over the limited future of his own children. But he also made plain that his heart was broken by other factors:

> Here I float 'round in the river of Ch'in,
> Wavering and drifting without end.
> In office and yet no official,
> Retiring and yet no farm to retire to.
> I face the jade past always as a wanderer,
> I sit on the long river to enter the evening of my life.
> My eyes are greeted by myriad disappointments
> And my broken heart yearns for the nine yellow springs [the grave].

When the *fu* in the hands of Yü Hsin had become a vehicle of lyricism to be followed by able poets of the T'ang and Sung Dynasties and after, it had departed clearly in spirit and in literary technique from its original Han prototype.

Although the dynastic span of the Southern Liang Empire was short, merely half a century, it represented the high-water mark in literary attainment among the six Southern Dynasties. One of the basic factors for the unusual flowering of letters was the effective leadership taken by its emperors. In the second place, many of the important court ministers who excelled in their literary writings were great masters inherited from the previous Ch'i Dynasty. As they grew into greater maturity in their ripe old age they became assets of unusual merit to the new dynasty. Moreover, the prolonged peace had relaxed the tension maintained by the southern courts, leaving literature as the natural field of creative effort. In this brief period of a half century of creative writing, literary criticism and the compilation of anthologies all exhibited new trends and new standards.

Among literary critics, Liu Hsieh (flourished 530) was probably the most outstanding. Before his conversion to Buddhism and his eventual ordainment as a monk, he had undertaken the writing of a systematic treatise of fifty chapters on literary criticism entitled *Wên Hsin Tiao Lung*, or *The Carved Dragon of the Literary Mind*, which may be loosely translated as *Secrets to Literary Success*. The first twenty-five chapters which constituted Book 1 were discussions of literary types ranging from each one of the Confucian classics as literary models of excellence to types of occasional literature. In this portion of this book he explored not only the literary types as such, but also their relationship to the cosmological totality. The remaining chapters, also twenty-five in number, were discussions of the varying levels of literary excellence. In this connection he entered into minutely detailed discussions of rhetorical principles and other literary traits and devices which determine the degrees of success. His definition of literature was formulated in strict conformity with the prevailing view of his age—that only rhythmic and parallel-structure prose writing and poetry might be regarded as *wên* or belles-lettres, whereas all other writing of a random and practical nature would be grouped under the general classification of *pi*, or prosaic prose. When this book was finished he submitted it to his senior contemporary, the great expert on phonology and phonological principles in rhetoric, Shên Yüeh, who valued it highly. As a piece of artistic writing, the work was by all standards an impressive tour de force. Utilizing the *p'ien wên* as a tool, a tool that was least conducive to clear exposition on account of its artificiality, the author succeeded not only in his work of exposition but even in the presentation of his arguments—a gift little short of positive genius.

Another critic of note was Chung Jung (flourished 504), author of *Shih P'in* or *Levels of Poetic Attainment*. Differing from Liu, Chung's approach was one of classification. In his treatise he built up a neat scaffolding consisting of three shelves, indicating his three levels of poetic attainment. Onto these three shelves, each subdivided into three pigeonholes, the critic assigned individual places for each of the poets from antiquity down. Although complaints and protests have been numerous since the completion of his work of classification, his verdicts indicated a number of novel points of view. His reaction, for example, to the current theory of the surpassing importance of phonological and tonal requirements was entirely different from the position taken by Liu Hsieh. Liu, in strict conformity with the principles laid down by the great master, Shên Yüeh, had written:

Among tones there are ones that fly and others that sink and among sounds there are ones that are alliterative and others that rhyme. Alliterative initials, when interspersed, would often be erroneous in their effects, and rhyming finals, when carelessly disseminated, would certainly run into conflict. Sinking ones would have their sounds explode and cut short; flying ones would have their cadence distant beyond return. All these come and go like pulleys and intersperse like fish scales.

This, obscure as it sounds and more felt than clearly understood, is well within the bounds of Shên's teachings. Against this convention, Chung voiced his protest:

What was called in antiquity *shih* and *sung* was all set to music; hence, without harmonizing the five basic notes in the musical scale, the singing would be all awry.... The three emperors [by which he meant Emperors Wu, Wên, and Ming of the Wei Dynasty] might lack perfect art in their verse writing and yet their songs all sounded well when sung. This is the real meaning of emphasis on the tonal scale which is completely different from what the world means when it discusses the musical scale. Now that literary writings are no longer sung to musical accompaniments, what good would it do and what purpose would it serve to correlate literature with music? The tradition was started by Wang Yüan-ch'ang of the Ch'i Dynasty and later developed and enlarged upon by Hsieh T'iao and Shên Yüeh. These three worthy men were all members of aristocratic families and had attained an enviable literary reputation when they were young, wherefore, the whole stream of scholars in its admiration for them made every attempt to be discriminating, faultless, expansive, and minute, one writer devotedly trying to outdo the other. The net result is that many taboos are set up in letters and real beauty is damaged. It is my opinion that literary compositions are written to be read and, therefore, should read smoothly. It is enough that pure and turbid sounds flow smoothly together and the lips and

speech organ can function fluently [in reading]. This is enough. As regards
[the intricacies in] arranging the four tones of even, rising, going, and entering,
I am sorry I am unable [to submit myself or conform]. And as to such taboos
as the bee waist and the crane-knee, men of the street all have.

Although the last sentence is so obscurely worded as to defy clear
understanding (possibly due to copying errors), his opposition to
the conventional standards in regard to phonology in rhetoric is
quite obvious.

In the second place, these two distinguished literary critics seemed
to disagree also in their attitudes toward classical allusions, those
short cuts in communication. When they are not hackneyed they are
valuable in making the abstract appear more concrete and have a
tendency to make language picturesque. When the sources are obscure, however, they invariably become a hindrance to communication. In the Liang Dynasty, however, classical allusions were the
literary order of the day. Hence Liu Hsieh made the following
comment:

Elucidating an argument by drawing upon a formulated phrase and seeking
significance by enumerating an actual human event: these are the grand patterns set by sages and the common principle followed by the classics.

To this, Chung Jung voiced his uninhibited opposition, thus revealing a new idea in literary criticism:

In the writing of important state documents one should explore extensively
into antiquity and in refutation of memorials past arguments should be fittingly
reviewed. When it comes to the writing of poetry to express feelings and emotions, what value is there in using allusions? "Thinking of you continuously like
a running stream" is only a recording of what is seen by the eye; "upon the
high terrace blows many a sad wind" again is a picture registered in the organ
of sight. "In a clear morning I climb the embankment" has no allusion behind
it. "The bright moon illumines the piled-up snow"—how can this line be based
on any Confucian classic or dynastic history? We can see that the winsome
sayings of the past and of today are mostly not borrowings but direct finds. Yen
yen-chih and Hsieh Chuang were especially rife in their use of classical allusions and their contemporaries, much overpowered, were influenced. Consequently during the reigns of Ta Ming and T'ai Shih [457 and 471] literary
compositions were practically patchwork consisting of quotations from books.
More recently Jên Fang, Wang Jung, and others, instead of trying for new expressions, compete in coining new allusions and contemporary writers, by following them, have crystallized a new fad with the result that no phrase within
the sentence and no word within the phrase is free from some allusion, seeming pinched here, crunched there, patched here, and strained there, corroding
letters in the extreme.

CHAPTER 13

The Songs of the T'ang Dynasty

WHEN the T'ang Empire was founded in 618 it achieved quick political and economic unification. From 623 to the eruption of the
An Lushan rebellion in 755 was a period of peace and prosperity
almost entirely free from internal disorder and external threats of
foreign aggression. The subversion of the dynasty and usurpation
by Empress Wu (690-705) who called herself "emperor" was only
a dynastic change that caused no derangement of the social and
economic scene. During this age the different facets of T'ang civilization achieved a free and rapid development; religion, the classical
studies, arts, and literature all flourished side by side. When Emperor Hsüan Tsung, also known as Ming Huang, ascended the throne
in 713, the cultural seeds sown at the beginning of the dynasty all
began to bloom.

When the second T'ang emperor, T'ai Tsung, ascended the throne
in 627, he had laid the groundwork of T'ang literature for, even
when he was still Prince of Ch'in, he had established a Hall of Letters to which he had invited eighteen learned scholars as his guests.
This good work was followed up not only during his own reign but
also by his extremely unconventional daughter-in-law Empress Wu
herself, and also her son Chung Tsung (684-709). Thus, early in the
eighth century the cultivation of literature had become routine at
the imperial court. An early entry such as we find in the *Ta T'ang
Hsin Yü* or *New Anecdotes of the Great T'ang* was typical:

> During the reign of Shên Lung [Divine Dragon, 705-706] lantern parties
> were the order of the day on the first full-moon night of the year in the capital.
> The constabulary regulations were relaxed and the curfew was held in abey-
> ance. Everybody, from the imperial relatives and aristocrats to mean artisans
> and tradesmen, all took part in night entertainments and parading in the streets.
> Horses and carriages would become so congested that people dared not turn
> their heads. Royal and princely families would play music on horseback in
> rivalry and competition. Men of letters would each write a poem to com-
> memorate the event. These composers numbered several hundred.

The following two paragraphs from *Ch'üan T'ang Shih Hua,* or
Poetry Anecdotes of the T'ang Dynasty, are equally revealing:

230

In the tenth month, Emperor Chung Tsung [nominal reign, 684-709] cele-brated his birthday in the Forbidden Palace with a banquet at which the ministers were to join the emperor in contributing lines to a poem. . . . The emperor said to his attendants, "Now that the world is peaceful and both court circles and the commoners enjoy many pleasures, I wish to share with you men of letters the pleasure of dining and verse-writing. Knowing my wish as you do, please don't avoid intoxication. . . ."

.   .   .   .

Chung Tsung graced the K'unming Lagoon with his presence on the last day of the first month and composed a poem to which over a hundred poems were written in response by his attendants and ministers. In front of his throne in a tent was a storied structure decorated with multicolored silk in which a court lady was to select one poem to be set to new music. Below it the participants had gathered. A moment later leaflets dropped down from the balcony, flying in different directions, and each one would seek out his own by identifying the signature for keepsake. The two poems written by Shên Ch'üan-ch'i and Sung Chih-wên, respectively, had not been dropped. In a moment one sheet flew down and the crowd scrambled to take a look and found that it was Shên's poem.

On Shên's sheet there was written a verdict, apparently in keeping with current usage, detailing why Shên's poem had been considered inferior to the one submitted by Sung.

Poems like these were necessarily mediocre even though they might have been written by first-class poets. The atmosphere in which this type of literature was born could not but savor heavily of the stuffiness of the court. Among poets of this school Shên Chüan-ch'i (650-713?) and Sung Chih-wên (660?-712) were hailed as the twin masters for flawlessness in observing all the regulations that had been set down. The main targets were rhetorical cadence, accurate symmetry, and appropriateness of antithesis with or with-out substantial content. The only redeeming grace of sonorous courtly poetry of this type was the occasional presence of a touch of the humorous. We must understand that prior to the rise of Neo-Confucianism in the eleventh century, Chinese society had not ac-quired the rigidity imposed upon it by that school's strict moralists. Jesting between monarch and subject was not only not frowned upon but provided general gaiety. Some cautious curtailment was evident, of course, for everyone seemed to know the limit beyond which no venture should be made in making fun of the emperor and his associates. But the general effect was entertainment for all.

For this kind of poems, at first mainly occasional in nature, new patterns were soon set, and it was for their faithful and successful observance of the rules governing these patterns that Shên and Sung were admired. In fact, they were credited with leadership in crystal-lizing the new verse forms which had been slowly evolving for nearly two centuries, and which, once universally adopted, were to be continually cultivated by Chinese poets down to contemporary times.

This new type of verse forms was *lü shih*, or regulation poetry.

Regulation poetry was built upon two rhetorical devices especially favored by the unique features of the Chinese language: (1) parallel structure facilitated by the monosyllabic pronunciation of each graph, ensuring easy recognition of the parallelism when the passage is read aloud, and enhancing the appeal to the eye when the passage is recorded in characters, each occupying exactly the same amount of space; and (2) intonation, which assigns a specific tone or pitch to each word, and which, therefore, may increase the euphony of the sentence or line of poetry by a tested arrangement of words differently intonated in proper sequence.

Originally resorted to mainly for the purpose of remedying the paucity of vocables in the Chinese language and of avoiding confusion between homonyms, intonation had grown in complexity before T'ang times also as a result of the introduction of Buddhist incantations and Indic phonology. By the seventh century, there were already in the language spoken in metropolitan Ch'angan, the T'ang imperial capital, eight different tones. These were, arranged in four pairs, as follows:

1. the upper even
2. the lower even

3. the upper rising
4. the lower rising

5. the upper going
6. the lower going

7. the upper entering
8. the lowering entering

Without going into the complexities and niceties of T'ang and post-T'ang prosody, all that we need to bear in mind is that they were grouped by T'ang poets into only two categories, namely, the even tones (1, 2) and the deflected tones.

The even tones are noteworthy because, according to T'ang pronunciation, if all eight tones were represented in musical notations, the upper even would represent the highest pitch, and the lower even the lowest pitch of the scale. Roughly speaking, the upper even and the lower even would approximate in intonation the two syllables in the English word "even" in normal pronunciation. Thus, the two even tones were valued as the cornerstone of euphony, and used to balance off the intermediate pitches of the deflected tones.

With parallelism and intonation thus capitalized upon, *lü shih*, or regulation poetry, was "regulated" by the following requirements: (1) Each poem or stanza was to consist of eight lines of uniform length, either five or seven syllables each; (2) The middle four lines were to comprise two couplets of parallel construction, with the fourth line answering to the third, and the sixth answering to the fifth; (3) Lines 2, 4, 6, and 8 were to have the same end-rhyme, usually in words of the even tones. Extension of the end-rhyme to the first line was optional; (4) Each poem or stanza was to follow a set pattern of tonal sequence. Deviations were permissible as a rule to only the first and third words of a line; and (5) There were two basic patterns each for *lü shih* of the five-syllable lines and the seven-syllable lines. In each pattern, there was a slight variation to accommodate a fifth end-rhyme, so that all told, there were only eight patterns.

The characteristic features of the new verse form may be summarized in a diagram, as follows (– = even tone; 1 = deflected tone; R = end-rhyme; P = parallel structure):

$$
\begin{array}{ccccccc}
- & - & 1 & 1 & 1 & - & -R \\
1 & 1 & - & - & 1 & 1 & -R \\
1 & 1 & - & - & - & 1 & 1 \\
- & - & 1 & 1 & 1 & - & -R \\
- & - & 1 & 1 & - & - & 1 \\
1 & 1 & - & - & 1 & 1 & -R \\
1 & 1 & - & - & - & 1 & 1 \\
- & - & 1 & 1 & 1 & - & -R
\end{array}
$$

(lines 3–4 braced as P; lines 5–6 braced as P)

To illustrate this pattern concretely, we shall examine a seven-syllable *lü shih* written by Shên Ch'üan-ch'i in 705 in response to Tu Shên-yen, Tu Fu's grandfather, when they were both living in exile in the northern part of present-day Vietnam. The romanized reading is in Cantonese, which among current Chinese dialects preserves most fully the feature of T'ang pronunciation. The even tones are indicated by small capitals, the deflected tones by small letters, and the deviation by italics.

TIN CH'EUNG tei   fut   ling   T'AU FAN
sky long   earth wide sierra head divide
The sierra divides the vast heaven above and the wide
     earth below

hui kwok　LEI　KA　kin paak　WAN
go country leave home see white cloud
Far away from country and home appear the same white
　　clouds

lok p'o　FUNG　KWONG HOH　soh　ch'i
Lokp'o local color what soever resemble
The sights and scenes of Lokpo, what do they resemble?

SUNG　SHAAN　cheung　lai　pat　HAM MAN
Sung mountain pestilence vapor not able hear
The pestilence vapors of Sungshan are unbearable to hear

leung　tei　KONG　SHAAN　*man*　*YUE* lei
two places rivers mountains milliard more li
Between the two places lie mountains and rivers for over
　　ten thousand Chinese miles

HOH　SHI　CH'UNG　kin shing　MING　KWAN
what time again see sage bright monarch
When are we to see again our sage and enlightened ruler?

Since even Shên, a master of the new technique, had to resort to
deviations (*YUE*), it is understandable that to some poets like Li Po,
the *lü shih* verse form presented no special attraction.

With the ascension of Emperor Hsüan Tsung in 712, T'ang prosperity was to reach its zenith. Much luxury and leisure were available to members of the upper classes in Chinese society. A natural
product of the age was the birth of superior art and literature.

The emperor himself was a lover of beauty and of the arts. He
not only personally supervised the building up of vast orchestras in
which traditional music was successfully blended with frontier and
Central Asian music in which many types of instruments were involved, but also undertook the training of singers and musicians.
For centuries he continued to be known as the founder of dramatic
music and entertainment, having himself not only written the words
for some forty dramatic songs but also having arranged the musical
scores for them. In many of these new musical compositions there
was a great intermixture of what was known as barbarian and
"narrow-alley" music.

This does not mean, however, that he was blind to the genius of
superior poets or that his tastes were confined to what was merely

popular. Toward the end of his reign, according to one dependable record, he ascended the storied building labeled Ch'in-chêng Lou, or Attention to Political Duties, to admire the moonlight. As though obviously to forget the exhortation intended by the name of the building, he ordered his court musicians to present a few songs. One was the quatrain written by the outstanding poet, Li Ch'iao (644-713):

> Mountains and rivers fill the panorama as tears are wetting my coat.
> Wealth and honor and luxury, how long will they endure?
> Do we see that now bedecking the surface of the river Fên
> Are only autumn's swans flying year after year?

As the emperor was already advanced in years and felt touched by the message of the poem, he asked who the author might be. When he heard that it was Li Ch'iao, he could not refrain from weeping and rising before the music was ended and exclaiming, "Li Ch'iao is a real genius!" Even when the emperor was younger he had made the acquaintance of Li Po, a much younger poet than Li Ch'iao; but as Li Po was much addicted to drinking, his presence at court was irregular. Each time the emperor had completed a set of new musical scores he wanted to have the lyrics done by Li Po. Frequently when the poet was alerted by the imperial messenger, he was snoring in a wine shop. Far from being displeased by this romantic conduct, the emperor would take special pleasure in seeing water splashed on the poet's face and in seeing him dash off lines of poetry rapidly after he had become clearheaded.

It was this kind of uninhibited creative activity that made this reign the golden period of poetry. Poets enthusiastically wrote lyrics for songs. Although they might use old titles they did not feel compelled to adhere to the letters of those titles or to follow the musical pattern of the original composition. Freedom of creation was further extended by the use of themes and cadences of old ballads as well as of current popular songs. It was this forthright experimentation in meter and theme, which had permeated the whole field of poetry writing, that gave the literature of the age of K'ai Yuan and T'ien Pao (713-755) an unusual brilliance.

Not only was high society universally interested in the writing of poetry, but even the common people in sparsely populated villages in frontier regions—"wherever water was drawn from wells"—were eager to convert the handiwork of poets into popular songs. The process of enrichment of T'ang poetry by folk literature might be divided roughly into three stages: the leading poets, aware of the value of folklore, wrote in imitation of popular songs; inspired by the titles of popular songs, the poets wrote new compositions, often deviating from the original scores as well as from the original themes; freeing themselves from established themes and patterns, the poets created new songs of their own in conformity with the traditional spirit of folk poetry. In this subtle manner there was a greater extent of interpenetration between the creative writings of the T'ang poets and the literary heritage of the common people.

This age of liberation of the arts was greatly strengthened by the cumulative effect of philosophical naturalism from the age of Lao-tzŭ and Chuang-tzŭ, on one hand, and by the merging of this naturalism with the spontaneity in Ch'an Buddhism, on the other. Ch'an Buddhism had been introduced from India by Bodhidharma (died *circa* 530) and stressed the importance of contemplation in contrast to dependence on books and ritual. By the middle of the eighth century, Ch'an Buddhism had not only matured but also was surprisingly Sinicized. The beginnings of the revolution in Ch'an Buddhism had been set in motion by an illiterate monk from southern China, Hui Nêng (died 713), who had hoisted the banner of rebellion to found the so-called southern sect. One of their shibboleths was "down with the obstructions of letters and rituals." All that came between the seeker of enlightenment and enlightenment itself was obstructionist in nature and was, therefore, to be completely eliminated. To them, all discipline and procedure purporting to train the prospective convert gradually was regarded as hindrance rather than aid. Even incantations and meditations were regarded as so many shackles because all human beings, according to their belief, were capable of sudden enlightenment and immediate attainment of Buddhahood. This revolutionary movement, which had been started at the turn of the centuries, had amassed such a solid following by the middle of the eighth century that it had come into sharp conflict with the northern orthodoxy and replaced the latter in legal apostolic succession by scoring a universal victory toward the end of the century. This revolutionary movement in Chinese Buddhism was also a great revolution in the history of Chinese thought, with its repercussions felt in practically all fields of human activities, art and literature included.

The reflection of the spirit of the age on the current philosophy of life was one dedicated to the breaking of all shackles in search of freedom and naturalism. We might use the famous poem written by Tu Fu on the "Eight Immortals of Drinking" as a mirror in this regard:

Ho Chih-chang rides his horse as though he were sculling a boat
And is quite willing to tumble into a well asleep.
The Prince of Ju-yang had his three gallons before going to court
Yet a passing brewer's cart makes his mouth water,
And his heart longed for a transfer as Prince of Wine Spring.
Ten Thousand coins a day our Second Minister spends
On the drinks he takes as a whale drinks the waters of the sea,
Yet says he, "I like the unmingled and avoid the split."
Ts'ui Tsung-chih—a young man, handsome and carefree—
With bland eyes lifts his cup to the blue skies
And stands like a sparkling jade tree in the wind.
Honoring an embroidered Buddha,
Su Chin is a vowed vegetarian;
But how he enjoys his lapses whenever he is drunk with wine!
A hundred poems Li Po will write for a gallon
And will sleep in a wine shop in the market of Ch'angan.
Disobeying the imperial command to board the barge,
He says, "Your majesty's servant is an immortal of the cup."
Give three cupfuls to calligrapher, Chang Hsü,
Even before dignitaries he will throw off his cap,
And draw clouds on paper with his brush.
Chiao Sui will need at least five gallons to be awake—
To startle the company with eloquence in discussion or debate.

(William Hung's translation)

This distinguished company, as we can readily see, was representative of high society; a prince royal, a prime minister, a Buddhist, a Taoist, poets and artists. On appearance, the conduct of this group seemed decadent, but decadence, in their case, was actually a protest against accepted rules and customs and a manifestation of a new kind of naturalism as expressed in a life philosophy.

The first of these eight immortals, Ho Chih-chang (659-744), was a leading figure in T'ang literature whose biography is worthy of our notice. A native of scenic Kueichi, close to Hangchow, he had enjoyed an immense reputation since young manhood. As he climbed up the hierarchical scale he succeeded in retaining his unconventionality. According to the *Old T'ang Dynastic History* (*Chiu T'ang Shu*), besides being romantic in nature and gifted in humorous discussion, he became even more untrammeled toward the end of his life, visiting out-of-the-way lanes and cities and scribbling rolls of poetry after intoxication. Although he seldom revised his writings, his first drafts were all readable. In 744, as he was suffering fits of dizziness, he memorialized the throne for permission to become a Taoist and to return to his native district where he would donate his own mansion as a Taoist temple. The emperor responded not only with permission but also with poems to bid him farewell. As he departed from the capital all dignitaries from the crown prince down saw him off. He died not long after his return home, in his eighty-sixth year. His life was a reflection of the age in that such an unconventional figure had commanded the profound respect of society at large, indicating that he had lived in a society of extreme liberalism made possible by the termination of authoritarian Buddhism and yet unhampered by anything like the new Confucianist puritanism that was to rise in the eleventh century. It is, therefore, no coincidence that the remnants of Ho's poetry, which was not carefully preserved, were indications of the liberal movement in poetry and its tendency to approximate the natural speech of everyday language.

Casually Written After Returning Home

I left my home when I was young; grown old I now return.
The village accent remains the same, but my temple-hair has thinned.
The children gaze, not knowing who I am;
"Oh, Guest," with smiles they shout, "Where are you from?"

Many are the years and months since I left home.
Most blurred are the affairs of recent times.
But before my gate lies the water of the Mirror Lake
And the spring breeze stirs the ripples as of old.

Although Ho Chih-chang did not leave to posterity his compositions written in conformity with popular ballads, many of his contemporaries were experts in ballad writing. One such distinguished poet was Kao Shih (700?-765), a native of Puohai County near the North China coast, who, when he was young, was not interested in earning his livelihood. He would not even exert himself in the writing of poetry until he had passed the prime of his life. Once he tried his hand at this dynastic art, his success was immediate. His poems were recited far and wide. Bending his nature to accommodate himself in various indifferent secretarial posts, he was finally discovered by Emperor Hsüan Tsung while the latter was in distress. Thence onward he held various high posts until his death in 765. Although his special traits as a poet cannot be revealed in translation, they can be summed up briefly as his willingness to benefit from the examples of old ballads and to use the same balladlike and carefree lines in the writing of even lyrical poems, and his experiment with the use of lines of varying length to simulate the irregularity of daily speech. While he aimed at elegance in diction, he did not hesitate in employing slang expressions.

A Song of the Yen Country
(*Written to music*)

(In the sixth year of K'ai Yüan, a friend returned from the border and showed me the "Yen Song." Moved by what he told me of the expedition, I have written this poem to the same rhymes.)

The northeastern border of China was dark with smoke and dust.
To repel the savage invaders our generals, leaving their families,
Strode forth together, looking as heroes should look;
And having received from the emperor his most gracious favour,
They marched to the beat of gong and drum through the Elm Pass.
They circled the Stone Tablet with a line of waving flags,
Till their captains over the Sea of Sand were twanging feathered orders.
The Tartar chieftain's hunting-fires glimmered along Wolf Mountain,
And heights and rivers were cold and bleak there at the outer border;
But soon the barbarians' horses were plunging through wind and rain.
Half of our men at the front were killed, but the other half are living,
And still at the camp beautiful girls dance for them and sing.

· · · · · · ·

As autumn ends in the grey sand, with the grasses all withered,
The few surviving watchers by the lonely wall at sunset,
Serving in a good cause, hold life and the foeman lightly,
And yet, for all that they have done, Elm Pass is still unsafe.
Still at the front, iron armour is worn and battered thin,
And here at home food-sticks are made of jade tears.
Still in this southern city young wives' hearts are breaking,
While soldiers at the northern border vainly look toward home.
The fury of the wind cuts out men's advance
In a place of death and blue void, with nothingness ahead.
Three times a day a cloud of slaughter rises over the camp;
And all night long the hour-drums shake their chilly booming,
Until white swords can be seen again, spattered with red blood.

· · · · · · ·

When death becomes a duty, who stops to think of fame?
Yet in speaking of the rigours of warfare on the desert
We name to this day, Li, the great general, who lived long ago.

(Translation by Witter Bynner)

Another poet who had attained great popularity was Ts'ên Ch'an (722?-770?). The fact that his poems, as soon as they were released, would be avidly copied by scribes was probably due to the fact that in them the readers found many new verse forms and new cadences. For example, Ts'ên introduced the new rhyming scheme of a complete change in each triplet.

Even more outstanding was Wang Wei (699-759) on account of his many-sided accomplishments. Besides being a major poet, he was also a great pioneer in calligraphy and painting, as well as music. Despite his involvement in politics and his imprisonment by the rebel, An Lu-shan, he seemed to be able to maintain his tranquillity through his years of storm and stress until his death in 759.

Wang Wei was an artist par excellence, never losing sight of his creative talents in watercolor painting while he was writing poetry, thus deserving the praise of posterity in its saying that there was always a picture in his poems. A great lover of natural beauty and enjoyer of leisurely living in his county villa, he was also a devout Buddhist. His love of meditation, of scenic beauty, and of pictorial art, is thoroughly reflected in his poetry, thus founding the school of nature poets. Before we examine his nature poetry, let us look at his ballads, which were extremely popular in his lifetime. Since his narrative poems written in the style of ballads were all carefully dated, three of his masterpieces were written before he was twenty-one. In him we see the key of the development of T'ang poetry as Wang Wei trained himself in his younger days as a narrative poet in conformity with the pervading tradition of the so-called new *yüeh fu*. He left this kind of composition for pure lyrics in the latter part of his life. Similarly, the trend of T'ang poets was first to seek liberation and training in *yüeh fu* and finally to outgrow this type. The following are among Wang Wei's best loved shorter poems.

Seeing a Friend Off

After seeing you off on the mountain
I close the wooden gate at eventide
When the grass is green again next spring
Will you return, my honored friend?

[No title]

Fresh wind and bright moon arouse my thoughts (of you)
My wanderer has been in uniform for over ten years!
My soldier, on parting, earnestly commanded me
"Write me often via the homing swans."

The Lodge on Chungnan Mountain

Since my middle age, I have taken to the cult of Tao,
But only lately have I been able to make my home by the hillside.
Whenever the spirit moves in me, I saunter forth all alone,
To feast my eyes and nurse my soul with the thrilling beauties of nature.

I walk along a water-course and follow it to its source;
I sit down and watch the clouds as they are just beginning to rise.
Sometimes when I chance upon an old fellow in the woods,
We would chat and smile and forget to return home.

(John C. H. Wu's translation)

Among Hills on an Autumn Evening

Windswept hills—after a fresh shower.
The weather—Autumn in eventide.
Bright moon shining through the pine trees,
A clear stream flowing on pebbles.
Bamboos noisy—washing maids returning.
A stir among water-lilies—fishing boats starting.
The Genius of Spring will stay with you for aye,
If you don't mind too much its going away.

(John C. H. Wu's translation)

Sitting alone in the quiet bamboo grove,
I play my flute and chant my poems.
None is aware that I am deep in this forest,
Only the bright moon comes to shine on me.

To Chang Shao-fu

In life's evening I love only quiet;
Things of the world no longer concern me.
Having no plan to lean on,
I yearn in vain to return to the old forest.
The pine wind blows as I disrobe;
The mountain moon shines as I play my lute.
You want to know about failure and success?
The fishermen's songs are penetrating deep into
    the other bank of the river!

Wang Wei's life was enriched by a younger contemporary whose poetry was more varied and more romantic. Li Po (701?-762?), who was claimed as a native son by many different regions, was born in present-day Shantung Province. All his life a seeker of freedom and a lover of wine, he had joined various groups in living as a recluse. We have noted before that to Tu Fu, Li Po was one of the great Immortals in Wine Drinking. According to the T'ang *Dynastic History*, he was, on one occasion, so completely drunken that he forgot all the basics of court manners and went so far as to order a commander of the imperial guard and a favorite of the emperor to remove his boots. Even the unconventional Emperor Hsüan Tsung felt offended by this violation of etiquette and decreed his dismissal. Later, during the An Lu-shan rebellion, he joined the staff of an imperial prince who had been plotting for political independence, and after the collapse of that princely court, Li Po was sent into exile to the far southwest to the country of Yeh Lang. After his eventual parole, he died of intoxication on his way back to the capital. Around the life and death of Li Po so many stories were spun by posterity that probably not a single one was reliable, including the one saying that he lost his life by plunging into the river in an attempt to grasp the reflected moon, which he felt was even more beautiful than the real one.

Probably more than any single individual, Li Po was the epitome and summation of his age, spending his life variously as he did in running away from the crowd to the mountains and forests, in drinking to intoxication at wine shops and the imperial court, in practicing alchemy to attain physical immortality, and in wandering in scenic areas close to rivers and lakes. Distinctly different from his contemporaries who sought eagerly to elevate themselves in the official hierarchy by advertising their talents in poetry writing, Li Po persistently sang in praise of freedom.

> How can I beat my brows and bend my back to serve the powerful,
> And deny myself the pleasure of a joyful heart and open smiles?

Li Po's gifts as the brightest star in the early T'ang galaxy lay in three traits: first, his discernment of the futility of superficial embellishments in traditional poetry, which he tried to correct by fully exploiting the possibilities of folk song. Second, while other poets were mindful of the earthly rewards which could be derived from successful versification, Li Po was entirely free from all such utilitarian considerations. In the third place, while most of his contemporaries would make a special effort to put up fronts of patriotism and heroism, Li Po was always forthright enough to reveal his own feelings and reactions unashamedly and unadornedly.

While we should not belittle the genius of Li Po, we must bear in mind that his gifts were those that belong to an otherwordly order. In spite of his rare moments of grave concern with the human world:

> Without a resolve to benefit the world
> What good will personal perfection do in solitude?

or:

> I am also a member of the human world
> Not without a desire to help others.

his preoccupation was always to transcend rather than to abet the evils of the human world. It is because of this transcendency that for all our admiration for him, we do not feel his nearness or his being one of us common mortals. For the same reason, although his models in poetic composition, the popular ballads, had come from the world of the people, singing their joys and sorrows, this very vehicle, once guided by Li Po's hand, had a natural tendency of rolling upward to the heavenly regions. Thus we feel that Li Po's songs, beautiful as they are, were not originally sung to us and for us. As we imagine him high in the clouds looking down upon his great contemporary, Tu Fu, we feel that the latter stands by us while the ethereal spirit of Li Po is, as Ho Chih-chang put it, a heavenly immortal in temporary exile on earth. Before we leave Li Po's company, let us enjoy a few more of his masterpieces:

The Song of Wine

Don't you see the waters of the Yellow River come from the skies,
And run endlessly toward the Ocean, ne'er to return?
Don't you see in the bright mirror in the high hall our white hairs make a
  sorry scene?
In the morning they look like black silk: in the evening they become snow!
In life, when you are happy, you must drink your joy to the last drop,
And don't let your gold goblets face the moon without wine!
Heaven has endowed me with genius, and will find a use for it:
As for money, a thousand pieces of gold scattered away will return some day.
Let us roast a lamb and slay an ox and start the music!
We shall drink, each of us, three hundred cups of wine.

You Master Ts'en, and you Tan-ch'iu dear!
To you I offer wine, and refuse me not!
I'll sing a song for you. Please incline your ears and listen!
Bells and drums and choice dishes are not what I prize:
My only wish—to remain drunk and ne'er to be sober.
The sages and savants of old, who remembers them now?
But the names of drunkards have resounded throughout all times.
Don't you remember the Prince of Ch'ên how he used to feast in his Palace of
  Peace and Pleasure?
What jolly and riotous times they had over endless measures of precious liquors!
Why should my host worry about his poverty?
Let us order more wine, and I'll drink to you.
Look! What nice roan horses and costly furs you have!
Ask the boy to take them away and barter them for sweet wine!
Let us drown in wine the sorrows of ten thousand ages!

(John C. H. Wu's translation)

Lines at a Farewell Feast to Shu Yün held in the Hsieh T'iao Memorial Hall

That which cast me off is gone—
Yesterday—has slipped my grasp, I could not hold it back;
And that which much disturbs my mind—
The day I simply call today—is full of troubled care.

The steady winds convoy the geese afar in autumn flight;
Content we watch they fly away, while we sit here and drink.
Indite your skilful P'eng-lai tales, your measure Chien-an lines.
While I, a lesser Hsieh shall, too, reveal my simple thoughts.

Alike we cherish hearts set free, the strength of mind to fly
High up where sky is clear and blue, to gaze at sun and moon!

I draw my sword to cut the stream, its waters flow right on!
I lift my cup to drown my cares, the cares but bigger grow!
In life man may not always win the goals of his desire:
Tomorrow, then, my hair unloosed, I sail my boat away.

(David Willard Lyon's translation)

To the City of Chinling (Nanking)

Already six kingdoms have risen and fallen here.
I drink three cups and sing thy praises forth!
Smaller thy fields than those of the State of Ch'in,
Yet many thy hills, as many as crown Lo-yang.
The ancient castles, flowering gardens of Wu,
The courts of Tsin, hung full with silk brocades,
With other works of man have disappeared,
Borne eastward, lost in depths of rolling waves!

(David Willard Lyon's translation)

To a Friend in Distress

Your horse was yellow,
And mine was white.
But our hearts were equally mellow,
Differ as the colors of our horses might!

What a grand time we had together,
Racing round the suburbs of Loyang,
Wearing a dazzling sword each like the other,
Flaunting our head-gears all along.
Guests of the great, and not meanly dressed either,
Our life was like a long carefree song.

Now like a tiger you writhe entrapped—
A fate common to the heroic and strong.
When my bosom friend in distress is enwrapped,
I feel like a lost sheep not knowing where to belong.

(Teresa Li's translation)

On His White Hair

Methinks my white hair has grown ten thousand feet long!
For it grows alongside of my sorrow.
I only wonder how all this autumn frost
Has entered into the bright mirror in front of me.

(John C. H. Wu's translation)

Tu Fu and Li Po were twin stars of the golden period of Chinese poetry—the T'ang Dynasty. They were both complete masters of the art of poetry, they were contemporaries, and they were devoted friends. But between them there was a great chasm—created not only by different personal circumstances but also by the emergence of political and social upheavals after Li Po's death in 762; these created a new age with which Tu Fu was to identify himself and of which Tu Fu was the major prophet.

We have seen how Li Po was intent on being himself—a hermit poet satisfying himself by creative activities and paying no attention to versification as a short cut to official honors. Completely dedicated to personal freedom and glorifying the liberating influence of the beauties of nature, he was unprepared to meet the challenges of political confusion and social injustice. As a consequence, the rebellion of 755 and its upsetting effects deepened his decadence into pessimism.

To Tu Fu, the shock of the rebellion was equally acute. Thus he sang:

> The tableaus of the K'ai Yüan reign
> Are still clear and distinct as though shining before my eyes.
> Suddenly the rebellion arose
> And suddenly years and seasons elapsed.

When the tumultuous mutiny led by An Lu-shan in 755 broke out and spread into a huge conflagration, mid-eighth-century China, which had been rhapsodizing in the plenty and peace of an age of prosperity, was caught completely unprepared. The northern half of the empire was soon set aflame, both the capital at Ch'angan and the co-capital at Loyang fell, and the dynastic superstructure was on the verge of complete disintegration. It was not until the inadequacy of the dynasty to cope with the situation had been clearly demonstrated and the assistance of alien tribes had been secured that the rebellion was subdued after years of strenuous effort. Even then, the prestige and power of the central government could not be restored and the peace and prosperity of the earlier reigns could not be revived.

The sudden arrival of the catastrophe had awakened only a relatively small group from their dreams of a perfect and orderly society. Many others continued to indulge themselves in wine and song while others strained their literary efforts in praise of the reigning dynasty. For those who had stopped dreaming, however, the universe had acquired an appearance of seriousness and their own philosophies of life had become profoundly realistic. This difference in response was naturally traceable to differences in personal temperament. Even a casual look at new literary trends after the rebellion, however, would convince us that they were, by and large, the products of a completely changed age. In Tu Fu's own words:

I Recall (II)

I remember that in the glorious decades, a quarter of a century ago,
Even a small district might contain ten thousand households,
And the glutinous rice was fat and the ordinary rice white,
And how they filled up the granaries both public and private!
No panthers or tigers paced the roads of the Empire;
Distant travelers never worried whether the day was lucky or not.
The fine fabrics of Ch'i and Lu could be seen on long lines of merchants' carts;
Men plowed the fields; women tended the silk worms; all were happy at work.
Our brilliant emperor stayed in his palace to enjoy good music,
While the whole world was a solid friendship.
Then, for over a century, people had no reports of calamities;
They had the best law and practiced the best etiquette.
Who ever heard of a roll of silk priced at ten thousand coins,
Or of people abandoning their farms for bloodshed?

(William Hung's translation)

Changes in literature thus reflect the transition to a new age. Literature of the latter half of the eighth century was cast in an entirely different mold from that of its predecessor. This is most clearly seen in the seriousness of attitude and the profundity of vision of the writers. Literature was no longer a pastime or a ladder to the imperial official hierarchy. Moreover, it was no longer a form of entertainment supplying the court musicians with lyrics for the amusement of the aristocracy. Nor did it consist in ventures into the unreal by imagining the toilsome life of military service, or by projecting pictures of an earthly paradise of the immortals. Leaders in literature now began to face life seriously—not imaginary life but real life—the suffering of the masses, problems of social change, challenges of state and government, and the realistic aspirations and fears of actual living.

Traditional historians of T'ang literature have failed to stress this sudden change on the Chinese scene and the incongruities of the reigns of K'ai Yüan and T'ien Pao when they refer to the middle decades of the eighth century as an indivisible unit. Actually the line of division made by the rebellion of 755 cut deep into the century. What had preceded it was a literature singing praises to peace and prosperity with romantic contents creating man-made scenes, whereas what followed it was a literature saturated with pain and suffering reflecting a disintegrating society—a literature deeply characterized by an all-pervasive realism. This new age was no longer the age of lighthearted songs sung to the accompaniment of music. What had been known as *yüeh fu*, songs written in imitation of the ones sung by the Music Bureau, had done its work as an effective training program in inducing the writers to attempt liberation in technique and in spirit. Instead of subjecting themselves to further discipline, the new poets were now eager to create, hence, we have what was publicly heralded as "the new *yüeh fu*"—a kind of new poetry to demonstrate the new life under a new age.

The pioneer, and the greatest representative of this new age was Tu Fu, with many new allies and followers to extend and magnify the new literary movement in the latter half of the eighth and the first half of the ninth centuries. Thus a most brilliant period in the history of Chinese literature was created.

We might be justified in saying that Chinese literature of the seventh century was the literature of childhood in which poetry consisted of games and play of a high order. At the imperial court and in the mansions of the aristocrats occasional poetry played even a positively inferior role. The literature of the K'ai Yüan and T'ien Pao reigns was only a literature of adolescence. In spite of the stylistic liberation, the contents of literature were still on the whole shallow and superficial, consisting largely only of the singing of heavy drinkers and self-appointed hermits. These decades might be justifiably labeled as *shêng T'ang* or the high tide of T'ang with reference to peace and prosperity in the political and social scene. From the vantage point of literature, however, the period of greatest glory came later and it was not until after the rebellion that full maturity in literature was attained. From the middle years of Tu Fu to the death of Po Chü-yi in 846, both prose and poetry embarked upon the highway of realism, returning from the romantic celestial realms to the world of man.

Tu Fu (712-770), also known by the courtesy name, Tzŭ-mei, was a native of the county of Hsiangyang in present-day Honan Province. His grandfather, Tu Shên-yen, was a famous writer in the latter part of the seventh century. In his youth, Tu Fu had to face greatly reduced family resources and was compelled to undertake extensive travels along the China coast, which travels widened his intellectual horizons and made a lasting impression on his plastic young mind as he recalled later in a poem addressed to Wei Tsi:

When I was still in my youth, I was a candidate for the imperial examinations.
With thousands of volumes worn by reading,
Whenever I took a pen, my thoughts were inspired.
My prose was thought to rival Yang Hsiung's,
My poetry was regarded as approaching that of Ts'ao Chih.
Even the great Li Yung wanted to make my acquaintance,
And the brilliant Wang Han wished to lodge near me.
I thought, of course, I was extraordinary,
And should immediately climb to an important position,
To help my sovereign to succeed better than even the best,
And to restore the purity of culture and civilization.

But all these hopes were sadly shattered.
I gleaned to live in an unwilling hermitage.
Now for more than three years on a donkey's back,
I have been fed on the spring air of the flowery capital.
Mornings, I knock on the doors of rich youth,
Evenings, I follow in the dust of the fast horses.
Left-over wine and the roast that is cold
I swallow together with my pride and my tears.
In answer to His Majesty's recent command,
I leaped in the hope of vindication.
But I was a bird dropped from the blue sky with folded wings;
I was a carp thrown upon a reef and not allowed to swim.

Though I hardly deserve your generosity,
I do appreciate your genuine kindness;
And I know that frequently among your associates,
You have quoted good and fresh lines of mine.
One moment, I rejoice in your recent promotion,
The next, I detest my own poverty.
I know I should not have allowed the heart to be restless;
But how am I to give rest to my weary feet?
Now I am about to go eastward toward the sea;
And that means I shall quit Ching-chao in the west.

I do still love the look of these Southern Mountains,
Many a time I shall remind myself of the clear Wei.
A grateful heart will find it hard not to remember a simple meal;
And still harder to forget a great statesman.
But when the white seagull disappears in the vast expanse,
Who will be able to tame him from afar?

(William Hung's translation)

At thirty-eight he submitted three *fu* compositions on the three imperial ceremonies after the reception of which he was offered an official post which he declined in preference for another minor position. Despite his humble circumstances, he befriended other poor poets like Chêng Ch'ien who were all concerned with the degenerating political and social situation. It was during these years that he wrote his poems of satire such as "The Ballad of the Beauties" and "The Ballad of the War Chariots." That he long remained in obscurity was probably a great blessing in disguise, for in his humble circumstances of riding donkeyback for thirty years he not only watched at close range but also actually participated in the deprivations of the masses. Hence, he was able to discover the latent dangers with which the T'ang Empire was faced before the actual volcanic eruptions, although in conformity with the taste of the time, he also was a member of the fraternity of the drinking poets. Even then, however, in his drinking songs, people heard his voice of sorrow:

> We only feel in our elated singing there are gods and spirits
> Without realizing starvation might lead to the filling of ditches.

At the end of the reign of T'ien Pao (755) he traveled to a distant county, Fênghsien, to see his wife and family:

> On entering the door I heard wailing—
> Our younger son had died of starvation.

It was in sorrowful circumstances like this that he sharpened his powers of observation and widened his care of the family into a grave concern for the state. Pouring out his mind without reservation he wrote a long poem of a hundred lines entitled, "On My Way from the Capital to Fênghsien County"—a poem in which he frankly unfolded the gloomy picture of the hard facts of life below the veneer of the so-called K'ai Yüan and T'ien Pao prosperity. Even before the ink of this poem had dried, general disorder accompanying the great rebellion had reached the state of absolute despair. Toward the end of the year Loyang had fallen. By the following summer in 756 the strategic pass of T'ungkuan was captured by the rebels. The emperor had no sooner left Ch'angan in great haste than the capital itself capitulated. A month later, a crown prince ascended the throne in Lingwu County to be known to posterity as Emperor Su Tsung. After resettling his family in a more secure place, the poet hurried to the emergency capital but was kidnapped on his way so that he did not arrive at Fêng-hsiang until the following year. Thenceforth, he busied himself partly by following the court in flight until it was back at Ch'angan, and partly by filling appointments away from the capital. He visited Loyang in ruins in 758 where he stayed for a while and wrote numerous poems—some strongly emotional—recording historic facts of the age.

After relocating himself in county after county as a result of rapid official transfers, he seemed to have been suspended by his superiors, which fact aggravated his problems of poverty even more. In 760 he traveled southward from Shensi Province in the north to present-day Szechuan Province where he lived in Chengtu from 760 to 765. It was during this short period of comparative rest that his talents were appreciated by the military commissioner, Yen Wu, who recommended Tu Fu's appointment as his staff adviser with the accompanying rank of counselor of the department of works, a position which gave rise to a popular appelation by which the poet is frequently identified—Tu Kungpu or Tu of the Ministry of Public Works. From 765 to 770 he again found himself busy with constant relocation in different parts of Szechuan Province and along the Yangtze River eastward to the present-day Honan Province, where he died in Hêngchow at the age of 58.

Tu Fu's poetry shows three stages of development and progress in chronological order: (1) poems written before the great rebellion, (2) poems written during the rebellion and its aftermath, and (3) poems written toward the end of his life after his relocation in Chengtu.

Tu Fu's life in the first period was that of "donkeyback riding for thirty years." Even after his elevation to an official post following his submission of the three *fu* compositions, his poverty seemed to have persisted. But in spite of his poverty he always retained his bountiful humor, the kind of humor which was ingrained in him and was never consciously or artificially cultivated. Frequently, while the themes of his poetry were serious in the extreme, a few lines would precariously border on the pattern of limericks.

While he was facing poverty while holding a lowly position in Ch'angan, his most intimate friend was Chêng Ch'ien, a doctor in the Kuang-wên Kuan, or the Hall of Liberal Arts. Between the two of them there were frequent exchanges of verses written in mutual friendly ridicule, of which the following is an example:

> The Professor arrives at the college;
> He ties his horse before the steps of the hall.
> When drunk, he mounts his horse to leave,
> Leaving his superior officers to curse after him.
> Though he has had literary fame for thirty years,
> He is still too poor to provide cushions for visitors.
> It is good that there is Dean Su Yü
> From whom he can beg money for wine.

(William Hung's translation)

Even when he was describing his own impoverishment he never failed to see the humorous side of poverty. In the group of three poems entitled "Sighs During an Autumn Rain," he wrote:

> During the downpour all herbs are rotting in the autumn. . . .
> The blooming flowers are like numberless golden coins.

During this first period of his literary activity he was in the prime of manhood and extremely eager to make his contributions to society. In moments of complete frustration he would express feelings of impatience with the lack of justice and would consider giving up everything to become a hermit.

> Don't you see that the falcon on the perch once sated would fly and soar?
> How could it become a hall swallow carrying tidbits to increase the warmth
>   of the influential?
> A man of the wilderness unhampered and uncaged who knows of no blushing
>   mood
> How can he prolong his company among dukes and princes?
> Though I have never tried the diet of jade in a container
> Let me enter the Blue Field Mountains tomorrow.

The allusion to the jade diet was to Li Yu of the Later Wei Dynasty, who was said to have pulverized seventy pieces of jade for his daily diet to ensure physical immortality. The best jade was said to have come from the Blue Field Mountains. That was why Tu Fu was eager to go there for his experiment. Although he had no cooked rice, he would think of living on jade. This was a typical example of how Tu Fu would suggest disapproval of hermitage and at the same time distill from it any possible fun. It is this spirit of positivism that distinguished him from his eminent friend, Li Po.

In those days of apparent peace and prosperity, the pride of the world was the powerful Yang family. The main pillar of the Yang house was the beautiful Yang Yühuan, the imperial consort elevated to the position of *kuei-fei,* or noble consort. Her cousin, Yang Kuo-chung, had been made prime minister and her two sisters had been ennobled the Princess of Kuo and the Princess of Ch'in. It was the sparkling brilliance of these girls of the Yang family which supplied Tu Fu with the theme of his "Li-jên Hsing" or "The Ballad of the Beauties."

There is a freshness in the air this Third of Third, a spring festival day.
I see by the Meandering River of Ch'ang-an many fair women
With distant looks but frequent smiles, sweet and real.
With delicacy of complexion and symmetry of form,
They appear in silken dresses embroidered with golden peacocks
Or silvery unicorns, dazzling in the sunshine of late spring.
What do they wear on their heads?
Kingfisher head-dresses with jade-leaves over the temples.
What do you see on their backs?
Pearl-trimmed capes cut perfectly to fit.
You can spot the Imperial relatives among those rainbow-screens,
Among them the Lady of Kuo and the Lady of Ch'in.
The purple steak of dromedary hump, broiled in a shining pan,
The white meat of raw fish served on crystal plates,
Are not inviting enough to the satiated palate.
All that is cut with fancy and prepared with care is left untouched.
Palace messengers come on light steeds, galloping without dust,
Continuously bringing the rarest delicacies from His Majesty's kitchens.
Strings and pipes now accompany the feasting with music, weird enough
To move ghosts—not to mention the hoard of guests and retainers, each of
  commanding importance.
You see the last comer, who approaches leisurely on his horse,
Dismounts near the screens, and steps on the flowery carpet.
Willow catkins drop like snow to confuse the white frogbit;
A blue bird flies away with a pink kerchief in its beak.
The Prime Minister is so powerful, his mere touch will scorch.
Approach not, lest you anger him.

(William Hung's translation)

In satirizing the excessive power of the imperial relatives, the poet clearly maintained large measures of artistic restraint. He could have but did not say more. In spite of the semblance of peace and prosperity latent troubles all along the frontier were already obvious. Disturbances of a political as well as a military nature were being created by the Khitan, Hsi, and Turkic tribes in the north and by the Turfans in the west, each ravaging and plundering frontier towns, periodically necessitating many a punitive expedition. For the year 751 a major military defeat of the Chinese imperial forces was registered in their attempt to quell a rebellion of barbarian tribes in Yünnan. The fatalities involved had mounted to sixty thousand. When imperial rescripts were issued to the citizens of the two metropolitan districts and to Honan and Hopei for volunteers for rebuilding the expeditionary force, popular reaction was completely negative. Consequently the prime minister, Yang Kuo-chung, instructed the agencies of the imperial censorate to resort to pressure and violence in obtaining recruits, and injustices and corruption became widespread. The resentment of the common people which Tu Fu had witnessed was well expressed in his "Ballad of the War Chariot." When we compare this poem with Li Po's "Fighting South of the City" we see clearly that Li Po's was an imitation of ancient ballads and Tu Fu's poem was an indictment of current politics. Indictments as bold and unadorned as this were something new since the age of the *Book of Songs*. In this light we might say that Tu Fu was a founder of a new tradition. Even some of the folk songs and literary ballads descriptive of the destructiveness of war do not measure up to the directness and clarity that Tu Fu had exhibited in accusing the government and even the emperor of misrule:

From border areas blood is flowing to form sealets
And yet Emperor Wu ["my emperor," according to another version] has not
　　suspended his plans of extending the frontier.

This mention of Emperor Wu of the Han Dynasty to dull the edges of criticism against the reigning T'ang emperor did not carry boldness to the extreme. In "The Ballad of the Beauties" the Princesses of Kuo and Ch'in were forthrightly mentioned by name.

Tu Fu's most unreserved criticism of contemporary political and social corruption was expressed in an even greater poem, the poem in which he described his travels from the capital to Fênghsien County. This poem, formerly subjected to misdating and misinterpretation, was really not written before the eruption of the An Lu-shan rebellion. Although, when this poem was written, the T'ang emperor, Hsüan-tsung, and his imperial consort, Yang Kuei-fei, were wintering in comfort and luxury in the Hua Ch'ing Palace, a mountain resort in Li Shan away from the capital, the T'ang empire was far from being the utopian society that some of the court circles thought it was. Tu Fu, on arriving home, had heard of the tragic news of his youngest son's starvation. His sense of deep personal bereavement immediately reminded him of the many injustices to which he had been subjected and the social iniquities which he had seen with his own eyes. It had also reminded him of the excessive luxury and unjustifiable extravagance he had witnessed at the winter capital through which he had traveled on his trip home. Further restraint being now beyond him, he gave full expression to his feelings in this unprecedented indictment in the form of a long narrative entitled, "On My Way to Fênghsien County."

The war drums were soon sounded in Yüyang, the center of the An Lu-shan rebellion, and Tu Fu was to enter his second period of literary production which ended with his relocation in Szechuan in 765. In this period of great confusion and reversal of the scales of value, Tu Fu's powers of observation became keener, his art more realistic, his views more profound, and the vistas opened up in his poetry more comprehensive and humane. In this regard he was a forerunner of the poet with a social conscience.

When he was marooned in Ch'angan he saw the different facets of the tragedy and plight of the imperial capital. These impressions were organized and recorded in two of his most famous poems. One was the "Lament of the River Bank" ("Ai Chiang-t'ou") and the other was "Lamenting of the Imperial Heir" ("Ai Wâng-sun"). The first was a poem of twenty lines in which the poet described the Ch'üchiang, or the Winding River which skirted the city of Ch'angan. The second presented the sole remnant of the imperial family as an imaginary literary vehicle for the presentation in dialogue form of all the destruction and cruelty brought upon the imperial clan. By elaborating one episode in the life of an individual, the poet succeeded in recreating the general atmosphere surrounding the tragic fate of an imperial clan facing extinction. This technique of using a narrow canvas in suggesting the contents of a whole panorama was a technique begun by the writers of the ancient ballads but not brought to perfection until it was touched by the genius of Tu Fu. His concentration on one episode and, through that episode, his ability to create a well-rounded but unique impression, furnished the most effective means to arouse an intense emotional response on the part of his readers. This technique was not only consistently utilized by Tu Fu himself in his later narrative poems but also adopted by such leading poets of later generations as Po Chü-i (also Po Chü-yi) and Chang Chih in similar compositions. Thus was formed the common technique for the so-called New Lyrical Ballads or hsin yüeh-fu. Upon Tu Fu's arrival at the emergency capital of Fênghsiang in 756, he had the written permission of the new emperor to go on a trip to Fuchou (in present-day Szechuan Province) to visit with his family. The experiences of this trip were woven into a long poem entitled "Pei Chêng" or "Northward Travels." This poem was apparently an artistic effort beloved by the poet. The artistic attainment of this poem, however, was not as great as the labors that the poet had put into it. On the other hand, in the midst of many stretches which are prosaic descriptions in verse, the poem sparkles with a rare sense of humor and insight into human nature which contrast sharply with and palliate the innate feeling of tragedy.

The Trip North
[Excerpt]

On top of a slope I gaze at the highlands of Fuchou,
At mountain peaks and deep valleys winding in and out.
I hurry on to the bank of the river,
My servant is still at the edge of the woods.
Strange owls hoot among the brown leaves of mulberry trees,
Field mice peep from scattered holes.
At midnight we pass a battlefield
Where the cold moon shines on the white bones.
I wonder why an army of a million men at T'ung-kuan
Should suddenly be scattered in the past,
Why half the inhabitants this side of the Yellow River
Should perish as a result.

Even I had the experience of falling into the Tatar dust;
And now I return with my hair completely white.
More than one year it took me to reach the thatched hut again—
To find my wife in clothes with a hundred patches.
Her cries when she saw me wailed like a sharp wind through the pines;
Her subdued sobs were like a gurgling brook.
The boy that has been the jewel of my life,
Wears a face paler than snow.
He turned his back to me and wept;
I saw that his feet were dirty and without shoes or socks.

Before my couch my two little daughters stand
In patched robes that barely cover their knees.
The waves of the ocean do not match
On the embroidered pieces cut from an old dress.
The sea monster and the purple phoenix
Are inverted on the short skirts.
Who can blame an old man for feeling ill at heart?
Nausea confines me for several days in bed.
Of course, I have some cloth in my bag
That may be used to spare my family from the cold.
There are also some cosmetics in little packages;
And the bedding may be taken out of the luggage.
Once more my poor wife's face is glowing;
The silly girls are trying to dress their own hair.
Imitating their mother, they will play with anything;
They smear their hands in the jars of the morning make-up.

In a minute, powder and rouge color their cheeks.
And the eyebrows are painted askew and too broad.
To return alive and be with these children
Enables me to forget the hunger and the thirst.
They shower me with questions, they pull my beard;
Who has the heart to make them stop?
When I recall my weary days among the rebels,
All this noisy pestering I joyfully accept.

(William Hung's translation)

This passage is outstanding because it illustrates how concrete the poet was in presenting his imagery and how under circumstances of absolute distress, Tu Fu, the man, could well afford to joke with tiny boys and girls. This sense of humor, which was intimately a part of his personality, and a philosophy of living which he had cherished ever since his boyhood days, was also visible in his other poems written during this time. While his long poem, "Northward Travels," especially in its humorous elements, reminds us of the poetry of Tso Ssŭ; Tu Fu's shorter poems of this period, especially the three poems entitled, "Chiang Ts'un," or "Chiang Village," resemble the poems of T'ao Yüan-ming. Both T'ao and Tu were amply fortified by their appreciation of the humorous in adverse circumstances. Thus fortified, even hunger and penury would not lead to loss of mind, on one hand, and degeneracy, on the other.

His trip to Loyang and his observations of the ruins and destitution there inspired him to write numerous narrative poems in which were recorded the different facets of the scars of warfare. Among these masterly poems on social problems, which have been collectively labeled *New Lyrical Ballads*, probably the most admired was "The Sheriff of Shih-hao Village." It was a short narrative poem describing how a sheriff was recruiting able-bodied men in a small community. He came to one family where an old man had made his escape by climbing over the yard wall and the aged woman left behind to plead her case with the sheriff.

In the evening, I found a lodging place at Shih-hao Village.
A recruiting officer came to take men at night.
My old host scaled the wall and fled;
His old wife went to answer the gate.
The officer was raging;
The old woman cried bitterly.
I listened to what she said:
"My three sons went to the camp at Yeh;
A letter came from one of the boys,
Telling of the death of his two brothers in battle.

The dead ones are forever gone.
How long can the living one last?
There are no more men now in the household
Except a suckling grandson.
His mother has stayed here because of the son—
She hasn't a whole skirt to put on.
Though I am an old woman and have not much strength,
I will go with you, officer, this very night.
Let me answer the urgent call from Ho-yang;
I can at least cook meals for our men."
Voices of talking ceased late in the night,
I seemed to hear only subdued sobbing.
At dawn, I resumed my journey;
Only the old man waved farewell.

                         (William Hung's translation)

The literary technique of this poem was unique and surprising. When a draft officer resorting to compulsion decided to kidnap an aging grandmother, the other aspects of social and political injustice may well be imagined.

In 759 Tu Fu was dismissed from office. Wandering all the way to far-away Szechuan in his forty-eighth year, Tu Fu began to realize what official life was like and where he, as an individual, stood in a withering society. In his twenty poems written during his sojourn at Chinchow, he seemed to feel a keen disappointment in current politics. Thus he wrote:

> Emperor Yao of the T'ang Dynasty was really a sage.
> How can a rustic oldster claim to know anything?

Again, his disappointment was expressed in another poem entitled "Hsi Ping Ma," or "Purging of the Woes of War." In this he referred to those who climb on the bandwagon of the national heroes; of how everybody had become princes and dukes; of how according to dynastic flatterers all tiny kingdoms outside of China were submitting tributes, thus reiterating his disappointment with the young emperor whom the poet estimated to be a mediocre ruler. Thenceforth, he made up his mind that there was not much he could do and that he should not entertain any further hope of "elevating the emperor above Yao and Shun." From that time on—especially after his arrival in Szechuan—he finally resolved to live the life of a poet for the rest of his life.

In the third period of his literary production, his life was a little more composed, although as yet not entirely free from extreme poverty. Nonetheless, he had a little more rest and a little more leisure compared with his constant flight in the previous period. The heart of the T'ang Empire was still exposed to a whole series of emergencies. The An Lu-shan rebellion was prolonged by a new rebellion led by another insubordinate semi-Chinese general, Shih Ssŭ-ming; the Turfans, dissatisfied with their share of the war booty, pressed their invasion to the wall of the capital; and the central government was dropping daily in prestige and real power, making it possible for the different war lords stationed in the frontier regions to become so many petty kings. China was destined to experience another period of political disintegration and division. Realizing what history had decreed for the future, Tu Fu confirmed his belief that what was open to him was nothing more than the life of a poor but dedicated poet. As before, he had no liking for reclusion and so he did not seek to leave the world, seeking only contentment and regularity in life as he found it. Hence, his poems written in this third period were ones descriptive of the simple life. The echoes of war and devastation were still audible and political dependency was still attended with hardships but he was never deprived of his ability to elicit smiles and poetry from adverse circumstances. With the ripening of his age, his verse forms became absolutely mature. His short poems of this age were the natural overflow of his personality recorded at random without adornment and without conscious artistry but all palpitating with poetic flavor. They were continuations of the tradition of T'ao Yüan-ming and vanguards of the poetry of the Sung Dynasty. What he was experiencing during this stage was real rustic life and not the life of self-styled farm hermits of the earlier part of the T'ang Dynasty. As a result, his poetry was real poetry dedicated to the appreciation of nature.

The Autumn Gale Tears Off My Thatched Roof

The madly howling wind of a matured autumn in September
Has rolled off the three layers of thatch on my roof.
Most of the stalks flew across the river and dropped along the bank.
Some are caught and entangled in the treetops;
Others tumbled along the ground until they sank into the hollows.
The boys of the southern village take advantage of my age and infirmity
To steal my property before my eyes,
To carry openly armfuls of thatch into the bamboo grove;
I shout, I protest until my mouth is dry and my lips are parched;
Then I return to the house, I lean on my staff, and I sigh.

Soon, the wind subsides, and the clouds, ink-black,
Cover the autumn sky to hasten the dark night.
The cotton quilt after many years' use is as cold as an iron sheet

And is torn inside because our spoiled children sleep restlessly and kick their feet.
The roof leaks over the bed, and there is no dry spot.
The streaming rain streams like flax fibers without a break.
Since the rebellion, I have lost much sleep;
Now I wish quick end to such a long and drenching night.
Would it be possible to build a huge house with many millions of rooms
To give shelter to the poor scholars of the whole world, who should all be happy
Even in a rainstorm; for the house should be as unshakable as a mountain?
Oh, if I could only see this house suddenly appear before my eyes.
Let my hut be smashed, let me die alone in exposure and I shall die content.

(William Hung's translation)

In the above poem we can see that Tu Fu, while lamenting the fate that had befallen the various impoverished scholars of the empire, could still see the humorous side of poverty. In this we see most clearly Tu Fu's indebtedness to the humorous treatment of the tragic phases of life so common in folk songs—a type of literature which he had never despised. In many of the titles to his poems he indicated clearly his intention of writing humorous verse. Even when he was writing long historical poems of a serious nature like "Pei Chêng," "Northward Travels," there are injections of lines and phrases that revealed the poet's fondness of the humorous and jocular.

This lighthearted side of Tu Fu's poetic temperament did not preclude his frequent manifestations of seriousness in life and his deep-seated concern with and sorrow for his age. As a poet, however, he did not put on any air of dressed-up solemnity or venture to be purely didactic. Just as he could laugh heartily, his occasional efforts to swallow his own sorrows were all the more touching. The sadness he felt in the evening of his life is most clearly revealed in the poems in which he reminisced about incidents and feelings of his younger days.

Although he never succeeded in detaching himself completely from the many basic difficulties threatening the reigning dynasty and the T'ang Empire as a whole, he was, after all, living the life of a retired scholar, spending his leisure on a farm. His daily schedule consisted in planting vegetables and picking mushrooms. While on one hand he lamented that he would fail to sleep at night on account of his inability to stop wars and to rectify the universe, he could in the daytime find much that was poetic in the chores of daily living. These little discoveries of what was meaningful and pleasant he recorded in his many "little poems." These poems, recording small episodes of farm life, small reactions and impressions, were patterned into a verse form that was known as the *chüeh chü,* consisting of four

lines composed of seven or five syllables. This verse form was not
subjected to the limitations of tonal sequence or elaborate rhetoric.
Externally it had a good deal in common with the quatrains of the
yüeh fu type which Li Po had written with the greatest dexterity
and which were originally intended to be sung to music. In spirit
it was an entirely different vehicle completely detached from musical accompaniment and, therefore, peculiarly adapted to language
of the common people. Tu Fu was able to breathe so much new life
into this convenient verse form that many major poets of the following Sung Dynasty continued to cherish this *chüeh chü* form.

The following are some interesting examples of Tu Fu's "impressionistic" little poems:

The river and the hills are beautiful in the lingering sunlight;
The flowers and the herbs are fragrant in the spring wind.
The swallows are flying with soft mud in their beaks,
While the ducks still slumber on the warm sandy beach.

The gulls look whiter against the blue river,
And the flowers glow against the green of the hills.
This spring too will soon be gone:
In which year will occur the days of my homecoming?

Light and dark compete to shorten the day toward the close of the year.
Snow has stopped, and we have a clear cold night in this remote corner of
    the world.
The drums and bugles of the fifth watch before dawn sound especially im-
    passioned,
While the stars in the Heavenly River above the Three Gorges are twinkling.

Willow catkins, sprinkling the road, spread a white carpet.
Lotus leaves, dotting the stream, form a string of coins.
A small pheasant hides from view among the bamboo sprouts,
While a few tiny ducklings sleep by their mother on the sand.

In Madame Huang's garden, the flowers crowd out the walks;
Thousands upon thousands are pressing the branches low.
Playful butterflies now and again stay to dance among them,
And orioles accompany them with appropriate notes.

Short poems, it should be noted, were no innovation. In many of
the short poems—actually folk songs of the third century—we find
many similar records in which simple incidents and feelings were
caught and registered. All the so-called "little songs" are attempts
to seize fragments from nature or from human life and reveal their
quintessence. This mood and this technique made a special appeal
to Tu Fu in his old age and in these little gems we see the dexterity

of his mature hands in oning the short, crisp lines until they were artlessly natural an unexpectedly stunning. He would accuse the spring wind of iling into his garden without permission and of breaking the bran of his flowers. He would poke fun at his neighbor's willow tre having flirted with the spring wind and losing its longest bray way of penalty. He would recognize the cormorant on the sameach as an old acquaintance and urge the latter to visit him a hed times each day. These little poems, which appear to be most ial and effortless, were really the crystallizations of a long-pracl artistry.

We must now examine Tu's compositions in the form for which he has been most famous. ; verse form, which had been perfected in the early half of the ng Dynasty, is known in Chinese as *lü shih,* or regulation poetin its normal form, a poem of this type consists of eight lines withd-rhymes at the end of the first, second, fourth, sixth, and thst line. Regulation further stipulates that the two pairs of the mle lines should contain couplets which are balanced in structure.n additional requirement is the tonal sequence prearranged for ch line based on the classification of tones into two main categos known as the even and the inflected. Despite these imposing regtions a verse writer trained in the discipline would find it relatiy easy, instead of hopelessly difficult, to observe all the regulatis and yet find enough room for free manipulation. A verse formvented to test the ingenuity of the verse writer by harassing hi at every turn, it was a form based on gymnastics not too dissimilto other literary games or even non-literary games, such as chesand checkers, in which rules must be observed. As a result, this rse form was most fitted for use in competitive literary examinaon and for occasional poetry required by Chinese popular usage sth as poems expected to be written in welcoming friends or sendinthem off on a trip. Literary historians have noticed that Tu Fu wro profusely in this form in his old age. According to his own confeson these poems were attempted as a means of cultivating his spiritual nature by which he probably meant that he felt attracted by this verse form to see how he could successfully transcend the discipline called for. The very fact that he enthusiastically subscribed to the artificialities of regulation poetry lent considerably dignity to this verse form and, therefore, effectively prolonged its life span to the twentieth century.

Tu Fu's regulation poems at their best are unsurpassed because in his hands rules and regulations ceased to be threatening pitfalls and served as so many springboards to spontaneity and naturalness. Thus Tu Fu could manage to write in the manner of actual everyday speech securing freedom in bondagl spontaneity in discipline, making his readers feel as if there been no rules for him to observe. A good example is the one ed "Facing an Accumulated Desk on a Hot Day in Early Autum

On the sixth of the seventh mooneat is unbearable.
Facing my meal, I find it hard ev rush it through.
I am worried scorpions will spreamselves after nightfall,
And the swarming of flies with thly turn of autumn.
Tightening the sash makes you wo yell
And the piling of papers seems to? no end.
To my south I see a green pine sjing a narrow gorge,
And I wish I could go barefooted tread on ice.

Observance of the rules in this manrs tantamount to a breakage of all the rules of verse.

This technique of transcending thiles, of following the grammar of natural speech in writing regtion poetry, paved the way for one of the major schools of poen the succeeding Sung Dynasty. In Tu Fu's hands all the possibies of observing and breaking of rules had been exhausted. In this isee the consummation of his art of poetry.

Our discussion of T'ang poetry wld not be complete without a passing mention of the women poe

Women poets had cropped up ar distinguished themselves in nearly all the previous dynasties. Altugh there had been attempts made to discourage higher educatiofor women and to block out a special curriculum for them in whh domestic duties and ethics were emphasized, daughters of distiruished scholarly families had acquired from time to time eruditionnd developed creative talents by virtue of family association. Besid; this, the voices of unlettered but naturally gifted women singers wre registered in the collections of folk songs and popular ballads. Noetheless, women in China until very recent times were disfavored by ultural conventions as in other parts of the world.

T'ang China, however, was an exception to the rule in more ways than one. In the first place, the art of versification was singled out by the successive emperors as the foremost mode of artistic creation and, hence, became the vehicle for social and political advancement. As a result, nearly all educated people in China tried their hand at the writing of poetry. T'ang poetry, especially that portion which was written in the so-called newer styles, was all set to music and actually sung on diverse occasions. Professional singers, most of them young women, thus maintained frequent social contact with the major poets and many of them succeeded in expressing their emotions and narrating their experiences in verse form in simple but attractive language.

In the second place, many of the empresses of the T'ang Dynasty were enthusiastic patrons of literature, especially Empress Wu, who declared herself "emperor," and Empress Wei, who after she became empress dowager had a direct hand in the promotion of verse writing both at court among the ministers and in the Forbidden City among the court ladies. Although the poems now attributed to these two empresses were probably written by proxy, the example they set must have exerted a profound and extensive influence. Thus it was recorded that in the reign of K'ai Yüan (713-741), the golden period of T'ang poetry, the emperor decreed a special award of padded garments to the officers of the frontier garrisons. These were all made by court ladies. A certain cadet in the frontier garrison discovered in his package of a padded robe, a slip of paper on which was written the following poem:

> You warrior on the sandy fields
> In bitter cold please sleep well.
> With my hand I make your warrior's robe,
> How am I to know on whose side it will fall?
> Purposely I increase the stitches
> And for good measure I add a little more cotton.
> This life will soon be over
> May we be united in the next life span.

When the soldier submitted the poem to his general, the general returned it to the imperial court, whereupon Emperor Ming searched through the six harems with the instruction that the composer should not hide her identity, since she would not be punished. One court lady confessed, saying her error would merit ten thousand deaths. His majesty was greatly moved and decided to give her in marriage to the recipient of the poem, saying, "I will materialize your union in this life."

There was another tradition of the T'ang Dynasty which illustrates the large number of talented women in the Forbidden Palace and their pent-up emotions resulting from their life of segregation from the outside world: the practice of their writing poems on red leaves and dispatching these lyrical messages onto the streams which flowed out to the larger world by way of the imperial moats. No wonder many of the aspirants to literary honors in Ch'angan would frequently take strolls along the imperial moats in late autumn where the leaves would turn red and the sequestered poetesses would become exceptionally emotional. There are at least three cases recorded in which poets and poetesses were happily united as a result of special imperial grace by these propitious red leaves.

In the third place, the T'ang Dynasty was one which would provide the most favorable climate and environment to the birth of women poets. Ch'angan was without doubt not only the most brilliant cultural center of the whole world but also the most liberal melting pot of the diverse cultural streams from all directions. Entertainments and games of all conceivable origins were merged in Ch'angan, the eternal city of the east, and were enjoyed alike by both women and men. There was no puritanism of the Neo-Confucian type such as we find in China from the late twelfth century on, so that social mixing of men and women was more liberal in China than elsewhere, Europe included, and the cult of the dutiful daughter and the completely domesticated wife was no universal formula. No privileges that men enjoyed were deliberately denied to women. Since polo had become a game in which T'ang women took their greatest delight, versification could not be construed as a masculine monopoly. As men had their literary clubs, so women could enjoy considerable intellectual and artistic companionship in the popular establishment of Taoist sorority houses (at other times misinterpreted as nunneries). The members of these sororities, usually known as women Taoists or *nü kuan* (literally "hatted women"), were often divorcees of distinguished poets and painters who claimed careers in their own right, although quite a number of them were fairly lax in their individual lives.

Among women poets of T'ang times, two deserve special mention. Yü Hsüan-chi (flourished 850-870), an extremely gifted girl, began her literary life as a concubine to a poet-official, Li Yi. As she grew older she failed to retain the attention of her husband and decided to become a *nü küan*. Hence she sang principally of her disappointments in life.

> As compared with a devoted man
> The getting of a priceless jewel is easy.
> On my pillow I let my tears stream
> And among flowers I feel my heart break silently.

Although her volume of poems is slender, it is all readable. But she did not live long. She killed a tender maidservant accidentally and had to pay for the act with her own life.

Even more celebrated than Yü Hsüan-chi was Hsüeh T'ao (flourished *circa* 780-810). A gifted girl on an impoverished Ch'angan family, she early became a professional singer. With the spread of her reputation, she toured one province after another, winding up eventually in present-day Szechuan where she became a *nü kuan* in a "hermitage" near a stream known as Flower-Washed Stream. She would write her poems on her own stationery over fir flowers painted on it in subdued colors. This stationery started an artistic tradition in China kept to this day and greatly prized in her own time. Once during a penalty tour to the frontier regions in the northwest, she sent the following poem to one of her patrons:

> I have heard life in the frontier is bitter,
> I didn't realize it until I arrived here.
> And I feel ashamed to sing my own songs
> To boys of this rugged plateau land.

Among poets of her own age, Hsüeh T'ao maintained frequent literary contacts and exchanges of poems with Po Chü-yi and Yüan Chên. From them she must have learned many lessons of poetic art. Thus to a friend whom she did not name she sent the following:

> Among the reeds in this water country
> There is frost at night.
> The moon is cold, the mountains are colorful,
> And they share their green.
> Who says the separation of a thousand miles
> Begins only tonight?
> My dream of separation is long, long
> Like the great wall.

In the collected anthology of T'ang poetry there are recorded poems written by women whose station and reputation did not even measure up to the level of Hsüeh T'ao. These were professional singers. Their poems all have a directness of expression that remind us of the simplicity of folk songs. These singers had no face to save, no social position to defend, and no need to write deviously. Nonetheless, many of them led highly moral lives. For example, the famous Hsü Chou (her professional name was Kuan P'an-p'an) had been promised by one of her patrons, a high official, Minister Chang, that he would immediately come back to marry her. For ten years she waited with devotion and patience in her own Yentzu Lou, the Swallow Lodge, finally dying of a broken heart.

The Pei Wêng Cemetery locks its sorrowful smoke in rows of firs and cypresses.
In a storied Yengtzu [swallows] tower, now deserted, I long listlessly.
My dancing sword and slippers are now buried
And the music of my singing is scattered.
The fragrance in my red sleeve has disappeared now for ten years.

CHAPTER 14

The Dawn of Chinese Fiction

THE rise of prose fiction in China was surprisingly late and slow. Pre-eminently practical though the ancient Chinese had been, they were not so close-minded as to be able to resist the attractiveness of indulging in the nonreal and fictitious. Myths and legends must have existed in fairly large numbers among the common people although their preservation in China was extremely imperfect.

As primitive people noticed the endless variations of climate and vegetation and appreciated their being beyond the control of man, they developed explanations in the form of stories which have been generally described as myths. In a myth a superhuman being was usually the key of interpretation. Around this key there were woven numerous events bringing out the chief attributes of the deity to which obedience and submission were owed and for whom glorification and worship were invoked. With the development of culture, these narrations and descriptions became more complex, involved, and prolonged. Besides enriching the content of primitive religion and fostering the growth of primitive art, myths were also the early inspirers of folk literature. On the other hand, although literature was engendered by mythology, the early poets were actually the defacers of the original myths since these poets, in tampering with the recording of these myths, usually would embellish them with efforts of their own imagination, therefore altering the contents of the original. In the later myths, the principal characters had an increasing tendency to resemble human beings. As deities gave way to men, ancient heroes and heroines began to loom large in these primitive narratives. Thus arose the origin of hero worship as developed in legend.

The myths and legends of ancient China have never been collected into a compendium but there are remnants still widely scattered and embedded in ancient writings of diverse types. Thus, in the *Book of Songs* we read of the supernatural births of the founders of the Shang-Yin and Chou Dynasties. In the *Tso Commentary* on the *Spring and Autumn* we read that Emperor Yao ordered the exe-

cution of the unsuccessful flood controller, K'un, at Yü Shan or
Feather Mountain, and that the spirit of the latter was transformed
into a yellow bear which entered into Yü Yüan or the Feather Abyss.
And, in the *Book of Mencius*, we read that Emperor Shun in his
youth was ordered by his father to repair the roof of a barn and
that while the repairing was going on the barn was set afire by
Shun's younger brother. This was elaborated upon by Ssŭ-ma Ch'ien,
possibly on the basis of folk tales which were still in circulation
among the humble folk, to the effect that Shun had saved himself
by jumping down while holding two huge straw hats in his hands.
The *Shan Hai Ching* or *Mountain and Sea Classic* was particularly
rich in preserving little bits of early myth and legend. In it numerous
fragmentary references were made to a principal superhuman being
by the name of Hsi Wang Mu, or Western Queen Mother. It was
said that she lived on Jade Mountain, that she had the face of a
human being, the tail of a leopard, the teeth of a tiger, and was an
expert in whistling. Another version stated that south of the western
sea beyond the edge of the floating sands, behind the red river and
in front of the black river, there was a mountain called K'unlun;
that living on it was a deity with a human face, a tiger's body and
tail, all white; that encircling it below was an abyss of weak water;
that beyond it was a mountain of fire which would at night burn all
things thrown onto it; that there was a human being with a tiger's
skin and a leopard's tail living in a cave known by the name of Hsi
Wang Mu. The disappointing thing about this peculiar treatise is
that there is no general description of Western Queen Mother, only
conflicting details and attributes.

The fragmentariness of Chinese myths and heroic legends has
been explained in the light of the strenuous mode of living to which
the early Chinese were subjected. Living along the bend of the
Yellow River in the northern portion of the temperate zone where
the gifts of nature were unbountiful, they had to work hard to maintain their livelihood. Stressing practicality, they were limited in
their imaginative wanderings and were not interested in piecing the
widely scattered myths and legends into harmonious and continuous
elaborations. Secondly, the emergence of Confucius and his followers, who taught principally ethics, ordering of the family, government of the state, and pacification of the world, purposely avoiding
discourses on the realm of the gods and spirits, naturally encouraged
a tendency to discredit and discard all early records and hearsay of
the fabulous and fantastic. Hence the poverty of ancient Chinese
mythical and legendary lore. Moreover, there was a peculiar tradition in ancient China which was almost unique; namely, the faint

line of demarcation between deities and spirits. In theory there had been the nominal separations among the nonhuman beings of heavenly gods, terrestrial deities, and ghosts. This segregation, however, was purely theoretical. Instances were numerous to show that the departed spirits of men might become gods and deities on one hand, and gods and deities were weighted down to the level of the human world by their human attributes. When gods and men were thus endlessly confused, the original myths and legends were prevented from running their full course of evolution. The result was that new gods were created in China from no previous background and that the old gods might undergo physical changes but no organic evolution.

In the bibliography section of the Han dynastic history, *Han Shu*, there is a section labeled "Hsiao Shuo," literally, "Small Talk"—a term now equated with fiction. According to the commentator, our literal translation is correct. *Hsiao shuo* meant "petty speech," like backyard gossip and discourses in tiny alleys. Under this heading there were listed the titles of twenty-seven works. Unfortunately all of these were lost except for fragments. Even more discouraging in this regard is the fact that all six works of fiction type now extant and attributed to Han writers are nothing but forgeries by much later hands.

After the disintegration of the Han Empire, however, books were written in large numbers in which the strange, the miraculous, and the supernatural were recorded. This was no mere coincidence. Ancient China had followed the cult of the *wu*, a kind of shaman who, besides being a medium between the gods and men, were also practitioners of the dance and of singing and posturing in order to induce the descent of the spirits. During Ch'in and Han times, speculations regarding the immortals or *shên hsien* had grown immensely in volume and in influence. At the end of the Han Dynasty, the cult of the *wu* was greatly revived and its preoccupation with ghosts and ghost stories enhanced by the teachings of Buddhism from India through Central Asia. The new collections of stories about gods and ghosts were thus partly written by followers of the new religious cult for edification and also by writers for entertainment. In other words, neither group of authors was consciously bent on literary creation. Among these collections was *Lieh Yi Chuan* or *Strange Tales*, of which the authorship is uncertain, probably written before 300. The following anecdote is typical:

> When Tsung Ting-po of Nanyang County was young, he met a ghost while he was out one night. "Who is it?" he asked. "Ghost," replied the ghost, "and who are you?" Trying to fool him, Ting-po said, "I am also a ghost." The ghost

then asked where he was going. He said he wanted to go to the market-town of Yüan and the ghost said, " I want to go to Yüan, too."

After traveling together for several *li*, the ghost suggested that walking was too strenuous and that they should take turns carrying each other. "Very good," replied Ting-po, whereupon the ghost took the first turn and carried Ting-po for several *li*. "You are too heavy," observed the ghost, "Could it be that you are not a ghost?" "I have newly died," said Ting-po, "and that's why I am heavy."

Then, in his turn, Ting-po carried the ghost but the ghost had scarcely any weight. Thus they shifted turns two or three times. "I am newly dead," said Ting-po again. "What do ghosts detest most?" "Oh, just human spittle," replied the ghost. Traveling forward a little while, they came to a stream. At Ting-po's urging the ghost waded across first but made no sound. Then Ting-po himself waded and the water made a swishing sound. "Why that sound?" asked the ghost. "Why that sound?" "Oh, I am just newly dead and not yet accustomed to wading. Don't feel surprised."

When they were about to get to the town of Yüan, Ting-po raised the ghost up over his head and held him fast. The ghost yelled aloud with a gutteral sound demanding to get down but was disregarded. When they reached the center of town, [the ghost] changed into a sheep on reaching ground. Ting-po offered it for sale and for fear it would transform itself again, spat at it twice. It was sold at one thousand, five hundred cash.

A writer who was frequently identified with this type of narrative writing and to whom similar collections have been, therefore, attributed, was Chang Hua (232-300). An expert in the occult sciences of his day and widely read in literature pertaining to the supernatural and its special meanings, Chang was recognized for his encyclopedic learning. It was recorded that he had combed the whole body of existing literature in his lifetime from the beginnings of antiquity to his own age, consulted the oral sources prevailing in districts far and wide, and embodied his cullings into a work of four hundred books submitted to Emperor Wu (reigned 264-290) of the Tsin Dynasty. The pleasant work which bears the same title as Chang Hua's collection and contains various bits of information extracted from old preserved literature and, therefore, little that is new and surprising is probably the patchwork of a much later age and does not represent the original collection.

Another teller of stories of the supernatural and miraculous was Kan Pao (flourished 323) of the Tsin Dynasty. Author of *Tsin Chi*, or *Annals of the Tsin Dynasty*, in twenty books, Kan Pao is now remembered as a historian. Absorbed also in the cult of the Yin-Yang school and in folklore as so many contemporaries of his were, he was deeply moved by the death and coming to life again of one of his father's bonded maidservants. Later on, his elder brother also came to life again after apparent physical death and told weird stories of having met the heavenly hosts. Whereupon he felt compelled to write a collection of stories of this nature in twenty chapters to "make clear that the way of the gods are not a lie." Again, what we have today bearing the same title is most likely not Kan Pao's original work.

Among the many collections of similar stories attributed to eminent writers of the period, the only one in which touches of the original writings are preserved is the *Hsü Ch'i Hsieh Chih* (*More Inelegant Tales*) by Wu Chün of the Liang (one of the Southern Dynasties, 502-556). Wu Chün (469-520) enjoyed a good reputation in his day as a poet and so his work in narrative fiction was also praised by subsequent writers. A good sample is his story of the goose coop.

Hsü Yen of the district of Yanghsien was walking along on Sui-An Mountain. On the road he met a student of about seventeen or eighteen lying on the roadside and saying he had a pain in his leg and begging to be put into the goose coop. Yen thought he was joking but meanwhile the student had already entered the coop though the coop didn't look any larger nor the student any smaller. He simply sat with the pair of geese and the geese were not afraid of him. Yen carried the coop on his back but he felt no additional weight. When Yen had walked to a tree he rested himself in the shade. The student then came out of the coop and said to Yen, "I want to treat you to a simple meal," and Yen replied, "Good." The student then produced from his mouth a brass tray containing different items of food. . . . After they had taken a number of drinks he said to Yen, "I have a woman with me, I want to call her now," and Yen said, "Good." Thereupon he produced a maiden from his mouth aged about fifteen or sixteen, clothed in exquisite silk garments and looking beautiful indeed. The three sat down to continue their meal. After a while the student felt sleepy after the drinks and went to sleep. The girl said to Yen, "Although I am wedded to the student as his wife, I really am not pleased with him. I have stolen a man to travel with me. Since the student is asleep I will call him. Please don't say a word." Yen said, "Good." The maiden then produced from her mouth a young man aged about twenty-three or twenty-four who looked intelligent and likable. The young man chatted with Yen. Meanwhile the student showed signs of waking up and the maiden spilled out an embroidered curtain screening the student and the student insisted that the maiden lie down by his side. Then the young man said to Yen, "Although this girl likes me, she is not singly devoted. I have stolen a woman to travel with me. Now I want to see her for a while. Please do not say anything." Yen said, "Good." The man in turn produced a woman from his mouth aged twenty-odd years. They ate and drank and conversed together for a long time and they heard the sound of the student moving about. The man said, "They are both waking up." Whereupon he took the woman and swallowed her. A little while later the girl came out from behind the screen and told Yen, "The student now wants to get up," and she swallowed the man facing Yen alone. Then the student got up and said to Yen, "I have slept longer than I meant to, didn't you feel sad sitting alone? The sun is also setting, I shall say goodbye." Then he swallowed the maiden and all the utensils except the big brass tray about two feet in width which he left to Yen as a souvenir, saying, "I have no better gift for you to remember me by." Yen became an imperial historian in the reign of Ta Yuan and at a dinner entertaining imperial secretary Chang Shan, he used the very same brass tray and Chang Shan saw the inscription saying, "Cast in the third year of the reign of Yung P'ing."

This kind of theme was definitely un-Chinese. The T'ang critic Tuan Ch'êng-shih (flourished 860) observed that it was modeled after a Hindu tale. The passage which Tuan quoted from what he called Buddhist sacred literature is an abbreviated summary of a similar story, in the old miscellaneous fables translated by the Buddhist monk, Sêng Hui, of the late third century, now fully preserved in the Tripitaka. This is a clear illustration of how a motif in the narrative literature of India, transmitted to China through the translated texts, found its way into popular literature of a nonreligious nature.

More directly indebted to India were the Buddhist writers of Chinese stories to aid the cause of Buddhist propagation. Such a collection is *Ming Hsiang Chi* written by Wang Yen of the fifth century. Ordained as a Buddhist monk in Cochin-China when he was young, he was a devout Buddhist especially impressed by the Buddhist miracles. Although the original collection is now lost, a large part has been preserved in quoted form in later collections. Most celebrated is the following story about the entry of Buddhism into China:

Emperor Ming of the Han Dynasty saw a godly being in his dream with height over twenty feet, a body revealing the color of yellow gold and with his neck surrounded by a halo of sunlight. The emperor asked his ministers about the dream and one of them answered, "In the western regions there is a god whose name is Buddha and who answers to the description given us from your majesty's dream. Isn't it likely that this is it?" Then emissaries were sent to India for the purpose of procuring and copying classics and likenesses. These were made manifest to the Central Empire, all revered by the son of heaven, by kings and by noblemen. When these had heard that man's soul did not perish after his death, all were inspired with awe and a sense of possibly being lost. When the chief of the commission had returned from the western regions with the Buddha's likeness, the emperor valued it for bearing resemblance exactly to what he had seen in his dream. Then he had court painters make several duplicates of the likeness and distributed them to the southern palace, to the K'u palace, to the gate of the high sun, and other places for worship and reverence. In addition, at the Monastery of the White Horse the emperor decreed the painting on a wall of a mural showing a thousand chariots and ten thousand horsemen in three circuits surrounding a pagoda.

In competition with Buddhist writers, Taoists made similar narratives and for a similar purpose. Most curious among the Taoist writers was Wang Fo, who flourished at the turn of the third and fourth centuries and who, after his defeat in a debate by the Buddhist monk, Pai Yung, proceeded with the forgery of a purported Buddhist classic about Lao-tzŭ. The following was a typical story in his collection of Taoist tales entitled *Shên Chi* or *Records of the Miraculous:*

> Ch'ên Min, who served as the prefect of Chianghsia during the overlordship of Sun Hao, was traveling to his post from Chienyeh [Nanking]. As he had heard of the miraculous powers of a wayside temple at Kungt'ing, he went in to pray for safety in his tenure and promised the tribute of a silver staff. After the tenure had been filled, he had a staff made to fulfill his promise at the temple. He ordered the staff to be made of iron and plated with silver. Soon he was summoned to hold a new position in the capital city as imperial attendant and he called at the temple to present the staff. As the ceremony was over he resumed his journey. At nightfall a spiritual medium appeared to announce: "Ch'ên Min promised me a silver staff. Now I am presented with a coated staff. It should be dropped into water to be returned to him. His sin of deception, however, will not be tolerated." Whereupon the medium produced the staff, opened it up, saw the iron stem, and dropped it into the lake. The staff floated on the surface of the water and floated forward with the speed of flying. It floated finally against Min's barge and the barge capsized.

As contrasted with this major trend among Buddhist and Taoist narrative writers who were preoccupied with the presentation of the supernatural and miraculous in support of their respective faiths, there was another tradition which, following the indigenous Sinitic emphasis on what was authentic and actual, concerned itself with incidents and anecdotes in the world of men. In spite of their divergence in the selection of subject matter, both of these schools claimed that they were recorders of actual occurrences and, therefore, made no overt claim to the writing of fiction. The handiwork of the former, however, was of such a nature that in the eyes of the readers, at any rate, it was closer to invention than matter-of-fact recording.

With the increase of social disorders in China resulting from the breakup of the Han Empire and with the introduction of Buddhism from Central Asia, members of the scholar class found it increasingly attractive to agree with the Buddhists and Taoists in fleeing as much as possible from the world of affairs and traditional values. This is clearly borne out by the fact that among Confucian classics studied and discussed the one that received the greatest attention was not the *Spring and Autumn* with its rectification of names, nor the *Classic of Li* (rites) emphasizing the importance of correct usages and attitudes, but the *Book of Changes,* which could be and was actually interpreted in such a way as to rival the mysticism and other-

worldliness of Buddhism and the new religious Taoism. Though the
scholars outwardly and consciously took the position of defending
Confucianism against the encroachments of the other two faiths,
they were actually traveling the same road as their opponents. The
new vogue thus created and shared in by all the members of the
intelligentsia irrespective of external and nominal philosophical or
religious affiliations was that of *Ch'ing T'an*, that is, "unsullied discourse" or "pure conversation." We have noted that preoccupation
with the gain and losses of this world and concern with what was
correct and incorrect would sully discourse or render conversation
"impure." *Ch'ing T'an* was an escape from the duties and values
which had been held as almost sacred. The contribution to literature
made by this vogue of *Ch'ing T'an* was probably much more substantial than its contribution to philosophy or mere speculative thinking.
In the first place, it had a tendency of minimizing the importance
of long and formal essays as vehicles for the expression of opinion.
In the second place, as it was rooted in conversation and discourse,
relying on the speech organ rather than the writing brush, it led to
and promoted the search for choices of appropriate words and clever
phrases. It had a high disciplinary value in the improvement of diction comparable to the value of salon conversation to the writers of
prerevolutionary France. In the third place, it frankly acknowledged
the natural limitations set by the very nature of "small talk" upon
what it undertook to do, and made no pretense to rival the glory
and dignity of such stately literary efforts as the formulation of a
long memorial, the protracted construction of an elaborate *fu*, or
the compilation of a dynastic history, leave alone the painstaking
labors of writing a hundred-thousand-word commentary on two or
three characters extracted from one of the Confucian classics.

The recording of anecdotes goes back to a much earlier age, of
course. These anecdotes had been utilized, for example, in the *Book
of Han Fei* and the one attributed to Lieh Yü-k'ou (Lieh-tzŭ), but
their recording had been done for nonliterary purposes; by Han Fei
to support his political theories and by Lieh-Tzŭ to elucidate his
expositions on *tao*. Anecdotal literature of the Han period was of a
similar nature. During the third century, after the gradual rise of
Ch'ing T'an, compilations of anecdotes were made clearly for entertainment and were, therefore, far removed from utilitarian objectives. An early example of such compilations was the *Yü Lin* or *The
Forest of Sayings* recorded by P'ei Ch'i in 362. Although the collection was denounced soon afterward as containing inaccuracies, and
therefore was not preserved in its entirety, many of its entries found

their way into other collections. The following entry from the *Forest of Sayings* is indicative of its style:

Emperor Wu of the Wei Dynasty once said, "While I am asleep do not rashly come close to me. If you do, I might slaughter you unaware of what I am doing. You who are on my left and on my right had better beware." Later he feigned falling asleep and one of his favorite boy attendants secretly covered him with a comforter, whereupon he killed the young guard with his sword. Thenceforward nobody dared to go near him (while he was asleep).

Better known and more influential was another compilation entitled *Shih Shuo* or the *Sayings of the World,* compiled by Liu Yi-Ch'ing (403-444) with a commentary by Liu Hsiao-piao. This collection, transmitted through many hands and with its title elongated more than once and with its contents occasionally rearranged, was a work highly treasured principally for entertainment. The commentary was not one in the ordinary sense but contained similar anecdotes either in refutation or in support of the stories in the main text, representing cullings from over four hundred titles of which many have been lost. The original compiler was described by contemporaries as a man of few words and literary gifts but, extremely fond of company, he was able to play host to many gifted writers, some of them coming for his hospitality from afar. Since the entries in this collection of anecdotes were mainly selections from what already had been committed to writing in other literary works, it is possible that the compilation was the work of multiple hands.

Juan Chi once had an exquisite carriage when he was in the county of Yen. This carriage he loaned freely to people who asked to use it. There was a man who wanted to borrow it for the funeral of his mother but dared not to make his wishes known. Later on when Jüan heard about it he sighed, "I have a carriage which other people dare not to borrow. What is the use of having a carriage?" Then he had it burned.

. . . .

Tsu Shih-hsiao was fond of riches, and Juan Yao-chi was fond of clogs (for mountain-climbing), and they usually were engaged in their hobbies. These were both hindrances but their relative values had not been determined. People called on Tsu and found him checking on his valuable belongings. When the guests arrived the checking was not over, there being two little baskets left unchecked. He pushed them to the rear and inclined his body to hide them, being unable as yet to tranquilize his mind. Other people called on Juan and found him blowing a fire to wax his clogs and sighing, "I wish I knew how many pairs of clogs I need for this one life span." While saying this both his mind and his complexion were restful and carefree. Then people knew who was the winner.

. . . .

Juan Chi had an enviable reputation and the prime minister, Wang Ti-t'u, asked him when the two met, "What are the similarities and dissimilarities of

Lao-tzŭ and Chuang-tzŭ and the holy teachings (of Confucius)?" The reply was, "Aren't they similar?" The prime minister was delighted at the response and elected him to a secretaryship. Hence, the world called him the Three-Word Secretary.

Dedicated purely to entertainment rather than to edification were the numerous collections of jokes, of which the best known was the *Hsiao Lin* or the *Forest of Smiles* compiled by Han-tan Shun at the turn of the second and third centuries. Although the work is now lost, over twenty entries have been preserved in quotations in later works.

There was a native of the state of Lu who tried to enter a city gate carrying a long bamboo pole. First, he held it vertically but could not go in, then he held it horizontally but again he could not go in. He was unable to figure out a way. Soon an elderly man arrived and said, "I am not a sage but I have seen many things. Why don't you saw it in two in the middle and go in?" His advice was followed.

· · · · · · · · · · ·

A and B fought over a quarrel and A bit off the nose of B. The court officials had to settle the case. A claimed that B had bitten off the nose himself. The judge said, "But a man's nose is higher up than his mouth. How could the mouth bite off the nose?" A said, "He [in Chinese the same word as "it"] climbed up on the couch to do the biting."

These many collections of jokes and little anecdotes that might provoke laughter were mostly lost. It was natural that they could not survive the acid test applied to books during the later ages of the rise of Confucian puritanism. On the other hand, for centuries they enjoyed a fairly wide circulation.

With the reunification of the T'ang Empire, fiction, like other branches of literature, underwent major changes and developments. As in previous centuries, T'ang fiction adhered to the pattern of the miraculous and weird. Similarly, T'ang fiction was recorded, as before, in classical prose instead of in the vernacular, although often in presenting dialogues and in repeating jokes attempts were made to approximate the living speech of the characters. The new forward step taken in T'ang times consisted in a more sustained and longer narration and an inclination on the part of the writers to create stories. In other words, admissions were freely made of the presentation of what is imaginary. The new name invented for these longer prose narratives was *Ch'uan Ch'i* or "transmission of the strange," originally a term of disparagement. Many of these short prose romances provided the nuclei of the narrative elements utilized in the dramas of the Yuan and Ming Dynasties which will be discussed in a later chapter. The earliest example now extant of this new type of romantic narrative is "Ku Ching Chi" or "The Tale of the Ancient Mirror," usually attributed to Wang Tu, who flourished around 600. It was a story of how the narrator had obtained a miraculous mirror from one of his friends and how, with the aid of the mirror, he could cause genii to descend from the ethereal spheres to perform various services at his command, and how his younger brother had borrowed and used the mirror in his extensive travels for the subduing and elimination of various malignant ghosts and spirits, and how, finally, the mirror vanished of its own accord. This lengthy and episodic narrative set a new pattern in literary composition, although in substance it still continued the previous tradition of recording the unusual and the unbelievable. That the new taste was no longer frowned upon by the world of the learned, could be borne out by the fact that the author, Wang Tu, was the younger brother of Wang T'ung, the author of the philosophical treatise *Wênchungtzŭ*, one of the few noticeable Confucianist philosophical writings of medieval China, and the elder brother of Wang Ch'i, author of another philosophical treatise of a serious nature, entitled *Tungkaotzŭ*.

Another long narrative was "Pai Yüan Chuan" or "The Biography of the White Monkey." The full title in Chinese was "The Biography of the White Monkey Written to Fill the Default of Chiang Tsung," suggesting that Chiang Tsung should have written this but did not. This was by an unidentified author describing how a general of the Liang Dynasty, Ou-yang Chi, in following his military exploits in Ch'anglo County in present-day Fukien Province, had penetrated deep into the unexplored mountain regions. His wife was captured by a white monkey and when she was rescued by his troops she returned home pregnant. A year later she gave birth to a son whose face resembled that of the monkey. This general was a historical person known for his military career and remembered for his heroic death when he was captured by the founder of the Ch'ên Dynasty which succeeded the Liang. His son, Ou-yang Hsün, was adopted by Chiang Tsung and attained a huge literary reputation at the beginning of the T'ang Dynasty. He was reported to look like a monkey and apparently one who was jealous of his literary pre-eminence had written this narrative to blacken his name. The utilization of fictional and semi-fictional writing for personal vengeance thus is no modern invention.

As we have pointed out before, the grip of convention on prose style was a firm and deadening one. Although writing mainly for entertainment, no fiction writer had been bold enough to discard the archaic language of the bygone age and to adopt the free and easy vernacular spoken universally. We conclude, therefore, that these stories were written by the literati for the literati.

This feature of stylistic conservatism was carried even further in fiction writing by Chang Chu (660?-740?), a hot-tempered and reckless man despite his literary reputation. Besides numerous collections of anecdotes, Chang wrote a lengthy narrative entitled "Yu Hsien K'u" or "The Cave of the Traveling Immortal." It was an account of how he in his young manhood traveled to Hoyüan on official duty and how on his way he had sought lodging in a huge mansion one night where he met two young women with whom he had a pleasant banquet and wrote poetry through the night. The story had no plot worthy of the name but had a style that was entirely unconventional. Instead of using simple, classical style, Chang resorted to a medium least suited to narration, namely, the stilted balanced prose known as *p'ien wên*. Sentences, in other words, had to be written in pairs with strictly equated structure. Although this peculiar composition had been forgotten in China itself, it was well preserved in Japan where it had an immense influence. To point out the stylistic peculiarities of this narrative, we need to add that each time the stilted, florid, and artificial *p'ien wên* failed the author in its function, he would jump to the other extreme of using the vernacular.

It was not until after the T'ang Empire had been plunged into civil war which ravished it permanently that fiction writing in prose was attempted by an ever increasing number of authors and was to constitute one of the main facets of a conscious literary reform in the ninth century. Among writers of fiction who flourished in the later half of the eighth century was Shên Chi-chih (flourished circa 780), trained both as a classicist and a historian. He was respected for his accomplishments in both of these highly esteemed fields of authorship. That he wrote feelingly in creative fiction proved the popularity of the new genre. His *Chên Chung Chi* or *Record of the Inside of a Pillow*, also entitled in another anthology *Lu Wêng* or *The Old Man Lu*, tells of an incident which had happened in 719 to the principal character. Traveling on the highways of North China, the Taoist, Lu, sought rest in a public inn. He met a young man at the inn who seemed sad and listless. The Taoist reached into his traveling bag for a pillow and presented it to the young man. Thereupon the latter dreamed a long dream that he married a girl of the Ts'ui clan, one of the four or five powerful clans of the empire. Then he won the highest literary degree after which he was appointed governor of Shensi Province and subsequently mayor of the imperial capital. He was then made a commander of the imperial troops to fight the barbarians and the records of his decisive victories elevated him to the top ranks in the imperial official hierarchy.

Laudatory rescripts were received three times on one day from the throne which praised him as a virtuous minister for his contributions and recommendations to the emperor. Then his colleagues, inspired by jealousy, accused him on false grounds of having formed secret agreements with frontier generals to foment a rebellion. He was destined to a prison sentence. The county sheriff arrived at his door with numerous followers for an imminent arrest. He was shaken with fear and anxiety for the unpredictable outcome and said to his wife and child, "My family has many acres of good farming land in Shantung. Enough to ward off cold and hunger. Why should I have sought official distinction and immolument at the start. Now here I am unable to wear a summer shirt and ride a greenish pony on the highways of Hantan even if I wished to."

He drew his sword to commit suicide but was stopped and saved by his wife. Those who were involved in the criminal case were all sentenced to die except him who had been saved by the intercession and guarantee of the eunuchs. With his penalty reduced, he was sentenced to exile in Huan County. A few years later the emperor became fully aware of the frame-up and ordered him to be restored to the secretaryship of the empire and given the noble title of the Duke of Yen and showered with other unusual favors. . . . He had five sons, all taking wives from the eminent families of the empire. . . . Later on, in view of his advancing years and declining health he repeatedly petitioned the throne for retirement without avail. In his illness, eunuchs dotted the roads to inquire after his health and famous physicians and superb drugs all arrived. . . . Then he died, whereupon he yawned and woke up finding himself lying in a bed in the inn.

The old Taoist, Lu, was sitting beside him and the innkeeper was steaming the rice which was not yet fully cooked. The other things he saw were as before. He jumped up and said, "Could it have been a dream?" The Taoist said in an aside to the innkeeper, "Thus are all experiences in human life." The young scholar sat pensively for long, then he broke out in gratitude, "The ways of elevation and humiliation, the courses of passage and obstruction, the meaning of gain and loss, the feeling of life and death, I have now thoroughly learned. With this, you, my master, have trimmed my desires. How dare I neglect your teachings?" He bowed low and took leave.

This moral, even in the T'ang Empire, which was inundated with a flood of desire for distinction and reputation, was nothing new. In Kan Pao's collection of strange stories we find the following:

In Chiao Hu Temple there was a jade pillow. In the pillow there is a tiny crack. A man from the County of Shanfu by the name of Yang Lin had come to the temple as a traveling salesman asking for blessings. The temple priest asked him, "Do you want to be happily married?" Lin answered, "I would consider that very lucky." The priest then urged Lin to go near the pillow and he entered the crack where he saw a red storied building with rooms decorated in jade. Inside was Governor Chao who gave his daughter in marriage to Lin. Six sons were born and all became imperial secretaries. For decades he had not thought of returning home. All of a sudden he felt as though he were waking up from a dream and found himself still at the side of the pillow. He felt sad for long.

Whereas the fourth-century anecdote as translated above in full was a narrative of one short paragraph, the late eighth-century version was not only more than twenty times longer, but was also told with the characters and events much more fully developed with characterization and description. In the four centuries, fiction writing had outgrown the stage of laconic and matter-of-fact recording to become a consciously cultivated art.

The dignity of the prose romance, as we have pointed out previously, was suddenly heightened by the support given to it by leaders of the literary revolution headed by Han Yü. It was only natural that Han Yü's pupils should try their hands at the writing of prose romances. Among them might be mentioned Shên Ya-chih (flourished 825), a native of Chekiang who distinguished himself as a *ku wên* writer. Unlike his master, however, who considered literature principally if not exclusively as a vehicle for tao, or the Confucian way of life, Shên proudly claimed he was good in creating subtle and involved love stories. Steeped in the tradition of Chinese folklore, he suggested in nearly all of his tales that genii and ghosts also had limited life spans. In his tales he used this device to lend charm to his narratives. In a prose romance entitled *Hsiang Chung Yüan* (*Sad Romance on the Hsiang River*) he told of a young scholar by the name of Chêng who had fallen in love with the humanized spirit of a fox in the form of a beautiful maiden—a popular theme in Chinese folklore. Living together happily for years they were to be parted because she had exhausted her span of existence. Over ten years later, however, he saw her again in a beautiful pleasure barge. In the brief meeting she sadly sang a song, wept, and then a few minutes later disappeared as stormy waves began to rock the barge violently. In his other tales he would create imaginative characters and project them into remote historical backgrounds in which touching episodes of romantic love had been suggested but never elaborated by early writers.

A contemporary of Shên Chi-chih in the writing of love stories is Po Hsing-chien (died 826), younger brother of the major poet, Po Chü-yi. His most celebrated romance, which was adapted many times in dramas of the Mongol and Ming Dynasties, was *Li Wa Chuan* or *The Life of the Maiden Li*, written in 795 when the author was a relatively young man. The story concerns the son of a provincial governor who, on his way to Ch'angan for the competitive examination, fell in love with a sing-song girl, Li Wa, on whom he squandered all his personal fortune including his carriage and horse. Finally, he was expelled by the owner of the house of prostitution and became a professional mourner in funeral processions. When he returned home after a long period of wandering, his father drove him out of the house, forcing him to live the life of a beggar. By accident, while he was begging, he met the young maiden again. With her inspiration the young man began a new page in life, not only winning high honors in the competitive examination and an enviable position in the government, but also succeeding in regaining his father's love. Based, possibly, on the actual life of a real person, the author wove his tale with such dexterity that it enjoyed immense popularity. The following passage describing the young scholar's reaction on entering the apartment of the singer is representative of the narrator's art:

When [the young man] was led to the side of a lonely wall he saw a matron going up a staircase and found that she was the maiden's mother. Bowing and kneeling he went forward and said: "I have heard there is a vacant room here ready for rent, is it true?" The matron said, "I am afraid it is too narrow and humble and unequal to your elevated status. How dare I mention the rent?" Then she led the young man into the guest house which was beautiful and well appointed. In the course of a conversation she said, "I have a little spoiled daughter who, in spite of her lack of accomplishment in the arts, is fond of meeting my guests. I hope you will not mind meeting her." Then she ordered Li Wa to come out. Her dazzling eyes, her handsome wrists and her graceful gait were such a surprise to the young man that he did not dare to raise his eyes. After exchanging greetings and remarks about the weather he began to realize that he had never seen such a beauty before. Then they resumed their seats. Tea was prepared and rice wine was served, all in immaculate services. In a while night was falling and the drums announcing nightfall were heard on all sides. The maiden asked where he was living and the young man purposely deceived her by saying, "Just a few miles outside of the Yen-p'ing Gate," hoping that an invitation might be extended to him on account of the great distance he had traveled. The maiden's reply was, however, "The drums are being sounded. You should make haste lest you might run into the curfew." The young man said, "I was so enchanted by the graciousness and gaiety with which I have been received that I didn't realize the sun had already set. Now I have to travel a long distance as I have no relatives in the city. What am I going to do?" Whereupon the young maiden interceded, "If you don't mind the modesty of the place, what objection can there be to your staying here?" Repeatedly the young man eyed the matron and the matron finally said, "Yes, indeed."

Equally celebrated was the tale of *Huo Hsiao-yü* or *The Little Jade of the Huo Family,* written by Chiang Fang (flourished 813). The heroine, Hsiao-yü, was the daughter of Prince Huo who had read and admired the poetry of Li Yi. Through the introduction of a matchmaker she met and fell in love with the poet. Meanwhile a betrothal had been arranged by the parents of the poet to another girl. Li Yi, accepting his fate, submissively decided to stop all communication with Hsiao-yü. As Hsiao-yü had been disowned by her family after the decease of her father, she now had to sell all her jewelry, including her purple jade pin, in order to live. Even after she had fallen seriously ill, Li Yi continued to avoid her. One day while he was admiring the peony gardens of a Buddhist monastery he was virtually kidnapped by a ruffian wearing a yellow jacket and was, perforce, brought to the humble lodgings where Hsiao-yü was lying seriously ill. Touchingly, the young maiden recalled for his benefit how he had repeatedly jilted her and then passed away. All of a sudden the poet felt penitent but it was already too late.

Li Yi was a poet of good repute in the latter part of the eighth century and his biography in the *Dynastic History* recorded him as extremely fickle and suspicious, having divorced three wives. Nothing, however, is said of a love affair with Huo Hsiao-yü. The following passage represents the minuteness with which the incidents were narrated in the romance:

Hsiao-yü realized that his return had been long overdue and she tried all within her power to get news. Instead all she got was rumor which differed from day to day. She extensively sought the assistance of priests and fortune-tellers without avail. Alone she embraced her sorrow and her regrets for over a year. Lying weakly in her inner apartment she was finally laid up with a serious illness. Although the young man had remained completely silent, Hsiao-yü's hope and trust remained firm. She would make expensive presents to friends and relatives soliciting them for assistance in urging him to write. As she was extremely earnest and eager in her search, her resources began to dwindle. From time to time she had to ask her maid servant to sell the finery and ornaments in her trunks, most of which were entrusted to the pawnshop run by Hou Ching-hsien in the western market. One day she asked Wan Sha to sell her precious purple jade pin at Ching-hsien's shop. On the street an old jade-smith saw what Wan-sha was holding in her hand and came forward to identify it by saying, "This hairpin is my own handiwork. Many years ago when the youngest daughter of Prince Huo was about to wear her hair for the first time as an adult, orders were issued to me to have this made, for which I received 10,000 cash. Through all these years I have not forgotten it. Who are you and from where have you gotten this?" Wan Sha answered, "My mistress is none other than Prince Huo's daughter. Her family went bankrupt and she had promised her love to a man. Her husband left some time ago for the eastern capital and to this day has sent no message. On this account she has been ill for the last two years. I am now instructed to sell this so that she will have money to give to people who might help her to get letters from him." With tears the old jade-smith said, "How can the offspring of a nobleman be fallen into such a lamentable state as this. My last years are approaching their end. But as I witness this fluctuation of fortune, my grief is limitless." Then he led her to the mansion of the Princess Yen Hsien where she told the princess the story of the jade hairpin. The princess sighed with grief for a long time then offered for it a price of one hundred twenty thousand cash.

While the romantic tales of this type were increasing in popularity, the central government was becoming more and more powerless, taxation became heavier, and the rights of the citizen were shamelessly trampled upon. Old standards of justice were completely abandoned and hopes of the restoration of peace and order had completely vanished. To beguile the tedium of hopeless existence, writers gifted with imaginative powers tried to rouse a little hope by creating fictitious champions of social justice. These champions usually took the form of expert swordsmen and dedicated themselves to the righting of all social and personal wrongs. These tales of "supermen" were nourished by the prevalence of Buddhist and Taoist tales. Although many of such tales were not elaborated into full-fledged romances but only briefly summarized into short tales of a few paragraphs, the attractiveness of the subject matter did not fail to win the attention of romance writers. As in the case of the tales of romantic love, the narratives eulogizing superhuman swordsmen of the late T'ang Dynasty later inspired many plays.

One of the many prose romances of this type which might be mentioned was *Wu Shuang Chuan* or *The Tale of Peerless*, written by Hsieh T'iao (830-872), who was known for his extreme handsomeness even more than for his literary talent. The romance tells of the heroine, Liu Wu-shuang, daughter of Liu Chên, a minister at the imperial court in the 780's. Engaged to her cousin, Wang Hsien-k'ê, she was estranged from her fiancé by widespread mutiny. Later on, by a peculiar twist of circumstances, she was drafted into the imperial harem and her fiancé though shocked and enraged, was entirely helpless. Finally he made the acquaintance of the heroic swordsman Ku Ya-ya, who volunteered to rescue her. Unfortunately Wu-shuang had been killed and her fiancé gave up hope. One night, however, the swordsman succeeded in secretly taking the body of the girl from the Forbidden City and a miraculous potion was administered which revived her. The pair then took flight from the human world. Despite the unreasonableness of the supernatural elements, the narration was charmingly unfolded.

Another writer of prose romances was P'ei Hsing (flourished 880). In the collection of romances he wrote, the best known and the most influential on later playwrights was a piece entitled *Kunlun Nu* or *The Negrito Slave*. The Negritos, who had been imported into China in large numbers, must have struck the imagination of fiction writers not only on account of their jet black complexion but also because of their diminutive stature, and soon they were being credited with supernatural talents. P'ei Hsing's tale made of an alien bonded slave a convenient mechanism in resolving the complications of a love story rather than a corrector of social wrongs. The setting is the late eighth century in T'ang China and the hero a young scholar of the Ts'ui clan who had been instructed by his father to inquire after the health of a state official of first rank during the latter's illness. During the call the young scholar had occasion to notice three beautiful singers. One of these, clad in a graceful silk dress, signaled to him as he left the nobleman's mansion by holding up three fingers, turning her palm three times and pointing to a small mirror which she was wearing as a pendant. Puzzled by the gesture, the young scholar was so troubled that he fell ill. Fortunately he had a Negrito slave by the name of Moleh who, probably because he had learned Chinese the slow, hard way, had become an expert in sign language. According to his interpretation the three fingers indicated that the singer lived in the third court, revolving her outstretched hand three times meant fifteen and the round mirror to which she had pointed indicated the full moon which, according to the Chinese lunar calendar, invariably falls on the fifteenth day of the month. A secret meeting was indicated but one great obstacle was the fierce hound guarding the nobleman's house. Moleh not only got rid of the dog but also carried the scholar as he leaped over walls, then both the scholar and the singer in their escapade. When the Cha'ngan constabulary was ordered to arrest the Negrito, Moleh flew away to Loyang where he lost his identity by disguising himself as a herb seller in the market place.

The best-known T'ang romance of this type was *Ch'iu-nan K'ê Chuan*, possibly a corruption of *Ch'iu-hsü K'ê Chuan* or *The Curly-Bearded Guest*, a tale distinguished by sharp characterization and dialogue. Its author was most probably Tu Kuang-t'ing (850-933), who after repeated failures in the competitive examinations decided to become a Taoist at the famous T'ient'ai Mountain. After the collapse of the T'ang Dynasty he entered Szechuan where he was offered various honors, but denying himself all of these he spent the rest of his life as he had before, as a Taoist recluse.

The hero of the tale of *The Curly-Bearded Guest* was the historic figure of Li Tsing around whom many romantic tales were woven. Li, who flourished at the turn of the Sui and T'ang Dynasties, had met a beautiful singer in the family of General Yang Su. As she usually held a red duster, Li remembered her as Hung Fu, the Red Duster. Knowing Li would have an extremely brilliant future, Hung Fu decided to elope with him. On their way to the city of Taiyüan they met a stranger with a curly beard. As the stranger and the maiden had the same surname—Chang—they decided to become sworn brother and sister. Curly Beard not only escorted the pair but also gave them his entire personal fortune, urging them to support the major hero of the age, Li Shih-min, who was to help found the T'ang Dynasty and become the second monarch as Emperor T'ai

Tsung. Curly Beard had tried to distinguish himself as a leader of men during the crisis of a social and political upheaval. After interviewing Li Shih-min, however, he convinced himself that he had better yield leadership to the man on whom was descending the Mandate of Heaven. After seeing the fortunate pair comfortably settled, he flew away. Although this episode was never given official recognition in the *T'ang Dynastic History* it became the nucleus around which were woven many prose adaptations and a synopsis of many popular plays. The following scene introducing Curly Beard is elaborated in all such plays:

When they had arrived at the inn in the town of Lingshih, they tidied up the couch and cooked meat on the stove. Miss Chang (Red Duster) had to stand in front of the couch to comb her hair as it was so long that it touched the floor. The hero (Li Tsing) was currying the horse. All of a sudden there appeared a man of medium height with red and curly beard who had arrived on a decrepit donkey. He threw his leather bag in front of the stove, laid his head on a pillow on the couch and looked at the maiden intently as she combed her hair. Li was furious but was undecided what to do, so he went on currying his horse. Miss Chang looked at the face of the stranger fixedly, held her hair with one hand and waved her other hand which was shielded by her body from the sight of the stranger to indicate to her lover that he should not be rash. Hastily she finished her hairdressing, curtsied to the stranger as she adjusted her dress, and asked who he was. The stranger, still lying on the couch, said, "My name is Chang." She said, "My name is also Chang. It is proper I should be your younger sister." Thereupon she knelt and bowed to him. The girl asked him what his order was among his brothers and sisters. He said "Third. And what order are you, younger sister?" She replied, "Oldest." Then gladly he responded, "I am glad to be fortunate enough to meet a younger sister." Then Miss Chang called out, "Li, you had better come in to meet third elder brother." He came in and saluted the stranger graciously. Then they sat around the table. "What meat is it you are cooking?" "Mutton. It is about done." The guest said, "Hungry." The host then went out to the market and bought some foreign pancakes. The guest pulled a dagger from his belt, cut the meat, and together they ate. After eating he chopped up the left-over meat and delivered it to the donkey, which ate it up with great rapidity.

These romances of the T'ang Dynasty, it should be pointed out, were all written in classical prose, and their circulation was obviously limited to the small segment of the Chinese population which was literate. In due course stories like these were told to large audiences in a language which was understood by all. To facilitate smoothness of transition a new type of narrator's notes had to be prepared and a new literary type was born. Even then the vogue of prose romances written in laconic classical style continued, although it is admitted by all literary critics that the post-T'ang prose romances do not compare with the compositions of the high tide of this art in T'ang times.

CHAPTER 15

The Literary Reform

It is an interesting fact that Li Po and Tu Fu were not only contemporaries but close friends. Although Li Po probably did not rate Tu Fu too highly as a poet, Tu Fu had nothing but eulogy for his friend, the drinker-poet. For this, Li Po was not entirely to blame because instead of forming a team, the two great poets of the T'ang Dynasty exemplified two differing literary tendencies and epochs. Li Po was the culmination of the romantic movement in poetry for whom he had no successor, whereas Tu Fu, the exquisite artist baptized in the vicissitudes of life, was the founder of the realistic school of poetry and thus the forerunner and accelerator of a new trend. Whereas the romantic poets, elevated in their imagination and excessively impressive in their diction, had their feet planted in the floating clouds far removed from the solid earth of realities, the realistic poets were immediate, concrete, easy to understand, and compelling in their power to make their readers feel a sense of affectionate camaraderie. Between these two schools at mid-eighth century, there lay a deep abyss: the abyss of an extremely disruptive and destructive civil war.

This civil war caused by the rebellion of An Lu-shan and continued by the rebellion of Shih Ssŭ-ming (755-762) had shaken T'ang society from its very foundations with inevitable repercussions in the world of literature and art. Just as the rebellions were not fomented in one day, the new trends engendered and accelerated by the many-faceted disorders of the post-rebellion period were not completed in a short time. In the case of Tu Fu, for example, such poems as "The Song of the War Chariot," "The Song of Beauty," and the poem he wrote on his way from the capital to Fênghsien County, which were all written before the rebellion of An Lu-shan, were forebodings of the catastrophe that was to come and, therefore, distinctly different from those writings of the romantic poets in which only the glories of prosperity, peace, and joy of life were reflected. Besides Tu Fu there were also minor pioneers of the new realistic school who had seen the unhealthy effects of excessive romanticism

285

upon literature. It was only Tu Fu's surpassing genius which had made him outstanding among new voices of his age.

If the desire for change had been felt by the poets, urgency for reform in prose was also apparent. Straightforward prose, bold enough to disregard the use of parallel structure and the observance of tonal juxtaposition for artistic effects, was used only in the writing of fiction, a class of writing that was considered to be immensely inferior to the formal essay type and, therefore, cultivated only as a diversion. In the more respected genres of prose composition adherence to rigid formulas was the prevailing rule. Behind the dazzling regularity of sentence structure and the sonorousness of carefully selected syllables, there was an alarming emptiness in content. This was true of the essay, of the memorials, of the imperial rescripts, and above all, of funerary eulogies. This last-mentioned prose type had assumed a unique social as well as literary importance in China where filial piety had long been held up as the cardinal virtue. In each tomb and each ancestral temple there would be found one or more compositions summarizing the chief events in the life of the deceased to be made permanent for posterity. Such compositions naturally presented a challenge even to expert writers when the demand for them was universal. As the lives led by the average citizen were so similar to that of his neighbors hardly anything could be done to distinguish one composition from another. As a result, the numerous examples which have been recovered from the various T'ang burial sites bear such great resemblance to one another that the situation borders upon the ludicrous. What was followed was a set form into which blanks would be filled with the name, dates, and geographical origin of the deceased. Hardly anyone among the common people was distinguished, or was even distinguishable.

This formulization of prose writing demanded a change. The change took the form in a negative way of discontinuing the use of the balanced style or *p'ien wên*. With the dropping of one style, there came the problem of the search for a substitute. And the selection of a substitute was a more complicated and sensitive problem to contemporaries for it had to be both effective and acceptable. Curiously enough, the solution of the problem took the form of a revival of "ancient prose." Hence, this movement was known as the *ku wên* movement. In theory, it was dedicated to a revival of early Han and pre-Han prose style. Thus the leader of this movement, Han Yü (768-824), was credited with resurrecting the dignity of prose after its decadence through eight dynasties. Actually, this so-called "ancient prose movement" was no more a resurrection of what was dead than the European Renaissance was a rebirth of European antiquity. Literature, just like other realms of human activity and creativeness, never repeats itself. What seems to be a backward retracing of the steps of a bygone past and what sounds like retrogression is oftentimes revolution in disguise.

Strange as it may seem that none of the reformers had thought of the possibility of blazing new trails in literature by adopting the spoken language of the common people as a vehicle for creative writing, the situation is not difficult for us to understand, especially with the advantage of hindsight. In the first place, speech and writing had traveled widely apart, and the spoken language, despite its liveliness and its vigor, had failed for so long to receive systematic refinement that it was universally regarded as a vehicle unworthy of recording. In the second place, reading and writing were the privileges of the learned and the tools of the privileged were expected to bear the hallmark of distinction—the sign of superiority to what was universal. Against this accepted standard, complaints and grumbles were few, and diminished with the expansion of educational opportunities in the empire. Under these circumstances it is easily understandable that even village children in rural schools in frontier provinces were eager to climb the ladder of distinction by attempting to write in the style of the textbooks which they were trying to learn. Thus, the sanction of keeping the written style distinctly different from the folk speech was an established fact universally welcome. Who among students in the medieval universities in Europe would have thought of submitting a thesis written in his mother tongue instead of universal Latin?

With the vernacular thus disposed of with affection (because even the most erudite and the most pedantic would continue to use it with relish and feeling in everyday life), and with the stilted *p'ien wên* outworn and threadbare, the only way out was the reactivation of early Han and pre-Han prose style. This was the most natural and easy course to win approval, for in spite of the cultivation of an artificial style for over a thousand years, the scholars of the empire had maintained a universal and enduring contact with early Han and pre-Han writings. The core of a formal education had always consisted in committing to memory one or all of the Confucian classics, the number varying in accordance with the length of formal schooling. In other words, even pupils in rural areas, with only one year of formal schooling, would have been exposed to the Confucian classics. In addition, many of the folk sayings and adages circulated among the illiterate had been quotations from the Confucian classics and the writings of the early Han and pre-Han philosophers and essayists, especially Lao-tzŭ and Chuang-tzŭ.

It was one thing to appreciate a new medium as more conducive to creative writing, and another thing to demonstrate ability in wielding the new tool. Experimentation was necessary, but experimentation could be applied only to a form of writing in which no serious offenses would be committed. What was then more natural than to test the usability of the new vehicle in the writing of fiction. It was no coincidence, therefore, that Han Yü, the chief exponent of the literary reform concurrently as he was being hailed the defender of orthodox Confucianism and authoring essays and memorials in which Buddhism and Taoism were unconditionally condemned with dignity and persuasion, should cultivate the seemingly incompatible technique of writing stories of the prose romance type.

In a purely historic sense the literary reform led by Han Yü and his associates was not without precedent. The first instance of the advocation of such a reform without the label *ku wên* was started in the eleventh year of the reign of Ta T'ung (545) of the Western Wei Dynasty. The chief advocate was a northern Chinese Su Ch'o (498-546), who was in the service of the alien Topa monarch, Yü-Wen T'ai, who had instructed him to write a proclamation of the dynastic policy in a style directly imitative of the *Book of Documents*. This revolutionary attempt did not bear fruit in the field of literature because it was mainly a political move, although it was not completely devoid of cultural significance. The northern half of China was then split into the Eastern Wei and the Western Wei. Having inherited the old cultural area of Shantung, the Eastern Wei had far surpassed its western competitor culturally; thus the Western Wei felt compelled to impress its subjects with a positive cultural program and policy. Steps were taken to rebuild its official hierarchy in conformity with the specifications of the Confucian *Chou Li* and as a literary accompaniment decided to have its official documents written in the style of the *Book of Documents*. In substance, the whole undertaking was the spreading of a cultural smokescreen to consummate its dual policy of the antiquarianizing of its cultural policy and the barbarization of its political and military program.

Another similar attempt at restoring the prose style of antiquity took place in the early years of the Sui Dynasty even before China was again reunified. In 584 Emperor Wên instructed his secretaries to be truthful in all their private and public writings. In response, his minister, Li O, submitted a memorial to elaborate the meaning of the imperial decree in which the ornate prose style of the Six Dynasties was reviewed in disparaging terms, criticizing its deviation from the models of the great sages. The recommendation was reinforced by a leading northern Confucian philosopher, Wang T'ung, (585-617), whose book, *Chung Shuo,* had been written in the style of the *Confucian Analects.* This proposed reform was also abortive in a literary sense, for, at this time, the southern half of China had already become aware of its precariousness. This launching of a literary movement from the north was, therefore, interpreted as political propaganda in disguise. The south, despite its military weakness and political confusion and corruption, was convinced of its cultural and literary superiority to the north. This feeling was not only universal among the literate citizenry of the south, but also secretly shared by the northern leaders. As soon as the political unification of China had become an established fact in 589, all Sui emperors and aristocrats succumbed to the cultural hegemony of the south. Emperor Yang not only wrote songs in imitation of the southern style, but also was so fascinated by the luxury and softness of the Yangtze Delta that he chose to die south of the Yangtze.

Even after the T'ang Dynasty had been founded in 618, the attempt was not abandoned to replace the excessively artificial and ornate prose style of the Six Dynasties with a kind of writing more simple, more direct, and more terse. In other words, the need continued to be felt that there should be a frank prose style to replace *p'ien wên,* which had always straddled both prose and poetry. These isolated warnings, however, produced no appreciable results because theories on the necessity of the stylistic change would usually attract no attention.

When Han Yü held up the banner of revolt, however, the situation had been completely changed. In addition to suggestions for stylistic changes and actual sustaining of such suggestions there was a massive struggle as a consequence. For, whereas the two previous literary reforms had been initiated by the monarchs, this time the incentive came from the writers themselves to radiate upward.

Let us take a look first at the central thought pattern and the slogans of the literary reform. In the words of Han Yü, the leader, we see his claim to cultural orthodoxy. In his essay entitled "Yüan Tao" or "The Origin of Tao," he wrote:

> What Tao is this Tao? The answer is, this Tao is what I call Tao and not an inquiry into what Lao-tzŭ and the Buddha have meant by Tao. This is what Yao transmitted to Shun, Shun transmitted to Yü, Yü transmitted to T'ang T'ang transmitted to King Wên, King Wu and the Duke of Chou, King Wên, King Wu and the Duke of Chou transmitted to Confucius and Confucius transmitted to Mêng K'o. When Mêng K'o died there was no one to transmit it to . . . . Now the ways of the barbarians have been elevated above the teachings of the ancient kings. How far are we from degenerating into barbarians ourselves?

In his memorial submitted to the throne in 819 he wrote:

In the fourteenth year of the reign of Yüan Ho ... there was a protective relic pagoda in Fa Mên Monastery in the county seat of Fênghsiang and inside the pagoda there was a finger joint of the Buddha which purported to open up once in thirty years. ... Emperor Hsien dispatched a special palace commissioner, Tu Ying-ch'i, to escort thirty palace maidens to welcome the relic into the Forbidden Palace with fragrant flowers. After remaining in the Imperial Palace for three days it was escorted back to the monastery. At this, princes and noblemen, scholars and citizens marveled and sighed and ran in haste to report to one another. Han, Vice-Minister of the Board of Punishment, submitted a memorial in remonstration:

"In your servant's opinion, Buddhism is only one of the ways of the barbarians. It was introduced into China in the Later Han Dynasty and was never heard of in antiquity. ... When Emperor Kao first accepted the empire from the Sui Dynasty on its abdication, he proposed to ban it. His ministers in those days, however, did not have farsighted knowledge and talents. Hence, they did not know the way of the ancient kings, propriety according to old and new standards, and therefore were unable to extend the illumination of his majesty to terminate that piece of malpractice. There the matter rested—and your servant has always regretted it. ... As regards the Buddhists, they are originally barbarians, speaking a language other than Chinese and wearing clothing of a different style. They ... know nothing about the propriety between monarch and subject, nor the affection between parent and child. If the Buddha himself were still alive today and had received the orders of the state to come reverently to the imperial capital, and if your majesty condescended to receive him, what would result would be the granting of an audience, the arranging of a dinner by your subordinates, the gift of a suit and the sending of an escort to accompany him back as far as the frontier without letting the multitudes be misled. ... The common citizens, however, are uninformed and slow of under-standing, easy to mislead and difficult to enlighten. If, seeing your majesty doing what has been done is interpreted as your majesty truly serving the Buddha, the people will unanimously say, 'Even the son of heaven with his great sageness respects and believes with an undivided mind, who are we, the people of the hundred surnames, to care and hesitate about our bodies and lives? ...' They will fear being behind time and the young will vie with the old in abandoning their professions and their sense of precedence. If nothing is done to suppress and prohibit this ... the mores will be hurt and the people's customs will be ruined as the report will spread in all directions as a laughing-stock. This is not a small matter."

This campaign against Buddhism rested mainly on the preconceived and emotional assumption of China's cultural orthodoxy. Logic and objectivity were completely lost sight of. It is no surprise that his efforts in behalf of Chinese cultural orthodoxy ended in complete failure. The T'ang imperial house was at least partly descended from Central Asian "barbarians" and had adopted the very common Chinese clan name of Li which they shared with pride with Li Erh, the legal name of Lao-tzŭ, founder of Taoism, the keen rival to Confucianism. Furthermore, it was no surprise that after his political banishment to Chaochow in northeastern Kwangtung Province, Han Yü submissively mended his ways by singing only praises of the imperial crown. Despite the persecution of 485, the influence of Buddhism on late T'ang society was strengthened impressively.

If the source of inspiration for the literary reform had been confined to a claim of China's cultural superiority and orthodoxy, the movement would have ended in complete failure. But the more concrete target had always been kept in sight and this was the preoccupation of the literary reformers with factional strife arising out of the intricate relationship between politics, literature, and the procedure of official recruitment. The prevailing mode of recruitment for civil service positions was a simple one. Competitive examinations were held periodically and successful candidates were rated and selected by examiners appointed by the imperial government. These candidates were granted the title or degree of *chin shih* or advanced scholars and were appointed by the government to official positions. Important officials of the empire including the members of the prime ministry and the supervising examiners themselves were almost invariably holders of the *chin shih* degree. Simultaneously they were also the most outstanding members of the writing profession. The upshot of the situation was the identity of the politically influential and the literarily pre-eminent. Those who were in power in politics were the wielders directly or immediately of literary influence. The more numerous were the disciples and pupils of a political boss, the more firmly and extensively he entrenched his political tentacles. The one power that the administrators of the empire were most reluctant to let go was the supervision of the competitive examinations. Occupation of literary leadership and seizure of power in the examination halls were the surest steppingstones to the fulfillment of the highest political ambitions.

In 821 factional strife between two groups in their attempt to seize the examination field had come to a head. The event was summarized thus in the *T'ung Chien*, a summary of Chinese History year by year written by Ssŭ-ma Kuang (1019-1086):

In the sixth year of the reign of T'ai Ho (832) Niu Sêng-ju (leader of the Niu faction) was appointed co-prime minister to serve as the regulator-general of the Huai-nan circuit. . . . Before 827 the regulator of the Hsi Ch'uan circuit, Li Tê-yü (leader of the Li faction) had been appointed president of the board of defense. . . . On Li Tê-yü's return to the capital, Li Tsung-min (supporter of Niu) tried to block it in a hundred ways without avail. . . . Tu Tsung said, "I have a plan to dissolve the long-harbored grievances, but I am afraid you could not use it. . . . Li Tên-yü is well versed in letters but did not go through the normal channel of the examinations and always feels sorry for it. If we let him head up the examination board, he will feel happy." Li Tsung-min remained quiet for a while and said, "Think of something else. . . ."

The foregoing summary of a protracted and complex struggle for power thus underscored a number of signal facts: (1) that a man of letters despite his accomplishments failed to rate in the eyes of the literati; (2) that even though one faction was eager to make concessions to its oppoent for a political truce it would not abandon its hold on the examination organ; (3) that abandonment of the examination organ would lead to a loss of influence among men of letters and eventually to loss of support by members of the civil service.

In this light it is easy to understand that the Li faction, mindful of the fact that its leader was not a holder of the *chin shih* degree, advanced as a counterstroke the proposition to the throne of terminating the *chin shih* examinations or changing the subject matter of those examinations from belles-lettres to Confucian classical studies. These recommendations, made many times during the reigns of two emperors (827-846), were obviously blocked by the Niu faction.

These two specialties of classical studies and creative writing in belles-lettres had parted company for a long time. When China was split in 318, the leading families of the Shantung area did not migrate in large numbers to the south and with the establishment of alien dynasties in the north; they continued the cultivation of the study of the Confucian classics and became the training center of Confucian commentators. This tradition was piously maintained through the centuries of north-south opposition to the golden period of the T'ang empire. In the south, where the purportedly orthodox Chinese cultural traditions sought refuge and were maintained, studies on the Confucian classics had been neglected on account of the prevalence of Taoism and Buddhism and scholarly activities were replaced by the cultivation of imaginative literature in prose and verse. Despite the fact that the Confucian writings were universally read in all schools, the approach followed in the two halves of the Chinese Empire was entirely different. The south studied them as storehouses of literature alongside Taoist and Buddhist books, even possibly rating them as inferior to the latter in philosophical content. The north, on the other hand, regarded the Confucian canon not only as the fountain of all wisdom and the standard of ethics, but also as a weapon with which to fight or convert their alien rulers culturally. While the south was blooming with esthetic elegance, the north remained firm and solid with its erudition. In the Niu-Li factional strife, the first group allied itself with the southern tradition and the Li group was a continuator of the northern tradition. With this understanding of the background we can assess the significance of the literary reform headed by Han Yü.

According to contemporary records both official and private, Han Yü was known to have attracted a wide following of the *chin shih* candidates. When the leader of the new faction, Niu Sêng-ju, arrived at the capital from his native circuit in central China, he called on Han Yü with his literary exercises. Han Yü was at home with his friend, Huang-fu Chih, another prominent writer, and received him at leisure. After examining the young man's writings, the two literary giants were enthusiastic and lavish in their praise, saying, "Your writings will entitle you not only to success in the examinations but also to enduring fame." Soon after, ascertaining that the young man was not home, they called at his house and left a note on the door saying, "Han Yü and Huang-fu Chih called together." On the following day those officials who had stopped to admire the note were as numerous as to have made a "solid wall." These were eager to make the acquaintance of a successful candidate and thus Niu Seng-ju won fame all over the empire even before he had taken the examinations. Thus the little note paved the way not only to Niu's successful candidacy but also, eventually, to the prime ministry for nineteen years. Another cornerstone of the literary reform was the peculiar practice of submitting sample compositions to the leaders of literature, including the official examiners. This practice, known in Chinese as *wên chüan,* literally means "warming up scrolls," or "reviewing scrolls." This would be done intermittently before the examination time. Those to whom the scrolls or sample writings were submitted were leaders in the realm of letters who invariably were leaders in politics at the same time. Whatever they favored would set a literary trend and whoever they approved would become successful candidates. The official examiners, naturally, would be influenced by prevailing literary opinion. It was, therefore, a usual phenomenon that even before the entry of the candidates into the examination halls, it was already determined as to which candidates would be successful, and among them which ones would receive special distinctions and honors. The formalities of the examination itself were, therefore, only a gesture. The only exception was during the reign of Empress Wu (684-701) when the names of candidates on the books were sealed off and success depended entirely upon performance.

Aware of the burden of sample writings they had to read—and sample examination papers are usually no more interesting than actual ones—a number of the literary grandees of the T'ang Dynasty purposely and openly stated that no more than three would be accepted from any one candidate; but these warnings were usually disregarded by the young aspirants. Hence it was a common occurrence that the gatehouse of a literary leader would be filled to overflowing with these scrolls. As screening was difficult but necessary, an urgent problem that had presented itself was, what kind of writing would demonstrate the talents of the candidate and minimize the ennui of the reader? The demands made by the imperial government and the general public of a good writer were threefold: the fluency of a historian, the clarity of an administrator, and the adornment of a poet. An ideal composition would be one in which all three classes of the candidate's talent could be brought forth for exhibition: a narrative, usually imaginary in character, with its purple patches emotionally recapitulated in verse, followed by a little essay pointing out a moral or assessing the ethical excellence or depravity of the major characters. This, then, became the prototype of the "warming-up" scrolls which permanently set a pattern for a new literary genre, the *ch'uan ch'i*, loosely translated as "romances."

Would this not be in conflict with the high purpose which Han Yü had set for himself—the transmitting of orthodoxy of the ages, left dangling since Mencius and ready to fall like a cloak upon the shoulders of Han Yü himself? Riding the double horse as he did, Han Yü had not only written serious essays on the defense of Confucian Tao, but also had written a fictitious biography of the writing brush in the style of current short fiction. This had elicited a protest from a friend, Chang Ch'i. To Chang's criticism, Han Yü replied with embarrassment that he was only doing it "for fun." In further protest, Chang wrote: "A superior man is never removed from *li* in his words or his deeds. I have never heard that he would undertake mixed-up writings for fun. You have seen these writings. You exclaim, you laugh, you follow suit. That means you have drifted away from what is right in rectifying your good nature and in repelling the temptations of temperament." To this Han Yü wrote in reply: "You are blaming me for writing what is mixed-up. I have answered fully and I hope you will reread my letter. In former times even the master had his fun. Doesn't the *Book of Songs* say, 'One who is good in making fun will never allow himself to become cruel'? And it is said in the *Book of Rites*, 'Tension without relaxation is something beyond the ability of King Wên and King Wu.' How could it be damaging to the Tao?"

There must have been others critical of the new trend generally and of Han Yü particularly. That is why the second leader of the literary reform, Liu Tsung-yüan (773-819), wrote in Han Yü's defense: "Mr. Han has read extensively in the books of antiquity and is fond of letters. He approves the ability of Mr. Writing Brush in developing his theme and volunteered to write the biography to express what has been harbored in his mind for the benefit of scholars. Isn't it helpful to the world?"

Both answers were probably correct. When Han Yü said "for fun" he probably meant for experimentation, and when Liu Chung-yüan said "beneficial to the world" he meant that fiction might be an effective vehicle for the spreading of Tao.

Experimentation was necessary because the type was so new. The problem that remained now was, for the storytelling part, whether straightforward prose should be used or the prevailing florid p'ien wên. To contemporaries, what was known as ancient prose was much more wordy than the laconic style of p'ien wên. For the telling of a story, however, the use of more words to make the recording detailed and accurate was evidently much more appropriate because events usually do not happen in pairs to resemble the structure of balanced prose. Even after p'ien wên has been eliminated as a possible vehicle, there was yet another choice—that between the revival of Han and pre-Han prose style and the using of the spoken tongue. After all, the new type was not so new. For at least two centuries Buddhist stories had been told in prose, and in fact, in a type of prose not only far removed from p'ien wên, but actually approaching the naturalness of the daily speech of the common people. These narrative portions of the Buddhist stories in addition were recapitulated in verse and chanted to the great satisfaction of the pious audience. The only difference between these Buddhist recitals and the new type lay in the lack of a moral tale for the former which would rather become an advantage from an esthetic point of view. This example was not followed partly because Buddhism had been so vehemently attacked by Han Yü and partly because Han Yü, by temperament and by training, could not have made his choice otherwise.

One great difference between the T'ang romance and the Buddhist recitals lay in the conscious cultivation in the former of an esthetic prose style in place of the casual narrative prose used in Buddhist writing in which no special attempts were made to emulate the style of the Han and pre-Han prose masters. In view of this, it is historically accurate to regard the ninth-century romance as a new literary genre which won extensive contemporary approval and extended its influence upon the writers of later ages. With this movement should be identified the literary reform with its far-reaching effects.

The new pattern was adhered to by Han Yü himself of combining prose narration and poetry in the same composition. His "rotative poetry on a stone vessel" with its preface illustrates our point. The preface which precedes the poetry is a narrative in prose. And the story told is briefly as follows.

In the seventh year of the reign of Yüan Ho (812) a Taoist from the Hung Mountain, Hsien-Yüan Mi-Ming, had arrived at the capital and called upon his old acquaintance, Liu Shih-fu, holder of the *chin shih* degree. It was after nightfall that the two met in the studio in the company of a young scholar, Hou Hsi, newly known as an accomplished poet, who had come to call on the host to discuss poetic art. By his side the Taoist looked extremely unattractive with his white beard, dark-complexioned face, long neck, protruding knot of hair and his awkward southern accent. The young poet disregarded him completely. All of a sudden the Taoist flared his robe, opened his eyes wide and pointed to the vessel inside the furnace, addressing the scholar, "You are reputed to be a poet. Could you write a poem collaboratively with us on this as a topic?" The host had heard reports of the Taoist's age as being over ninety and of his ability to exorcise evil spirits and tame wild beasts; he had never had a chance to check on the veracity of such reports, but had respected him only for his age without even knowing whether the old man had an education, and was greatly delighted with the suggestion. Without hesitation he took hold of a writing brush and wrote two opening lines of poetry on the given subject and passed the sheet on to the young poet. The poet in turn actively accepted the challenge and continued the poem. Then the Taoist laughed uproariously and said, "Is your poetry just like this?" He then struck his shoulders, clasped his hands inside the wide sleeves of his robe, leaned on the northern wall of the studio, and said to the poet, "I cannot write in the current worldly style. Please do the writing for me." Whereupon he chanted two lines which sounded unlabored but connotative of a satire of the poet. The two literati looked at each other, trying to embarrass the Taoist guest by outstripping him with quantity.

When the sheet was again passed by the host to the poet the latter tried desperately hard to surpass the Taoist but when he chanted his lines his voice sounded sad and when he held his writing brush, ready to write, he hesitated more than once. After the lines were committed to writing they did not seem to be distinguished. When it came to the Taoist's turn he elevated his sitting position and shouted his lines aloud. They seemed more effortless but the artistic effects were more out of the ordinary and his connotations all the more satirical. This went on until the middle of the night when the two literati felt that their poetic inspiration had been exhausted. They rose in apology and said, "You, elevated teacher, are not an ordinary man of our world. We feel subdued, willingly become your pupils and dare not discuss poetry with you any more." Energetically the Taoist answered in reply, "Not so. The poem must be finished." He said again to the host, "Get your brush. I will finish it up for you." Then he chanted eight lines of five syllables each and when these were recorded he said, "Isn't the poem finished now?" and the two answered in unison, "It is now finished." The Taoist said further, "What I have done is really not writing. I have done it only on your level. What I can do neither of you is prepared to listen to with understanding. This is true not only of writing. My words themselves you are not prepared to understand and so I will close my mouth at this moment."

Profoundly frightened, the two younger men prostrated themselves before the couch. "We don't dare to raise any questions except one. You told us you could not do the current handwriting of this world. May we ask what script it is that you can write?" To this the Taoist remained quiet as though he had never heard the question. The same silence prevailed although the question was repeated more than once. Completely lost, the two retired to their seats. The Taoist, leaning against the wall, fell asleep, snoring thunderously. The two scholars were so shocked that they didn't even dare to pant. In a little while the dawn drum was sounded rhythmically. As the two scholars were also tired, they fell into a sleep while sitting in their chairs.

When they awoke the sun was already up. They looked around in surprise in search of the Taoist who was no longer there. They asked a boy servant and the latter said, "At daybreak the Taoist got up and went out of the door as though he would soon return. And when I wondered why he had not returned, I looked for him outside the door but could not find any trace of him." The two scholars felt disappointed and reprimanded themselves. They told this to me but I wasn't able to tell what Taoist that had been although I have heard of a superior hermit named Mi-ming. Could it have been he?

Following this prose part, signed by Han Yü himself, was the purported poem of composite composition—a literary practice recorded of the early Han imperial court but revived for the first time by Han Yü. The procedure reminds one of a literary game with participants taking their turn in the composition of a poem. While it is indisputably a form of literary gymnastics, yet some of the results happily, are clever. In the case of the poem on the stone vessel, however, instead of a poem of rotative authorship, the whole poem most probably was Han Yü's handiwork, although attempts were made to vary the style to fit the station and attainment of each composer. The over-all technique betrayed the authorship of Han Yü as was attested by the discernment many centuries later of Chu Hsi.

In keeping with the major trends of Chinese culture, the literary reform went far beyond the limits of the prose romances, which will be more fully discussed in the following chapter. Attractive and entertaining though these prose romances were, they could not be endowed effectively with dignity comparable with the upholding of Tao—the orthodox Way of Life in China transmitted through the ages of antiquity to which Han Yü and his associates in the literary reform had dedicated themselves. As supporter of the orthodox Tao and as leader of a movement to retrieve the dignity of letters from the disrepute into which it had fallen for eight dynasties, Han Yü had to hoist a more glorious official banner than the composition of fictional narratives "for fun."

Han Yü, despite his unique place in T'ang thought and letters, was a fascinating bundle of contradictions. Often during the third decade of his life he relied for support and education on a sister-in-law. His youth was precocious and his acquaintance with Chinese traditional literature was unusually extensive. At eighteen he went to Ch'angan, the imperial capital, where he won the *chin shih* degree six years later. It was not until he was twenty-eight that he was appointed to a public office. His rise in the official hierarchy was steady and rapid. In 817 he had distinguished himself by participation in a military campaign against rebels in the Huai Hsi region under the generalship of the prime minister, P'ei Tu. In response to an imperial decree to compose a memorial tablet for the military victory, he wrote a composition in which the merits of the prime minister were eulogized and no mention was made of the heroic feats of Li Su, who actually did more than other officers in bringing about the capture of the chief rebel. Dissatisfied with the official document, Li Su's wife appealed to Emperor Hsien who, after a careful inquiry was made, ordered the effacing of Han Yü's composition and the substitution of a new piece to be written by Tuan Wên-ch'ang (772-835). After this dishonor he memorialized the throne on the impropriety of honoring the Buddhist relic, whereupon he was demoted and exiled. From this time on, he seemed to have lost his fighting spirit totally and submitted himself docilely to the whims of the emperor. After less than one year in exile, he steadily regained his official honors. With the coronation of Emperor Mu in 821, he was appointed to the presidency of the imperial university at the capital. Then he was promoted to the vice-ministry on the board of defense and the board of civil service successively.

As we have noted before, the core of the literary reform initiated by Han Yü was the revival of what was called the ancient prose style, in opposition to and deviation from the florid and trivial artificialities of balanced prose which had held sway during the six dynasties of political disunion and continued to hang heavily on the literary horizon during the first 150 years of the T'ang Dynasty. In form as well as in substance, this literary movement was officially a return to the past. In keeping with this spirit, Han Yü handed out to his younger contemporaries the orthodox advice of Han and pre-Han writings harboring only those thoughts which had been taught by the ancient sages. Those he held up as models for imitation in writing were all masters of the pre-Christian centuries in China, omitting mention of even the leading writers of the Eastern Han Dynasty itself. Knowing that he was swimming against the tide when he advocated the literary reform, he said in his letter to Fêng Hsü:

I have been writing for long. In each self-assessment, I have found that whatever I consider good, will invariably be considered bad by others. What gives me slight satisfaction will elicit slight wonderment by others; what gives me great satisfaction will elicit great wonderment by others. I have frequently responded to requests by writing what is in conformity with vulgar taste, and I feel ashamed when I apply my brush; by the time I show it to others it is considered good. What I am slightly ashamed of has similarly been labeled slightly good; what I am greatly ashamed of is considered invariably greatly good. I do not know what forthright use there is of ancient style in the current world but I am willing to wait for those who really know to know. Formerly Yang Hsiung wrote T'ai Hsüan and was universally laughed at by people and Yang Hsiung's words were, "It does not hurt if the world doesn't know me. If there is another Yang Hsiung in future generations, he will love it."

He was thus willing to brave opposition and to sustain disregard in his promotion of the new "ancient" prose style. In his irreconcilable attitude we see clearly his leadership. He was capable of demonstrating his theories by outstanding examples. The result is the attainment of a prose style at once direct, lucid, and yet charming in its archaic unconventionality. While his argumentative pieces in which he tried to defend China's cultural orthodoxy have been highly respected, his success in literature was more fully demonstrated in his familiar essays and epistolary pieces. His farewell words to his dead friend and colleague in the literary reform, Liu Tsung-yüan, written in accordance with a peculiar Chinese genre (a kind of eulogy to be read and then burned by the side of the bier or at the grave to be communicated to the deceased), are extremely touching:

> Alas, Tzŭ-hou [Liu's courtesy name], and have you come eventually to this state? People ever since antiquity have invariably come to this state, why do I need to grieve? Man's life in the world is like a dream followed by waking up, thus what need is there for one to check his loss and gain? While the dream is on there is sorrow and joy, but after the dream is over what is there worthy of clinging to remorsefully? . . . You have now gone to your eternal home and will not return. I spread these sacrifices before your coffin and I offer my message with an affectionate heart.

This piece, written in prose except for intermittent end-rhymes, is less free from conventions than a similar piece addressed to his deceased nephew. This epistolary message written in down-to-earth prose, contains passages like the following:

> Henceforth my gray hairs will grow white and my strength will fail. Physically and mentally hurrying on to decay, how much longer will it be before I follow you? If there is knowledge after death, this separation will be for only a little while. But if there is no knowledge after death, this sorrow will also be for only a little while and then no more sorrow for the rest of eternity. . . .
>
> Oh, you blue heavens, when will my sorrows end? From now on the world has no charm for me. I will get myself a few acres on the banks of the Ying River and there I will wait for my end, teaching my son and your son if they grow up and my daughter and your daughter until they get married. Alas, although words may fail, love always endures. Do you hear me or do you not hear? Woe is me, may heaven bless you.
>
> Last year when Mr. Mêng Tung-yeh went to you, I wrote a letter to you saying, "I have not yet reached the age of forty and yet my eyesight is blurred, my hair is graying, and my teeth are loosening. I recall that my father and my uncles and my elder brothers are short-lived in spite of their good health. Now that my health is ailing, how can I expect to last long?" I could not go to see you, you did not wish to come to see me, and I was afraid that I would die of a morning or evening and you would harbor a boundless sorrow. Who would say that the young would perish and the old would continue to live? That the strong would die prematurely and the sickly is still preserved intact? Alas, is this real or is it a dream?

In his more formal writings in prose, however, when he was probably more on guard, he would occasionally relapse despite himself into the beaten paths of parallel prose:

On the Origin of Man

What takes form above is called Heaven; what takes form below is called Earth; and what has life between the two is called Man. Those that take form above—the sun, the moon, the planets and the stars—are all Heaven; those that take form below—herbs and trees, mountains and rivers—are all Earth; those that have life between the two—barbarians and savages, fowls and beasts, are all of the realm of Man. One may ask: "That being the case, may I call fowls and animals men?" The answer is no. When you point to a mountain and ask whether it is a mountain you may answer yes, in which case all the herbs and trees, fowls and beasts which are on the mountain are included; but when you point to a blade of grass on a mountain and ask whether it is a mountain, the answer should not be affirmative.

Therefore, when the Way of Heaven is confused, the sun, the moon, the planets, and the stars will fail in their course; when the Way of Earth is confused the herbs, the trees, the mountains, and the rivers will lose their equilibrium; and when the Tao of Man is confused, the barbarians, the savages, the fowls, and the beasts will lose their true qualities. Heaven is the overlord of the sun, the moon, the planets, and the stars; Earth is the overlord of herbs, trees, mountains, and rivers; Man is the overlord of barbarians, savages, fowls, and the beasts. When the overlord abuses the overlordship it loses the way of the overlord. Hence, the sage regards them as one and loves them with equal kindness, cares for the near, and elevates the distant.

What Han Yü was aiming at, according to his own protestations, was more than the restoration of an archaic prose style. This prose style, important as it was to him, was only to serve as a new vehicle for something more vital than literary reform:

When I do ancient prose, how can it be that I merely value it for its rhythms being dissimilar to the current style? When I think of the ancients without being able to see them, I study the ancient way and wish also to be perfectly at home in their writing style. My eagerness to be at home in their ancient style is deeply rooted in my resolution to understand the Tao of antiquity.

Therefore, his ancient prose cultivation was a means to an end, and that end was "to walk in the paths of human-heartedness and propriety and to swim in the source of the ancient books of songs and documents, without losing the path and without damming up the source." This preoccupation with the upholding of the traditional way in defiance of heterodoxies was frequently lost sight of in his literary career. Violent though he was in his denunciations of Buddhism and Taoism, he not only would glorify a Taoist at the great disadvantage of Confucian scholars as he did in the case of the "Stone Vessel" poem, but he also maintained long-lasting friendships with Buddhist monks and Taoist initiates. This is particularly evident in his poetry. He would spend a delightful afternoon admiring the beauties surrounding a Buddhist monastery and he would write long poems to bid farewell to departing monks. Thus, to a Taoist who had sent him some huge mushrooms, he would write a poem in response using Taoist allusions in which he felt perfectly at home.

On another occasion he would adorn the living quarters of a Zen Buddhist with the following lines:

> I walked a hundred paces through a bridge flanked by water pines,
> And arrived at a monk's abode with bamboo couch and mat covers.
> I bent my arm to support my head for a little nap,
> Then fetched my fishing rod and went to the beach sands.

In his long poem sending off the eminent monk, Chêng Kuan, he wrote among other things:

> Regretting I am too old to catch up,
> I sit gazing at you with tears in vain.

Speaking of Han Yü's poems, we must point out that his influence on late T'ang poetry was just as immense as it was on the prose style. As he had liberated prose writing from the shackles of the rules and regulations of parallelism and balance, he recommended a similar freedom to writers in verse. He had developed a complete disregard for poetic diction and he recommended writing verse as one would prose. He would adopt in his own poems the word order of straightforward prose, and yet he was aware of the basic difference between prose and poetry. This difference, however, he envisaged in what he considered to be the difference in levels of flatness. The flavor of poetry was not derived from the artificial choice of poetic diction for adornment but from deviation from what was flat. As a result, his contemporaries agreed in describing his poetry as strange and precarious. Strangeness actually meant something that was not flat and precariousness meant deviation from beaten paths. To him the writing of poetry was comparable to scaling the Alps, whereas prose writing was comparable to walking along an open boulevard on a business trip. In both instances, however, one's gait should be natural. The following poem is about an obscure person who flourished around 800, and whom the poet admires.

> In the morning Tung Shêng goes out.
> In the evening he returns to read the books of the ancients.
> For the whole day he gets no rest;
> Sometimes he gathers firewood on the hills,
> Sometimes he goes to the streams to fish.
> He enters the kitchen to prepare food,
> And ascends the hall to inquire on the health of his parents.
> His father and mother never feel sad,
> His wife and children never sigh.
> Tung Shêng is filial and kind.
> Men don't know him,
> Only Old Man Heaven does.

The Chinese original of the poem paraphrased above was written not only in sentences that could have been punctuated as prose, but also in lines varying in length from two to six characters.

As a child of his age, Han Yü showed considerable dexterity also in writing poetry in the traditional pattern. The liberty that he attained in prose and verse was the liberty that came as a reward and outgrowth of discipline.

Han Yü's literary pre-eminence was assured by the support given him by Liu Tsung-yüan (773-819). A native of present-day Shansi Province, Liu attained literary prominence when he was barely twenty. As his reputation steadily grew, the political leaders of the empire vied with one another in providing him with patronage. In his official career, especially when he had to attend to administrative chores, he developed an aversion for routine contacts with his superiors and colleagues who were more concerned with advancement and promotion than with efficiency and contribution of welfare to the common people. On account of his intimate association with a political leader whose reputation was questionable, he lived many years in exile to minor positions in far-off regions in the Chinese Empire. His following, however, did not dwindle as a result of these political setbacks. When he was a prefect in Liuchou in far off Kwangsi in 815, the most prominent scholars in the extreme southern region of the empire would travel hundreds of miles to visit him and honor him as their teacher and patron. He died in 819 in his forty-seventh year.

Unlike bureaucrats of his time, Liu Tsung-yüan took a definite stand on the political struggles of the age. When the imperial censor, Wang Ch'ang, was exiled by the emperor on account of his political attacks on a favorite minister, two hundred imperial university students demonstrated against the decree by kneeling at the entrance of the imperial palace. Liu, in this instance, exerted his independence of judgment and action by writing a long letter to the demonstrators approving of their bravery.

Moral integrity was not a common characteristic among T'ang scholars and officials; intent on personal advancement, they showed little hesitancy in seeking the patronage of the great and powerful. This gave rise to factionalism among scholars during the whole span of the T'ang Dynasty. In this regard, Liu distinguished himself by supporting a political leader, Wang Shu-wên, who was brave enough to sacrifice his own public career by advocating drastic changes. When Wang fell as a prime minister, Liu undauntedly faced the inevitable consequences by accepting demotions, and he never regretted it. During his magistracy in Liuchou he banned the corrupt practice prevailing in this southern fringe of the T'ang Empire of the selling and buying of young slaves. Within a twelve-month period he was able not only to terminate that terrible practice but also to restore to full freedom almost a thousand slave boys and girls.

Distinctly different from his literary colleague, Han Yü, Liu exhibited the same independence of judgment in his attitude toward the religions. Whereas Han Yü had made it his mission to attack the Buddhists and the Taoists, Liu, in spite of his Confucianist upbringing, continually fraternized with Buddhist monks, and he openly admitted, "I have been attracted by Buddhism ever since I was a little boy and I have searched for its truth for close to thirty years." On another occasion, going even further, he said that the teachings of Buddhism "are in harmony with the *Book of Changes* and the *Analects*—even if the Sage were resurrected I would not refute them."

More dedicated to literature and less concerned with political influence, Liu sustained Han Yü's position in the literary reform. Like Han, he believed in freeing prose style from the artificialities of the Six Dynasties and that the most effective way to attain freedom was to return to the simplicity of ancient times. Like Han, again, he believed that the cause of literature should be made dignified and valuable by its preoccupation with the perpetuation of Tao. On this point, however, he also parted company with Han. To Han, Tao meant the "way" of the Confucianists, the "way" of ethical living measured by the yardstick of Confucius and Mencius, and the "way" also of ordering the state and pacifying the world as advocated by the chief spokesman of the Confucian school. To Liu, a great lover of Buddhism though not a confirmed Buddhist, while study of the Confucian classics was inherently a valuable asset to writers, Tao itself was universal. To Han, the value of the Confucian classics lay primarily in the gem within the mounting—the message of Tao in the books. To Liu, the gem was valuable, but the mounting itself enhanced the beauty of the jewel and therefore should not fail to receive the attention of men of letters. Thus Liu's assessment of the value of ancient letters was twofold, paying equal attention to both the manner and the matter of the Confucian classics. Moreover, he advised writers to study the *Book of Documents* for substantiality, the *Book of Changes* for rhythmic pulsation, to supplement his training with Mencius and Hsüntzŭ to attain fluency, and with Laotzŭ and Chuang-tzŭ for poignancy. His position, therefore, was that of a man of letters not entirely unmindful of the philosophical wisdom contained in ancient classics and was not the position taken by Han Yü who considered himself a member of the sagely succession regarding literature as a mere chambermaid to ethical moralism which he equated with Tao.

Liu's keenness for the esthetic was greatly abetted by his extensive travels, especially in the counties of Yung and Liu in Kwangsi Province. The greatest examples of Liu's writings are found in his little descriptive pieces in which he succeeded in drawing miniatures of landscape in words. Following is a description of the little rocky pool west of the Tiny Mount:

Walking a hundred twenty paces westward from the Tiny Mount, we were confronted by a screen of bamboo growth. We heard the sound of water like the tinkling of jade pendants which made our hearts delighted. We cut down some bamboos to blaze a trail and saw a little pool underneath. The water was excessively clear and cool with rocks at the bottom. Near the side of the pool rocks protruded out of the surface in the forms of little banks, harbors, islets, and overhanging precipices. Green trees were in luxuriant growth covered with nets of wavy vines, irregular in shape and rolling in undulations. Inside the pool were about a hundred fishes swimming as though in the void supported by nothing. Sunlight beams downward casting shadows on the rocks which stand staunchly immovable. . . . The fish swim hither and thither far and near seemingly to enjoy the company of the human travelers. As one looks away southwestward from the pool, the landscape twists like the stars of the polar constellation and winds at times like a serpent clearly visible in all its outline. The banks of a stream zigzag in dents like rows of a duck's teeth with its source well hidden. Sitting at the pool's side, we saw the pool embraced by trees and bamboos in four directions. The quiet was absolute, chilling one's spirits and cooling one's bones. There was stillness and solitude, there was seclusion and remoteness. On account of excessive coldness we did not tarry long and left after the short description was made.

The movement gathered momentum and magnitude with the immense following that Han Yü had gathered around himself. Among his associates and pupils two names are particularly worth mentioning: Li Ao, who, misled slightly by Han Yü's proclamations, dedicated himself to learning Tao instead of letters from the latter; and Huang-fu Chih (flourished 793-840), proud of his originality and independence of style, who would not hesitate to take pride also in accepting payment for his writings. Although Huang-fu's literary taste followed the tradition of Han Yü, he was mainly interested in cultivating distinction in literary style without diverting his attention in search of Tao. With the tradition thus perpetuated, the literary reform was soon to gain permanency with the formation of the Ku Wên school.

The literary reform started by Han Yü was to find its fullest expression outside of the field of formal essay-writing in the creative work of a group of poets under the informal leadership of Po Chü-yi

(772-846). This group is of unique significance in China's history because it initiated a new pattern in literary comradeship. The formation of literary clubs, formal or informal, was nothing new. We have noted that in early Han times literary artists would cluster around the various feudal courts and that during the time of the south and north dynasties, literary and philosophical clubs were especially numerous and popular. Though these were organizations to encourage comradeship in support of a cultural trend or to uphold a literary creed, they paid relatively little attention to mutual discipline in literary craftsmanship. Even between Han Yü and Liu Tsung-yüan there was relatively little give and take and we have no information that one had made a deliberate attempt to learn the technique of writing from the other. With the Po Chü-yi coterie, however, certain new practices were established. Among them there was collaboration and competition, as well as conscientious mutual criticism. All were contemporaries of Han Yü. All were cultivators of the new type of creative writing of a composite kind involving prose narration, recapitulation in verse, and the pointing out of a moral; confirming the common belief that in this type of writing the talents of the historian, the poet, and the philosopher-essayist could be successfully blended and brought out. The center of the coterie was Po Chü-yi. Born in present-day Shensi Province, Po, like so many of his contemporaries, was of part non-Chinese extraction. The Central Asian origin of many a writer or statesman could be disregarded except in setting the genealogical record straight because the process of Sinicization had been at work in the family for so long and so thoroughly that the person involved was hardly distinguishable from any normal full-blooded Chinese. In Po Chü-yi's case, however, the part-alien origin of the clan had a telling effect on the temperament and style of the poet through his family environment and circumstances which lasted throughout his whole life. In his prose writings, which describe his parentage directly or by implication, he subtly hinted to those who would be patient and curious enough to work out the data graphically, that his father had violated the strict current T'ang law by marrying his own niece, the daughter of his sister. According to T'ang law this was punishable by a three-year jail sentence or exile to an area five hundred *li* from home when brought to the attention of the court. Despite the fact that no such penalties had been meted out, the irregularity of the marriage alliance must have been well known and had resulted in voiced or silent disapproval. It goes without saying that the children of such a marriage suffered.

It was probably in his attempts to offset such inevitable adversity and to minimize public disdain that he capitalized on his unusual native intelligence and added to that his unusual application. Having been born in the northwestern part of the T'ang Empire, he would see all the more reason for associating himself with the Li faction in politics in opposition to the Niu faction largely composed of and supported by the Shantung scholar-gentry whose chief specialty was the upholding of Confucian standards of propriety. Whether his failure to win the *chin shih* degree until his twenty-seventh year was due to prejudice on the part of the examiners and those who could influence the decision of the examiners cannot now be determined. Once awarded that degree, he obtained a high rating, being a successful candidate of the first class. From that time on he was appointed to various executive posts which gave him chances to travel to different areas of the T'ang Empire, and his rise in the imperial hierarchy was steady. He had won a titular dukedom by the time of his death in his seventy-fifth year. In his long life, unusual for a T'ang poet, he never forgot the circumscribed status of his youth and continued to show a boundless sympathy for the underprivileged and impoverished. In politics he believed in the urgency of establishing a government responsive to the needs of a people in an empire which had been badly wrecked by civil war and repeated armed rebellions. In literature he advocated the utilization of the writing brush to eliminate social evils, attack unenlightened policies, reflect the crying needs for social and political reforms, and oppose the esthetic theories of art for art's sake.

Like Po, his close associate and rival, Yüan Chên (779-831), a native of Loyang, the eastern capital, had struggled through poverty to attain pre-eminence. For a short time he was even a member of the prime ministry, but on account of his involvement in factional strife had to leave the central government post to become governor of different provinces.

In 804 Yüan Chên wrote a prose romance entitled *Ying-ying Chuan* or *The Story of Ying-ying*. According to the story there was a scholar, Chang by name, who lived during the reign of Chêng Yüan (785-804). Handsome but studious, he had stayed away from the company of women although he had frequently taken part in many of the literary banquets in which, in T'ang times, the gifted singers played a very important and active role. While he was traveling in the county of P'u, he had sought lodging in a Buddhist monastery, P'u Chiu Ssŭ. Staying in the same monastery was the widow, Mrs. Ts'ui, on her way home to the capital, Ch'angan. After casual conversation with her, Chang found out that she was a distant aunt from a remote branch of the same clan.

Meanwhile the death of a war lord had resulted in the forays of armed banditry and general disorder in the countryside. Mrs. Ts'ui was greatly worried. Fortunately the young scholar, who knew the commanding officer of the local guards, succeeded in obtaining protection for the widow. After the restoration of order and in gratitude, Mrs. Ts'ui invited Chang to a dinner at which her daughter, Ying-ying, was also present. Immediately infatuated, the scholar sent the young maiden two love poems by a maid servant, Hung Niang. In reply, on the same evening, Chang received a poem from Ying-ying promising to meet him. When Ying-ying arrived, however, she appeared in full formal dress and reprimanded the scholar for violation of the rules of etiquette. In due course, however, Ying-ying fell deeply in love with Chang. They met regularly at night for over a month. This meeting place was one to be famed in Chinese drama and fiction as The Western Chamber. At last Chang had to leave for Ch'angan ahead of her to take part in the competitive literary examinations. After his failure he continued to reside at the capital but frequently wrote love letters to Ying-ying, to which she faithfully replied. These letters from her were shown by Chang to his friends. They became the theme of many beautiful poems written by the poets at the national capital, including Yüan Chên himself. While Chang's friends were admiring him for this good luck and fortunate union, Chang had grown indifferent to the girl. After the lapse of over a year, Ying-ying was married to another man against her own wish. Meanwhile Chang was also married. One day Chang was going past her home and had the desire to see her as her cousin. Despite repeated pressure, this request was denied by Ying-ying. A few days later Chang was about to leave the capital and Ying-ying sent him a poem urging him to forget the past. Thenceforward there was no communication between the two.

This formed the narrative part of the new type of composite writing and although the prose style was not of the highest quality, there were extremely touching passages because of the autobiographical nature of the narrative. Finishing the job where Yüan had left off, two poets of the same coterie, Li Shên (died 846) and Yang Chü-yüan (flourished early ninth century), both wrote poems elaborating the narrative. The moral was tacked to the end of the narrative in an imaginary conversation between Chang and Yüan Chên. Chang was made to observe:

Any unique feminine creature ordered by providence will bring ruin to others if it does not wreck itself. If the Ts'ui girl had been united to a man of wealth and influence and had ridden high on her charm and favors to reach the height of clouds and rain in the company of heavenly dragons, I would not know what transformation she would have undergone. Formerly King Hsin of the Yin Dynasty and King Yu of the Chou Dynasty each presided over a kingdom with a myriad chariots and sat securely on their thrones. [In each case] a single woman ruined him, scattering his following and depriving him of life, causing him to be a laughingstock even to this day. Since my virtue was not sufficient to win over what was seductive and weird, I decided therefore to curb my passion.

Though this moral was in extremely bad taste, the composition fulfilled the physical requirements of the newly popular composite genre.

That the members of the Po Chü-yi coterie kept constant contact with one another and studied the creative compositions of one another critically, was obvious from a letter written by Po to Yüan Chên. In that letter Po said: "When you and I are in favorable circumstances we submit poems for mutual edification; when in distress we do it for mutual encouragement; when in solitude we do it for mutual consolation; and when together we do it for mutual entertainment." Again in a poem describing how he benefited his fellow poets, he referred to how his technique of versification was frequently stolen by Yüan Chên and how his narrative poems had subdued the pride of Li Kung-sui. Although Li's poems were not as carefully preserved, there is still plenty of internal evidence to prove that he had taken an active part in competitive writing in that small literary fraternity. The pattern of composition was roughly as follows: One member would write a poem on a given subject and have it circulated among his friends, who in turn would try to surpass the original composition by efforts of their own.

To illustrate this point with a concrete example inspired by the immediate success and wide popularity of both long narrative poems on Yang Kuei-fei, Yüan Chên continually thought of utilizing a historic episode of contemporary interest for the theme of a competitive piece. Twelve years later in 818 he had completed his poem on Lien Ch'ang Palace. This was a poem describing the emotional response felt by the poet as he was traveling past the grounds of a temporary palace built in the days of national emergency to accommodate an emperor in flight, but now lying in total ruins. Following the pattern approved by the coterie, the poem begins with a statement of the theme in clear terms and ends with the pointing out of a moral. Although the established pattern of a composite pair of compositions, one in prose and the other in verse, was now abandoned for a well-justified and easily understandable reason (that of concentrating on one focus and of the avoidance of repetition) this poem is obviously one written expressly for the cultivation of poetic art rather than one written as a result of a creative urge aroused by an actual experience.

A careful study of the biographical details of the poet's life proves that the poem was a composition done in the manner of a literary exercise in the poet's studio. This process reminds us of the popular practice followed by many a Chinese landscape painter who, after drinking in the beauties of nature of a given scenic spot to satiation, would return to his studio quietly, and a few days or even months later, paint the scene from memory. The Lien Ch'ang Palace lying in touching ruins had been visited by Yüan on previous occasions but the beautiful illusion created by the poem that the poet was actually standing on the midst of the palace units deep in meditation and recollection of the tragic events connected with the palace grounds were attributable to his memory and artistry rather than to immediate realism.

Aside from these longer narrative poems for which the poets of this group were celebrated, the contributions made by the coterie were also noticeable in a new type of poetic composition which the members advocated.

In the collected works of both Po and Yüan are found poems grouped together under the general label of "New Yüeh Fu." *Yüeh fu*, as we recall, were poems sung to music in Han times and collected for preservation by a special bureau of the government bearing the same name. These *yüeh fu*, or Music Bureau songs, originally of anonymous, popular authorship, were destined to attract the attention of the leading poets of subsequent times, who consciously wrote in imitation of that style. All through the intervening centuries *yüeh fu* poems were written by nearly all the poets. The style had become so self-conscious and so stereotyped that the simple beauty of folk songs had been almost entirely lost sight of. Realizing that new vitality had to be instilled and new philosophy had to be established if that type of poetry was to be successfully revived, Po and Yüan purposely prefixed the word "new" to the classification. In the creation of this new type of what we might call pseudo-folk songs, Po was the greater master. As regards the formulation of theories, Yüan had been the forerunner. In his preface to an anthology of ancient *yüeh fu*, Yüan wrote:

From the *Book of Odes* to the later songs sung to music, the theme was invariably the singing of contemporaries in criticism of current events to be left to posterity. Later compositions written on conventional themes and eliciting similar compositions by way of response may bring out certain excellences in literary artistry. These compositions, however, have no new message to give, being only echoes of the voices of the ancients and, therefore, are inferior to poems written on ancient episodes from which new significance may be deduced for the benefit of a later age. . . . Among recent poets, Tu Fu alone had sung in such pieces as "The Lament of a River Bank," "The War Chariot," "The Beauties," etc., of contemporary events without dependence on past models. In my youth I discussed this with my friends, Po Chü-yi and Li Kung-sui, and we all approved of this practice and decided no longer to write in imitation of ancient *yüeh fu.*

Similarly, Po Chü-yi expressed the same admiration for Tu Fu when he wrote to Yüan Chên:

Among great poets of our age the world has acclaimed Li [Po] and Tu. Li's compositions are doubtless talented, unusual, and unmatchable. But the moment one looks for special messages such as the *Book of Songs* abounds with, one doesn't find it in one of Li's poems among ten. Tu's poems are surpassingly numerous of which over a thousand are worthy of permanent preservation but when we look for lines such as

> While wines and viands are spoiling inside the crimson doors
> Bones of frozen people lie on the roadside,

we would find them only in three or four poems.

On another occasion when he was memorializing the throne on the necessity of collecting folk songs for the guidance of government, he emphasized the "faultlessness of the speakers and the great value derived by the listeners." This glorification of the purposefulness of the ancient poets, especially the composers of folk poetry included in the Confucian classic *The Book of Songs,* was not to be confused with excessive moralization of the traditional commentators, because Po and Yüan meant by purposefulness only the linkage of art to life and the avoidance of creating poetry in an artistic vacuum.

Before we proceed to present some outstanding examples of the new folk songs, it may be interesting to examine the new metric pattern adopted. Although Li Kung-sui's compositions of this type are now irrevocably lost, it is likely that they were similar to Yüan Chên's in metric pattern, which was to use the seven-syllable line as a basic framework with occasional shorter or longer lines to obviate monotony. Instead of following this set pattern, Po worked out a new scheme which was to achieve a more energetic rhythm by using two three-syllable lines or repeating one three-syllable line and ending the stanza with a seven-syllable line. This three-three-seven arrangement was in a way nothing new. It was a combination frequently occurring in ancient ballads and used by Tu Fu himself with remarkable results in his "War Chariot." Nonetheless, it would be unfair to say that Po, in this regard, was merely capitalizing on a conventional usage, because unlike Tu Fu and the earlier folk song writers who had used this rhythmic pattern only occasionally, Po held onto it as a basic formula. With the discovery of medieval popular songs at Tunhuang of which the most popular line arrangement was the three-three-seven, we can safely say that Po Chü-i's stanza form was a new product into which the patterns of the *Book of Songs*, of Han *yüeh fu*, and of Tu Fu were intermixed with the prevailing pattern of the folk song. In this light, we must conclude that Po's movement in initiating the new *yüeh fu* was really an extension of the revolutionary spirit of Han Yü's literary reform into the realm of versification.

Po's leadership in this field was evident in another way. In Yüan Chên's compositions the normal phenomenon was the criticism of several political and social phenomena in one poem. But, whereas the indictment might be effective and convincing, the significance of the issues was frequently blurred by complexity and repetition. Po's new folk songs, on the other hand, were a definite improvement as these demerits were avoided by concentrating on one focus in each poem. This same care, exercised by Po to achieve artistic effect and critical clarity, was further demonstrated in the arrangement of his fifty poems of the new *yüeh fu* category. Whereas Yüan Chên's poems were grouped together casually, as is evidenced in his collected works, Po's compositions were obviously arranged in strict chronological order. In "The Old Man with the Broken Arm" an aged man leaning on the shoulders of his great-grandchildren is asked how he acquired his injury. In reply he explains that when he was still young he was drafted to fight a thousand miles from his home:

We heard it said that in Yünnan there flows the Lu River;
As the flowers fall from the pepper-trees, poisonous vapours rise.
When the great army waded across, the water seethed like a cauldron;
When barely ten had entered the water, two or three were dead.
To the north of my village, to the south of my village the sound of weeping
     and wailing,
Children parting from fathers and mothers; husbands parting from wives.
Everyone says that in expeditions against the Min tribes
Of a million men who are sent out, not one returns. . . .
In the depth of the night not daring to let any one know
I secretly took a huge stone and dashed it against my arm. . . .
Bones broken and sinews wounded could not fail to hurt;
I was ready enough to bear pain, if only I got back home.
My arm—broken ever since; it was sixty years ago.
One limb, although destroyed—whole body safe!

(Arthur Waley's translation)

This poem describing the woes of warfare and the hardship of military service is moving because the presentation of the theme is concrete. Instead of theorizing on the destructiveness and futility of war, the poet presented an actual experienced veteran. In other pieces of this group, however, Po occasionally would slip in his art on account of the stand which he took in the philosophy of poetry. In a number of these new folk songs he would occasionally border on overdidacticism as a result of his eagerness to get his message across. The saving grace was his outstanding directness and simplicity. Going even beyond Tu Fu in his attempt to approximate the language of the common people, he appeared thus to be the first poet to make a conscious attempt to write poetry in plain language, if not quite using verbatim the so-called vernacular. According to well popularized traditions, he had adopted an unmistakable yardstick. It was reported even during his time that each time he finished writing a poem he would seek out an elderly woman, not too educated, and slowly read to her line by line. Then he would ask her if she had understood everything. In case of a favorable answer, what was read would be the final form. Otherwise the poem needed revision. Although this rule could not have been followed by the poet in every single instance on account of the large amount of time involved, the anecdote must have been based on occasional specific instances.

In his last years he pushed this trend of using unadorned language even further. This plainness did not detract from the beauty of his poems. In the case of Han Yü, who tried hard to erase the line of demarcation between poetry and prose, the use of prose syntax was made purposely to achieve the result of surprise and so rugged phrases would be introduced into his poem to shock his readers into attention. Such artificialities do not occur in Po's poetry. Typical is the following poem in praise of himself:

You have done well, you have done well, Po Lo-t'ien,
You have been seconded to Lo-yang for thirteen years!

.   .   .   .

To household matters for two years I have not given a thought
The kitchen stove is seldom lit, grass grows at my gate,
The cook's boy said this morning there was no more salt or rice;
The serving maids were complaining tonight that their dresses were full of holes.
My wife and children are not pleased, my nephews are depressed,
While I, lying drunk in my bed, could not be happier than I am.
However, let me sit up and tell you about my plans—
How I mean to dispose step by step of the little that I possess.
First I shall sell those ten acres of field near the eastern wall.

After that I mean to sell the house in which we live
And shall get in a round sum of two million cash.
Half of this shall go to you for food and clothing;
The other half I shall keep myself and spend on meat and wine.
It is likely enough that having reached my seventy-first year,
Dim of eye, white of lock, and dizzy in the head,
Long before I have had time enough to use up all this money
Like the morning dew when sunshine comes I shall vanish to the Realm of
　　Night.
But if I have to wait for a while, I shall raise no objection—
Shall sup when hungry, drink when I choose and sleep sound in my bed.
There is much to be said for being alive and much for being dead;
You have done well, you have done well, Po Lo-t'ien.

(Arthur Waley's translation)

Even his longer poems such as the "Song of the Everlasting Sorrow" were widely known. According to Po's own records in a letter he wrote to Yüan Chên, when he revisited Ch'angan on one occasion, he heard that a general of the army, Kao Hsia-yü, was looking for a woman singer to furnish entertainment to his troops. One, when interviewed, said with pride: "How can you rate me as an ordinary singer? I can sing scholar Po's 'Everlasting Sorrow.'" Whereupon her pay was immediately raised. Then he continued in the same letter:

Again when I was going through the city of Hannan, I went to a dinner party where special entertainment was provided for the other guests. When the singers saw me coming they remarked to one another, "This is the author of 'Everlasting Sorrow.'" In my travels from Ch'angan to Kiangsi, over a distance of three to four thousand *li*, I have seen my poems written on the walls of village schools, Buddhist monasteries, and wayside inns as well as on the boards of passenger boats. And I have heard my songs sung by students, monks, widows, maidens, and men in the streets.

According to Yüan Chên's witness:

In Szechuan in the middle reaches of the Yangtze as well as in Ch'angan, young people try to compete with one another in writing new poetry according to the style we have set, calling them poems of Yüan Ho style. For over twenty years the walls of offices, temples, post stations, are decorated with the writing of these poems and singing of these poems is common among princes and dukes, ladies and peasant women, teamsters and cowboys. Pirated editions are printed or copied for sale in big and small markets and some of these are surrendered in payment of tea or wine. . . . Extreme cases there are of forging our poems for sale and there is nothing we can do about it. Once I noticed in a haymarket town on the shores of Mirror Lake how village boys in the rural school were competing in reciting poems from memory. I summoned them and asked what they were reciting and they all answered, "Our teacher has taught us the poems of Po Chü-yi and Yüan Chên," not realizing that I was Yüan Chên himself.

This claim was probably trustworthy because it was borne out by the comments of the poet Tu Mu (803-856?) who had no use whatsoever for the poetry of Po and Yüan:

Since the reign of Yüan Ho there has been a type of poetry identified as poetry of the Yüan-Po school, petty and extravagant and completely out of line. Except in the cases of serious scholars and men of elegant taste, degeneration of taste was the result. This kind of poetry was widely circulated among the common people, written on screens in private households and taught to children by their parents. Irrespective of season, bitter winter or burning summer, these vulgar and gossipy lines penetrate to the bones and marrow of men and their eradication is well-nigh impossible.

After the subjugation of the rebellion of 755, the T'ang Dynasty lost its vigor and glory but it still had one and a half centuries in which to wind its course through multiple difficulties to reach its complete disintegration. Despite political disorder and military weakness, however, it was to witness further progress in the cultural realm. There was also an outburst of minor poets, with whom we can deal only briefly. Their emergence in large numbers was doubtless due at least partly to the diffusion of literature made possible by a sudden increase in block printing. Although we are unable to confirm the tradition that Tu Fu's poems had been printed from blocks, we know for sure—on the basis of an essay by Yüan Chên, written to preface one edition of Po Chü-i's collected poems—that many of his own poems as well as Po's had been printed from engraved blocks and sold in the book market on the East China Coast. Printing centers began to develop in four or five areas, the most important of which was in present-day Szechuan Province. Although many of these early printed books are now known only by titles recorded in occasional notes and essays, many nonreligious works such as collections of poetry and reference books were printed and circulated. When the Japanese monk, Sosui, returned to his own country after three years of residence in China in 865, he took back to Japan over a hundred scrolls of Buddhist sūtras and commentaries, which might or might not have been printed from blocks, and at least two reference works which he clearly indicated were printed editions—a rhyming dictionary, *T'ang Yün,* by Sun Mien (751), and a dictionary by Yeh-wang (543), *Yü Pien.*

There were many lesser poets who looked back to Wang Wei as their model. Among these might be mentioned Liu Chang-ch'ing (710?-780). Like Wang Wei, he was fond of Buddhist literature and cultivated the friendship of eminent Buddhist monks. In many of his poems presented to such followers of the Buddha he followed the example of the master in capturing the beauties of nature.

Another minor poet of distinction was Wei Ying-wu (735?-830?) a native of Changan, who was said to have served Emperor Ming. Moving from one locality to another as required by civil service traditions, he took his poetry with greater seriousness than his official assignments and continued to write all through his long life span. He, like Liu Chang-ch'ing, preferred the old-fashioned five-syllable line and possibly on account of this he looked back to T'ao Ch'ien for inspiration.

A lesser poet who took special delight in adapting the themes and diction of folk songs was Liu Yü-Hsi (772-842). Poems of this nature he entitled "Songs of the Bamboo Twigs." The following song was primarily built around a pun:

> Green, green grows the willows;
> Evenly flows the river
> I hear your singing voice on the river.
> "On the east rises the sun
> And on the west the rain is falling."
> Is this sunshine or no sunshine?

The word "sunshine" in the song is *ch'ing*, which is a homonym to a word meaning "love."

Liu Tsung-yüan (773-819), whom we have discussed as a great participant in the prose revolution and a chief supporter of Han Yü, was also a charming poet. The following five-syllable-line poem has been chanted throughout the ages in China by country school boys and girls:

> Amidst the thousand mountains the flight of birds has vanished;
> On the myriad trails the footsteps of men are erased.
> An old man in rainwear on a lone boat,
> Is fishing alone on the snowy cold stream.

An ill-fated poet who distinguished himself in spite of a short life was Li Ho (790-816). Winning recognition at an extremely early age, he proceeded to the capital as a candidate for the much coveted degree of *chin shih*, but his ambition was blocked by Yüan Chên.

Li Ho's technique in writing poetry was peculiar. He did not seem to be satisfied with his handiwork until he had thought of all the possibilities of revision. According to a contemporary legend, he would go out on horseback in the morning, asking a manservant to walk by him with an embroidered black bag. Each time he had jotted down a line of poetry he would drop the slip of paper into this bag. On his return home at sunset, he would empty out the bag's contents and weave them into complete poems. He would never think of a topic first for a poem and then go about its composition. One day his mother, finding the bag full of slips, exclaimed, "My boy won't stop until he has vomited his heart." His poems were admired for their special elegance in diction—such as the phrases "ancient blood," "sorrowful red," and such as the line: "Autumn rain poured as though the rocks had been split and heaven itself had been shot."

Tu Mu (803-856?) was usually referred to as Little Tu in contrast to Tu Fu. He became chiefly a poet of desolation. Thus, musing in one of the pleasure parks near Ch'angan which occupied the same site as a pleasure garden of the Han Dynasty, he wrote the following poem:

> Into the pale stretch of heaven a lone bird has vanished.
> In this we find the end of myriad ages.
> What are the accomplishments of the Han House?
> Only the autumn wind rises on the five barren mausoleums.

Li Shang-yin (813-858) was noted for two special characteristics, elegance and obscurity. By elegance the critics have meant compactness of composition and colorfulness of diction. The poem by which he is best known may illustrate both characteristics—his regulation poem on the inlaid harp:

> I wonder why my inlaid harp has fifty strings,
> Each with its flower-like fret an interval of youth.
> . . . The sage Chuangtzŭ is day-dreaming, bewitched
>   by butterflies,
> The spring heart of Emperor Wang is crying in a cuckoo,
> Mermen weep their pearly tears down a moon-green sea,
> Blue fields are breathing their jade to the sun . . .
> And a moment that ought to have lasted for ever
> Has come and gone before I knew.
>
> (Witter Bynner's translation)

This poem has confounded the interpretation of commentators for over a thousand years. Some of the allusions make sense individually but the message intended has remained unrevealed. Even the opening lines are obscure. Could they mean he was fifty years of age when he wrote the poem? But he died in his forty-sixth year. Again, in Chinese, reference to broken strings of a musical instrument symbolizes the death of one's wife. Could it be that his wife died either in her, or in his, twenty-fifth year? These are questions that will remain unanswered to the end of eternity.

CHAPTER 16

T'ang Popular Literature

In the mid-twentieth century one can speak with much greater certainty about the popular literature of the T'ang Dynasty on account of the huge data recovered from the hidden caves of Tunhuang, a rediscovery almost equal in importance, for the literary and cultural historian, to the unearthing of the oracle bones.

This library, containing a huge quantity of manuscripts in Chinese as well as Sanskrit and other lost Aryan languages of Central Asia, was found in the beginning of this century in the northwestern tip of China proper. Around the year 1900 an itinerant Taoist priest from Shansi came to this area almost by chance and took up lodging in one of the temples in the Caves of the Thousand Buddhas. The entrance to this temple was almost completely blocked with fallen rocks, debris, and drifting sand. Having established his temporary quarters here, he decided that his cave could be made really habitable and consequently made numerous tours in the neighborhood to solicit funds for its restoration. In the course of preliminary repairs, one of the workmen noticed a crack in the frescoed wall of one of the passageways connecting two caves. Once his attention was called to the crack, the Taoist priest did further prying and discovered to his pleasant surprise an opening leading to yet another room, a small chamber hollowed out from the rock. Within this little chamber he found heaps of manuscript rolls. A Chinese official traveling in this vicinity in 1902 heard of the discovery and received as gifts on various occasions manuscripts and paintings from Tunhuang in 1903 and 1904. Apparently much of the hoarded material had been taken out of the hidden chamber and circulated in the neighborhood. When the viceroy heard of the rediscovered materials, he asked for specimens to be sent to his headquarters at the provincial capital of Lanchou. Complying with this viceregal order, the priest submitted a few scrolls of Buddhist texts together with some bronze statuettes which were found in the chamber. As the bronze statuettes were of no great antiquarian or commercial value and as Buddhist

318

literature was usually not held in high esteem by Chinese official-dom, the importance of the find was not appreciated. Orders were issued merely to stop the shipment as it was expensive and to have the other manuscripts of the collection deposited in the original chamber under the custodianship of the priest. Soon afterward, how-ever, the unusual artistry of the statuettes began to draw attention from expert collectors and so many requests were made for them that the collection was soon exhausted.

Meanwhile, word of the peculiar rediscovery had spread even outside of China. At the suggestion of Professor L. de Loczey, head of The Geographical Society of Hungary, Sir Aurel Stein, a Hungar-ian on the staff of the Indian Archaelogical Survey, visited the Caves of the Thousand Buddhas on his second expedition to Central Asia under the auspices of the Indian government in May of 1907. His avowed purpose was to make a survey of Buddhist art. On his ar-rival at Tunhuang, however, he heard from a Turkish trader from Urumchi (Tihua in Chinese, capital of Sinkiang) a vague report of the discovery of the manuscripts. Failing to find the Taoist priest, he was shown around by a Tangutan monk who took him to the library and showed him a genuine specimen to prove the reliability of the report.

When Stein returned to Tunhuang in May, 1907, from his field work in Sinkiang, he succeeded in contacting the Taoist priest through a Chinese interpreter. From this point on, positive action became rapid. With bribery in the form of a generous donation and with persuasive diplomacy, the Hungarian adventurer succeeded in examining the hoarded manuscripts. Stein and his interpreter were not only given lodging in one of the nearby temples, but also shown diversified types of hidden treasures: manuscript rolls of canonical Buddhist texts, mixed bundles containing the convolutes of miscel-laneous papers such as painted banners, sacred drawings, religious paintings, and block prints. While these were passing through Sir Aurel's hands those which were considered most valuable were laid aside for close inspection. At nightfall more promises of generous donations were proffered and in return concessions were made by the priest to have those items which had been picked for further inspection brought to the lodging of the visitors.

Still later on, the priest became more generous in his response. More hidden treasures from the tiny chapel were transferred to the spacious hall of the cave temple: about 1050 bundles of Chinese rolls, each containing an average of more than a dozen separate manuscripts, eighty packages of Tibetan rolls and convolutes and eleven huge Tibetan hangings as well as a large quantity of superb paintings on silk and beautiful textiles. Fascinated by what he saw, Sir Aurel decided to demonstrate his real generosity by offering a donation of forty ingots of silver—valued then at about $1500—for the whole collection. Unexpectedly the priest resisted, for despite the offer, he knew that once it was known the sacred books were gone, he would certainly lose his position. Early the following day, the collection was moved back into the hidden chamber.

Greatly tantalized by the items he had closely examined, Stein urged his secretary to attempt further bargaining. Finally, upon payment of four ingots or horseshoes of silver (about $150) the Hungarian was permitted to take fifty compact bundles of Chinese manuscripts and five rolls of Tibetan texts plus a selection from the "mixed bundles." Hurriedly the Taoist left the caves again to go on his mendicant tours. Upon his return a week later he had to yield to Stein's further pressure and another appropriate donation, for which twenty more bundles of manuscripts and more selections from the miscellaneous papers were surrendered.

This, however, is far from the end of the story. Stein tactfully took his leave after having instructed his interpreter to go on with the secret mission. Further success of this circuitous negotiation yielded 230 more compact bundles of Chinese and Tibetan manuscripts. All told, the British Museum was enriched with twenty-four cases of manuscript rolls and five cases of paintings and other art objects all surreptitiously shipped across the border to India, thence transshipped to the British Isles. After the exit of Sir Aurel Stein, Professor Paul Pelliot of the École Française d'Extrême Orient at Hanoi came on the Tunhuang stage. He had been sent by the French government and a number of learned French organizations on an archaeological mission to Central Asia in 1906. As he had learned from his readings of the Caves of the Thousand Buddhas he decided to include Tunhuang in his itinerary when he left Paris. Arriving at Urumchi in the autumn of 1907, he heard of the finds at Tunhuang. In Kansu Province he received from the Manchu Duke, Tsai Lan, a roll of Buddhist sūtras dating back to before the ninth century and was told that it was one of the specimens of the hoarded treasures from the Caves of the Thousand Buddhas.

As soon as he arrived at Tunhuang, Pelliot was greatly dismayed to hear that Stein had already been there. He feared he would only find empty caves. A talk with the guardian priest served to allay his fears and convince him of the immensity of the hoard. In March of 1908 he was shown the treasures and he still found intact the remainder of the manuscripts, which he estimated to be between fifteen and twenty thousand rolls. He immediately negotiated with the priest for a purchase. After the deal was concluded, Pelliot felt perplexed by the vastness of the job of selection. Even a cursory examination of those manuscripts one by one would take him at least six months, as the rolling and unrolling of the scrolls would be time-consuming. Consequently, criteria were set up for selection: (1) all the non-Chinese manuscripts; (2) all manuscripts of Chinese secular literature; and (3) all Buddhist manuscripts containing colophons. According to his own record, approximately a hundred rolls passed through his hands each hour and at the end of the first ten days he had inspected close to ten thousand rolls. After working thus feverishly for slightly over three weeks, Pelliot departed with selected gems for the donation of two hundred dollars.

In order to complete his secondary mission of book buying, Pelliot had to proceed to Peking. When he arrived in the old capital early in 1909, the news of the Stein and Pelliot negotiations had already been widely spread. According to his own claims, Pelliot immediately called it to the attention of the Chinese imperial government. Furthermore, he had brought along with him certain specimens of the rare manuscripts and showed them to Chinese scholars. He was even approached by Viceroy Tuan Fang of Chihli Province with an offer to buy them back, which offer he naturally declined. A group of influential Chinese scholars immediately urged the Ministry of Education to have the rest of the Tunhuang library transferred to Peking for safekeeping. An official order was issued in 1910 with a substantial provision for the livelihood of the custodian. According to the Taoist, however, the remuneration was never received. The whole collection was packed away in carts and the bundling was extremely careless. Shipment was delayed and the cartloads waited idly for some time in the compound of the magistrate's office at Tunhuang where some pilfering was reported. On the road to Peking the inefficiency of the convoy guards resulted in further thefts. The exact amount of loss was undetermined but eight thousand rolls finally arrived in Peking.

The words of the Taoist were apparently not to be trusted altogether. He had not surrendered all the remaining collection to the government. When the third Otani Asiatic Expedition arrived at Tunhuang in 1911, purchases of treasure manuscripts were made. Then, when Sir Aurel Stein visited Tunhuang again in 1914, he succeeded in inducing the same priest to surrender as many as five more cases of Chinese manuscripts. It is still an open question whether the Tunhuang treasures have been exhausted by now.

Besides unspecified numbers of these manuscripts which have found their way into the private collections in China and Japan, the main bulk is scattered but well cared for in various public libraries all over the world, with approximately 10000 in the British Museum, 2500 in the Bibliothèque Nationale in Paris, 8579 manuscript rolls and 192 detached pieces in the National Library of Peking, and about 1000 rolls at Ōtani University in Japan.

Situated as it was close to the imperial borderline, Tunhuang had its distinct disadvantages. In time of armed conflict between China and her western neighbors, it would be the first town to suffer from disorder and devastation. It was not surprising to find it occasionally occupied by non-Chinese, such as the Tibetans or the Tangutans. During the tenth century, confusion began to grow in the Tunhuang area and prosperity began to decline. For fear of an armed invasion, a local prince at that time ordered a spacious sanctuary to be dug in the rocky hillside where these valuable manuscripts, documents, and sacred objects could be preserved. The room was about eight feet square and ten feet high, enclosed by thick rock on the barren hill on four sides, and could be easily covered up with drifting sand. Moisture was completely shut off in this manner and the air inside the chamber underwent but very slight changes of temperature. These natural protections had been almost ideal in preserving the manuscripts for over eight centuries.

Many of the manuscripts found in this library bear colophons. From the dates indicated in these, the Chinese manuscripts extend from the beginning of the fifth century to the end of the tenth century of the Christian Era. The oldest manuscript in Chinese is dated 406 and the latest 995. In none of these do we find any mention of the frontier kingdom of Hsi-Hsia, the Tangutan kingdom, which has induced Pelliot to conclude correctly that the deposit must have been walled up in the early years of the eleventh century, probably shortly before the conquest of Tunhuang by Hsi-Hsia in 1035.

The chief feature of the contents of the manuscripts is not difficult to guess at. Since the establishments were Buddhist, most of the manuscripts reflected devotion to that religion. In numerous cases, duplicate copies of the same Buddhist sūtra were made and donated to the temple by the pious as tokens of faith or as good deeds for salvation of themselves or their dear departed relatives. Some of the manuscripts revealed high attainment of artistic handwriting and most of the texts had been carefully proofread two or three times by different scribes. Nonetheless, the majority of the texts are full of errors that are equivalent to misspellings and the penmanship is below par. When the transcription of sacred texts for deposit in the

Buddhist temples had become a fad, many poorly trained scribes were hired for economy, including schoolboys and uneducated monks. Even these manuscripts, from the antiquarian point of view if not from the literary, are still treasures, as they are the oldest specimens of Buddhist literature in Buddhist Asia. Other religions represented in the library are Taoism, Manichaenism, Nestorianism and other Central Asian cults besides Confucianism. Equally diversified are the languages used in these manuscripts. Besides Chinese there are manuscripts in Tibetan, Sanskrit, Khotanese, Kuchean, Sogdian, Turkic, Uighur, and other languages now extinct. Besides manuscripts there are specimens of woodcuts (among the earliest in the world); a printed roll dated 868, the oldest survival of early printing; and an abundance of silk remains, many of which indicate the presence of Persian influence.

Among those manuscripts that bear on Chinese literary history, brief mention must be made of word books, rhyming dictionaries, and practical manuals for writers which reflect current usages and range of vocabulary. Among the pieces in creative literature, those written in conformity with standard usage and imitation of well-established masterpieces were in general of a fairly low quality, comparable to what the results might be if an average fourth-grade pupil had attempted to write in the style of John Milton or Alexander Pope. These are only interesting in that they reflect a trend on the part of the less educated populace to try artificially to raise their literary level, a trend in reverse to that of the major poets in listening to the voices of the common people.

The most striking literary genre rediscovered in Tunhuang and uniquely representative of a branch of popular literature during the centuries encompassed is the *pien wên*. These long narrative pieces, generally written for recital before an audience, often have as their principal narrative thread a series of connected episodes from the Buddha's life, very much in the style of similar pieces in the Tripitaka. Once these had become popular, similar compositions were made utilizing non-Buddhist stories. Among the Buddhist *pien wên* one of the most popular is the "Pien Wên of Mu Lien (Moggallâna)." In this connection we should note that technically the Chinese term means literally, "changed composition or writing," indicating a slight deviation in the telling of a story from the version recorded in a Buddhist sutra. *Pien wên*, in this light, is a creative narrative based on but not limited by the official recording of a Buddhist story.

To return to the Mu Lien piece, we recall that as far back as the ninth century that type was already highly popular among the common people as well as among the literati. Of the three recorded versions of this *pien wên*, the British Museum manuscript is fuller than both the Paris and the Peking version. This manuscript, finished in the seventh year of the reign of Chêng Ming (921), as is recorded in the colophon, retells the well-known and often repeated story of one of Buddha's disciples.

Mu Lien (Moggallâna), who had decided to leave home and family to become a Buddhist monk, succeeded in attaining enlightenment and with the help of the Buddha had become an arhat or Buddhist saint. When he ascended to heaven, he saw his father but could not find his mother. Having been told by the Buddha that she was in the infernal regions, Mu Lien went through all the depths of hell in search of her. His journey in itself was a series of impressive tableaus and full of surprises in narrative elements. Finally, in one of the layers he found his mother who, thanks to the assistance of the Buddha, succeeded in making her escape. Nonetheless, although she was now out of hell, she was unable to extricate herself from the way of the Hunger Devils. Each time she saw food, it would turn into burning fire; thus she felt eternally famished.

Deeply touched by her plight and consumed with deep grief, Mu Lien tried all he could to save her but to no avail. The Buddha then told him to make a special feast on the fifteenth day of the seventh month, to which all the Hunger Devils should be invited so that she, in their company, might at least allay her hunger on that one occasion. After she had eaten her hearty meal, however, she vanished suddenly, having been born again into the world in another reincarnation inhabiting the body of a black dog.

After various attempts had failed again, Mu Lien appealed to the Buddha anew for assistance and succeeded in releasing her from doghood to go up to heaven to receive eternal bliss. This *pien wên*, although not as magnificent in conception and execution as some of the similar pieces, has exerted its influence upon the Chinese mind most profoundly by its detailed description and narrative of the hero's journey through hell. In literary influence it is almost comparable to the *Odyssey* and the *Iliad*.

Among the non-Buddhist *pien wên*, three pieces have been preserved in almost their entirety. One is the *Lieh-kuo Pien Wên* in which is told the story of a devoted minister of the Warring States period in subjecting himself to various disciplines for the revival of a vanquished state. Another one is the *Ming-fei Pien Wên*, telling of the Han court woman who was sent as a result of court intrigue to the northern desert regions to be married to the Count of Hiung-Nu. Chao Chün was a beautiful maiden in the Han harem from a humble family and thus was devoid of any influence at court. The Count of Hiung-Nu, in accordance with established practice, had asked for the hand of a Han princess. The Han emperor, enraged by the demand, had decided to send the most ugly girl available as counterfeit for a royal princess. All young maidens at court were thus to have their likenesses painted by court painters for the selection. Mao Yen-shou, the chief court painter, seized the opportunity for the extortion of bribes; as Chao Chün was unable to offer anything at all, he painted her portrait as the ugliest in the whole collection. She was selected as the unfortunate candidate, and when she took leave of the emperor the error could not be corrected, as her selection was already well known among the Hiung-Nu envoys.

Better known even than these, was *Shuntzǔ Chih Hsiao Pien Wên,* probably the earliest fictionization of the legendary Emperor Shun, supreme embodiment of the virtue of filial piety. It is a series of incidents telling how Shun's father, Ku-shou, lending a ready ear to the plottings and intrigue of Shun's stepmother, tried to kill the son by various means such as burning the farmhouse while Shun was repairing the thatched roof or pushing huge rocks into the well when Shun was down there dredging it. Into this framework, which was already built in Mencius' time and recorded in substance by Mencius himself, were woven many folk stories.

The prose narrative of this *pien wên* itself followed set patterns. For example, each time the stepmother was hatching a new plot, she would say in the *pien wên:*

Ever since my husband left home for Liaoyang, I have been entrusted with the management of the home. The offspring of my predecessor, both boys and girls, however, are unfilial. . . .

Each time Ku-shou listened to his second wife's projection of the new plot, he would invariably break out in approval as follows:

Although you are a woman, the plans you lay down are magnificently careful and foolproof.

As we shall show in later chapters, both the style and composition of the *pien wên* considerably influenced the recital literature of the common people for many centuries.

Next in importance is the folk poetry retrieved from the Tunhuang manuscripts. Among the Chinese scrolls there is an anthology of popular songs entitled *Yün Yao* or *Cloud Songs.* These tens of songs, all anonymous, reflect the emotions of the common people, of men and women limited in their formal education, and are touching in their expression. Such lines as:

> Dust and earth covering all my face,
> I have been a victim of men all day long.

> I do not apply rouge and powder before a mirror stand,
> I only burn my incense and pray to heaven.

are fair samples of the sentiments expressed by the little people of medieval China.

There were also folk songs that described and sang of the different periods of the night and the twelve double hours of the day, a type of composition in which lines of different lengths and varied patterns were used, which eventually led to the rise and growth of a new manner of versification to be known in later ages as *tz'ŭ*.

In prose there are specimens of the fictionization of historical and semihistorical personages and episodes, which technique prepared the way for the eventual development of the prolonged types of prose fiction. Most curious and instructive among these is a *fu* composition entitled "Han P'êng Fu." The very title of this piece confirms our observation that there was a process of mutual penetration between the handiwork of established literary men and that of the obscure common people. The *fu* form which was originated by the supporters and exemplifiers of the courtly kind of elaborative poetry was apparently used also by the people, who as a rule looked up to their social superiors for guidance in taste, whether it was within their reach or not. Slavish imitation, however, was not the usual rule as nobody realized more intimately than the common people themselves that they were not equipped by education nor possessed of enough leisure to duplicate what they themselves considered the polite literature of courtly and aristocratic circles. Nonetheless, social fluidity in China would not recognize class barriers and the common people were always free to experiment in folk compositions as they were with methods of agriculture and of other so-called lowly occupations.

In the light of this it is easy to understand why the *fu* form was aspired to at the same time that the conventional artificialities in its craft were almost entirely dropped or boldly departed from. In the "Han P'êng Fu" no attempts were made to imitate the parallel structure of the Han *fu* or the intricate lyrical turns of the short *fu* of the Six Dynasties. To entitle itself to the name of *fu* it maintained a minimum of *fu* features. Its alternate lines were rhymed and its narration was indirect and suggestive so as to achieve a poetical effect.

The language itself, however, reflected the terse and simple vocabulary and syntax of the ordinary people and its figures of expression were reflections of the conversational art of the rural population.

The substance of its narrative was derived from a semihistorical episode which had been continually revivified by the imagination of folk-story tellers. The theme was simple: a country maiden had fallen in love with a farmer boy. On account of her unusual beauty she had attracted the attention of the royal agents and was brought to the royal court. Before she took leave from her lover they touchingly reaffirmed their troth to each other. At court she resisted successfully all the attempts of the king to make her submit. On a ceremonious state occasion she had been forced to mount a high terrace in the king's company for an elaborate program of entertainment. Suddenly she plunged to the ground from the height of the terrace, thereby killing herself. On hearing this, her lover, now deprived of all hopes of reunion with her in this life, also committed suicide. The two young people were buried in graves in the same neighborhood separated by a rural highway. The souls of the lovers first underwent a reincarnation in the form of mandarin swans, the traditional Chinese symbol of conjugal happiness and perfection. In a further reincarnation, they assumed the form of pine trees growing up from their respective graves. In spite of the width of the country road the trees climbed high with entwining branches to consummate their ideal to posterity.

The Ballad of Han P'êng

There once was a virtuous scholar
By the name of Han P'êng.
Lonesome were his boyhood days
For he had lost his father;
But to his aged mother he performed
All the duties of a pious son.

To serve the state was Han P'êng's desire;
But he was loath to leave his mother
Until he could marry
A perfect and virtuous wife.

Such a girl was Ching-fu,
A maiden of seventeen,
Lovely, sagelike and unaffected;
She used no adornments at all.

Beautiful were her face and form,
Equaled by none under Heaven.
Though she was young,

She knew the classics well;
And all her deeds
Followed the will of Heaven . . . .

Han P'êng then set out to travel
And became an official in Sung.
He had planned to be gone for three years,
But he did not return for six.

His mother longed to see him;
Depressed she was and sad.
His wife wished to send a messenger,
But feared men's tongues.
A letter then by bird—
But birds flew too high.
She wanted to send it by the wind,
But there was no wind.
The spirit of the letter felt moved,
And went of itself to Han P'êng. . . .

After reading the message
Han P'êng was filled with grief.
For three days he fasted,
Yet he felt no hunger.

He longed to go home,
And awaited an excuse.
He carried her letter in his bosom,
But dropped it unawares in the palace.

Prince Sung found the letter
And fell in love with the words.
He summoned his ministers
And his secretaries as well.

She was hurried off in the chariot
Which drove with the speed of wind.
The old woman wailed and wept,
And all the neighbors sighed. . . .

While people were conversing [at the palace]
Ching-fu arrived.
Her face like frozen cream,
Her waist like a silken skein
Surpassed all the ladies of the court.
She was beautiful and refined.

Three days and three nights
Of ceaseless celebrations
And unending ceremonies—
Ching-fu became the Princess of Sung.

Attendants followed her into the palace,
Rendering her all services.
Ching-fu did not feel at home;
She grew thin and fell ill. . . .

Liang Pê was summoned and said:
"I can offer you a solution.
Han P'êng is under thirty years of age,
Gentle and brave,
Handsome and refined.
His teeth are like chosen shells,
Earlobes like hanging pearls.
She cannot forget him and be happy.
If Han P'êng be deformed,
Her heart may change."

The Prince followed this advice,
Commanded Han P'êng to be beaten,
Two teeth pulled out, and rags to replace his robes.

In a new mansion of the Prince,
Han P'êng became a gardener.
Ching-fu visiting the new garden,
Looked at P'êng from a distance and wept. . . .

[She] . . . tore three inches of silk,
Bit her finger till it bled,
Wrote with her own blood on the silk,
Tied a message on an arrow,
And shot the arrow to Han P'êng.

When Han P'êng saw the note
He ended his life. . . .

Ching-fu then said to the Prince:
"Han P'êng is dead;
Will you now show him some kindness
By having him fitly interred?"

The request was graciously granted,
And Han P'êng was buried with pomp.
Ching-fu wished to be present;
She promised not to stay long.

A white chariot she rode,
With three thousand attendants.
She alighted near the grave;
Three times round the grave she went,
Wept, and called Han P'êng's name,
And her voice went up to the clouds.

She returned to the palace,
To her own apartment,
And drank bitter wine;
Dressed herself neatly,
Went near the window,
Looked left and right,
Waved her hands,
Then disappeared.

Aghast and bewildered the servants,
Beating their breasts.
Prince Sung heard the news,
Was enraged;
Drew a sword from the bed,
And heads fell;
Turned the flying wheel,
And summoned his officers.
A heavy rain was falling,
The fields were flooded.
Ching-fu had disappeared,
And could not be found.

Liang Pê said to the Prince:
"She cannot be alive,
With ten thousand chances to die,
Hardly one to survive."

Officers were sent in the rain,
But no trace of Ching-fu did they find—
Only two rocks,
One green, one white.

Prince Sung saw the rocks,
And threw them aside—
The white rock east of the road,
And the green one to the west.

The white rock grew into a cassia tree,
And the green one into a wutung;
Their branches face one another,
Their leaves intertwine,
And their roots unite underground,
With a flowing stream below.

Prince Sung went out,
Saw the trees, and asked:
"What trees are these?"
"The trees of Han P'êng,"

He was answered.
He asked again, "Who can explain them?"
"I," replied Liang Pê.
"With their branches they nod to each other,
For their devotion endures.
Their leaves intertwine,
For their love persists.
Their roots unite underground,
For their hearts are still one.
Underneath is a flowing stream,
For they still shed tears."
Prince Sung was displeased,
Had the trees hewn down.
For three nights and three days
Without cease, the trees bled.
Pushed then into the water,
They were transformed into mandarin ducks.
"Let us stretch our wings and fly high,
To return to our proper realm."

This long narrative poem which was entitled *fu* indicates the unhampered freedom with which the peasantry took it upon itself to tamper with a dignified established literary genre and symbolizes a kind of wry humor in poking fun at the literary taste of the great and powerful. That the ballad had been recited endless times among the common people for amusement and edification is obvious from the fact that the whole manuscript was preserved intact in the northwestern frontier town of Tunhuang.

Wang Fan-chih (590?-660?) was also represented at Tunhuang. Although all four rolls of his poetry are fragments, three in Paris and one in Japan, they reveal an unconventional bard who was not represented in the monumental *Ch'üan T'ang Shih* or *The Complete Poetical Works of the T'ang Dynasty*, published in 1706, containing nearly 49,000 poems by some 2,200 poets of the T'ang Dynasty. To his contemporaries and successors, Wang was not unknown. His poetry was quoted by masters of Ch'an Buddhism during the eighth century; penmanship books in current use during the earlier half of the tenth century in village schools presented calligraphic models written of his poems; poets and critics of the poetry of the Sung Dynasty (960-1279) spoke highly of his poetry. From the existing rolls, variously dated 949, 972, and 950, we can gather that his poems were widely popular during the tenth century. Unfortunately the biographical details of this poet are scanty. The only entry reprinted in the huge collection of stories and anecdotes, *T'ai P'ing Kuang Chi* or *Extensive Records Made in the Period of Peace and Prosperity* (completed 978, published 981), based on an unknown work entitled *Shih Yi* or *Historic Fragments*, reads as follows:

Wang Fan-chih was a native of Liyang District in the County of Wei (present-day Honan Province). Fifteen *li* (about five miles) east of the city of Liyang lived a man by the name of Wang Tê-tsu who, during the reign of Emperor Wên of the Sui Dynasty (581-604), had an apple tree in front of his home. On the tree there was a knot the size of a peck. Three years later the tree rotted. Seeing this, Tê-tsu peeled off its bark and saw a baby emerging from it holding the wood. Tê-tsu took care of the baby who spoke for the first time when he was seven, saying, "Who has cared for me and what is his name?" Tê-tsu told the truth and then gave him the name of Lin-mu Fan-t'ien meaning The Forest of Brahmanic Heaven. The boy later on shortened it to Fan-chih, adding, "Since I have been cared for by the Wang family, my last name might as well be Wang." From that time on Fan-chih wrote poetry to show people and it was full of wisdom.

This mythical anecdote contains information that might be authentic regarding his native district, the age in which he flourished, and the high esteem in which he was held. His poems in Book 1 are nearly all didactic, reminding us of the didactic poems of Ying Chü. The following is typical:

> Having power is not bothersome,
> But bullying others brings danger.
> Only look at fire coming from wood
> Which burns wood and all.

Book 2 now having been lost we can select a few poems from Book 3:

> I have ten acres of land
> All planted and lying on the slope of the southern hill.
> Of green pines there are four or five,
> Of green peas two or three nestle.
> I bathe in the pond when warm
> And sing at the edge when cool.
> Thus amusing myself, I feel contented.
> Who can take this away from me?

> .   .   .   .

> I saw that man die
> And my inside boiled like fire.
> I not only lamented that man
> But also thought of my turn.

> .   .   .   .

> My grass hat protects me from wind and dust.
> On my barren bed I quietly lie,
> I greet my guests when they come.
> Within I sit on the coarse floor mat.

There being no charcoal at home,
A fire is made of willow branches and flax.
There is white wine in the earthen jar,
There is the tripod with two legs gone,
There are three or four strips of dried venison,
There are five or six lumps of salt,
Thus I entertain my guests.
You may laugh at me if you please!

. . . .

Outside the city is an earthen bun [grave],
Inside the city is the meat dumpling,
One share for each person,
And don't complain there is no taste.

. . . .

Others ride on large horses,
I only ride a donkey.
I turn back and see a wood-carrier
And within my heart I feel slightly different.

. . . .

People don't live a hundred years
But they try to plan for a thousand.
While they cast iron for thresholds,
Ghosts clap their hands in merriment.

This Tunhuang poet, who sang in the manner of the people, although he was not long remembered, attracted the attention of posterity. In criticism of the fourth poem in this group, Huang T'ing-chien, one of the major poets of the Sung Dynasty, to be discussed in a later chapter, wrote the following comment:

Since one's self is nothing more than an earthen bun, who is there to eat it? So, I submit the following revision in place of the last two lines:

Let us pour libations in advance
To make it more tasty.

Again, impressed by the poem, the great Ch'an (Zen) master, K'ê Ch'in of the Southern Sung period rewrote it as follows:

Outside the city is an earthen bun,
Inside the city is the meat dumpling.
Weeping in a group, people send it off—
Off into the earthen bun.
In turn we become the dumplings;
In endless procession we see others off.
With this we sound a warning,
Don't sleep with our eyes wide open.

CHAPTER 17

The Five Dynasties

AFTER the final disintegration of the T'ang Empire in 906, China was plunged into more than a half century of political confusion during which five extremely short-lived dynasties claimed imperial paramountcy in rapid succession and ten separate kingdoms exerted their autonomy in outlying areas by way of challenge. During the sixty-seven years between 907 and 974 hardly a year passed without warfare being waged in considerable portions of the country. Among these so-called Five Dynasties the Post-Liang, the first and most long-lived, only enjoyed a span of fifteen years (907-922), whereas the Post-Han had only two emperors occupying the throne for a mere four years. In addition to disturbances within the confines of China, the confusion of the scene was further enhanced by continual encroachments of non-Chinese races upon the Middle Empire. Occasionally the so-called emperors theoretically claiming sovereignty over China had to be so humble in their dealings with the Khitans that in their official communications with that regime they bestowed upon themselves the titles of sons and grandsons. Nonetheless from the standpoint of cultural and literary advancement, the picture was not one of unremitting gloom.

A major cultural accomplishment of the period was the rapid progress in the art of printing. Beginnings of block printing in the reproduction of books had already made their debut in the eighth and ninth centuries and had accelerated the spread of both religious and secular literature. Although the exact date of the acceleration of Buddhist block printing cannot be accurately determined, huge collected and comprehensive serial publications of Buddhist sūtras had awakened in the minds of Confucian scholars the resolution to compete keenly. This competition reached a culmination in 955 when all the Confucian classics were published under the auspices of the state with Fêng Tao, a writer of some repute, in charge of the supervision. In the last years of the T'ang Empire the slowness of the process of making individual blocks must have been keenly felt but it was not until the eleventh century that movable type was invented. But the years of confusion in the first half of the tenth century saw an enormous increase in the reproduction of standard literary works.

Moreover, in a number of the outlying areas which had been organized into virtually autonomous kingdoms by local war lords, relative peace and order were maintained for longer stretches of time. It is to these unaffected areas that many of the prominent writers were attracted. Of these outlying areas, present-day Szechuan and the southern portion of Kiangsu Province were especially noticeable centers of literary activity.

In the literature of the Five Dynasties, poetry claimed more attention than prose. Among poets there was a concerted desire to cultivate a new type of versification which had been started in the declining years of the T'ang Dynasty. This new type of verse, which was written to be sung with musical accompaniment, had a number of distinctive characteristics. The lines were usually of unequal length with prescribed rhyme schemes and tonal sequences. Moreover, each pattern was conditioned by the musical scores and bore the name of a musical air. Since this song form had originated with the common people and numerous anonymous poets, it made full use of the language of the common people and often admitted colloquialisms and slang which would be taboo in the more formal poetry, *shih*.

Although many T'ang poets had tried their hands at this new song form and technique, the pioneer who exerted the greatest influence upon the new poets of the Five Dynasty Period was Wên T'ing-yün. He was admired primarily for his art in devious suggestiveness and in the creation of the atmosphere for a poetic mood rather than direct communication. The first evidence of the full flowering of *t'zŭ* poetry, as this new type was to be known, was the publication in 940 of an anthology compiled by a native of Szechuan, Chao Ts'ung-tsu, entitled *Hua Chien Chi* or *The Anthology Collected in the Midst of Flowers*. In this we have the works of eighteen new poets most of whom flourished during the Five Dynasties, although led by the late T'ang poet, Wên T'ing-yün. It is no coincidence that among the poets represented in this anthology fourteen out of eighteen were natives of Szechuan.

The book of the new poetry in Szechuan was promoted by Wei Chuang (860?-910). Though he was a native of the county of Ch'angan, it was in Szechuan that he spent the most glorious years of his life. A member of a once powerful official family, he was orphaned in early years but gradually distinguished himself for his intelligence and literary talents. As the T'ang Dynasty was rapidly declining and disintegrating he had to wander extensively from area to area for a livelihood. Failing to pass the literary examination in 893, he stayed in the national capital waiting for another chance. Meeting with better luck in the following year he embarked on his travels again. After having formed a secret tie of friendship with a powerful war lord, Wang Chien, who was stationed in Szechuan, he went there in 901 to become Wang's secretary. Later on as the war lord declared himself emperor, Wei Chuang was appointed prime minister. Discovering Tu Fu's old house in Ch'êngtu in ruins, he renovated the house and turned it into his own private residence. In homage to the major poet, however, Wei made a scrupulous point of not remodeling or expanding the old structure, so that he could feel the spiritual presence of Tu Fu.

Wei Chuang has long been recognized as one of the major *t'zǔ* poets in the last years of the T'ang Dynasty but it was not until after he had seen the collapse of the T'ang Dynasty that his fame as a poet was permanently established. During his many travels he frequently demonstrated the facility of his art in *t'zǔ* writing by recording fragmentary emotions aroused by what he had seen and heard. Thus on a painting of Chinling (Nanking) he wrote the following:

> The rain is pouring incessantly on the river,
> The grass is growing thickly on the banks.
> The Six Dynasties have vanished like a dream;
> The birds' cries sound hollow.
> The most heartless are the willows along the wall:
> They still sway carelessly in the midst of smoke and mist.

> (John C. H. Wu's translation)

Besides lending his personal support to the newly arisen *t'zǔ* poetry, he also wrote copiously in the older tradition of poetry with regular meter. His *shih* compositions were collected late in his life, as was frequently the case with Chinese poets. In Wei Chuang's case, however, the longest poem he had written and by which he was known far and wide, was deliberately excluded from the definitive edition of his poetry. Moreover it was reported that in a prose composition containing instructions to his survivors in the family, he emphatically warned his children and grandchildren against inscribing the poem on screens. That poem, long buried in oblivion, was written in 883 and was a narration of the experiences undergone by a maiden during the sack of Ch'angan by rebellious troops who had joined forces with organized banditry. Led by the terrible Wang Ch'ao they continually ravished different parts of the T'ang Empire for a whole decade from 874-884. The imperial capital, Ch'angan, had fallen in 881 driving the emperor and a few of his close attendants into flight. When the rebel entered the city court ladies numbering over two thousand greeted him on the main streets to hail him as King Wang. This king, however, was unkingly, and after a lapse of three days the personality of the bandit reasserted itself and what followed was looting and extortion, rape and arson. It was not until months later that the imperial troops were able to drive out the bandits. Peace and order, however, could not be restored, as the imperial troops could not be disciplined. Upon hearing this, the bandits returned and occupied Ch'angan for a second time. As the Ch'angan citizenry had given secret assistance to the imperial troops, Wang Ch'ao decided to give the imperial capital a series of blood baths, after which the bandits were deeply entrenched until 883. It was this dynastic disaster that formed the backdrop of Wei Chuang's long poem of 238 lines. Entitled "The Ballad of the Lady of Ch'in," the poem presented the devastating scenes in Ch'angan from the vantage point of a young woman in refuge. Thus, in the opening lines he presented the scene of the narrative:

> In the Kuei-mao year of Chung Ho [883], in the third month of spring,
> Outside the city walls of Loyang the blossoms were like snow.
> East and west, north and south, wayfarers were at rest.
> The green willows were still, their fragrant scent was departed.
> Suddenly, by the wayside I saw a flower-like lady,
> Reclining in solitude beneath the shade of the green willows.
> Her phoenix head-dress was awry, and a lock of hair lay athwart her eyebrows.
> I made bold to question, saying: "Oh, lady, whence do you come?"
> Looking distressed, she was about to speak, when a sob choked her utterance.
> Then, turning her head and gathering up her sleeves, she apologized to the traveler:
> "Tossed and engulfed in waves of revolution, how can I find words to speak?
> Three years back I fell into the hands of the rebels and was detained in the land of Ch'in,
> And the things that happened in Ch'in seem engraved in my memory.
> If you, sir, can loosen your golden saddle to hear my story,
> I for my part will stay my jade footsteps in your company."

Then she went on to draw a word picture of what had happened in Ch'angan:

> The year before last on the fifth day of the sacrificial moon,
> I had just shut the golden bird cage after giving a lesson to my parrot,
> And was looking sidelong in my phoenix mirror as I lazily combed my hair,
> Idly leaning the while on carved balustrade in silent thought,

When suddenly I beheld a cloud of red dust rising outside the gates,
And men appeared in the streets beating metal drums.
The citizens rushed out of doors half dazed with terror,
And the courtiers came flocking in, still suspecting a false rumor.
Meanwhile government troops are entering the city from the west,
And proposed to meet the emergency by marching to the T'ung Pass. . . .
Yet a little while, and my husband gallops up on horseback;
Dismounting he enters the gate; stupefied he stands, like a drunken man. . . .
Supporting the infirm and leading children by the hand, fugitives are calling
    to one another in the turmoil;
Some clamber onto roofs, others scale walls, and all is in disorder.
Neighbors in the south run into hiding with neighbors in the north,
And those in the east make for shelter with those in the west.
Our northern neighbor's women-folk, trooping all together,
Dash wildly about in the open like stampeding cattle.
Boom, and boom!—heaven and earth shake with the rumbling of chariot
    wheels.
And the thunder of ten thousand horses' hooves re-echoes from the ground.
Fires burst out, sending golden sparks high up into the firmament,
And the twelve official thoroughfares are soon seething with smoke and
    flame.
The sun's orb sinks in the west, giving place to the cold, pale light of the
    moon.
God utters never a word but his heart is surely bursting within him.

Then she describes how the women in her neighborhood in all directions react to the catastrophe, some being kidnapped while others commit suicide by jumping into wells and plunging into fires. Wandering alone she runs away from Ch'angan after going through heartrending experiences time and again. Then in recollection she asks:

Ch'ang-an lies in mournful stillness: what does it now contain?
—Ruined markets and desolate streets, in which ears of wheat are sprouting.
Fuel gatherers have hacked down every flowering plant in the apricot
    gardens,
Builders of barricades have destroyed the willows along the imperial canal.
All the gaily colored chariots with their ornamented wheels are scattered
    and gone,
Of the stately mansions with their vermilion gates, less than half remain.
The Han-yüan Hall is the haunt of oxen and hares,
The approach to the Flower-Calyx Belvedere is a mass of brambles and
    thorns.
All the pomp and magnificence of olden days are buried and passed away;
Only a dreary waste meets the eye: the old familiar objects are no more.
The Inner Treasury is burned down, its tapestries and embroideries a heap
    of ashes;
All along the Street of Heaven one treads on the bones of state officials.

Before she goes on to describe other details of the national disaster on her way from Ch'angan to Loyang, she presents a picture of what she has seen on leaving Ch'angan:

> Day was breaking when we arrived at the highway east of the city,
> And outside the walls wind-borne smoke tinged the landscape with the dismal hue of the frontier regions.
> Along the road we sometimes saw roving bands of soldiers;
> At the foot of the slope was heavy silence—no speeding nor welcoming of guests.
> Looking eastward from Pa-ling, we see no trace of human life or habitation;
> From Li Shan, bosomed in trees, the wealth of blue and gold had utterly departed.
> All the great roads are now become thickets of brambles,
> And benighted travelers sleep in ruined shells, under the light of the moon.
> Next morning at dawn, we arrived at San-feng-lu,
> Where of countless inhabitants not a single household remains;
> The desert fields and gardens show nothing but weeds;
> The trees and bamboos are destroyed, and everything is ownerless. . . .
> I turned to interrogate a Golden God in his wayside shrine,
> But the Golden God is silent: he is more melancholy than ourselves.
> Of the aged cypresses before the temple only mangled stumps remained;
> The bronze incense burners in the sanctuary secrete nothing but dust.

Finally when she was utterly confused as to a possible escape from desolation and hopeless poverty, as she has found out in other areas in North China "the aspect of the countryside would cause even a warrior to swoon, and the rivers and streams are half composed of the blood of murdered men," she ends her recital by holding out a ray of hope:

> Now I happen to hear that a visitor has arrived from Chin-ling [Nanking],
> Who reports that in Kiang-nan things are quite otherwise than here;
> For ever since the Great Brigand invaded the Central Plain,
> No war horses have been bred on the frontiers of that land.
> The governor there regards the extirpation of thieves and robbers as a work of heavenly merit,
> While he treats his people as tenderly as though they were new-born babes.
> His walls and moats often secure protection, as if made of metal and filled with boiling water,
> And with the levies and taxes that pour in like rain, he provides troops and ramparts.
> While the whole empire, alas! is in a state of ferment,
> This one district remains smoothly tranquil and undisturbed;
> It is only the denizens of the capital that must flee to escape calamity,
> So that in our yearning for peace we must envy even the ghosts of Kiang-nan.

—I pray, sir, that when you have plied the oar once more and journeyed
    back to the east,
You will present to his excellency this lengthy ballad that I have sung.

(Lionel Giles' translation)

"His excellency" appears to have been a military commander
stationed in a western part of present-day Chekiang Province, General Chou Pao, whose hospitality was enjoyed by the young poet.
The lengthy ballad he had sung he was later to regret profoundly.
The word pictures he had drawn of the lawlessness prevailing in the
desolated stretches of the empire, and especially of the national
capital and other important metropolitan areas, as well as the censure implied in the last portion of the poem exposed him to an
overwhelming amount of adverse criticism. Especially offensive to
sensitive minds were the two lines

The Inner Treasury is burned down, its tapestries and embroideries a heap
    of ashes;
All along the Street of Heaven one treads on the bones of state officials.

It was probably for this reason that he seriously wished to rescind
what he had written, leaving stern warning to his family never to
have it calligraphed on any screens and taking special pains himself
to delete it from his own collected works.

His wishes were respected and this long poem of 238 lines was
destined to fall into oblivion for over a thousand years. To his contemporaries, however, Wei Chuang's reputation as a poet was intimately linked to this poem. In fact, he was known far and wide
primarily as "the young scholar of the 'Ballad of the Lady of Ch'in' "
and the poem was so popular that many copies were transcribed by
hand in different parts of the far-flung tottering T'ang Empire, including the frontier regions. If most of such copies failed to survive
the ravages of time, at least five fragmentary ones were safely preserved in the cave libraries of Tunhuang. Luckily the five texts supplemented one another so that the text was reconstructed tentatively
by a Chinese scholar, Wang Kuo-wei, in 1924, and definitively by a
British scholar, Lionel Giles, in 1926.

A main literary type usually held up by literary historians and
critics as the distinguished poetic achievement of the Sung Dynasty
(960-1279) is the *tz'ŭ*. This form is characterized by a number of
external features: (1) lines of unequal length, (2) specific patterns
of rhyming scheme, (3) a sequence of finely distinguished words of
tonal variations, and (4) conformity to a song form bearing the

name of a musical air. These characteristics were the result of a close relationship with singing during the formative stage of *tz'ŭ* development. It must now be recalled that the emergence of all new types of poetry in Chinese history had been intimately connected with changes of taste in singing, particularly the singing of folk songs. As we have seen before, all through the T'ang Dynasty a considerable portion of the poetry produced was primarily written to be set to music or in conformity with musical airs that were already prevalent. The two most popular song forms in the T'ang Dynasty, the regulation poetry, *lü shih*, and the four-line form, *chüeh chü*, called for strict sequence of tonal patterns because they were written primarily to be sung to the accompaniment of specific airs.

Hence, capitalizing upon the tonal studies of the Six Dynasties, T'ang poets were all trained to classify Chinese characters phonologically into two main groups, as we have noted. This was not only desirable but strictly inescapable since the use of a word of high pitch in a line of poetry where the musical air would require a low note would either render the singing completely unintelligible to the listeners or else would change its meaning so completely that the result might be either ludicrous or fantastic. To be more explicit, the syllable *hu* pronounced in the medium pitch would mean *gate*, whereas if it were pronounced in a low pitch or tone it would mean a *lake* or *lagoon*. The interchange of tonal levels would cause a lagoon to be a gate or vice versa. So, to ensure clarity and enjoyment, the classification of all Chinese sounds in a syllabary into two tonal divisions, the so-called even and the deflected, was continued from T'ang times, but finer distinctions were made within each division.

T'ang poems, which were sung, were largely regular in their line length, usually with each line consisting of five, six, or seven syllables. No matter how attractive the musical airs might be—and there were many attractive melodies imported from Central Asia—the strict regularity of the line was found to be both a deterrent and a help. Both singers and audience came to recognize the monotony of regularity, and in order to improve upon the situation attempts were frequently made to scramble lines of different lengths in the same poem. This novelty immediately found an immense following. In addition, in many of the musical airs, especially those that were of foreign origin, there were notes, usually at the beginning or the end of a line, which were not accompanied by any words. These, in Chinese singing, were known as *fan shêng*, which may be loosely translated as "floating or unattached notes." Since these unattached notes added a great deal to the liveliness of the singing, they were held onto with great enthusiasm and to forestall the possibility that they might be lost sight of, an extra word would be injected into the line of regular rhythm to take care of the floating note. It was this interpolation of a word or two which gave rise to the irregularity of lines. It was no coincidence that in the first period of *tzŭ* composition, even before the invention of the label "tz'ŭ" itself, songs of this newer type were universally known as *ch'ang tuan chü*, literally, "long-short lines" or "poems of irregular lines."

To review what we have stated above, we shall quote Hu Shih:

The *tz'ŭ* differs from the older forms of poetry in several aspects. First, whereas the older poems were usually written in regular lines of either five or seven syllables each, the *tz'ŭ* are usually irregular in the length of the lines, varying from one syllable to nine or eleven. This variation makes the lines better suited to the natural pauses of speech.

Secondly, though irregular in the length of the lines, even the *tz'ŭ* is a song composed to a definite tune and is, therefore, necessarily limited by the pattern of the melody. There were thousands of tunes but all the songs written to a particular tune must conform to its particular pattern.

Thirdly, the *tz'ŭ* is essentially lyric in nature and very brief in form, and is, therefore, incapable of expressing big themes or epic narration or didactic meditation. Practically no *tz'ŭ* is more than two stanzas each and few of the tunes have over one hundred words or syllables. Some poets of the Sung Dynasty tried to use this new poetic form for purposes other than lyrical and a few of them actually succeeded in producing some well-known didactic poems in the strict form of *tz'ŭ*. But in general the *tz'ŭ* is only suited to small sentiments of love and concise passing reflections on life.

The beginnings of *tz'ŭ* are traceable to the second half of the ninth century at the very earliest. The traditional theory that Li Po was the initiator of the new literary type and that his example was immediately followed by T'ang poets of succeeding generations has now been found to rest on extremely doubtful grounds. Many of the *tz'ŭ* pieces attributed to these poets have now been verified as compositions of a much later date and many of the tunes for these attributed pieces were not introduced from Central Asia until fully a century later. Moreover, instead of the major poets being initiators and their compositions being imitated by the anonymous writers of folk songs, it was rather they who were imitators of a new folk taste. By the time the well-established poets had successfully improved the new literary type, the experimental stage of that type was already over. This hypothesis is now clearly borne out by three observations. In the first place, many of the popular melody patterns of the *tz'ŭ* were unmistakably importations from alien areas, mainly Central Asia, and had been extremely well known among the little people during the T'ang Dynasty. Under these circumstances, it is extremely likely that the late T'ang poets were stirred by these attractive tunes and, inspired by the popular music of alien origin, wrote new lyrics for them. In the second place, nearly all of the early *tz'ŭ* now authenticated as having come down to us from the late T'ang Dynasty and the Five Dynasties are short whereas the anonymous *tz'ŭ* verses preserved in manuscript in the Tunhuang cave libraries of unknown authorship, and with extremely simple wording suggestive of popular origin, are much longer by comparison. This seems to indicate that by the time men of letters were beginning to make use of the *tz'ŭ* form, that literary type had been fairly well developed by the folk singers. In the third place, in conformity to the genesis of new verse forms in the history of Chinese literature, a new form was usually born at the time when its predecessor had reached full maturity and was beginning to show signs of decline. If this hypothesis is sound it is likely that the beginnings of *tz'ŭ* writing among men of letters could not be earlier than the beginning of the ninth century.

At any rate the ten or more late T'ang poets who are represented as having had a share in experimenting with the new rhythm and the new melodies were all poets whose periods of creativity straddled the end of the eighth and the beginning of the ninth centuries. Moreover, all of these poets wrote the principal portions of their poetry in conformity with the established form, namely, poems composed of lines of equal length, and it was as a kind of diversion and side line that each of them would occasionally venture into experimenting with the *tz'ŭ* form. Moreover, all their early *tz'ŭ* writings consisted mainly of lines of three, five, and seven syllables, still deeply reminiscent of the rhythm and tonal patterns of the well-established, conventional poetry.

It was during the period of extreme political division and confusion of the Five Dynasties that *tz'ŭ* made its rapid rise in the realm of letters. In the half-century which saw five distinct short-lived dynasties rise and fall, orthodoxy of taste would naturally yield ground to the spirit of free experimentation. Among the so-called Five Dynasties it was only during the Post-T'ang (923-935) and the Post-Chou (951-959) that *tz'ŭ* flourished, whereas during the more native dynasties of the Post-Liang (907-922), the Post-Tsin (936-946), and the Post-Han (947-950), there were no *tz'ŭ* writers of any attainment. The fact that the new type of poetry was officially and unofficially patronized by the more alien of the dynasties and by the peripheral kingdoms less attached to cultural orthodoxy is a fact extremely provocative of thought.

In presenting the major writers at the dynastic courts we must first invite attention to Li Ts'un-tsu (885-936), known in formal political history as Emperor Chuang of the Post-T'ang Dynasty. He was a native of that portion of Chinese Turkestan known as Sato— the vicinity of the present-day Jekderck region in Sinkiang. Despite his family name of Li, which his forebears had received as a special honor from the T'ang imperial dynasty, his original clan name was Chu-yeh or Chu-ya. Ascending the precarious throne in 923 after avenging the wrongs done to his father by rival states, he continued his reign only for three years, dying in the midst of a mutiny in 926. In spite of his military career he excelled in dramatics, music, and singing, as well as being a successful gambler. He not only befriended singers and actors but also died for the troubles they gave him.

As setter of a pattern in literary taste, this interesting short-lived emperor left only three *tz'ŭ* to posterity. The tune names of all three pieces were identical with the first line of each. It was therefore extremely likely that the airs had been composed by the poet along with the lyrics. The following, composed of lines of three, five, and seven syllables, was sung to the tune of "One Leaf Has Fallen."

> One leaf has fallen.
> The crimson screen is drawn
> A scene is unfolding, withered and sere.
> On the, pavilion the moon shines cold,
> And the west wind blows on the silken curtain.
> It blows on the silken curtain,
> Recalling to mind what is bygone.

A poet identified with the Post-Chou Dynasty, Ho Ning (898-955) was one of numerous professional statesmen who not only survived but served all five of the short dynasties. A native of Shantung, he had wandered to many frontier regions as a result of his checkered political career culminating in the prime ministry. He was known to the Khitan Tatars, among whom he had many friends, as the singing prime minister. Unfortunately for posterity he cared so much for his posthumous reputation that after his appointment to the prime ministry he decided to recall all the copies of his collected poetry and have them burned so that his good name as a prime minister would not be defiled by the survival of the love songs that he had once written.

The most outstanding *tz'ŭ* writers of this period were to be found in the so-called Ten Kingdoms established away from the political center rather than at the dynastic courts. Among them the most outstanding was Wei Chuang (850?-910). His life was made colorful, if tragic, by his having been an eyewitness to the catastrophic decline of the glorious T'ang Empire. The political confusion of the time necessitated his extensive travels, partly for personal security and partly in search of livelihood. For over ten years he relocated constantly in different towns and cities along the course of the Yangtze River, finally seeking refuge in Szechuan in the so-called Kingdom of Shu. Even before the final collapse of the T'ang courts he tried to heal the wounds of his heart in a peripheral area and to plan anew a political career for himself. It could be said that the lyrics he wrote to the various melodies were records of his variegated life. Fair examples are the following:

The Dream
(To the tune of "Songstress")

At midnight last night
I clearly saw you in my dream.
For long we talked.
Your face was blooming, as before, like peach flowers,
And your eyebrows, when lowered, were like willow leaves.

You were half bashful and half glad,
Wanting to leave and yet lingering long.
When I awoke and knew it was only a dream,
Unbearable was my grief.

The South
(To the tune of "Bhosatman")

Everybody says the South is all attraction:
"You travelers should stay till you're old."
The waters in spring are bluer than the skies;
The sound of rain in a painted boat sweetens your sleep.

The barmaids are like the moon,
With white hands soft as snow.
Don't go home if you are still young;
Being back home will break your heart.

The greatest *tz'ŭ* writer of the age, however, was another monarch, Li Yü (937-978). The kingdom which he ruled was the expansive Southern T'ang, a kingdom that covered a huge portion of the present-day Yangtze Valley. On account of his ineptitude as a ruler, however, he saw the rapid weakening of his state. In the field of literature he was much less inept than in politics.

His reputation was so overpowering as compared to the fame attained by other poets of the period that many poems, often the best done by others, were attributed to him. Nonetheless, his own poetry had a uniqueness that was inimitable. The sad recollections could not be shared by anyone else of his age—the sadness of seeing his own regime overthrown and the facing of the most tragic evening of human life that could be endured. The following has been memorized by the schoolboys in China for the last thousand years in spite of the fact that its attractiveness had been greatly reduced by the loss of the musical score.

Parting Sorrow
(To the tune of "The Pleasure of Meeting")

Speechless I am up here alone in the western chamber.
The moon is like a sickle.
In utter loneliness the limpid Autumn is locked within a secluded
    mansion by the paulownia trees.

Scissors cannot cut,
Nor combs comb,—
That's parting-sorrow.
It has a taste of its own that's known to the heart alone.

(Teresa Li's translation)

Among the setters of the *tz'ŭ* tradition, Li Yü exerted the greatest influence in stabilizing the verse form and in inspiring later writers. Also known as the last monarch of the Southern T'ang regime, he was the sixth son of Li Ching (916-961) and succeeded to the throne in 961. By that time the commotion of the half-century of division and regional rivalry had subsided and the Sung Dynasty had been established the year before in 960. During the fifteen years of his reign, Li Yu saw the decay of his kingdom and when his capital, Nanking, was heavily besieged in 975, he surrendered. The fact that he did not submit to the new dynasty until the imperial armies were mobilized against him made the evening of his life exceptionally miserable. After his capture in 976, he was given the humiliating title "The Marquis of Disobedience" which he retained for over a year. In spite of the high official rank awarded him, the attitude of the imperial government toward him and his retainers was not exactly one of forgiveness or friendliness. Hence the often repeated legend that writing to one of his former servants at court in Nanking he feelingly confessed, "Where I am I only wash my face with tears mornings and evening." The austerity of his circumstances is clearly borne out by many references in the *Sung Dynastic History*.

Long accustomed to the ease and luxury of a monarch in a kingdom far removed from the centers of political storms, Lu Yü must have found the life of a prisoner intolerable. His recollections of happier days gave rise to notes of extreme sorrow and melancholy in his poetry. In this regard, Li Yü injected new modes into the writing of *tz'ŭ* which, as lyrics usually sung at gay parties and luxurious banquets, had frequently degenerated to the level of preciousness and frivolity. The tragic strains of Li Yü's songs not only elevated the status of *tz'ŭ* as a dignified literary type but also opened up many new vistas in behalf of its numerous followers. His continuing to sing of his lost kingdom and his frequent use of the word *east* were said to have aroused the suspicions of the second Sung emperor, T'ai Tsung, regarding his submission, and there were rumors after his death that he might have been poisoned by the emperor.

Although the subject matter of Li Yü's poetical compositions was not varied, yet monotony was completely avoided not only by his presentation of his sad recollections from different viewpoints but also by his use of divergent musical airs which had called for different types of metrical combination.

In the following poem, written to the tune of "Hsiang Chien Huan" or "The Pleasure of Meeting," the theme is obvious:

> Vernal redness is faded from the flowers.
> Ah, why so soon?
> But who could prevent the cold showers in the morning and the
> cruel blasts in the evening?
>
> How the tears, dyed in the rouge,
> Used to coax me to take more wine!
> When will this happen again?
> 'Tis as inevitable for life to overflow in sorrows as for the waters
> to flow toward the east.
>
> (Teresa Li's translation)

Precisely the same poetic sentiments were expressed in the following lamentation written to another tune—"Yü Mei-jen" or "The Beauty Yü."

> Spring flowers, Autumn moon, come and go—
> When will they know an end?
> What memories crowd into my mind
> As last night the East Wind stole once again into my garret,
> And the moonlight brought with it wistful thoughts of home.
>
> Carved balustrades—marble stairs—
> Surely they remain there still,
> But alas! the bloom of youth must have faded.
> How much sadness, you ask, is harbored in my breast?
> —Even as the swollen rivers in spring flowing toward the East.
>
> (Teresa Li's translation)

Written to the tune of another long-known folk song was the following:

> In life no-one is wholly immune from sorrows and griefs.
> But whoever felt as I do now?
> In my dreams I return to my fatherland:
> Upon waiting [a pair] of tears drop from my eyes.
> With whom can I go up the storied mansion now?
> I only remember how beautiful the fair days of autumn used to be.
> Past events have vanished without leaving a trace behind.
> They are no more than a dream.
>
> (John C. H. Wu's translation)

The pain of recall was presented even more concretely in the following written to the tune of "P'o Chên Tzŭ" or "Smashing the Battle Array."

> A country with a history of forty years,
> Possessing thousands of li of mountains and rivers,
> With phoenix pavilion and dragon tower towering to the skies,
> Daughters of jade with beautiful sprigs of precious gems—
> That was all I saw.
> How many times did I ever see the weapons of war?
>
> One day I became a captive slave.
> My graceful waist and delicate features have wasted away.
> Ah, I can never forget the day when, after I had taken leave of
>   my family temple,
> The Academy of Music played a doleful song of farewell,
> And I wiped my tears in front of the maids of honor.
>
> (John C. H. Wu's translation)

And yet another presentation was the following, written to another tune—"Lang T'ao Sha" or "Waves Washing the Sand."

> Beyond the screen the rain is falling.
> Spring is growing old.
> My silken quilt fails to withstand the chill of early dawn.
> I had forgotten while dreaming that I was a transitory guest.
> Thus pursuing pleasures of a few more moments.
>
> Now alone leaning on the balcony in twilight
> I see the endless stretch of my own country.
> Which it is easy to leave behind but hard to see again
> Amidst flowing waters and fallen flowers, spring will be gone.
> To heaven, or the world of men?

It should be pointed out that in spite of the well-justified prerogative used by translators in altering the length and number of lines, the original poems were all short songs of the *tz'ŭ* type. This brevity of the musical aspect of the songs was a characteristic of the first stage of development in *tz'ŭ* poetry. This brevity, of course, did not necessarily restrict the length of songs, for more than one stanza could be written to suit the tune. This, however, was practically never done as the contents of these songs were almost exclusively lyrical and never narrative or didactic. In the second place, what purported to be the title was actually the title of the musical air having nothing to do at all with the contents of the song. It was not to be wondered at that whereas the name of the tune might sound gay, the feeling expressed by the words might be extremely sad and vice versa. In other words, the situation in which the name of the tune also suggested the nature of the words had been outgrown at an early stage, a stage during which the new type of songs had not attracted the attention of well-established song writers.

On account of the fact that the same tunes were utilized by different writers for the creation of new lyrics during the late T'ang Dynasty and the Five Dynasties (from about the middle of the ninth to the middle of the tenth centuries), the practice of *t'ien tzŭ* was already established and recognized as good taste. This term literally means, the filling in (*t'ien*) of words (*tzŭ*), i.e., the writing of new words to fit the music of an old air. This type of activity was motivated by three factors: (1) lyrics were written to enhance the popularity of a tune for which no words had been composed, and (2) new lyrics were written for an old and established song of which the words originally composed by semi-illiterate musicians or women singers in a haphazard manner had failed to satisfy the esthetic taste of other singers or even to make much coherent sense. (3) A third motivation was later developed when established poets, attracted by the verse structure and cadence pattern of a lyric, wrote new compositions in accordance with the coveted pattern without giving much attention to its being sung or not.

It is possible that even the third type of composition had been initiated by professional musicians and women singers. When they admired a tune they felt naturally tempted to use that same tune for the expression of feelings or sentiments of their own. It was not until the vogue of the new songs had reached overwhelming proportions that their impact was felt by the conventional poets in China whose temperament was, in the main, conservative rather than experimental.

CHAPTER 18

Sung Literature:
Classical Prose

The Sung Dynasty, or to be exact, the two Sung Dynasties (960–1129–1279) marked an era in which China was unusually weak in national defense and diplomacy but astonishingly active in cultural development.

The weakness of the dynasty was traceable to the peculiar circumstances surrounding its foundation. After the disintegration of the T'ang Empire there was not only a rapid succession of five short-lived dynasties but also the carving up of China into multiple sections, most of which refused to recognize the legitimacy of the claimants to imperial authority. Out of this confusion there arose a peculiar practice of war lords' making attempts to usurp the imperial throne and spreading a political smoke screen to hide the usurpation.

Officials in the provinces, like their colleagues in the central administration, had their authority carefully split up and their procedure subjected to minute regulations, so that a new system of checks and balances effectively forestalled the amassing of power by any single individual. Despite the enormous size of the standing army, the dynastic military striking power was mediocre, and despite the complex governmental organization in which larger staffs were employed, administrative efficiency was greatly reduced by office-holders who glorified conservative behavior and personal contentment.

Besides the Khitan, who had arisen to power in the north, the Tangutans in the northwest were also covetous of prizes which they might be able to extract from China. They began plundering Chinese border towns around 1000 and in the course of three decades their inroads were so threatening that they had become a major threat. By 1030 the military stalemate again gave birth to a peace treaty in which annual gifts were stipulated. A new nomadic group, the Nüchen (Chin), had arisen in the northeast. In rapid succession it

350

exterminated the Khitan Empire in 1125 and liquidated the Sung Dynasty in North China in 1126.

Thanks to the immensity of the Sung Empire and the lack of preparation of the Chin Empire to annex a territory ten times its original size, the Southern Sung court was able to set itself up far, far in the south at present-day Hangchow. Kao Tsung, the founder of the Southern Sung Dynasty, felt perplexed by the immensity of his political problems. On one hand, he had to face the possibility of the return of the two northern Sung emperors who might deprive him of his crown, and on the other hand, he was worried that his excellent generals, once they had scored brilliant military victories, might blossom forth into powerful war lords. In this quandry, it was only natural that he loved the tunes of peaceful coexistence led by such ministers as Ch'in K'uei (1090-1155), and thus laid down the basic plan for the Southern Sung Empire of seeking contentment in the tucked-away little glorious court and of abandoning the northern half of China to the dust kicked up by the invading armies of the Chin Empire. The height of the ignominy suffered by the Southern Sung Empire was reached in 1141 when the patriotic general, Yüeh Fei, was recalled from the front and thrown in jail on account of "insubordination" and a peace treaty was signed in which, among other stipulations, the Sung emperor was to declare himself a subordinate to the Chin emperor.

Thus dictated by unenlightened self-interest, the Southern Sung court, which had begun as a promise to open up so many bright possibilities of national revitalization, was soon to lapse into increasing gloom and despair. With the execution of Yüeh Fei, the military genius and patriot, people became completely disillusioned with regard to the will of the emperor to rouse himself from temporary luxury and comfort to consider the reconquest of North China. In this political climate what was nurtured among the upper classes was indulgence in an aimless life of pleasure and excesses. The intoxicating natural beauty of Hangchow and the enchanting West Lake made the city anything but a tense emergency capital. Instead of temporary refuge the dynastic sojourn at Hangchow became permanent residence.

What was most ironic was the fact that beautiful Hangchow, which had lulled the imperial court in refuge into a stupor, had whetted the appetite of the Chin Tatars to capture it as an additional prize. Emperor Liang of Chin personally led huge army divisions, six-hundred-thousand strong, in his march southward. The invading army was finally beaten back and a peace treaty was renewed which permitted the Southern Sung Empire to work out a tentative and uncertain coexistence. Since armed opposition between north and south continued to exist, what was naturally expected of the intelligentsia of the south was a program dedicated to the problems of national defense and social and political betterment.

The philosophical trends of the times, however, had been directed to peculiar ends. What had been most influential in the main current of scholarly thinking was the building up of the so-called Neo-Confucian tradition. Scholars by and large were eager in their search for a new integration of Buddhist metaphysics and Confucian ethics. Practical problems were piously avoided by the bulk of the scholars. An exception to the rule was Ch'ên Liang, a scholar who was mindful of practical problems and was regarded by his contemporaries as a worthless heretic. Thus the situation drifted along unrealistically in spite of the warning served by the rise of an even more powerful nomadic group, the Mongols, who completely overpowered and exterminated the Chin Empire in 1234. In exactly forty-five years, the same tragedy was to be visited upon the Southern Sung Empire and upon the Chinese people who were now, for the first time, to be completely dominated by alien conquerors.

This tale of the dynastic woes of the two Sung empires should be balanced by a recital of the chief facts of history which brighten the picture in certain specific ways. Besides elevating Chinese attainments in art—especially in water-color painting and porcelain-making—the Sung Dynasty achieved remarkable success in the educational and publication fields. Aversion to military preparedness had led directly to the deflection of attention to more peaceful pursuits.

The founder of the dynasty, who had been fully aware of the ruthlessness and uncouthness of the proud military men of the Five Dynasties, had made it a basic policy in his empire to encourage military commanders to take up systematic reading so as to make them equally versed in the art of government. As a result, many notable generals of the early Sung period were seen in the imperial library as omnivorous readers. Moreover, the rapid progress made by the art of printing with movable type during the Five Dynasties had made publication of books easy and inexpensive. The imperial government, therefore, took the lead in this dynastic span in launching and completing sizable projects in compilation and publication. Five of such projects are particularly worthy of mention: (1) The *T'ai P'ing Yü Lan*, in one thousand books or *chüan*, an anthology and a digest of reference works of the Six and T'ang Dynasties, (2) *T'ai P'ing Kuang Chi*, in five hundred *chüan*, a treasury of pre-Sung prose fiction, (3) *Wên Yüan Ying-hua,* or *The Flowers of the Garden of Letters,* in one thousand *chüan,* a classified anthology of belles-lettres and poetry since the third century, (4) *T'se-fu Yüan-kuei,* or the *Grand Tortoise of the Libraries and Archives,* in one thousand *chüan,* a historical encyclopedia.

Besides these huge government-sponsored projects, book printing was stimulated by increasing demands for private copies of the Confucian classics, dynastic histories, and the basic texts of Buddhism. With rapid improvement in the quality of paper and printing ink, as well as wood blocks and movable type, editions also grew in size. Considerable progress in the art of printing was made as a result of the keen competition between government and private presses. It is not difficult to understand why extant sample pages of Sung printing have long been cherished as treasures by collectors.

Thus, with new and old forces at work, the Sung Dynasty was able to build upon the foundations of the T'ang and Five Dynasty achievements new superstructures. Just as in the field of art, progress in literature bespoke intensive, if conservative, efforts. Nonetheless, conformity to convention did not mean slavish imitation, for even in convention itself there had been conflicting currents and when these were studied in Sung times most writers were emboldened by convention itself to extend the barriers of convention. This freedom in trying out new experimentation in all fields of literature gave meaning and attractiveness to Sung literary developments.

The early Sung writers continued to cultivate and continued the vogue of *pien wên* as a literary vehicle most befitting the dignity of the newly established dynasty. All grand secretaries of the imperial court wrote exclusively in this artificial style, rendered even more artificial than during the Six Dynasties by late T'ang writers such as Li Shang-yin.

The basic structural unit of *pien wên* is a pair of sentences or clauses fulfilling the following requirements:

1. They both must have the same number of words, that is, the same number of syllables in the Chinese language.

2. They must be strictly parallel in structure to the extent that if the first word in Sentence 1 is a noun, the corresponding word in Sentence 2 must also be a noun, and so forth.

3. They must be similar in structure in the sense that if one is composed of two phrases of four syllables each, the other should adhere to this same pattern.

Although the English language is not monosyllabic, the general effect of *pien wên* is clearly suggested by the following lines from Psalm 19:

> The heavens declare the glory of God;
> and the firmament sheweth his handywork.
> Day unto day uttereth speech,
> and night unto night sheweth knowledge. . . .
> The law of the Lord is perfect, converting the soul:
> the testimony of the Lord is sure, making wise the simple.
> The statutes of the Lord are right, rejoicing the heart:
> the commandment of the Lord is pure, enlightening the eyes.
> The fear of the Lord is clean, enduring for ever:
> the judgments of the Lord are true and righteous altogether.

What rendered the *pien wên* style even more artificial by the end of the T'ang Dynasty was a set of new restrictions. First, each pair of sentences making up one unit had to consist of ten syllables, each set off by a comma after the fourth, thus justifying a new name for the style, "four-six style." Second, each word in Sentence 1 must be answered by a word of a different class of intonation in Sentence 2. For this purpose the eight pitches of intonation in Chinese were arbitrarily divided into two categories. The highest and the lowest constituted the first group known as the "even" tones. All the six intermediate pitches were called "deflected" tones. In observance of this ruling, if the third word in Sentence 1 were an even tone, the corresponding word in Sentence 2 had to be a deflected tone. The wonder of the matter was that when a *pien wên* composition was declaimed by an expert, its melodious tune was extremely pleasant to the ear. The great masters of this style at the founding of the new dynasty were Yang Yi (974-1020) and Liu Yün. Their writings, though mainly consisting of official documents and therefore devoid of inherent literary merit, became the universal models of composition, and all aspirants to official posts had to undergo special training to fortify themselves for public service. All decrees, proclamations, official announcements, and memorials addressed to the throne were written in this artificial but regularized style.

While *pien wên* dominated the literary scene in courtly and official usages, its limitations were already subjected to persistent criticism. The accompanying reaction which crystallized itself into a revolt and which recommended a healthy return to simple classical prose or *ku wên* was of course nothing new. The movement led by Han Yü in the ninth century indeed had not been forgotten. Between the two similar movements in favor of straightforward prose of the classical type, however, there was a major difference. Whereas Han Yü was uncompromising in his rejection of *pien wên*, his counterpart in early Sung times, Liu K'ai (flourished 940-970?), despite his strenuous efforts, won only a small following. When the so-called *ku wên* movement reached its high tide in the eleventh century with the support of six major writers who, incidentally, also distinguished themselves in poetry, a peculiar literary compromise ensued. All six masters contributed substantially to the cause of *ku wên* and prolonged its life for another thousand years. They also earned for themselves literary immortality as members of the so-called eight great masters of *ku wên* in T'ang and Sung times, enjoying the company and continuing the tradition of Han Yü and Liu Tsung-yüan. Unlike the T'ang revolutionary advocates, however, all six Sung masters of the *ku wên* were excellent writers, also, of the four-six style in conformity with official usages. Thus, in spite of themselves, they gave new life and vigor to a literary type to which they were not expected to avow allegiance. Nonetheless their attitude was not difficult to understand as they were not convinced of an inherent relationship between the style of any literary school and cultural orthodoxy. In transmitting any Tao they saw no reason why two techniques could not be cultivated at the same time to serve different functions. It is this spirit of unadvertised tolerance which differentiates the second *ku wên* movement from the first.

Another indication of the change of literary convictions and technique with reference to the *pien wên* in Sung times was that among these six masters there were unmistakable attempts to blaze new trails. Ou-yang Hsiu showed his mastery by obtaining a continuous flow of thought and argumentation, observing the rules of parallel structure in form but crashing them in spirit. In the case of Wang An-shih and Su Shih, blocked quotations from the Confucian classics and from the dynastic histories were accommodated in the parallel structure as though they had been the author's composition so as to breathe out a subtle spirit of easy, forthright prose. Among their followers even greater freedom was exercised. In place of the four-six structure the twin columns were so prolonged that often three and four units are stacked up in each member of the twin columns.

Despite their abilities to master the techniques of both schools, the so-called six masters of the Sung Dynasty were primarily remembered for their attainments as prose writers of the *ku wên* school. The beginnings of the second *ku wên* movement, however, were more dedicated to the orthodoxy and uncompromising attitude advocated by Han Yü. Its forerunner, Liu K'ai (947-1001), was so much of a purist that he revealed his orthodoxy by designating himself as Chien Yü, that is Shouldering Han Yü, and adopted as his second nom de plume, Shih-Yüan, namely, Continuing the Tradition

Started by Liu Tsung-yüan. Despite this enthusiasm, his influence was but limited. His successor, Shih Chieh (907-1045), was a propagandist of similar zeal. In an essay entitled "Kuai Shuo" or "Strange Theories" he attacked the leaders of the *pien wên* in a fictionlike tale. The great advocate of the new school, however, was Ou-yang Hsiu (1001-1060), who rose to great heights in his official career and through his influence succeeded in laying the cornerstone of the second *ku wên* movement. In his official career he was more than once appointed chief examiner and thus succeeded in lending his personal support to the popularization of Han Yü's writings. In his collected works, Ou-yang wrote a postface to the collected works of Han Yü in which he narrated how, as a youth, he discovered an imperfect copy of Han's collected works which he borrowed and succeeded in receiving finally as a gift. In those days, he said, nobody in the world remembered Han Yü and it was not until he had become an official in Loyang that he organized a small club for the publishing of Han Yü's works and for the promotion of *ku wên* writings in accordance with Han Yü's style.

Ou-yang Hsiu appeared to be the most orthodox among the six Sung masters. Like Han Yü he wrote an essay entitled "Pên Lun" or "On the Origins of Truth." In this essay he attacked Buddhism vehemently in continuation of Han Yü's tradition. He thus established the official stamp of *ku wên* writers as primarily defenders of Confucian orthodoxy. This formula, however, was not followed out in Sung times. With the naturalization of Buddhism as a Chinese religion, the time had passed when cultural orthodoxy would refuse to give recognition to the Buddhist faith. It therefore became almost superfluous for *ku wên* writers to engage in systematic attacks on heresies in China. Moreover, with Neo-Confucianism already in its embryonic stage, the holding of Confucian orthodoxy was soon to become the chief function of philosophers of the Neo-Confucian school rather than the burden of prose writers.

Even in the case of Ou-yang, his claim to fame as a prose writer rests on the pieces in which the defense of Confucian orthodoxy was not involved. In fact even the great opus of his life, the *Hsin T'ang Shu* or the *New Dynastic History of T'ang*, which was a revision of the standard dynastic history, *T'ang Shu*, compiled under the directorship of Liu Hsü (887-946) of the Five Dynasties, was received by posterity with mixed feelings. His upholding of Confucian standards as a historian has been questioned and his purported accomplishment in supplying more historic details with the use of fewer words has not been regarded necessarily as a virtue. His resort to summarizing important documents instead of quoting them at length has been regarded by some as a fault—the fault of excessive tampering with source material. Critics looking at his conscientious attempts primarily from the standpoint of literary excellence have defended him as a greater master of style than his predecessor and it was only for the great respect due him as a prose master that we have now in the dynastic history collections two universally acknowledged versions dealing with the same subject matter.

It was the poetic temperament in Ou-yang Hsiu that distinguished him as a prose writer. It is therefore no coincidence that his most admired pieces had little to do with the defense of orthodoxy on one hand or the meting out of praise and censure as a moralist-historian on the other. The poet in him was apparently nurtured in his young years when he had lost his father and had to depend on his mother for elementary education. On account of their poverty she taught him to write with a reed and prepared him well to achieve an enviable reputation by the time he was fifteen. This devotion of hers raised her to the level of the mother of Mencius as a model of motherhood.

One discipline to which he had continually subjected himself was that of tireless revision. According to tradition, when he wrote a short prose piece in the classical *ku wên* style in which he described the scenic beauties of a pavilion known as the Old Drunkard's Arbor he had written in his first draft a detailed description of the varying beauties of the different hills and mountains surrounding the County of Ch'u. Realizing that the beautifully phrased sentences had a distracting effect, he avoided the diffusion of focus by compressing all the sentences together. As a result we have the following in the opening paragraph:

The County of Ch'u is entirely surrounded by hills, and the peaks to the southwest are clothed with a dense and beautiful growth of trees from which the eye wanders in rapture away to the confines of Shantung.

Thus, in this revised form he succeeded in concentrating attention on the peaks in one specific direction. Then he went on:

A walk of two or three miles on those hills brings one within earshot of the sound of falling water, which gushes forth from a ravine known as the Wine Fountain; while hard by in a nook at the bend of the road, stands a kiosque, commonly spoken of as the Old Drunkard's Arbor. It was built by a Buddhist priest called Deathless Wisdom, who lived among the hills, and who received the above name from the governor. The latter used to bring his friends hither to drink wine; as he personally was incapacitated by a few cups, and was, moreover, well stricken in years, he gave himself the sobriquet of The Old Drunkard. But it was not wine that attracted him to this spot. It was the charming scenery, which wine enabled him to enjoy.

In elaborating the scenery with the eye of a poet he presented the following word picture:

The sun's rays peeping at dawn through the trees, by and by to be obscured behind gathering clouds, leaving naught but gloom around, give to this spot the alternations of morning and night. The wild-flowers exhaling their perfume from the darkness of some shady dell, the luxuriant foliage of the dense forest of beautiful trees, the clear frosty wind, and the naked boulder of the lessening torrent,—these are the indications of spring, summer, autumn, and winter. Morning is the time to go thither, returning with the shades of night, and although the place presents a different aspect with the changes of the seasons, its charms are subject to no interruption, but continue always. Burden-carriers sing their way along the road, travellers rest a while under the trees, shouts from one, responses from another, old people hobbling along, children in arms, children dragged along by hand, backwards and forwards all day long without a break,—these are the people of Ch'u. A cast in the stream and a fine fish taken from some spot where the eddying pools begin to deepen; a draught of cool wine from the fountain, and a few such dishes of meats and fruits as the hills are able to provide,—these nicely spread out beforehand, constitute the Governor's feast.

(Herbert A. Giles's translation)

Another landmark left in the *ku wên* movement by Ou-yang Hsiu was the liberation he gave to the *fu* type. All through the T'ang Dynasty the *fu* had run two parallel courses—the continuation of the short lyrical *fu* of the Six Dynasties and the formalization of the parallel *fu* structure we have described in a previous chapter. In either course there was no evidence of the free use of intermittent passages written in rhyme but liberated with the casualness of prose. Ou-yang Hsiu started a new trend of liberalizing the *fu* to such an extent that the lines became all irregular as in prose but punctuated with rhymes so as to enhance the beauty of recital. Thus, a new trend in *fu* writing was started by a brilliant example entitled "The Sounds of Autumn." While it is elaborative in technique which justifies the label of *fu*, it was no longer repetitive and accumulative to the point of monotony. Moreover, all the artificiality of Han *fu* and the frivolity of the Six Dynasty lyrical *fu* were successfully avoided. Thus opened the first paragraph of his "Sounds of Autumn" or "Ch'iu Shêng Fu":

One night as Master Ou-yang was reading he suddenly heard a sound from far away towards the southwest. Listening intently he wondered what it could be. On it came, however, at first like the sighing of a gentle zephyr . . . gradually deepening into the plash of waves upon a surf-beaten shore . . . the roaring of huge breakers in the startled night amid howling storm gusts of wind and rain. It burst upon the hanging bell, and set every one of its pendants tinkling into tune. It seemed like a muffled march of soldiers, hurriedly advancing, bit in mouth, to the attack, when no shouted orders rend the air, but only the tramp of men and horses meet the ear.

Then there followed a short prose passage completely without rhyme in which he asks his boy servant what noise it was and urged the latter to go out and see. Upon his return the boy answered:

The moon and stars are brightly shining: the Silver River spans the sky. No sound of man is heard outside: it is only the whispering of the trees.

In response the writer pointed out the special characteristic of autumn—the cruel and the cold, the season of rack and mist and cloudless skies, the season of desolation and blight:

For autumn is nature's chief executioner, and its symbol is darkness. It has the temper of steel, and its symbol is a sharp sword. It is the avenging angel, riding upon an atmosphere of death. As spring is the epoch of growth, so autumn of maturity. And sad is the hour when maturity is past, for that which passes its prime must die.

Then, taking a turn of mind that is more Taoist than Confucianist, he saw decline as being in harmony with the processes of nature and that men after all, as he told the boy, had no right to accuse these autumn blasts. The ending lines bespoke the artistic restraint exerted by the poet:

My boy made no answer. He was fast asleep. No sound reached me save that of the cricket chirping its response to my dirge.

(Based on Herbert A. Giles's translation)

The great towering figure in Sung literature, as in Sung politics, was the misunderstood and frequently downgraded Wang An-shih (1021-1086). Starting from extremely humble circumstances, Wang rose gloriously to the prime ministry. As a young man he was known for his intellectual brilliance, strong in his powers of retention and extremely facile as a writer. Even Ou-yang Hsiu, the great arbiter of literature, admired his writings and praised him in superlative terms. Rising steadily in the official hierarchy, Wang made political history in 1068 when Emperor Shên Tsung ascended the throne. As prime minister he addressed a famous document to the throne known as the Myriad-Word Memorial. The political, administrative, educational, and military reforms advocated and launched by Wang An-shih were drastic and comprehensive in nature, representing an all-embracing attempt to strengthen the weakened Sung Empire in its dealings with the increasing encroachments from the Tatar regime of the Liao in the north. In spite of the confidence of the emperor which he had won, he had unfortunately roused the opposition of some of the best minds of his age like Ou-yang Hsiu, Su Shih, and especially Ssŭ-ma Kuang. Self-reliant to the point of obstinacy, he brought about the ousting of all his opponents from public office. After five years of strenuous efforts his reform measures failed to win popular support and had to be suspended on account of a drought which was interpreted by his opponents as a stern warning from heaven. Consequently he was forced to resign as prime minister and to accept the post as governor of present-day Nanking. In spite of many subsequent honors bestowed upon him he was never returned to power. As a political leader he was exceptionally firm in braving the storms of opposition. On more than one occasion he upheld his famous dictum, "Astronomical anomalies need not be feared; imperial ancestors need not be followed; and the criticism of men need not be heeded." At the same time he was so forthright that he was transparent, making him, as a person, attractive even to his opponents.

His habits were so thrifty that he was suspected by some of hypocrisy, but Wang did not care. On one occasion when Emperor Jên Tsung (1023-1063) was still reigning before Wang's patron, Shên Tsung, ascended the throne, he was summoned into the palace to take part in a state banquet preceded by tours of the flower gardens and the fishing game. When the eunuchs placed before him a golden plate of bait, he unhesitatingly ate it up. Even after he had been made prime minister his personal habits were extremely thrifty. Once a relative paid him a special visit and was invited to stay for dinner. When dinner was served it consisted only of a few Central Asian wheat cakes and slices of wild boar meat. Disgusted with the fare, the guest only tasted the centers of the pancakes but the prime minister, mindful of the poverty of the numerous unfortunates, unblushingly ate up the outer parts left by the guest, to the great astonishment of the latter.

As a prose writer Wang An-shih has been regarded as the most outstanding among Sung writers. Unlike Ou-yang Hsiu, who was meticulous in his almost never-ending revisions, Wang wrote at a rapid speed as though he were engaged in drawing up a first draft. When the draft was finished, however, he would give it practically no retouching. One of the most outstanding prose compositions was the long memorial he addressed to the throne reflecting his enthusiasm for launching an all-comprehensive reform. The forcefulness of this memorial was due almost exclusively to his strong conviction. This alone was enough to make the piece great even without reliance on rhetorical devices. In spite of his extremely busy life as a public administrator, he ranged far and wide in his use of literary types. As an example of his extreme versatility may be noted his many biographical essays known in Chinese tradition as funerary inscriptions and usually engraved on stone tablets at the graves of the dead. In the case of most other prose writers a prescribed form was followed but in Wang's biographical essays he followed no specific pattern, varying his style and procedure as he felt they would best fit the subjects. The spontaneity might have been a natural reaction on the part of the author to the stereotyped form of similar compositions in previous ages. His claim to excellence in this regard lay in his absolute honesty in characterizing the dead person. The following example illustrates his complete lack of preconception in approaching the composition.

The Funerary Tablet of Mr. Wu Ch'ing of Chinch'i

This gentleman was easy to deal with but reserved in words. His exterior conformed to what was within him. He never mentioned the faults of others. As regards the good and bad of past generations and the causes of the successes and failures, the order and disorder as well as the rise and fall of states, his discourse was worth listening to. Numerous were the books he had read and he was particularly fond of the past ages and of imitating their literary art. And what he had thus learned in literary art he could wield with such dexterity that he succeeded in saying all he meant to say. When he was in his forty-third or forty-fourth year he took part in the competitive examinations as an Advanced Scholar but he never succeeded in passing them. He was buried in the sixth year of the reign of Huang-yu [1054] and his grave was on the elevated plains of Shih Lin of the village of Kueitê in the County of Chinch'i, about five li south of his home. At that time his mother was already aged but his sons, Shih Lung and Shih Fan, were both still young. Of daughters he had three, one of which had died before him and the remaining two were not yet married. Alas, when we compare what he had to the attainments of those who are distinguished, wealthy, and famous under heaven, doesn't it seem that heaven dealt with him meagerly? However it might be, this man did not succeed in accumulating enough emoluments to put into practice what he had intended to and he lacked even the means to offer sacrifices to his departed ancestors, to support his aged mother, and to bequeath to his descendants at the time of his death. This is why his numerous friends feel grieved for him. On the other hand, a scholar is dedicated to live in complete harmony with nature and when this harmony with nature is complete, he would know the meaning of what is usually represented as a dedicated life. If the meaning of the dedicated life is well known, what grief should there remain about his inability to fulfill his desires?

A rival in letters and an opponent in politics who crossed the path of Wang An-shih many times was Su Shih (1036-1102), better known by his courtesy name of Su Tung-p'o. Son of a great writer and a student of Ou-yang Hsiu, Su Tung-p'o succeeded early in attaining literary distinction. During the prime ministry of Wang An-shih, he was exiled to many provinces in which he tried successfully to feel at home. Equally influential as a poet, he distinguished himself as a prose writer by continuing the tradition of Han Yü whom he exalted as "a commoner who rose to be a teacher of a hundred generations and whose word deserved the following of the whole universe." In spite of his excessive admiration for the T'ang writer, he opened up new vistas for himself instead of following the beaten paths of Han Yü. For one thing, he was unable to contain himself within the bounds of traditional Confucianism, for despite his official adherence to the orthodox cult he derived special delight in befriending many a Buddhist monk. Again, instead of posing as a defender of Confucian orthodoxy in upholding the cardinal virtues demanded by traditional Confucianism, he would explain the Tao by resorting to the use of a parable. Thus, he evolved the original story of the blind man's idea of the sun:

> There was a man born blind. He had never seen the sun and asked about it of people who could see. Someone told him, "The sun's shape is like a brass tray." The blind man struck the brass tray and heard its sound. Later when he heard the sound of a bell, he thought it was the sun. Again someone told him, "The sunlight is like that of a candle," and the blind man felt the candle, and thought that was the sun's shape. Later he felt a (big) key and thought it was a sun. The sun is different from a bell or a key, but the blind man cannot tell their difference because he has never seen it. The truth (*Tao*) is harder to see than the sun, and when people do not know it they are exactly like the blind man. Even if you do your best to explain by analogies and examples, it still appears like the analogy of the brass tray and the candle. From what is said of the brass tray, one imagines a bell, and from what is said about a candle, one imagines a key. In this way, one gets ever further and further away from the truth. Those who speak about *Tao* sometimes give it a name according to what they happen to see, or imagine what it is like without seeing it. These are mistakes in the effort to understand *Tao*.
>
> (Lin Yutang's translation)

Like his predecessor, Ou-yang Hsiu, he confirmed the new Sung tradition of the *fu* in which the free flow of prose was adapted to the rhyming scheme of the traditional *fu*. Among many such attempts made by Su the best known was probably the twin composition he wrote when he was admiring the beauty of the historic site known as the Red Cliff. In the early autumn of the year 1082, Su went on a boat excursion to this famous historical spot in the company of a friend. In recapturing the unique experience the author drew delicate word pictures of the moonlit river and its environs. Together they recalled the decisive naval battle fought there during the Three Kingdoms Period almost a thousand years before their time. From lamenting the sad footprints of history with his companion, he moved on to a recording of the philosophic reactions that these reminiscences called forth:

Look at this water and this moon! The water passes continually by, and yet it is always here. The moon waxes and wanes but it always remains the same moon. If you look at the changes that take place in the universe, there is nothing in it that lasts more than a fraction of a second. But if you look at the unchanging aspects of things, then you realize that both the things and ourselves are immortal. Why should you envy this river? Besides, everything in this life has its proper owner; there is no use trying to take what does not properly belong to us. But this clean breeze over the river and this clear moon over the mountain tops are for everybody to enjoy. This life and this sensuous existence are here; they strike our eyes and become color, strike our ears and become sounds—truly a boundless treasure, the inexhaustible gift of the Creator, a feast for us to enjoy, free and costless.

(Lin Yutang's translation)

On another full moon night three months later, Su and two other guests visited the site again. With the change of season, the beauties observable were of a different kind and these were effectively caught by the poetic eyes of the author. Su asked his friends to climb up the Red Cliff with him but the friends declined and he went up alone. On coming down he entered the boat again and let it drift with the current. Instead of philosophizing again on the transiency of life, he ended his *fu* with a unique episode:

It was about midnight and all around was silence. It happened that there was a lone stork flying across the river from the east as though its wings were the wheels of a chariot. As though it had been like a Taoist dressed in a white garment over black flowing robes, it swept by my boat in its flight westward with a sudden and prolonged cry. A moment later the guests were gone and I also went to bed. In a dream I saw a Taoist priest dressed in a fluttering feather dress of an immortal who came to salute me under the Red Cliff and asked, "Did you enjoy the excursion to the Red Cliff?" I asked his name but he lowered his head without replying. "Ah," I said, "I knew it. Wasn't it you who flew past me wailing the other night?" The Taoist turned around with a smile and I woke from my sleep. I opened the door in an attempt to find him but I couldn't see where he was.

The three Sung writers immortalized in the Great Octet of T'ang and Sung prose writing included, besides Su Tung-p'o, his father, Su Hsün (1009-1066), and his younger brother, Su Ch'ê (1039-1112). The former was noted for his witty arguments, many of which did not make clear logic. For example, in his essay on understanding he wrote:

The things of the universe might be compared to the existence of ten things. I enumerate one among them but people don't realize I am ignorant of the remaining nine. They would recount the remainders from one to nine but publicly confess they don't know the missing one. They are not unpredictable as I who have enumerated one. This situation will hold true all the more in case of people who don't know as many as nine.

Su Ch'ê, as a prose writer, was not as witty as his father nor as expansive as his elder brother and yet in his simplicity there is a naturalness and lucidity unrivaled by his elders. Despite these differences between father and sons and brother and brother, the three Su writers seemed to exhibit a similarity in style, so they are usually grouped together as a team.

The last of the octet was Tsêng Kung (1019-1083), who was a minor administrator in many provinces. A pupil of Ouyang, he shared with his master a kind of beauty that is described by the Chinese as of the *yin* or soft quality. Whereas Ou-yang's prose was distinguished by its inestimable grace, Tsêng, as a stylist, distinguished himself by his ability to give his subject matter an unhastened and emotionalized treatment:

Note on a Southern Studio

After securing some unused land from a neighbor and burning the undergrowth, I planted some trees, bamboos, ferns, and vegetables, and built myself a small thatch-roofed building to rest myself. I was overflowing with happiness. Of course, there are those in the world who hold high honors at court and who command such private fortunes as to rival potentates of sizable states, but I would not trade my life with theirs. Realizing that men are different in their temperaments I have convinced myself that lying low with leisure and keeping quiet in obscurity suit my temperament best. Living a busy and complicated life by force of circumstance is not what I excel in and to go a step further, struggling for power and influence in the midst of love and hate, praises and censure would be even worse for me. On the other hand there are the problems of the lack of support for my parents and of my inability to entertain my brothers and cousins occasionally with simple meals which makes it impossible to stay here all the time as I need to labor for necessities. Sometimes eating in the field or camping in the wilderness, how can I avoid the feeling of dissatisfaction?

I have done a little thinking on this. I have come to the conclusion that there are objectives which have motivated me to go against my temperament and subject my body to bitter strain in order to labor for necessities. Scholars all have their strivings and relaxations and if one realizes that they have received these from their natural lot and accept it docilely one should feel happy wherever one may be. In which case, why should it be necessary for me to feel rested only here?

My aspirations, however, are far removed from these circumstances. The classics in the six arts and of the hundred philosophers, the various historians, the endless volumes of commentaries and all the writings praising the virtuous and censuring the wicked, emotionalizing the obscure and recording the remote, engravings on mountainsides as well as on funerary tablets on tombs, some of them weird and others extravagant, besides the many documents transmitted on military science and calendrical computation, on government and medicine, on agriculture and horticulture, on dialects and geography, on Buddhism and Taoism—I have them all here. In these are the theories from Emperor Fu Hsi down through the Ch'in and Han Dynasties to the sages and virtuous men of the present age—works in which years and months were exhausted and thoughts and meditations were distilled. By day and night each contributes its speciality in throwing light on the myriad things and problems comprehensively touching on the little and big problems of heaven and earth and all the contents in between and on the full significance of self-cultivation, of the government of men, of order and disorder, security and peril, and the rise and fall of states and empires. These with whom I live here—should they not be called my beneficial friends? From these I get glimpses of the teachings of the sages to dispel my doubts and to resolve my problems. I also get acquainted with the sayings of the virtuous and the wise, with the details of which I broaden my mind and nurture my heart so that I may hold on to my loyalty to life and stand ever ready to forgive others. Whenever I am at fault, I correct and surmount this with courage unending. This, which I have sought from my inner life, I shall act on in proper time and I would consider it erroneous to live reclusively or to refuse to serve the world by hiding myself on high mountains and in deep vales. When I am not favored by circumstance, I can live in contentment and would consider it equally erroneous to exert myself for the prevailing of my own way.

When I am lacking in propriety, praises that have arisen from partiality are superfluous. When I am not lacking in propriety, damaging remarks growing out of prejudice are also superfluous—what have these to do with me? This, then, is the way I rely on Heaven and live in harmony with myself. What I wish to learn is broad but what I wish to hold onto is simple. What I say is elementary and easy to understand but what I place on myself as responsibility may be called weighty. These words I write on the wall of my Southern Studio so that I may seek advancement in self-improvement by looking at them morning and night.

Aside from these six major Sung prose writers, there were others who were remembered as distinguished essayists. Worthy of mention were Fan Chung-yen (989-1052), who was reputed to be the first to worry over the world's problems and the last to share in its enjoyment, and Ssŭ-ma Kuang (1019-1086), the greatest opponent to Wang An-shih and the great author of *Tzŭ Chih T'ung Chien* or *The Mirror of Good Government*, a general history of China year by year for which he invented the Chinese counterpart of note-taking on cards. Both of these men were admired more for their moral and political stature than for their literary attainments.

Speaking of the moral stature of writers, we must not forget that the Sung Dynasty was the period that gave birth and nurture to a Chinese philosophical renaissance of great importance usually known as the Neo-Confucianist movement, in which the heterodoxies of Buddhism and Taoism were freely and subtly utilized for the enrichment of China's cultural orthodoxy.

The new Confucianist movement entered its period of full maturity after the northern half of China had been lost to the border tribes and the Sung imperial court had taken its flight from Kaifêng to Nanking in 1127 and resettled itself in Hangchow two years later. The greatest representative of this movement was Chu Hsi. Under his leadership the *ku-wên* movement, which had always advertised prose writing as a vehicle for the propagation of Tao or the ideal way of life, became merged with the philosophical aspect of the new age. Influential though he was, he did not succeed in silencing opposition in the literary realm, for the writers of the much reduced Sung Empire had now settled down to their major task: how to prepare the stage for the recovery of lost territories and how to strengthen the Chinese government for national defense. The second group, which might be loosely described as political writers, was headed by Ch'ên Liang. The interaction between these two schools did a good deal to stimulate the progress of Southern Sung prose writing.

Ch'ên Liang (1143-1194), a native of Yungk'ang in present-day Chekiang Province, was probably the greatest political theorist of his time. Dedicated to strengthening of the Sung house, he wrote extensive essays on a great variety of subjects related to political, economic, and military reforms. Though a devoted friend of Chu Hsi, he differed with him on nearly all major topics. In his memorial to Emperor Hsiao Tsung, who reigned from 1163-1189, he clearly drew a line of demarcation between his own school and the school of the Confucianist philosophers:

> The scholars of our generation claim to have achieved the erudition of a rectified heart and a sincere will but are actually people who are paralyzed and callous to itches and pain. They want to convert the whole world to complacency in spite of the urgency or the threats of the great enemy of monarch and parent, and with folded hands and elated eyebrows to discuss nature and life. I hardly know what they mean to say.

Chu Hsi (1130-1200), the son of an official from Anhui Province, was actually born in Fukien although he was usually identified with the place of origin of his clan. After taking the *chin shih* degree at nineteen and obtaining a civil service appointment, he studied Buddhist and Taoist teachings for many years, although the legend that he had once become a Buddhist priest cannot be verified. Later on in life, he came under the influence of a Confucianist teacher, Li T'ung (1088-1158), and he became an ardent Confucianist. In spite of the charges of his intimate friend, Ch'ên Liang, he was not an armchair philosopher, for he responded time after time to imperial summons to the capital in Hangchow to offer advice on governmental matters, and in 1180 he was appointed governor of Kiangsi where he vigorously translated his ethical theories into governmental practice. He repeatedly sought temporary retirement, however, to the celebrated Pai Lu Tung or White Deer Grotto near Kuling where he revived the activities of a well known academy.

In his tireless literary endeavors he wrote commentaries on the Confucian classics and also revised and brought up to date Ssŭ-ma Kuang's great general history of China arranged in chronological order. His writings were so voluminous that in spite of his central importance in China's intellectual history they have not been collected into definitive form. Possibly the most learned man of his age, his erudition was encyclopedic; he even speculated substantially on geology and astronomy.

As a prose writer he was distinguished by coherent thinking, logical reasoning, and transparent exposition. His many letters and prefaces, which seem on first reading to be ordinary, were actually written with great care and moving earnestness. His guiding principle seemed to be naturalness. As he once wrote himself, "The writings of the ancients are generally natural presentations but their messages are worthy of prolonged appreciation. Later writers, however, were preoccupied with the multiplicity of ideas and became sour and unsmooth. In the 'Li Sao,' for example, there are no strangely chosen words but only an attempt on the part of the poet to write as he had spoken. It was naturally good. Later on, poets like Huang T'ing-chien strenuously exerted themselves as they wrote and were, consequently, no good."

Writers in both of these schools, strangely enough, did not pay primary attention to the art of writing as such. Each school regarded something else as more important than literature. As the political reformers were interested in using literature as a medium for the propagation of their ideas, schemes and programs in social and political reform, the philosophers were bent upon the elucidation of the fundamental teachings contributory to the illumination of Tao and the betterment of the moral qualities of human life. The attainments of many of the philosophers, such as Chu Hsi, were exceptionally high and their critical theories in relation to literature were oftentimes more cogent than the traditional remarks of professional literary critics. Nonetheless, the philosophers would take their achievements in literature with only secondary concern; their real contribution to Chinese literature lay in ways which they themselves had never anticipated as contributions.

In their conferences with friends and pupils the philosophers naturally had used simple everyday language and these sayings were frequently recorded by some of the participants, often the pupils of the masters. Since the recorders were not interested in rhetoric or elegance of expression, such records were usually very close to the vernacular used and understood by the common people. This type of recording revived a literary genre later on to be known as *yü lu,* literally, records of sayings.

From the ninth century on, one sect of Buddhism known as Ch'an (Zen in Japanese) had begun to gain an immense following. Within the sect there arose many schools and these penetrated the different parts of China. Although Ch'an Buddhism deprecated book learning and reliance on the printed page more than any other branch of Buddhism in China, many of the Ch'an masters had had considerable discipline as rhetoricians. In fact, not a few of them even conformed to the artificial rules of writing such as those demanded in the writing of balanced prose. Most of them, however, avoided writing and their discourses when recorded by their disciples were verbatim reports written in the vernacular. Recordings of this kind were especially numerous during the Northern Sung Dynasty when Confucianist scholars were making attempts to establish points of contact with Buddhism.

In an age during which conformity to pattern was the first principle of literary composition and imitation of the well-established masters in prose and poetry was the only royal road to literary achievement, the unadorned verbatim records of sayings in the vernacular came to the general readers like the cooling breeze of spring into an artificially heated room.

It was no coincidence that the many collections of sayings by eminent monks attracted the attention of even non-Buddhists and that such collections not only increased in number but also gained in general circulation. We shall give one example from the sayings of a Northern Sung monk, K'ê-ch'in, also known as Yüan-wu:

I, the aged monk, once upon a time suffered from fever and lost consciousness for a day. I found in front of me a stretch of road that was totally dark and had no idea which way I was headed. When I came to I discovered, with a shock, the problem of life and death. Then I made up my mind to do extensive travel in search of someone who had real knowledge of the Way so I might pursue the problem thoroughly. First of all, I arrived at Takuei where I attended Abbot Chên-ju. I spent many full days facing a wall in meditation and reviewed the cases [*kung-an; kōan* in Japanese] of people of the past. Slightly over a year later all of a sudden I seemed to realize that I had come to understand something but that I only understood something illuminating and bright. But it was as if mules in front and horses behind were bringing their impact against a human body made up of the four elements. If I should be jolted from behind I would suddenly lose all I had perceived. Just to avoid being buried alive my belly was full of the ways of Ch'an. But these seemed real only from the standpoint of the Buddhist law and were nonexistent from the vantage point of the way of the world. Later on, I arrived at the place of old Abbot Pai Yün [Abbot White Cloud] and was told by him, "You haven't seen a thing." From that time on, feeling completely let down, I left him in great disappointment and confusion.

My mind was so full of doubt, however, I could not feel at ease. Then I went up to Pai Yün again and became his attendant. One day there came an official who was in search of the "way" and my late master said, "Your excellency, don't you understand the two lines from the love poem:

> Little Jade's name was called frequently for nothing in particular
> Except to make sure she recognized the voice of her lover."

That official was completely bemused but I, your aged monk, heard it and all of a sudden felt that the lacquer pail had been knocked through from the bottom. I had seen what I saw while standing on my own feet without help from anybody.

Then I realized that in the universe and the endless moving of time there was a treasure hidden in some mountain and all the births of the various Buddhas and the coming to China of all the pioneering saints had been directed to teaching man about this one thing. Those who have not learned but who have pretended that they know, raising their eyebrows and dilating their pupils, don't seem to have realized that they have only rubbed their eyes to create the illusion of flowers and that they have worn the cangue in serving a sentence. When have they ever obtained freedom and release? . . .

If one has actually attained this, then he could proclaim the great cycle of causality, erect a banner of the law and help all human beings by pulling out nails and wedges, releasing bandages and robes. Then he could illumine a thousand people, ten thousand people, like a bird with golden wings entering the sea directly to swallow up the dragon, like the many bodhisattvas plunging into the sea of life and death to salvage the sentient beings and place them upon the Bodhi Bank. Then what is done will remain done and what is finished will be finished. Sometimes a single yell is like a precious sword made of gold or diamond, sometimes a yell is like the roar of a lion resting majestically on the earth. Sometimes a yell is like waving a stick to shed its reflections on the grass and sometimes a yell does not function as a yell at all. Then, one could kill or spare with perfect freedom, doing and arranging at will and proclaiming, "I am the king of the Law and I am in the Law."

Although most of the recording of sayings was done by pupils of the masters, it was possible at least occasionally for a master to write his sayings himself. At any rate this same casual style of the daily language of the common people was used by some monks in their correspondence. Thus in the collection of writings of another eminent Northern Sung monk, Tsung Kao (1084-1163), there are many letters written in this very style. In answer to a letter he wrote:

I have received two letters from your elder brother, Chü-jên, and have learned he is very busy. He should be busy and hurrying. He is already sixty and has been an official. What else should he wait for? If one doesn't get busy in time, what could one do on New Year's Eve? . . . The poor pedant after spending a whole life boring into ancient scraps of paper wanting to know everything, to read every book, talking in high tones and on expansive subjects, telling us what Confucius was like, Mencius was like, Chuang-tzŭ was like, and the ups and downs of ancient and modern history were like; by these words and adages he was turned topsy-turvy. Whenever a single character was lifted out of the writings of the philosophers of the hundred schools, he would continue to recite from memory thenceforth until he had finished the whole book, illustrating that he was ashamed to confess ignorance even on a single thing. But when we ask him about the affairs in his own home, he doesn't seem to know a thing. He answers the description of one who "counts other's treasures all day long without having one farthing which is his own." He had come to this world in vain to exhibit a tour de force. . . . Those scholars who have read many books have much unenlightenment and those who have read only a few books have little unenlightenment. Those who have been small officials find small differences between their ego and others and those who have been great officials have found the differences great between their ego and others. Those who claim themselves to be clever and smart will find upon the challenge of a tiny problem of gain and loss that their cleverness has completely vanished and that of the books they had read for a whole lifetime, not a single character is of use on the occasion. This is simply because the error has crept in at the time they learned their ABC's.

The beginnings of this genre went back at least to the *Analects* of Confucius and the *Book of Mencius*, to confine ourselves to the Confucian tradition alone. After the introduction of Buddhism into China, Buddhist monks frequently had their sayings recorded, assembled, and circulated as *yü lu*. Although evidences of indebtedness are difficult to establish, it seems likely that the revival of this type of writing in Sung times among the Confucianist circles was due to their awareness of what had been done by their Buddhist rivals.

Among Sung writings that might be classified under this category —and there were many collections of sayings that were not entitled *yü lu* but actually belonged to this general type—the first one to attract public attention were the sayings of the two Ch'êng brothers, Ch'êng Hao (1032-1085) and Ch'êng Yi (1033-1107), who laid the cornerstones of Neo-Confucianism. Though respectable as *ku wên* writers, they touched the masses of Chinese students much more effectively through their recorded sayings. Although recorded often in short and choppy paragraphs, these came closer to the common people in the manner in which ideas were expressed:

Students are fond of being flighty in their words just as poor men would speak of gold, saying that gold is yellow in color and soft in substance. It wouldn't do to say they are wrong but on the other hand you feel tempted to laugh. We have never seen rich people describing gold in those terms.

Conversing with students is like steadying a drunkard. When you have propped him up on the east side, he would fall on the west side. But when you have propped him up on the west side he would fall on the east side. It is eventually impossible to make him stand up straight.

The most influential collection of sayings was the one composed of Chu Hsi's discourse with his pupils; partly because Chu Hsi was the central figure in Neo-Confucianism and partly because the collection, besides being most voluminous, was quite varied in contents and, therefore, absorbingly interesting:

Then it was discussed that the Buddhist sects have well defined and strict discipline whereas the scholars do not follow the stipulations of *li.* The Master said: "They have a way of concentrating their attention. Now on the part of the scholars, although there are some good ones who commit no misdeeds, it is accidentally due to their personalities. By and large, their minds are utilized nowhere. During each day there are many hours in which they are idle. When they wish to understand certain basic principles but have not quite succeeded, they will postpone their attempts for three or five days or even a half-month without feeling urgently challenged. In their attempt to bore into truth, if they don't get through, they will divert their attention to another area. Now it doesn't matter whether one bores in through a big issue or small issue from the east or from the west, because once you have bored into the heart of truth the result will be the same. But when one, after boring here and boring there without getting through, then gives up, there is nothing much to say for such attempts. When one has failed to understand something, one should get all the busier and work harder, then one will find there is nothing which he cannot understand. Suppose a man has lost a huge precious pearl. If he himself does not seriously go in search for it, how can he recover it?"

Although these sayings do not constitute elegant literature, the important stamp of approval given to them by orthodox Confucianists lent considerable dignity to the speech of the common people and indirectly paved the way to a revival of the vernacular language as a medium in serious writing.

CHAPTER 19

Sung Literature:
Traditional Poetry

Running parallel to the Sung continuation of the *ku wên* tradition in prose writing was the Sung retention of the T'ang heritage in the *shih* type of poetry. All the subdivisions of *shih* poetry developed in the seventh, eighth, and ninth centuries were followed by Sung poets. As a result of a decided change in the spirit of the times reflecting organized national life as well as individual reactions to it, Sung poets writing in the *shih* form did not exactly confine themselves to the ruts left by the T'ang poets in spite of the fact that they freely expressed their admiration for one or another of the leading T'ang poets as their masters and models.

In the first place, the most striking difference between T'ang and Sung poetry of the *shih* type is easily noticeable in the absence of pride in national defense and expansion during the latter regime. This is noticeable not only in the *shih* poetry of the Southern Sung Period but also in poems written at the beginning of the dynasty, when *shih* poetry failed to manifest the spirit of national pride.

Moreover, in spite of the tenuousness of international peace, Sung poets were fond of reflecting the tranquillity of the newly established empire. As a result, poems written protesting social and political injustice—poems that might be called problem poems—were almost completely neglected by Sung writers. Hence, many of the tragedies presented in vignette by such poets as Tu Fu and Po Chü-yi were totally lacking in the works of the Sung poets.

In addition, what is more surprising, love poetry portraying the soul-consuming sorrows of ill-fated women ceased to be a preferred theme of the new dynasty. As we shall see later, the only exception to this rule was the borderline case of Huang T'ing-chien who would occasionally write a love poem or two. But, many of his critics pointed out, he was prone to be licentious and might deserve punishment in purgatory. The warmth and fervor of T'ang poetry, as a whole, seemed to be noticeably absent from Sung poetry.

Although generalizations are apt to be misleading, a number of differences in the background of poetry writing might be mentioned in explanation of at least a part of this new spirit and trend in the technique and attitudes of the major poets. By and large, the Sung poets led fairly successful and comfortable lives. Of course there were outstanding instances of party strife, of political persecutions and exiles. In spite of these, however, most of the major Sung poets rose to high distinction in the official hierarchy and led long lives. At least when they were engaged in the writing of poetry they seemed to take considerable delight in the tower of ivory and their themes were relaxed in spite of disillusionment and tranquil in spite of personal misfortunes.

The intellectual background against which the Sung poets lived their relatively smooth lives was an increasingly moralistic and even puritanical society under the pervasive influence of Neo-Confucianism. In this atmosphere, which was saturated with the revival of the sagely ideals taught in traditional Confucianism, it was only natural that didactic poetry and philosophical poetry began to attract the eyes of readers. Disparaging the T'ang poets as forgetful of Tao, Sung poets regarded poetry which was an essential part of literature as a major vehicle for the propagation of Tao or "the Way" of life and the universe. This tinge of moralism was the vogue of the dynasty from beginning to end. Nonetheless, it would make no sense to claim that the Sung poets were devoid of emotion.

It should be pointed out in passing that there were more poets on record in the Sung Dynasty than in the T'ang Dynasty known as the golden period of Chinese poetry. If Sung poetry has to defer to its predecessor in quality, it is certainly not inferior in quantity. In the monumental collection of T'ang poets compiled in the eighteenth century under the general title of *Ch'üan T'ang Shih,* there are over 2,220 poets represented. Although no similar compilation has been made of Sung poetry of the *Shih* type, there are at least five thousand Sung poets on record with varying numbers of poems preserved. Moreover, the two most voluminous poets, Lu Yu (1125-1210) and Yang Wan-li (1127-1206), had each written more than ten thousand poems. Nonetheless, when the *shih* form of versification was resorted to among the great majority of these poets people saw little evidence of any outburst of forceful emotion.

The explanation for this disparity is not difficult to ascertain. As we have pointed out before, the status of *shih* had been elevated by the Sung poets so that *shih* might become a major vehicle for the propagation of a way of life. This, however, could not mean the damming up of emotional outlets for the poets for there was the convenient outlet available in the form of the newly developed *t'zŭ*. This new form was known in Sung times under many names, one of which was *shih yü*, literally, the remnants of *shih*. It became a new vehicle for those *shih* poets who were tired of the conventions. In spite of the fact that *t'zŭ* was the representative literary type of the Sung Dynasty, it was officially looked down upon by both writers and readers. *T'zŭ* was referred to as a bypath, a petty trick unrelated to the important functions of poetry—a little plaything which might be utilized as a pastime. Since neither Confucius nor any of his major followers had laid down specific rules governing such a tiny point and since this diversion had won universal admiration of little men and women in expressing their love and hate, hopes and fears, aspirations and frustrations, what harm could it do for the more dignified writers to try their hand at this petty craft of the masses? Hence, outpourings of the romantic feelings of Sung poets were diverted into the channel of *t'zŭ* and it was no coincidence that even in the case of the major poets they did considerably better in *t'zŭ*.

Its limitations notwithstanding, there were new attainments even in Sung *shih* poetry—new vistas opened up and new techniques evolved. One of the most impressive new vistas was the capturing of the beauty of paintings in word pictures. Of the possibility of this the T'ang poets had not been unaware, for Wang Wei had formulated the dictum that good poetry should have the flavor of good painting and vice versa. And Tu Fu started the long-followed tradition of inscribing poems on paintings. But it was not until Sung poetry had fully developed its own characteristics that we find the painting-poem developing into a major type. Thanks to the fact that many Sung poets were also accomplished painters, the number of painting-poems left to us by Sung poets outnumber the didactic poems by a ratio of at least two to one. The most striking characteristic of Sung poetry of the *shih* type was the adoption of prose technique in versification. The T'ang poets, like their predecessors, had been sparing in the use of what we call particles in the Chinese language, as these words have a peculiar co-ordinative and subordinative function, and their omission is often conducive to obscurity and ambiguity. While admirers of T'ang poetry still insist that suggestiveness is always superior to exhaustiveness in poetry, even they would readily admit that the communications of the Sung poets are easier to gauge even though they disparage the latter by saying that lucidity invariably means shallowness.

Aside from this, the Sung poets had the advantage of building their new technique upon the successes and failures of the T'ang poets. They seemed to know exactly what pitfalls to avoid and what virtues to cultivate. Their descriptive power, for instance, was developed to a new fineness unenvisaged by T'ang poets. And of the carelessness of versification committed by some T'ang poets, they were almost entirely free. They would avoid dissonance by purposely committing a similar violation of prescribed tonal sequence in an even-numbered line to counterbalance an unwarranted deviation in the preceding line.

In spite of the large number of poets of the *shih* type on record, it should be clearly pointed out that their writing, for all its variety of subject matter and accumulated volume, represented only a minor current in the total scene of the development of Chinese literature. Its importance lay mainly in keeping alive a tradition, a technique, and a literary type of expanding complexity which had been in progress for over a thousand years. This minor current was to flow on with dignity if not with universal popularity until very recently. It constituted a major highway in traditional literature and despite its general trend of conservatism, reflected changing tastes and experimentation from age to age. Among the thousands of Sung poets we shall examine the individual contributions of only a small number who used this type of verse form.

All through the Five Dynasties and the early decades of the Sung Dynasty numerous minor poets might be characterized in general as petty sentimentalists. Most of them had been overpowered by the new technique evolved in *t'zŭ* poetry and tried to transfer the new technique and new rhythm to the writing of traditional *shih* poetry. Somehow the mosaic type of artistry seemed precious and the new rhythm of the uneven lines sounded jerky.

Against this a reaction set in, comparatively short-lived but effective, in which the late T'ang poets, especially Li Shang-yin, were held up as models. If such models were not superlative poets at least they had held their own in the last days of T'ang poetry. This movement was known as the Hsi K'un school, a name derived from an anthology composed of selections of poetry written by members of that school led by Yang Yi (974-1020). The basic characteristics of this school were emphasis on diction and a conscious display of technical cleverness in perfecting the artistry of parallel structure. A representative example of this trend is a regulation seven-syllable poem written by Yang Yi himself on "Tears," which it is virtually impossible to translate into any foreign language. Instead of singing on the announced theme of tears, he chose deliberately to cull from Chinese classical literature all the scenes and stories in which the shedding of tears was involved. In the poem *tear* was never used but all the allusions pointed out to those who were learned enough that it was tears that the poet was talking about. To one unfamiliar with the obscure sources of the allusions, all the poem presented was an assemblage of colorful and ornate diction. In substance, therefore, the poem was nothing more than a riddle.

This excessive preoccupation with the display of flowery phraseology called forth a reaction which stressed naturalness and readability. Among the leaders of the new poetry in Sung times the most outstanding was Ou-yang Hsiu, whom we have already noted as a major prose writer. As he was dedicated to the purging of ornateness and obscurity, it was no coincidence that he had a natural aversion to regulation poetry in which such matters as tonal patterns and antithetical construction were of primary importance. In four-line poems, however, he was a true master.

The Pavilion of Abounding Joy

Red trees, blue hills, and the setting sun—
Outside the city stretches an endless expanse of green.
The wanderers, hardly mindful of the decline of spring,
Trample on the fallen flowers as they walk past the pavilion.

Even when Ou-yang tried deliberately to write in imitation of poets who had preceded him, his own voice and feelings were unmistakable. In a poem entitled "Returning Home in the Rain," a poem of only twenty syllables arranged in four lines, he wrote:

In the morning clouds hover above a storied building,
And at sunset it rains south of the city wall.
On the long road the fragrant chariot travels slowly,
Going, going, I wonder where it is headed for.

Again, in imitation of an early medieval ballad entitled "Night After Night" he wrote another twenty-syllable poem:

The floating clouds emit the bright moon,
Shedding shadows on the jade balustrade.
Though we share the moonlight over a thousand miles,
How can one's thoughts be known, the same thoughts night after night?

Rivaling Ou-yang Hsiu, Wang An-shih excelled especially in quatrains of twenty or twenty-eight syllables known respectively as five-syllable quatrains (*wu chüeh*) and seven-syllable quatrains (*ch'i chüeh*). In a poem entitled "On the River" he wrote the following five-syllable quatrain:

> The river water responds with ripples to the western wind,
> The river blossoms shed their fading red,
> Sorrows of departure are being carried
> By the sound of the fife eastward beyond the rolling hills.

For a quatrain of the seven-syllable variety we may note the following occasional poem that he wrote on the studio wall of a friend:

> Underneath the thatched roof it is clean-swept, silent, mossless;
> There are rows of flowers and ferns planted by the master himself.
> A stream protects by encircling the green field;
> Two mountains radiate through the gates to deliver their verdure.

Among his longer poems was one highly praised, written on the historic theme of Lady Wang of the Han Dynasty who was sent by mistake to become consort of the Hunnish Khan because a court painter had purposely disfigured her face in an album of portraits of the court ladies as a result of her refusal to bribe him.

> Lady Wang was married to a Hunnish youth.
> In a hundred cushioned chariots were Hunnish ladies.
> She was clamping up her emotions as she found none to talk to,
> She could only confide in the p'i-p'a and herself.
> With a golden plectrum her hand plucked the strings like a spring wind.
> She played as a maestro during the serving of wine.
> Her former maids from the Han Palace wept silently;
> But travelers on the desert turned their heads around.
> "The grace of Han is scanty and the Huns are kind;
> The joy of life may yet be found in comradeship."
> Her green tomb now lies pitiably in ruins.
> Yet the doleful strains of her zither are still alive.

No matter what versification form Wang An-shih was writing in he invariably showed a terseness, a deep philosophic insight, and a melody of leisure.

The real vitality of Sung poetry was not completely released until Su Shih wrote his many songs. In his *shih* poetry as well as *t'zŭ*, Su manifested a surpassing energy and a disregard for rules and regulations. Creative writing he compared to the movement of floating clouds and gushing streams. Slightly reminiscent of Li Po but more consciously dedicated to freedom from discipline, he wrote poetry as he would prose. Although he was extremely effective in his short poems of four lines, he found special delight in longer poems. In a poem in which he sent off his good friend, Chang Chia-chou, on a long journey, he exhibited his forthrightness:

> In my youth I aspired not to marquisates of a myriad families,
> Nor to the patronage of a powerful minister at court;
> But I would not mind the magistracy of a district like Chiachou,
> Where, equipped with wine, I could often visit the Temple of Rising Clouds.

> A great name is useless, now that my hair is white;
> In my dreams I would only climb the Dragon Cliff.
> Worldly honors, like fleeting clouds, are dispensable;
> Mountains and rivers alone are truly to be coveted.

> "Autumn's half moon on top of Mount Omei
> Shines into and flows with the water of P'ingchiang River."
> These lines of Li Po how few have fully understood?
> Go up to the top floor when you see the moon.

> What of the many things laughed and talked about?
> Let them one and all be consigned to the pale white wine.
> You will soon be back after serving the grateful people,
> Fulfilling the best wishes of an aging friend.

It was because Su Tung-p'o and his followers were consciously dedicated to the creation of a new type of poetry by following the traditional use of versification that they consciously tried to deviate from the masters they followed. For this reason, typical Sung poetry of the *shih* type came to be looked upon as literary heresy by many a subsequent poet and literary critic. T'ang poetry in its almost endless facets had come to be so unconditionally admired that any departure from its trends seemed unwarranted. Actually, it is unfair to identify Su Tung-p'o as the first innovator, for Wang An-shih had already paved the way. But, since Wang had been noted principally as a statesman and because he did not organize any literary coterie around himself, he was sometimes forgotten as the first rebel from the standpoint of chronological sequence. In contrast, Su Tung-p'o not only broke out of the limitations of T'ang poetry more deliberately and spectacularly but also re-enforced his stand and convictions by drawing to himself a number of the outstanding poets of his age to perpetuate his technique. This school of poets with Su Tung-p'o as its initiator and nucleus was to dominate the *shih* poets for the remainder of the Sung dynastic span for over two centuries.

There is no question that at least in the formative period of Su Tung-p'o's literary career he had studied as his models various major T'ang poets. Critics have pointed out that he was heavily indebted to Tu Fu, whom he fervently admired. Aside from Tu Fu he also showed considerable admiration for Han Yü as well as for his senior Sung contemporary, Ou-yang Hsiu. Nonetheless, admiration did not result in slavish imitation. Having been born in the expansive province of Szechuan noted for its famous scenic beauties, and having been nurtured in a family of long established literary reputation harking back to the T'ang Dynasty, he was destined by heredity and circumstance to outgrow all cultural conventions, including the literary. A man with strong tendencies toward romanticism, expressing himself in excessive drinking, in succumbing to the temptation of plural concubinage and frequenting houses of prostitution, he could not allow himself to be bound by any conventions. In this light it is readily understandable that he excelled in those types of *shih* poetry in which regulations and rules counted least. In other words, besides the long poems in which versification patterns were left to the choice of the poet he also excelled in seven-syllable quatrains. It was in these two types that he could write poetry as though he were writing prose. His relative freedom thus gained, he never allowed himself to abuse it. With self-imposed discipline and artistry, he took delight in enjoying his freedom. Hence his shorter verses reveal a naturalness behind which there was considerable artistic restraint—a restraint which was never imposed from without. The following quatrain on the "Midautumn Moon" might be taken as an example:

The clouds have disappeared to increase both the clarity and chill of the evening.
Silently stands the Milky Way as the Jade Disc turns.
This life and this night will not last forever.
Where will I see the bright moon next year, I wonder?

The last couplet in the original was written in conformity to the principle of parallel structure. The fourteen characters literally translated would read:

This life, this night, not forever good;
Bright moon, bright year, which place see.

By taking advantage of the fact that "bright year" in Chinese literally means next year or the following year, the two lines, instead of being quietly parallel, gave the effect of continuous thought and expression.

In other, shorter pieces, he would forego the difficulties of parallel structure completely. In the following poem written in response to a friend who had sent him a poem on "Peach Flowers on the Eastern Hedge," he wrote:

The peach flowers are pale white and the willows are deep green.
When the willow floss flies about, the flower petals will scatter over the whole city.
In melancholy stands the snowy tree near the eastern hedge.
How many spring festivals can one see in a life-time!

Su Tung-p'o succeeded in communicating to a number of his contemporaries this resolution of blazing new paths and opening up new vistas for poets of the new age. Aside from four pupils whom he had won over completely to his views and technique, he also took special pains to cultivate the friendship of an established poet, Ch'ên Shih-tao. The master not only exerted influence over all of them, however, but succeeded in surpassing them with his poetic attainments.

Among the followers of Su Tung-p'o, we shall mention only one in passing, partly because he had written voluminously but more especially because he was in due course to become the purported founder of an influential school of poets known as the Kiangsi school after the birthplace of its founder. This poet was Huang T'ing-chien (1045-1105), a native of Hungchou in Kiangsi Province. Like Su Tung-p'o, his master, Huang had a checkered career in public life. As a result of repeated disillusionment, he sought solace in the arts and letters. He distinguished himself not only as a prose writer and a poet utilizing both the *shih* and *t'zŭ* forms, but also in diverse forms of calligraphy. When, as a young man, he presented himself to Su Tung-p'o with his prose and verse compositions, the master exclaimed in great surprise and gave him the credit of being able to rise above many a generation. Although his name was frequently linked with that of his master by his contemporaries and immediate successors, Huang, as a poet, seems to have fallen short of Su Tung-p'o in originality and independence. He seemed to have been less successful in shedding the influence of the master poets whom he had adored, especially T'ao Ch'ien, Tu Fu, and Han Yü. He was little indebted as a poet to his master, to whom he was sentimentally attached. On one occasion he is reported to have said, "There are people whose literary reputation pervades the whole world but whose poetry cannot quite catch up with that of the ancients. Su probably is one of these."

As contrasted with the dexterity with which Su could rise above discipline and regulations, Huang's poetry exhibited meticulous tempering and retempering. According to the observation of a contemporary, when Huang reached middle age he had accumulated over a thousand poems. Two-thirds of these failed to satisfy the poet and were pitilessly burned. Those left were circulated in a slender volume entitled *Salvages From the Fire*. Later on, as the remnants increasingly pleased him, he changed the title of the collection to *Collection of Worn-Out Brooms*, utilizing an old saying from one of the ancient Chinese philosophers who remarked that sentimental attachment could sometimes be so overdeveloped that one would so prize a worn-out broom to which he was attached that he would consider it worth a thousand pieces of gold. To epitomize his tireless revision he summarized his sentiments in two lines of a poem:

> Of ten times I wanted to speak, I held back nine times.
> In a multitude of ten thousand, one would understand.

On another occasion while discoursing on the art of poetry, he compared it to alchemy where one touch on a piece of iron would transmute it to pure gold.

The outstanding characteristic which Huang continuously and conscientiously cultivated was oddity, in which such qualities as rawness, apparent dissonance, obscurity, and crudity were the most noticeable. This characteristic was not unknown among T'ang poets when they tried to do something unusual. In Huang's hands, however, what was casual with the T'ang poets had become a cultivated habit.

While Huang's regulation poems and his so-called *ku shih* (ancient style poems) were regarded as his most representative compositions, actually his charm as a poet was best exhibited in the shorter poems. In a four-line poem which he wrote to a friend in place of a letter, he wrote:

> The color of the mountains and the sound of the river exchange
>   their clarity.
> With the screen rolled high, I await the rising moon.
> The doleful tune being played now in a neighboring boat
> Sums all up my sorrow of departure from my old friend.

Again, when he wanted to ask for a few branches of a special variety of plum flowers known as wax plums, he addressed the following to a friend:

> I have heard the wild plums are flowering behind your monastery,
> And fragrant wax has dyed them to a noble shade of yellow.
> I am asking for cuttings not to please my aged eyes,
> Only to be sure that the colors of spring are pervading your ponds.

The movement started by Huang was generally known as the Kiangsi movement. The movement crystallized itself into a well-defined school. Within this school twenty-five or twenty-six poets were included. Poets in China, as elsewhere, had for a long time formed themselves into coteries, but coteries did not necessarily make schools. Within the so-called Kiangsi school it must be pointed out there were certain types of heterogeneity. In the first place, at least half of the poets counted as members were not natives of Kiangsi. In the second place, although they all claimed Huang T'ing-chien as their leader, many of them publicly proclaimed that besides Huang they had other masters. In the third place, within the school itself many styles were stressed. Nonetheless, all the poets had one point in common, namely, the oddity which Huang so fervently sought.

Without mentioning these minor Sung poets one by one, we shall present the most outstanding representative, Ch'ên Shih-tao (1053–1101). Like Huang, whom he claimed as his master, he was fond of burning the poems he had written which failed to please him. To his contemporaries he is remarkable in that he would shut himself up for days in search of an apt line in poetry. It was also reported among his contemporaries that whenever Ch'ên found inspiration on an excursion he would hastily leave his company for home, hurriedly climb into his bed, and cover himself up with a quilt. The bed was thus nicknamed "the poetry bed" and during such periods of self-imposed confinement, members of his family would chase away all cats and dogs. At times babies and young children would even be escorted to some neighborhood family for temporary lodging. In spite of his readiness in destroying poems he succeeded in distilling 765 poems out of his poetic life span. According to later critics, Ch'ên was at his best in regulation poetry, mainly because the regulations were effective aids to him for endless revision. Since he was a slow writer the discipline required in regulation poetry seemed to have appealed especially to his genius. In a poem of five-syllable lines of the regulation type, he wrote:

> The mountain opens up two banks of willows,
> The river circles villages of a few families.
> The land is inclined, tipping itself into a chasm;
> The windy billows chew at the roots of rockeries.
> To the distant woods frost has added its color,
> On the sandy banks the tide has left its traces.
> I still shed tears for being away from home.
> How can I summon my scattered soul?

The same characteristic of drawing word pictures with carefully selected vocabulary is revealed in a similar poem on "Autumn Emotions":

> The mountain breaks open to yield room to an expansive wilderness,
> The river winds to slacken off its rapids.
> Climbing and loitering are best toward eventide;
> Wind and rain are most fitting in autumn.
> Swiftly, the slow-flying swans try to gain speed;
> And lingeringly the seagulls circle without alighting.
> The boat is awaiting yet awhile in the eventide
> But the ricebirds at dusk have vanished into the far horizon.

This type of technique so fondly cultivated by Huang and Ch'ên came to be known as "pecking at poetry lines." While it was appreciated as valuable discipline, it was a discipline submitted to in order to be outgrown.

Among the minor poets of the Northern Sung period, real literary charm is to be found first in *t'zŭ* poetry which will be discussed in a separate chapter and second in the works of people who were primarily known for scholarship, miscellaneous information, and philosophical speculation. These often left to posterity many little gems of exquisite beauty not to be found in the collected works of the so-called Kiangsi poets.

As Northern Sung poetry lost its brilliance in the hands of poetasters who imitated the technique of line-pecking, the fate of the empire was also rapidly running downhill, culminating in the conquest of northern China by the Chin Tatars and the hasty flight of the imperial court to the Yangtze Valley in 1127. Taking part in the great exodus were many poets of high attainment who were wise enough to avoid the pitfalls of the Kiangsi school. These, in a sense, had only paved the way for the rise of a real poet of great vitality in the Southern Sung period.

The first Southern Sung poet who deserves mention was Lu Yu (1125-1210), a native of Shanyin County in present-day Chekiang Province. Distinguished as a writer of both prose and verse in his twelfth year, he began to attract attention not only from the poets but also from the dignitaries of the state including Emperor Hsiao himself. Victim of irresponsible gossip, he went through many rises and falls in the official hierarchy. When another great poet, Fan Ch'êng-ta, was commander-in-chief in Szechuan, Lu was invited to join his staff. He met his superior as a fellow poet and was blamed by his colleagues for his unconventionality. Whereupon he gave himself a new pen name, Fang-wêng, namely, the Unconventional Old

Man. Many-sided in his literary gifts and almost unequaled by other poets in his long life span, he left to posterity a huge volume of poetry. In spite of his romantic nature, his refusal to conform, and his great love for travel, Lu Yu distinguished himself primarily as a poet of patriotism. In the evening of his life, he summed up his life's ambition in a poem he wrote on the occasion of examining a painting of Ta-shan Kuan, one of the most important strategic passes over a precipitous mountain. The poem was not an autobiography but rather the dream of a lifetime. The dream was one of the complete recovery of all territories lost to the Tatars, a dream which was never realized. This feeling he exhibited most naturally in many of his poems. An example is the following:

> Even if one is not an An Ch'i-shêng—the immortal of old,
> Who after hearty drinks would go ride the whale on the Eastern Ocean,
> One can emulate the heroic Li Hsi-p'ing
> Who slew the rebels and regained the old capital.
> The golden seal of authority I have not yet won,
> But crispy white hair has stealthily crowned my head.
> As I lie in late fall in this Chengtu monastery,
> The monk's window is flooded with the light of the setting sun.
> Can't I mount my horse and smash the enemy troops?
> Should I hum my poems with a cold cicada's voice?
> Thus aroused I buy up all the wine at the bridge market,
> Piling long jars helter-skelter on my big wagon.
> The doleful music helps me down my drinks
> Like the plains of Chüyeh sucking up the Yellow River's inundation.
> As I have never before taken a single drop,
> My inspired capacity stuns a thousand friends.
> My country unavenged yet, but lo! I am growing old;
> So at night my sword in the sheath makes a stirring sound.
> When will victory come, and when the grand banquet?
> When will midnight snow overpower the town of the Flying Fox?

This yearning for the reconquest of the North China plains was sometimes symbolically and hiddenly expressed:

The Herd-Boy

> In the southern village the boy who minds the ox
> With his naked feet stands on the ox's back.
> Through the hole in his coat the river wind blows;
> Through his broken hat the mountain rain pours.
> On the long dyke he seemed to be far away;
> In the narrow lane suddenly we were face to face.

> The boy is home and the ox is back in his stall;
> And a dark smoke oozes through the thatched roof.
>
> (Arthur Waley's translation)

On another occasion after he had been intoxicated on a high pavilion he wrote the following poem:

> A real man is never born in vain,
> I am bent on defeating the barbarians
> And recovering our lost lands.
> In my struggles I have failed to fulfill my hope—
> For eight years I wandered in Liang and Yi only to grow old!
> One midnight as I fondled my pillow I loudly exclaimed,—
> "I have recaptured the Pine Pavilion Pass!"
> On waking I sighed, "We have lost many chances,"
> I found in my bed traces of tears the following morning!
> In this official mansion at Yichou wine is ever flowing like the sea,
> I come here daily to buy my share,
> And when I feel warm I play a game for joy
> And yell my dices until I win.
> While gambling my eyes flash like lightning.
> I look mad but I know myself better.
> How dare a minister forget the imperial ancestors in the nine temples
> With the spirit of the emperors hovering around the supreme God?

Lu Yu has been praised for being possibly the only poet after A.D. 200 who saw dignity in the warring profession and who regarded warfare as a necessity in national defense. This attitude, which stemmed from his deep-seated patriotism, must have been re-enforced by his love of country, inspired by the beauty of the various areas which he had visited. Besides many long poems which he wrote in the midst of towering peaks of high mountains he also recorded inspired moments in shorter poems. On one occasion when he was riding on donkeyback in a drizzling rain on his way to Szechuan passing through Chienmên or the Sword Gate, he wrote:

> The marks of travel and of drinking are mixed on my garment.
> Wandering far from home I find all places depressing.
> I wonder now if I am really a poet,
> Riding a lone donkey in a drizzling rain through the Sword Gate.

Although his poetry was voluminous, he had consciously cultivated that art with unstinting care as he recorded his experience on one occasion,

> Smile if you like but this old poet cuts short his sleep
> And his little poems are oftentimes completed during the
> uncanny hours.

The last poem that he wrote was a message he transmitted to his son on his deathbed:

> I know to die is to be dead to the world.
> Still I am sorry not to have lived to see a united China.
> On the day when our royal troops have recovered the lost lands,
> Don't fail to tell your anxious father at your ancestral altars!

(Teresa Li's translation)

Lu Yu seemed to be the only poet during the national emergency when the last Sung emperors had been carried off by the Chin troops as prisoners of war to remember that there was a national shame to be removed.

A contemporary of Lu Yu, who more actively participated in government in the Southern Sung administration and who yet was able to identify himself with the quietude of the beauties of the universe was Fan Ch'êng-ta (1125-1193). A voluminous writer even in prose on many varied topics, including bibliography, Fan distinguished himself primarily as a poet leaving close to two thousand poems to posterity. Attaining official recognition in his early years and rising steadily in the official hierarchy—including the leadership of a diplomatic mission to the Chin court—he succeeded in keeping his life close to the rhythm of nature. He frequently used his courtesy title of Shih Hu to remind himself of his exceptionally attractive manor with a lagoon surrounded by a unique rockery.

In his self-imposed discipline as a poet, he had for a time identified himself as a follower of the Kiangsi school, and yet from his own notes attached to his poems he frequently admitted having taken various T'ang Dynasty poets as his models. The imitative period of his poetic career, however, was not a long one. His masters and models were early outgrown and his own style and preferences emerged. While his regulation poems of the *shih* type were frequently stilted in style and his longer poems on the whole lacked distinctiveness, he seemed to be especially gifted in his four-line poems. This vehicle he continued to employ in his own particular manner. Instead of expressing intensely emotional reactions, he devoted himself almost exclusively to a delineation of the beauties of farm and garden. In his role as a poet of nature, he was distinctly different from his great predecessor, T'ao Ch'ien, because while T'ao merged himself with nature and revealed strong personal emotions through the different facets of nature, Fan's approach was one in which he would leave himself out. Thus, whether consciously or unconsciously, Fan as a nature poet might be described as an exponent of objective realism.

His most typical group of poems consisted of sixty quatrains written in 1179 on the four seasons with their changing scenes in farm and garden. He was then spending the year in recuperation from an illness in his country manor and recorded his observations of the changes of nature from time to time. The following poems give us glimpses into Fan's attainment as a major poet of his era.

Early Spring

Deep in the lane lined with willow flowers, the cockcrow breaks the mid-
day quiet.
The tender tips of the mulberry leaves are not yet fully green.
Waking from my doze in the chair, and having nothing to do,
I watch the newborn silkworms by the side of the sunny window.

Late Spring

Butterflies in pairs fly into the vegetable flowers.
A long day in the farmhouse; I expect no callers.
Suddenly the dog barks, the hens hop over the fence—
The pedlar has come to buy some more tea leaves.

Summer

A sweating stranger has come from amidst the yellow dust
To quench his thirst at my fragrant well.
To him I lend my seat—the millstone at my door,
Where, in the shade of willow trees, blows a cool breeze at noon hour.

Autumn

New frost at dawn augurs the arrival of late autumn,
Converting the green forest into a forest of beige brocade.
Inside the orange grove a different picture emerges—
Emerald clusters bedecked with countless dots of gold.

Winter

Drifting in my boat, I admire the bright snowy hills.
The wind subsiding, the air turns freezing cold at nightfall.
A queer sound made by the pole, like shattering of jades and pearls
Tells me the surface of the lake has turned into a sheet of ice.

While Fan Ch'êng-ta had concentrated upon poetry of nature of his own style, excelling in little else in his poetry, his devoted friend and contemporary, Yang Wan-li (1127-1206), who had paid Fan the highest of tributes as a poet, was more voluminous, more varied in style, and more experimental than anyone else in the Sung Dynasty. Yang shared with the Neo-Confucianists the conviction that moral rectitude and unflinching integrity counted above everything else. As a member of the civil service he resolutely refused to compromise himself with political leaders whose character was in question. As a poet he laid himself open to periodic but drastic changes, including periods during which he would regard verse writing as absolutely meaningless. According to his own admission he was fond of writing poetry when he was young and then after a while he felt bored. It was not until he had changed his style that he was again pleased and a little later again bored. These intermittent periods of resignation from verse writing were mainly due to his dissatisfaction with any given form or style. All the time he was in search of something the nature of which he himself did not quite know. Imitation of T'ang poets irked him and he turned to the Sung poets of the Kiangsi school. Another period of imitation convinced him he wasn't any longer himself. Treading in the well-worn steps of his predecessors led him nowhere. Then he suddenly realized, after reading Po Chü-yi, that the language of the people would open up endless vistas. Now that he had outgrown imitation and all preoccupation with masters, he could write as he chose. This discovery had come to him almost accidentally or in his own words, "as though I had suddenly awakened to something." Then he continued:

I tried asking my sons to have their writing brushes ready while I recited a few poems orally and the result was that the lines came flowing as though from a life-water without the stuttering of previous years. From then on each day after the noon hour, with the clerks dispersed and the offices vacated, I would take with me a fan and stroll around the rear garden or climb the ancient city wall picking berries and chrysanthemums, climbing bamboo groves and turning around clusters of flowers. The myriad phenomena seemed to be assembled to present me with materials for poetry in such rapid succession that I could not wave them away. Before I could dispense with one graciously I was already confronted with another. In complete relaxation I did not feel the difficulty of writing poetry.

Keeping Po Chü-yi remotely as his model and reading him with thorough enjoyment whenever he could afford the time, he evolved his own independent style. Looking at the moon on a frosty night in a fishing boat he wrote the following:

Standing a little while beside the creek waiting for the moon
I found the moon rising late as though purposely.
I came home, shut my door, too sated to take another look.
All of a sudden it flew up above a thousand cliffs.
Then I boarded my fishing boat to take another glance,
And found the icy orb neatly suspended from a twig of pine.
Poets love the moon at midautumn.

My response to that is a sideward-swing of my head.
A year's most beautiful moon is in the winter
When it is washed clean with snowflakes and frosty water,
When there is an endless stretch of blue sky,
Shining upon an azure lake with a white jade disc floating.
As its companion I would invite the plum blossoms.
Isn't this something surpassing the midautumn scene?

Most of these casual impressions expressed in everyday language
are to be found in his shorter poems:

The Morning Walk Along the Fir Path

After the rain, coolness has engendered itself in the forest.
With wind winding its way, the morning is surpassingly clear.
Following my nose, I have wandered into unvisited spots
And frightened myself by frightening the wild fowls.

Crossing the Takao Ford in the Morning of the Fifth Day in the First Month, 1180

Hidden in a thick fog, mountains and rivers are not clearly
    discernible
And so I have only the sounds of dogs and cocks to guide me to
    the village beyond.
On the deck of the ferry the frosty sheet looks like snow
Now impressed with my footprints as its first pattern.

Besides the trio of Southern Sung poets we have just mentioned, there were many minor poets of high quality. Divided as they were in many rivaling and opposing camps and schools, they continued the tradition of *shih* poetry to the end of the dynasty. Although the volume thus produced was impressive, the attractiveness of conventional poetry of this type had long been eclipsed by the rise of a freer and subtler technique of versification which was to be recognized as more representative of the temperament of the Sung Dynasty.

At the end of the Sung Dynasty there was a curious reaction against the Sung trends in *shih* poetry. All four participants in this movement happen to have the character "Ling" in their courtesy names so they are referred to as the four Lings. These were Wêng Chüan, Chao Shih-hsiu, Hsü Chao (died 1211), and Hsü Chi (died 1214), all from the County of Yungchia in present-day Chekiang Province. Dissatisfied with the fact that Sung poets by and large were long-winded, they decided to cultivate literary economy and return to T'ang standards. They were particularly appreciative of late T'ang technique. On the surface, therefore, the movement promised itself to be a sort of return to the past. When late T'ang models were resorted to, however, no one could escape the liberalizing influence of Po Chü-yi and his readiness to use the common speech of the common people. As a result, this actually was a liberating movement from the artificial standards which had been set up in Sung poetry. This is why in the short poems of the four Lings, we find many charming short verses composed in simple and unadorned language.

> In the yellow plum season, rain falls everywhere.
> In the ponds surrounded with green grass frogs croak all over.
> My guest has not arrived in spite of his promise.
> A casual knot of a chess piece drops the lamp flower.
>
> Chao Shih-hsiu

> Numberless mountain cicadas are chirping at the setting sun,
> While I sit in the cool of the shade thrown by the high peak.
> Near the rockery the clear spring drips incidentally
> And the fragrance of pine needles is faintly borne to me by the
>   passing wind.
>
> Hsü Chi

Besides this movement led by the four Lings, the last years of the Sung Dynasty also saw the rise of the eminent critic, Yen Yü, who in his well-known discourses on poetry attacked Sung poetry in preference for the golden periods of the T'ang and of the Han and Wei dynasties. He advocated the singling out of the major poets from the third to the eighth centuries as masters. While he was right in pointing out the greatest weaknesses of Sung poetry—the equating of poetry with linguistics, erudition, and argumentation, resulting in a lack of emotional depth and intensity, he proposed a faulty solution which he regarded as the only way out, namely, the avoidance of using one's own ideas in poetry and the return to T'ang and pre-T'ang models as perfect yardsticks of excellence. This killed all chances of a truly creative age in late Sung poetry.

CHAPTER 20

The Golden Period of the Tz'ŭ

With the establishment of the Sung Dynasty in 960, the *tz'ŭ* had already come to stay. In fact, signs were apparent that *tz'ŭ*—poetry to be sung to music as contrasted with *shih*, poems written to be read, recited, or at most chanted, but not sung—was to be a more typical expression of the literary genius of the new dynasty. Nonetheless, literary conservatism was still strong. In spite of the natural fondness felt by the poets for *tz'ŭ*, nearly all of them continued to write poetry of the *shih* type to dignify their status if for nothing else. Moreover, *tz'ŭ* continued to be taken lightly on the surface and was, therefore, referred to by the established poets as *shih yü*, which means literally, as we have noted, the left-over crumbs of *shih*, faintly suggesting that poets would resort to the composition of *tz'ŭ* by way of afterthought or extra diversification. Even the noncommittal and neutral appellation for *tz'ŭ* of *ch'ang tuan chü* or "long and short lines" did not reveal the actual enthusiasm with which *tz'ŭ* composition was secretly taken up by the great poetic minds of the new period. Among the early proponents of the new verse form was Yen Shu (991-1055). Known as a child prodigy when he was thirteen, he was summoned to the imperial court and awarded the *chin shih* degree. His life was characterized by his profound respect for talented scholars and by his steady rise in the official hierarchy culminating in his premiership. In spite of his reputation for thrifty living, he was known to be a charming host who entertained frequently, especially at dinner parties at which music and songs were always presented. When his guests had been satiated with the musical program he would call for writing materials for the composition of the traditional *shih*. Although he was reputed to have excelled in both *shih* and *tz'ŭ* it was in the latter that he distinguished himself and made permanent his literary reputation. Thus, to the tune of "Su Chung Ch'ing" or "Pouring Out the Heart's Contents," calling for lines of three, four, five, and seven syllables, he wrote the following:

The hibiscus flowers rival the chrysanthemums in fragrance
The year is rolling on to the Double Nine Festival.
As in a painting the distant village shows its autumn colors
With red trees interspersed lightly with brown.

The waters flow clear and shallow,
The azure sky is vast,
The roads are endless.
Looking far from on high
As the swans fly by
Arouses unending thoughts and sentiments.

When the *tz'ŭ* form had become an accepted type of new poetry, the early Sung poets tried to expand the scope of their canvas by trying to utilize longer tunes to accommodate more turns in the development of emotion. Making use of a popular tune again, Yen Shu wrote the following on the "Listless Beauty," which happened also to be the name of the tune:

The spring wind blows in this second moon
On the catkins blooming all along the road.
The pain of parting now is just unbearable!
Hiding her tears with her silken handkerchief,
Letting it be stained with powder, if it will,
She wonders why there's no way at all to have
　　him detained.

The jade cups are filled time after time;
Her eyebrows are heavily laden with sorrow.
Soft parting music now only breaks her heart.
"As for our next meeting—
Who knows where it might be!
But in my dreams, I will often fly to your side."

The artistic restraint and arrested emotional expression shown in this poem seem to be a carry-over of the technique he used in his *shih* poems. While in the traditional type of poetry he often erred in excessive floridity, his *tz'ŭ* poems seem to belong to a higher order of accomplishment. The *tz'ŭ* form during the Northern Sung period gained increasing dignity from the hands of major literary figures who excelled in multifold forms of literary composition. One such literary giant who did not consider it beneath his dignity to make full use of the *tz'ŭ* form was Ou-yang Hsiu. As we have noted elsewhere, Ou-yang was highly revered not only as the main supporter of the so-called *ku wên* or classical prose reform movement but also as an outstanding upholder and continuator of the orthodox Confucian tradition. For this reason, Ou-yang's *tz'ŭ* of the love song type have disturbed later conservative critics, who tried to shield the eminent Confucianist from unwarranted attacks by saying that those love songs were composed by petty writers and erroneously attributed to Ou-yang. Such a policy was entirely unwarranted, for the puritanical tradition of Neo-Confucianism had not been established in Northern Sung times, during which the writing of love songs was never considered a hindrance to scholarly worth.

Continuing the tradition of the Five Dynasties rather than blazing new trails, Ou-Yang's *tz'ŭ* poems are largely of the shorter type, and his style had a good deal in common with his predecessors of the Five Dynasties, especially the style of Fêng Yen-chi. In fact, there are many poems attributed to both and included in the collected works of both, making it virtually impossible for the most careful critics to clarify the problem of authorship.

The best known of Ou-yang's love songs written in *tz'ŭ* style was the following composed during the New Year lantern festival—an occasion to celebrate the first new moon of the year:

> Last year at the Lantern Festival
> The flower-market lights were bright as day;
> When the moon mounted to the tops of the willows,
> Two lovers kept their tryst after the yellow dusk.
>
> This year at the Lantern Festival
> The moon and the lights are the same as then;
> Only I see not my lover of yesteryear,
> And tears drench the sleeves of my green gown.

> (Teresa Li's translation)

The above-quoted poem in the original was rather like the late T'ang and Five Dynasty tradition because it was composed of eight lines with five syllables in each, reminiscent of the five-syllable *shih* form but distinguishable from the latter by greater care for tonal sequences for musical effect. The following poem, written to the tune of "Yü Lou-ch'un" or "Spring upon the Jade Pavilion" consists of eight lines of seven syllables each, again bearing striking resemblance to the regularity of the *shih* form with seven syllables to the line. Bearing in mind what the original rhythm would sound like, we might read Miss Li's translation:

> Since you left, I know not whether you are far or near,
> I only know the colours of nature have paled and my heart is pent-up with
> infinite yearnings.
> The more you travel, the farther you go and the fewer your letters.
> The waters are broad, and the fish sink deep; where to find any news of you?

In the depth of night the wind plays on the bamboos an autumnal tune,
Echoed by the direful song of the endless leaves.
Leaning upon the single pillow, I try to conjure up the Land of Dreams
　　　where to seek for you.
Alas! no dreams come, only the dim lamplight fuses with the shadows!

(Teresa Li's translation)

It happens that this poem might make some sense in a word-for-word translation into English so that the reader might be aided in appreciating the rhythm of the original:

After parting know not you far near
Greet eye melancholy listlessness
More go more far more no words
Water wide fishes sink [mail carriers] whither ask

Night deep windy bamboo rap out autumn tune
Myriad leaves thousand sounds all are sad
Recline single pillow in dreams seek
Dreams don't materialize lamp goes out

As in the case of classical scholarship in the Northern and Southern Dynasties and in T'ang times, the gift of *tz'ŭ* writing seemed to run in distinguished families. The reason for this is not difficult to find, as classical scholarship was effectively aided by good-sized family libraries. So, aptitude in song writing would be stimulated by family environment. All through the Sung Dynasty well-to-do families in their attempt to cultivate proper taste for poetry and music would maintain groups of singers and musicians. It was no wonder that Yen Shu's younger son, Yen Chi-tao (died 1100), whose ears were early attuned to *tz'ŭ* singing, rose as one of the great stars in this field, although he had no luck whatsoever in his official career. He was evaluated by another Sung poet, Wang T'ing-chien, in the following words: "Not only a jewel among men, his naïveté is unsurpassed. . . . Handicapped in his official career, he would not lean on any political leader for support: naïveté number one. Holding the basic principles in literary criticism he would not utter a sentence, like a newly successful doctoral candidate: naïveté number two. Having squandered millions and millions, exposing his family to hunger and cold, his face still reveals the innocence of a child: naïveté number three. People could betray him a hundred times and yet against them he would bear no grudge as he maintains a perfect faith in man and never suspects their betrayal of him as a possibility:

this is an additional naïveté." In the following poem part of this quality is revealed:

> Raindrops fallen are parted from the clouds;
> Flowing waters never return to their springs.
> When will my enduring sorrow end?
> My heart is bitter like the kernel of a lotus seed.
>
> Swallowing my tears, I cannot sing.
> I'll try to speak through the cither strings.
> The strings seem to murmur "meet again";
> Of that how can I be sure!

Among Northern Sung *tz'ŭ writers*, Liu Yung (flourished 1034) distinguished himself for learning incessantly from singers and musicians and for writing songs of a type that were admired not only by fellow poets but even more by the illiterate common people. While he was a candidate in the Northern Sung capital in K'aifêng, he was tireless in visiting the professional musicians and women singers. To reciprocate their courtesy, whenever new melodies were available, conductors and musicians would approach him for appropriate lyrics. Thus, his reputation as a lyric writer spread so universally in China that it was said his lyrics were sung by people wherever there was a well. In consequence, he has been hailed as a Po Chü-yi singing in *tz'ŭ*. Indeed, like Po Chü-yi, he was a past master in using the language of the common people for creative writing. Thus to the tune "The Butterfly Loved the Flowers," he wrote:

> Upon a high balcony I lean alone.
> The silken wind blows mildly.
> I strain my gaze afar.
> The sorrow of separation oozes dimly from the horizon.
> The colour of the grass and the light of the mountains
>   glimmer in the waning sun.
> No one can divine the feelings that surge in my bosom.
>
> I too have thought of drowning my sorrows in the ocean of wine,
> And singing out the burden of my mind.
> But forced joys leave no taste in the mouth.
> What if my robe and girdle should grow looser every day?
> Is it not for *her* that I am suffering?
>
>   (Teresa Li's translation)

In the following, written to the tune of a widely sung song, he combined the simple language of everyday speech with elegant poetic diction in such a harmonious way that it was admired by both the sophisticated and the illiterate:

A Farewell to My Love

The shivering cicada wailed heart-rendingly.
A long road stretched out before me in the eventide.
A sudden shower had just stopped.
In the tent by the city gate, I drank farewell to my love in a
    gloomy mood.
Just where I wanted to linger a bit,
The boatman came to hasten my departure.
Her hands in mine, we gazed into each other's tear-filled eyes.
Mutely we gulped down our frozen sobs.
Ah, how many miles of mists and waves I have to travel through!
The boundless sky of Ch'u merged into the deepening shades of
    the night.

(Teresa Li's translation)

A contemporary of Liu Yung who shared with him his great love for music and singing and who, like him, lent support to the new verse form with his enormous reputation was Su Shih (1036-1101), better known as Su Tung-p'o. Excelling both as essayist and calligrapher of the highest order, Su Shih was a giant in diverse forms of poetry. It was his literary creed that creative writing was comparable to a floating cloud and a running stream in that its course is neither frozen nor predictable; it should go on as it goes on and stop when it has to stop. In Su's hands *tz'ŭ* poetry was to undergo a number of changes. In the first place, the spirit of careful embroidering and the atmosphere of cosmetic fragrance were now brushed aside. It was reported in contemporary anecdotal literature that the poet once asked an expert singer on his secretarial staff about the difference in style between himself and Liu Yung as *tz'ŭ* writers. The answer was, "Liu Yung's *tz'ŭ* would sound best if sung by a teen-age girl to the rhythm of ivory castanets dyed red, and your *tz'ŭ* calls for a big fellow from the region west of the Grand Pass marking time with iron clappers and chanting your 'Eastward Flows the Huge Yangtze.'" Although this comparison was presented in a jocular manner, it was a good indicator of the difference between the two schools and the two periods represented by Liu and Su. Before Su Tung'p'o's time, *tz'ŭ* writers were primarily concerned with love and complications between men and women with a few of them not entirely free from the presentation of the sensuous. The highest level attained was that of surpassing sorrow of an empathetic kind. With the coming of Su Shih new possibilities were unfolded, possibilities of outgrowing what is imprisoning and delimiting in the everyday life of man, or in the words of another Sung poet, Lu Yu, "After singing it one would feel the impact of a heavenly wind or an ocean rain."

Critics averse to the *tz'ǔ* style of Su Shih blamed him for drawing no distinction between *tz'ǔ* and *shih*. While this verdict is true, it should not be regarded as a demerit, for both types of poetry had grown out of popular songs. In the same way that *shih* had completely detached itself from musical scores there is no reason why *tz'ǔ* should be permanently tied to musical considerations. Su Shih's disregard for the minute regulations had almost achieved the effect of freeing the *tz'ǔ* style from all its previous musical and phonological commitments. Consequently, the *tz'ǔ* form could be utilized for meditative as well as didactic poetry. Some of Su Shih's contemporaries explained his unconventional style in the light of the fact that Su himself was never a good singer. Be that as it may, the convention was established utilizing the *tz'ǔ* for the writing of poetry with complete disregard for musical potentialities. In other words, it had become an orthodox practice to recite instead of singing *tz'ǔ*. Thus in the year 1076 he wrote the following *tz'ǔ* on "Full Moon Festival," affixing the following note to the tune selected: "On Mid-autumn Festival day in the year 1076, I drank merrily through the night till dawn. While greatly intoxicated, I wrote this lyric partly remembering myself to Tzu Yu [his younger brother]."

> How rare the moon, so round and clear!
>   With cup in hand, I ask of the blue sky,
>   "I do not know in the celestial sphere
>   What name this festive night goes by?"
> I want to fly home, riding the air,
> But fear the ethereal cold up there,
>   The jade and crystal mansions are so high!
> Dancing to my shadow,
>   I feel no longer the mortal tie.
> She rounds the vermilion tower,
> Stoops to silk-pad doors,
>   Shines on those who sleepless lie.
> Why does she, bearing us no grudge,
>   Shine upon our parting, reunion deny?
> But rare is perfect happiness—
> The moon does wax, the moon does wane,
>   And so men meet and say goodbye.
> I only pray our life be long,
>   And our souls together heavenward fly!
>
> (Lin Yutang's translation)

It must be pointed out that by this time the contents of the words had become farther and farther removed from the connotations of the title of the musical tune, so that it was necessary as an aid to readers for poets to supply what might be regarded as long subtitles. In the foregoing poem the poet had found it necessary to disclose the circumstances under which the poem was composed. These subtitles in a later period began to be attended to with such artistic concentration that they had a tendency of vying with the poem itself in artistry. In this regard, Su Shih or Su Tung-p'o may be regarded as a forerunner of the tradition of the elaborative subtitle. Thus, to the following tune of the musical score "Lin Chiang Hsien" or "The Fairy at the Riverfront," the poet had to attach the following subtitle: "Composed on my way back to Linkao under the influence of liquor after a drinking bout one night in Snowy Hall."

> After a drink at night, Tungpo wakes up and gets drunk again.
> By the time I come home it seems to be midnight.
> The boy servant is asleep snoring like thunder
> And does not answer the door.
> Resting on a cane I listen to the murmur of the river
> And feel with a pang that I am not master of my own life.
> When can I stop this hustling about?
> The night is late, the air is calm,
> And the water a sheen of unruffled light.
> Let me take a small boat down the river hence
> To spend beyond the seas the remainder of my days.
>
> (Lin Yutang's translation)

At the time of the composition of this poem the poet was living in exile in Huangchow. After this poem was composed it was sung by the poet and his friends in several rounds before the party was scattered. The following day it was rumored that after writing the poem the previous night he had hung his official hat and robe on the branches of a tree by the riverside and had made his escape to an unknown destination. The county chief who was in charge of the banished officer was greatly concerned about the rumor and sent his personal guards out to determine the whereabouts of the poet. To his great satisfaction the county chief learned that Su was still sleeping undisturbed after the intoxication. But when the song was later relayed by singers to the imperial capital, the Sung emperor was a bit suspicious of what had happened.

No matter how inept Su Tung-p'o might have been as a student of music, his boldness in breaking the rules of $tz'\breve{u}$ poetry led him on to new enterprises, namely, working out song patterns of his own and experimenting with vernacular phrases as raw material for *tz'ŭ* composition. Thus we find a new tune of his own—"There Is No Sorrow to Untie"—to which he added the inevitable elaborate sub-title:

The great musician, Hua Jih-hsin, has composed a new tune entitled "The Untying of Sorrow." Lu Yi of Loyang, whose courtesy name was Po-shou, has heard it and is extremely fond of it, trying for fun to write lyrics for it in the vernacular language. The whole world has been singing it, praising it as an approximation to knowing the meaning of life. Master Lung Chiu [Su himself] maintains a smiling attitude toward it. In that composition although sorrow is untied, it still proves that there is something to be untied. As regards those who travel with and delight in the company of nature and rely on the standard of inevitability, feeling happy with others' happiness and sad with others' sadness, would they have anything at all to untie? Whereupon the attitude of the composition is now reversed for this song, "There Is No Sorrow to Untie."

A hundred fleeting years
And people called it a life span.
Having tasted sorrow,
I wonder where sorrow comes from?
And what there is to dispel?
Things are always like wind passing by my ear,
What need is there to take things to heart?
You say, "Cheer up and you will be an optimist."
I fear I can't agree.

This thing is really hard to talk about.
How can we say loafing is just as good as success?
To say it may be all wrong;
Not to say it is not necessarily right.
Neither you nor I really exist here;
What then could we mean by arising above the world of
    material things?
If you say we need drunkenness to dispel sorrow,
How can we be drunk without wine?

In the evolution of the technique of *tz'ŭ* poetry, Su Tung-p'o's position was unique. As critics have repeatedly pointed out, all the artificiality and refinement of *tz'ŭ* language was set aside to make room for boldness and forthrightness. This change was warranted by a desire to widen the range of contents of *tz'ŭ* poetry. *Tz'ŭ* before this time had confined itself mainly if not exclusively to the sentimentality common among love songs. Even the poems written by Li Yü in which he lamented the collapse of a kingdom were presentations of the emotionalized aspects of court life and how court life was abruptly terminated by political upheavals with the passage of time. Now, first attempts were made to make the *tz'ŭ* form the vehicle for the expression of heroic feelings and even philosophical communication. It was Su Tung-p'o who made this possible not only by precept but also by example. Aptly had a later poet, Lu Yu, remarked that at the end of the recital of a Su Tung-p'o *tz'ŭ* one would feel an impact similar to that of a heavenly wind or an ocean rainstorm.

In the second place, from this time on, at least among the followers of Su, the fine distinctions between *tz'ŭ* technique and the traditional *shih* technique were deliberately scrapped. For a long time this was held against Su and his followers as a weakness and a regrettable failure. It had been upheld as a universal truth among poets that *shih* and *tz'ŭ* had their respective spheres and should never be allowed to merge. *Tz'ŭ* should be intimate, personal, subdued, indirect, and mosaic, whereas *shih* should be forthright in a subtle manner, beautiful without artificiality, gentle without femininity, and dignified without officiousness. According to this school of opinion, *tz'ŭ* should have the quality of chamber music and *shih* that of a symphony orchestra. These fine differentiations were actually called for by one practical difference between the two types of prosody. *Shih* were written in dissociation from music, but *tz'ŭ* were, at least originally, written as lyrics to well-established melodies. With the lapse of time, however, the *tz'ŭ* form had been increasingly monopolized by professional poets, many of whom knew scarcely anything about the intricacies of music and singing. Thus, they began to be written without reference to music and singing. In other words, the practice had been established already that a *tz'ŭ* poem could be written by following a mechanical formula without knowing the musical score. Under these circumstances there was no reason why the *tz'ŭ* form should not be regarded as simply a new verse form.

Su Tung-p'o was a pioneer of the school which disregarded the numerous restrictions upon the *tz'ŭ* style; one of his associates, Ch'in Kuan (1049-1100), on the other hand, perfected the technique advocated. He adopted a more natural type of poetic language without violating or disregarding musical requirements. Besides being a poet of no mean talent, Ch'in was exceptional in that he was an accomplished student of *tz'ŭ* music. This is probably why, in the eyes of their contemporaries, Ch'in seems to be a greater master of the new technique.

While Ch'in Kuan was a past master in writing short poems in conformity to established *tz'ŭ* patterns, the new vistas opened up by the new technique could be better illustrated in his longer *tz'ŭ* pieces. The following poem, written to the tune of "Man T'ing Fang" or "Fragrance Throughout the Yard," is a good representative poem by Ch'in:

Fickle Youth

With the mountains touched up with traces of clouds,
And the horizons bordered with withered grass,
The painted bugles murmured intermittently from the
    watchtower.
I stop my journey here for a while
And drink my parting wine.
Endless memories of old fairyland
Are now recalled
Faint and fleeting like haze;
Beyond the setting sun,
A few specks of cold crows,
A stream flowing around a lone hamlet.

Soul-stirring recollections:
Especially the moment
Her sachet was detached
And her sash loosened!
All I've won is
The long-lasting name of the "fickle one";
Once departed when will I see her again?
My sleeves and lapel are still tinted with her tears.
Steeped in sadness,
The tall city, now barely visible,
Already glows with its dim yellow lamplights.

Another distinguished member of the new coterie was a pupil of Su Tung-p'o's, Huang T'ing-chien (1045-1105). Known equally well for his *shih* writings, in which he was the founder of a new school, his accomplishments in *tz'ŭ* writing seem to be more impressive. His *shih* poems were written primarily for circulation among the learned scholars of his age, making it almost imperative that he give evidence of his erudition; his *tz'ŭ* poems, however, were primarily intended for the use of women singers. That is exactly why the latter bubble with spontaneity. The following *tz'ŭ*, written to the tune "Hao Nü Erh" or "Good Girl," is among his better-known pieces:

Where is Spring gone?
It was so quiet, no footprints were left.
If anyone knows where Spring is now,
Call it back to reside here.

Who would know since Spring left no traces here,
Unless we ask the Oriole?
Its warblings that no one understands
Are borne by the breeze to the roses.

The *tz'ŭ* form by this time, partly on account of its inherent attractiveness and partly because of its novelty, had engaged the attention of nearly all writers, including such epoch-making leaders of the age as Wang An-shih and Ssŭ-ma Kuang, who towered above their own age.

In spite of the theory logically developed that *tz'ŭ* could be written by filling words into a diagram or pattern without reference to music at all, the divorce of the two failed to materialize for a long time. In the first place, there is no doubt that the charm of *tz'ŭ* was invariably enhanced when sung to the accompaniment of music. In the second place, the tradition had already been well established so that most of the masters in *tz'ŭ* composition were also experts in folk music. The great writer who confirmed this tradition worthily was Chou Pang-yen (1056-1121), who was not especially respected by his colleagues because of his erratic behavior but who won various official posts in the government as a result of his specialization in music. During the reign of Emperor Hui Tsung (reigned 1101-1125), himself a connoisseur of *tz'ŭ* music, an outstanding water-colorist, and a patron of art, Chou was even appointed director of the Music Bureau. It was at this time, too, that he got himself into an embarrassing situation. He had developed an intimate friendship with the most noted woman singer of the age, Li Ssŭ-ssŭ, who happened to have attracted the attention of the emperor himself. One day when Chou was visiting in her home, the heralds of the emperor announced the arrival of his majesty. The poet hastily ducked under the bed. The emperor had brought a new orange from the Yangtze Valley as a gift, and there followed an exchange of witty repartee. This badinage Chou, having overheard, wove into a *tz'ŭ*. This fun at the emperor's expense resulted in Chou's expulsion from the capital. The singer naturally saw him off. It happened that on that same day the emperor arrived at the home of Li Ssŭ-ssŭ and had to wait until after dusk before she returned. Knowing the cause of her absence, the emperor asked what new *tz'ŭ* she had learned from the exiled poet. The singer feelingly sang the lyric describing the sorrows of his departing and his regrets at his own misdemeanor. Much impressed, the emperor saw fit to retract the penalty and summon the poet back to the imperial court.

Chou's poetry was praised by contemporaries for "fitting the musical scores." This consisted principally in his ability to select his diction with reference to its tonal qualities so that no word pronounced in normal speech at a low tone or pitch would be correlated with a high note. The natural result was that his lines would be readily understood when sung and for this reason he could freely use the phraseology of everyday language to enhance the intelligibility of his songs. The subject matter of Chou's poetry naturally reverted back to the norm of the tête-à-tête expressions of the pain and pleasures of youthful love and the melancholy of parting between lovers. Chou was one of the poets most widely read in T'ang poetry, so he could utilize passionate excerpts from the best of T'ang poetry and weld them into his own songs without leaving any impression of patchwork. The following poem, written to the tune of "Kuan Ho Ling" or "The Song of the Pass and the River," is one of the best remembered among Chou's compositions:

> The autumn sky frequently turns gloomy
> Changing my courtyard to a stretch of chilly sadness toward
>   nightfall.
> Here I stand listening to the voice of cold weather.
> The thick clouds conceal all traces of the flying swans.
> The night is deep, the guests gone, everything is quiet.
> Only a lone lamp is shining on the wall and me.
> Completely sobered from my drinking,
> How am I to spend the long, long night?

Equally representative of Chou's ability in varying the length of his lines is the following:

> The slanting sun shines below the leaves at the water,
> Rolling up light ripples that seem to stretch for a
>   thousand li.
> The sour wind on the bridge shoots at my eyeballs.
> I stand there long
> Looking at the dusk
> And the lighted market place.
>
> Beneath a cool window of an aged house
> While listening to the falling paulownia leaves
> I leave my light coverlet to get up again and again—
> But who knows
> It is to her
> I am filling a page?

A great rival to Chou Pang-yen is Li Ch'ing-chao (1081-after 1141), a women poet, among the greatest literary geniuses of China. A native of Tsinan, now capital of Shantung Province, she was the daughter of Li Kê-fei, who was highly praised by Su Tung-p'o as a writer, and granddaughter of Wang Kung-ch'ên, who had captured supreme honors at the highest level of the competitive examinations. She was married in 1101 to an imperial university student, Chao Ming-ch'êng, who was a serious scholar and a noted antiquarian, author of the well-known treatise *Chin Shih Lu* or *Records of Metals and Stones*. Their married life was obviously extremely happy. In the short summary feelingly written many years later (1132) in the postface to her husband's learned work she recapitulated the little details of their younger days:

My husband was then in his twenty-first year, a student at the imperial university. . . . At the beginning and the middle of a month he would pawn a robe for a half-thousand cash, walk into the Hsiang Kuo Monastery, and buy some rubbings and books, fruits, and nuts to bring home. The two of us would open up the books and rubbings and exchange remarks of appreciation while munching the food, calling ourselves citizens of the utopian period of Ko Tien in antiquity. Two years later he went out to fill an official post. He had made up his mind to be satisfied with simple meals and coarse clothing but to explore the unvisited areas in the extremities of the universe thoroughly, exploring all specimens of ancient scripts and weird diction in the universe. . . . After that when he occasionally saw paintings and calligraphic masterpieces by noted hands, and rare articles of the three ancient dynasties, he would also sell his coat to purchase them. . . . During his tenure as chief executive of two counties he exhausted his earnings to finance his publication. Each time he found a rare book he would do the collating with me as well as other preparation for reprinting. Each time he got a rare book, a good painting, a valued tripod, or some other sacrificial vessel he would invariably fondle his new prize in my company, trying to discover flaws and imperfections, if any. The normal rule was working in the evening with me until a candle had burned out. . . . After each meal we would sit in the living room named the Returned Year Room where we would make tea. We would utilize the heaps of books, old and new, by naming an event or topic and by guessing in what line on which page in which chapter the material was to be found. The winner would be the first to drink tea. Sometimes the winner would raise the cup with hearty laughter so that the tea would spill into the lap, leaving none for the drinker. We were content to live there until our old age.

Peace was not to last long for them, for the Chin Tatars were making active preparation for their southward invasion. In 1126 the Chin troops surrounding the capital of Kaifêng for many months finally succeeded in forcing a surrender. In the following year the artistic Hui Tsung, who had abdicated in 1125, his successor Ch'in Tsung, and their imperial consorts together with the whole imperial household, were rounded up and herded north as prisoners of war. The only member of the Sung royal house left behind was the aged empress dowager who had been deprived of her regalia some time before and therefore was regarded by the northern invaders as no more than a commoner. It was in her name, however, that the official proclamation was declared for the southward removal of the imperial court to the Yangtze Valley and an imperial clansman crowned as the new Southern Sung emperor in Nanking in 1127.

In the confusion and catastrophe of the dynastic collapse the poetess and her antiquarian husband hastily made their escape southward with what they could salvage from their art collection. In 1129 her husband died a premature death. Fleeing alone, she visited one coastal city after another until she had reached the new emergency capital at Hangchow, having sold most of her art objects for maintenance. When she wrote the postface to her husband's antiquarian manual, she was already fifty-one years of age and living in Hangchow. Two years later she had to flee Hangchow for Chinhua where she probably died around 1150. Unfortunately practically all her writings, including seven volumes of essays and six volumes of *tz'ŭ*, are now lost. Her *tz'ŭ* poetry is preserved only in fragments.

Being the most noted among Chinese women writers, Li Ch'ing-chao had obviously invited the jealousy of men. Many attempts were made to smear her reputation, including the baseless rumor that after the death of her husband she was remarried to a Chang Ju-chou. Recent researches have amply demonstrated the fictitiousness of the charge. Actually, in the Northern Sung Dynasty the remarriage of widows was not only a common but also an honorable custom. It was not until after puritanical Neo-Confucianism had established itself that the practice was frowned upon. This seems to indicate that the rumor did not arise during the life span of the poetess and so the jealousy she had aroused seems to have continued for a long time. This is perfectly understandable because the poetess herself had been also a keen critic when she was alive, having concretely pointed out the shortcomings of nearly all of her predecessors in the *tz'ŭ* field, including such literary idols as Ou-yang Hsiu, Su Tung-p'o, Ch'in Kuan, and writers of lesser stature. Nonetheless, in her own time her poetry was highly rated by the leading poets. Her fellow townsman, Hsin Ch'i-chi, would occasionally write *tz'ŭ* of a high order and plainly label them in a subtitle as "in the style of Li Ch'ing-chao." The two following poems have long been acknowledged as precious gems in Sung poetry:

I

Seeking seeking fumbling fumbling
Cold cold pale pale
Chilly chilly cheerless cheerless choking choking

After a sudden warming up the weather has turned cold again
I can find no rest
A few cups of wine
No match for the blast that rages at dawn
The wild geese are passing over my head
My heart is aching
They are my familiar acquaintances.
The ground is piled all over with yellow flowers
I am worn out with melancholy
Who will pick the flowers for me now
Clinging to the window
How can darkness come to a lonely watcher
The paulownia trees are veiled behind the finespun rain
Drop after drop drips in the yellow dusk
At this point
What can I do with this word Sorrow?

(Teresa Li's translation)

II

The wind has stopped; the earth is fragrant with fallen petals.
At the end of day I am weary to tend my hair;
Things remain, but he is not, and all is as nothing.
I try to speak but the tears will flow.

I hear it said that at the Twin Brook the Spring is still fair,
And I, too, long to float in a light boat.
Only I fear that the "locust boat" at the Twin Brook
Cannot move with a freight
Of so much grief.

(Teresa Li's translation)

Among the poets who migrated southward there were two of great distinction besides Li Ch'ing-chao. One of these was Chu Tun-ju (1080?-1175?). A native of Loyang, he enjoyed a huge reputation in his younger days for staying away from corrupt politics. Even after the removal of the imperial court in 1127, he declined the imperial summons persistently. Once responding to government appointment, his rise in the hierarchy seemed to be rapid. Ch'in K'uei was then at the helm of the state and advocated a policy of peaceful coexistence with the Chin Tatars against the patriotic faction led by General Yo Fei. Ch'in was a patron of letters as was his son, Ch'in Hsi, and both looked upon Chu as a past master in letters and recommended him for high positions. After the death of Ch'in K'uei in 1155, Chu seemed to disappear completely from all records, public and private. As posterity had looked upon the name of Ch'in K'uei as synonymous with the word *traitor*, it was natural that Chu failed to receive public applause for guilt by association. Hardly anything other than information which may be extracted from his poetry is on record concerning his life.

In spite of his political associations—and there is no evidence that he was ever involved in treason—Chu was a distinguished *tz'ŭ* writer of his period. His collected poetry is entitled *Ch'iao Ko* or *Woodcutter's Songs* in three *chüan* or volumes corresponding to three periods of his life. It is in Volume 3, consisting of songs written in the later days of his life, that he was completely disillusioned with the ways of the world and rededicated to harmony with nature and its rhythms, reminding us in many ways of T'ao Ch'ien. The following poem combines the simplicity of a folk song with the freedom from care of medieval Taoism:

The Fisherman

Swinging his head, he leaves the busy world behind,
Drunken or sober as he pleases.
For a living—with coarse raincoat and rain hat
He is a veteran in facing snow and frost.

When in the evening calm he is not fishing,
He enjoys the crescent moon and its reflection.
Where for a thousand *li* sky and water blend in one hue,
A lone swan would fly in and out of sight.

Ever since he became fisherman,
His rod has been his best friend.
He rows his boat back and forth at will,
Leaving no trace on the water as though flying through the air.

The water rushes flower and fade as they will,
Long drunkenness is always his chief delight.
The wind and rain on the river the night before
Always left him unperturbed.

Around his little boat and short oar
The evening mist spreads a purple screen.
Here the frontier swans and seagulls part company,
Here he is lord of the autumn hues—waters and sky.

With a basketful of radiant, splashing fishes,
He gets his quota of wine.
Now sailing home with a favorable wind,
None could detain him even a little while.

Forthright he is home in this direction
Contented with his certain lot.
Provided by Heaven with rod and line,
He is prince of endless misty waves.

The red dust of untold ages swirls around his bow,
Like seagulls and egrets disappearing into space.
He roves in the world unhampered,
North or south, east or west.

CHAPTER 21

Metamorphosis and Decline of the Tz'ŭ

In the early twelfth century the *tz'ŭ* type of poetry had firmly established itself as the dominant type for lyrical expression. Although the major singers had not abandoned the cultivation of *shih* and continued in their attempts to open up new vistas so as not to fall into the beaten paths of T'ang poets, they had diverted the greater portion of their attention and energy to perfecting the art of *tz'ŭ*, for the charm of its irregular meter had captivated readers and hearers at all social levels. Their primary concern was to keep the lyrics in line with the musical scores, stressing intonation with all its fine distinctions so that a word of low pitch would not be used in a line of a lyric where a high note would be called for in singing. This preoccupation with prosody and intonation was so emphatically stressed that the single line was apt to become the test of a poet's power of concentration. Oftentimes this conformity with strict regulations would necessitate the use of classical and antiquated allusions and bookish language to fulfill the minute requirements of tonal patterns. As a result, *tz'ŭ* language became more and more florid and the lyrical theme became less and less apparent. With patchwork being recognized as standard usage, a *tz'ŭ* poem when sung or read aloud would become at times unintelligible except to expert ears. One of the leading critics of the time observed that many of the masterpieces were comparable to highly ornate and jewel-bedecked storied buildings which dazzle the admirer's eyes when they were erected but which when taken apart would be extremely difficult to reassemble as they did not contribute to a unified theme.

This tendency had been counteracted first by Su Tung-p'o, whose genius, as we have seen, ran contrary to strict rules and regulations. Though himself possessed of considerable book lore, Su would write *tz'ŭ* poems as though he were trying to write prose. Or, to use another analogy, he refused to use dance steps in traveling between two points, instead of plain walking. Su's example was admired but not followed, mainly because in his attempts to use plain language in poetry writing he had distinguished himself in the eyes of his contemporaries only by the dexterity with which he could violate accepted principles of composition.

With the birth of another major *tz'ŭ* poet, heterodoxy almost became orthodoxy. This new poet was Hsin Ch'i-chi (1140-1207), an outstanding patriot and soldier who was forced by circumstance to become a poet. Fourteen years before he was born, the Northern Sung Dynasty had been on the verge of complete disintegration. The Nüchen or Chin Tatars had carried away the last two Sung emperors, the remnants of the court had fled to the south, and the emperor of the new Southern Sung court had agreed to negotiate a most dishonorable peace. Shantung, now a Chin province, was the birthplace of Hsin Ch'i-chi, who was brought up under the tutelage of a grandfather who had been unable to seek refuge in the Southern Sung area but who had utilized every opportunity to prepare his grandchild to avenge the oppression of the enemy. He became one of the chief advocates of the use of force in dealing with the Nüchen people. This young tactician, hardly twenty years of age, was not only a soldier of unusual physical prowess but also an extremely systematic theoretician in national defense. In spite of all the memorials which he submitted and which proved beyond doubt that he was a great master of Chinese prose, the Southern Sung court was bent upon the policy of negotiation and coexistence. His career as a public administrator consisted of brilliant strategies and patient struggle in support of his policies, but in 1164 a new peace treaty was negotiated between the Sung and Chin Empires which was to frustrate Hsin's ambition for good. He was recalled in 1192 and impeached in 1194. After that, realizing that his official career would at best be a very unsteady one, he responded to official summonses only in a half-hearted manner. The last years of his life were spent in retirement, during which he divided his time evenly between reading and writing and keeping in rhythm with nature. His financial resources made it possible for him to live in comfort in some of the most scenic areas in the Sung Empire. In the county of Shangjao in present-day Kiangsi Province he built himself an attractive home facing a long and narrow lake called Tai Hu or Sash Lake. In his home he had a studio which he named Chia Hsien, which name was to become to his readers and admirers his new courtesy name. *Chia* means farming and *hsien* means a building with many windows. Whether he actually did much farming could not be determined, but the meaning of the studio was, in his own words, an attempt to hold up an ideal.

> Man's life should stress intelligence and should hold the cultivating of the soil as a foremost duty. People in the north do not depend on others for livelihood and so are not sharply differentiated between extreme wealth and hopeless poverty. Southerners usually try to avoid agricultural labor and the concentration of farming lands in the hands of a few absentee landlords arises, thus resulting in sharp contrasts in economic status.

Hsin's home and gardens were so artistically and extensively laid out that many of his friends were impressed. Among these was the most eminent philosopher of the age, Chu Hsi, who, after calling on the poet during the latter's absence, exclaimed in a letter to another friend that he had seen something which he had never seen before. Particularly famous among the many beauties in the garden was a spring with brickwork built around it in the form of a spoon; hence the spring was given the name of P'iao Ch'üan (Spoon Spring). It was in this new home that he lived as a major poet of his age besides holding inspiring political discussions with many leading thinkers of the age.

As a poet, he deliberately chose the medium of *tz'ŭ*—the medium that had become universally indulged in by emperors and very many commoners alike. In productivity he ranks first among some eight hundred writers of *tz'ŭ* poetry whose names have been preserved from 960 to 1279. His 623 poems of this type constitute about one-thirtieth of the whole Sung dynastic output and yet while he was prolific he was never careless. He would frequently give parties for his literary associates and while reciting his own poems to the prescribed musical accompaniments, he would persistently force his guests to become critics and ask them for suggestions for improvement. It was not infrequent that he would change the lyrics of a song more than ten times within a day. His poetry was a full manifestation of his personality, hence he would use the adopted vehicle for description, argumentation, and narration as well as for the expression of lyrical emotions. As a result, the language of his poetry covered an unusually wide range, from the recasting of emotional passages in classical literature into new allusions to the purposeful adoption of everyday language. To the tune of "Shên Yüan Ch'un" or "Spring Permeating the Garden" he wrote the following with a short subtitle:

> (Being on the verge of entering into complete abstinence,
> I warn the wine cup not to come near me.)

Cup, you come forward.
Today your old master
Is tidying up his conduct.
I used to crave for drinks all year long,
Panting like an overheated cauldron.
But now I am happy,
And strong like thunder.
Now you quote Liu Ling—
Wise man of all ages:
"What matters if burial follows intoxication."
Be that as it may, I still wonder
How you to your best friend
Could be so ungrateful.

Relying on dances and singing as inducers
What you contain is still poison.
All faults big and small
Are born of what is loved;
All things good or bad
In excess will bring catastrophe.
Now this one agreement:
Get out and don't stay,
I'm still strong enough to smash you.
The cup bows on its exit
Saying, "I will disappear at the wave of your hand
But will gladly return on special orders!"

A poem in a similar vein in which current slang was used follows:

What is hard is unfirm,
What is soft isn't destroyed easily.
If you don't believe, open your mouth.
Your teeth will fall while your tongue will endure.

The two end chambers are vacant,
The middle one is also gone.
Don't laugh at your old man, my children,
This dog hole you are welcome to use.

Literary historians have invariably emphasized the new trend in *tz'ŭ* writing which Hsin started, namely, the trend of unrestrained vigor and an attempt to transcend rules. This, however, was only one aspect of Hsin's poetic art, which was a natural expression of his personality; this had taken definite form while he was in active combat on battlefields. Besides this there is an aspect of Hsin's poetry which amply illustrates his meticulous observance of prosodic rules of the *tz'ŭ* to show his complete mastery of the intricate art. While these features cannot be easily brought out in translation, the following might suggest evidence of careful composition:

> To the tune of "Mo-yü-erh" ("Catching fish"), written in 1179 on his transfer from Hupeh to Hunan.

> How many more storms can we stand?
> Hastily spring will leave us.
> Spring lovers loathe the sight of early flowers
> How much more the sight of petals of fallen red?
> Spring! Stay with me!
> I've heard that fragrant grass has covered your homeward path!
> Spring does not answer.
> Only the obliging cobwebs beneath the painted cornice toil all day to catch the catkins.

> Dance no more;
> Don't you see that supreme beauties of Han and T'ang end in common dust?
> Most unbearable is listless sorrow!
> Don't go out onto the lofty balcony;
> For the sun is setting where mist and willows symbolize the broken heart.

Even in those poems in which he is celebrating the contentment of his retirement we notice a departure from the major beaten paths of *tz'ŭ* writing, the minute embroidery of emotional patterns. In poems of reminiscence he demonstrated the new trend all the more eloquently. In a poem written on the occasion of a caller's discussing the development of distinguished careers, he recalled his own youthful days with semiplayfulness which did not succeed in covering up his real nostalgia:

> In my younger years I commanded a myriad men;
> Wearing an embroidered cape
> I dashed through the enemy line to cross the
> Yangtze River.
> Tatar troops readied their silver quivers at night:
> Chinese gold arrows flew on the morrow.
> Recalling these happenings of the past
> I sigh at my present self.
> Even spring winds will not dye my white beard.
> Now I have traded my disquisition on leveling the barbarians
> For a homey book on gardening.

On another occasion when his houseboat was anchored at the waterfront near the strategic city of Hangchow, he feelingly recalled his younger days:

At sunset dust arose outside the Great Wall—
The Tatar horsemen were hunting in the crisp autumn.
The Chinese Empire with troops a hundred thousand strong,
Had also rows of warships displaying storied towers.
Who would boast a horsewhip would dam the river to facilitate
     a lightning invasion?
Who would forget that once after his whistling arrows were
     stained with blood,
A Tatar chieftain was saddened by a threatening storm?
I was then in the prime of my youth,
Galloping round dressed up in black sable.

Now I am old;
And running my fingers through my white hair
I am coming through Yangchou.
Tired of wandering, I want to go near the riverside
And grow oranges by the thousand.
But both of you, my friends, I've met in the lovely southeast
And devoted to both learning and careers,
May I offer you my counsel:
Leave the details alone—even the shooting of tigers,
And set your sight on the prime ministry.

In spite of Hsin's great attainment in *tz'ŭ* writing, his failure to conform to conventions and traditions has elicited some unfavorable criticism. An outstanding weakness of his was his fondness of classical allusions and quotations. In this regard his critics seemed to have missed his great creative fervor which gave him complete mastery over his cullings from classical literature. All his borrowings from previous poets are so thoroughly digested that there is no offensive artificiality. A mere comparison of his technique with that of his contemporaries will easily reveal that the lesser poets of his age were nearly crushed by the heavy load of classical phraseology. The difference lies in the fact that Hsin's poetry was a manifestation of his dynamic personality. He wrote because he had to express himself and to give full vent to his towering personality.

Another line of criticism leveled against Hsin has been made on the grounds of accompanying music. This charge seems at first sight to be a serious one. It has been repeatedly pointed out that Hsin's poems, when sung to the accompaniment of musical scores called for by the various tune patterns he had used, would not sound right. All forms of Chinese versification had evolved from a musical origin; they were at first sung. Invariably after the lapse of time there came a parting of the ways. A given verse form would become so universally popular that it would continue to be used by poets without reference to music. In other words, the verse form was released from the binding regulations of accompanying music and attained a maturity of form of its own. *Tz'ŭ* writers like Su Shih and Hsin were more interested in experimenting with the new verse form than in writing poems for professional singers.

In Hsin's collected poems we find reflected a prevalence of the longer tunes. This was in keeping with the trends of the time. When the *tz'ŭ* form was first developed only shorter tunes were produced. When the new form was patronized by professional poets as new tunes were being composed, there was a tendency to increase the length of the tunes not only to bring out more fully the talents of the musicians and singers but also the gifts of the poets. With the prolongation of the musical scores and hence, concurrently, of the lyrics, the undesirable trait of padding became more and more obvious, especially among minor poets. Even great masters like Hsin were not entirely free from this fault in the longer lyrics. In most poets padding took the form of repetition couched in a number of rhetorical devices which would contribute to the looseness of composition and the blurring of the major theme. It is therefore in Hsin's shorter poems that we found him at his best. In the following lyric written to the tune of "Hsi Chiang Yüeh" or "West River Moon" there is a touch of the inimitable humor of Hsin's *tz'ŭ* poetry:

> In drunkenness I crave joy and laughter.
> As for sadness, where would I find time?
> I have just found out that literal acceptance
> Of the writings of the ancients
> Would lead me totally astray.
>
> I lay drunken near a pine last night.
> I asked: "How drunk am I?"
> Then I thought it was moving to lend me a hand,
> I pushed it and cried, "Go away!"

Toward the end of his life it was in his poetry that he manifested his disillusionment with the externals of life. On hearing the midnight peals of a monastery bell, he wrote the following to the tune of "Lang T'ao Sha" or "The Waves Washing the Sands":

> Ah for a whole life spent with the wine cup!
> Everything else is inanity and vanity!
> The heroes of the past, I can count them on my fingers.
> But the gorgeous temples and palaces they built for themselves
> Have not weathered the rain and storm of endless seasons.

Last night in a dream I found myself among a group of young men;
Dancing and singing, what a riotous time we had!
But in the midnight the old monk rang the bell by mistake;
I was awakened from my dream and could sleep no more.
Outside the windows, a strong West Wind was sweeping the ground.

(Teresa Li's translation)

Even during his lifetime Hsin was branded as unorthodox in his *tz'ŭ* writing. His uniqueness, however, won him many admirers who seemed to fail to understand that uniqueness defies imitation. For this reason his school of technique was repeatedly pointed out by critics as a stumbling block to novices, and the many imitators succeeded only in repeating his outstanding foible which was disregard for set rules. Whereas such a feature might be a tour de force when exhibited by Hsin, it would become horseplay when performed by lesser talents.

We have pointed out more than once that there has always existed an intimate relationship between singing and poetry in China, and that in the genesis of new verse forms and their accompanying technique, the usual inspirations were popular songs. Each time the common people were inspired by frontier or alien music they would burst out in new types of songs. Aside from the music, upon which we can pass no judgment, because in nearly all cases it was soon lost, the wording of the songs was usually characterized by a simplicity of diction and a forthrightness in presentation. Many of the songs would even betray the influence of nearly illiterate singers. Despite these elements of crudity and rusticity they manifested so much of the vital strength and unadorned charm of the populace that they invariably caught the imagination of the most sensitive among the poets. Those poets who capitalized most thoroughly on the new discoveries and added their creative genius and their cultivated artistry to improvements the new models became heroes of a new age and major poets of the new genre. Their greatness was often due at least in part to their willingness to learn from the folk art of the ordinary people. Once they had risen to prominence and become the advocates of a new taste they would rapidly inspire a huge following. Nonetheless, their own compositions as compared with the folk originals were still songs in the full sense of the word —they could be and were actually sung to music. Because of their greater artistry, they gradually replaced their folk prototypes as models for composition. By this time the new verse forms had already taken permanent root.

In turn, these new models were to become the representative

patterns after which new imitations would be composed by literary novices. Among these, not a few would be bold enough to consider the new verse form strictly on its own merit, that is to say, purely as poetry, not only detachable but also detached from its accompanying music. Many new compositions thus conceived might be good poetry but they were no longer true to type in that they were no longer songs because they were no longer singable. With this separation between lyrics and musical scores, the new verse form had virtually made its declaration of independence and its new masters would cease to pay attention to the musical aspect of the composition. Simultaneously the new verse form would lose its contact with the common people, as its lyrics were no longer sung. Thus, the new verse form might improve along the lines of greater sophistication and finer technique but in due course it was destined also to lose all of its vitality. With the accumulation of generations of technical imitators there might emerge a few exceptional talents who would by chance recapture some of the spirit of the proto-types, but by and large the practiced form would become so thread-bare that really creative poets would turn their ears again to the common people in search of new tunes.

This process of metamorphosis is true of the five-syllable verse form of the late Han Dynasty which had been inspired by the folk songs, marching songs, and sacrificial hymns collectively known as *yüeh fu*. It is also true of the rise of the seven-syllable-line poetry of the T'ang Dynasty which was again inspired by folk songs of a similar pattern.

When the *tz'ŭ* form of poetry had been completely divorced from singing and music in the last years of the Sung Dynasty, *tz'ŭ* writers wrote their compositions by following accepted models bearing the common title of a once popular tune. All they needed to do was follow a pattern faithfully, using a five-word line to conform to a five-word line of the model and writing an eight-word line where an eight-word line was called for with no reference to music or singing. A few of the masters still bent on imitation, who happened to have had training in music, would go a step further and pay attention to the tonal qualities of each word in the model to guide their own choice of diction. These latter examples, if they had the virtue of being singable, were also handicapped by the artificial attempts made toward tonal conformity. Instead of natural mani-festations of deeply felt emotions, they became highly gifted at-tempts at duplicating the art objects of the past. Under such circum-stances even the subject matter of *tz'ŭ* poetry was changed. Instead of writing on spontaneous and meaningful themes, many of the minor Sung poets would write new *tz'ŭ* poems in conformity with an accepted tonal pattern on such subjects as the cicada or a newly ripened peach. The artistry involved is undeniable, for an extensive search would be conducted by the poets to look up all the anecdotes and allusions connected with the subject matter in order to draw a pleasing word picture of the subject under assignment. At this time the *tz'ŭ* compositions had cut themselves completely loose from the joys and sorrows of the common people.

Thus, after the age of Hsin Ch'i-chi, *tz'ŭ* poetry underwent a drastic change. The *tz'ŭ* of the poets was to be replaced by the *tz'ŭ* of the technicians. These technicians, many of them experts in music, were not necessarily mere poetasters, for some of them were really gifted in their own way and took their art with great seriousness. Nonetheless, their efforts in re-emphasizing the subtle relationship between *tz'ŭ* versification and the musical notations of the established *tz'ŭ* tunes were expended in a distorted direction. Instead of listening to the songs of the common people, and learning from the spontaneous technique of the women entertainers as their predecessors had done, they relied on their own erudition in musicology and their own literary creed in which classical elegance was the foremost requirement.

An anecdote may be retold in this connection to illustrate to what length some of the poets would go to subordinate poetry to the consideration of music in *tz'ŭ* writing. Chang So, who flourished in the middle of the thirteenth century when the new trend was in high vogue, and whose son Chang Yen was to achieve even greater fame, had once written a *tz'ŭ* poem in which a three-syllable line did not seem quite right when sung to music. The line was *so ch'ang shên,* meaning "the precious window is deep." The Chinese word *shên* (deep), of the upper even tone, had the highest pitch in the intonation scheme, and so conflicted with the low note called for in the musical score. *Shên* was then changed to *yu* (dim), but this was unsatisfactory, for the same reason.

After further deliberation, the line was emended to read *so ch'ang ming.* As *ming* was a word of the lower even tone, or the lowest pitch in the intonation scheme, it sounded perfect, and was adopted as the final choice. The word *ming,* however, means "bright," and the line now would read "the precious window is bright," exactly the opposite of what had been intended in the original version.

Before we conclude our brief review of the evolution of *tz'ŭ* poetry, we shall note several more great names in passing.

The first important advocate of musical precision in *tz'ŭ* writing was Chiang K'uei (1155?-1235?), whose life was spent along the middle and lower reaches of the Yangtze River. An outstanding authority on music, he not only contributed important treatises for the reformation of court music, but also created many new tunes for his own *tz'ŭ* writing. These musical scores, written in the notation system of his own age and printed alongside his poems, are still highly valued for the reconstruction of *tz'ŭ* music despite the many errors which have crept in as a result of careless transcriptions.

The following *tz'ŭ* poem was written to a tune of his own composition, "The Light Yellow Willow":

> At dawn the horn blows
> From the empty city onto the willow bedecked road.
> Lightly clad, I feel the chill on horseback.
> Around me is a familiar scene south of the River—
> An endless expanse of light yellow and pale green.
>
> Lonesomeness is everywhere.
> Tomorrow comes the Spring Fast.
> I fetch wine anyway to the house near the little bridge,
> For the fallen pear flowers suggest autumn's face.
> The swallows have flown here,
> But where is Spring?
> Only the ponds are green, by themselves.

Swimming against the tide of his contemporaries to prolong the tradition of Hsin Ch'i-chi and Lu Yu as *tz'ŭ* poets was Liu K'ê-chuang (1187-1269). Scion of a Fukien family which had rendered distinguished service to the state, he had a long and checkered career in the Southern Sung official hierarchy, and finally retired only after he had lost his eyesight.

A distinguished poet writing both *shih* and *tz'ŭ*, he was noted for naturalness and fluency:

> With the coming of age,
> I pique myself on the hardness of my heart!
> And yet a lingering tenderness still remains,
> For I am obsessed with the love of flowers.
> How often I have worried lest cold weather should delay their coming,
> Lest hot weather should hasten their fading!
> Alas! The boisterous wind and the ruthless sun are too heartless!
> What can I do with these kill-joys?
>
> Time and again I have lit candles
> To look at them tenderly.
> I request the ivory hands
> To pick them softly.
> Some more showers, and these gorgeous clouds will vanish without
>   a trace!

If you do not come tonight to drink under the flowers,
Tomorrow you will seek them in vain on the sprigs!
You will only hear the orioles wail over their red corpses,
Adding loneliness to the scene!

(Teresa Li's translation)

A music expert who wrote a sizable volume of *tz'ŭ* poetry but whose merits are extremely controversial was Wu Wên-ying (1210?-1270?). Little was known of his life except that he was a native of Ssŭming County in Chekiang Province and befriended a few of his contemporary writers and poets. Among them, some admired him for his strict conformity to established patterns of *tz'ŭ* music, while others regretted his excessive fondness for patchwork. His *tz'ŭ* poems were so heavily laden with classical allusions and artificial purple patches of his own coinage that few were intelligible even to his average contemporary readers without detailed commentaries.

Another member of the same school and a contemporary of Wu Wên-ying was Wang Yi-sun (1240?-1290), also a native of Chekiang. After the fall of the Southern Sung Dynasty in 1379, he entered the civil service of the new dynasty under the Mongols as an educational administrator. Known especially for his minutely descriptive *tz'ŭ* poems, he was prone to be devious and obscure like Wu Wên-ying.

> The fragrant woods now drenched clean by last night's wind
>   and rain—
> I have hastily bid farewell to Spring.
> Having barely seen Spring off,
> I need to see you leave at the southern bank!
> Please hear my plea:
> I think by now Spring must be on the roads of Wu as it is
>   homeward bound.
> When you get there,
> Make haste to break a thousand willow twigs,
> And with them fasten Spring secure.
>
> Even if Spring could be stayed,
> No need to seek out singers of Spring tide,
> The fallen petals have turned to dust.
> Far away in the mist and ripples around Kusu Terrace,
> Convey my greetings to our lady the West Lake.
> Will you call out to her?
> I fear Spring will leave no trace of its arrival!
> Pray invoke your magic powers,
> And for my benefit,
> Weave Spring with its flowers and willow leaves
> Into verdant poetry.

Chang Yen (1248-1320?), a native of Hangchow and son of Chang So the musician-*tz'ŭ* poet, had spent over forty years on musical studies. Descended from an early Southern Sung nobleman, he suffered many reverses. For a time, he was so poor that he tried to earn a livelihood by setting up a fortuneteller's booth at the market place in the city of Ningpo.

As a *tz'ŭ* poet, he was famous for his descriptive pieces on scenery and animate and inanimate objects, such as the one on white lotus flowers containing the following lines:

> Misty moonlight flooding the lake,
> Seagulls and egrets dotting the lake shores,
> In a tiny boat on that quiet night,
> Surrounded by glimmering waves and fragrance borne
> from afar,
> I did not see even faintly the flowers in bloom.

When Chang was freed from the rules and mechanisms called for by meticulous delineation, he could burst out in pure lyricism.

Spring on the West Lake

> In thick leaves nestle the orioles.
> By smooth ripples the floss is rolled away.
> The Broken Bridge, the slanting sun, the homeward-
> bound barge.
> How many more outings,
> Then, farewell to flowers for another year.
> O East Wind! caress the roses a little more.
> With roses here, Spring itself is withering.
> Even more saddening—
> Over the boundless verdure there at Hsiling,
> Spreads a sweep of desolate-looking haze.
>
> Where are now the swallows of bygone years?
> The Wei Clan's Bend is covered thick with moss;
> The Slanting Stream looks dim with faded grass.
> Even the seagulls, it is said,
> Have felt the spread of the new sorrow.
> No more desire to resume the dreams of merrier days,
> I close my doors to lie idly in my light drunkenness.
> Don't draw the screens:
> I loathe the sight of flying flowers
> And the sound of wailing cuckoos.

Despite the erudition and dedication of Chang Yen, the curtain was falling on *tz'ŭ* poetry. He witnessed not only the gradual dimming of the light of the Chinese cultural tradition as a result of the Mongol conquest, but also the fading out of *tz'ŭ* as the central genre in poetry. The language of the *tz'ŭ* poets had for long drifted away from the language and the hopes and fears of the common people.

Now in violation of the chronological order which we have generally followed, let us take a look at how the *tz'ŭ* form was to undergo a reincarnation.

The people by this time had woven new patterns for their own songs. These new songs, with their new melodies, were now to be known as *ch'ü* or *ch'ü tzŭ*.

The term *ch'ü tzŭ*, it must be emphatically pointed out, was not a term of late origin. On the basis of the Tunhuang manuscripts, we know for certain that a number of the songs of irregular meter, songs which were written to conform to established musical patterns identical with the ones that were to be known later on as *tz'ŭ* patterns, had already been labeled in those manuscripts as *ch'ü tzŭ*. These songs to all intents and purposes are indistinguishable in their structure, style, and prosodic pattern from the *tz'ŭ* of the great masters. But when they were sung to the accompaniment of music in the frontier region of Tunhuang in the last decades of the ninth and the early decades of the tenth centuries, they were recognized by the populace as *ch'ü tzŭ*. Even more interesting than the lyrics of these songs, which later on were to be collectively described as *tz'ŭ*, there have been rediscovered (and are now preserved in Paris and London) three sets of musical scores, two sets containing the musical notations of six and eight songs respectively and the third consisting of two long scrolls on which is recorded a fairly complex sequence of dance music. When these musical records are unraveled and actually played on musical instruments, considerable new light will be shed not only on late T'ang music but also on the prosody involved in the experimental stage of the writing of *tz'ŭ* poetry.

To return to the term *ch'ü tzŭ*, it is obvious that as soon as the new verse form was dignified by its official adoption by the literati, the early nomenclature of *ch'ü tzŭ* was dropped. It was not until centuries later when the *tz'ŭ* form had again become stereotyped and far removed from the interests and creative activities of the common people that new attempts were again made by unknown singers to present new songs with new lyrics. In exactly the same manner that the *tz'ŭ* form had been invented and espoused to supplement and to replace in part the irregularity of the *shih* form, the new *ch'ü tzŭ* were invented for the amusement of the common people who now had no share in the enjoyment of the unsung *tz'ŭ* writings.

While sporadic attempts of this kind at the creation of songs mainly for the benefit of the common people had been made even during the golden period of *tz'ŭ* development, it was not until the beginning of the thirteenth century that *ch'ü tzŭ* began to win an ever-widening recognition and following. Although the new verse form had its popularity immensely enhanced by its adoption into the musical dramas of the Chin and Yuan dynasties, its emergence preceded the development of musical dramas. In fact it might be considered the cornerstone of the development of the new musical drama. Its repertoire of musical tunes was immense, including all musical tunes that had been preserved, new as well as old, alien as well as native, those emanating from court circles as well as the ones in vogue among the people. Among these, however, it was the popular songs and the newly introduced alien music which sustained the new art which was equally cultivated by theatric troupes as well as by individual singers.

Since both *tz'ŭ* and *ch'ü* had originated from the songs of the people, how were the two genres related and what major difference was there between them? And why should *tz'ŭ* have yielded ground to *ch'ü* as its successor? These questions are interrelated and should be examined in their respective historical backgrounds.

After *tz'ŭ* had reached its full maturity it had already been so refined that the lyrics were far removed from daily speech. The type had become a monopoly of the literati and minute rules had been laid down in versification. This may be illustrated by the fine discrimination drawn between the various tones in the Chinese language. Instead of the five tones in *shih* poetry, there were seven governing *tz'ŭ* versification, and conformity to tonal patterns had made the language unnecessarily style-conscious and artificial. In other words, creative impulse was stifled in the hands of expert versification craftsmen. Some of the results achieved in spite of the pitfalls and road blocks were nothing short of stunning. Nonetheless, such manifestations of artistry could no longer be shared by the slightly literate, and *tz'ŭ* became the exclusive vehicle of literary amusement for the privileged classes.

Meanwhile, not only had people continued to sing tunes of their own, but the spoken language itself had begun to simplify itself, particularly with reference to actual pronunciation. The fine distinctions between the upper and lower scales of the second or rising tone and also of the third or passing tone had completely disappeared. At the same time, thanks to the infiltration of northern tribes which had found Chinese pronunciation too complicated, the final consonants in words of the fourth or entering tone were completely eliminated. To illustrate, the standard pronunciation for the Chinese character for "eight" in T'ang and Northern Sung times (roughly from 600 to 1150) was *pat*. After 1200, the final "t" completely disappeared so that it was now pronounced *pa*. With this curious disappearance of the final consonants in the fourth tone an even stranger thing happened and that is the disappearance of the old entering tone. To make a complicated situation simple, we may summarize our observation by saying that now the number of homonyms had increased and the number of tones reduced to only four, making it, therefore, a simpler operation to secure proper words for end-rhymes. At the same time, to avoid misunderstanding as a result of the increase of homonyms, the Chinese language began to see the coinage of new polysyllabic compounds. All these linguistic changes were widely utilized by and fully reflected in the new songs of the people now designated as *ch'ü*. In spite of the fact that the latest span of *tz'ŭ* ran concurrently with that of the popular *ch'ü*, the more refined and sophisticated genre had refused to recognize and utilize these linguistic changes. Thus a *tz'ŭ* writer even in the twentieth century would have to honor tradition by pretending that "eight" was still *pat* and would not allow it to rhyme with "flower" which is pronounced *hua*—a practice which has been sanctioned in *ch'ü* ever since the new genre had come into being.

This illustration typifies the parting of the ways between *tz'ŭ* and *ch'ü* in relation to pronunciation. But the difference between the two genres does not stop here. The *tz'ŭ* patterns were completely frozen during the tenth and eleventh centuries so that a given air would call for a specific number of lines and each line would call for a specific number of words with sanctioned tonal sequences. Any deviation from this set pattern and procedure would have to be sanctioned by time, in which case the violations would give rise to an alternate air bearing the same title. In the case of *ch'ü*, since all the compositions were to be set to music, set patterns were also a logical necessity. The key words of each line had to correspond to music but between these, extra syllables sung rapidly might be interpolated to bring out more clearly the meaning of the line. In Chinese, where these auxiliary syllables (commonly called particles) have played an important part in conveying moods and even in taking over the role of punctuation marks, their free use in a song was a definite step forward. Such a usage also facilitated the incorporation of provincialisms and slang in the text of the lyrics so as to keep it in close contact with the sentiments and aspirations of the people. These points, which cannot be borne out in translation of the texts, may be a help toward understanding the emergence of a new genre when the *tz'ŭ* had become fossilized as far as the illiterate people of China were concerned.

To be distinguished from the singing parts in full-fledged musical dramas which were written to the same musical tunes, the non-dramatic *ch'ü tzŭ* was given a special name—*san ch'ü*, namely, un-attached songs.

As China had been cut in two from 1127 to 1279, these isolated and unattached *ch'ü tzŭ* were composed in two styles in accordance with the folk music which prevailed in the two regions. In the north the indigenous *tz'ŭ* songs of the Chinese people were gradually modified, especially in rhythmical and musical aspects, by the impact of music introduced by the Chin Tatars and later on by the Mongols. Meanwhile, in the southern half of China we witness the introduction of *tz'ŭ* singing with the southward flight of the Sung court and its merging with the popular songs of the southerners. In both south and north the *ch'ü tzŭ* songs developed along two separate lines, namely, the *hsiao ling* or small songs and the *t'ao su* or serial cycles. The small songs in *ch'ü tzŭ* were short songs sung to the tune of moderate length at times when novelty was desired by the composers; the so-called syncretic tunes would be the result, selecting attractive bars from familiar tunes to form a new whole. At other times four or eight stanzas would be written to take care of the four seasons of the year or eight aspects of the scenic beauty of a famous landmark.

The *t'ao su* or serial cycles are composed of several separate tunes to form an organic whole. Irrespective of the number of tunes involved in each unit, the lyrics were written generally with one rhyme. In both cases the introduction of everyday speech is obvious. The insertion of particles was a great help in making the lyrics intelligible even to relatively illiterate ears. As these syllables were auxiliary in nature, they were often recited rapidly between the key words, which were sung to music. This feature, first initiated by the early *tz'ŭ* writers of the ninth and tenth centuries, had now been deliberately exploited so as to make the songs more like the utterances of the common people.

In the first century of the emergence of *ch'ü tzŭ* as a new literary genre, especially from 1234 to 1300, its cultivation and popular appeal were eclipsed by the rapidly expanding influence of musical drama. It was almost universally felt, although not necessarily justified, that poetry sung to music was the logical property of drama. All the major writers of these *san ch'ü* or unattached songs were dramatists. They invariably regarded the writing of these non-dramatic songs as an avocation. After 1300, however, there came the clear parting of the ways between the playwrights and the song writers.

Many writers dedicated themselves to the writing of songs without aspiring at the same time to become dramatists.

Among writers of the first period nearly all leading song writers were dramatists. Some would use the common vehicle for the writing of parting songs. Many of such songs were doubtless sung to music at farewell dinner parties. Thus from the pen of the great dramatic poet Kuan Han-ch'ing comes the following, written to the musical tune of "Ts'ên Tsui Tung Fêng" or "The Intoxicating East Wind":

> The southern tip of heaven and the northern edge of
>   the earth
> Might appear to be no longer than a foot.
> When suddenly it is felt that the moon ceases to be round
> And the flowers fall apart,
> I should be holding a glass at this send-off party.
> And restraining my tears of departure.
> Barely I say
> "Take the best care . . . ,"
> The pain is so acute that it is hard to let go.
> Go and travel well,
> Lying before you are myriad miles.

Occasionally the same dramatist would utilize his favorite tunes to draw word pictures that he wanted to celebrate.

> The powdery snowflakes
> Are dancing like pear flower petals
> Obscuring the four or five houses of the misty village.
> As the snow thickens it makes the scene all the more paintable.
> Listen to evening crows in the shrivelled forests,
> And the yellow reeds wavering below the sparkling stream
> Slantingly embracing the fisherman's boat.

Surpassing Kuan as a song writer was the famous Ma Chih-yüan (1265?-1325?), who in spite of his distinction as a dramatist was preeminently a lyric poet. The individuality of his personality permeated all his writings. In spite of the loss of the accompanying musical scores, many of his little lyrical songs have come down to posterity mainly as poetry. Like a master sketcher he could suggest moods and emotions by the use of a few aptly phrased lines. Thus, in his "Mood of Autumn" he wrote:

> Withered vines, old trees and evening crows,
> Small bridge, flowing stream, rustic homes,
> Old paths, westerly wind, thin horse.
> The sun setting in the west
> Leaving a heartbroken man at earth's end.

Among song writers of the second period, the most outstanding was Chang K'o-chiu (flourished 1275-1325), who filled various minor positions in the civil service of the alien Mongol Empire. Many of his songs were expressions of his disappointments in life and of his conscious attempts at self-consolation.

(To the tune of "The Narcissus")

The white swans are sky-writing on the cold clouds near the horizon.
The mirror reflects the emaciated face of the beautiful one.
Last night's autumn wind whipped up my sorrows into formation.
I think of you but cannot see you.
Singing slowly I open the wine bottle by myself.
With the lampwick exhausted,
And the wine half intoxicating me,
What an evening!

(To the tune of "Clear River")

Clouds screen off all the lovely mountains in front of my gate;
For a whole day there is no human trace.
The pine trees roar in response to the pale blue waterfalls.
As the master slumbers after drinking
The lonesome spring is growing old.

Most capable of wielding the language of villagers and laborers was the song writer Hsü Tsai-ssŭ (Owner of the Sweet Studio), who gave himself that courtesy name because he was fond of candy. In Hsü's imitations of popular songs we discern clearly the influence of folk motifs such as we find in the following:

Each sound of a paulownia leaf dropping is a sound of autumn.
Each drop dripping from the banana plant is a drop of sorrow.
During the third watch I dreamt of home.
And I see the chessboard still spread under the flowerlike snuff of
    the lampwick.

This repetition of phrases for echoing effect reminds one of the numerous folk songs sung by the Chinese people during the period of Mongolian domination.

With the emergence of Chang and Hsü we see the beginning of a new trend in the development of the technique of the unattached songs or *san ch'ü*. Before them, songs of this nature were primarily written by dramatists as a diversion. There was no question that the principal playwrights were masters of this type of poetry since the same musical tunes which were used in the musical dramas of the period were well known to them. Whenever they wanted to express their own feelings in poetic form, they would naturally write in conformity with the established popular tunes. Their creative energies were almost exclusively centered on the production of musical drama and to them the writing of nondramatic lyrics was only an afterthought. Chang and Hsü were epoch-making in that they were the first poets who, on the one hand, gave full attention to the limitless possibilities of these unattached songs and, on the other hand, refused to be lured into the field of dramatic writing.

During the golden period of the *san chü* many of the first-class writers were of non-Chinese descent: Chin Tatars, Mongols, and Central Asians. This is not surprising, partly because many of the new tunes for popular songs were of alien origin and partly because new songs of this style freely adopted the speech of the common people; a speech which, with the rapid Sinicization of non-Chinese groups relocated in China proper from the peripheral regions, had been completely mastered by these respective partakers of the newly enriched Chinese civilization. In spite of the fact that many of these new masters of the Chinese art of letters—musical drama and classical prose, as well as the detached songs—had thoroughly identified themselves with the main current of Chinese cultural trends, and had discarded their original names in favor of typical Chinese family and given names, quite a number were forthright enough to reveal their racial origin by signing themselves as Hara Pucha, Al Wei, Arudin, or Odun.

When the Mongol Dynasty was beginning to crumble in the middle of the fourteenth century, the northern school of *san chü* appeared to have reached the zenith of its power and productivity. Writers were still numerous and the songs they turned out were still vigorous and forceful. Nonetheless all the great masters were so impressively correct and true to form that they give us the impression of faultless training on one hand and rigid conformity on the other. Like *tz'ü* in Southern Sung times, the *san chü* had become a well-formulated and almost perfected art.

At about this time a new trend was being quietly but unmistakably developed in the far south. This southern school had nurtured a few novel voices singing new songs and developing new themes. Before the northern school retreated from the stage it was further strengthened by numerous highly accomplished writers in the Ming Dynasty (1368-1644). By this time, these northern tunes were no longer sung by the common people; hence the outstanding representatives of this art were masters of rhetoric, setting a new standard in literary elegance in the composition of their lyrics. The features of casualness and the frequent adoption of slang and localisms were totally absent from their works. Nonetheless these great masters were not formalists but real creative talents manifesting their individual originality even in what is generally described as occasional poetry, such as songs of felicitation and songs sung at memorable banquets. Of these late masters of that art which was soon to fade out at least three deserve recognition.

K'ang Hai, who flourished in the latter half of the fifteenth century, and Wang Chiu-Ssŭ (1468?-1550?) were close rivals in the estimate of subsequent critics. K'ang, who was exiled in his middle age, continued to raise the voice of protest. In many of these protests there was a note of harshness, but after addressing questions to Father Heaven and Mother Earth, he would occasionally settle down to admire the beauties of nature:

> The heavens are clear and the high fog is gone;
> The clouds are leisurely; the rain has stopped.
> The water is rising, the waves are coming in,
> Forests and gardens reveal an endless stretch of green.

His contemporary, Wang, was also criticized for his intentional crudity and for the obscurity of his diction, but he was capable of forgetting artificial rhetoric when he preferred to sound his notes of Taoist contentment:

> Riding in a fishing boat on the Lake of Beauty,
> Living in a thatched pavilion on the Purple Mountain;
> My wife and my child and I are happy together.
> Sharing the refreshing breeze and the bright moonlight,
> No one quarrels with us.
> The green mountains and the blue waters are ours to enjoy
>   and sing about.
> After heartily drinking we sing a song of peace.
> Though no longer young, I am still romantic.

Another memorable figure among northern song writers was Ch'ang Lun (1492-1528), who wrecked his official career by ranting at and reviling his superiors when intoxicated. After his dismissal from public life he continued to excel in drinking bouts and in archery. It was during such moments of completely uninhibited living that he would burst out in new songs. His short life came to an abrupt end after he had decorated the graves of his ancestors. After drinking to his capacity, he dressed himself in red and while whirling a pair of swords on horseback he galloped at a reckless speed toward the ford in the river. His horse, frightened by his reflection in the water, fell down and Ch'ang's sword pierced through his body. All his lyrical songs were reflections of the mode of life he led; samples could be picked at random, such as the following:

> A real friend is a real friend, wherever he may live,
> In the royal city or in a hermitage.
> Who is to say where one should be?
> I just follow the lead of my walking staff,
> I call on whomsoever I yearn to see.

The towering figures in song writing were two extremely versatile virtuosos who excelled in various branches of the humanities. T'ang Jen (1470-1523) was celebrated even in his own lifetime as calligraphist, painter, and poet. In popular song writing he was equally at home in both the northern and southern traditions. His official life, which had risen rapidly, was cut short by his inadvertently revealing official secrets. This disappointment was to leave an indelible mark on his poetry, especially upon his *san ch'ü*. In his poetry, as in his paintings, he took special delight in merging himself with nature and in extricating himself from all rules and commitments. His whole life might be epitomized in the following lines:

> Leisure cannot be bought with mere gold,
> Why weigh the self down with mental chains?
> When one lives to beyond a hundred,
> He will have risen above all the three realms.
> Besides this, there is no other way out.

He developed the same sentiment further in another poem:

> Wealth and honor are unenduring,
> The unenlightened bear this in mind.
> Orchids and weeds in the last analysis
> Are both grasses.
> Phoenixes and owls likewise
> Are both fowls.
> The way to the cemetery provides no escape!
> True enjoyment may come too late.
> Let us down ten thousand glasses
> And sing three thousand songs.
> We would wish for more when our call comes.

Another eminent humanist who had dedicated himself to song writing was Yang Shên (1459-1529), who had risen to the highest rank in the official hierarchy but was reprimanded and dismissed when he failed to please Emperor Chia Ching, who had been adopted into the imperial succession from a collateral branch of the emperor's family and who, therefore, had adamantly insisted that

his deceased natural father should receive retroactive canonization
as an emperor—a controversy which generated both heat and color
but contained extremely little sense. Yang, who had spent the
greater portion of his life collecting official honors and circulating
obscure literary rarities, including many items of his own forgery,
amused himself with *san ch'ü* of the southern school later in his life.
Many of the songs reveal a return to the casual note:

> The wind has subsided, preventing the sky from clearing,
> The rain has stopped, but clouds are still appearing.
> For a few moments I rejoice to see
> The flowers playfully casting their shadows.
> The birds singing responsively,
> I have, unawares, completed writing a poem.

These southern song writers were nearly all natives of the south
and as such were familiar with the tunes which provided them with
their song pattern. All literary men, after they had broken the co-
coon of the stereotyped Eight-Legged Essay, joined in strengthening the *san ch'ü* tradition. Even the great epoch-making scholar-
statesman, Wang Yang-ming, was an enthusiastic participant:

> In confusion the crows and magpies emit their squawking;
> Blocking the roads are fierce jackals and wolves;
> Careless and excessive speeding exhausts the fat of the land;
> How can one bear to see families scattered?
> And to hear them exchange news with aching heads and knitted brows.
> Emblems and decorations fill the Audience Hall;
> Arms and weapons throng the country roads; allow the empire to be
>   shaken to its foundations.

Soon after this the vogue of southern *san ch'ü* became so universal
and unchallenged that it became the chief form of occasional writing, gradually detaching itself again from the original folk prototypes and becoming the monopoly of the literary elite until the end
of the Ming Dynasty.

CHAPTER 22

Liao and Chin

DURING the period of temporary disintegration and division between the T'ang (618-906) and Sung (960-1279) empires there developed another restive redistribution of power among the nomadic groups to the north of China, resulting in the hegemony of the Khitan group which in later times came to be known as the Liao people. Declaring himself the Khan of Khitan in 907, Abaoki decided to build himself an empire. Apparently aware of how the Topa and southern Hunnish groups had been completely swept into the orbit of Chinese civilization, he ordered the invention of the Khitan script in 920. This, made up of trimmings from Chinese characters, in the long run failed to replace the Chinese language. According to Chinese records, the first specimen of Khitan writing done on silk was recorded in the year 928 during the Post-T'ang Dynasty. When the Emperor Ming Tsung (reigned 926-933) showed the specimen to his ministers in the audience hall there was not a single one who could read it. There was a script among the Liao people themselves, but there is no reliable information on it. From a recent discovery of stone inscriptions in which the Khitan script was used and the Chinese version engraved in parallel, it was probably likely that the independent use of the newly invented phonetic alphabet was extremely limited.

As soon as he had succeeded in sacking Loyang in 921, Abaoki made a special point of preferring maps and books as well as the Confucian classics to jewelry as his rightful war booty. Even before the establishment of the Sung Dynasty in 960, the pattern had been determined for the Khitan regime to Sinicize itself in preparation for larger conquests. That some wavering was intermittently felt was clearly indicated in the change of the name of the country frequently between Khitan and Liao. This same wavering was manifested in formulation of basic policy on how much Sinicization was necessary for dynastic dignity. Whether the importation of Chinese culture should be limited to the Chinese subjects or be made free for all continued for a long time as the basic point of controversy.

432

In 988 an innovation was introduced: holding the competitive literary examination in Chinese style. The propaganda value of the move was beyond expectation. Immediately in the following year a group of distinguished Sung literati who held doctoral degrees migrated to the Liao kingdom with their families. To their great amazement these seventeen southern doctors discovered that it was merely an experiment and that the frequency of holding such examinations was as yet undecided. Moreover, they found out that the examinations were staged for the benefit of Chinese residents only. As late as 1043, when a Khitan, Yalu Koru, succeeded in winning honors in the third series of examinations and won the doctor's degree, the Liao Emperor, Hsing Tsung ordered the successful candidate's father to proceed to court to receive two hundred bastinadoes. After a lapse of approximately half a century, the taboo was apparently lifted because the Liao records show that in 1115 Yalu Tashih had already won his doctor's degree in the midst of applause and festivities. That the dual policy would not work was already felt in 1044, the year in which a historical bureau of the Chinese type was being organized for the editing of Khitan historic records.

In spite of the fluctuation in dynastic policy with regard to the adoption of Chinese standards in literature, we know for certain that there was writing in Chinese style among both Liaos and Chinese. Many of the literary records in the Liao area, however, were irrevocably lost on account of a strict regulation barring books from exportation. According to Sung notices any attempt to smuggle a Khitan book written in any language, presumably in Chinese, would involve a death penalty. This probably explains why only three works have been preserved from the Liao period, namely, a dictionary, a fortunetelling handbook, and a book of anecdotes.

The dictionary in four volumes entitled *Lung-an Shou-chien* compiled by Hsing Chün in 997 is still treasured as a lexicographical work for the clear indications of pronunciation of Chinese characters. The main entries of characters were 26,433 in number, containing numerous variant forms current in popular literature of that age. It was worthy of notice that the author was not only a Chinese in descent but also a Buddhist monk in vocation. Whether the compilation was done mainly for the benefit of non-Chinese-speaking citizens of the Liao Empire or for Buddhist novices, there is no way to tell.

The author of the *Book of Anecdotes* was also of Chinese descent. Wang Ting (flourished 1065-1089) was a native of present-day Honan Province who had won high honors in the competitive literary examinations and who had distinguished himself as the most capable imperial secretary, drafting decrees in Chinese. His involvement in dynastic politics had sent him more than once into exile and it was during the years of his loneliness in frontier areas that he began to realize the injustices and complexities in court intrigues. *Fen Chiao Lu* (*The Tragedy of an Empress*), a book of anecdotes, which he wrote in 1089 when he was in semiretirement, contained a long narrative in which he volunteered to leave to posterity an accurate record of the innocence of Empress Hsüan-yi, a distinguished poet and calligrapher. The empress, who was extremely talented as a poetess, had offended various members of the Liao court and was eventually incriminated to such an extent that she was forced to commit suicide. Wang Ting, on the basis of firsthand information which he had obtained from reliable ladies in waiting at the Liao court, proved to his readers' satisfaction that the accusation that the empress had carried on an illicit love affair with a court musician had been a fiction and that the poems which had been presented as evidence had all been forgeries. Thus he compared the injustice of the case to a huge inky cloud covering up all heaven so that even the white sun was unable to pierce through it. Although the authenticity of the piece has been doubted by a few literary critics, there are no discrepancies between the anecdote and the official dynastic history.

The development of the intrigues leading to the empress' suicide was due to the cultural conflict inherent in the merging of two widely divergent life patterns. A number of elements in this tragedy could have come only from the seminomadic culture of the Liao people, such as the casual entry by court musicians and maidservants into the palace building for responsive playing sessions with the empress. Certain other elements, however, were undoubtedly derived from the Confucianist traditions inherited from historic China, such as the submission of memorials by the empress remonstrating the emperor for preoccupation with hunting trips and on topics of imperial administration. Also belonging to this category was the empress' attempt to win back the favors of the emperor by writing and submitting poems of her own composition. The public accusation of an empress and the inability of the emperor to determine the authenticity of literary evidences against the empress could not have happened in orthodox Chinese society.

Empress Hsüan-yi's attainment as a poet writing in the Chinese language can be gauged only from such remnants as have been preserved by Wang Ting, as her other writings must have been destroyed after the tragedy. The first group of poems, ten short pieces written in the irregular meter of the *tz'ŭ* style, were written in 1074 after she had lost the imperial favor. After these poems were written, they were set to music and sung in the hope that they might catch the attention of Emperor Tao Tsung. They were all addressed to the emperor. The following may illustrate the themes in general:

I

I sweep the spacious palace hall,
As the golden ring on the door has tarnished after long disuse.
The cobwebs are filled with gossamer and the dust has grown to heaps,
The green moss has heavily coated the steps.
And so, I sweep the spacious palace hall,
For your majesty to dine in.

VIII

I trim the silver lamp
So it might recover its persistent luminance.
But on your majesty's arrival
It produced a variegated aura,
And shines on me with a bluish shimmering.
And so I trim the silver lamp to bid your majesty farewell.

When these poems were finished, there were only two who could play the newly composed tunes on the stringed instrument like a harpsichord and known in Chinese as *chêng*. One was the court musician, Chao Wei-yi, and the other was the maidservant, Shan Têng, who had been confiscated into the imperial household from the family of a rebellious imperial uncle. As the empress by now had fallen into disfavor she could not summon the maidservant; moreover on a previous occasion the maidservant had claimed she was a better *chêng* player than Chao and to rate her properly, the empress herself invited her to responsive playing at which she honestly admitted that her own playing was inferior to that of the servant. Knowing the maid to be a good *chêng* player, Emperor Tao Tsung later on summoned her for a performance, but upon learning this the empress called it to his attention that she had come into the imperial household from the family of a rival prince and that she might turn out to be an assassin in disguise. This bit of counseling antagonized not only the emperor but also the woman musician. Immediately Shan Têng became the medium of a complicated plot which brought about the suicide of the Empress.

On the day the empress was to take her own life, the crown prince and his sisters let their hair down in token of extreme sorrow and tearfully petitioned the throne to die in their mother's place. The emperor refused the petition and rejected the request of the empress to make one statement to him before her death. Then, after prostrating herself in the direction of the imperial palace, the empress wrote her last verse in *ch'ü tzŭ* style and hanged herself with a piece of white silk. The last lines of her farewell poem were the following:

> I was about to carve open my heart in self-elucidation,
> Hoping thus to reverse the rays of the white sun.
> But the various witches had their own shames
> And caused the flying frost to descend and hit in force.
> As I see my sons and daughters in sorrow and exhaustion,
> I turn left and right in writhing pain.
> I am now to set with the western sun,
> To be gone forever from my abode.
> I invoke heaven and earth in extreme unction,
> And I lament the thousand ages without end.
> Now that I know that life is always accompanied by death
> Why should I love to tarry for another day?

Although the section on the biographies of literateurs in the *Liao Dynastic History* is exceptionally short and uninformative, it does not follow that there were no writers of importance of Liao descent. Nonetheless, it is true that the Liao regime was slow and uncertain in its policy of encouraging Sinicization and that conscious attempts were made in the early part of the tenth century to prevent the loss of tribal vigor resulting from a large-scale cultural and literary change. Even as late as the early years of the eleventh century, a Liao Emperor, Shêng Tsung (971-983-1031), took the trouble to translate the poems of Po Chü-yi into the Liao language or Khitanese for the benefit of those tribesmen of his who could not read Po in the original. There was little evidence, on the other hand, that any such translations were either necessary or favorably received. It is true, however, that many of the members of the imperial house as well as of the aristocracy were extremely well versed in the writing of the Chinese language and particularly in the composition of poetry.

An outstanding example was Crown Prince Pei (872-926). When he was invested in an elaborate ceremony as Crown Prince in 916, the founder of the Liao dynasty, Abaoki, his father, asked the dignitaries in the audience hall what god he should offer sacrifice to. When the answer came unanimously in favor of Buddha, the crown prince protested by saying: "Confucius is a great sage and has been honored throughout the generations. He should, therefore, receive priority." Whereupon the first Confucian temple in the Liao Empire was erected by imperial decree. The crown prince was appointed chief officiator at the semiannual sacrifices. That the crown prince had been profoundly touched by the reading of ancient Chinese history was clearly borne out by his decision to forsake the imperial throne and to abdicate in favor of his younger brother in 927. He knew he was following in the footsteps of the elder brother of King Wu of the Chou Dynasty. According to reliable traditions, his personal library had more than ten thousand Chinese volumes with which he had succeeded in educating himself in many fields of learning, including Taoist alchemy and Chinese medicine as well as music and painting.

When the Khitan Empire was conquered by and absorbed into the Chin Empire in 1124, the cultural scene in the northern half of China underwent a sudden and thoroughgoing change. A group closely cognate to the Liao people, the Nüchen, builders of the Chin Empire, had come from the same general area, namely, present-day Manchuria. Unlike the Liao, who were gradual in their rise to power as well as in their decline, the Nüchen did not attract any great international notice until their first defeat of the Liao armies in Manchuria in 1114. Thus in ten years they had built up a vast empire which was to last for 120 years and then almost as suddenly be completely conquered by the Mongols. Despite the relatively short span of their empire, the Chin regime has left much greater contributions to the mainstream of Chinese literature. Replacing the Liao Empire as the dominating regime over the northern half of China, the Chin imperial court early adopted the policy of encouraging free cultural intercourse with the Sung Empire to its south. Thus it encouraged the amassing of all civilizing influences no matter from what quarters they might be forthcoming. It was under the patronage of the Chin emperors that many Sung literary practices were taken over by the northern regime and conscientiously cultivated. Especially distinguished were the Chin attainments in the writing of serial songs and the experimentation with sustained musical drama.

Before we examine the Chin drama and dramatic songs, we shall review the northern attainments in traditional prose and poetry writing. According to a bibliography compiled of Chin writers by Ch'ien Ta-hsin in the eighteenth century, over seventy Chin writers are listed as having had their collective works published. Unfortunately for our purpose the great majority of these works are now lost. This scarcity of material is not due to any government legislation prohibiting the free circulation of literary works outside of the Chin Empire. There was no deep-seated ill feeling between the writers of the opposing empires of the Chin and the Southern Sung. The widespread destruction of Chin literary works can therefore be ascribed only to the well-known enmity between the Chin and the Mongolian Empire.

The stiff resistance put up by the Chin fighting forces against the encroachments of the Mongols from 1205 to 1234 had aroused so much antipathy among the Mongols that after the liquidation of the Chin Empire at the last-mentioned date, the new conquerors for decades not only hated their new subjects but even their writings. No special attempt was made, as far as we know, to salvage the literary remains of the fallen Chin Empire. In fact, the dynastic histories of both the Liao and the Chin Empires were so sloppily edited and hastily published by the Mongol authorities that they have remained the most defective works of this kind to this day.

Moreover, when the Mongols were ousted from China proper in 1279 by the Han Chinese, the problem of salvaging the lost literary materials of the Chin regime no longer appeared to be urgent. The founders of the new dynasty had considered themselves full-blooded Chinese and therefore looked upon the Chin people as border tribes far removed from the pale of Chinese civilization. The lapse of over a century after the subjugation of the Chin people by the Mongols had also rendered the work of literary reclamation difficult. It is not difficult to understand that during the entire Ming Dynasty (1368-1644) no single attempt was made to preserve Chin literature either by re-publication or by the inclusion of outstanding Chin work in standard anthologies.

As distinctly different from the Liao policy, the Chin imperial house was well represented by its various members in its assimilation and appropriation of Chinese literary lore. We might mention an imperial prince, originally named Wuya, whose Sinicized name was Wanyen with the given name of Tsu and who was nicknamed "the scholar" by his own people. When K'aifeng, the Northern Sung capital, had fallen to the Chin invaders in 1127, he was sent there as a special envoy to share in celebration ceremonies. When the two commanding generals asked him what he wanted as souvenirs his answer was, "I love books." And so a few cartloads of books were wheeled away for him. In the following year the Chin court, in order to build up its imperial dignity, was eager to collect all biographical data of the imperial ancestors in preparation for the writing of its dynastic history, and Tsu was appointed chief editor. As a result, three volumes were written covering ten generations of the imperial house. About 1145 he completed an important literary undertaking, the *Veritable Records* of the founder of the dynasty in twenty volumes, thus pioneering the adoption of the Chinese usage of compiling the day-to-day records for each of the reigning emperors.

Unfortunately his collected prose writings and poetry, although printed, were soon lost to posterity.

Another Chin prince rendering distinguished service to Chin letters was Prince Kushên, whose Chinese name was Wanyen Hsi Yün. Besides being an excellent soldier, he also turned his attention to literary and linguistic matters. Now that the Chin regime was rising in international importance and had to carry on diplomatic relations with neighboring states, it resorted to the only medium easy to use, namely, the Khitan script of the Liao people. Soon it was realized that it was not commensurate with its rising status for the Chin Dynasty to use the written medium of a rival state and Wanyen Hsi Yün received imperial orders to write out its own alphabet, known as the *nüchên* alphabet, which was based on the radicals in Chinese characters and submitted to the throne in 1119. Although a simpler script known as the "little script" was adopted by imperial order about 1140, the original big script continued in use on ceremonious occasions.

As in the case of the Khitan script adopted by the Liao Dynasty in 920, these two Chin systems of spelling were never widely used although they were made available mainly for the promotion of dynastic respectability. The reason for which these three scripts were soon to fall into desuetude was their lack of support by any body of existing literature. Unlike an artificial language all three could have been capable of success if they had been utilized in recording the literary traditions of the peoples concerned. Since no such efforts were made the acquirement of the apparatus would not of itself lead to the use of that apparatus. When there was very little of interest available in any one of the three scripts it was only natural that they died a timely death when they failed in their competition with the Chinese script as a literary vehicle. The Manchus later on, as we shall see, were faced with the same situation and artificial efforts were made to sustain a newly created alphabet by having Chinese novels and poems as well as the Confucian classics translated into Manchu and written in the newly devised script. Even these efforts could not resuscitate the decline into which the new script was plunged. For, as long as Chinese was available as a common literary medium, few Manchus would care to read the Chinese masterpieces in Manchu translation. Even stern decrees forbidding the learning of Chinese by any Manchu were of no avail, particularly as the emperors issuing those decrees were themselves violators of the decrees in spirit and in letter. There being the same sort of situation in Liao and Chin times, writers of any standing had written exclusively in Chinese.

The greatest exponent of Chinese art and literature among the Chin aristocracy was Wanyen Ch'ou, who was more interested in reading and writing than in participation in public life. It was reported that he had read the voluminous general history of China written by Ssŭ-ma Kuang over thirty times. He was also noted as a collector of specimens of Chinese calligraphy and painting, having amassed a collection as extensive as that owned by the imperial household.

Among Chinese scholars in the Chin Empire probably the most famous was Wang Jo-hsü (1174-1243). Benefiting from an excellent home environment, especially the tutorship of a maternal uncle, Wang was noted even as a young boy for his remarkable power of memory. He could recite by rote over a hundred thousand Chinese poems and a similar number of the well-known essays. His literary influence was great not only because his poems were simple and touching like those of Po Chü-yi but also because he conducted himself as an open-minded student all through his life. Although he would not remain silent when problems of an ethical nature arose, he would receive struggling scholars from obscure origins and remote quarters as though they were his own equals. When he died he was lamented as the last arbiter of public opinion in classical studies as well as in literary taste and ethical standards.

While the Liao Empire was haphazard and hesitant in its basic literary and cultural policy with regard to the civilization of historic China which it was supposed to have inherited, the Chin tribal leaders were fully aware of the importance of Sinicization before they embarked upon their programs of territorial conquest and expansion. Special efforts were made to draw Chinese literary talents to work for the vigorous young empire in its infancy. Fully aware of the importance of the cultural aspects of empire building, the early khans of the Chin Empire had consciously appointed themselves the legitimate successors to the Northern Sung Dynasty, which had relocated itself in Nanking in 1127. Such an awareness of their cultural policy was clearly reflected in the clean and dignified prose style of the Chin official papers in which the floridity and frivolity of the southern style had been clearly barred.

Besides cultivating traditional polite literature in continuation of the Sung tradition, the Chin writers were particularly successful in keeping alive the development of a literary type in semipopular literature whose origin, though obscure, probably went back to Northern Sung times before the flight of the imperial court in 1127. The immediate source of inspiration was obviously the *pien wên* (not to be confused with the *p'ien wên* balanced prose, let us remember). These Buddhist narrative poems sung to music were fostered by the Buddhist church in China for the edification and entertainment of large audiences. Adopting the technique but changing the subject matter, Sung writers were gradually to evolve a number of new song forms. One of these was known as *ta ch'ü* or "grand songs" using various musical tunes in series, for the telling of a complicated story. Another derivative type was known as *ku-tz'ŭ* or "drum songs." Of these there are practically no extant specimens except in fragments.

From such fragments, however, evidence is deduced that it was a direct imitation of its Buddhist prototype. For, besides the use of sung parts there are also passages in prose which were narrated. Both these grand songs and the drum songs are short as compared with the *pien wên,* which were composed of thousands of lines apiece. The grandiose structure of the *pien wên* with its complexity of subplots and digressions knit together by stretches of prose narrative was most closely copied in a new literary type known as *chu kung tiao* which literally means "a song of narrative nature in which musical airs of various keys were used." The most successful composer in if not the originator of this new genre was a gifted singer, K'ung San-ch'uan, who was a native of Shantung Province and flourished in the last decades of the eleventh century. Beyond this little was known about the man except that his writings were committed to memory by members of the gentry.

This new type of narrative poem was partly sung to musical accompaniment and partly recounted in attractive but simple prose— exactly the same way that the *pien wên* compositions were presented in open courtyards in front of Buddhist monastaries. Between the two, however, there was a noticeable difference in the structure of the sung parts. In the first place, in the Buddhist songs the lines were usually of seven syllables with an occasional dispersal of three-syllable lines for variation. The *chu kung tiao* were composed of songs after the patterns of currently popular musical airs, varying the length of each line to suit the music. Moreover, whereas in the drum songs and the grand songs one tune was repeated many times in the telling of a story, the *chu kung tiao* would use not only many different tunes but tunes with divergent keys. It was, therefore, no surprise that once this new composite conglomeration made its appearance it almost immediately replaced its rival types.

The new type reached its apex of popularity in the Chin Empire at the end of the twelfth century. The most noted author was a gifted writer whose family name was Tung and who was generally referred to by contemporaries as Tung Chieh-yuan, who flourished at the turn of the twelfth and thirteenth centuries. The term *chieh-yuan* attached to Tung's name should not be literally interpreted in the light of later usage meaning "the first successful candidate in the literary examinations." In the age in which Tung lived it was a courtesy title which could be applied to any writer who had won the respect of his readers. This "Scholar" Tung, who had won an immense reputation in his own day but who has lost his identity almost completely to posterity, has become not only an important landmark in the annals of Chinese literature in the Chin Empire but also an important link between long narrative poetry sung to music and romantic musical comedy in later times. Tung's immense literary reputation rests on one single work, namely, a *chu kung tiao* in which a T'ang prose romance was developed and transformed into a long narrative poem with prose transitions, known as *Hsi Hsiang Chi* or the *Tale of the Western Chamber*. The *Hsi Hsiang Chi* is based on the original story written by Yüan Chên in prose in which he told of his romantic love with Ts'ui Ying-ying which we have summarized in a previous chapter. From the original prose romance of a few thousand words, Tung expanded the story to four books in which all the principal characters were fully delineated and many of the details in the narrative were magnified. Moreover, in the original story the scholar Chang, after his long romance with the heroine, Miss Ts'ui, accepted the admonitions of his friends and heartlessly jilted the heroine, thus winning the approbation of his contemporaries for his "bravery in repairing his mistakes." This ending of the narrative, despite the moralistic theorizings, leaves a feeling of oddness and discomfiture on the part of the readers. In the enlarged version, however, this shortcoming was effectively corrected. Although the reunion was persistently blocked by the schemings of a villain, the scholar Chang remained loyal to his love and at the suggestion of another fictitious character not found in the original version—the White Horse General—the story was given a happy ending, an ending which was warmly welcomed by the audiences who heard the recital.

Another type of popular entertainment related to literature which the Chin Dynasty inherited from the Sung and elaborated upon was early indigenous Chinese drama known in those days as *tsa chü*. As this is a link in the chain of reactions in which the first stage of Chinese dramatic development was nurtured, we shall defer its discussion to a later chapter.

The culmination of traditional poetry during the Chin period was represented by its major poet, Yüan Hao-wên (1190-1257). A native of Shansi, he transferred his traditional sense of loyalty to the

alien dynasty in which he was born and brought up. He also participated actively in the Chin official hierarchy. When the Chin Empire
was overpowered by the rising Mongols in 1234, Yüan Hao-wên was
still at his prime but, unable to satisfy his conscience by serving two
masters, he resolutely retired from public life. It was in the latter
part of his creative life that he distinguished himself as a poet.
Knowing the rules of Chinese versification thoroughly, he exercised
singular discretion in avoiding those types which would hinder his
freedom of expression. Thus, in his collected works we find few
poems of his in which parallel structure was called for. In his longer
poems the reader finds a note of naturalness expressed in lines of
varying length and in an obvious lack of all artificial attempts at
cleverness. A typical example is the following poem entitled "Writing After Intoxication":

The fragrance of three cups of Fukien tea reminds me of ice and snow.
The "Li Sao" and the "Nine Songs" shine forever like the sun and moon.
With gold around my belt I shall again ride a stork to go to Yang-chou
And self-contented I do not envy being a lamp in the retinue of grand
    officials.

The mountain ghost standing on one leg
Applauds me and laughs by my side!
Like Ch'ü Yüan I have come home to lament a fallen country;
The green mountains and the old trees are still on the terrace.
I close my books and deeply I sigh,
"How is the night?" The night is young.
My eastern neighbor's daughter in an embroidered dress
Is serving wine from a silver flask, inviting me to drink.
My love of tea and love of books will not end with death.
Please come fill me with ice-clear wine.
In this world only wine has a flavor unforgettable.

In his shorter poems he also exhibited a freshness and the pic-
turesqueness reminiscent of the flavors of the painter-poet Wang
Wei. Among his group of poems entitled "Living on the Mountain"
is the following quatrain in which he tried his hand at parallel structure without feeling the binding effects:

On the lean bamboos vines hang curlingly;
Among the quiet flowers grass grows in confusion.
In the tall forests the wind blows in style;
The moss is smooth and the stream flows quietly.

A dominant literary figure unsurpassed for upwards of thirty years,
Yüan Hao-wên was the last great poet of the Chin Dynasty and the
pioneer of Yüan Dynasty literature.

CHAPTER 23

The Rise of Drama in China

IN THE last decades of the Sung Dynasty both Chinese literature and Chinese politics rapidly declined. In 1141 Emperor Kao of the Sung Empire had gone so far as to call himself in a peace treaty "servant" of the Chin Empire. Less than a century later this haughty Chin Dynasty in the north was completely crushed by a new group, the Mongols, in 1234. In the earlier half of the thirteenth century, the Mongols liquidated the Chin or Nüchen people to their south and invaded what is now Russia to their northwest. As a result of the brilliant military victory of the Mongols, the name Genghis Khan became a household word in Europe and Asia. The Southern Sung, however, did not attract the immediate attention of the Mongols and was, therefore, spared until 1279. During this one hundred and forty years—from 1140 to 1280—China once again went through a period of political division, with the north dominated by the Chin for about a century and by the Mongols for over forty years. With the conquests of the Sung Empire by Kublai Khan, China not only was reunited but also became the nucleus of a far-flung empire. This new process of reunification, however, was more apparent than real. The cultural split between north and south in China itself was to continue with the southern half again a place of temporary refuge for China's classical civilization. Since there was no fusion of the races, there was no lasting change in Chinese civilization in the south. In the north, however, storms were rising and changes were far-reaching and rapid. We have noticed that even during the Southern and Northern dynasties, many new races were absorbed by Chinese civilization. After the decline of the united T'ang Empire into which many alien racial strains and cultural assets had been assimilated, the invasion and occupation of North China by the Khitans, by the Nüchen, and now by the Mongols, were to produce changes that were even more violent in nature and more varied in scope than during the T'ang Dynasty.

From the standpoint of orthodox Chinese culture, the north was continually regarded as inferior to the south. The center of Chinese philosophy and Chinese literature was supposed to have left the north. And yet from a larger view, the north had sustained no great losses. First, the population in the north had benefited from the racial fusion made possible by the inroads of the conquering groups. Second, the migration of these invading races and their assimilation by the Chinese in varying degrees had created a common medium for the spoken language in the north. The inability of the new conquerors to master the intricacies of Chinese intonation and pronunciation was to result in a simplification of the spoken language. The number of tones was permanently reduced to four instead of the puzzling eight or ten current in Changan at the height of the T'ang Dynasty. All final *k*'s, *t*'s, and *p*'s were dropped and all final *m*'s became final *n*'s. This linguistic simplification, similar to the phonological changes in French from the thirteenth to the fifteenth centuries, should not be looked upon as a barbarization, for it provided northern China with a common language with only minor local variations, thus laying the cornerstone of a national language for the whole of China. In the third place, traditional classical Chinese literature, such as had been conscientiously cultivated by China's conservative literati, despite occasional innovations, had migrated southward to the Yangtze region, which was to become its headquarters.

As a result, the dignity and authority of what was old and conventional in literature was to suffer a decline in the north. In the eyes of the conquerors, the old literature meant even less than to the Chinese residents. During the Liao and Chin Dynasties, the competitive literary examinations were continued only in a purely perfunctory manner. After the Chin Empire was overrun by the Mongols, there was only one competitive examination held (1237). After that the hoary institution was held in suspension for almost eighty years. It was not until 1314 that the system was revived. But even then the subject matter on which candidates were examined was so radically changed as to make it almost unidentifiable with what had gone before. From this one instance it can be clearly seen that traditional literature had lost its grip on the populace. This lamented fact again was not an unconditional catastrophe but a blessing in disguise. The literature cherished by the common people of the north under these circumstances gradually became raised in status and was to receive unprecedented attention and nurture. What had been frowned upon now became universally acclaimed. Long novels written in the vernacular, folk songs sung in series, and full-fledged dramas were all products of the north during this age. Although these new tastes were cultivated by a few in the south, they were never taken up as seriously as by northerners. It was during this period, therefore, that the real vernacular literature of the Chinese people, written in the living language of the people, was fully developed and assigned the position it deserved for the first time in China's cultural history.

The greatest achievement by the Chinese people in vernacular literature during the second period of political disunion and especially during the ninety years of complete domination by the Mongols was the sudden attainment to full maturity of the Chinese drama.

Like the ostensible absence of the epic tradition and lack of interest in epical grandeur in China, the belated rise of the drama has been singled out as another striking anomaly in China's literary history. Despite the obscurity in which the origin of the Chinese drama was for long beclouded as a direct result of the traditional belittlement of dramatic writings by China's scholars, considerable progress has been made in the last half-century in tracing the ancestry of Sung and Yüan drama. Now we know for certain that the rise of the full-fledged Chinese drama of the Yüan dynasty was preceded by numerous forms of ceremonial and entertainment, advancing from the participation of early Chinese shamans assuming the roles of supernatural beings to vaudeville acts, one-act plays dramatizing historical personages or legendary episodes, and the short skits especially popular during the T'ang and the Five Dynasties period. In addition, the Chinese drama was also indebted to the so-called drum songs, the episodic song-dances, the puppet shows, and the shadow plays.

The origin of the early Chinese shaman, called *hsi* if a man, and *wu* if a woman, must have gone back to early antiquity. During the period of the *Spring and Autumn Annals* these spiritual mediums were widely scattered and recorded in China, especially in border states outside the core of the so-called Middle Kingdoms. Clothed in dazzling ceremonial robes and headgear, these people, the majority of whom were women, would assume the role of the gods and goddesses in their revelations to the worshipers. In this particular regard they might be loosely described as the earliest actors and actresses in China.

At the same time in the central parts of the Chinese cultural circle where supernaturalism was played down and where shamanism was reduced to the minimum, there grew up a peculiar practice in connection with ancestor worship. As an important item in the semi-religious ceremony of doing reverence to the memory of a departed ancestor by the descendants of the deceased, a member of the clan, usually a minor, would be selected as a living symbol of the ancestor.

This symbol would be dressed in the attire of the deceased person to be honored and would assume a seat at the sacrificial table to accept the offerings of food and drink as well as prostrations by the clan members. It was generally expected that this person, called *shih*, would go through the ceremony motionless and emotionless to simulate a corpse, which is the etymological meaning of the word *shih*. Although no acting whatsoever was assumed by the person in that capacity, the role was definitely one of impersonation.

In the state of Ch'u, where Ch'ü Yüan touched huge audiences with his new songs, these two traditions of the *wu* and the *shih* were interestingly merged. The shaman in that semi-Chinese region was not only the impersonation of a spiritual being during the short period of trance in which messages of revelation were enunciated, but continued to play the role of the god or goddess throughout the religious service. With music, song, and dances going on during the colorful and impressive ceremony, the atmosphere of a theatrical performance was closely approached, although technically speaking the Chinese drama was not yet born.

In the nonreligious spheres of human activity, professional entertainers had also gone beyond the limits of storytelling and joke cracking to assume the roles of other people, historical or contemporary. These entertainers were particularly valued and appreciated at the feudal courts, with many of them often traveling from one state to another on special occasions. Thus it was recorded that at the international convention between Ch'i and Lu in 500 B.C. at which the chiefs of the states were present, the Ch'i government presented a court jester from the feudal state of Tsin by the name of Shih who had apparently traveled to Chia-ku, the site of the conference. When his appearance was announced, he walked over to the canopy of the Lord of Lu. While he was dancing in prelude to the presentation of the spoken parts, Confucius intervened with firmness and dignity, saying "According to international usage one who commits a *lèse-majesté* to a monarch is punishable by death." Thus the performance was cut short and the humiliation to which his own monarch might have been subjected was avoided by the Chinese sage.

Again, it was recorded in the state of Ch'u that there was an actor-entertainer of unusual talent by the name of Mêng. An extremely meritorious prime minister of the state had died in office and the prince of Ch'u missed his virtuous minister so much that he ordered Mêng to enact particularly memorable episodes from the life of the deceased prime minister. Mêng, donning the clothing of the minister, was so perfect in creating the desired illusion that the prince decided to appoint the actor prime minister. These professional entertainers, usually referred to as *p'ai yu,* were doubtless the forerunners of the professional actors of later ages. In all these presentations of songs, dances, and episodes of either a jesting or serious nature, there was no unfolding of any well-developed plot— not even the telling of a sustained story. It was not until the Han Dynasty that the *p'ai yu* presented stories.

The first recorded example of combining singing and dancing with theatrical presentation seems to have been an innovation at the Topa court of the Northern Ch'i kingdom in the fifth century. Prince Lan Ling was a warrior of unusual valor but he was so handsome that he decided that his refined and sensitive facial features would be a liability instead of an asset in close combat. In consequence, he had various huge and fearsome masks made for his military exploits. Thus armed, he rushed repeatedly into the enemy formations of the Chou state and overpowered his foes. In admiration for his bravery, his people invented dances to celebrate his victories. Invariably the impersonator wore a huge mask which came to be described as *ta mien,* meaning "big face," or *tai mien,* meaning "substitute face" or, in plain language, a mask. This custom of impersonation was popular also among the common people themselves.

According to another record there was an odd character in the Northern Ch'i state by the name of Su. He had a strange-looking button-shaped nose, called himself an officer although he was a plain commoner, and was extremely fond of drinking. Each time he was intoxicated he would give his wife a terrible beating and the wife would make her woes known to the neighborhood in an extremely touching manner. The neighbors were so amused by the husband and moved by the wife that they invented a dance accompanied by special songs. Both dance and songs were so popular that the menfolk in the community taking part in the song-dances began impersonating Mrs. Su telling her sorrows. Their singing invariably elicited participation by the onlookers. Later on, to increase the realism of the performance, Su himself was impersonated beating the men disguised in women's clothing—a beating which was more comic gesticulation than a real chastisement. Although these are far from being real dramatic performances, the fact that they arose in the northwest corner of China close to the Central Asian frontier regions deserves close attention. The Topas were an alien group dominating a part of North China. It was during this time that intercourse between China and the countries of the so-called western regions had been accelerated and increased. As we have noticed before, most of the Buddhist sacred books had been introduced into China through this overland route. Coming into China with Buddhism were the musical instruments and musical scores of Central Asia and India. It was the music of Kucha, above all, which had distinguished itself to Chinese ears and it is no coincidence that Kuchan music enjoyed pre-eminence at the imperial court as well as among the common people during the Sui and T'ang dynasties. It was quite natural for short skits from Central Asia accompanied by Central Asian music and dances to be introduced into China in large numbers during this period.

A very frequently recurring expression found in Chinese literary records of the period of the South and North Dynasties was *pai hsi* or "the hundred forms of entertainment." Among these hundred forms we could discern such items as acrobatics, magic, wrestling, and masquerade parading as well as singing and dancing. With the establishment of the T'ang Dynasty, these so-called hundred forms of entertainment became more popular and more elaborate. During the reign of Emperor Ming (reigned 713-755), founder and patron saint of the two Pear Gardens, foundations were firmly laid for a type of entertainment composed of singing, dancing, and a slight element of story-telling known as *ko wu hsi,* later on to be transplanted to Japan from the T'ang Empire and to influence the kabuki of the Japanese people.

Since the element of humor was most emphasized and appreciated, the progress most noticeable on the T'ang stage was mainly in the direction of farces. That theatrical presentations were not entirely independent of the miscellaneous entertainments is obvious from historical records. In the sixth year of the reign of T'ai Ho (832), for example, a special imperial banquet was given on Cold Food Festival in one of the palace buildings. Among the entertainers who appeared at the banquet there was a jester poking fun at Confucius by playing the role of the sage. Emperor Wên, seeing that the subject matter and the presentation were incongruous, ordered the performance banned and the jester driven out of the palace building. Not all T'ang emperors, however, were so serious-minded. During the reign of another emperor, a player, Li K'o-chi, had distinguished himself by his clever comic remarks. On one festival day when representatives of Buddhism and Taoism had finished their orations on the two respective cults—an incident anticipating what Marco Polo and his contemporaries from Europe were to witness at the court of Kublai Khan—theatrical entertainments were presented. Thereupon Li ascended the pulpit in full Confucian regalia. In an affected and artificial tone he announced his subject as a fair-minded estimate of the three religions. An assistant sitting at a corner of the audience asked, "Since you claim to be thoroughly informed in all

three religions may I ask you what sort of person was Sakyamuni?"
The answer was, "The Buddha was a woman." Then an explanation
was made in response to a surprised exclamation by the assistant,
proving the point by relying on the use of puns from quotations in
Buddhist texts. A similar procedure was followed with regard to
Lao-tzŭ and later on to Confucius. By the use of clever puns Li
demonstrated to the satisfaction of his audience that all three religions were founded by women.

Another instance where more action was involved is recorded.
Ts'ui Hsien was so fond of theatrical entertainments that he had
built up his own family troupe under the instruction of a director.
One day he invited his wife to see the dress rehearsal of a new
skit. Knowing that Ts'ui's wife was extremely jealous and suspicious,
the writer of the skit assigned some boy actors to play the roles of
husband, wife, and concubine. The details of the skit were such
that Ts'ui's wife soon noticed the close parallel between the actions
and feelings of the wife in the play and herself. As she suspected
that the troupers would not be so bold as to offend her purposely,
she kept quiet and watched on. The satire became more and more
realistic so that she finally broke out into loud protest, "How dare
you be so impolite? I have never been as bad as that." Her husband
was so amused that he almost fell from his seat with laughter.

These comic skits first attained popularity during the reign of
Emperor Ming, but toward the end of the dynasty they were so popular that they were very strong rivals to the musical skits or *ko wu
hsi*. They were continued into the Sung Dynasty and were popular
mainly because of their value in criticizing current politics. This
they did, keeping the sharpest edges of their criticism hidden behind
the façade of a purported historical episode. Their chief purpose,
besides dispensing criticism, was the provoking of laughter, not the
unfolding of a dramatic story with a definite rising action, climax,
falling action, and denouement.

Sung plays, with the embryos of dramatic plots, were inspired by
a new type of folk entertainment which had become a universal
vogue. This vogue, extending storytelling to a popular audience in
public squares in front of temples or near a market place, will be
discussed more fully in connection with the development of prose
fiction in the vernacular language. It is appropriate to point out in
this chapter that the most effective storytellers would occasionally
shift from third-person narration to first-person presentation, accompanying dialogues of the principal characters with appropriate actions and gesticulations to heighten the interest of his audience,

especially before asking for contributions. As these animated story-tellers had to face keen competition from their rivals, the tendency was natural for them to lapse frequently into dramatization. While it is obvious that their attempts were still far removed from the actual presentation of plays, their primary emphasis on the unfolding of a dramatic plot was of clear significance.

A step closer to dramatic production was the presentation of puppet shows. Probably already fairly well developed during the Han Dynasty, puppet shows were presented, strangely enough, in connection with funerals to alleviate the sorrow of mourners. It was not until the Sung Dynasty that puppet plays became perfected with greatly improved mechanism, although even when Han Yü was staging his literary reform in prose writing, the puppets were being described as "lifelike." By Sung times puppet productions were classified into the following varieties: Puppets suspended from silk threads, puppets moved by running threads, puppets on sticks, puppets moved by gunpowder, "flesh" puppets, and water puppets. It is also recorded that in all these types of puppet shows the chief interest was the narration of complicated stories.

A close cousin to the puppet show was the shadow play originated in the Sung Dynasty. With the removal of the Sung court from K'aifeng to Hangchow, shadow plays became even more popular in the national capital. Paper figures, usually in white, were now replaced with translucent sheepskin figures painted in colors. The stories presented were usually identical in substance with those narrated by storytellers—namely, a fictionization of historical incidents.

The influence of the early puppet show and its twin brother, the shadow play, upon Chinese dramatic conventions is clearly noticeable. From Yüan times down to the present in Chinese traditional drama, there have been three conventions which examined in the light of general dramatic technique seem odd and unreasonable: (1) the practice of players' announcing their respective roles on their first appearance on the stage; (2) the ramification of conventionalized masklike make-up in which individual historical personages presented in theatrical productions could be identified at a glance by connoisseurs; (3) the development of artificial and stereotyped gesticulations and gaits for individual classifications of players such as the heroes, heroines, jesters, and villains, as well as minor parts. These special features, which have lent uniqueness to Chinese dramatic productions, have elicited apologies from the supporters of the orthodox conventions. Actually the apologies are superfluous ex-

cept by way of minimizing the unnaturalness of dramatic development in China, namely, the slowness of full-fledged Chinese drama
to outgrow the shackles placed upon it by its predecessors, the
puppet show and the shadow play.

Another form of entertainment allied to the development of
drama in China was the presentation of short dramatic stories by
a troupe making a round of the main thoroughfares of a city. The
presentation of the story was made by members of the troupe continually as they went through crowded streets, which became even
more crowded with the spectators following them from beginning to
end of the presentation. Except for a stationary stage, Chinese
drama had almost come into existence.

As Chinese drama, even in its earliest stage of development, was
never aware of the possibility of cutting itself loose from music and
singing, we must now turn to another influential factor—the development of a series of songs with a common key. These long musical
compositions in series were called in Sung times, ta ch'ü, literally,
"big songs." The term ta ch'ü originated during the period of the
South and North dynasties. Although the details concerning these
early ta ch'ü are now lost, many of them were of foreign, mainly
Central Asian, derivation. Moreover, it is especially significant that
the types which had successfully stood the test of time were all
alien music or Hu music. This type of song writing, of course, was
not necessarily geared to the production of drama. The songs are
equally adaptable to lyrical or descriptive singing of a special kind,
as we have mentioned in a previous chapter. Nonetheless, the availability of lengthy musical scores was an important factor in fulfilling
the requirements for the emergence of the Chinese classical type of
drama in which the audience expected to be entertained with both
spectacle and music.

Since the early plays of the Sung and Chin dynasties are now all
lost except for their titles, we can only venture guesses at their compositions and style. Generally speaking, they were probably different from the later full-fledged plays of the Yüan Dynasty, as their
titles suggest they probably contained a good deal of nondramatic
entertainment such as dancing, guessing games, and other interludes
of the olio, or vaudeville, type. It is also fairly safe to make a guess
that the principal characters in these pre-Yüan plays—called tsa chü
in the Sung Dynasty and yüan pên in the Chin Dynasty—were already stereotyped as hero, heroine, jester, villain, and so forth.

Lacking reliable data on plays prior to the Yüan Dynasty, we are
justified in saying that it was in the thirteenth century that Chinese
drama in its full-fledged form was born. This contention has been

strengthened by the complete loss of all earlier plays. Their disappearance may have been due largely, if not unconditionally, to the marked superiority of the Yüan productions over all their predecessors—a tenable conclusion in view of the painstaking care the Chinese people have exercised in preserving their literary heritage.

Before we discuss Yüan drama we must point out the new climate created in China by the establishment of the far-flung and vast Mongol Empire of which China was only one unit. In this new climate the long-established tradition in China of appropriating cultural assets and of assimilating literary importations from Central Asia and regions beyond was followed and magnified. When Chang Ch'ien had returned to China in 126 B.C. from his grand tour of the western regions, he brought back two Indian musical scores entitled the "Moho Touli" in Chinese. According to P. Y. Saeki of Japan this was the "Mahâturya," an Indian musical composition transmitted through various Central Asian states to become a source of revitalized musical activity in China. With the availability of Buddhist treatises and sūtras in translation, knowledge of Indian literature was incidentally diffused. The *Rāmāyana,* for example, is referred to in the *Vibhâhâ-Sâstra* with its two translations, one of which came from the pen of the eminent monk Hsüan Tsang himself. Indian musical entertainment—nataka—was mentioned in such translations as the *Buddhacârita.* The *Lalita Vistara* even suggests that the Buddha himself took part in entertainments of a dramatic nature.

Although the exact extent of indebtedness of the Chinese drama to the Indian cannot as yet be determined, pending further researches, there are several striking similarities between the two which demand our attention as they cannot be disregarded as mere coincidence. They are: (1) the religious or semireligious prelude; (2) the interspersal of songs and dialogues; (3) the singing parts carried normally only by the hero and the heroine; (4) the careful discrimination in the use of the elegant language (Sanskrit) and popular language (Prakrit) to suit the social stations of the divergent characters; (5) the frequent use of remarkable stories well known to the audience for the skeleton of the stories, either the Prakhyāta in Indian plays or the *chüan ch'i* (literally meaning "transmittal of the strange and miraculous") type of Chinese prose romance; (6) the emphasis on the poetic quality of the composition. Besides this the minor characters in both Indian and Chinese dramas were given stock names. In the case of the Chinese plays of the Yüan Dynasty, for example, nearly all the maidservants were given such names as Autumn Fragrance.

These observations on the indebtedness of Chinese drama to Indo-Iranian predecessors are fragmentary because most of the historic documents have been lost. Their loss was partly due to the narrow-mindedness of the typical Chinese cultural historian who, on account of limited acquaintance with alien lands and peoples, made brief and unenthusiastic recordings in most cases. The loss was also partly due to orthodox Confucianists after the T'ang Dynasty who grew increasingly puritanical and looked upon anything playful with absolute disdain. The Chinese term *hsi chü* unfortunately was synonymous with the word meaning "play" or "playfulness." As a result, none of the early dramas were listed in any of the bibliographical sections of any of the dynastic histories.

This being the temperament of Chinese scholarship with regard to drama, it is easily understandable that we are ignorant not only of the exact dates of the infiltration of alien influences from India and Iran through Central Asia, but also of even the principal stages of the growth of dramatic presentations and playwriting. Without reviewing the process of laborious researches by recent scholars into the origin and early development of Chinese dramatic literature, we can briefly summarize the findings in the following terms. First, although the generic name *ta ch'ü* was used in T'ang and Sung times as well as in the Yüan Dynasty, it is obvious that this common label designated different types of compositions. Whereas in T'ang and Sung times *ta ch'ü* represented a suite of melodies sung in narration of stories, animated occasionally with dances, in Yüan times the term was used for songs interspersed in full-fledged drama. The only justification for the continuing use of that label is due to the fact that the *ta ch'ü* meant complicated singing without reference to the contents of the song. Second, before the Mongolian conquest of the Chin Dynasty, which had dominated the northern half of China, there had been specimens of dramatic compositions both in the Chin Empire in the north and in the Sung Empire in the south. Unfortunately these early pieces of dramatic literature in Chinese, many of which had been actually presented on the stage before 1234 (the year of the collapse of the Chin Empire), as well as those that continued to be written in the Sung Empire until it was conquered by Kublai Khan in 1279, were all destroyed except for their titles. We know for sure these were playlets, thanks to the preservation of anecdotal records describing some of the performances and the reactions of the audiences to them. Beyond this our information is nil, so that we are unable to determine the exact relationship between these and the well-constructed dramas of the Yüan Dynasty, which strike the casual reader as finished products that had simply dropped down to earth from the sky.

For long the plays written at Tatu (the great capital of the Mongol Empire—present-day Peiping) have been regarded by the scientific literary historian, in defiance of the sneering attitude of the traditional critic, as dynastic literature of the Yüan period comparable to the *fu* of the Han Dynasty. Its sudden emergence, apparently without foundation and predecessors as a result of the loss of the Sung-Chin dramatic writings, was once explained as a forest of literary monuments in the vernacular language to suit the taste and understanding of the uncultivated new conquerors, the Mongols, who were purportedly poor linguists. Again, the sudden blossoming forth of a fully developed dramatic literature was interpreted as an unusual but understandable phenomenon resulting from an innovation introduced into the competitive literary and civil service examination system by the new conquerors who, against convention, had decided to use playwriting as the yardstick. Interesting and feasible as these two theories appear to be, a minute search into contemporary historical records reveals that these hypotheses have been erected on pure hearsay and clever speculation.

The rise of dramatic literature in North China after 1234 was meteoric and the number of playwrights of full stature was remarkably impressive, with at least half a dozen masters of the technique competing for the reader's admiration. Although over six hundred full-length plays consisting of four or five acts each were written and produced between 1234 and 1368, and although over a hundred names of dramatists have come down to us in connection with their literary productions, in no single case has it been possible to reconstruct a continuous biography of a dramatist. In nearly all cases even their dates of birth and death are unknown. It is on the basis of such scanty records that we have to reconstruct the growth of Yüan drama.

Thanks to the curious labors of Chung Ssŭ-ch'êng, who compiled a book in 1330 entitled *Lu Kuei Pu*, literally *A Record of Ghosts* (i.e. a record of deceased personages in the theatrical profession), we are informed of the names of dramatists who belonged to the generation older than the compiler, dramatists who were contemporaries of the compiler but who had died before the year of compilation, and those of the compiler's generation who had not become ghosts yet. This peculiar work has furnished us with a milestone for the periodization of the development of Yüan dramatic literature. It is obvious that in the early period the outstanding dramatists were natives of Tatu or writers at Tatu, there being hardly any southerners. The majority of those of the second period seemed to be southerners coming from the Hangchow area. Even northern authors of the second period seem to have had important connections with southern China such as relocating in Hangchow, serving long terms of office there, etc.

The first leader, in regard to both chronology and technique—if priority could be assigned to any one person at all—was Kuan Han-ch'ing (1220?-1307?), a native of Tatu (Peiping), and at least for a while a member of the Academy of Imperial Physicians. Anecdotal records indicate it was likely that he had also served in the Chin court before 1234 for he was classified as a literary ghost of the first generation by Chung. The date of his death must have fallen before 1300, so we are probably not far amiss in assuming that he flourished between 1220 and 1280. Besides excelling in *ch'ü* of the lyrical type, he had written sixty-five plays, or perhaps sixty, if we discount the five that have been considered by critics as of questionable authorship. Unfortunately only fourteen of these are extant.

On the basis of these fourteen we can readily see his varied gifts in dealing with themes of different types and in the development of diverse dramatic personages. Six of his plays may be described as comedies of love, four as mysteries (in the contemporary sense and not in the sense of mysteries at the time of the morality plays), and two of them heroic dramas, which can also be loosely described as historical plays. Concerning his character delineations, Kuan was unique in making all his principal characters heroines. In the treatment of plots he was able to instill new life and fresh vigor into themes that had become almost threadbare in the hands of professional storytellers. His mysteries, for example, were all based on traditional stories of how capable magistrates had succeeded in solving riddles of crime. These plots, like the ones in typical detective stories, would lose their charm and elements of surprise when retold. In Kuan's hands, however, so many new incidents and twists were introduced and so much analysis of motivations was brought out in the monologues and dialogues that to the modern reader they seem anything but trite. To contemporary audiences who saw the plays unfolded on the stage, the magnetism of a master playwright must have been even more compelling.

In *Hutieh Mêng*, or *Dream of the Butterfly*, for example, Mother Wang, refusing to see her two stepsons die for a crime which they had not committed, decided after a painful process of rationalization and moralization to sacrifice her own son, Wang San. But when she found out that her stepsons had been acquitted and that only her own son was being held responsible for the crime and faced capital punishment, her real emotions could no longer be suppressed. Later on she broke out into bitter tears when she saw the remains of her own son and yet as she noticed that her two stepsons were weeping just as bitterly, she decided to strengthen herself and said to them, "Stop. Merely to see you two still here—" then she broke into song— "even if I myself should have to die, I would remain contented."

In another piece, *T'iao Fung Yüeh,* or *Breeze and Moonlight,* he describes a young girl who, on account of her lowly station, was forced to consent to her lover's betrothal to a girl of higher social standing. She was sent by her old mistress to approach the young lady with the proposed marriage alliance and to seek the latter's agreement. Maddened with jealousy, she secretly prayed that the marriage proposal would miscarry. Unexpectedly the young lady gave her consent and all preparations for the wedding proceeded smoothly. On that fateful day she had to assist the young lady in dressing for the wedding. Although she had to be dutiful in her assignment, she could not but recall her love for the bridegroom. It was in presenting such complexities of conflicting emotions in young womanhood that Kuan particularly excelled.

Besides his exquisite delineation of feminine psychology, Kuan was also a master in presenting heroic episodes taken from history. In a word, Kuan's multiple talents were unswervingly devoted to his immediate task irrespective of the nature of the play he was writing. His realism was so unequaled that his own personality was almost never projected into the play. It is true on certain occasions he would lapse into the conventionalities of Yüan drama and to a modern reader some dialogue would sound stereotyped. In this connection it should be pointed out that Yüan audiences, like Chinese audiences of subsequent ages, went to the theater in search not only of surprises but also of the recurrence of the familiar. As we shall see in our presentation of other dramatists, Kuan's plays were much more varied in type than those of his contemporaries and successors. The only theme from which he purposely shied away was the glorification of the life of the recluse and the otherworldliness of Buddhism.

Another dramatist of distinction was Wang Tê-hsin (1250?–?), better known by his courtesy name, Wang Shih-fu. Less productive than Kuan, Wang was the author of twenty-two plays besides a number of sets of lyrical songs sung to the *ch'ü* type of music. Of his plays only two are now fully preserved with another two existing only in fragments. His reputation rests on the *Western Chamber* or *Hsi Hsiang Chi,* a play converted from the well-known prose romance

The Record of Ying-ying by Yüan Chên. Tradition tells us that when Wang was writing the drama he concentrated so intensely upon the project that after writing the closing lines

> Blue clouds in the skies,
> Yellow flowers on the ground.
> The west wind is blowing hard
> And swallows are flying south,

he felt his genius had been exhausted and died of a stroke. Although such legends are unreliable, they bespeak the extent of popular appreciation of the exquisite writing in this drama. Actually, of the five acts of this drama, Wang had composed only four, the final act being completed by his friend and contemporary, Kuan Han-ch'ing. The authorship of this piece has been a topic of controversy for nearly six hundred years. The concensus today is that it was a work of collaborative authorship as stated above.

The striking feature of this play is its excessive length—roughly speaking, two or three times longer in its written form and its presentation time than the average Yüan drama. The circumstance warranting such a lengthy production is not hard to understand. The romantic story line, ever since the prose romance had been written in the ninth century, had received so much popular acclaim that it had become the common property of writers in both prose and the diversified forms of verse. Meanwhile the incidents had been adorned with so many details and subplots that according to an entry in a work of bibliography, one popular play version written by a scholar named Tung, prior to the end of the Chin Dynasty, had taken up two folio books. Once elaborated into a lengthy form, it was difficult for any playwright to satisfy the anticipation of an audience by a process of abbreviation. The technical problem with which the authors were faced was how to present an unduly long play in a manageable form. The result was that the five acts could be presented as five separate programs or either read or witnessed on the stage as a pentology.

The first unit of this five-act play deals with the romantic exploits of the hero, Chang Chün-jui. Being a temporary lodger at P'u Chiu Ssŭ, or the Monastery of Universal Redemption, Chang met in the main hall of the Buddhist temple, Ts'ui Ying-ying, daughter of the Prime Minister, who was residing in the house near the monastery. Electrified by her, he decided not to resume his journey. One evening as the young lady was offering incense to the Buddha in the monastery, Chang recited a poem dedicated to her to which she responded with a poem using the same end-rhymes. On the thirteenth day of the third moon, according to the Chinese calendar, Madam Ts'ui requested a special Buddhist high mass to be celebrated in memory of her deceased husband, the Prime Minister. In the name of a sharer of the charities offered on that occasion, Chang took part in witnessing the colorful ceremonies of the high mass and formally met the young lady. At this point the first unit ends.

In this way the original romance was cut up into five different parts, each with the constituent elements leading up to a climax and concluding with a minor denouement. The fourth unit, which was the last unit written by Wang Shih-fu, ended with the parting between Ying-ying and Chang. When Chang had traveled twenty miles from the monastery and was trying to rest at a wayside inn, he saw Ying-ying arriving at the inn in search of him. Suddenly there appeared a group of disbanded soldiers who tried to grab the girl. Chang intimidated the soldiers into submission and surrender of the young lady, but, when he was about to embrace his lover, found a wooden harp in his clasp and realized it had been a bad dream. Later critics were of the opinion that this was the most esthetically satisfying ending for the play and that any continuation was tantamount to attaching a dog's tail to a mink fur. Actually, without the fifth act, in which the original prose-story ending of tragedy was changed into a happy ending with the marriage of the two lovers, the expectation of the average theatergoer would not have been satisfied.

Among Yüan dramatists of the first period, mention should be made also of Pao P'o (1226-after 1291), a man slightly younger than Kuan, who, on account of his devotion to the Chin Dynasty, refused to serve under the Mongols. He was only seven when the Chin Empire fell. Nonetheless he moved southward to Nanking where he associated himself intimately with other "survivors" of the old dynasty in retirement, devoting himself to literary activities and declining all recommendations to public life. Of his sixteen plays, only two are now preserved, and he is remembered mainly for his dramatization of how Emperor Ming of the T'ang Dynasty sought but failed to obtain a reunion with his consort, Yang Kuei-fei.

Ma Chih-yüan (1265?-1325?) is best remembered for his *Han Kung Ch'iu* or *Autumn in the Han Palace*, among his fourteen extant plays. The story was a well-known one of how a Han court lady during the reign of Emperor Yüan was sent by mistake to the encampment of the Hsiung-nu, already celebrated many times in prose romances as well as poetry. In the Yüan drama, historic incidents were fictionized so that the emperor himself became a chief character who had fallen in love with the young lady of tragic fate. As the dramatist was a man first eager in his search for official honors and then completely disillusioned in life, he wrote other plays in which the transitoriness of human life was successfully dramatized with the aid of Taoist tales and episodes.

Probably best known to the Western world through translation as a Yüan dramatist of the first period was Chi Chün-hsiang (flourished 1260-1280) of Ta-tu, author of six plays, of which only one is now extant—*Chao Shih-ku erh* or the *Orphan of the Clan of Chao*. This play, translated by Father Joseph Premare and published in France in 1735, became immediately popular in Europe and served as the basis of revisions by William Hatchett and Arthur Murphy in Great Britain, Voltaire in France, Metastasio in Italy, and Goethe in Germany. The story was based on a record of the Spring and Autumn Period of the feudal state of Tsin. T'u-an Ku, in his mad pursuit for power, had succeeded in killing all three hundred members of the rival house of Chao. The only survivor was the wife of Chao Su, who was spared because she was the daughter of the feudal prince. After she had given birth to a son, T'u-an had her house guarded to eliminate all chances of the survival and continuation of the Chao clan. A devoted servant smuggled the child out in a basket with the consent of the military guard, who immediately committed suicide. The villain ordered all infants within the state between the age of one month and a half year to be surrendered to be killed. The devoted servant hastily got together with another devoted supporter of the Chao clan and decided to surrender his own son as substitute for the Chao infant.

After the arrangements were made he accused his friend of hiding the Chao baby. An official search was conducted, and both the substitute infant and his abductor were executed. The servant now had won the confidence of the villain who, having no male issue himself, adopted the servant's son—actually the Chao infant—as his own. Twenty years later when the Chao orphan had grown up, he found a scroll of paintings purposely left on the floor by the servant. Upon learning of the tragedy which had befallen his own house, he appealed the case to the feudal prince and justice was done. Irrespective of the imperfections seen by its European adapters, this play enjoyed popularity in China because of its confirmation of the Chinese tradition of importance in the continuity of the clan and the righteous indignation of refusing to live under the same roof with the enemy of one's father.

Without enumerating other Yüan dramatists and plays, it is appropriate that we point out the one single feature of Yüan plays as a whole. While certain phrases of the classical language were retained in many of the plays, we see for the first time in Chinese literary history a mass production by many hands all utilizing the vernacular language. This vernacular language, while retaining the best qualities of directness and simplicity of folk speech, had been beautifully enriched and sensitized by the playwrights with their training in belles-lettres. This situation was made possible by the rise of a peculiar set of political circumstances emanating from the complete domination of China by the Mongols. In previous ages alien conquest of China had never been complete and so the alien dynasties set up in the north had been affected by varying degrees of Sinicization in their rise to power, and, later on, in their competition with a domestic Chinese regime in the south, had to utilize Chinese scholars as assistants, if not as full participants, in their government.

In nearly all cases, partly to check up on the reliability of their Chinese secretaries and other subordinates, and partly to try to partake of the enjoyment of Chinese literature itself, alien royalties and aristocracies had taken up Chinese studies with avidity. Knowledge led to fascination and fascination crystallized into love and admiration. The net result was complete Sinicization of the conquering tribes. In the case of the Mongolian conquests of China, the situation was different in a number of ways. First, China became only a part of the empire and so Chinese could not be used as the official language to replace the role of Mongolian. Second, there was no southern Chinese court in existence with which the Mongolian court had to compete in the matter of cultural orthodoxy. Third, as the southern half of China, the last territorial acquisition of the Mongolian Empire, had put up stiff resistance to the southward march of the Mongols under Kublai Khan, southern Chinese, described by Marco Polo and other European travelers of his day as Mangi, became members of a fourth estate and were discriminated against as inferior to the Mongols, to the Shê-mu or colored-eye folk, and even to the Han group, meaning northern Chinese who had been incorporated into the population of the Mongol Empire in 1234.

Members of the Chinese intelligentsia could not have failed to recognize this unprecedented discrimination leveled against them and except for a few who would seek honor by any means or who were dragged into office against their own wish, sought solace in nonco-operation. As a result, their creative energies were directed into two nonpolitical channels: namely, water-color painting, in which the Yüan artists ranked extremely high, and the writing and production of dramas.

This diversion of creative energies into the channels of painting and literature resulted, in the literary realm, in the acceleration of two belated but dormant developments: the rise of long prose fiction, which we are going to discuss in a separate chapter, and the full flowering of sustained drama with which the dynasty has been identified. The record of production is an impressive one. Despite the large number of dramatic works allowed to fall into oblivion and possibly permanent loss, at least 733 plays can still be accounted for. Of these, 591 were written by known authors but 437 have not been recovered; 32 exist only in fragments; and 122, fortunately, have been preserved intact. Of the remaining 142, by unknown authors, 48 are extant, 12 preserved in fragments, and 82 lost. Of dramatists of the dynasty, 108 names have come down to us. Of these, 57 are represented by works which have remained intact, 7 by fragments, and 44 by titles only.

These data, it should be pointed out, represent only our present state of knowledge. Both the number of writings and the number of plays are likely to increase with the progress of further researches and rediscoveries. Even according to our present state of knowledge the scene of literary activity in typical Yüan drama, that is to say in what was then called *tsa chü*, or miscellaneous plays, represented only one half of the picture. It was in this half of the picture that we have discovered the sudden rise of creative dramatic writing which had been stimulated continuously by the inflow of alien influences from India and Persia through Central Asia. And it is this branch of Yüan drama which had spread from the north to the south as we have clearly seen from the removal of the center of creative writing from Tatu to Hangchow.

In the south of China, however, where Mongolian domination was delayed for over four decades, southern drama went ahead in its own way. To all intents and purposes, indigenous Chinese drama developed beyond the scope of vaudeville acts and narrative skits and was already popular in its embryonic form about the eleventh century. By the early half of the twelfth century, scripts were already being used. After the occupation of the Northern Sung capital, Pienching, now known as K'aifeng, northern drama was rapidly developed. To the best of our knowledge the writing of abbreviated scripts for play production was begun during the reign of Hsüan Ho (1119-1125), but the earliest scripts now preserved go back only to about 1220.

This purely native branch of early Chinese drama was first called *hsi wên*, or play script, and was principally popular among the common people of the south and, naturally, utilized the folk songs of the south. Between these two branches of Chinese drama there were striking differences which confirm our hypothesis that the northern branch had been more exposed to foreign influences than its southern counterpart. First, in *tsa chü,* or northern drama, the singing was carried exclusively by the principal character, either the hero or the heroine, from the beginning of the play to the end. In the *hsi wên* or southern type of drama, the singing could be assigned to any character and any number of characters. Second, in northern drama the prologue was a part of the play itself, whereas in southern drama the prologue consisted of greetings to and blessing of the audience with an explanation of the purport of the drama and a synopsis of the story—features entirely lacking in the northern *tsa chü.* Third, whereas in northern drama the component parts were normally a prologue followed by four acts, in exceptional instances, the main part of the play could consist of five acts. These exceptions were extremely few. In southern drama the change of scene was multiple, often numbering beyond fifty and later on extended to more than a hundred. On account of the scantiness of historical materials, we are unable to describe in detail what the early *hsi wên* plays were like. We only know that even after the collapse of the Sung Dynasty in 1279, these plays were not completely replaced by the northern dramas. Originating as a local school of playwriting, the *hsi wên* first dominated the southern half of China, but with the southward penetration of *tsa chü,* it was likely that this southern drama also spread northward, making the two schools both nationally influential even if they did not interpenetrate as much as might be expected.

From cullings of anecdotes it is safe to assume that at least 150 of these southern plays were written before the end of the Yüan Dynasty. Unfortunately, except for three southern plays hidden in their entirety in the imperial encyclopedia, *Yung Lo Ta-tien,* completed in 1408, and one play preserved on account of its great popularity, all the remnants of the early specimens have been completely lost. The most popular piece, entitled *P'i P'a Chi* or *Record of the Balloon Guitar* (a musical instrument of decidedly non-Chinese origin), was written by a famous litterateur, Kao Ming (flourished 1345-1375, at the end of the Yuan Dynasty). Kao Ming was not only a southerner forced to serve the Mongolian court more or less against his own wish, but also slightly involved in the rebellion against the Mongols. This play, written in a language which combines the simplicity of folk speech and the elegance of refined rhetoric, was a great masterpiece dealing with a well-known but greatly distorted legend.

The hero was a historical character, the great writer Ts'ai Yung (132-192) of the Han Dynasty. Scarcely two months after his marriage he had to face a choice between his filial piety, following the advice of Confucius not to travel while one's aged parents were still alive or making one's itinerary definite and specified if travel one had to, and the persuasive talk of his father, who was preoccupied with the young man's future. After much debate Ts'ai left for the capital to take part in the competitive examination. After his departure the family resources were sharply reduced and, threatened by famine resulting from a crop failure, Ts'ai's wife volunteered to apply for charity rice. Waylaid on her way home, she decided to plunge herself into a well but was saved by her father-in-law, who happened to be traveling close by. Despite her efforts to increase the nourishment of her parents-in-law, she was suspected by them of hiding the best foods for her own consumption. One day she was spied upon and found to be eating the husks of rice, which discovery so profoundly moved her parents-in-law that the elderly pair died of self-reproach.

After taking care of the funeral services and the completion of the tombs with the assistance of supernatural beings, the wife decided to travel to the capital in search of her husband. She embarked on the long journey with very little money, a balloon guitar, and a portrait of her parents-in-law. Meanwhile Ts'ai had succeeded in obtaining the highest possible honors in the literary examination and had been commanded by the emperor to marry the daughter of Prime Minister Niu. Although resolved on declining all honors, he failed to bypass the firm decision of the emperor. While he was living in the capital unhappily in his new status, he was called upon by a swindler with a forged letter from his parents, who promised to carry his reply as well as his remittances back to his native district. Realizing his inner grief, the prime minister's daughter proposed to return with him to his native district but failed to win the consent of her father, who preferred to dispatch a messenger to fetch Ts'ai's parents to the capital.

One day, when Ts'ai was riding listlessly outside of the city, he crossed the path of his first wedded wife, Chao Wu-niang. As neither had expected to meet the other they failed to recognize each other. In her haste to yield the road to the formidable procession of the prime minister's son-in-law, the wife dropped the portrait on the roadside, and by the time Ts'ai's retainers submitted the picture to him she had already traveled far. Meanwhile, however, she had discovered she had missed her husband on the highway.

On the following morning she called at the Niu mansion and was presented to the prime minister's daughter, who showed her great hospitality and asked her to stay as her guest. By special arrangement she was shown Ts'ai's studio where the missing portrait was already hung on the wall. On the margin of the portrait she wrote a short poem and left. When Ts'ai returned to the studio he not only succeeded in meeting his first wife but also in obtaining imperial consent for an immediate return home with his two wives, purportedly to do homage to his parents at the graveside. Upon learning of their sudden departure, the prime minister memorialized the throne in detail, which resulted in the conferring of honors on all concerned.

This treatment of the life story of an eminent Chinese scholar of the Han Dynasty was not as flat as it might sound. For over a thousand years, for some unknown reason, Ts'ai had been misrepresented in Chinese folklore in stories and ballads as a person unloyal and unfilial. Kao Ming's play was the first attempt to set the historic record right.

Although the earliest recorded specimens of *hsi wên* were all committed to writing in the county of Wênchow, the birthplace of Kao Ming, the vogue soon spread to other areas. Like northern drama, the center of literary creation gravitated finally to Hangchow. Unfortunately, materials are entirely lacking to show the possible merging of these two branches of early Chinese drama in that southern metropolis.

CHAPTER 24

Early Fiction in the Vernacular

Aᴌᴛʜᴏᴜɢʜ its name was forgotten by posterity, the influence of *pien wên*—the Buddhist narrative poems for recital—was extremely profound and many-faceted. The phonology emphasized in the recital had sharpened Chinese ears to a wider range of possibilities in intonation and led directly to the creation of new poetry forms and types. The intermixture of prose narrations and poetic incantations inspired the T'ang romances in prose as well as the peculiar school of group authorship in T'ang narrative poetry. The emphasis on the unexpected and supernatural (*pien* means "change") gave added impetus to narrators and poets in capitalizing on the miraculous and weird.

As noted in a previous chapter, the T'ang prose romances of the *ch'uan ch'i* type had reached great vogue in the ninth century of the Christian era. Although the illiterate were just as fond of a good story as were the sophisticated, their lives were not intimately touched by these well-constructed tales of the unusual and supernatural because such compositions were almost entirely written in the classical language by members of the scholar-gentry class for their own amusement. The common people, meanwhile, had to content themselves with listening to the recital of the Sinicized versions and secular imitations of the Buddhist *pien wên*—recitals in which native Chinese stories and personalities had taken the place of their Indian prototypes.

At the time the Mongols were making preparations for the final conquest of South China, the telling of popular stories with the interspersal of songs continued with increased vigor. Nonetheless, the name of *pien wên* had all but disappeared from the Chinese language. Evidences were numerous that the cultural loan had been completely assimilated and appropriated. The recitals were not limited to the vast terraces and yards adjacent to temples and monasteries, but also took place in market places and centers of entertainment bearing a striking resemblance to modern amusement parks. These semipermanent quarters in which the popular story-

466

tellers would erect their lecterns were called *wa shê* in Sung times, possibly indicating areas sheltered from wind and rain by a tiled roof because *wa shêh* simply means "tiled roof quarters." In addition, storytellers had grouped themselves into schools.

Naturally there were still those who continued to teach popular Buddhism to the listeners in story form, thus keeping up the tradition without the name of *pien wên*. More popular than these were the "elaborators of history." And just as popular were the narrators of fiction, with the smallest following being attracted to a group specializing in *ho shêng*. Although we don't know the exact nature of this fourth specialty, imperfect records seem to indicate that it allotted more time to moralization than narration. From the names recorded of the greatest practitioners of this new profession, collectively described as *shuo-hua jên* or "speech makers," quite a number were women. The two cities in which these professional reciters abounded were K'aifeng and, later on, Hangchow.

Since we are primarily concerned with the contributions made by these reciters of literature, we shall confine ourselves in the present discussion to the "elaborators of history" and the narrators of fiction.

Narrators of fiction, even the most eloquent of them, used a type of prompt book to aid their memory, which was actually a synopsis of the narrative. These booklets were at first called *hua pên* or "story roots." Some of these were also called *tz'ŭ hua* or *shih hua*, "poetry and speech." Their earliest prototypes go back to the T'ang Dynasty if not earlier. Among the manuscripts salvaged from the archives of Tunhuang we have a piece entitled "T'ang T'ai Tsung Ju Ming Chi" or "The Tale of Emperor T'ai-tsung of the T'ang Dynasty in the Nether World," a piece narrating in a language close to that of common people the experiences of the T'ang Emperor in the nether world during a trance.

The greatest *hua pên*, however, seems to have been produced in Sung times, because it was during that period that the art of oral narration and recitation attained new levels of perfection as an art. Thus the recorded outlines of those narrations and incantations revealed a new mastery of technique in wielding the language of the people in oral communication as well as writing. Whereas the Tunhuang manuscript uses an intermixture of classical and vernacular Chinese in an extremely hesitant, ineffective, and crude manner, the Sung "story roots" show the full florescence of a new technique.

Unquestionably it was during the Northern Sung period (960-1127) that the new technique was developed to maturity in the national capital of K'aifêng. Listening to long narratives interspersed with songs had become a universal vogue throughout the empire with the best-tested talents assembled at the capital. There, not only imperial families but also the great majority of the populace would spend idle afternoons and evenings listening to such recitals in the midst of diverse other types of entertainment and would amuse themselves by flocking to the well-known and advertised lecterns scattered throughout the city in its various amusement centers. Parents who were annoyed by the running about of small children would herd them off regularly to a tile-roofed shelter where they could learn at least the rudiments of the most dramatic episodes of Chinese history and where they would gather a few themes for improvising of games among themselves after they had returned home.

Despite the large number of "talented hands" in this fascinating art, as reported by travelers from different parts of the empire to the capital, there was no mention of the circulation of the storytellers' books either in print or in manuscript. The earliest specimens of these reminder books have been lost in China. Luckily five have been preserved in perfect condition in the government library in Japan. All five of them deal with selected exciting episodes from Chinese history, such as the launching of the punitive expedition against King Chou of the Shang-Yin Dynasty by King Wu of the Chou Dynasty, or the annexation of the Six Kingdoms by Ch'in.

Besides these five, other stories of the same type have been preserved in anthologies of prose stories but are concerned with the Sung Dynasty. Altogether, we have approximately thirty such stories preserved for us. Their dates vary between 1127 and 1279 so that we are justified in saying at least tentatively that the Southern Sung period was the golden period of the first stage of development of Chinese fiction.

These divergent samples of Southern Sung fiction, although advanced beyond the rudimentary recordings of the original *hua pên*, were still reminiscent of the crudity of the latter. Also they apparently were by many hands, as they distinctly reveal divergence in style. For the first time in China the use of the vernacular language for narration was a proven success. They were equally epoch-making in subject matter, in that they were now synthetic. Before this time storytellers had either wholly emphasized the ways of the world or concerned themselves only with the miraculous and supernatural. Now hardly a single sample was recorded in which a realistic presentation of everyday stories was free from an admixture of the strange and weird. Besides this, there was a new type of fiction making its full-fledged debut in Chinese literature, and that is the emergence of the earliest detective stories. The best one among these was so skillful in its presentation that the mystery increased as the story went on until the very end of the narration in which the solution was presented when the listeners or readers least expected it. Even the less distinguished ones, in which elements of the mystery would unwittingly give themselves away, were highly successful in portrayal and description and in their use of the vernacular language with great effectiveness.

Among the narrations from history there is one piece of fictionization that is particularly outstanding. Its substance was the reign of Hsüan Ho (1119-1125) of the Sung Dynasty and it presented a fictionized elaboration of the capture of two Sung emperors by the Chin Tatars and the southern flight of the Sung court to Nanking and Hangchow. Most striking was the fourth part in which was told the assembling at Liangshan Lagoon of a number of underground leaders in defiance of the corrupt local government. This episode became the nucleus around which later accretions clustered to give rise to the great cycle of the *Water Margin* heroes.

The most regrettable fact about the earliest storytellers is that all their names except three have been completely forgotten and that their writings, if any, have not been recovered. Their influence on later Chinese fiction, however, is easily recognizable. Even the Southern Sung stories, which were written and printed primarily for individual perusal, preserved the original coloring of the story roots by the presence of an audience. In the first place the question-and-answer form was occasionally preserved, such as, "What was the name of this gentleman and what was he about to do?" In the second place all chapters end with a stereotyped statement such as the following: "If you are interested in knowing what is to follow, please listen to the further explanation of the subsequent chapter." This influence was so profound upon later Chinese writing that these two conventions, and a number of others, were not dropped by some Chinese fiction writers until after the introduction of Western literature in translation at the end of the nineteenth century.

The transition between the *hua pên* and full-fledged Chinese fiction is to be seen in five early specimens of *p'ing hua* all preserved in their original editions in Japan. These, all printed during the reign of Chih Chih of the Yüan Dynasty (1321-1323), furnish us with the Yüan versions of the "story root." All five were printed in the coastal province of Fukien and three of them imply by their titles that they were parts of larger wholes. In fact, their titles seem to indicate that there might have been in existence or in project a serial publication of the fictionized history of China from antiquity to the end of the Sung Dynasty. The arrangement of the printed page in these five rarities of printed Chinese fiction is also interesting. On each page is to be found a picture occupying about one-fifth to one-fourth of the printed text. This practice must have gone back to earlier times to serve the double purpose of arousing the interest of the none-too-literate reader and of aiding the memory of the master storyteller who could, by a glance at the picture at the top of the page, recall the details of the text below.

Of these five, which are obviously by different hands representing different levels of literary attainment, the third deserves special mention. It was the story of the unification of China resulting from the conquests of the six rival states by Ch'in. It is a pure historical novel without the involvement of the supernatural and miraculous, easy though it obviously was to magnify the latter elements for the narration of such a world-shaking incident as that series of military conquests. Moreover, on account of its close adherence to actual history and on account of its presentation of a summary of Chinese history down to the end of the warring states period, it was obviously an independent work intended to stand by itself instead of being a portion of a serial publication. It was effective in dramatizing the intense struggle between the legalist state of Ch'in intent on its consecutive conquests of its rival states, one by one, and the anti-Ch'in coalition dedicated, with varying degrees of faithfulness by the Six Kingdoms, to the basic policy of collective security and solidarity. It was equally effective in capitalizing on individual incidents and magnifying each into a full-scale canvas.

All the early forerunners of this literary type written in a language close to the daily speech of the common people were anonymous. In a few cases the author would dare to go far enough to identify himself in a rather faint way by resorting to the use of a nom de plume, a kind of pseudonym which involved no similarity to a real name such as George Eliot or George Sand, but vaguely suggested the temperament of the owner by such assemblages of words as "The Lover of Mists and Waves" or "Lone Fisherman." This practice was in vogue partly in conformity with the tradition long adopted by the painters, who considered it vulgar to claim credit for creative work by projecting their names on any part, no matter how obscure, of the paintings themselves. Besides this, the anonymity of the early prose fiction also indicated the lack of reader interest in the authors. In fact, most of the authors were people of little literary training and attainment, as the crudity and awkwardness in the use of the vernacular language fully revealed. As a result, all contemporary writers of anecdotal literature and recorders of folkways had paid closer attention to the actual reciters of ballads and narrators of long romances whose names they did record, than to the authors of the story roots whom they did not mention by name in a single instance.

This negligence of the identity of storytellers persisted so firmly and for so long that its effect was still felt at the time of the emergence of the real masters of the narrative art. The name of Lo Kuan-chung, author of the *Romance of the Three Kingdoms*, did not appear in any of the biographies of the dynastic histories of the Yüan and Ming periods. The only entry worthy of note was found only in one book and that book itself was considered to be of such little moment that it was scarcely read. According to this sole literary source, he was a native of T'aiyüan in Shansi Province, his nom de plume was "A Wanderer on Lakes and Seas," despite his attainment as a poet he had and cared for few friends, he flourished around 1364, and at the time of the recording of this scrap of anecdote, some sixty years later, nothing had been heard of him since. This entry in the obscure work entitled *A Continuation of the Records of Ghosts* by Chia Chung-ming attracted practically no attention and later admirers of the *Romance of the Three Kingdoms* continued to speculate upon the name and origin of Lo.

It was obvious that Lo was one among many who, refusing to co-operate with the Mongol conquerors purposely tried to bury themselves in obscurity but who, sparked by their gifts of genius, had to seek expression in fine arts or belles-lettres. In the case of Lo Kuan-chung the problem of livelihood was an additional hurdle to be surmounted. Thus, in presenting historical narratives of his own composition, he would incorporate representations of the social injustices of his own age. He was so exhaustive and yet so subtle in the voicing of his social criticism and in the delineation of corruptions and wickednesses that the legend early grew to the effect that as a result of his overexpressiveness in divulging the basic mysteries of life and the universe, his descendants were all born dumb for three generations. This legend, obviously a fabrication inspired by jealousy, could be taken as a most eloquent though unintended tribute to Lo as a novelist.

Lo Kuan-chung's bequest to posterity in the realm of fiction was vast. The exact volume of his writings is as yet difficult to determine because many have been reprinted anonymously and others have been so badly tampered with by editors that they hardly represent Lo's original works. Principally he wrote fiction of the historical type, of which the most distinguished examples were *San Kuo Chih* or the *Romance of the Three Kingdoms* and the *Shui Hu Chuan* or the *Story of the Water Margin* (retitled *All Men Are Brothers* in Pearl Buck's translation). On occasion Lo would also indulge in long tales of the miraculous of which the most successful was the

P'ing Yao Chuan or the *Story of the Subjugation of the Evil Phantoms.*

The *Romance of the Three Kingdoms* is the most popular among the works of Lo Kuan-chung and possibly also the least tampered with by later editors. The recent discovery of various "early" editions of this romance has revealed extremely few variant readings, thus tending to establish the fact that we have a version close to the original work. In this work the author's originality was displayed more in his novelty of presentation rather than in his inventiveness of a theme.

Traditional Chinese prose fiction has a good deal in common with the metrical romances of medieval Europe. In both cases the substance was conventional, utilizing stories that had been told and retold many times, such as the cycle of Charlemagne, the cycle of King Arthur and his knights, and the cycle of Alexander and his military exploits. In the hands of a real master, such as Chrétien de Troyes, a well-known story was never allowed to be threadbare. There were always methods of presentation to make the familiar attractive and there were always new episodes, subplots, and tricks of characterization which would make an old story and its heroes and heroines appear refreshingly new and vigorous.

Thus, capitalizing on an old cycle which had not only been told many times by the professional storytellers at centers of public entertainment, but even committed to writing, Lo was successful in instilling new personality into the old vehicle. In the first place, he refined the narration by purifying the language, eliminating the vulgar elements of the folk speech by introducing a more refined vocabulary that was still not above the understanding of the common people. In the second place, he minimized the falsification of authentic history by twisting and reshaping some of the folk tales worked into the mosaic of the romance so that they would embellish the main thread of the narrative but not contradict the official historical records. That he had exercised immense artistic restraint was obvious from the daring way in which he would delete portions of the popular version which bordered upon the miraculous and superstitious. Some students have felt justified in calling him a mere editor or redactor. While these labels may be justified on certain grounds, it may be more nearly accurate to call him a recreator.

According to the earliest version of the *Three Kingdoms* story root preserved today, the scaffolding of the story was erected upon the theme of retribution. The disintegration of the Han Empire into three separate kingdoms had been, according to folk interpretation, the result of the great injustice done to three supporters and co-founders of the empire; and the reunification of the three kingdoms into the Tsin Empire was the reward of heaven to the Ssu-ma clan, one of whose ancestors had been unswervingly just in his administration of the law. The first drastic change introduced by Lo Kuanchung was the scrapping of this piece of retribution. Besides purging the work of all its elements of primitive and childish folk concepts of reward and punishment, he eliminated all minor episodes which did not tally with history and utilized many incidents in the authentic history of the period which had not been made use of in the folk narrations.

Lo's genius as a storyteller is especially noticeable in the pains which he took in selecting incidents capable of dramatization and in magnifying them manyfold with new embellishments for full artistic effect.

One of the best-loved episodes in the historical romance was how Liu Pei, also known by his courtesy name Liu Hsüan-tê, the hero among heroes who was reigning as the King of Shu, in his great eagerness to avail himself of the great wisdom of a hermit scholar, Chu-ko Liang, took the trouble to call on the latter in his thatchroofed hut three times. During the third visit to the Sleeping Dragon's (the hermit's nickname) retreat he waited a long time for the return of his host. No impatience was shown by the caller while he was exchanging remarks with the younger brother of the host, Chu-ko Chün, although his short-tempered companion, Chang Fei, saw no point in prolonging the waiting. The following passage presents the various characters with sustained realism:

"What forthright poor luck have I had!" exclaimed Liu Hsüan-tê. "Twice have I failed to meet the great virtuous man."

"Please sit down for a while," replied [Chu-ko] Chün, "so that I may offer you a cup of tea."

"Since the master is not home, Elder Brother," said Chang Fei, "please mount and let's be on our way."

"As I am already here," said Hsüan-tê, "why should I leave now without having exchanged a single word with him?"

Thereupon he asked Chu-ko Chün, "I have heard that your elder brother, Master Sleeping Dragon, is extremely learned in military tactics and strategy, studying the classics on war every day. Can you tell me a little more about him on that score?"

"I don't know," Chün replied.

"Why bother to ask him at all," said Chang Fei. "The snowstorm is getting worse and worse; we had better go home quick."

Hsüan-tê ordered him sternly to stop gabbling.

"Since my elder brother isn't home," Chün said, "I dare not detain you any longer. In a few days, I shall return your call."

"How dare I to expect such courtesy from you, sir," replied Hsüan-tê. "I myself will call again before long. I wish you would lend me writing brush and paper so I might leave a note for your elder brother, telling him how earnest and eager I am [to meet him].

Chün then produced the four treasures [of a scholar's studio]. Hsüan-tê thawed the frozen ink on the ink-slab with his warm breath, spread out the nice sheet of paper, and wrote. . . .

.   .   .   .   .   .

The letter now written and handed to Chu-ko Chün, Hsüan-tê bowed and took his leave. Chün escorted him out and repeatedly urged him to take good care of himself. As soon as Hsüan-tê had mounted and was ready to go, he saw the houseboy waving his hand outside the hedge, yelling, "Here comes the old master!"

Hsüan-tê looked up, and saw a man wearing a winter hat and fur coat, riding a donkey west of the bridge, and jogging along on the snow-covered path. Following him on foot was a youngster in green, holding a gourd of wine. As the donkey rider crossed the bridge, he began to hum a song.

.   .   .   .   .   .

On hearing the song, Hsüan-tê assured himself, "Now this is the real Sleeping Dragon!" Then he hurriedly slipped out of the saddle and dismounted. Stepping forward, he saluted the man and said, "Master, it must have not been easy to ride through this cold wind. My companion and I have been waiting for you a long time." That man dismounted in a hurry to return the courtesies. Chu-ko Chün, standing behind him, said to Hsüan-tê, "This is not my elder brother the Sleeping Dragon, but his father-in-law Huang Ch'êng-yen."

(Chapter 37)

Although Lo's attainments were high in his remodeling of historical romances, he must have felt hampered by the limitations imposed on him by the very nature of that type of work. Circumscribed by considerations of historical authenticity, his genius could not enjoy unlimitedly free play in his creative work. Moreover, the large time scope comprehended in historical romances must have also been a hindrance to him. Thus, he looked with greater eagerness to a related field, that of narratives built around semihistorical heroes projected against the backdrop of authentic history. Lo's masterpiece in this category is the *Shui Hu Chuan* or *Water Margin*, which he modestly disclaimed as his own. On the title page of the earliest extant copy of this semihistorical romance are printed in bold type the following characters: "The True Edition of Shih Nai-an of Ch'ien T'ang, edited by Lo Kuan-chung." We have no information whatsoever as to who Shih Nai-an was nor whether he was a contemporary of Lo's. It is possible that Shih's original work was an unpublished manuscript since there was no mention at all of the work in printed form prior to the appearance of Lo Kuan-chung's edition. We are also uncertain as to Lo's contribution to the edition as editor. From the style of the prose of the 115-chapter edition, which is current today, even a casual reader can detect the similarity of its style to the *Three Kingdoms* romance, so that we are justified in crediting Lo with the rewriting of the original. The many editions of this novel which are now currently circulating are traceable to two early versions, one full and one brief. Pending the rediscovery of the original Lo edition, we are tempted to conclude that the fuller edition published during the reign of Chia Ching of the Ming Dynasty (1522-1566) was of a later date of compilation and revision than the brief version which, despite evidences of emendations, bears greater resemblance to the Lo original. The prose style of the *Water Margin* is obviously more developed than that of the *Romance of the Three Kingdoms*, representing a compromise between the vernacular and the classical. Nonetheless, Lo's characteristic of expending more space on narration than on description and characterization is common to both works. In the presentation of characters, however, Lo's technique had apparently progressed, as his characters are more fraught with liveliness and individuality and the arrangement of details in narration was done with a keener eye upon artistic effect. The following passage is a typical illustration:

Let us now return to the people of the Clear Wind Village and see how they had been making preparations for lighting their lanterns in celebration of the First Full Moon festival. With the money collected from each family and other donations for the occasion, they had erected in front of the Temple of the Great-God-of-Earth a bamboo scaffolding in the shape of the Sea Turtle Hill. On it were flower decorations and colored ribbons, besides some five or seven hundred flower lanterns hanging here and there. Inside the temple gates, there were various kinds of fireworks contests in the open yard. In front of every house there was a frame-like awning from which floral lanterns were hung to compete with those of the neighbors. In the streets could be found all sorts of amusements and entertainments. Even though it could not compare with the imperial capital, it was nonetheless a little bit of heaven on earth in the eyes of the inhabitants.

At that moment Sung Chiang was drinking wine with Hua Jung in the stockade in celebration of the feast. The day had been sunny and clear. About two hours before noon, Hua Jung mounted his horse and went to his office where he selected several hundred soldiers to keep peace and order in the village that night. Besides these, he also appointed numerous other soldiers to guard the different gates of the stockade. Two hours after midday, he returned to the stockade and invited Sung Chiang over for some light refreshments.

"I have heard that tonight this village is going to celebrate the lantern festival," said Sung Chiang to Hua Jung, "I am eager to go out and take a look."

"I have meant to accompany you, Elder Brother," answered Hua Jung, "but I have my official duties to attend to, and won't be able to take a stroll with you. You will please go see the lanterns with two or three members of my household, and come back early. I shall be waiting for you at home, and we shall drink three cups to celebrate this fine festival."

Sung Chiang said, "Superb!"

Soon the sky was dark, and on the east the bright full moon was beginning to rise. Sung Chiang and the two or three household men of Hua Jung's family walked out leisurely in a group. When they arrived at the market place of the Clear Wind Village to admire the lanterns, they found lantern awnings in front of all houses and flower lanterns hanging everywhere. Some of the lanterns were decorated with pictures from famous stories, others with pasted-on or cut-out figures and patterns. Still others were shaped like peonies, hibiscus or lotus flowers, and in other odd forms and motifs.

Thus walking hand in hand, the three or four of them came to the Temple of the Great-God-of-Earth, where they looked around for a while in front of the Sea Turtle Hill scaffolding and then followed a winding road to the south. After no more than five or seven hundred paces, they saw a cluster of dazzling lights ahead of them, and a crowd surrounding a gate to a walled court, enjoying something exciting. Responding to the sounds of a gong, the crowd noisily shouted approval.

After taking a look, Sung Chiang knew it was a troupe playing the popular dance-farce of "Pao Lao" [in which the masked actors would dance around barefoot and periodically emit small fireworks through the mouth openings of their masks]. Sung Chiang was short in stature and could not see well, standing behind other spectators. One of his companions, however, happened to know the man in charge of the festival entertainments, and so he requested the latter to tell the crowd to yield room so that Sung Chiang could see the play.

The principal actor playing the role of Pao Lao twisted his body in a rustic and artificial manner, and Sung Chiang, seeing him, laughed a hearty and prolonged laugh.

Now it happened that inside the courtyard, Magistrate Liu, his wife, and several other women were also watching the show. The moment the magistrate's wife heard Sung Chiang's laughter, she recognized him at once under lantern light. She pointed him out to her husband and said: "Look! that black, short fellow who is laughing—he is the chief of the robbers who seized me the other day on Clear Wind Hill!"

(Chapter 32)

This type of narrative art is a long step forward from similar passages in the *Romance of the Three Kingdoms*. This same episode in the Chia Ching edition is presented with greater sophistication and finer rhetoric but yet retains the basic technique of the brief version. We feel fully justified, therefore, in believing that Lo should be regarded at least as the coauthor with Shih Nai-an of this immortal semihistoric romance.

Lo's other writings in the field of historical or semihistorical romances have been so radically revised by later hands that it is unfair to pass judgment on his merits as a novelist on the basis of these. For example the trilogy of *Shuo T'ang Chuan,* or the *Popular History of the T'ang Dynasty,* is at best either a new edition of an old manuscript brought out by Lo Kuan-chung or a later radical revision of Lo's own writing.

Probably it was in the writing of *P'ing Yao Chuan* or the *Story of the Subjugation of the Evil Phantoms* that the author derived most delight, in spite of the fact that readers of his own time were probably much more fascinated by prose fiction dealing with historical events. Like all other early Chinese novels, this romance has two versions, a brief one with twenty chapters representing the original; and a fuller version with forty chapters revised and "supplemented" by a much later writer—Fêng Mêng-lung (died 1645)—of the end of the Ming Dynasty, an addition in which the original version was completely defaced.

The brief version, probably representing Lo's original handiwork with few emendations, tells of the strange experiences of an entirely fictitious character, Hu Hao of the County of Pien or K'aifeng. After he had obtained a painting done by an immortal fairy, he showed it to his wife who, failing to appreciate the art piece, decided to reduce it to ashes. While the painting was being burned its ashes circled around her body for long before they fell onto the ground. Soon afterward she gave birth to a daughter, Yung Erh. When the latter grew up she met the phantom spirit of a fox presenting itself as Miss Sheng or Holy and learned from her certain forms of magic for turning paper figures into human beings and bees into horses. She was married to Wang Tsê, destined in folklore to receive in a few years the mandate of heaven. With numerous individuals coming to him repeatedly to urge him to fulfill the mandate of heaven, he hoisted the banner of rebellion and Wên Yen-po was nominated by the imperial dynasty as commander-in-chief to suppress the rebellion. While Wên (1006-1097) is a real historical character, all other personages and incidents are fictitious. From this point on the narrative grows in complexity and in interest with the unfolding of the contest between the two groups in the utilization of all possible magical formulas. Interest of the readers keeps mounting with each introduction of the unexpected, and the denouement with the capture of the rebel and his collaborating wife is rapid and decisive.

As a literary milestone, Lo Kuan-chung's significance is not to be minimized. He was to see no successors for over two centuries, partly because he had so clearly outdistanced his contemporaries that competition seemed unrewarding and partly because the storyteller's art was eclipsed by the expanding development and influence of the drama and the attraction of its cousins, the shadow play and the puppet play. The populace enjoying its holiday at an amusement center on festival days would naturally feel more attracted to theatrical performances than to the lectern of a storyteller. This made it necessary for the storyteller's art to seek retreat onto the bookshelf, thus accounting for the increased volume in printing of novels and romances on inexpensive paper casually bound in broché. As literacy was still the acquirement of but a small percentage of the Chinese population, such publications were scarcely profitable. Hence, the poor engraving of the printing block and the creeping in of misspellings and misprints in books of fiction was a normal phenomenon leading directly to the alarming loss of literature of this type, and to the complete disregard of them by book collectors and bibliographers.

After the passing of Lo Kuan-chung, Chinese prose fiction written by the scholar for the common people and utilizing the language of folktales for literary creation was destined to experience a long lull before it was again revitalized.

CHAPTER 25

From Hua-Pên *to Novel*

THE evolution of *p'ing hua* seems to have paralleled the development of southern drama. Both types of literature appealing to the populace began making their appearance during the Sung Dynasty (960-1279). Both reached their zenith in the sixteenth and seventeenth centuries and gradually declined after the establishment of the Manchu Dynasty, which made it an overt policy to sponsor research scholarship and classicism—even antiquarianism—in creative writing. Whereas southern romance was continually sponsored by outstanding men of letters, the *p'ing hua* type of fiction, usually written in the plainest type of vernacular, remained the main attraction to the common people of Chinese society with the result that even outstanding compositions were largely published anonymously. The origins of this type of popular fiction were diverse, some of the plots being taken from the story-root notebooks of professional storytellers of Sung times. Other plots were more original in that they had been built up by contemporary storytellers with all the characters and incidents woven out of pure imagination. Their contents are likewise varied, with a considerable number of them continuing the ancient tradition in China of using historical incidents, expounding the obscure meanings of classical texts by use of appropriate narratives, or elaborating the obscure doctrines of religious scriptures. Although these narrative prose pieces were usually short they were all attempts to tell a rather complicated story in a compact manner. Each one could be expanded enormously to the length of a full-fledged novel; hence this type was distinctly different from the short story in modern Western literature, in which only one episode or the mood of one personality is intensely developed to the exclusion of all else in a manner almost worthy of Maupassant or O. Henry.

In its external form the *p'ing hua* of the Ming Dynasty retained all the formalities of its Sung predecessor. At the beginning of each piece there was usually a prologue in which was briefly summarized a well-known story analogous in meaning to the main tale which followed it. It was in the prologue that the moral of the piece was either subtly hinted at or elaborately pointed out.

These stories, revised freely each time they were retold, were best known in their collected forms. Of these collections, the best known are the *Three Yen* and the *Two P'ai*. The *Three Yen* are actually three collections of such stories under three titles in each of which is found the Chinese word *yen* meaning "speech" or "words": (1) the *Yü Shih Ming Yen* (literally, "illuminating world, clear words," i.e., *Clear Words to Illuminate the World*), (2) *Ching Shih T'ung Yen* ("warning world, ordinary words"), and (3) *Hsing Shih Hêng Yen* ("awakening world, plain words"). Similarly, the *Two P'ai* are two collections with titles containing the word *p'ai*, meaning "slap": (1) *P'ai An Ching Ch'i* ("slap table, surprised by the strange"), and (2) also called *P'ai An Ching Ch'i*, Second Series, because the new compiler was so elated over the success of the first series that a new title seemed superfluous.

The *Three Yen* collections were made by an extremely unconventional Chinese writer who deliberately disregarded traditional literary trends and dedicated himself to the writing of popular songs of the *ch'ü* type. Fêng Mêng-lung (died 1645), native of present-day Soochow, deserves our gratitude for the labors he undertook to collect these popular stories for posterity.

The first Yen—*Yü Shih Ming Yen*—according to Fêng's own preface, was a selection of twenty-four tales out of a previously published but obscure collection consisting of several tens of such narratives originally entitled *Ku Chin Hsiao Shuo,* or *Prose Fiction, Ancient and Modern,* published by Lü T'ien Kuan or "Green Heaven Studio." Since the character indicating the number of sets of tens is missing we don't know the exact number of stories included in this anthology. At any rate we were told by Fêng that the circulation of the original anthology was not wide. It was in view of this that he decided to edit those tales which appealed to him most for inclusion in a new edition under a new title in which he intended to bring out the tales that were not only easy to understand but edifying in character.

The second series, also edited by Fêng, was a collection of forty stories, and the third series contained tales of a similar number. The second series was preserved intact only in libraries in Japan, having failed entirely to attract the attention of book collectors in China. This fact is indicative of the lack of attention given by traditional Chinese scholars to popular fiction. The third series apparently suffered the same fate in China. In these three outstanding collections of short prose fiction there were no new compositions by the compiler. In spite of the fact that all three collections were soon forgotten by critics and book collectors as well as literary historians, they did exert considerable influence in China while the printings were still in circulation in the 1620's. While Fêng did not try his hand at creative writings of this type, his painstaking care in circulating the three collections did arouse considerable interest in the type by late Ming writers of an unconventional turn of mind.

Among these story writers who purposely followed the lead of folk taste was the author of the two *P'ai* collections, Ling Mêng-ch'u (1584?-1644). Like Fêng Mêng-lung, Ling was also a noted author of southern drama and known for his interest in the reprinting of outstanding titles in literature. In his two collections of thirty-six and thirty-nine stories respectively he not only preserved meritorious narratives from T'ang times but also wrote numerous tales of his own. In many of the tales that he himself had written, Ling daringly exposed the sophistication and unscrupulousness of contemporary social life.

Although the impact of these five collections was immense, there being numerous collections published in the 1620's and 1630's in imitation of the prototype, the flowering of these short prose tales was extremely short-lived. As many of the tales were written in surprisingly realistic manner, local bureaucrats in different parts of China saw fit to impose a censorship of their own initiation and put many of the collections on the index. As far as the Chinese reading public was concerned, prior to their reproduction in recent years, the *p'ing hua* as a type had almost completely fallen into desuetude. The only remnant of this great vogue was a collection of forty of what had been regarded as the less objectionable and more edifying tales known as the *Chin Ku Ch'i Kuan* or *Wonderful Sights, Ancient and Modern*. Even this digest of digests was published under the pseudonym of Pao Wêng Lao Jên (literally, "hugging jar old man"). We have no information as to who this old man hugging the jar was or when he lived. Posterity is grateful to him, however, for preserving forty of the hundreds of *p'ing hua* tales.

While these shorter pieces of prose fiction were being popularized by a rapid succession of anthologies and by concerted attempts made in the early seventeenth century to propagate the type, longer fiction was being continued, prolonging tradition on one hand and exploring new possibilities on the other.

It is pertinent to observe that sustained prose fiction in China had, from the early Sung Dynasty, deviated from the prose romances and anecdotal literature of the Six Dynasties and of T'ang authorship by resolutely adopting the language of the common people as its sole medium of expression. T'ang and pre-T'ang anecdotes and romances, which might be described collectively as literary diversions written by the literati for the literati, had held onto the style of classical prose and therefore had made relatively little appeal to the general reading public. Taking its inspiration from the living art of the story-teller, long fiction was not only unconsciously competing with the technique and art of professional storytellers in public squares but also consciously perpetuated that style to conform to the taste of the meagerly educated.

Once prose fiction of the *chang hui* type—that is, "chapter division" type—had established itself, two clear tendencies of further development were soon obvious with regard to the choice of subject matter.

A fiction writer might decide to revert to perennial type by sticking to the pattern set for him by his predecessors in the professional storytelling field, of capitalizing on history, legend, or folk tale for subject matter and giving the theme of his choice an imaginative treatment in regard to details and supporting characters. This technique was to become a tradition unique in Chinese literary history—to tell again and again the same complex of historical or folkloric events, depending on a common pool for inspiration and trying to satisfy listeners or readers by supplying main threads of narration with which they were familiar, then delighting them with occasional surprises in the form of little departures from the conventional mold. This explains why the various editions of a well-known novel vary so much not only in the number of chapters but also in huge parts of the contents, making it a most trying experience for the literary historian to single out any one edition as its definitive form. In fact, strictly speaking, there is no definitive edition to Chinese fiction of this type, there being only different editions or, at best, preferred editions according to individual tastes. This trend of redecorating and reinterpreting old tales the gist of which was known to practically every serious reader, uninteresting as it might seem at first sight, did present an intriguing challenge to fiction writers. Their primary concern was how to make old wine taste good in new bottles.

On the other hand, the resourcefulness of such writers as might respond to the challenge and the liberty which they might take in reshaping and even distorting historic versions of the narratives, sometimes even to the extent of inventing completely fictitious characters as principals and unfounded incidents at important turning points in the unfolding of the plot, were bound to reach their natural limits. The awareness of these limitations made other fiction writers mindful of the relatively unrewarding nature of writing historical fiction. This same awareness made them turn their attention to the possibility of building up long narratives entirely independent of history and folklore.

This second type of prose fiction, drawing principally on the novelist's imaginative powers and on contemporary social life and events, was developed at a relatively late date and at first primarily as an experiment (if not an afterthought), as compared with fiction of the traditional historical type. Once tried and found successful, however, the second trend not only rapidly increased in volume and influence but also attracted by far the great majority of creative writers, who warmly welcomed the opportunity of giving free rein to their imaginations. Both of these trends were continued down to literally yesterday in China. Although retelling of a well-known story or a cycle of stories in the form of a popularized dynastic history that has already been well told by fiction masters of the past has never been considered plagiarism, the latest samples of such traditional historical romances, those of the late nineteenth century, for example, are works satisfactory as to type but far from distinguished by the side of their great predecessors. In order to avoid the flatness of a historical narrative and often to obviate the requirements of delicacy in presention of recent or contemporary persons, some writers tried to benefit from both formulas of fiction writing by purposely mixing up the chronology or by presenting contemporary history heavily diluted with completely imaginative subplots and fictional names for the characters.

Having thus discerned the main currents in the development of fiction in China in the last eight or nine centuries, we shall analyze and summarize a few more pieces of distinguished fiction.

A romance of the late Ming Dynasty which closely rivals the *Romance of the Three Kingdoms* was *Hsi Yu Chi* or *Travels to the Western Regions,* written by Wu Chêng-ên (1500-1582), a native of Huai-an in northern Kiangsu Province. *Hsi Yu Chi,* translated into English by Arthur Waley as *The Monkey,* was based on numerous versions, historical as well as fictional, of the famous pilgrimage to India made by the eminent Chinese Buddhist monk, Hsüan Tsang (602-664). Some of these early sources were the *ch'uan ch'i* romances by numerous T'ang narrators, the *hua pên* by an anonymous writer of the Sung Dynasty, the northern play bearing the same title by Wu Ch'ang-ling of the Yüan Dynasty and above all, the "Western Travels" portion of a novel written by a senior contemporary of Wu's, Yang Chih-ho, in which the eminent monk was presented in his travels in all four directions. These previous attempts had furnished the distinguished novelist with the raw materials and the framework of his narrative, but it was his own literary genius that succeeded in instilling charm and life into the attractive fictional travels.

Wu's dedication to fiction writing in the vernacular did not come to him as the fruit of a sudden inspiration but rather as the culmination of a long process of intellectual and literary growth. His first attempt at storytelling was a conservative imitation of the great T'ang writers. In his preface to a now lost book of short stories written in the classical language, the author told an interesting story of his personal experience with and fondness for prose fiction. It is an important document in that it reveals an intimate picture of how fiction of any type was once universally frowned upon by members of the scholarly world.

I was very fond of strange stories when I was a child. In my village school days, I used to buy stealthily the popular novels and historical recitals. Fearing that my father and my teacher might punish me for this and rob me of those treasures, I carefully hid them in secret places where I could enjoy them unmolested.

As I grew older my love for strange stories became even stronger, and I learned of things stranger than what I had read in my childhood. When I was in my thirties, my memory was full of these stories accumulated through years of eager seeking.

I have always admired such writers of the T'ang Dynasty as Tuan Ch'êng-shih and Niu Sêng-ju, who wrote short stories so excellent in portrayal of men and description of things. I often had the ambition to write a book [of stories] which might be compared with theirs. But I was too lazy to write and as my laziness persisted I gradually forgot most of the stories which I had learned.

Now only these few stories, less than a score, have survived and have so successfully battled against my laziness that they are at last written down. Hence this *Book of Monsters*. I have sometimes laughingly said to myself that it is not I who have found these ghosts and monsters, but they, the monstrosities themselves, which have found me!

Although my book is called a *Book of Monsters*, it is not confined to them; it also records the strange things of the human world and sometimes conveys a little bit of moral lesson.

(Hu Shih's translation)

As Dr. Hu Shih has rightly observed:

All this he might have written of *The Monkey*, had he cared to write a preface to it under his own name. He had apparently grown dissatisfied with his monster stories composed in the classical style in imitation of the T'ang writers. At long last he decided to carry out his great literary ambition by writing a great book of monsters in the language of the "vulgar" literature of his time. But it was such a great disgrace for a man of literary reputation to produce a novel in the vulgar tongue that the story was published anonymously. And nothing in the two volumes of his collected writings gives the slightest hint of his connection with the book. Just as he in his early boyhood could only enjoy the novels and stories in secret hiding places, so he in his old age had to conceal the authorship of his great masterpiece in anonymity.

A little later in his introduction to Waley's *Monkey,* Hu Shih says again:

The literary evolution of Wu Ch'eng-en is typical of many an author of Chinese novels. He loved the vulgar novels in his boyhood; he went through his classical education and training and became ashamed of his boyish delights; he wrote his imitative poetry and prose in the classical style; he tried to write his stories in imitation of the story writers of T'ang and Sung; finally, in his mellow old age he took the bold step of producing his masterpiece in the language of the street and the market place and published it anonymously.

The anonymity of *Hsi Yu Chi* was so complete that for over three centuries the general reading public actually believed that the story was written by the Taoist patriarch, Chiu Ch'u-chi (1148-1227), who in 1219 was invited by Genghis Khan to visit him in Central Asia and who left a record of his travels under the title of *Hsi Yu Chi* which is still regarded today as a valuable contribution to the geographical knowledge of the time. In fact, when the first translation into English was made toward the end of the nineteenth century, the translator attributed it to Chiu the Taoist.

In this novel of a hundred chapters there are three rather uneven divisions. The first seven chapters present the story of the monkey, how he had been born of an egg-shaped rock, how he had traveled and studied under expert guidance to learn the seventy-two ways of transfiguration and to turn somersaults that would span 108,000 Chinese miles. Furthermore, the story is told of how he entered the Palace of the Dragon and secured the golden ring, a sacred relic from the days of King Yü who had controlled the grand deluge. As he was summoned heavenward, he was dissatisfied with the lowness of his official rank and started two major disturbances, but was finally subdued by the Buddha and was placed in confinement underneath the Mountain of the Five Elements. The second section, consisting of the next five chapters, was the story of Hsüan Tsang and the origin of his mission to India. The remainder of the book is an extended narration of Hsüan Tsang's pilgrimage to India. In eleven chapters (13-23) details are recorded of how the eminent Chinese pilgrim accepted his pupils, the monkey included. Thenceforth, the pilgrim and three of his pupils were to continue traveling for fourteen years in India, going through eighty-one major and minor trials before they reached India where they succeeded in collecting 355,048 scrolls of Buddhist sūtras with which they returned to China before their final attainment to Buddhahood.

This long novel is a lively and rapid-moving narration. In all the eighty-one episodes of trial and tribulation, no two are alike. Among the almost endless number of monsters, each had his unique individuality. As a sample of the good humor which abounds in this book, the following paragraphs as translated by Arthur Waley are typical:

> Monkey wished to detain the planet and give a banquet in his honor. But the planet would not stay; and they both set off together for the Southern Gate of Heaven. When the "monkey groom" was announced the Jade Emperor said, "Come forward, Monkey. I hereby proclaim you Great Sage, equal of Heaven. The rank is a high one, and I hope we shall have no more nonsense." The Monkey gave a great whoop of delight and thanked the Emperor profusely.
>
> Heavenly carpenters were ordered to build the office of the Great Sage to the right of the Peach Garden. It had two departments, one called Peace and Quiet and the other, Calm Spirit. In each were Immortal Officers who attended Monkey wherever he went. A star spirit was detailed to escort Monkey to his new quarters, and he was allowed a ration of two jars of Imperial wine and ten sprays of gold leaf flowers. He was begged not to allow himself to get in any way excited or start again on his pranks.
>
> As soon as he arrived, he opened both jars and invited everyone in his office to a feast. The star spirit went back to his own quarters, and Monkey, left to his own devices, lived in such perfect freedom and delight as in Earth or Heaven have never had their like.
>
> And if you do not know what happened in the end you must listen to what is told in the next chapter.

That the readers would invariably pursue the story from chapter to chapter was not only borne out by the extreme popularity of the *Hsi Yu Chi* itself but also by commentaries upon it from various angles as well as by many attempts to continue or supplement the original story. This latter group of continuations and supplements were varied in length and in merit. All of them did not measure up to the spontaneity and artistry of Wu. Of these, only one entitled *Hsi Yu Pu* deserves special mention. This work, which purported to be a supplement to *Hsi Yu Chi*, was written by Tung Shuo (1620-1686) of Chekiang Province. A child prodigy in an extremely well-to-do family, he was exposed to Buddhism before he studied the Confucian classics and achieved considerable success in the competitive literary examinations. During the reign of the last Ming emperor, Ch'ung Chêng (1628-1644), he had anticipated the imminent fall of the dynasty from astrological calculations in which he was also an expert. Thus realizing that the amassing of unwarranted wealth could not be justified, he liberally gave away his family fortune, including his large collection of precious gems and golden wares as well as stores of grains, for the benefit of the poor. After the Ming Empire had been overrun by the Manchus in 1644, he by-passed the new Manchu requirement imposed on the menfok of the vanquished Chinese to wear cues by having his head shaven clean in conformity with Buddhist practice. This was a prelude to his full ordainment as a Buddhist monk in his thirty-fourth year. Living from then on as a Buddhist recluse, he wrote poetry and recorded his meditations in the style of *Yü Lu*. His one great piece of creative work was a supplement to *The Monkey*.

This supplement, which contained sixteen chapters, was really an attempt to give an alternate ending to the original story. Detaching the last thirty-nine chapters from the main body of the original novel, he developed the story from chapter sixty-two on in his own manner. While the monkey was fasting he was led astray by a spell cast over him by the spirit of a mackerel and while he was spellbound, he was led into an illusory and phantom world created for his confusion by the mackerel. Going up and down the ages he had first thought of borrowing a huge bell from the first emperor of the Ch'in Dynasty with which to scare away a volcano. Before he had time to do that, however, he wandered into a tall storied building known as the Building of the Myriad Flowers in which he saw what had happened in the past as well as what was in store for the world in the future. At times he would find himself transformed into a beautiful woman playing the role of Lady Yü, who was celebrated in literature as the companion of the great warrior and aspirant to the imperial throne, General Hsiang Yü, who was defeated by the founder of the Han Dynasty.

On another occasion he saw himself transformed into the king of the Buddhist nether world. It was not until he was roused by the thunderous voice of the Lord of Vanity that his imaginative ventures came to an end and he was transported to the level of full enlightenment. Among the historical figures depicted was the famous medieval warrior, Yüeh Fei (1103-1141), who on account of his patriotism and brilliant victory over the northern Tatars had now become a national hero. By the use of homonyms, which were abundant in the language, Tung Shuo gave vent to his anti-Manchu feeling but escaped the atrocities of the literary inquisition under the Manchu regime by his clever use of a flowing and humorous style so that even his readers might have been deceived as to his more serious intentions.

Another novel of similar character but utilizing a completely different set of historical materials, was *Hsi Yang Chi* or *A Record of Adventures into the Western Ocean,* a novel of adventure of a hundred chapters written by Lo Mao-têng (flourished during reign of Wan Li, 1573-1620). The novel was a fictionalization of the historic travels of the eunuch, Chêng Ho, who was sent abroad on special missions. Chêng Ho was a native of Yünnan and a follower of the Islamic faith, who was sent in 1405 by Emperor Yung Lo in search of his nephew whose throne he had usurped and who had been reported to be at large since the coup d'état of 1402. Leading an armada of more than sixty seaworthy ships built especially for the purpose, armed by 27,800 officers and men, he set sail from the Fukien coast on a grand tour of the countries in present-day Southeast and South Asia, announcing the establishment of a new dynasty and exacting vassalage from the rulers of countries he visited. Returning from his first mission two years and three months later, Chêng reported to the imperial court with such a glorious account and such booty in men and goods, including the chieftain of a Sumatran tribe, that the original target of the mission was gradually lost sight of and he was instructed to repeat the mission for six other times between 1408 to 1430 during the reigns of three emperors. He sailed as far as the northeast coast of Africa on his longest voyage.

Capitalizing upon this major overseas exploit of the early Ming Empire, the Buddhist novelist, while holding onto the basic sequence of historic facts and personalities, gave such free play to his imagination and fancy that his final achievement was a peculiar combination of *Gulliver's Travels* and *Robinson Crusoe*. According to the novelist, all the military victories scored by the leader of the expedition were blessed with the assistance of two supernatural figures, the Buddhist Abbot of the Bluish Peak and the Taoist deity, Chang the Heavenly Teacher. The first fifteen chapters of the novel in which were narrated the birth, the ordainment, and the miracles of the former as well as his contest and reconciliation with the latter, were completely devoid of historic fact.

From Chapter 15 on, the author presented a systematic itinerary followed by Chêng Ho into which were woven a huge admixture of fact and fiction. Each time the hero was in trouble in his attempts to carry out his plans and score his victories, he would be assisted by the two supernatural personages. Aside from reliance on unhampered imagination, Lo freely utilized the historic records of the expeditions as well as folk tales and anecdotal literature for accuracy of description as well as for general embellishment. While he fell short of Swift and Defoe as a writer, he succeeded in perpetuating his handiwork mainly because he was inspired by a resolution to advocate stronger national defense. As he pointed out in his own preface, the past glories of China's naval power contrasted sharply with the military weakness into which the empire had fallen in facing the menace of Japanese pirates and Manchu marauders.

While the novelists were fully exploiting the possibilities of the supernatural and the miraculous, attention to the realistic presentation of contemporary life was not totally lacking. Attempts were made to portray life in all its facets, unpleasant as well as pleasant, the ugly as well as the beautiful. The most outstanding composition of this latter type was the problematical *Chin P'ing Mei.*

This long work of a hundred chapters was written by an unknown hand. As it enjoyed great popularity and was unique in many respects, various conjectures were circulated regarding its authorship. The most popular among these was its attribution to a scholar of many-sided learning, Wang Shih-chêng (1526-1590). Although this conjecture has been proven to be definitely groundless, the details woven into the original hypothesis were so full of human interest that they deserve a summary.

It all began, according to the legend, with a famous water-color scroll presenting a panoramic view of the diverse activities of the people at the imperial capital of K'aifeng during the Sung Dynasty on a late spring festival, Ch'ing-ming—the Clear and Bright Festival —which corresponds roughly to Easter of the Western world. Painted by Chang Tsê-tuan before 1120 and purported to have been lost but continuing to be admired through its various early and later copies, it has been regarded as a prototype of a whole genre of panoramic paintings describing the daily life found in a metropolitan area. As copies increased in number and varied in quality with the lapse of time, it had become a mystery how and when the original had been lost. The question had also been raised whether it had been lost at all and whether or not the rumor of its loss had not been invented to protect the owner of the authentic original.

At any rate, Wang Shih-chêng's father, Wang Shu, was supposed to have owned this rare treasure, "Ch'ing-Ming Shang Ho T'u" or "Flocking to the River at Ch'ing-Ming Festival," known far and wide for its surpassing exquisiteness. Having heard of this, the corrupt but powerful prime minister, Yen Shih-fan (died 1565), demanded to see it and Wang Shu hired an expert copyist to make a reproduction, which he presented to the extorter. Yen felt so outraged that he decided to avenge himself. Capitalizing on Wang Shu's military reverses in fighting the Mongol invaders of the Yenta tribe, Yen instigated a censor to impeach Wang, resulting in the latter's imprisonment and execution. Although continuing the family feud, Wang Shih-chêng called on Yen one day and was asked by the latter if there were any unusual novels in the book market. Taking advantage of the situation Wang glanced around in the parlor and was struck by a golden vase holding clusters of plum blossoms, so he replied that there was a fascinating novel entitled *Golden Vessel Plum Flowers* but that the print was poor. He asked for a few days' leave to hire some scribes to make a clean copy which he would submit as a gift. After the visit, Wang elaborated a chapter from the *Shui Hu Chuan* (*Water Margin*) into a full-length novel. When the final copy was made he poisoned the corner of each page so that anyone who, like Yen, habitually turned the pages of a book with fingertips periodically wetted by his tongue would slowly poison himself. Wang's objective was attained.

This hypothesis of the authorship of the novel, interesting as a story, is no longer tenable. Even with the rediscovery of the satisfactorily printed 1617 edition all we know of the author was his nom de plume, Lan-ling Hsiao-Hsiao-shêng or the Laughing Laughing Student from Lan-ling. The Lan-ling part of the signature has been borne out by the peculiar dialect of the text, for Lan-ling is a county in Shantung Province and the vernacular Chinese used in the novel was clearly of the Shantung Province variety. This bit of evidence has the negative virtue of proving conclusively that the writer could not have been Wang Shih-chêng, whose native district was T'aits'ang, near Shanghai, where the *wu* dialect, far removed from the Shantung vernacular, prevailed, as it still does.

The title of the book, which on the surface can be interpreted to mean "plum blossoms in a golden vessel," was actually compounded of parts of the names of three feminine characters, namely, P'an *Chin*-lien ("P'an Golden Lily"), Li *P'ing*-erh (Li, "Little Vase"), and Ch'un-*mei* ("Spring Plum Blossom"). Of these three, only the first feminine character appeared in the semihistorical romance of the *Shui Hu Chuan* or *Water Margin*. In the twenty-second chapter of that novel, the story was narrated of how Wu Sung's sister-in-law, P'an Chin-lien, carried on an illicit love affair with the villain, Hsi-mên Ch'ing, how the two poisoned her husband, Wu Ta-lang, and finally how, to avenge the wrongs done to his elder brother, Wu Sung succeeded in killing off the shameful pair. Using this chapter of the older novel as framework, the unknown author built up a complicated story.

Hsi-mên Ch'ing, the villain who overshadows all other characters in the new novel, was a satanic character from the district of Ch'ingho who had built up and presided over an underworld. One day he was impressed with the beauty of P'an Chin-lien and persistently plotted to acquire her. After poisoning her husband, Wu Ta-lang, he married Chin-lien as a concubine. When Wu Sung came to his household to kill him a mistake was made and someone else was killed. From this point on, the villain became all the more extravagant in his debaucheries. In spite of his having several concubines, he made various amorous sorties wherever he went. He murdered his henchmen, Hua Tzu-hsün, and married the latter's wife,

Li P'ing-erh, as another concubine. He debauched one of his own slave girls, Ch'un-mei, and through her acquired some illegitimate wealth. His fortunes kept mounting. He had a son born to him by Li P'ing-erh so that he was now a proud father. Through bribery he acquired a military official title and was recognized not only for his wealth but also for his high social position.

Family intrigue then began to develop and he lost his only son as a result of the viciousness of Chin-lien. The son's mother, P'ing-erh, soon died of grief, and the villain himself also died suddenly as a result of his debauches. Chin-lien was expelled by Hsi-mên's wife as she was caught in illicit amorous relations with her own son-in-law, and while she was living in refuge with a family of an old Mrs. Wang, she was slain by her husband's younger brother, Wu Sung. Thus two of the three feminine characters making up the title of the novel were now disposed of. The third, the former slave girl Ch'un-mei, was soon to be sold to a military commander, Colonel Chou, to be the latter's concubine. Finally, the Chin Tatar troups were descending upon the Sung Empire and Hsi-mên's legitimate wife, Yüeh-niang, or Madame Moon, fled from the Chin soldiers with her son, Hsiao-ko, who was born after Hsi-mên's death. While they were stopping at an inn in the city of Tsinan, she had a dream in which she saw the whole life of her wretched husband from birth to death with all the complexities of causal relations. On awakening, she came to the realization that her own son was none other than the reincarnation of Hsi-mên. For the redemption of the sins of his past life and for the benefit of his future, she prevailed upon her own boy to leave the world to become a Buddhist monk. Thus ends the biography of an incorrigible villain rising steadily as his villainy steadily increased.

Although the narrative was projected against the backdrop of the Sung Dynasty, this novel was the first attempt in Chinese fiction to depict realistically the temperament of the current age. In an extremely charming and persuasive style, the details of the political, social, economic, and psychological situation in sixteenth-century China were so faithfully portrayed that it could be read almost as a documentary social history of that age. An impressive array of representative characters at all levels of late Ming society was fully presented with photographic accuracy. Fearless in presenting all phases of contemporary life as it was, the author was unprecedentedly bold in delineating with exhaustive details all aspects of social degeneracy and personal corruption. As a result endless details of the principal characters' sexual perversions were gone into without reserve, surpassing even the most radical trends of French naturalistic fiction. For this reason, the novel has ever since its first appearance been deprecated as pornography. As Arthur Waley has pointed out:

The Ming code contains no injunction against such fiction (i.e., "licentious fiction") chiefly no doubt because until well into the Ming Dynasty fiction had not advanced beyond the very elementary stage. But Confucianism was, especially since the Sung Dynasty, a Puritanical and aesthetic creed, teaching that man's only spiritual concern should be the restoration of his Natural State (*hsing-ming*), the primary beauty of which is marred by every stirring of the appetites or emotions. Now Confucianism, with whatever impatience it may at various periods have been regarded at court, was always during the period in question the official creed of the bureaucracy; and the fact that at the time when the Chin P'ing Mei was written and for a hundred years afterwards licentious novels were permitted, does not mean that the government during this period took a lenient view of this sort of fiction or indeed of fiction in general. It merely means that during the close of the Ming Dynasty the popular development of the novel was too new a thing to attract the attention of the Government.

(Introduction to Miall and Kuhn's English translation)

In spite of the lack of an official ban against the *Chin P'ing Mei,* popular opinion had no doubt been averse to it. For this reason copies of the first edition of 1610 soon were completely destroyed and few copies of the second edition of 1617 are extant. Moreover, a legend came into circulation that the publishers of the novel in Soochow and Yangchow had met with major catastrophes resulting in the total destruction of the blocks from which the novel was printed. On the other hand, public censure on this title fell short of its objective and led to a mutilation of the original in two different ways: expurgated editions, and purposely corrupted editions in which the spicy passages were rewritten and magnified in their filthier aspects.

As an illustration of the care with which contemporary life was recorded, the following passage presents the villain, Hsi-Mên, calling upon the chancellor before acquiring an official title:

The Chancellor gave a sign to those about him to bring a chair for Hsi-Mên, and invited him to take a seat, which he did, with a bow. While he was offered tea, Ti hastily ran to the entrance, and gave a sign to the porters, who were waiting outside with the gifts. Now they appeared with their twenty loads, opened the woven bast cases, and laid out the treasures contained in them before the dais on which the Chancellor was seated. Here were piles of magnificent garments and bales of cloth, sparkling golden goblets, gleaming jade beakers, ten great pearls, splendid jade girdles, and the yellow glitter of two hundred ounces of gold ingots.

The Chancellor, with the list of presents in his hands, regarded with satisfaction the treasures heaped up before him, deigned to utter a brief word of thanks, and graciously commanded his intendant to have the presents taken to the treasury. He also, as a mark of distinction, had wine set before the donor. But Hsi Mên knew that it was not fitting that he should linger, since the Chancellor was expecting many more visitors. So he contented himself with sipping the wine as a matter of form; then he rose and begged leave to withdraw.

(Miall and Kuhn's translation)

Equally realistic is the description of Hsi-Mên's ecstasy on the birth of his son by his sixth wife. After the midwife had been rewarded with five ounces of silver she was also invited to attend the feast in celebration of the washing of the newborn child:

Now he [Hsi Mên] himself went at last to the mother's bedside, in order to inquire into the welfare of his wife and child. His delight in the beautifully formed little creature, who was distinguished by an exceptionally fair complexion, was boundless. He spent the whole night in the pavilion of the Sixth, and was never weary of gazing at the child.

Early the next morning servants were dispatched in all directions to publish the joyful news to kinsfolk and neighbors. For this reason they had to distribute no less than twenty ceremonial boxes of noodles. The first visitors to present their congratulations, covering two full paces at every stride, were Beggar Ying and Hsia Hsi Ta. Hsi Mên shared a dish of "long life noodles" with them in the belvedere; then he sent them away. That day there were all sorts of things to be seen to. Above all, a suitable wet-nurse had to be engaged. She was soon found. The wife of Neighbor Pi brought to the house the young wife of a servant of hers. She had lost her child a month earlier, and now her husband, who had been enrolled for military service, had to leave her and proceed to the front. Moon Lady took a fancy to this strongly-built, neatly dressed young woman of thirty, so she bought her from her neighbor for the price at which she was offered—namely, six ounces—and established her in Mistress Ping's pavilion, where she was to feed the child night and morning. She was given the name of Ju I—"As you like it."

(Miall and Kuhn's translation)

The popularity of *Chin P'ing Mei* is well attested by the numerous imitations called forth. As these were as a whole far inferior to the original and greatly more licentious in content, they produced a reaction in the form of love stories of another type in which were depicted what might be regarded as ideal love matches. In these, the hero was usually virtuous and talented and the heroine incorruptible and beautiful. Of these a typical example was the *Hao Ch'iu Chuan* or *The Story of an Ideal Marriage,* the first Chinese novel to be translated in abbreviated form into any European language. Based on a fragmentary translation in part in English and in part in Portuguese brought back to England in 1719 by a trader whose name was Wilkinson, Thomas Percy edited the manuscript in 1761 and had it published as *Hau Kiu Chuan* or *The Fortunate*

Union. This in turn was translated into many other European languages and attracted the attention of Goethe and Schiller.

Like numerous other novels of this type which were published either anonymously or pseudonymously, the *Hao Ch'iu Chuan* was attributed to a certain Ming Chiao Chung Jen or "A Follower of Orthodox Confucianism." In eighteen chapters the story was told of a handsome, righteous, and learned scholar, T'ieh Chung-yü, a native of Taming Prefecture in Chihli Province, the son of T'ieh Ying, a member of the imperial censorate. As the father had offended many high-ranking officials by his forthrightness in carrying out his duty of impeachment, the hero decided to proceed to the capital to urge his father to temper his impeachment documents. After righting various social wrongs on his way he went on to the neighboring province of Shantung as a wandering scholar. In the capital of that province, there was living in retirement a vice-minister of the Board of War, Shui Chü-yi, who was living a simple life with his only child, a daughter named Ping-hsin, noted for her beauty, learning, and practical wisdom. A fellow townsman, Kuo Ch'i-tsu, capitalizing on the political influence of his father who was a prime minister at court, had repeatedly asked for her hand in marriage but had been repeatedly rejected. In desperation a decree was counterfeited ordering the marriage, but the plot was exposed by the hero, who had just arrived from the imperial capital.

After this incident the heroine gradually developed an admiration and love for the hero. Very soon he was taken seriously ill and was nursed back to health by Ping-hsin. The Prime Minister, at the instigation of his son, memorialized the throne on the irregularity of conduct between the virtuous pair. After various tests to which the hero and heroine were submitted, they were vindicated and were formally wedded with the emperor's special approval.

The characterization and description are less stereotyped among novels of this class because the hero was represented as more than a bookworm and the heroine instead of being a sickly beauty was talented in letters and seasoned in the ways of the world. Although the tough-minded type of realistic description in which the uglier aspects of nature and human nature are delineated with photographic detail, if not enlargements, is not resorted to, there is usually a sufficient portrayal of the social usages and mores of the Chinese people to make a novel of this category interesting to foreign readers.

It was no coincidence that after the Thomas Percy translation of 1761 in which many passages of the original had been left out untranslated, a new translation was made from the Chinese original by

John Francis Davis under the title of *The Fortunate Union* in 1829 and a similar one was done in French by M. Guillard d'Arcy in 1842. Besides these there were at least four other translations into English in the latter part of the nineteenth century, some complete and some hardly going beyond the first chapter. In 1925 a new rendering into French was undertaken by George Soulié de Morant under the title *La Brise au Clair de Lune,* which was translated into English the following year as *The Breeze and Moonlight.*

Another novel of this type similarly enjoyed by Chinese and Western readers was *Yü Chiao Li.* Like the *Hao Ch'iu Chuan,* the *Yü Chiao Li,* sometimes retitled *The Strange Romance of the Beautiful Pair,* was a late Ming novel by an unknown hand. According to an early edition preserved in Japan, the nom de plume of the author was Ti Ch'iu Shan-Jen or "A Wanderer Among Autumn Weeds." The story was projected into the reign of Chêng T'ung (1436-1449). A minister at the imperial court, Po Hsüan, who was approaching old age, found solace in his only child, a daughter named Hung-Yü—which means Red Jade, a beautiful poetess. A member of the Board of Censors, Yang T'ing-chao, had expressed an interest in having the girl as his daughter-in-law. Since the proposed marriage alliance seemed worthy of approval, the young man, Yang Fang, was invited to parties so that Minister Po could have the literary attainments of the young man tested by the girl's maternal uncle, who was a member of the Hanlin Academy. Young Fang failed the tests miserably and the negotiations were broken off. Meanwhile a Mongol tribe had invaded the northern border and the emperor, who had personally led an expedition against the invaders, was disastrously routed and carried off as a prisoner of war in the autumn of 1449. After negotiation for a whole year the captors agreed to return the emperor whose throne now, however, was occupied by his younger brother. Harboring a deep-seated hatred against the father of the gifted girl, censor Yang decided to avenge his loss of face by recommending that Minister Po Hsüan head a delegation into Mongolia to complete negotiations for the redemption of the temporarily deposed emperor. Preparing for the difficult mission and his possible failure, Minister Po entrusted his daughter to the care of her maternal uncle who saw fit to take her south to her home town, Nanking.

In their travels, the uncle had read a beautiful poem written on a wall of the hotel room with the signature Su Yu-pai and was so fascinated by it that he took the trouble to locate the poet through a middleman and offered his niece in marriage. The proposal was declined. Angered, the uncle, Wu Kuei, exerted his influence upon the superintendent of higher studies and deprived the haughty young poet of his scholarship.

After losing his scholarship, Su Yu-pai decided to continue his studies in Peking where an uncle of his was holding office. On his way to Peking he ran into a company of several young scholars tearing their hair in a desperate attempt to write poems on the subject of new willows by using the end-rhymes of a poem already completed and signed by Po Hung-yü. Su was pleasantly surprised to find that attached to the signature of the poem was a postscript saying that whatever young man met the requirements of the challenge with greatest satisfaction would automatically win her hand, without realizing that it was the same girl he had rejected unwittingly, thanks to the statements of the matchmaker. The more he read the poem the more he admired the poetess. Offhand, he wrote two poems in response. These were picked up by two worthless scholars who presented the poems as their own and tried to claim the poetess in marriage. The plagiarism was easily exposed on account of mutual accusations and the farce ended to the amusement of all except the plagiarists themselves. Meanwhile Su tried to locate the poetess, but she had not revealed her family name and could not be found. As Su Yu-pai resumed his journey he met another young scholar, Liu Mêng-li, who soon became an intimate friend and entrusted his younger sister in betrothal to Su.

After the completion of his difficult mission, Minister Po Hsüan asked leave to travel southward to see his daughter. One day while wandering about admiring the scenic beauties in Chekiang incognito, he made the acquaintance of a young scholar in a monastery —a Mr. Liu Mêng-li—who was so impressive and peerless in appearance and in literary gifts that he felt sure the young scholar would immediately rise to great distinction. Perplexed for a while as to whether the young man should espouse his own daughter or an orphaned niece, both of whom were of marriageable age, the minister cut the Gordian knot by resorting to an accepted Chinese usage of proposing to give both in marriage.

The reputation of Su Yu-pai had made such a lasting impression on the two girls that they both felt exasperated when they were informed of a marriage proposal to an unknown man. The whole situation happily resolved itself when Mr. Liu called to reveal that he was none other than Su Yu-pai and to discover to his great surprise that the young scholar whom he had met as Liu Mêng-li had actually been a girl in disguise—the orphaned niece of the minister—doing her own proposing.

Translated into French by Jean Rémusat in 1826, this novel was widely read and admired in Europe. Not only were retranslations made into English and Dutch from the French but the story in one medium or another attracted the attention of many an eminent European writer. Goethe spoke of it approvingly and Carlyle was so enthusiastic that he wrote penciled comments on the margin of a copy loaned him by Leigh Hunt.

These full-length novels, which made their appearance in large numbers in the latter part of the Ming Dynasty, were no mean literary attainments. To contemporaries, however, including the authors themselves, they did not constitute contributions to the main currents of the literature of the age. For one thing, they were all written in the daily speech of the ordinary people which had drifted far away from the standards of the classical language. The contents, in addition, had nothing to do with the direct elucidation of China's cultural orthodoxy in spite of the fact that most of the authors had meant to produce an edifying effect, if not in delineation of details and the presentation of minor episodes, at least in the basic observance of poetic justice. Nonetheless, they were so diffident of the reception their handiwork might receive that none of the authors had dared to identify themselves publicly.

CHAPTER 26

Ming Prose and Poetry

As COMPARED with previous dynasties, the Ming period (1368-1644) in Chinese literary development has certain peculiarities of its own. In the first place, publishing activities began to flourish so that not only were writings of secondary importance now preserved in print but also obscure manuscripts handed down from previous periods were generously perpetuated for posterity. This was possible with the springing up of new centers of publication, especially in Szechuan and in Fukien where block-printing technique was developed with meticulous care. Texts began to appear all over China in which the basic reading was printed in black with comments and recommendations for textual changes superimposed in multiple colors. In the case of fiction and drama most of the printed copies were much more amply illustrated with full- or half-page woodcuts than during the Mongol Dynasty. This sudden progress in printing technique served as a most effective stimulus to writers of nearly all types of literature.

In the republication of older texts many works that would have been irrevocably lost were happily preserved. This credit, however, was vitiated by two malpractices on the part of the editors. In the first place, literary forgeries were probably more rampant than in any other period of Chinese cultural history. To satisfy the curiosity of a reading public obsessed with an interest in antiquarian literature, many lost works which had been recorded in bibliographies merely by title now confronted the readers with full texts. Of this nature are numerous Han and T'ang romances or popular utilizations of historical events and court intrigues, fabricated by Ming authors who were first-class writers and prominent book collectors in their own right. This reminds us of the temper of eighteenth-century Europe during the genesis of the romantic movement, in which the search for the long ago and far away succeeded in recapturing masterpieces of folk literature but also in nurturing some of the most outstanding literary forgeries.

This enthusiasm for preservation of the obscure works of literature also gave rise to the publication of works by different authors on widely varied subjects bundled together under the one generic name of *ts'ung-shu*, "collectanea." In these Ming collectanea are to be found many rare books of previous ages and of contemporary authors in far-off regions. While the contribution made to the diffusion of literature was great, the compilers often exercised prerogatives which were extremely doubtful. In the first place, many of the titles included were reprinted only in part without any kind of indication of omission or editorial emendation. In the second place, the original readings would be changed at random, again without indication. Once the practice was started by reputable scholars it was imitated by semiliterate publishers who went into the field mainly for profit.

In the case of poetry, many of the new renderings were disastrous and hardly fair to the original authors or readers. For example, one line of Sung poetry: "The banana plant shares its greenness with the window screen" was emended by an editor to read: "The banana plant divides its greenness and climbs up the window screen." Again, in the following line of a T'ang poem: "At autumn's end in Kiangnan, the grass has not withered" apparently the poet's idea was to suggest the mild climate south of the Yangtze River. But in the emended edition the line became, "At autumn's end in Kiangnan, the grass and trees wither." This type of license was, of course, directly due to the peculiar nature of the Chinese written language, in which one character could substitute for another without disturbing the rest of the text and in which one character easily could suggest another character that looked like it in construction. For example, the character for "not yet" (*wei*) with one stroke taken out would read "trees" (*mu*).

The craze for the publication of collectanea which dominated the literary scene in Ming times and continued with increased vigor to current times was started at the beginning of the dynasty by Yung Lo (reigned 1403-1424), the third emperor. Emperor Yung Lo, fourth son of the founder of the dynasty and born of a Korean mother, was a man of limitless energy. After he had occupied the throne in 1403 he not only led numerous military campaigns against the Mongols in the north but also championed the cause of the arts of peace in humanist ways. One of the monuments which he decided to erect to immortalize himself was the compilation of the greatest collectanea recorded in Chinese history, originally entitled *Wên-hsien Ta-ch'êng* but later changed to *Yung Lo Ta-tien* (*The Great Collectanea of Yung Lo*). The undertaking was begun in the seventh moon of the year 1403 and was not completed until the end of 1408. The editorial board, which had originally consisted of a hundred scholars, was expanded to over two thousand as the scheme in progress was to become more and more comprehensive and ambitious. When it was completed, it comprised 22,937 sections bound in 12,000 stitched volumes. It was so voluminous that the original plan of printing it had to be dropped. When the imperial capital was transferred from Nanking to Peking in 1421 the collectanea was moved northward to be housed in a special building. It was not until 1562 that two additional copies were made under the direction of a hundred scholars. When these were completed, about 1570, the original copy was returned to Nanking. At the time of the dynastic collapse in the 1640's, the Nanking copy and the second copy in Peking were completely destroyed. The first Peking copy was preserved intact until the sack of Peking by British and French troops in 1860.

This Yung Lo collectanea was important mainly because its editorial procedure was extremely crude. Instead of breaking up the contents of existing works of importance for reclassification, large subdivisions of each work were copied in full and arranged by the first word of the title in accordance with the scheme of the prevailing rhyming dictionary. Although the three copies were never widely circulated and had little influence on the learned world, it was known by reputation throughout the empire. Many works which were no longer available in any other form were thus carefully preserved for posterity. In the latter part of the eighteenth century, when another great attempt was made for full inventory of China's existing literature, a total of nearly five thousand separate works were salvaged from the Yung Lo collectanea. Not only were many valuable titles on the classics, history, and philosophy retrieved from its pages, but even many a Ming play which otherwise might have been completely lost.

Aided by publication facilities and by interest in the diffusion of literature, Ming writers were not only more numerous but also more prolific in their literary production. In terms of volume the records of the T'ang and Sung dynasties were completely shattered. The incomplete bibliography of the *Ming Dynastic History* alone records 949 titles in 8746 books (*chüan*) on the classics, 1316 titles in 28,051 books on history, 970 titles in 39,211 books on philosophy, and 1398 titles in 29,966 books in belles-lettres. These figures, however, are no guarantee of the quality of Ming writing. We have already mentioned that Ming authors were especially interested in forgeries, but forgery was not the greatest sin of the age. Plagiarism in extremely subtle forms seemed to have been a fairly common foible among

Ming writers. Many of the titles noted above were merely compilations without due acknowledgment, hence the exaggerated form of a statement of evalution to the effect that the securing of a hundred books of the Ming Dynasty may not be as rewarding as one book from Sung times.

Another literary phenomenon of the Ming Dynasty worth mentioning is the preparation and preservation of the so-called *Shih Lu* or *Veritable Records*. These records, a detailed day-to-day chronicling of the most important events and personalities of the empire, went back in origin to T'ang times. Although most of the earlier records of this type are now lost, the surviving specimens seem to indicate that the chronicling was extremely brief as compared with the Ming records which, discounting the gaps especially toward the end of the dynasty, number almost three thousand books. In these we find the full text of many of the lengthy and important memorials submitted to the throne as well as the lengthy decrees issued in response. With this tradition reverently kept until 1908, with a short accompaniment extending the records to the end of 1911, we have an impressive body of records of the Chinese Empire for over five centuries.

As is the case with government-sponsored literary activities, collaborative attempts mark another feature of Ming literary life. More fervently than in previous ages, Ming littérateurs were fond of organizing literary societies. While most of these societies were of a regional nature, many of them were nationwide in scope. It was under the sponsorship of such literary coteries that many literary movements and critical theories were espoused. Occasionally these organizations would sponsor political platforms and acquire the coloring of political factions, but most of them were of a purely literary nature. Their principal purpose was the study of literary technique in response to requirements set for competitive literary examinations.

These literary examinations were, of course, no innovations of the Ming Empire. Ever since the overthrow of the Ch'in Dynasty in 206 B.C. numerous efforts were made to seek out special talents in the empire for the recruitment of the civil service. We have noticed that in T'ang times such examinations were organized around regulated poetry as a nucleus. In Sung times, by way of reaction to T'ang usage, new emphasis was laid on the applicants' familiarity with the Confucian classics and the applicants were examined on their ability to write long exegetical essays on passages from the Confucian canon.

The innovation was introduced originally with a serious purpose by the great statesman-reformer, Wang An-shih, in 1071, in view of the inefficacy of the old system inherited from the T'ang Dynasty whereby the candidates for civil service had been examined and evaluated on their compositions in *shih* poetry and in *fu*. As he was not only prime minister and originator of the extensive reforms known as the "new deal" but also a leading figure in literature, he wrote a model essay which later on came to be regarded as the forerunner of a stereotyped essay form.

The title of the essay was lifted from the first chapter of the fourth book of the Confucian *Analects:*

> The Master said, "It is virtuous manners which constitute the excellence of a neighborhood. If a man, in selecting a residence, does not fix on one where such prevail, how can he be wise?"

Instead of writing on the whole chapter, he had singled out the first sentence as his topic, "It is virtuous manners which constitute the excellence of a neighborhood," or to be more literal to the Chinese original, "It is the humaneness of the neighborhood which makes it good and beautiful." In five brief paragraphs Wang tried to expound and exhaust the latent meanings of the Confucian saying.

> To do good and to be good one has to be careful of what he gets accustomed to and it follows that he should be selective in planning where to live. Goodness rests inherently in one's self. What can others do to diminish it? The reason for which a superior man makes a special point of selecting his abode is the care with which he plans his surroundings. Is it not for this that Confucius said, "It is the humaneness of a neighborhood that makes it good and beautiful?"

Then in the second paragraph he made use of several allusions to other classical works to build up his argument that associations and environment exert a most potent influence. The first was from the *Tso Commentary* on the *Spring and Autumn Annals* to the effect that if a fragrant grass and an unpleasant-smelling one were kept together the latter would so overpower the former that even after the lapse of ten years there would still be an unpleasant odor. The second allusion was from the *Book of Mencius* where Mencius emphasized the importance of consistency of efforts by saying that if one were to expose a plant to sunshine for one day and keep it away from the sun for ten days even the most rugged vegetation could not survive. The third allusion was similarly to the *Book of Mencius* where he taught by using the following parable:

> Do you want your king to be good? Let me speak to you frankly. Here is an official in the State of Ch'u who wants his son to learn the speech of Ch'i. Should he ask a Ch'i man to be his tutor or a Ch'u man? The answer is he should employ a Ch'i man. But while he is being tutored by a single Ch'i man and shouted at continually by numerous Ch'u men, even though he were given

a flogging every day to force him to learn the Ch'i speech, the results would be unobtainable. Whereas if he should be placed in the midst of the Chuang Mountains [in Ch'i] for several years, even if he should be flogged daily to force him to speak the old Ch'u speech the situation would also be impossible.

On these allusions Wang's second paragraph was built thus:

A fragrant grass and an odoriferous one would leave an offensive odor even after ten years. Is it not because the one has overpowered and changed the other? One day of sunshine and ten days of sheltered coolness would not permit anything to grow. With few tutors but numerous distractors even a daily flogging will not facilitate the learning of the Ch'i speech. Is it not because of the overweighing of the damaging factors that the possibility of good being overpowered by evil is not a new story? If one were to try to live a good life without seeking an environment conducive to goodness, then even before one succeeds in preserving what he has already attained he would be confused and overpowered by bad habits and surroundings. For this reason failure to select one's abode in the midst of a humane neighborhood could be described as unwise. And a neighborhood that is humane would be true and beautiful.

The third paragraph further elaborated the importance of environment:

If one actually lives in an environment of humaneness [jên] one's contacts at all times of the day are nothing but jên. One's points of agreement in discussion are nothing but jên. What one hears is all the speech of people of jên and what one sees is nothing but the deeds of men of jên. As a result of mutual influence and mutual re-enforcement one would grow in goodness without realizing it. Is this not good?

Living in the village of Po Yi, even a covetous man might become incorruptible; living in close proximity to Hui [Liu-hsia Hui], even a mean person might become magnanimous. Living in a neighborhood saturated with humanity, how could one become inhumane even if he wished to the contrary. If even Mo Ti had places which he did not care to visit and if even Mencius had his home removed three times, how could an ordinary person afford not to be selective in locating his abode?

The laconic style of the foregoing paragraphs summarized four interesting episodes with which Wang's readers were all familiar. Po Yi was the son of a feudal prince who lived at the end of the Shang Dynasty. He and his younger brother were remembered for having given up the inheritance of their principality. They were followers of King Wên of the Chou State. When King Wên's son, King Wu, decided to launch a war of conquest against the Shang Dynasty in 1111 B.C., the two brothers reprimanded the warrior king to no avail. After the conquest they considered it shameful to partake of the cereals produced in the Chou regime, hence they sought refuge in the far-off mountains and fed themselves with wild growths. When the supply was exhausted they died of starvation.

Hui the curer of meanness, or Liu-hsia Hui, whose real name was Chan Ch'in, was a native of the state of Lu, who decided not to give up his public career after he had been dismissed three times from office as a judge. Asked why he had made the decision and swallowed the injustice, he replied, "When you are upright in serving men, where could you go to avoid being dismissed three times; and if you serve man in a way that is not upright, why is it necessary to leave the country of your parents?"

Mo Ti's avoidance of certain places referred to the tradition that when he was a member of the civil service in the feudal state of Sung, he was appointed magistrate of Chao Ko, literally, the County of Morning Songs. The county acquired its name, so tradition said, in the last days of the Shang Dynasty when, under the influence of King Shou Hsin, people were encouraged to sing during the morning hours instead of working as they should. As an advocate of the wastefulness of music, Mo Ti feared that the unsavory customs of the district might weaken his conviction and so he decided to decline the appointment.

Similarly, the removal of Mencius' home went back to early traditions. When the Confucian philosopher was a boy his home was near a cemetery and he was fond of playing undertaker. Mencius' mother exclaimed, "This is no place for me to bring up my child." She moved to another house near the marketplace and her son began to play tradesman. Again dissatisfied with the environment, she moved to the neighborhood of a school, whereupon her son became interested in rituals and etiquette and his mother decided not to move any more. Wang's essay ended with a short final paragraph:

> Those who are supreme in virtue, however, are never subject to change and those who are supremely pure cannot be tarnished. Those who have truly attained *jên* are so from their nature and not from artificial efforts and they are at home in it without forced discipline. While in action they move with *jên* and while at rest they abide by *jên. Jên,* then, is wherever they are. For these how can there be any more need of being selective?

The remarkable thing about this model essay in five paragraphs is that despite its brevity it contains the basic parts of a statement of the problem, an enlargement of the problem, its further exploration, and its conclusion. Its seemingly contradictory final paragraph was intended to make the argument complete by singling out Confucius and his peers as completely above the standard affirmed. Although this essay was widely copied as a model there was no freezing of the essay style. It was not until after the Mongols had completely consolidated their position in China that in 1313 a regulation was proclaimed whereby the essay subjects in the competitive examinations should be quotations from the Four Books of Confucius and that the interpretation of the Four Books should be based on Chu Hsi's commentary. Aside from the fact that such essays were not to be shorter than three hundred characters there was no specification regarding the construction or pattern of the essay. In the early years of the Ming Dynasty candidates were required to write three essays on the Four Books and four essays on the Five Classics. But it was not until 1487 that the details of the composition of such essays were clearly specified. This, then, was the real birth of the so-called Eight-Legged Essay.

The first leg, technically described as "the breaking open of the title," was a subtle disclosure of the candidate's knowledge of the provenance of the essay title. The originality of the candidate would be demonstrated by his dexterity in handling no more than the quotation without reference to what preceded and followed it. The second leg, technically called *ch'êng t'i* or "accepting the title," was an announcement of the general treatment to which the title would be subjected without divulging the intricacies of the later contents. On the other hand, an excessively general handling of this second leg would make it not only too colorless but also too loose a fitting for the main body of the essay. The third and fourth legs, known as the *ch'i chiang* (introductory discourse) and *ch'i ku* (introductory corollary) respectively, consisted of two paragraphs, one parallel to the other not only in rhetorical structure but also harmoniously contrasted. This technique was only possible in a language like literary Chinese in which all the basic units were monosyllabic and therefore susceptible to the most regular pattern of scanning. In other words, the pair of paragraphs are not only equal in the number of words but also exactly identical in the number of words in each part making up the total paragraph. The secret of developing the introductory pair of paragraphs was to build up a kind of rising action without exhausting the philosophical content inherent in the subject or title of the essay.

Following the introductory pair of legs were the middle pair, in which the most brilliant ideas of which the candidate was capable were brought out in full vigor, following the architectonic technique of the parallel structure design. Finally, the last two legs were to wind up the whole composition, bringing out the denouement and exhibiting completeness of the performance without betraying any sign of exhaustion.

As though these regulations were not sufficiently strict, the whims of the examiners of the essays were also expressed in the limitation upon the length of the essay. For example, in the 1640's the essays were limited to 450 words. During the reign of K'ang Hsi (1662–1722) the limit was set at 550. There were other specifications later on extending the limit to six hundred. Even when such bans were lifted in the eighteenth century, convention dictated that a good solid essay of this type should be written with approximately six hundred words.

As the Eight-Legged Essay was the principal royal road to literary honors, experts were legion. It would be pointless to survey the variation of technique and style from age to age. It suffices to examine a representative piece by one of the great craftsmen during the golden period of its crystallization—the latter part of the fifteenth century.

The author was Wang Ao, who rose to great distinction in his official career in the last years of the fifteenth and the early decades of the sixteenth century. Winning first honors in both the metropolitan and the palace examinations, he was hailed as the leading master of the Eight-Legged Essay of his age. The topic of the essay under scrutiny was entitled: "If the hundred surnames enjoy sufficiency how could the ruler suffer from insufficiency?" This was part of the answer given by one of the disciples of Confucius according to the ninth section in the twelfth book of the *Analects:*

> Duke Ai asked Yu Jo saying, "If the year is one of hunger and there is not enough for expenditure, what is to be done?" Yu Jo replied, "Why not tithe the people?" "With two-tenths," said the Duke, "I still find it not enough. How can I manage with one-tenth?" Yu Jo answered, "If the people have enough how can the prince be left in want? And if the people are in want, how can the prince enjoy a sufficiency?"

In handling this relatively simple title, Wang "broke" it with one sentence: "When the people below are rich, the prince at the top will naturally be rich." While the logic was far from flawless, the rhetoric in the eyes of the examiners was probably very impressive. Then, in confirming the breakage of the title, the essayist re-enforced his position with a short explanation:

> This is so because the wealth of the prince is something disseminated among the people. If the people are rich, how can it stand to reason that the prince alone is destitute?

Further to complement it, the third unit was added, known as the "unit of initiation of the lecture" or "elaboration":

> Yu Jo spoke from profundity the idea of the oneness of the ruler and ruled in his special message to Duke Ai. The suggestion was that the Duke's proposal to increase the taxation was due to the insufficiency of his revenues for state

expenditure. To guarantee the sufficiency of state expenditure, what could take priority over attempts to guarantee sufficiency for his people?

Following this came the so-called Initial Leg:

If the farming lands were tithed with a sincere wish to be thrifty in expenditure and to be considerate in showing love to the citizens; and taking one-tenth of the agricultural produce with neither exploitation of the people nor excessive luxury for the person of the prince himself; then the exertions of the citizens would not be burdened with excessive taxations and the accumulation of the people's property would not be exhausted by exorbitant demands. Within common households there would be savings and accumulation leaving little worry over caring for parents and raising the young; in the ordinary farms there would be plentiful harvests and well-stocked granaries forestalling the anxieties of nurturing the living and of honoring the dead.

In the foregoing unit were displayed the rhetorical attainments of the writer by the harmonious construction of double columns to evidence the charm of what we call balanced structure. To bring this feature out in full relief, a short unit now followed:

If the hundred surnames are enjoying sufficiency for what conceivable reason should the prince be left alone in destitution?

This one sentence, purposely unprolonged for rhetorical effect, constitutes what was known as the "vacuous or rhetorical question unit." As though the first major unit had not been punctuated, the essayist would now proceed to the middle link or leg:

What was disseminated among the common households would all be available to the prince without its being hoarded in the treasury to enable the prince to claim, "This is my wealth." What is stored in the farms and fields is accessible to the prince without its being stored in vaults in order to enable the prince to claim, "These are my possessions." With inexhaustible availability what worry is there for failure to respond to demand; with inexhaustible supplies, what anxiety is there for lack of preparedness in emergency?

Immediately taking up the subject for further elaboration where the middle left off, the final unit or final leg was expected to bring up the rear with further elaboration:

The sacrificial animals and ritual cereals to be used in religious offerings; and the jades and textiles to be used as tributes and diplomatic gifts: even if these were insufficient, the people of the hundred surnames will supply them in full. Wherein will there be a shortage? Breakfasts and dinners, beefs and drinks for the entertainment of state guests; carriages and horses, arms and equipment for the preparation of wars and defense: even if these were insufficient, the people of a hundred surnames will take care of the needs. Wherein again will there be insufficiency?

Then with an epilogue by way of a grand conclusion introduced
by an exclamation, the writer furnished the finishing touches:

The establishment of the tithe was originally for the good of the people
but in this very usage lies the sufficiency of national expenditure. Where then
is there any need to increase taxation to attain national wealth!

Despite the possibility of communicating to the emperor and
those who happened to be in power subtle suggestions for the solution of political and economic problems, the Eight-Legged Essay
was destined to fall into ruts with the formalization of the titles and
the freezing of rhetorical devices. Even with massive learning behind him the candidate would find it almost impossible, within the
limits of these accumulative regulations and bandages, freely to express any original ideas. In the end this type of composition was
to become a systematic play with words. The only virtue that it
could have was that its composition was clearly defined and its
architectonics definitely unified, making it easy to conform and easy
to learn and allowing no room for unbridled deviations. From the
standpoint of the examiners its virtue lay in its brevity minimizing
the time required for reading as well as the uncertainty in grading.
Any student with native intelligence could produce an essay of this
type of acceptable quality after the memorization of a few dozen
models from which a general tone would emanate. For what was
really tested was agility of mind rather than literary creativity.

This tradition was carried on into Ming times with certain new
requirements imposed. The point of view taken by the candidate was
no longer that of a commentator or humble pupil of the sage, but
that of the sage himself.

The question has been raised, why the exegetical essay on Confucian doctrines of Sung times should have undergone such a peculiar contortion to become the Eight-Legged Essay. To most literary historians the phenomenon was so irksome and the resulting
products were so repulsive that even an answer was not attempted.
In fact, most histories of Chinese literature had considered it below
their dignity even to mention the rise and fall of the Eight-Legged
Essay. Conservatism in the Chinese mind was certainly not a full
answer. According to an unconventional but scholarly critic, Chiao
Hsün (1763-1820), the Eight-Legged Essay did not rise out of a
vacuum. It had its main inspiration from the growth of the Chinese
drama, substituting Confucian classics for fictional material, elaborating on Confucian doctrines instead of the supernatural and
weird, and building up its own rules of euphony in place of dra-

matic musical tunes. The writer of the essay, assuming the role of Confucius or Mencius, was none other than an actor. The breaking of the title and the summarizing of the essay were comparable to the prologue. The paragraphs in pairs were counterparts to the dramatic lyrics arranged in cycles. Those who had practiced in it for long had never been aware of its origin. It is, therefore, the fascination of dramatic performance which sustained this peculiar literary type for over five centuries in the Chinese literary arena.

A more plausible-sounding survival factor may have been sentiment. To successful candidates the years of toiling and sweating spent in the mastery of its intricacies would conjure up recollections that were at least partly pleasant. To a third group, those who had been so completely subjugated and conditioned by the limited range of its literary craft, the Eight-Legged Essay had acquired the charm of a fetish, and to them the mere reading of a masterpiece would resemble the exhilaration of listening to a superb symphony. Nonetheless, in spite of the official stamp of approval, compositions of this type were seldom given a place of equality in the collected works of writers. It was only in a few rare cases that such compositions were collected into appendices of published writings. Even then they were deleted in subsequent printings; hence one has to search far and wide for samples of these essays and scarcely any attention has been paid to the historic evolution of this special literary type.

There is no question that the Eight-Legged Essay holds no place whatsoever in China's intellectual history except as a glaring example of demerit. Aside from intellectual content, the circumstances in which one's ability to write such essays on short order—in the competitive examination hall—were in the experience of the huge majority of scholars extremely unpleasant. Such painful experiences were frequently exchanged among scholars with sighs of relief and it is easily understandable that such reminiscences were seldom committed to writing. They were experiences the sooner forgotten the better.

In spite of the consuming interest in the Eight-Legged Essay, Ming writers kept their eyes intent on the continuation of the tradition of classical prose, the movement started by Han Yü and kept up during the Sung and Yüan Dynasties, the movement upholding the free construction of prose in conformity to the style of the Confucian classics and the pre-Ch'in philosophers. The question that arose in the Ming Dynasty, a period full of controversies of all types, was the search for models. Should *ku-wên* or "ancient prose" be an imitation of T'ang and Sung writers or of Chou and Han writers?

Since prose writers of the Ming period are legion, we shall only concern ourselves with a few representative writers to indicate trends of the different movements. Among the literary men sought out by the founder of the Ming Dynasty to lend dignity to the new regime after the expulsion of the Mongols, the best known was Sung Lien (1310-1381). Disciple of the Neo-Confucianist Wu Lai (1297-1430), Sung Lien had refused to serve the Mongolian court. With the founding of the new dynasty he responded to court summons and assumed the editorship-in-chief in the redaction of the *Yüan Dynastic History*. The imperfection of that history was partly due to the careless style of the original drafters and partly due to the great haste in which the work of redaction was brought to an end. Sung Lien, therefore, should not be held entirely responsible. Moreover, he was not trained as a historian and most of his associates were indifferent to an alien dynasty which had been expelled. As regards his own writing, he showed remarkable signs of naturalness and forthrightness. Since he was not a founder of any literary school, he seemed to have culled from the technique of all previous prose writers without setting up any definite target for imitation.

The first conscious founder of a school of prose writing was Li Tung-yang (1447-1516), who advocated the continuation of the school founded by Han Yü. Rising to premiership before his death, he exerted great influence on the writers of his age in revitalizing interest in the so-called eight masters of T'ang and Sung prose. With a new discipline thus set up, what he and his associates accomplished was the reduction of prose writing in length and avoiding prolixity.

This trend was soon reversed by his namesake, Li Mêng-yang (1472-1529), who advocated a return to archaic models before the T'ang and Sung writers. The standard thus heralded was not unjustifiable. Since *ku wên* meant "ancient prose" it was legitimate to ask, "Why not return to high antiquity?" Thus came Li Mêng-yang's advocacy of prose writing based on the pattern of Ch'in and Han writers and poetry on the model of the golden period of the Han Dynasty. Buttressed by six others of his own age, Li Mêng-yang started a movement of artisanship in which imitations of early Han and pre-Han writings rivaled in their archaic patterns the flavor of the original. His predecessor, however, was less emphatic in his theories of imitation. In fact, Li Tung-yang had certain ideas about the theory of imitation which sounded extremely original in his own age:

In writing poetry an attempt to make it all intelligible to an old country woman is, of course, not an absolute necessity. On the other hand, when attempts are especially made to confound the understanding of learned people, one also wonders if it is reasonable.

Though an advocate of the T'ang and Sung masters in prose, he was firm in his belief in the limitations of time and clime:

The poetry of the Han, Wei, the Six Dynasties, of T'ang, Sung and Yüan, each follows its own style. Comparing it to dialects, the languages spoken in Shensi, Shansi, Kiangsu, Chekiang, Fukien, and Honan as well as other places, the tones and tunes vary according to locale, one without influencing the other. From this one sees that in the universe what are motivated by local customs and inspirations express themselves in utterances according to time and place, differing from one another without infringing on one another. Isn't it difficult that we who are nourished in the spirit of the universe should try to transcend the limitations of age and climate?

This belief in the intrinsic molding influence of age and environment was scrapped by the imitative movement started by the younger Li. Whereas many people belittle the writings of the Ch'in-Han school by calling them exquisite counterfeits, the movement was important in that it won wide support and exerted influence as the first organized school of literature.

Li's antiquarian movement was given strong support by a poet, Ho Ching-ming (1483-1521). According to Ho, antiquarian literature was valuable because it meant the magnifying of the voice of antiquity. In spite of his theories, however, Ho had his own originality. Reacting against the powerful influence of Li and Ho were Wang Shou-jên, better known as Wang Yang-ming (1472-1529), in prose, and a group of painter-poets of the Soochow area in poetry. In spite of the fact that Wang was close to Li and Ho, he declined to recommend imitation of any style. While he was best known in Ming philosophy and politics, Wang exerted an influence through his numerous students upon literature. Untainted by the literary theories of his associates, Wang's prose style was one revealing unmistakably a high degree of general discipline. Best known among his prose writings are his long letters to his friends and pupils in which his philosophical and ethical theories were elaborated. In them we hear the clarion voice of one who sought unison with the whole universe. He distinguished himself as the great prose writer whose artistry was expressed in a complete freedom from concern with art and artificiality.

Wang Yang-ming was unquestionably distinguished as a writer in prose and verse in conformity with the orthodox literary pattern not because he was a successful imitator of any single master or a merger of the excellences of several schools, but because he was a real man who had distinguished himself in politics as well as military strategy and who asserted his full measure of independence in his thought. His writings were great, in other words, mainly because he had something substantial to say.

His greatest experience in life was undergone in 1507 when, after having offended a powerful group of eunuchs who had usurped the supreme powers of the crown, he was bastinadoed and sent into exile in the far-off province of Kueichow which had been converted into a part of the Chinese cultural circle not long before and which was still largely inhabited by non-Chinese tribes. Living in solitude in the tiny town of Lungch'ang buried in the midst of hilly country in the northwestern part of that province, which was badly infested with many unknown diseases, he had to play nurse for a long time to three servants who had been taken ill. Meanwhile the powerful eunuchs pursued further plans to get rid of him. After preparing for himself a stone coffin to symbolize his resolution not to run away from death, he spent many days in meditation.

In his earlier scholarly career he had dedicated himself to literary studies in which he excelled but found no lasting satisfaction. Then following in the footsteps of Chu Hsi and reading all of Chu's writings accessible to him, he devoted himself to a minute study and observation of the myriad objects in the physical universe. Nonetheless he found it difficult to identify the way of things with the reason in his heart or mind. Further searches led him into Buddhism and Taoism without furnishing him with an ultimate answer. While living in exile, he came to sudden enlightenment one night and found for the first time that the way of the sages was all within his own heart or mind. He reread Chu Hsi's writings only to discover that his new findings were all contradictory to what the twelfth-century philosopher had taught.

At the end of this period of exile in 1510 and with all the vicious eunuchs now eliminated, he returned to his civil service career and steadily rose in the official hierarchy, scoring important military victories in 1519 and 1520 over a feudal prince who had started a rebellion. Meanwhile he shared his philosophical theories with many scholars who flocked to him as pupils, and as the leader of a new idealistic movement within Neo-Confucianism his influence was exerted for many future generations in China and eventually in Japan.

More revealing of his personality than the essays and poems he wrote were the records his disciples kept of his sayings in the tradition of the *yü lu*. The following extracts from the *Ch'uan Hsi Lu* or *Records of Transmission* may throw light on facets of his philosophical system:

One day Wang Chi returned from a stroll and the Master asked him, "What did you see in your walk?" and the pupil answered, "I saw the streets were filled with sages." The Master said, "You saw the streets were filled with sages but at the same time the people who filled the streets thought they had seen a sage in you, too." On another day Tung Yün had returned from the town and went to see the master saying, "I have seen something strange today." "What was so strange?" the Master asked. "I saw the streets were all filled with sages." The Master said, "There is nothing strange in this, it's an ordinary sight."

.   .   .   .

When Huang Chêng-chih and Chang Shu-ch'ien returned from the competitive examination in the capital in 1526 they told the Master when they lectured on the new concepts of the Way in their travels there were believers and non-believers. The Master said, "You people betook with you a sage to lecture to people. When people saw a sage coming they were all scared away. How could you succeed in lecturing to them? You should have tried to identify yourselves with an ordinary man or ordinary woman before you could lecture to others."

Aside from those writers who were directly or indirectly connected with Wang Yang-ming, nearly all prose masters around 1500 were excessive worshippers of Ch'in and Han philosophers. But in their attempt to imitate archaic style they all had a tendency to make their writings almost impossible to punctuate so that instead of communicating ideas and feelings, their writings had the net effect of presenting riddles to their readers. Unintelligibility, besides being a besetting sin for writers, was bound to evoke a rebellion.

A leader of such a rebellion was Kuei Yu-kuang (1506-1571), a new advocate of T'ang and Sung prose. He denounced the pseudo-Han prose of the opposing camp as "so much nonsense" and following the style of later medieval writers he was particularly noted for the clarity of his narrative prose. He was so highly respected by continuators of the *ku wên* tradition that he was regarded as a major link between the eight masters of T'ang-Sung times and the great prose masters of the Ch'in Dynasty. Thus, between these schools of controversy were evolved numerous groups of Ming writers who fluctuated between the Ch'in-Han models and the T'ang-Sung models. Aside from the towering example of Wang Yang-ming, who rose above his age almost in every respect, few writers were aware of their own intrinsic creative abilities.

The only other voice of protest was raised by the three Yüan brothers, namely, Yüan Tsung-tao, Yüan Hung-tao and Yüan Chung-tao, who flourished at the end of the sixteenth century and the beginning of the seventeenth century. They openly objected to the imitation of all ancients and to the setting up of any defense of any orthodoxy. Their contributions lay in the arousing of interest in literature for its own sake. As a result, some of their best writings were familiar essays close to the style of Robert Louis Stevenson. Their shortcoming was that they were so concerned with the commonplace and the trivial that they could write extensively on any petty subject.

Among these three brothers who founded a movement named after the place of their origin, Kung-an, the most distinguished and most influential was the middle brother, Yüan Hung-tao (1568–1610), better known by his pen name, Yüan Chung-lang. Fearless of adverse criticism, he challenged all the prevailing trends of creative literature in his age, believing that literature should change with the lapse of each age and that any attempt to erase the special stamp of an era would result only in slavish imitation.

This same intransigence which he wanted to incorporate into his writings was frankly cherished in his philosophy of life. Although he was sentimentally attached to his elder brother, Tsung-tao, whose early death was lamented for a long time, he had no scruples about being different from his brother. While Tsung-tao believed that "living in the midst of men one should smooth one's sharp edges to be in perfect harmony with the human world as it rises and falls, in the interests of providing comfort for one's parents as well as for self-preservation," the middle brother, Hung-tao, insisted that "phoenixes do not share the same nest with common birds nor would unicorns share the same manger with ordinary horses. A real man should come and go alone as he pleases. How could he smile and weep with the world, allowing himself to have his nose pierced and his hair netted by others?" On the positive side of his literary creed he singled out two qualities as of foremost importance: substantiality and fidelity. For this reason he would frequently rate the popular songs far above the counterfeit antiques of ancient prose and poetry produced by his contemporaries. On one occasion he wrote:

I say the poetry and prose of our age will not be preserved. Those pieces that are preserved in one chance out of ten thousand are probably such compositions as "Break the Jade" or "Beat the Grass Lawn" as they are sung by women and children in little lanes and alleys—compositions by real people making no claim to knowledge and erudition—people who would not learn to frown according to the patterns of the Han and Wei Dynasties or walk according to the pattern laid down in the golden T'ang Dynasty. These people still understand the happiness and sorrow, the anger and joy, the wishes and desires of the common man, and this is a happy thing.

It is largely this aversion of his for the stereotyped and conventional that discovered for him petty subjects which no enshrined literary figures before his time had cared to notice, such as the arrangement and watering of flowers. It is in these little essays that he exhibited many an intimate and personalized note making his readers feel that he was very earnestly chatting with them. From his long essay on the care and enjoyment of flowers, the following paragraph is typical of Yuan's style:

I have found that all the people in the world who are dull in their conversation and hateful to look at in their faces are those who have no hobbies. . . . When the ancient people who had a weakness for flowers heard there was a remarkable variety, they would travel across high mountain passes and deep ravines in search of them, unconscious of bodily fatigue, bitter cold or scorching heat, and their peeling skins, and completely oblivious of their bodies soiled with mud. When a flower was about to bud, they would move their beds and pillows to sleep under them, watching how the flowers passed from infancy to maturity and finally dropped off and died. Or they would plant thousands in their orchards to study how they varied, or have just a few in their rooms to exhaust their interest. Some would be able to tell the size of flowers from smelling their leaves, and some were able to tell from the roots the color of their flowers. These were the people who were true lovers of flowers and who had a true weakness for them.

(Lin Yutang's translation)

The spirit of revolt against convention and against imitation was shared by another school known as the Chingling school led by Chung Hsing (1574-1624) and T'an Yüan-ch'un (flourished 1627). Chung and T'an, however, in their conscious efforts to be different from all previous writers, were characterized by their peculiar sentence forms. Their rebellion was carried so far that they purposely tried to explore the limits of ungrammaticalness. These, then, were the only eddies in the huge stream of antiquarianism permeating all Ming Dynasty prose.

Ming poetry, like Ming publications in other fields, was outstanding in volume. This was partly due to the increase of facilities for publication and partly due to the fact that there was a relaxation in standards. Just as Ming authors were fond of compiling appealing passages from previous authors, adding scanty comments of their own and publishing them with new titles under their own names, so most of the Ming poets were tireless in producing verses imitative of past masters of one age or another.

At the beginning of the dynasty, the only outstanding poet was Kao Ch'i (1336-1374), a native of Ch'angchow County near present-day Shanghai, who had refrained from co-operation with the

Mongols. After being appointed by the first Ming emperor to help edit the dynastic history of the vanquished regime, Kao had to pay the heavy price of being cut in half for revealing palace secrets in his poems. Writing verses in both the *shih* and the *tz'ŭ* forms, he was more interested in painting simple word pictures suggestive of varying moods than treading in the footsteps of the T'ang or Sung major poets. The following quatrain in five-syllable lines is typical of his poetry:

> The hanging lanterns are shining on our cool robes.
> Leaves are dropping and the rain is falling in the courtyard.
> My friend now drunken has ceased talking,
> And the autumn insects are carrying on the conversation by themselves.

Unfortunately, from 1400 on, a new trend was started by three high-ranking officials who insisted upon the importance of stateliness and elegance in verse writing, and for a whole century poetry reflected eagerness for rhetorical correctness and verbal floridity rather than originality. In the sixteenth century, however, a reaction set in under the leadership of Li Tung-yang, who has been mentioned earlier as a noted Ming prose writer. According to Li Tung-yang, Tu Fu was the supreme master of poetry and the only one worthy of being a model. Li Mêng-yang, his pupil, thought Li Tung-yang had not gone far enough and advocated that no one should read any books written after the T'ang Dynasty. While the influence of the two Li's were waxing with only minor modifications, the only voices of dissent were to come from the painters of the age, but their voices were feeble.

Thenceforth so-called groups of masters, sometimes in fives and sometimes in sevens, emerged from the literary scene, but they were all alike in that few of them could take any original stand in the art of poetry and were only differentiable one from another by their deep-seated preoccupation with one or another master as their supreme idol. During their own life spans their literary reputations were often enormous but their attainments were principally those of superb literary craftsmen. This tendency was continued throughout the Ming Dynasty and it was not until early in the seventeenth century that a mild form of dissension was expressed by the Kung-an school which we have heard of before in connection with prose development. As spokesman for the school, Yüan Hung-tao emphatically remarked:

> The T'ang Dynasty has its own poetry of the *ku shih* or ancient pattern type, and it is not necessary to go back to the *Wên Hsüan* anthology; the middle and late periods of the T'ang Dynasty have their own poetry, and it is not

necessary to insist on the early period or the Golden Age; Ou-yang Hsiu, Su Shih, Ch'ên Shih-tao and Huang T'ing-chien all have their own poetry and it is not necessary to eulogize the T'ang poets. T'ang poetry exhibits colors and hues that are fresh and bright as though they had been written only the previous evening; but the poems of today are all hackneyed and threadbare the moment they are written down. Isn't this a clear indication that what flows out from the heart and soul is different from what is pilfered and copied?

In this quotation and in his insistence on singling out Po Ch'ü-Yi as the foremost T'ang poet and Su Shih as the foremost Sung poet, we see that the Yüan brothers even as rebels were unable to extricate themselves from a preoccupation with the past. Nonetheless, inspired by unconventionality, Yüan Hung-tao was able to succeed as a poet beyond his own preachments.

The Ferry at Hêngt'ang

At the ferry at Hêngt'ang you arrive from the west,
And I depart for the east.
Thank you for that precious look—worth a thousand pieces
    of gold.
My home is at the Red Bridge,
Crimson doors facing the crossroads.
Remember the magnolia flowers, and don't go beyond the
    willow tree.

At other times he would go so far as to use the vernacular:

Unprepared I found white hair on my head.
I wanted to weep but smiled instead.
Delighted with the idea of smiling,
I smiled again and jumped for joy.

Pushing his unconventionality to its limit, he wrote one day:

West Lake

One day I walked by the lake,
One day I sat by the lake,
One day I loafed by the lake,
One day I slept by the lake.

As his critics have pointed out, such poems were hardly poems but they were precious fun-poking coming from the Ming Dynasty.

What is true of Ming poetry of the *shih* type was also true of poetry of the *tz'ŭ* type. The only exception to the rule came at the end of the dynasty.

Ch'ên Tzŭ-lung (1608-1647), a native of Chekiang, was involved in the last-ditch fights against the inroads of the Manchus. He was caught by special agents when he was organizing resistance forces at the great lake, Taihu. He ended his own life by plunging into the lake. In the *tz'ŭ* poems of his last years one detects many a tragic tone.

The Fifth Watch

With a light coolness pervading half my pillow, my tears slip out
   unconsciously.
My moments of sorrow are like a dream and my dreams are filled with
   bits of sorrow.
The bugle sound now reaches my little red pavilion.

The wind flickers the flame of my dying lamp and sways my curtain,
And the faint moon behind a screen of flowers shines palely on the hooks
   of my curtain.
Suddenly the old pains of tragedy surge up in my heart.

When Ch'ên took his life the Ming Dynasty was losing its last battles.

CHAPTER 27

Ming Drama

W E HAVE noticed in a previous chapter that full-fledged Chinese drama had its earliest beginnings during the Sung Dynasty and that in the Sung Dynasty two schools differing in technique as well as in their spheres of influence had already existed. The handiwork of these two schools was later on known by different names as though they were completely different literary types. One type upheld by one school was known as *tsa chü,* or miscellaneous plays. The other type, upheld by another school, was known as *ch'uan ch'i,* literally "transmission of the strange," or, in other words, romantic drama. The speed of their development was noticeably uneven. The first type, *tsa chü,* which was brought to full fruition in the north during the Yüan Dynasty, began to show signs of aging and decline with the exodus of the Mongols after their military defeats in China on many fronts. The second type, *ch'uan ch'i,* which was tenuously maintained in the south during the glorious development of the miscellaneous plays, suddenly revitalized itself with the founding of the new native dynasty. It conspicuously replaced its rival type as the major vehicle, monopolizing the attention and endeavors of the best creative writers of the age.

These two branches of Chinese drama—*tsa chü,* also called northern drama, and *ch'uan ch'i,* also called southern drama—differed from each other not only in the chronology of their golden periods and the locale of their diffusion. Even in construction they were dissimilar. Whereas the northern drama was usually divided into four parts or four acts preceded by a short prologue, a typical southern drama would contain from forty to fifty changes of scene. In the second place, the songs in each act, according to the northern tradition, had to follow one single rhyming scheme; in southern drama although the "acts" were necessarily much shorter, there was no set pattern with regard to rhyming among its songs. Not only was a change of rhyme permissible within one act, but also within one individual song itself. In the third place, northern dramas were written with the burden of singing to fall on one principal actor, and when an effort was made to avoid monotony the maximum number of singers was two. In southern drama all such scruples were completely dispensed with, allowing actors playing practically all parts, large or small, singing parts. In the fourth place, southern drama had done away with the prologue, calling its first act *k'ai ch'ang* or, literally, "the opening of the stage," in which the master of ceremonies prepared the audience with a synopsis that aroused the curiosity of the spectators without giving away its surprises and subtleties. Besides this, there were also differences in the classification of tones and in the labeling of the different roles.

The maintenance of southern drama during the period of Mongolian domination in which northern drama ruled supreme, was largely the effort of the common people in the south. The tradition was kept alive by amateurs in what might be loosely described as a sort of little-theater movement. There were no major playwrights comparable with the authors of the best-known Yüan plays. In fact, many of the performances were the result of a peculiar type of collective authorship. Not only were the dialogues spoken in the everyday tongue but even the interspersed songs were phrased in such simple language as to make their every syllable readily understood by the casual and illiterate. This folk coloring in the dramatic scripts was preserved in the southern drama of the first period when literary men began consciously to take over the authorship of the southern plays.

The period of the revitalization of the southern drama boasts of four masterpieces. The first of these is *Pai Yüeh T'ing* (Moon-Worshiping Pavilion), in forty acts or changes of scene. Its author, according to some literary historians, was Shih Chün-mei of Hangchow, a merchant operating a store in front of the temple of the city god. The fact that the authorship of the play is not clearly known indicated that at the beginning of the Ming Dynasty southern drama as a literary type was not yet seriously considered by the learned.

The scene of the play was laid in the years of military contest between the Chin Tatars and the Mongolians. While a young scholar, Chiang Shih-lung, and his younger sister, Jui-lien, were studying at home the political situation in the Chin Empire was rapidly deteriorating. With the threat of the Mongolian invasion ever increasing, the Chin court held a session to deliberate on the best way out. The prime minister, Haiya, argued against the majority of the court counselors who had advocated removal of the imperial capital and recommended his two sons To-mên and Hsin-fu as military commanders at the front. This appeal was dismissed by the Chin emperor, who, listening to scandals of a courtier, ordered Haiya's execution. Haiya's son, Hsin-fu, in order to evade possible arrest, escaped from his father's mansion and concealed himself in the garden of the Chiang family. Chiang Shih-lung, after finding out about the plight of the prime minister's son, agreed to become a sworn brother to the young man in distress. Hsin-fu immediately went underground and was soon elected by the underworld as a leader.

In the meantime, Wang Chên, the minister of war at the Chin court, had received imperial orders to inspect the military frontier for the collection of intelligence and left his daughter, the heroine of the play, Jui-lan, at home with her mother. With the victorious southward march of the Mongolian forces, disorder prevailed all over the Chin Empire. Chiang Shih-lung and his sister, Jui-lien, as well as Mrs. Wang Chên and her daughter, Jui-lan, had left their homes to seek refuge in the countryside and both pairs were broken up by the large number of fellow refugees traveling on the highway. When Wang Jui-lan heard someone calling "Jui-lien" she mistook it for her mother's voice and hastened to where the caller was surrounded by a crowd. She then found out it was not her mother who had been calling but Chiang Shih-lung. For the protection of the young girl, the two agreed to represent themselves as husband and wife in continuing their search for a place of safety.

Coincidence would have it that Chiang Shih-lung's younger sister, Jui-lien, had found the company of Jui-lan's mother. When Shih-lung and Jui-lan reached the Hill of the Tiger Head they were accosted by highway robbers whose chief, they were surprised to find, was none other than Hsin-fu, who sent them away in safety with ample gifts. When these two young refugees arrived at the town of Kuang-yang, they asked the hotel owner to join them formally in wedlock. On the morrow the bridegroom was taken ill. It happened that the minister of war, Wang Chên, had finished his frontier inspection tour and was registered in the same hotel. When Jui-lan told her father she had been married, the general refused to give his approval and forced his daughter to return home with him. When father and daughter arrived at the relay post of Mêngtsin they met Mrs. Wang and Jui-lien.

After the withdrawal of the Mongolian invaders, the prime minister's son, Hsin-fu, was paroled. On his way to the national capital to take part in the competitive examinations he met Shih-lung, whereupon the two of them continued their trip to the capital where they won the highest honors, one in the literary and the other in the military field. Soon, Wang Chên received an imperial decree to give his daughter Jui-lan and his adopted daughter Jui-lien to the winners of the two highest honors. Jui-lan refused to take orders from her father, but later on found out that all her protestations were much ado about nothing, for the winner of the highest literary degree was none other than the man to whom she had already been married at the hotel. Thus, a double wedding scene served as the finale of the play. The popular appeal of this romantic drama lay principally in the charm of the songs and dialogues rather than in the mechanically prearranged plot.

The greatest playwright of the southern school in its first stage of development in the Ming Dynasty was Kao Ming (1310?-1380?), a native of Yungchia County in present-day Chekiang Province. Most of his life he was a recluse spending his time on drama and song writing. He was noted principally for a play entitled *P'i P'a Chi* or the *Record of the Stringed Instrument*. (The *p'i p'a* is an instrument introduced from the western regions in early Han times.) The founder of the Ming Dynasty is reported to have been extremely fond of this play and to have remarked, "The Five Classics and the Four Books of Confucianism are necessities like the five staple cereals but the *P'i P'a Chi* is comparable to delicacies and rare condiments from afar. How can a wealthy family do without it?"

This play, consisting of forty-two changes of scene, was built around an extremely well-known story of the Han poet, Ts'ai Yung, and "Chao Wu-niang," or "The Fifth Young Miss of the Chao Family." This story had been so celebrated among the people for so many generations that in the Southern Sung Dynasty it had become one of the most popular narratives recited by blind singers in market places or in front of temples to the accompaniment of a drum.

The adorned story of the hero of the play is as follows: Ts'ai Yung, a classicist of the Han Dynasty equally versed in prose and poetry, married in his twenty-third year the fifth daughter of the Chao family. While the young married couple were celebrating the beauty of a spring day with his parents at home, it was learned that the prefect of the county had submitted Ts'ai's name to the imperial court and that the date was drawing near for him to proceed to the capital. Though the young scholar was not interested in official honors, his father re-enforced the pleas of their neighbors that he should not forgo the opportunity to win distinction for himself and for the family.

After entrusting the affairs of the family to his most respected neighbor, Grandfather Chang, Ts'ai left home and his new bride of two months. After his arrival in the capital he won supreme honors in the literary examination. The prime minister, Niu Sêng-ju, had received imperial decrees instructing him to give his only daughter in marriage to the successful candidate. Ts'ai declined the honor on the plea that his parents were at home and that he had already been married. This plea, instead of freeing him, only angered the prime minister and his compeers at court. Yielding to pressure, Ts'ai became the son-in-law of the prime minister.

Meanwhile, various misfortunes had befallen the Ts'ai family. Chao Wu-niang, Ts'ai's wife, tried to support the family of three as well as she could. But in spite of her best efforts the old people died. After taking care of the burial of both her parents-in-law, she was encouraged by Grandfather Chang to proceed to the capital in search of her husband. To identify herself she had painted the likenesses of her parents-in-law which she bore on her back and for traveling expenses she played the *p'i p'a* several times a day on her way.

After much difficulty she reached the capital, Loyang. One day she begged for alms in front of the Amida Buddha Temple where she hung up the portraits of her parents-in-law. Upon the arrival of an official party all the peddlers and beggars had to hurry away. The portraits were collected by the retainers of Ts'ai Yung. After the official party was gone, Wu-niang found out that one of the official visitors had been her husband. With mixed feelings of happiness and shame, she decided to go to the new mansion on the following day as a beggar to collect information. Since the prime minister's daughter was daily expecting the arrival of her parents-in-law she felt she needed a new maidservant, and Wu-niang was employed. From this point on the denouement was rapid. The prime minister's daughter found out everything and was profoundly moved. Fortunately, polygamous marriages were sanctioned by Chinese society, so all three were able to live happily ever after.

A peculiar specimen of southern drama at the beginning of the Ming Dynasty was *Sha Kou Chi* or *Record of a Dog Slain,* written by Hsü Chi, who flourished in the last decades of the fourteenth century. Noted for having declined official honors, he was admired by his followers for his devotion to literature, art, and leisurely living. This drama is exceptional in that in its preserved version the lyrics are written in a language highly colored by the unpolished expressions of the everyday speech, and are almost completely devoid of the rhetorical devices and florid phraseology usually found in southern drama. Moreover, the plot is almost entirely based on a northern drama of the Yüan period, thus illustrating an extremely common characteristic in Chinese dramatic literature of writers drawing from the same common pool of popular versions of history and folklore. Playwrights have never been accused either of plagiarism or of lack of originality for this practice. The spectators, on their part, apparently derived considerable satisfaction from anticipating the familiar—no less than from being completely surprised by the unexpected. Instead of feeling bored by what might be considered threadbare, the audience would sit tensely in anticipation of what they knew for sure would happen. To understand this bit of psychology the Western readers of Chinese plays of this type would be interested in the minor changes introduced. The *Record of a Dog Slain* under discussion, for example, became a success on the stage for its expansion of the original theme to over four times the length of the northern play, thus necessitating as many as thirty-six changes of scenery.

The principal character in this play is Sun Hua of Loyang who, with his immense family fortune, indulges himself in drinking parties and associates with women of questionable character. Since all his acquaintances are people of a similar cast of mind, he is estranged from his virtuous younger brother Sun Yung, who frequently remonstrates with his brother against the latter's vicious ways. The younger brother is finally ousted from the family. After a suicide attempt which is foiled by devoted friends, the younger brother seeks temporary lodging in an abandoned shack. On a snowy day the two brothers meet accidentally on a highway, and Sun Hua, who is intoxicated, vituperates his younger brother. Later on the drunkard is overpowered in the snowstorm and is carried home by the younger brother, and yet, after he has come to, he suspects the younger brother of ulterior motives.

Sun Hua's wife, Yang Yüeh-chên, has meanwhile thought of a strategem whereby to reform her husband. Knowing that he invariably comes home at night completely drunk, she has a big dog slain, dressed in man's clothing, and deposited near the main door of their home. Upon his return his wife quietly suggests he do something about the dead body so suspiciously close to their house. Disturbed, the drunkard seeks assistance from two of his friends to get the body removed and buried. Failing to get the help he desires, he follows the advice of his wife and goes with her to appeal to the disinherited younger brother who responds by handling the unpleasant task single-handed. The brothers are soon reconciled. Then the two drinking companions who had refused to help call on Sun Hua and demand an elaborate drinking feast. On being coldly received, the degenerate companions decide to expose the crime that they think Sun Hua has committed. The denouement, which is a rapid one, consists of the autopsy of the buried body, which results in the punishment of the blackmailers.

This play, which was hailed during the Ming Dynasty as one of the four great masterpieces of southern drama, has evinced more unfavorable criticism from literary critics than any southern play. Actually it is a reflection of the folk nature of the early Ming dramas of the southern school. Moreover, since it was staged much more frequently than contemporary compositions, it was also likely that the players had taken great liberty in revising the original text to suit popular taste. What is considered its weakness may in fact be claimed as its virtue inasmuch as the lyrics, when sung to the accompaniment of orchestral music, were probably more intelligible to the theatergoing public than the dramatic songs in other plays of the period.

Although the beginnings of southern drama might be traced back to the eleventh century, its development continued to be interrupted, as it was for a long time completely overshadowed by the growth of northern drama which was much more influential than the southern dramatic tradition. It was not until the sixteenth century during the reigns of Chia Ching (1522-1566) and of Lung Ch'ing (1567-1572) that the cause of southern drama was bolstered by the rise of a new style of singing developed by a great actor, Wei Liang-fu, of K'unshan County near present-day Shanghai. Wei's new technique, which unconditionally condemned ranting and shouting, necessitated a total reorganization of the dramatic orchestra, involving the replacement of noisy instruments with subtler, quieter counterparts which remind us of chamber music. The formation of a new and powerful school was made complete by the efforts of Wei's friend from the same county, Liang Ch'ên-yü (1510-1580), to write a special play to illustrate the newly envisaged art. This is the beginning of the K'unshan school of dramatic singing, also known by its abbreviated name, K'un school—a school whose influence continued until the end of the nineteenth century. The great success of Liang's participation in the movement was due to his being not only a poet but also a great singer.

The play that Liang wrote for the movement, entitled *Huan Sha Chi* or *The Laundering of the Silken Stole,* was admired principally for its elegant songs and dialogues rather than for its story. Based on the history of the national rivalry between the states of Wu and Yüeh in the warring states period, the plot has practically no novelty except for the little details of adornment. The hero, Fan Li, was the prime minister of Yüeh who went through all the vicissitudes of state collapse and recovery with the Yüeh king and who for ten years continually dedicated himself to the revival of the fallen kingdom against its rival and enemy, Wu. With the success of the revival of Yüeh brought to fruition, Fan had the personal satisfaction of declining all official honors in preference for the life of a recluse upon the beautiful Five Lakes. He also rescued the woman he loved, the famous Hsi Shih, from bondage at the Wu court, and spent the remainder of his life in her company. It is easily understandable that southern drama at this stage of its development relied heavily for its success on three factors: the rhetoric and melody of the songs, the quality of the singing, and the accompaniment of fine soft music.

Another outstanding dramatist of the first period was Wang Shih-chêng (1526-1590). Like most Ming dramatists, Wang was a southerner, a native of T'aits'ang near present-day Shanghai. He was primarily remembered by posterity for his accomplishments as a poet, essayist, and literary critic. Moreover, he had distinguished himself among his contemporaries as a devoted son who willingly faced long prison terms for protesting against the incriminations of the powerful prime minister, Yen Sung, who had sent Wang's father to the execution grounds.

The injustice of this court-martial became the synopsis of Wang's southern dramatic composition, *Ming Fêng Chi,* or the *Record of the Singing Phoenix.* The main villain of the play was the corrupt and oppressive Yen Sung, and the heroes were the opponents of the prime minister against many political and military measures which the latter had advocated. The climax of the drama was the fight between the two factions regarding the strategy to be used in dealing with the Mongolian threat around the bend of the Yellow River. The complications and elements of suspense were compounded out of the maladministration of justice to silence the opposition of the dictatorial premier. All the loyal ministers of the Ming court were successively incriminated and imprisoned. The denouement was the downfall of the Yen house in accordance with actual history.

When this play was first presented on the stage a magistrate was invited to sit in the dress circle. As the plot was thickening and as the political significance of the piece was being unequivocally revealed, the official was so much taken aback by the unadorned invectives against the prime minister that he asked to be excused, whereupon the author produced a copy of the court chronicle and reassured the magistrate by saying, "The Yen house has already fallen." As a specimen of southern drama, this play was far from perfect, as has been pointed out by many critics. Yet it was outstanding on two counts. In the first place it was an exception to the rule in that its principal theme was a major national issue as contrasted with the love dramas of the age. In the second place it was probably the first attempt to utilize current history in playmaking.

By the second half of the sixteenth century, southern drama of the *ch'uan ch'i* type had attained full maturity. It had become the principal literary type, in which the greatest authors of the age showed no hesitation in investing their talents. Both in rhetoric and in technique of dramatic composition, great progress had been made as a result of competition among a larger number of dramatists.

Among dramatists of this third period the most outstanding was undoubtedly T'ang Hsien-tsu (1550-1617), again a southerner, born in the Province of Kiangsi. Besides excelling as a playwright, T'ang was also admired by his contemporaries for his great personal integrity and for the naturalness of his prose style, adamantly opposed as he was to the artificial and imitative pseudoclassical style upheld by most of his contemporaries. Among the five dramas he wrote, the best known is *Mao Tan T'ing*, consisting of fifty-five changes of scene. Like most of the historical southern plays, *Mao Tan T'ing* or *The Pavilion of Peonies* was based partly on history. The principal character was the heroine, Tu Li-niang, daughter of Tu Pao, a prefect of Nan-an and a descendant of the great poet Tu Fu. After a tour of a deserted garden the young girl was enveloped in a sudden feeling of fatigue and melancholy. As she was resting, she dreamed that a young man beckoned to her to revisit the garden and the pair met at the pavilion of the peonies. At this point she awakened from her dream. From that time on, Li-niang yearned in vain to meet the young man she had seen in her dream. Finally she was taken ill and realized the ailment was one that was extremely hard to cure, as it was a peculiar form of lovesickness. For lack of better expression of her feeling of lovelornness she painted a portrait of herself and laid it inside the pavilion. After that her illness suddenly turned worse and she died on a misty autumn night.

Meanwhile the Chin forces were invading the Sung Empire from the north and Tu Pao was transferred to a more responsible position as defense commissioner of the great metropolitan district of Yangchow. Before his departure he buried his daughter in the rear garden beneath a plum tree and memorialized her with a tablet in a small temple.

After Li-niang's death, as her soul journeyed down to the nether regions, she was given special permission to return to the world of living men. Meanwhile a descendant of the great T'ang prose writer, Liu Tsung-yüan, by the name of Liu Ch'un-ch'ing, who had been born in the district of Nanhai (present-day Canton) and who had distinguished himself in the literary examinations, had seen in a dream a beautiful girl underneath a plum-blossom tree. To commemorate the peculiar experience he gave himself the nom de plume of Mêng-mei or Dreamer of Plums. Inspired by a conversation with a former servant, Kuo the Hunchback, now a peddler of fruits, Liu decided to sojourn to the Southern Sung capital in Hangchow to take part in the competitive literary examinations. While he was in Nan-an one wintry day, he obtained temporary lodging in the Plum Blossom Temple where he accidentally picked up the self-portrait left there three years before by Li-niang.

From that time on the two met happily in dreams. With the lapse of time the young lady confided in Liu what actually had happened and informed the latter of the permission she had received from the Hadean judge to return to the world of the living at the opportune moment, whereupon arrangements were made to exhume Li-niang. After administering of the first dose of herbal medicine, Li-niang was immediately revived. The couple then traveled on to Hangchow, the capital. As a result of military tension in Yangchow, Madam Tu, the girl's mother, had arrived in Hangchow for temporary refuge. Thus mother and daughter were unexpectedly reunited. Liu by this time also arrived in Hangchow, called on Tu Pao, and was sent to prison as a possible spy on account of his incoherent talk about Tu's daughter. With the repulsion of the invaders and the arrival of news from the capital that the purported spy was actually the recipient of highest honors in the literary examinations, came the happy ending of the play.

While the plot savors of the conventional tale of the miraculous, the delineation of individual characters was unique in Ming drama; all the principal characters, instead of being stereotypes, were highly individual.

Let us now examine the structural and stylistic features of southern drama, aside from the excessive number of scenic changes that we have already noted in replacing the strict rule of four major acts preceded by a prologue in northern drama. The most striking characteristic feature of southern drama lies in its exclusive adoption of southern tunes for the singing parts. This involved not only the preponderance of softer musical instruments but also an almost unlimited freedom in the choice of tunes in building up song sequences. Unlike northern drama, in which the opening song had to be written to a specific tune, southern drama might begin with any tune irrespective of length or musical key. This liberty, however, had its limitations. While the chamber-music type of accompaniment would be ideally suited to situations where lyricism and intricate delineation of emotions were called for, it was found to be too soft and too smooth for the presentation of the violent emotional and physical struggles. Hence the southern dramatists boldly crossed the barriers of convention and adopted musical tunes from both schools to suit the dramatic situations. Although we could not call this an innovation in the Ming Dynasty, as there had been clear cases in Yüan drama in which musical tunes were drawn from both north and south, yet it must be admitted that what had been merely exceptions had now become the rule.

In the second place southern drama in its golden age saw fit to revert to the convention of the prologue, which had been dropped from usage for nearly a century. In the case of dramas in which the plots were not historical, a brief synopsis would be presented in the prologue, often with the morals artistically hinted at if not mechanically presented. In the third place, the distribution of the singing parts to more than one actor had now become the prevailing mode. In Yüan drama the singing was exclusively carried by the principal actor or actress while the other members of the cast were restricted to speaking parts. The advantages of the innovation are obvious, as a larger number of gifted actors could now be happily accommodated to the great satisfaction of players and audience alike. In addition, both the singing and the songs had become more spirited, as characterization was now more varied and the emotional interpretations of the dramatic action was definitely less monotonous. As a result, naturally, from the purely literary standpoint the challenges presented to playwrights were now more exacting as they had to reorganize their dramatic technique so as to assure evenly distributed attention to the development of the leading characters instead of concentrating upon just the hero or heroine.

Another interesting innovation in southern drama was a somewhat unexpected reaction against the almost limitless freedom that was exercised in splitting the drama up into changes of scene. This unexpected reaction was the emergence of short plays in which only four or five changes of scene and ten or twelve musical tunes would be called for. This mutation of a peculiarly shortened version of the master type, comparable to the emergence of the short tale during the golden period of long voluminous fiction, had been known at an earlier date in China but had failed to attract public attention as long as it had remained a mere mutation. Such an innovation had been regarded only as a side dish to be completely obliterated by the glamour of the elaborate banquet. After 1506, short plays were no longer mutations but widely accepted typical performances. Their popularity was due to the increase in numbers of elaborate dinner parties in the sixteenth century, where formerly full-length southern dramas had been a heavy burden to hosts and guests alike. The subject matter of these short plays was usually drawn from historical anecdotes, and themes could be easily selected to suit the special occasion.

A leading playwright who contributed much to the new vogue of the short play was the scholar of many-sided accomplishments, Yang Shên (1488-1559). A native of Szechuan Province, Yang had traveled extensively in his young manhood and had gained wide recognition after he had won first honor in the palace competitive examination in the year 1511. In spite of the fact that he was not successful in his official career and that after many years of exile he had to spend his last years in the frontier area of Yunnan, he had exerted an immense influence upon the writers of his age, leaving an enormous amount of writing to posterity. Besides two short plays and a wide assortment of prose and poetry written in traditional style, Yang is also remembered for the pseudoclassical literature which he had produced, or in plainer language, which he had forthrightly forged. Several exquisite Han and T'ang pieces which had been known to have been irrevocably lost were "rediscovered" by Yang. Although not all readers could be easily fooled, they were almost unanimously gratified by the "rediscovered" pieces. In this respect, Yang belonged to the distinguished company of many confreres in the Western literary world that included Thomas Chatterton and James Macpherson in eighteenth-century England.

Of the two plays written by Yang, one was lost soon after his death. This piece, well known among his contemporaries, was originally entitled *Tung Tien Yüan Chi* or *An Original Tale from Primeval Heaven*. The plot, according to one literary critic who had seen the piece, was the story of how a Taoist priest had converted and reformed two highway robbers of the Kunlun mountain area— an exposition of the basic teachings of popular Taoism. According to another early reader of the play, the piece consisted of twenty-four sections to correspond to the twenty-four subdivisions of the year, in each of which was presented a tableau depicting the most touching scenes from the life of twenty-four different virtuous people of antiquity, and the bandits, instead of being enlightened by abstract expositions of Taoist doctrine, were simply shown these tableaus without comment by the Taoist and allowed to draw their own conclusions.

Less unconventional in its technique of presentation was the other play written by Yang Shên, *Wu Ling Ch'un* or *The Spring in Wu Ling*, based on the interesting essay written by T'ao Yüan-ming in which was depicted a utopian society which had been built up by refugees in a little-known area entirely cut off from the world of political turmoil. The other pieces that Yang Shên was purported to have written were of the same category, short plays depicting selected episodes from the lives of great Chinese writers.

Instead of being known as *ch'uan ch'i* or romantic drama, which was the collective name given to southern drama, these short plays of southern authorship, which were themselves an outgrowth of the southern tradition in dramatic production, were given the label of *tsa chü,* which was the name borne by the Yüan dramas. This interchange of names was less confusing and unreasonable than appears on the surface. Since these shorter plays were episodic in character and, therefore, lacked the feature of sustained development, they had to be introduced to the audience with the aid of short prologues which was a reversion to Yüan methods. In addition, to make the drop of the curtain less abrupt, the conclusion usually took the form of a short poem either chanted or sung, again in accordance with Yüan dramatic tradition. Hence it is understandable that they were called *tsa chü* or miscellaneous plays so as to be distinguished from the long-drawn-out fuller southern dramas which still held the center of the stage.

Once the shorter plays had come into vogue, there were many writers of this school. Almost all major writers of the age in other fields felt tempted to try their talents on short southern drama. All the intricacy of playmaking technique could be bypassed and extensive knowledge of musical tunes and technicalities was unnecessary. All that was involved in the writing of a short play was a kind of literary embroidery upon an attractive episode, imaginary or historical. The songs written for embellishment could be written to whatever tune the author happened to know best. Hence, among the large number of such plays written and produced, their merit ranged from really superb literary creations to a mere perfunctory fulfillment of prescribed formulas for amusement and pastime.

One outstanding author was Huang Fang-yü (flourished 1560), who utilized his short plays exclusively to delineate the world as one devoid of truth, of goodness, and of beauty. He was a kind of Zola in Ming drama, exposing all the cruelties, crudities, and injustices of the actual world. He was particularly penetrating and effective in exposing the heart-rending cruelties to which Ming women singers were subjected. So thoroughgoing was the development of his tragic scenes that he was almost un-Chinese in providing practically no relief in the presentation of the tragic aspects of human life.

Another unconventional writer was Yeh Hsien-tsu (1566-1641). Known to posterity mainly as a fighter against the inequities of the Ming eunuchs and as a writer on ethics, he produced nine short plays. These were partly romantic dramas built upon well-known themes in the private lives of T'ang literary men which were fairly stereotyped or short heroic dramas. It is in the second type of short plays that Yeh distinguished himself above his contemporaries. He would select such characters as defeated generals and unsuccessful assassins and present them against the emotional backdrop of history. The songs written for these characters were unconventional in the sense that they broke the natural limitations of the soft chamber-music type of accompaniment that was used in southern drama with the result that the singing, in order to do justice to the themes of the songs, had to be done in such a way as to drown out the accompanying music.

After the collapse of the Mongol Dynasty, northern drama, generally speaking, had virtually disappeared. Nonetheless, a popular form of literature seldom could die an abrupt death. In the case of northern drama in China, although no new plays were written, many of the popular tunes continued to be sung by the northern Chinese. While the southern drama was rapidly expanding its influence and its production there were echoes of the melodies of northern drama. A few specimens, nearly all written by unknown writers, have been preserved as evidence that northern drama did survive the dynastic change. On these, however, the influence of the new school was obvious. Adherence to structural rules had been relaxed. Although the four-act tradition was not entirely abandoned, there were northern plays of the one-act variety while there were others written in as many as seven acts. In the handling of the singing role some plays followed the typical convention while others would provide singing parts for more than one principal actor. Yet, in spite of these deviations from the basic rules of Yüan drama, these were not southern plays because in the first place the tunes utilized were northern tunes and the rhyming scheme was formulated in accordance with northern pronunciation in which the entering tone was totally absent.

The writer who most completely epitomized the purposeful merging of the techniques of the northern and southern schools was Hsü Wei (1521-1593), who by his courtesy name of Hsü Wên-ch'ang, was a massive figure in sixteenth-century folklore. To the common peasants, old and young, as well as to many other illiterate elements in Chinese society, he was the greatest wit of his age, who would use his humor to embarrass learned scholars in defense of the less fortunate. A native of Chekiang Province, he had not only distinguished himself in his divergent types of creative writing but also acquired an eminent reputation as a student of military tactics and strategy by making important contributions while on the military staff of General Hu Hsien-tsung in repelling the mass attacks of Japanese pirates who were then infesting the East China coast and the lower reaches of the Yangtze River.

After Hu had been incriminated unjustly and sentenced to a long prison term, Hsü Wei seemed to have lost his mind for a time, attempting to commit suicide by piercing his ears with a huge awl. Finally he was imprisoned on suspicion of having had a part in killing his wife. After he had served his period of imprisonment he traveled to many far-off regions, dissipating himself in heavy drinking and singing songs of his own composition. In his old age he suffered from extreme poverty but he refused persistently any offer of financial assistance by shouting behind a latched door, "Hsü Wei is not here." On one special occasion, however, he broke his own rule by accepting some ten bolts of superb woolen textiles sent him by General Hu, whereupon he called a tailor and made himself many suits, the first new clothing he had had in many years. Soon afterward he sold them all along with his collection of books and fine paintings. As a student he was extensively read in Taoist and Buddhist literature and had drawn up elaborate plans for the writing of new commentaries on several of the basic texts. As an artist he was unsurpassed in calligraphy and in sketches of flowers and ferns, bamboos, and rockery.

Among his writings there are four plays under the general title *The Four Shrieks of the Monkey* or *Ssŭ Shêng Yüan*. This peculiar title was based upon a tradition in Chinese folklore to the effect that when a monkey had lost its baby it uttered four shrieks and then died brokenhearted. Of these four plays, the last one is the most famous. This play, entitled *Nü Chuang Yüan* or *The Woman Chuang Yüan*, was based on the folk tale of the tenth century. A *Chuang Yüan* was the recipient of the highest honors at the top-level contest in the competitive literary examination system. The heroine, Huang Ts'ung-hu, was a gifted writer who was very fond of appearing in public in man's attire, although she never took part in a competitive examination as was represented in the play. However, she seemed to have been an extremely unconventional person who had served a prison sentence on account of her involvement in a case of arson.

While in prison her identity had not been revealed, since at the time of her arrest she had been mistaken for a young man. The magistrate of the county was impressed by the literary reputation and good looks of the prisoner and as he himself was unconventional he was eager to have the latter as his son-in-law. In a poem addressed to the magistrate, the prisoner disclosed her identity. When she was summoned by the magistrate it was discovered that she was the daughter of a distinguished commissioner, orphaned when she was a baby, and had been living with an aged maidservant. After continuing in man's attire and serving the magistrate as secretary-councilor for a time, she resigned her post and was not heard of thereafter.

Using this historic anecdote as the basic framework, Hsü Wei, the dramatist, did his eloquent embroidering. The complications of the plot were enhanced by sending the unconventional girl in man's attire to the competitive examination and having her come out as the most successful candidate. By employing subtle puns and injecting clever jokes into the superbly humorous dialogues, Hsü Wei succeeded not only in unfolding a charming story on the stage but also in substantiating his theme that there was no irrefutable reason why a woman was necessarily inferior to a man.

In his long years of solitary retirement prior to his death, he had one constant caller, a devoted pupil, Wang Chi-tê, himself a southern playwright of considerable reputation. Between the two there were many discourses on the musical dramas of the period. From the records made by Wang it was apparent that both master and pupil realized that the drama of the southern school had already passed its prime and could not be completely revitalized. The forthrightness and unconventionality of the northern school, however, were features worth cultivating. Hence, a compromise was reached —to use northern tunes for the songs and southern dialects in the dialogues.

This lingering interest in the musical dramas of the northern school toward the last half century of the Ming Dynasty brought about a revived interest in the reprinting of Yüan plays. Between 1599 and 1632 there were published no fewer than seven sizable collections of Yüan plays, the most famous being the *One Hundred Yüan Plays* reprinted in a collection in 1616. With this fervor in diffusing the best samples of Yüan drama, northern plays newly written in conformity with the Yüan tradition consumed the creative efforts of nearly all playwrights, including those whose special talents lay in the realm of orthodox southern drama.

Although in recent decades many of these late Ming dramas of both schools have been rediscovered and reprinted, they are in the main reflections of the most glorious days of Yüan drama. Historically speaking they are important as a link between Ming drama and the new drama that was to emerge after the beginning of Manchu domination in China in 1644.

Besides the new trends started by the eclectic school of dramatic writers in merging the music of north and south, in extending the freedom in playmaking with regard to the number of changes of scene, enlarging the range in cast of characters, and in enlarging the number of participants in singing as well as the style of singing, Ming drama is particularly noticeable for a number of other departures from the beaten path. In the selection of plots, whereas Yüan dramas relied chiefly if not exclusively on history and legendary fiction, Ming drama looked persistently if not exclusively to contemporary events for inspiration. Thus, in a sense, as far as the plots go, Ming drama was on the whole much more realistic, reminding us of the rise of middle-class comedy in eighteenth-century England as well as continental Europe. Ming drama was relatively free from the muzzled protests of the Yüan playwrights against the oppression of alien rule. Thus it has a tendency to utilize the vehicle for mere entertainment with no philosophical message, or as a convenience to parade the rhetoric and learning of the author.

CHAPTER 28

Early Ch'ing Poetry

In 1644 Chinese history seemed to repeat itself. As in 1279, China was again conquered by a foreign tribe from the northeast, the Manchus, who were to dominate all parts of the vast empire. This repetition of history was more apparent than real. Whereas the Mongols had developed little respect for Chinese civilization when they became the masters of the millions in China, the Manchus were already deeply Sinicized when they drove on to Peking and set young Emperor Shun Chih, a boy barely six years old, on the dragon throne. Moreover, the Manchus were actually the remote descendants of the Chin Tatars who had miraculously risen to power in 1115 and upset the Liao Dynasty in the brief period of a decade to dominate the northern half of China, thus having acquainted themselves fully with the special traits of Chinese civilization. Calling itself the Post-Ch'in regime, the Manchu Dynasty in 1616 adopted a program of conscious and accelerated Sinicization which laid the cornerstone of its expansion to areas inside of the Great Wall. In the second place, the Mongol Empire was a vast bicontinental setup, regarding China, especially the southern half of it, only as a constituent, though probably the most prized constituent, of its world empire, whereas the Manchus entertained no such pretentious ambition, were intent on China itself, and were even surprised at their own success.

Kublai Khan had completely disregarded the aspirations and welfare of his Chinese subjects when he took the southern half of China and was ready to apply the rule of the mailed fist and to set up a purely military government of occupation. He was awakened by the advice of his Liao Tatar advisor, Yalü Ch'u-ts'ai, to the effect that though one could conquer the world on horseback, one could never rule over an empire on horseback. Even after concessions were made by the Mongol administration to Chinese traditions and mores, Mongol sympathy for Chinese culture was to remain merely perfunctory and skin deep throughout the decades of the Yüan Dynasty. The Manchus, on the other hand, had decided so discreetly to impress their Chinese ministers and subjects with the worthiness of their acceptance of the Mandate of Heaven that they seemed sincere in upholding Chinese cultural orthodoxy intact. Secretly they were mindful of the fearsome consequences of such a policy—the possibility of the complete absorption of the conquering minority eventually by the vast subjugated majority.

This may have prompted them to follow the example of the circumspect Mongols, who had invented a Mongol script for the building up of a written vehicle for the official imperial language, which was Mongolian. The Manchu script was thus invented in 1610, to be revised several times subsequently, and was utilized in the translation of Chinese classics and belles-lettres for Manchus so as to obviate the danger of over-Sinicization of their own clansmen. Nonetheless a modicum of systematic training in the Chinese language, both oral and written, was needed by the Manchus, partly to enable them to check on the loyalty and fidelity of their Chinese subordinates, and partly to create the illusion for the benefit of the conquered that the new masters of the empire were serious in their adoption of Chinese culture.

As happens so often in the world of human affairs, a long-sustained pretense developed into a psychological and behavioral fact. Once a Manchu prince had tasted the first lessons in written Chinese, he had been exposed to a world of fascinating literature with which he had had no previous acquaintance, and with the joy of discovery he would gradually realize that reading Chinese literature in Manchu translation was insipid and comparable, as one of them observed, to "washing one's feet with socks on." Despite stern rescripts issued by the early Manchu emperors forbidding excessive preoccupation with Chinese literature and unwarranted personal intercourse with Chinese members of the official hierarchy, the Manchus continued to drink with increasing fervor and satisfaction at the fountain of Chinese civilization. Many of them became not only conversant with Chinese letters in the varied fields, but also major writers in Chinese themselves.

If this was true of the Manchu aristocracy and gentry, it was even truer of the Manchu emperors themselves, despite the guarded policy which was periodically renewed and supposedly followed. While this phenomenon prolonged the period of Manchu domination to three times the length of the Yüan dynastic span, it was also largely responsible for the almost complete disappearance of the Manchus as a distinct tribal and cultural group. When the Yüan Dynasty collapsed in 1368, all the Mongols resident in China proper, mainly as members of the garrison units, retreated en masse back to

Mongolia. When the Manchu Dynasty was replaced by the Republic of China in 1911, however, only a handful could speak Manchu and even they were more fluent in Chinese than in their ancestral language.

The decades of the integration surrounding the dynastic change and the foreign invasion produced far-reaching social and economic upheavals. Many populous cities were sacked and many millions were killed by the various organized bandit groups of the late empire. And the military operations and so-called pacification measures of the early Manchus were extremely cruel and devastating, often involving wholesale massacre, as in the case of the fortified town of Chiating, and the continued slaughtering of innocent citizens, children and women included, for days after the surrender of a city as in the case of Yangchow. These catastrophies and tragedies left many a scar on Chinese literature. And yet in a peculiar and subtle manner, the convulsions of the dynastic change did not disturb except in minor ways the main currents of literary trends in the empire. Many of the official posts both in the central and in the provincial governments were held by political turncoats who were veteran survivors of the foreign dynasty, and being men of letters of varying degrees of attainment and pre-eminence, they would naturally do their best to maintain the status quo.

Moreover, fully aware of their traitorous conduct and despicable record, they would try to make themselves less unpresentable to posterity by dragging as many of their friends and acquaintances as possible into the mud-pool of slavish and abject submission by collaborating with the new rulers in their policy of hunting down all noncollaborationists and forcing them to partake of the new dynastic honors. All through the latter part of the seventeenth and the whole of the eighteenth century, numerous special honors examinations were periodically set up to trap these unsullied elements of the Chinese literary world who had intended to have little to do with the new alien dynasty. The high-sounding labels of these special examinations, such as "the examination to honor profound erudition and magnificent literary style" (po-hsüeh hungt-z'ŭ) had only an irksome effect upon the noncollaborationists. Even the simplification of procedure made scarcely any new appeal.

The candidates, all named by imperial invitation, were to take part in the highest level of the competitive examination system without going through the intermediate stages. Those who were loyal to the Ming court were adamant in their refusal to respond to such invitations. Some would feign paralysis while others would threaten to drink poison. Still others would achieve the double purpose of by-passing the hairdressing regulation and of continuing nonrecognition of the new dynasty by seeking refuge and sanctuary as monks in Buddhist monasteries or ordained priests in Taoist temples, thus enjoying freedom to shave their heads clean or let their hair grow long in accordance with the long-established practices of the two respective cults, to obviate the ignominy of shaving the hair around the edge and wearing pigtails.

To complete the picture, however, it should be mentioned that not a few of the younger members of the literary and learned professions were dazzled by the offer of imperial largesse and submitted with only a slight reluctance to the temptation. The conformity and submission of these, just like the indifference and nonco-operation, did little to disturb the continuation of the Ming trends.

Under the strict surveillance of a suspicious alien dynasty, innovations were not the order of the day. As the Manchus had risen to power from obscurity in the unenlightened and peripheral region of Manchuria and as the direct ancestors of the Manchu imperial house had been recipients of official appointments and honors from the Ming Dynasty as guards of the military marches, they were interested in purging historical records of such references to their origin as might be derogatory and harmful to their new prestige. Sensitized by their suspicion, they were also rendered uneasy by the possible existence of Chinese writings which might be hostile to their domination of China.

Thus special efforts were organized repeatedly to comb the whole body of recent and contemporary literature in search of evidences of *lèse-majesté*. Many cases were brought to court and the offenders punished with extreme cruelty which might include the extermination of a whole clan. Among these cases were several in which the offenses seemed unintentional, but the incrimination was so deviously and intricately developed that the accused were unable to prove themselves innocent. To cover up the evil and cruel intent of these searchers, the imperial court tried repeatedly to make such exposures of guilt seem purely coincidental by launching huge programs of compilation and publication.

The two notable examples of editorial enterprises of encyclopedic scope were (1) the *T'u-shu Chih-ch'êng* (synthesis of books), under the reign of K'ang Hsi, in which all the representative and major writings extant in the empire were cut up and classified according to a prefabricated system, extending from the heavenly bodies and astronomical phenomena to the details of everyday activities in the world of men; and (2) the *Ssŭ-k'u Ch'üan-shu* or the *Complete Works of the Four Divisions of the Imperial Library*, which was so voluminous that it was never printed but of which seven copies were made by hand by the most conformist calligraphers of the empire. In this work the major writings of the empire from the earliest times down to the prevailing era were re-edited for inclusion and arranged in accordance with the four divisions of bibliography, namely, the Confucian classics, the histories, the philosophers, and the writers of belles-lettres. Works of secondary importance were not included but mentioned and summarized by title in the general catalogue.

According to one estimate made by experts in the Western world, it has been said that at the time of the conclusion of this second monumental collection (at the time of the American Declaration of Independence), the total repository of Chinese books in print was approximately the same size as that of all books of the non-Chinese world put together. These enormous labors were launched to guard against the diversion of literary energies into antidynastic and subversive channels and the continuation of well-established literary traditions, and avoidance of innovations seemed to be the most reliable guidepost for steering away from the tabus of an unreasonably sensitive censorship.

In the first century and a half of the Manchu Dynasty, the polite literature of China continually charted a safe and conventional course. Except for a few pieces registering the heartfelt tragedy of a lamentable dynastic collapse and except for the appearance of a larger number of writers who wrote creditable essays and poetry following traditional models and using the classical language with great dexterity, the light of literature seems to have been largely dimmed by the glow of scholarship. For evidences of real literary creativity we must look beyond the scope of polite literature to drama and fiction.

And yet, before we discuss attainments of the Ch'ing Dynasty in drama and in fiction, we should re-examine briefly what was accomplished in polite literature, because to contemporaries essay writing and poetry were still the primary concern of literary men.

Although there was relatively little that was new as compared with the vistas to be opened up in fiction and drama, Ch'ing literature of the traditional type was an impressive summing up of what had gone before. In the field of scholarship, continued efforts were made to conduct objective researches in such a way as to uncover the real face of antiquity, eliminating all the accumulations of guesswork and misinterpretations in spite of the fact that these might have been motivated by the best of intentions. The conscious adoption of the historical and inductive methods not only enlarged the horizon of scholarship but also objectified the attitudes of the research scholars. As a result, scholars of the Ch'ing Dynasty were omnivorous readers of all kinds of previous writings and their careful analysis in the study of archaic language usages and stylistic peculiarities stood them in excellent stead in duplicating and imitating masterpieces of the past. All previous literary types were revived with vigor during the Ch'ing Dynasty.

Thus, the *fu* of the Han Dynasty, the parallel prose of the Six Dynasties, the poetry of T'ang, the *tz'ŭ* of Sung, the *ku wên* or archaic-prose movement documents of the T'ang and Sung Dynasties, the dramatic as well as the lyrical *ch'ü tzŭ* of the Yüan Dynasty, and the prose fiction of the Ming Dynasty were all resurrected with increased vigor. Their Ch'ing imitators were actually more than merely imitators, for after mastering the technique required for successful imitation, they succeeded in wielding the old weapons with such dexterity that they could breathe a new spirit and a new distinctive personality into their creative writings. To sum up, these writers brought to a glorious summation old literary types of the past ages as though they were anticipating the emergence of an entirely new era.

Traditional poets of the Ch'ing Dynasty, like Ch'ing writers in other fields, did not free themselves from the age-old practice of following in the footsteps of great masters. In fact, each outstanding poet would exalt one or more idols of his own. Nonetheless, those who succeeded in rising to great heights were entitled to fame because of the irrepressible upsurge of their own originalities in spite of their professed homage to the respective masters. Among early Ch'ing poets, two stood out most prominently as Janus-headed figures spanning the two dynasties. In spite of the fact that they were both political turncoats, they exerted considerable influence upon their younger contemporaries.

The first of these, Ch'ien Ch'ien-yi (1582-1664), a native of Ch'angshu County in Kiangsu Province, had risen to great official distinction as minister of the board of rites when Peking was overrun by the Manchus in 1644. He soon fled southward to Nanking where Prince Fu was crowned and carried on resistance for a while. When Nanking was captured by the Manchu forces he openly surrendered to the enemy and was appointed by the latter as associate director of the board of historiography, becoming, therefore, a servant of two masters. As a poet he advocated a return to the T'ang and Sung masters and bitterly attacked the late Ming poets. Aside from his merits as a conscious imitator of Li Po and Tu Fu, he sang clearly with his own voice, especially after he had come to realize that his participation in the activities of the new alien dynasty were unworthy of a man of his attainment. The cloak under which his touching reminiscences of the fallen dynasty were then expressed was seen through by the Manchus and gave rise to a strict ban placed on these writings and their eventual destruction by decree.

Equally distinguished as a poet was Ch'ien's younger contemporary, Wu Wei-yeh (1609-1671), a native of T'aits'ang County near present-day Shanghai. A pupil of the famous ethical philosopher, Chang P'u (1602-1641), he had achieved great fame in 1644 when the Ming Dynasty fell. Having made a resolution not to have anything to do with the alien conquerors, he was forced by the local authorities and by even his parents to revoke his oath and to respond to the official summons of the Manchus. He was so unhappy at Peking, where he had been made president of the imperial college, that he decided to retire soon afterward. This unhappy event and tragic decision left an indelible mark upon him as a poet. Unlike other verse writers of his age, he excelled in the writing of long narrative poems of reminiscences. Most celebrated among these was the "Song of Yüan-yüan" in which he depicted with the charm and subtlety of Po Chü-yi one of the incidents related to the dynastic downfall.

Yüan-yüan was a beautiful singing girl who had become the favorite concubine of the Ming general Wu San-kuei (1612-1678), who was stationed at Shan Hai Kuan, the easternmost strategic pass of the Great Wall separating Manchuria from China proper. When he had heard that Peking had fallen to the forces of the bandit rebel, Li Chih-ch'êng, and Yüan-yüan had been carried away as a prisoner of war, he was so enraged that instead of fighting the Manchus he invited them to come in to help him avenge the personal wrong that had been done him. Presenting the vicissitudes to which the beautiful girl was subjected after her capture by the bandit-rebel, the poet's namesake, Wu Wei-yeh's art was chiefly one of devious narration and characterization which lent considerable charm to the treatment. In the remorse felt by the principal character the reader found unmistakably the reflection of the feeling of tragedy which also was the poet's own. His criticism of the traitorous general was voiced with restraint:

> In bitter tears the six armies all wore their mourning white,
> While the general felt an irrepressible rage for a beautiful woman.

It was reported that when the general saw these two lines, he offered the poet a valuable gift for their deletion, which gift the poet adamantly rejected. In some of his shorter poems he dedicated himself to two themes, namely, lamenting the fall of the old dynasty and regretting his own surrender to the alien conquerers. Thus, when he traveled close to the homestead of a deceased friend to whom he had pledged his continued loyalty to the Ming imperial house, he wrote:

> To my floating life what I owe now is mere death,
> In this old world I know of no way to retract my steps.
> Unlike the dogs and chickens of Prince Huainan of old,
> I failed to ascend heavenward; I ended by dropping into the world of men.

The third poet of great distinction was Wang Shih-chêng (1634-1711), a native of Shantung and a great admirer of the two T'ang poets Wang Wei and Mêng Hao-jan. He upheld inspiration as expressed in harmonious diction as the most important factor of poetry. In short, according to Wang, the writing of poetry amounts to the catching of spiritual inspiration embodied immediately in words. His use of the two terms *shên* and *yün*, in Chinese, needs some explanation. *Shên*, the word meaning "god" in ordinary context, connotes spirituality as well as the experience of spirituality and thus the going through of an inspiration which would transport one from the level of daily living to heretofore unacquainted planes. The Chinese word *yün*, which means "cadence," connotes in this context the subtle effects of a inner and lingering melody. To ensure this, it was Wang's advice that poetry should only be suggestive, never exhaustive. This would involve not only artistic restraint but also happy unconventionality of diction. On one occasion he commented, "Poetry is comparable to the divine dragon which when it allows its head to become visible will make its tail invisible. At times it would only reveal a single scale or a single claw. How can we expect to see it in its entirety such as would be revealed by a cheap sculptor or painter?"

Other poets of distinction carried on worthily the historic tradition of Chinese poetry. One was Chu Yi-tsun (1629-1709), a native of Chekiang Province, known for his extensive travels and his comprehensive scholarship. As he excelled in *tz'ŭ* writing, we shall defer mention of him for the moment. Another was Cha Shên-hsing (1650-1727) also of Chekiang Province. Pupil of the philosopher Huang Tsung-hsi, Cha was famous as a scholar besides being a major poet of his time. While erudition was a basic characteristic of nearly all Ch'ing Dynasty poets, he wisely stayed away from the use of classical allusions and the use of out-of-the-way words and phrases. Hence, beside the floridity and heaviness of his contemporaries, he impressed his readers with his unusual lucidity, making his poetry normally understandable without the assistance of explanatory notes. A typical example is his seven-syllable-line poem entitled "After a Rain."

> A plentiful year is expected of a single shower;
> We common folk desire immediate rewards.
> Compared with the peasants I am even more shortsighted—
> My only hope is a good sleep this cool evening.

A clear voice of protest raised against the powerful Wang Shih-chêng and his theory of *shên yün* was that of Chao Chih-hsin (1662-1744), Wang's fellow provincial neighbor, and husband of his niece. His dedication to poetry was forced on him by his unconventionality —drinking and dining during a period of universal mourning following the decease of an empress. Thus free from official life before he was thirty, he evolved his own theory of superior poetry. Instead of relying on inspiration, he recommended the studious approach to the set pattern of past masters. To make concrete his theories, he compiled a collection of tonal patterns of versification on the basis of the masterpieces of previous poets. He also wrote a collection of essays entitled *T'an Lung Lu* or *Notes on Discussing the Dragon* to refute the theories of his senior relative.

Wang Shih-chêng's surpassing quality as a poet was in part due to his extensive travel. Unlike the traditional verse writer who was closeted in a study trying to see the problems and the meaning of the universe as reflected in the literary gems of the past, he had firsthand contacts with the living conditions of people in far-off regions and the beauties of nature in those outlying areas. The high esteem in which he was held by his senior contemporaries was doubtless due to his ability to capture inspiring moments when he was on the road. Lines such as:

> Sailing with the cold evening tide, I crossed the Yangtze.
> Yellow leaves are filling the woods and the swans are singing.

or,

> Autumn's color is glowing outside the city walls;
> The fragrance of lotus leaves and of cereals are blending.

could not fail to impress sheer imitators of T'ang or Sung poets.

When Wang's influence had reached its heights in southern quarters and been challenged in other quarters, the cultural scene in China under the new alien dynasty was rapidly changing. The new ideal cherished by the world of scholarship was sound and extensive learning. Although the principal writers of poetry did not pretend to emulate the examples of the erudite classical scholars, they would often fall into step with the major trend in spite of themselves. One of the many-sided intellectuals of the age who was held up as the major poet of the first half of the seventeenth century was Shên Tê-ch'ien (1672-1769), a native of Ch'angchou near present-day Shanghai. It was not until he was close to seventy that he succeeded in passing the palace examination. At that time he was already well known as poet and anthologist. He had many pupils among the younger poets and was particularly well known for his ability to doctor badly written verse. One of his patrons was Emperor Ch'ien Lung. As he unwittingly revealed this information he was banished in the evening of his life and after his death the Manchu emperor was so unforgiving as to order the smashing of his tombstone.

Shên's influence was more extensively felt through his anthologies and his incidental critical remarks than through his own poetry. A believer in all the niceties of Chinese prosody, he emphasized what he called methodology and phonology. The most perfect poet in his estimation was the poet-painter of the T'ang Dynasty, Wang Wei. Distinctly different from his contemporaries, he did not eulogize Tu Fu unconditionally, on the grounds that Tu Fu's poetry was too ornate. His own attainment in poetry writing did not attract much attention on account of his involvement in a case of literary inquisition in which a minor poet had been accused of antidynastic thoughts in his writings.

When Emperor Ch'ien Lung was sitting on the Chinese throne, the control of the alien dynasty of the conquered people had already been made secure. The lingering memory of the tragic fall of the Ming Dynasty had grown dim. As a result, the inquisitional activities of the new dynasty was being given a comprehensive inventory in the compilation of the monumental collection known as the *Ssŭ-k'u Ch'üan-shu* or *The Complete Library of the Four Divisions of Literature.* This epoch-making piece of editorial work had been carried out supposedly as a stimulation to general learning but actually for the main purpose of combing the whole body of extant literature in Chinese for any anti-Manchu thought. Chinese scholars during the eighteenth century, fully aware of the cruelties inflicted upon the violators of the dynastic tabu, had discreetly steered themselves away from practical learning and from the discussion of contemporary topics in preference to historical and philological studies. Reflecting this trend in literature was the many-sided Yüan Mei (1715-1797).

A native of Ch'ien-t'ang, the present-day Hangchow, Yüan Mei rose to distinction early as a precocious child. Reading omnivorously in the bookstores of the city, he early mastered the intricacies of the Eight-Legged Essay, which he soon outgrew. In his own confession in a letter to a friend in which he recalled his early youth, he wrote:

> Ever since my boyhood days I have loathed the composition of the Eight-Legged Essays. Although I was admitted as a scholarship student of the county and although I was highly recommended by my examiners, deep down in my heart I did not feel I was doing the right thing. What I slighted in my mind was fully revealed in my ink and my candles so that as soon as the examination question was distributed and as soon as I seized hold of my writing brush, I refused to submit myself to the commands of the usual rules. Thus, I battled through examinations of this type in four autumns without satisfying myself or my examiners.

His luck was not any better when he had been recommended to take part in the special honors examination. It was then that he decided to brace himself to do what the rest of the world had addressed themselves to. In his twenty-fourth year he finally surmounted the hurdle and passed all the examinations in rapid succession. His next assignment was the intensive study of the Manchu language in both its spoken and written aspects. Since there was nothing interesting to read in Manchu he went through the course perfunctorily and was graduated with the lowest possible grade. In consequence, he was sent to Nanking as an executive of a county. Eleven years of civil service confirmed his decision to retire from public life.

His failure to climb in the official hierarchy was a blessing to him in disguise. Having bought a house with a charming garden at the price of 300 taels of silver, he renamed his charming retreat "Sui Yuan" or "Random Garden." Capitalizing on his literary reputation, he enjoyed an enormous patronage from people who were willing to pay him high prices for occasional writings both in prose and in poetry. Soon he succeeded in building up a magnificent library and an impressive following of pupils, including many gifted women. In his sixty-third year, after the death of his mother, he made extensive tours to all parts of China to enrich his experience.

As a writer, he was distinguished by his high native intelligence and by his daring in transcending many traditions. Naturally, he had invited severe criticism not only from conservative scholars but also from some of the best minds of his age, including the great historian and critic, Chang Hsüeh-ch'êng (1738-1801).

A great spokesman against inhibition, Yüan Mei glorified in what he called *hsing ling* or spirituality in poetry. By spirituality he meant the forthright expression of what the poet felt in the way of an urge from his inmost nature. This would be intensified by moments of inspiration raising the contents of the form to a high emotional level. Relying for his arguments on the dualistic aspect of the life of any animate being, he advocated intelligence as the quiet or passive element and emotion as the active and dynamic element. When these two elements were ideally brought into mutual play, the result was good poetry. Furthermore, as all emotional contents of the human mind were natural voices of man's personality, such emotions as anger and hatred were fit subjects for poetry. Hence, moralistic yardsticks did not apply in the field of creative writing. In a letter he addressed to Shên Tê-ch'ien he even went so far as to suggest that the theory advocating poetry as conducive to an elevation of moral standards was the fabrication of pedants. The mere recording of emotional outbursts, according to Yüan, would not necessarily make for superior poetry, because poetry by its very nature had to be selective and had to rely on concrete images. This is borne out in a quatrain of verse:

> Poetry exists where poetry is sought.
> A spark of inspiration is the poet's true teacher.
> Sunset and green grass and other ordinary things,
> To one who knows how to use them, will make poetry.

Again, in a four-syllable-line poem on the gradations of poetry, he wrote:

> Poetry is like playing the lute,
> Each sound revealing the mind.
> And the mind being a musical instrument
> Expresses what is felt from within.
> When my mind is in perfect peace
> My words have neither smoke nor fire.
> But when my mind is overpowered with emotions
> Readers will shed tears.

His theory of poetry accounts for his voluminous production. Some of his best poems were records of passing moments of inspiration. A typical example is the following short poem written casually on a spring day:

> A thousand branches appearing red in rain and shrouded in
>   layers of mist
> Depict the beauties of nature to the poet's satisfaction.
> The spring cloud on the hill is lazy like myself,
> Remaining drowsy irrespective of sunshine.

As in the case of poetry of regular meter or *shih,* the early Ch'ing Dynasty abounds with accomplished poets whose medium was that of irregular meter or *tz'ŭ.* Most of the *shih* poets whom we have reviewed were also superior writers of *tz'ŭ.* As compared with similar writers of the Ming Dynasty, the early Manchu Dynasty poets were aided by researchers who had formulated basic principles governing *tz'ŭ* writing in its most glorious period. In an age in which conformity to great masters was the sole guiding principle in the recreation of past types of literature, accurate analysis of historical techniques was understandably an important key to success. Another demand of the age, namely, general acquaintance with divergent types of previous literature, made all major writers of the last three hundred years successful cultivators of more than one literary genre. Hence, nearly all verse writers became masters or near-masters of various disciplines in versification.

In reviewing early Ch'ing attainments in *tz'ŭ* technique, we shall select a few writers who represented the major trends in this type of imitative literature.

The first *tz'ŭ* poet of the new dynasty was Ch'ên Wei-sung (1625-1682), a native of Yihsing County in Kiangsu Province. A many-sided literary man as well as a participant in the redaction of the *Ming Dynastic History,* he is above all to be remembered for his *tz'ŭ* writing. He is entitled to fame by virtue of both quantity and quality, his *tz'ŭ* writings being more voluminous than those by any other single hand. Apparently having shown little interest in the stereotyped Eight-Legged Essay, he won official distinction very late in life, after he was fifty. His avoidance of what had been considered the main channel to literary honors gave him considerable time to cultivate what he really loved to cultivate. His untrammeled literary habits had led him to the school of *tz'ŭ* writers of the Su Tung-p'o school, the school which preferred forthrightness to strict conformity to discipline, and the school which deliberately disregarded the musical minutiae of the technical aspects of *tz'ŭ* writing.

Autumn Moon

(To the tune of "Moon Over the City Wall")

The west wind blows over the icy disc and makes it pale.
The shadow of the cassia tree is even like a mat.
The washboard sounds in a deep lane,
And rumbling of the watchtower drum,
Contribute to the sadness of the voice of autumn.
Under moonlight the red banners waver and shine,

As the city wall is heavily dyed with silver frost.
Castles and rivers spread over ten thousand li,
A review of the past projected against centuries
Induces me to listen to the lapse of time
As reported by the watchman's bells and drums.

Another outstanding *tz'ŭ* poet among the tens who were busily engaged in cultivating this particular field of artistic writing in the late seventeenth century was Chu Yi-tsun (1629-1709), a native of Hsiushui County in Chekiang Province. Having developed a deep-seated aversion to the regimentation of the Eight-Legged Essay when he was merely sixteen, he devoted his entire life to classical studies and travel without winning any of the traditional honors. Finally, with the growth of his reputation, he was accorded special recognition by Emperor K'ang Hsi in 1679. Appointed to the historiographical bureau to edit the *Ming Dynastic History,* he was granted many imperial favors, including participation in banquets in the imperial palace. As a scholar he is best remembered for his *Ching Yi K'ao,* a carefully annotated bibliography of all the works which had appeared on the Confucian classics. As a poet, he distinguished himself in the writing of *shih* as well as *tz'ŭ.* His meticulous scholarship was utilized in the compilation of an anthology of *tz'ŭ* poetry in which were represented the collected works of more than a hundred *tz'ŭ* poets before his time. Among *tz'ŭ* poets of the Sung Dynasty he showed the greatest admiration for Chiang K'uei (1155?-1235) and Chang Yen (1248-1320?), whom he studied dutifully as models and from whom he learned the basic lessons of elegant diction and strict conformity to tonal patterns demanded by the various tunes. His high attainment in this field made him the founder of a *tz'ŭ* school known as the Chekiang school. In his ten volumes of *tz'ŭ* poetry one hears the charming echoings of the voices of the Southern Sung masters. The following, written to the tune of "Yi Hsiao Nien" or "Youth Recalled," could have come from the pen of a Southern Sung *tz'ŭ* poet:

A crescent moon,
A song of the swan,
A courtyard of autumn dew.
The yellow flowers have just begun blooming
In the form of numberless golden bells.

The swallows have left the autumn altar,
Leaving fragrant traces of mud on windows and screens.
With the approach of the double-nine festival
    [ninth day of the ninth month]
Again the city is swept by rain and wind.

These two *tz'ŭ* poets shared with a number of their contemporaries the ability to reproduce the flavor and atmosphere of the *tz'ŭ* poetry of the Sung Dynasty. Their expertness in reviving a bygone art form is unquestioned. Their reputation rested largely on their remarkable imitative technique which had been universally accepted as a yardstick in measuring literary excellence. Nonetheless it must be borne in mind that the early Ch'ing Dynasty was no longer the Sung Dynasty and poetry written in duplication of the work of the great masters of a previous period was at best only a perfect replica. No matter how admirable the copies are, they are the handiwork of craftsmen rather than creative artists. This observation might be made of other types of literary writings of this period which, with its great emphasis on massive learning, extensive acquaintanceship with the literary productions of past ages, and a sensitized technique in the analysis of literary style, had produced an impressive number of imitative writers who seemed unable to appreciate the fine distinction between first-class duplication and real creation.

The most outstanding case of conformity to the imitative technique which finally proved itself to be an exception which confirmed the rule was a young Manchu poet, Nara Singde (1655-1685). Like Ch'ên Wei-sung and Chu Yi-tsun, with whom he was intimately associated, he, as a *tz'ŭ* poet, also had his models and idols—the *tz'ŭ* masters of the late T'ang and the Five Dynasties, masters of the art before it had taken a crystallized and systematic form. In spite of his wholehearted acceptance of the prevailing literary discipline demanded of poets and prose writers, the young Manchu went beyond the limits of his literary apprenticeship. In his poetry there were doubtless echoings of the voices of his revered masters but in the midst of these there were notes which could be clearly discerned as the young poet's own. For this reason, Nara Singde was not only a striking case of the rapid Sinicization of a young Manchu aristocrat but also of how the vigor of a border tribesman blossomed forth in an old cultural environment. As Hu Shih has aptly remarked, "Singde was undoubtedly one of the best and most popular poets of the Ch'ing Dynasty."

Singde's father, Nara Mingju, who had entered Peking in 1644 as a member of the new nobility at the tender age of nine, became in due course an avowed patron of Chinese scholarship and literature. By the time his eldest son, Singde, was born, he had not only wielded the greatest political power in the empire but also set the example of hearty Sinicization by associating himself with high dignitaries from the Wu dialect district, noticeably Hsü Ch'ien-hsüeh (1631-1694) and his two brothers, nephews of the intransigent devotee to the fallen dynasty, Ku Yen-wu (1613-1682). Nara went so far as to adapt his clan name according to the Wu dialect, giving himself two characters, *Na lan*—acceptance of the orchids—in place of the purely phonetic characters *Na la*. *Lan* in the Wu dialect was pronounced *la*, so he not only tried to make his name Chinese but even southern Chinese.

It is no surprise, then, that as Singde grew up he was placed under the guidance of Hsü, and that he counted among his best friends practically no Manchu but a whole group of the most distinguished Chinese writers of his age, especially those from the Wu dialect area —an area which Singde himself said he "had constantly dreamed of in the past and would wish to be native of in my next reincarnation."

Singde's profound interest in traditional Chinese culture and his association with Hsü crystallized in the publication of a voluminous set of reprints of commentaries and studies on the Confucian classics, mainly by Sung and Yüan writers—the *T'ung-chih-t'ang ching-chieh*, noted for its extremely fine printing and its inclusion of many rare and inaccessible titles. This publication, purportedly prepared for him largely by his tutor and his staff but financed solely by his father's money, had given him such recognition in the scholarly world that later on after his premature death and the eventual fall of his father, it was to elicit a strong feeling of jealousy on the part of Emperor Ch'ien Lung. Be that as it may, the Manchu poet was more than a bookworm. For in conformity with early Manchu tradition, he also fulfilled his duties as an officer of the imperial bodyguards and betook himself in that capacity to many parts of north and east-central Asia on the various imperial inspection tours made by Emperor K'ang Hsi, who had a high regard for him. On one occasion he was even commissioned by K'ang Hsi to accompany two Manchu generals to the Amur River region to investigate the extent of penetration by Russian agents and their manhandling of Chinese hunters and trappers. These experiences were to serve him well as a budding poet. His ramblings in areas outside of the Great Wall gave his poetry a feeling of grandeur seldom met with in the writings of sedentary poets. Thus, he sang on one occasion, "Late at night a thousand camp lights glow" and on another occasion:

> Men lie drunken in a myriad tents;
> The stars shine vacillating above
> As though they were about to fall.

It has been suggested by several critics that Singde's high attainments as a poet utilizing the *shih* form and especially the *tz'ŭ* form with complete mastery was due largely to the fact that living in Peking as a second-generation Manchu, he had not been thoroughly steeped in the cultural traditions of China. With spiritual eyes still unblurred by the conventions of Chinese poetry, he was able to observe the beauties of nature at first hand and to express his emotions and reactions with fresh vigor. It was more than coincidence that he had taken as his models the *tz'ŭ* poetry of the initial period in pre-Sung times when the niceties of the technique had not taken a well-formulated and therefore frozen form. Although he wrote frequently without hesitation long lyrics in accordance with the longer tunes current in Sung times and had shown complete dexterity in this particular regard, he was probably at his best when he sang in the style of the shorter lyrics in *tz'ŭ* form after the manner of the ill-fated princes of the Southern T'ang regime.

As a poet, Singde is admired for two groups of poems, those addressed to his intimate friends, nearly all Han Chinese, and those in which he lamented the death of his wife. Of his numerous poems addressed to his intimate friends and fellow poets, the following one written in *tz'ŭ* form to the tune of "Ch'ing P'ing Lo," addressed to the young poet, Ku Liang-fên, is typical:

> Just listening to a bit of autumn rain
> Makes me feel that autumn is so much here.
> Surrounding the stone steps are insects chirping as I remain quiet.
> Even if I have dreams, there is no way to retain them.
> Across the river lie hills in confusion in a thousand rows,
> I wonder where my friend may be resting from wandering now.
> Does he know the red candle in front of the little window
> Shines on me this night with endless sorrow?

Of his many poems lamenting the early death of his wife, the following was especially celebrated because it was written on her death anniversary.

> When will this grief end?
> The dripping rain in the empty courtyard
> Has ceased on this chilly night,
> Such weather befits the burial of flowers.
> For three long years dreams have been scanty,
> And from this long dream I should have awakened.
> Probably you also have sensed
> The lack of meaning in this world of men—
> Not comparable even to the Terrace of Night.

Cool and cruel is this earth
Only fit for the interring of sorrows.
Our mutual oath
Is now abandoned.

If a message could be sent to the nether springs
I would wish to know
For the past year on whom you have leaned for support.
Throughout the night I turn and toss
Unable to bear the playing of old familiar tunes.
Is it possible to meet again in our next incarnation?
Still I fear we will face tragedy
And again will
Be separated in pale moonlight and dying breeze.
As my clear tears run dry
The ashes of the sacrificial papers swirl up.

Again, in another *tz'ŭ* poem written to the tune of "Yi Chiang-nan"
or "Remembering the South," Singde registered his feeling of tragic
loss:

Nocturnal Thoughts in a Temple

The fire in my heart is turned to ashes.
I feel like a monk;
Only my head is still unshaven.

O poor heart!
How the wind and rain have worn you out!
How the partings from friends, dead and alive,
Have torn you to pieces!

This orphan-like candlestick
Appears like an old friend to me.

There remains one thing alone
That keeps me from a complete Awakening:—
Love still smoulders in the ashes of my heart!

(Teresa Li's translation)

In Singde's collected works there is a third group of poems which
record in a language purposely befogged with classical allusions
and other rhetorical devices the heart-rending experience of his
early life. Though mistaken by the casual reader to be poems addressed to his wife, these had been inspired by his frustrated love
for a cousin who had been taken into the palace and whom, therefore, he was unable to marry. It is to be noted that misinterpretation
and confusion in the case arise easily, as the forbidden palace was
just as inaccessible to Singde as the other world and hence his rec-

ollections of the endearing moments he had spent with his living cousin are misconstrued as his remembrance of his deceased wife. A good example is the following *tz'ŭ* poem written to the tune of "Ts'ai Sang Tzu" or "Plucking Mulberries":

> In her gardens we stood
> Till the dead of night.
> The swallows were sleeping
> On the sculptured beams
> And moonlight climbing over the silvery walls.
> I could hardly see
> The flower clusters;
> Still less could I
> Discern their fragrance.
>
> The scene has long since become
> One to be sought only in memory.
> Scattered are the lovebirds.
> Following the rain,
> A mild chill.
> And to recall this dream—
> A dream of eleven years ago.

If the foregoing poem could have been one written in memory of his deceased wife, the following could hardly be interpreted similarly:

> Only now do I realize
> How wrong we were in those days!
>   With hearts burdened and broken,
>   With tears quietly streaming,
>   With a hundred things amiss,
>   That greeted our eyes in the spring breeze.
> Knowing we could not meet another time,
>   Yet against fate we set another date.
> Since we parted, it has been all like this:
>   Pear blossoms falling;
>   In the west the moon is hastily going down.
>
> .   .   .   .
>
> My loved one is gone,
>   Yet her image is clear.
> And now I face the pearly lamps
>   Of yester years.
> The moon is setting and
>   My fragrant company is gone.
> In this wide, wide world
>   Where can one find Han P'êng?

Han P'êng, a name frequently occurring in Singde's poetry, is a celebrated figure in Chinese folklore—a minister in the kingdom of Sung, he failed to survive the tragedy of seeing his own wife abducted by his sovereign. After he had taken his own life in protest, his wife swallowed bitterness with fortitude until one day when she was attending the prince in a party held on a high terrace. In the midst of merriment she plunged down into the depths of the ravine below. When the royal guards tried to grab her, she was suddenly transformed into a butterfly.

Singde would not have dared to communicate to any fellow Manchu this heartbreaking experience forced on him by regulations of the Manchu court. This feeling of continual frustration explains not only his devoted friendship for his Han Chinese friends but also his self-imposed Sinicization and his attainment as a major poet of his era.

CHAPTER 29

Early Ch'ing Prose

O<small>NE</small> of the outstanding seventeenth-century prose writers who deliberately bypassed the literary examination requirements was Hsü Hung-tsu (1586-1641), a native of Soochow whose ancestors traced their origin back to the County of Hsinchêng of Honan Province almost at the very center of the North China plains. Unlike most of his contemporaries who had distinguished themselves as great writers according to the traditional viewpoints, he has seldom been taken seriously by literary historians. In this sense he might even be labeled an outcast, because he never published even a single volume of his collected essays or poems. Though most of his contemporaries in the literary world spent their whole lives in the cultivation of style and rhetoric, he did not follow any set pattern. Least of all would he bother to write the normal types of essays to conform to tradition. As a result, he won no degree and held no office, real or titular. But write he did. What he wrote was, technically speaking, nothing novel—merely travel records. The novelty of his life work lies in the fact that he wrote practically nothing else.

Born of a family known for its wealth but subjected to many financial reverses, Hsü reaped the benefit of the wisdom and acute economic sense of his parents. Thus he was able to befriend a good many literary giants of his age, to collect a library of rare books, and to undertake extensive travels on his own resources. He lost his father when he was eighteen, but in his mother he found an unusual source of inspiration to pursue his one great interest in life —to visit all parts of the vast Chinese Empire. As it was against Confucian teachings to travel far while his widowed mother was still alive, the mother and son reached an interesting compromise. The Chinese sage had openly taught that a son's travel should be definitely limited in specified areas and this became the guiding principle to Hsü. As long as his mother was still alive he never failed once to return home ahead or behind schedule. Thus, with the blessing of his mother, who had made a special hat for his trips, he began his life as an unmatched traveler in 1607 when he was twenty-one years of age. From that time on he widened his circle of travel until the year before his death he found himself engaged in travel all over the different provinces of China. These were all carefully recorded, sometimes in diary form, sometimes branching out into detailed geographical and ethnographical descriptions and research essays.

The huge volume of writing that he did might be illustrated by his notes made in 1637 when he was fifty-one. That year he went from his home on the East China coast to the far recesses of Kwangsi Province in the southwestern part of China proper, a trip which started during one New Year season and lasted until past another New Year's Eve. Discounting the parts missing, he had written more than eighty thousand characters, averaging over two hundred characters a day. Taking into consideration the fact that he was ill for a time on the road, that he had to impose upon himself short periods of rest, and that he would pay no special attention in his writing to well-known cities and towns, we note that the average amount of writing he did while traveling was over four hundred characters a day.

When he visited the western sacred mountain in 1623, one of the five sacred mountains of China proper, he entered the following:

> The Hua Mountain is surrounded by stone cliffs on all sides so that there are no spectacular branches either on its top or in the foothill regions. As one climbs to the very top, however, one would find many of the pines and firs are so huge it would take three men with outstretched arms to encircle each. All the pines are of the five-maned variety and their cones are as large as the seed cases of the lotus. I picked some of the unfallen ones and found their flavor had a freshness unequaled.

His descriptions are superb mainly because of the minuteness of his observation. In describing his boat trip in Kwangsi Province he observed:

> Coming from Nanning and after passing the mouth of Yuchiang tributary, we noticed for the first time that rocks protruded from the banks. It was not until we reached the confluence of Yangmei River that the rocks began to assume unusual forms. It was not until we had passed the northern city wall of Hsining that the right bank confronted us with peaks in pairs. As our boat wound its way through the peaks of the rocky area, it was like a shuttle going through the threads, confronted with more scenery than we could leisurely absorb. Moreover, at this point not only were the rocky mountains beyond comparison but also the stone cliffs presented themselves with endless variations. All this is caused by the river water smashing at the mountains. The

mountains after continual washing take the form of sharp cliffs. As the water winds its way and carries with it the sandy sediments, steep rocks protrude where they are least expected, some presiding over the center of waves and others looking as though they were thrown across the water's surface to lie there flatly. All these form a vista with endless gradations and with foldings revealing many patterns. As the river meanders its way in endless directions, the rockery on the two banks and the steep mountains behind the rockery behave as though they feared they might be left behind. All of which enhances the competition between waters and mountains in excelling the other in unexpected grotesqueness.

To appreciate Hsü's unique place in the history of Chinese literature—or even in the general intellectual history of China at large—one should recall that Chinese writers were all addicted to sedentary habits and that in most cases traveling was undertaken only when it was mandatory, as would be inevitable in participation in a competitive examination held at the provincial or imperial capital and the filling of administrative posts. Even then the strain was keenly felt and only occasionally rewarded by the appreciation of scenic spots and historical monuments. Hence, the great scarcity of geographical explorers and travelers for pleasure. In the case of Hsü we find a reversal of the normal attitudes of Chinese literati. This is clearly borne out by the following entry in his travel records for the year 1639:

I rose early in the morning in preparation for a trip to the upper reaches of the river. Yüan K'ang [Ma Yüan-k'ang, his host] had two horses, one of which had been dispatched to the mountain regions, and so he asked me to postpone the trip until the following day. I told him we did not need to travel on horseback nor in company and that his general directions would be even more valuable than his generous attempt to see that I was not lost. What I really feared was his coming along and my desire to go it alone was due to my fear that he would insist on riding on horseback.

So he went alone and on foot. His fear of the delimitations of a traveling companion was well justified. Very few people in the scholar-gentry class would be willing to run the risks that he frequently did. Earlier in the same year, while he was exploring a certain number of rock caves high up on a mountain, he had had some thrilling experiences which he recorded in the following notes:

I looked up and climbed up. The top of the mountain was extremely steep. After half a li [one-fifth of a mile] the ground was so deep that it would not hold my feet, so I had to use my fingers to grasp the lichen roots as I ascended. After a while even these roots refused to be grasped by my fingers, but luckily I had reached some rocks. These rocks, however, were rather loose. As I stepped on one it would slide down; and as I tried to hold on to another it would slide down. It was only occasionally that I could discover a steady one that would permit the hanging of my fingers and the treading of my feet. My position would look as though I had been flatly pinned to the cliff. For a moment I felt I could not alter my position at all, there being no support for me to climb up and no ground for me to descend to. I had never experienced any more perilous situation than that.

This same venture involved other difficulties. Since it was unsafe for any traveler to carry any large amount of money, he had to face shortage of funds. Before he climbed the cliff in order to get to the rocky caves he had in his possession only thirty cash which he had hidden in one of his sleeves, an amount that would buy him enough rice for one day. After the perilous climb he discovered that in his excitement he had dropped all thirty cash somewhere. Then he had to offer three articles of clothing for sale by hanging them up in front of the inn. After a long wait a man came along who bought his pair of silk trousers for two hundred-odd cash, whereupon he happily bought wine and meat to celebrate the occasion with his servant.

But something else was to happen later on in the year—the desertion of his servant. He was staying in a Buddhist monastery and having an extremely pleasant time with two monks. One of the monks urged him to stay overnight. Realizing that there might not be sufficient bedding in the monastery, Hsü ordered his servant to go along with another monk who had to go down the mountain, fearing his servant might feel cold. The servant asked for a key and Hsü gave him the whole bunch. As he was descending the mountain the following day, he saw a third monk rushing up in great haste whom the abbot had sent to tell him that his servant had fled. When he reached the foothill monastery at noon:

> I opened my baskets and trunks and found everything had vanished. The abbot wanted to send two monks in pursuit but I stopped it. "The pursuers," I said, "might not be able to overtake him and even if they could they might not be able to force him to return." The only thing to do was to let him go as he pleased. Nonetheless for three years after we had left home, master and servant had mutually relied one upon the other like a body and its own shadow. Now that he would desert me, ten thousand li away from home, what a hardhearted man!

Undaunted by these unhappy incidents he went ahead with his explorations. Going ahead on foot he finally came in the following year to Chinsha Chiang (River of the Golden Sand) where he made a very important geographical discovery, namely, that this Golden Sand River was actually the upper reaches of the great Yangtze. He wrote a long dissertation on the sources of the Yangtze River which, unfortunately, was only preserved in part in quotations in the local history of the County of Chiangyin, and the discovery was buried in oblivion. When, at the end of the seventeenth century, numerous Jesuits were sent by Emperor K'ang Hsi to the different provinces in preparation for making a new map for the Chinese Empire, they proudly announced to the world that for the first time in history they had discovered that the Golden Sand River was part of the Yangtze tributary system.

Hsü's travel notes were for long circulated in manuscript and copies. As they were highly prized by his many friends from all parts of the empire, they were relatively well preserved, although by no means in a perfect state. However, the tradition that five-sixths of his writings were lost was unfounded rumor. We have reason to believe today that only 140 days of his travel records are missing out of a total of 1070-odd days. So that only about one-sixth is lost to posterity. The uniqueness of his writing and the uniqueness of the man who wrote practically nothing but travel literature was recognized soon after his death by a few literary critics. When a major poet of the age, Ch'ien Ch'ien-yi, urged the leading scholar-publisher, Mao Tsin, to have printing blocks made for the publication of Hsü's travels, he gave an apt dictum by saying, "Hsü is a unique man of a thousand ages and his travels are a unique book of ten thousand ages."

During the latter half of the seventeenth century, poets and essayists who distinguished themselves as superb imitators and adapters of past traditions were numerous. More deserving of mention than these conformists was a peculiar cultural dissenter, Chin Jên-jui (died 1661), who is now remembered as an unconventional literary critic. He was born probably about 1610; his childhood was spent in poverty and loneliness until his tenth year, when he suddenly blossomed forth in remarkable aptitude in his studies of the Confucian classics. When he took his first competitive examination it was reported that his papers, which were written in the form of the traditional Eight-Legged Essay, were couched in such obscure and antiquarian language that the official readers could not punctuate them.

After this spectacular failure he completely reversed his style in the next examination in which he sat and won first honor for his rigid conformity to the traditional patterns. Even then, however, he found greater pleasure in reading novels and dramas than in plying the Confucian classics. He ridiculed his fellow scholars continually for their commonplace literary interests and their lack of real esthetic appreciation. Still, he could also write copiously on the Confucian classics when he chose to. An unusual example was his commentary on two chapters of the *Book of Changes*—a commentary exceeding a hundred thousand words which his contemporaries could not understand.

Frequently in bad financial straits, he freely leaned on his devoted friends for support. From one of them he received a loan of three thousand taels of silver, promising to repay it in due course with interest. In less than one month, however, the sizable sum had been completely squandered, whereupon he approached his debtor and bravely declared: "If you had kept the money it is likely you would have acquired the reputation of a miser. I have absolved you of that charge." His eccentricity was also expressed in his profound interest in Buddhist literature and his lasting friendship with a number of cultivated Buddhist monks.

As an impressionistic critic, he singled out six books as *ts'ai-tz'ŭ shu,* books of genius, or masterpieces. These were the *Book of Chuang-tzŭ,* the *Li Sao* of Ch'ü Yüan, the *Shih Chi* of Ssŭ-ma Ch'ien, the Regulation Poetry of Tu Fu, the *Romance of Shui Hu* or the *Water Margin,* and the *Western Chamber* of Wang Tê-hsin. He had dedicated himself to the task of writing critiques of all six but he lived only long enough to finish his critical comments on the last two. This choice of his must have shocked all his contemporaries by elevating a work of prose fiction and a play to places of equality with the established masters. He even went so far as to compare the *Shui Hu* to the *Spring and Autumn Annals* and the *Western Chamber* to the *Book of Songs.*

In selecting and praising the historical romance he must have been attracted by the sympathy of the author for the poor peasants who, living under the oppression of officials, organized themselves into bands of robbers. This political conviction he finally translated into organized political action involved in the famous case of "weeping in the temple" in 1661 after the news had been received of the death of the first Manchu Emperor, Shun Chih, in the city of Soochow. This participation by Chin and friends in a political protest veiled in the form of mourning the death of the emperor at the local branch of the Confucian temple was finally to incriminate him in a case of *lèse-majesté* as a demonstration against the dynasty. Later on he was also accused of supporting Chêng Ch'êng-kung, better known in Western literature as Koxinga, the last defender of the Ming Dynasty on the island of Formosa. On the evidences of various trials in which he was involved Chin was executed in August of 1661. Before his execution he sent a short note to his family saying: "Beheading is most painful and the confiscation of property is most tragic. Isn't it strange that I have gotten both casually!"

His work of literary criticism followed a peculiar pattern. He would write a summary critique of the whole work and then proceed to make comments and asides on each subdivision down to the details of a single sentence or even a single phrase. It is in these minute and highly personalized and impressionistic marginal notes that he voiced his own sentiments and peculiar reactions to the writing of the author under criticism. Going beyond this he would even take the liberty of emending the original text and cutting out chapters and paragraphs which he did not like. His critical work in a sense was revision of the work under consideration. While opinions differ as to the quality of his emendations and redactions, it is agreed that he was not faithful in preserving the merits and demerits of the authors whom he reviewed. In his numerous comments Chin made it plain that his revisions were intended to give him a version of the work as he would prefer to have it written in the first instance.

As a rebel against the Confucian orthodoxy, Chin made the greatest contribution by elevating imaginative literature to the dignity of the Confucian classics. Although very few Chinese literary men dared to uphold his revolutionary point of view in literary criticism, nearly all of the less orthodox-minded writers continued to derive immense delight from his unconventional remarks.

Partly because of the threat of the literary inquisition which was about to grow in extent and intensity and partly because of the unsystematic way in which Chin went about his creative writing, the major portion of his essays and poems have now been lost. Nonetheless, as there was no ban placed on his so-called critical editions of the novel *Water Margin* and of the *Western Chamber*, many long digressions which were little essays in themselves have been preserved intact, sandwiched between his so-called critical remarks. For example, in his critical commentary on the *Western Chamber* he took time off to give an enumeration of the happy moments which he had counted together with his friend, when they were shut up in a temple for ten days on account of rainy weather. These he elaborated into thirty-three paragraphs describing the thirty-three types of happy moments which he had enjoyed in his life. It is needless to point out that they have no inherent connection with the *Western Chamber* or with his criticism of the play:

On a hot day in the sixth month of the year when the sun hangs stagnant in the firmament, when there is not the tiniest bit of breeze or even a speck of a cloud, when the front and back yards of my house are hot like ovens, and when not a single bird dares to fly around, perspiration drips down my whole body like streamlets. Lunch is spread before me, but I cannot eat it on account of the heat. I have asked for a mat to be unrolled on the floor so that I could lie down, but it is moist and flies gather around me to perch on my nose and could not be driven away. When I thus feel wholly frustrated, there comes a roaring of thunder, and huge stretches of black clouds cover up the sky and roll on like an army formation pushing forward to the battle line. Rain comes pouring down from the roof like waterfalls. My sweating has stopped. The moldiness of the floor is gone. The flies have completely disappeared and hidden themselves. And now I can eat my meal. Isn't this a great satisfaction indeed?

It was in an equally casual and facetious tone that he wrote his eighty-one paragraphs of prefatial notes on how to read the *Hsi Hsiang Chi* (*Western Chamber*), which he acclaimed as the sixth book of genius in Chinese literature:

He who says *Hsi Hsiang Chi* is pornography deserves only flogging. It is unnecessary to lecture him. Why not? Because he has merely heard those words in his youth from a village schoolmaster, and registered them permanently in his heart [mind] ever since. Actually his eyes have never been set on the *Hsi Hsiang Chi*. Even flogging him is a bitter waste of effort. (4)

One day, while I was eating rice porridge, I wanted to write an essay. For some reason I could not do it, and had to wait until my meal was over before I could fulfil my desire. Then I regretted having lost the piece I would have written during the porridge hour. This is comparable to throwing of dice. Any slight variation in timing, in using energy, and in choosing a direction has a telling effect. And yet stupid people still think they can always win. This is indeed laughable! (21)

When I was young, someone told me a joke. Once there was a man suffering from utter penury; but as he had worshiped the Taoist Patriarch Lü [Tung-pin] with great reverence, the latter was touched by his piety and descended upon him in his home. Seeing that he was penniless, the patriarch pitied him and decided to help him. As soon as the patriarch's finger was stretched and pointed at the millstone in the courtyard, the stone was immediately transmuted into radiant gold. "Do you want it?" the poor man was asked. The man bowed low and replied, "I don't want it." Patriarch Lü was greatly pleased, and said, "If you are really like this, I am ready to transmit to you the great Tao." The man said, "No, what I really desire is your finger. . . ." Now this *Hsi Hsiang Chi* is the very finger of Patriarch Lü. Whoever gets it will find gold wherever he points. (24)

Thus in his literary criticism, which left a great deal to be desired as to method, and in his own creative prose writings, most of which have been lost, Chin Jên-jui subtly deviated from the beaten paths of orthodox Confucianist writers who regarded literature as a mere vehicle to transport and extend Tao, the supreme way of life. While to this long line of traditionalists, literature was a chambermaid of morality in its widest sense of application, Chin's approach was avowedly amoral. This is why his heterodox views on literature were secretly admired if not publicly upheld. For more than two hundred years all readers of the *Water Margin* and the *Western Chamber* allowed their literary tastes submissively to be shaped by Chin Shêng-t'an—the courtesy name by which our erratic critic has been known. According to his own confession, he adopted this courtesy name which means "the sage sighed" because there was a legend in his native district that when he was born the statue of Confucius in the county temple sighed audibly.

Less interesting but much more influential was the continuation during the early part of the Ch'ing Dynasty of classical prose or *ku wên*. The first important classical prose writer was the famous survivor of the fallen Ming Dynasty, Ch'ien Ch'ien-yi (1582-1664), whose influence upon the poets of his day was equally profound. When the new dynasty was set up Ch'ien's literary reputation had been long established. Modeling his own compositions after the masterpieces of the two Sung writers Ou-yang Hsiu and Tsêng Kung as well as the Ming prose master, Kuei Yu-kuang, he made a special point of avoiding slavish imitation to achieve a distinctive style of his own. In criticizing current literary trends he singled out three prevailing symptoms in his diagnosis of the literary illnesses of his time. These were, in his words: lodging, pilfering, and slaving. The literary lodgers were compared to impoverished squatters lodged temporarily in corners and corridors of a huge mansion who would, in their daydreams, feel as though the expansive halls and perfectly appointed rooms were their own although actually they did not own even a single thatch with which to cover their heads. The pilferers rested during the day but were active after nightfall and, forgetting the dignified sources of livelihood, would freely appropriate what belonged to others as their own. Lastly, the literary slaves would reduce their ears and eyes as hired help and circumscribe their imagination and aspiration. They sighed and moaned and talked in their sleep without being their real selves. They breathed in the foul air that others had exhaled. Even if they should succeed in building up a reputation for themselves they were in actuality no more than slaves of the eternal ages.

On the positive side he advised young writers to be simple and natural, because to him "the ways of literature of ancient and modern times, the different crucial points of an essay, its pulses, its source of strength, its effective conclusion, its turns in development, and its meandering development of an idea or feeling are always found in simple, clear, and natural writing."

A younger contemporary of his who distinguished himself primarily in historiography and political thought, Huang Tsunghsi

(1609-1695) was a prose master in his own right. Refusing persistently to serve the newly founded alien dynasty, he continued to
work for the restoration of the Ming imperial house and only narrowly escaped the literary inquisition. One of his best-known essays
is "On the Origin of Kingship," in which he fearlessly expounded
the theory that kings were made by the people to serve their needs.
In the essay he wrote:

In antiquity the people of the world were regarded as hosts, and the
sovereign as guest. Everything that the sovereign devoted himself to throughout his life was for the benefit of the world. Now the sovereign is regarded
as host and the people as guests. Any lack of peace and order under heaven
the sovereign is responsible for. Before his objective is attained, he sacrifices
the livers and brains of the people and scatters the families in the world to
gamble for his personal fortune, saying to himself without grievance, "I am
building up an estate for my descendants." After his objective is attained, he
grinds out the world's bones and marrow, and again scatters the families of the
people to ensure his own personal wanton pleasure, approving himself as a
matter of course: "This is the interest of my estate." Hence, the sovereign is the
sole source of the world's greatest evil.

In ancient times it was no wonder that people loved and looked up to their
sovereign for leadership, regarding him as father and heaven. It is also appropriate, however, that in modern times people resent and hate their sovereign,
consider him a bandit and a public enemy, and call him a lone and deserted
individual. And yet, the petty followers of the Confucian school, bewildered
by their own narrow vision, would claim that the relationship between sovereign
and subject is a cardinal principle inescapable in the universe, and would go so
far as to criticize King T'ang and King Wu's punishment of the despots Chieh
and Chou and to invent the fiction of Po-yi and Su-ch'i [protesting against
the punitive expeditions], with the result that in their estimation, the blood
and flesh of the millions of people and of the myriad families were nothing
more than the body of a rotten rat. How can it be that in the vast expanse of
the universe, any single person or any particular clan should be partially
favored [against all the rest]?

Besides being a political essayist of distinguished talent he also
took time off to expound his own theories on writing. A slender
volume entitled *Lun Wên Kuan Chien* or *Humble Views on Literature,* this work consists of individual entries written at various
times.

Narrative writing should be endowed with rhythm and charm and should
avoid matter-of-factness. When people of this age see this statement of mine
they might consider it to be a mere trickery of fiction writers. Why don't we
look at the biographies of the *Tsin Dynastic History* and the histories of the
Southern and Northern Dynasties? In these biographies there are frequent in-
clusions of appearingly irrelevant episodes but these episodes made the subjects animated and lifelike as though adding breath to a portrait.

Literature, of course, should have logicality as its backbone but without
emotion even the backbone becomes that of a skeleton. . . . Throughout the

ages a number of writings are destined not to perish and they suggest that if even Heaven is endowed with emotion, Heaven itself will have to age. On the other hand there are compositions regarded as masterpieces comparable to a formidable army formation and the imposing atmosphere of a huge band. But oftentimes in their contents there is nothing which might sway man's emotions and these might be described as absolutely devoid of content.

Other prose writers of the early Ch'ing period form an impressive number. The peace and prosperity of the late seventeenth and eighteenth centuries made it possible for Ch'ing writers to outdistance their predecessors of the preceding four centuries. With the diffusion of large editions of heretofore rare or unavailable works, the past ages were effectively marshaled for the service of the new age. A similar situation existed also in the field of rhythmically balanced prose or *p'ien wên*. With the literary law of the past now easily accessible to writers, the *p'ien wên* of all previous schools and dynasties were resurrected as models and the new writers took delight in making their own choice and excelling in their own ways by imitating and often equaling the models which they had chosen. Many of these writers were disciplined in scholarly researches on the Confucian classics and had their logical thinking sharpened by the methods and tools of the scientific method. As a result, the balanced prose of the early Ch'ing Dynasty had a lucidity and logical sequence almost unknown in previous ages. This was brought about effectively by the additional use of connectives to clarify transitions and subordination. In the hands of the great masters balanced prose had a naturalness, clarity, and forthrightness which entirely transcended the binding effects of the basic *p'ien wên* mechanism. The rich imagery, the economy made possible by classical allusions, and the meticulous use of rhetoric gave to this literary type a charm that was definitely unsurpassed.

During the eighteenth century this new literary tide had reached a climax but this climax also indicated an innovation. Practically all the classical masters had been outgrown and imitation was made only to serve a transitory apprenticeship. Thus Chao Ch'i-t'ao (1718-1769) insisted that good balanced prose should be "clear, new, elegant, and attractive." K'ung Kuang-shên (1752-1786), a direct descendant of Confucius who was highly distinguished for his classical scholarship in spite of his early death, spoke as a master of *p'ien wên*, saying that the type should be utilized to communicate ideas as well as to elucidate arguments and that its manipulations should serve all purposes as though one were writing in plain prose. Another great master, Tsêng Yü (1759-1830), went even further. He said, "When *ku wên* is devoid of reality it is much inferior to *p'ien wên;* and *p'ien wên* when purged of vulgarity is none other than *ku wên* itself." This theory was a deliberate attempt to minimize the line of demarcation between the two different types of prose, in spite of the fact that historically the two had parted company for close to two thousand years.

What Tsêng Yü had advocated in theory was already put into practice by a very outstanding scholar-poet, Wang Chung (1744–1794). A native of the County of Chiangtu (Yangchou) he failed to win any signal honors in the competitive literary examination and for that reason was compelled to earn his livelihood by working on the secretarial staffs of high-ranking administrators. Among his extensive circle of acquaintances and friends he distinguished himself in classical and philological scholarship, but unlike most critical scholars of his age he succeeded in welding the prose style of the best Han and post-Han writers into a unique style of his own. His attainment in literature as a prose writer was so unique that his friend, Wang Nien-sun (1744-1832), the eminent classicist, declared him unequaled since the Sung Dynasty. Nonetheless, Wang Chung's volume of writings, collected posthumously, was exceptionally slim. In his collection of essays, however, he not only gave a unique literary flavor to his scholarly writing but also went so far as to fuse the styles of prose and poetry. To him, plain prose and *p'ien wên* were just so many tools which he could use at random. As he had to live the life of a wanderer, never completely relaxed from the emergencies faced by a poor scholar, his prose writings of the non-scholarly type are characterized by outbursts of emotionalism and by bold challenges to accepted standards of social justice. Thus he wrote a rhymed piece in praise of an ancient highwayman recorded in the book of doubtful authorship attributed to Lieh-Tzŭ. The short preface summarized the early folk tale:

In the *Book of Lieh-Tzŭ* there was a man in the eastern areas whose name was Yüan Ching-mu who was about to embark on a journey but was so famished with hunger that he had to lie feebly on the roadside. Then came a highwayman from Hufu by the name of Ch'iu. He saw the victim and fed him with pots of food. It was not until after the third feeding that the poor man regained his eyesight. Impressed by the episode I write this eulogy:

> There was once a robber of Hufu
> Whose given name was Ch'iu.
> Amusing himself after a good meal,
> He was reposing by the roadside.
> Coming from the east was a man
> Whom people called Yüan Ching-mu.
> The man was stumbling along,
> Felt famished, and collapsed.

Then, our Master the robber—
He gazed, he stared, he pondered:
"You are no kin of mine
Nor indeed even an old friend.
Except for your build, you are no longer man!
Your body is here, but your soul is nearly gone.
Your feeble breath is barely audible.
The fire of hunger is eating you up from within.
I have not caused you all this,
But still I pity your plight."

He fetched a basket in his left hand,
And a square kettle in his right.
"With this you will live;
Without it you will die.
In this petty simple meal
Lies the difference between man and ghost!"
"In this wide, wide world below,
I have no one at all to lean on.
Only you, Robber, have fed me
As a loving mother would her own child."

O you robber,
How did you get your food?
Outside you fought your foes in the royal city;
Inside you worried over your own den.
Brave knights are ever vigilant,
Hunting down outlaws like yourself.
Against you is the state penalty—
Capital punishment without parole.

You forgot about all your hazards;
You neglected even your own safety.
You washed that rice, you cooked that food
Just to help a stranger on the open road!
Who would have blamed you for ignoring him?
Who would now reward you for saving him?
But as compassion roused you from within,
You acted bravely without swerve!

O you robber, my Master!
Who else is compassionate like you?
With the spread of your way of life,
Human apathy may disappear.
You have treated a mere chance acquaintance
With a heart heaven-endowed!

Where is a robber of your kind in my days?
To him I shall entrust my whole life.

The same unconventionality was fully expressed in a commemorative message on a late Ming courtesan who was distinguished as a painter of orchids:

> In the year 1783 I was living as a visitor in the southern suburb of Chiangning [Nanking]. As I went in and out of the city I went past the Monastery of Reflected Light. At its left there was an abandoned garden where a small creek flowed by clearly and coolly and where wild groves studded the fields. All the houses were in ruins but an ancient fir was standing half alive in the midst of floating mists and a few odd-shaped rocks were jutting out in confusion from amidst the wild weeds. In this ruin was the old residence of the late courtesan, Ma Shou-chên. The waters of the Ch'in Huai River flowed by as time passed, but even though she was gone forever from the human world, her reputation remained. Her beauty, her artistic attainments, and her graceful living are still told by many an aged survivor of the past basing their remarks on transmitted oral tradition. Her paintings I have seen and have found her clusters of orchids and slender bamboos in their unsurpassable delicateness exhuming traces of elegance and inspiration completely transcending the limitations of paper and ink. On those occasions I dearly appreciated her talent and regretted that I was born too late to see her.

Then he went on subtly to point out that her sad fate was the result of a combination of circumstances and that it was unfair to reprimand her for failing to die to evade her lowly station. He even went one step further saying that literati who were ill-fated like himself and who moved from one secretarial staff to another responding to orders beyond their own choice were hardly any more honorable. Then he broke out into rhapsodic measures in the *ch'ü tzŭ* tradition to lament the ill fate which had befallen the songstress—an image of himself.

Joining Wang Chung in experimenting with the new *p'ien wên* type was the poet Hung Liang-chi (1746-1809), who was equally respected for his scholarship in historical geography and the Confucian classics. Having attacked political corruption and criticized even the personal behavior of the reigning emperor, Chia Ch'ing, Hung was exiled to Chinese Turkestan for a time. It is generally believed this exile accelerated his nonconformity in literary taste. Actually, even before the catastrophe of distant exile Hung had toyed with the idea of liberalizing the requirements of *p'ien wên*. He had used the *p'ien wên* style in conformity with early medieval usage for the writing of personal letters. Some of these letters were lyrical in nature and some were even expository and argumentative such as the letter he wrote on friendship. In these letters he chose the four-character or four-syllable line so as to obtain the effect of crisp uniformity. It was only on rare occasions that he would introduce into his lines the parallel structure device for variety. Thus he wrote to his friend Sun Hsing-yen (1753-1818), himself a master in the *p'ien-wên* art:

> I have traveled a thousand miles but have not met a single scholar. During the day I spread my books to traverse up and down the ages; and at night I occasionally light a candle to drive away sleepiness. Yesterday was the beginning of winter and the cold was especially oppressive. Once the wild wind blew and whiffed my book outside of the door. I was slightly late in catching it so it had already flown past the surrounding wall. In my southern neighbor's house there is a decaying mulberry tree with insects covering it over an inch thick. When the withering leaves have been exhausted will they feast on humans? When I hear the rumbling of carriages through the streets my couch and my tables both shake. As the soil is not hard, holes appear suddenly on the ground. Clinging southernwood unexpectedly covers the corner of the house yet the vacant lot of an acre will not grow grass. As the location is distant I can close my gate to avoid guests. On occasions when I go out socially, my trips result in unhappiness. After thinking the matter over once and again I still don't understand why.

Thus far there is little evidence of parallel structure. Then he goes on with four-character clusters in plain prose style to describe his eagerness to return south to be near his native district and his good friend, the addressee:

> But my farm is hardly one ch'ing [fifteen acres] and the pine trees hardly an inch. The ditch waters are not yet alive and the creek bridge is not yet built. For these several reasons I need to wait another year. Then I would move to be near my ancestral tombs seeking shelter near my elder sister. . . . The forest flowers will gladden my soul and the water fowls will enrich my spirit. I will entertain oldsters and youths and I will shoo away the neighbor's dogs. . . . The doors all open to the east so as to greet easily sun and moon and my tomb will face the west so as to be close to my deceased parents. Underneath the shade of a sole pine I will plant plum trees. In my fish pond of a few acres I will erect a crab trap. Furthermore I hope you could come and share the grounds. Then I would erect a house of several rooms next door for you. For our bodily needs we shall depend on the garden vegetables and for our postmortem comfort we can look up to the forest trees. Whenever there is frost or dew we shall enjoy chicken and pork. After offering it to the spirit of the ancestors, we can utilize the same to feed our guests. After a few years of such enjoyment even if we should then breathe our last, we shall leave few regrets. . . .

Although Hung was brave enough on occasion to deviate from the strict regulation of *p'ien wên* he was, nonetheless, equally fond and capable of writing in the traditional style of perfectly balanced prose. In fact, he voluntarily submitted himself to all the deviousness of convention required by that literary type. Thus, in a preface to a long *fu* in which he lamented the passage of time and the losing of dear friends, he wrote couplets like the following:

> The age of [your humble servant, comparable to] a dog
> or horse has now surpassed the life span of the
> commander-in-chief of the Ch'i Dynasty;
> And the years of wandering and roving have exceeded
> the sojourn abroad of Duke Wên of the Tsin state.

While the couplet in its Chinese original exhibits a pleasing structure and a rhythmic consonance in the tradition of *p'ien wên*, it also exemplifies the deviousness and obscurity inherent in that technique. What he actually meant to say in the two lines heavily laden with classical allusion was merely that he was already approaching forty and that he had been moving from place to place for more than nineteen years. The commander-in-chief referred to was Wang Chien (452-489) of the Southern Ch'i Dynasty who died in his thirty-eighth year. Less obscure is the allusion to Duke Wên of Tsin who, prior to his return to his ancestral state in 636 B.C. to claim his ducal crown, had been wandering about for nineteen years.

The artificiality of the traditional balanced prose in its most traditional pattern became increasingly obvious with the lapse of time and even in the hands of the best masters could not be entirely eliminated. As compared with straightforward plain prose, such as had been advocated by the champions of the so-called ancient prose or *ku wên* style, it was at best like an exhibition dance in relation to natural walking. Yet it did not completely recede from the Chinese literary scene in spite of its many handicaps as a clear vehicle for the conveyance of thoughts and emotions because there always were some people who derived delight from the staging and watching of exhibition dances.

The most influential advocate of the revival of the classical prose style of *ku wên* was Fang Pao (1668-1747) of the county of T'ungch'êng in Anhui Province. By the name of his birthplace the school which he founded was thenceforth to be known as the T'ungch'êng school of prose writers. Its guiding principle in reviving the ancient tradition of prose was that "the writings of the Chou and Ch'in dynasties and before contained everything in the way of basic principles in writing. Writers of the Han and Sung dynasties were not without faults although they had watched every single step they had taken." On the basis of this Fang Pao held up as a slogan the importance of the basic meanings and methods of ancient classical prose. In spite of his extensive writings and his numerous comments, he failed to lay down any specific rules for what he called *yi fa* or the guiding mode.

A successor of his, Yao Nai (1730-1814), also a native of the same district, tried to set the pattern by example instead of precept. Yao compiled an anthology of classical prose classified into various literary types which influenced subsequent prose writers and which called forth numerous supplementary anthologies of a later date. In literary theory he evolved the basic concept of the alternation of the *yin* and the *yang* or the hard and the soft, a theory recommending the alternation of tenseness and relaxation of effort and naturalness to suit the occasion. Actually, these views and comments of Yao and his master, Fang, belong to the category of rhetoric rather than real literary criticism. As Yao had numerous pupils who were proficient writers, the school of T'ungch'êng, which opposed the artificiality and ornateness of *p'ien wên*, was not only firmly established but also responded to by a branch school.

This branch school, known as the Yanghu school of prose writers, was named after the birthplace of its chief advocate, Hun Ching (1757-1817), a native of the county of Yanghu in Kiangsu Province. Hun was re-enforced by Chang Hui-yen (1761-1802) of the county of Wuchin, adjacent to Yanghu. Chang, like his friend Hun, followed in the footsteps of the T'ungch'êng school but as he was eminent in his classical scholarship and general erudition, he gave to that movement an unprecedented prestige. A younger contemporary, also of Yanghu, Li Chao-lo (1769-1846), continued the tradition of this school, on one hand, and pointed out its compatibility, on the other, with the best traditions of *p'ien wên*. Both schools would have faded out if it had not been for the emergence of a towering figure in literature and politics, Tsêng Kuo-fan (1811-1872), the distinguished soldier-statesman who fought for cultural orthodoxy more enthusiastically than for the weakened alien dynasty although his military campaigns finally crushed the T'aip'ing revolution in 1863. To broaden the base of the T'ungch'êng school and to instill into the *ku wên* style more eruditional substance, he compiled an anthology which was much larger in scope than the one compiled by Yao Nai. Furthermore, he elaborated upon the literary beauties of the *yin* and *yang* types. The virtues of the literary beauties of the *yang* or strong type were inumerated as: grandeur, perspicacity, oddity, and elegance. And the virtues of the literary beauties of the *yin* or soft type were: amiability, remoteness, neatness, and fitness. Despite the vagueness of these terms, Tsêng's subscription to the views of the T'ungch'êng school and his pre-eminence as the national hero of his age combined to prolong its life span and influence, until the emergence of a new age made the continuation of the school untenable.

CHAPTER 30

Ch'ing Fiction

As we have noted in a previous chapter, the prose romances of the T'ang Dynasty did not regain their popularity until the early sixteenth century. It was during the first half of the sixteenth century that they were reprinted in large numbers by booksellers. This gave rise to a new vogue, unashamedly subscribed to even by conservative writers of the conventional-essay type. Giving free reign to their imagination, nearly all late Ming writers expended their energies upon the production of semifictitious biographies of unconventional and erratic men and women, and even of unusual tigers and dogs, insects and ants, and proudly had these included in their collected works. They also diverted part of their energies to the collection of tales of the horrible, the weird, the miraculous, and the supernatural. An author would often compile book after book and anthology after anthology of tales of this type.

One who concentrated on this sort of short fiction written in the highly respected classical style almost to the exclusion of traditional literary activities was P'u Sung-ling (1640-1715), a native of Shantung Province. P'u had no luck whatsoever in his participation in the competitive literary examinations. It was not until after he was seventy that he won a minor literary degree in 1711. Apparently despite his divergent interests and his multiple literary talents he had not regimented himself to the discipline of the Eight-Legged Essay—the chief criterion in rating candidates. Besides writing for relatively illiterate persons, compiling a manual of vocabulary for the underprivileged, and writing essays and poetry in the traditional manner, though with distinguished individuality, he devoted his attention over decades to recording of the unusual, culminating in his collection entitled *Liao Chai Chih Yi* (*Records of the Strange in the Liao Studio*—translated by Herbert A. Giles as *Strange Stories from a Chinese Studio*), a work which gave him permanent literary fame. This collection, completed in 1679, consists of 431 tales, sometimes divided into sixteen books. By his own confession in the preface, he had been interested in listening to ghost stories and weird tales ever since he was young and, in response to his peculiar interest, friends and acquaintances would mail him pertinent materials from all parts of the Chinese Empire. That he was not entirely unmindful of his great predecessors of the T'ang Dynasty is evident from the fact that the themes in a few T'ang romances were retold with new embellishments and minor changes. By and large, his originality was so marked and his interest was so genuine and varied that the legend early grew up—probably no more authentic than hearsay—that he would habitually sit on a couch in front of a store offering tea and tobacco to rural passers-by who could offer him tales of the unusual.

P'u's distinction partly lies in his unusual command of the classical language in describing people and events of petty types and partly in his ability to make the improbable and impossible seem probable. Moreover, distinctly surpassing his predecessors, P'u had a special gift of making his supernatural characters almost human. Such non-human beings as the spirit of a flower and that of a fox for the first time in Chinese fiction appeared to the readers not only humanized but even likable. In one tale, for example, a fox spirit appearing in the guise of a young woman just married to an East China merchant was so humorous that she won the admiration of all his friends before she identified herself and departed. In another tale, the wife of Ma Tzŭ-ts'ai was an expert accountant and a shrewd businesswoman. Nobody suspected that she was really a chrysanthemum spirit until her younger brother fell down on the floor after intoxication at a party whereupon, beyond his control, he resumed the appearance of a flower.

In depicting the world of men, P'u had enough literary discipline never to overdo his characterization and description. For example, in a tale entitled "Ma Chieh-p'u" he described a shrew who maltreated her father-in-law, despised her guests, and frightened her brothers-in-law.

. . . About half a year later, Ma one day called at the house of Yang with his servant. Old man Yang [the father-in-law] was sunning himself in front of the door catching fleas. Mistaking him for an aged manservant of the house, the caller announced his name so that his call could be reported to the master of the house. The old man put on his rags and left. A stander-by told Ma, "This is the master's father." When he was still dazed in his surprise, the Yang brothers came out to welcome him. As the three ascended the hall and saluted each other the guest asked to see the host's father. Wan Shih [the husband] declined the honor by pleading a slight illness [on the part of the old man]. They continued chatting and joking and it soon was evening. Wan Shih repeatedly said, "Dinner will soon be served," but nothing happened. The host and his younger brother took turns in going in and out and later a thin servant brought in a flask of wine. The contents of the flask were soon exhausted and there was another long wait. Then Wan Shih jumped up and shouted his command to the servant while he was perspiring on his forehead and his cheeks. Thereupon the thin servant appeared again with portions of ill-cooked, inferior rice, hardly palatable at all.

These 431 short tales of the unusual and marvelous attracted considerable attention and revived the tradition of short T'ang romances for nearly a whole century, giving inspiration to numerous imitators among whom were many scholars and men of letters of high repute. The medium used was the conventional classical style, and in spite of the attention paid to characterization the pieces were usually much shorter than T'ang romances. The limitations of this type of fiction were obvious. Although the collection appealed to an unprecedentedly large number of readers, its influence was mainly exerted on people of leisure with a certain amount of literary training.

Unwilling to be hampered by the archaic medium of classical prose and the relative short length of the conventional tale type, P'u proceeded to write a novel in the vernacular of a million words. This longest piece of Chinese prose fiction, based neither on legend, history, nor mythology, the author wrote under a pseudonym, Hsi Chou-shêng, or Scholar of the Western Chou Period. This novel, entitled *Hsing-shih Yin-yüan* (*The Tale of a Conjugal Union to Arouse the World*) was a carefully knit narration of the experiences of a shrew and her henpecked husband. The shrew would punish her parents-in-law as well as her husband's friends in a widely assorted number of ways. So far as her husband was concerned, his very appearance would arouse hatred in her. She would not only beat him frequently but on a certain occasion she poured the red-hot charcoal from her iron on her husband through the collar of his robe. On another occasion she hit him with the laundry beater over six hundred times and nearly killed him. This sustained presentation of the torturous experiences of an unhappy marriage strangely enough did not suggest the possibility of a solution.

What was implied philosophically was that unhappiness in this life span was, in conformity with folk beliefs, the inescapable result of one's karma of a previous incarnation. The victim of domestic cruelties was supposed to have been the inflictor of injustices in a previous existence. In spite of this bit of unreasonable popular superstition the novel was a work of distinction. In the first place, it was a monumental piece of fictional creation in which the dialect of a special county in Shantung Province was elevated into a literary medium. In the second place, the pathos of the somewhat depressing narrative was periodically and effectively relieved by the introduction of the truly humorous. In the third place, its realism was so highly developed that the pictures drawn of contemporary society were almost photographic, particularly in such passages as the ones describing the tragedy of a vast famine.

This remarkable novel, which remained anonymous for two centuries, has been convincingly proven by Dr. Hu Shih to be the handiwork of P'u. The problem of domestic unhappiness resulting from ill-fated marriages had always haunted the author. The nucleus of what was developed into the million-word novel can be found in a nutshell in one of the short tales entitled "Chiang Ch'êng" ("River Town") in the strange-stories collection. In spite of the fact that he was happily married for fifty-six years and in spite of the fact that he was continually devoted to his virtuous wife even after her death, P'u had special reasons for magnifying the awful picture of a shrew. In his early life he had seen how his own large family was wrecked by a sister-in-law. Also, among his closest literary associates he had a friend who was so completely overpowered by a shrewish wife that he dared not care for the funeral of his own father. Thus his accumulated resentment against shrews in Chinese society was vented on the singular character of the heroine of this novel.

Besides experimenting with the use of a rural vernacular dialect in the production of a long novel, P'u also wrote various types of poetry in the language of the common people. The most distinguished pieces of this type were his drum songs, intended to be sung to the accompaniment of a small drum. At least six of these drum songs were dramatizations of his shorter tales in prose. One of these, entitled "Exorcising Against Jealousy," was a dramatization of the tale "River Town." While the tale was written in elegant classical prose of 2900 words, the drum song was prolonged to about seventy thousand words. What was described briefly in the tale in laconic prose was now given free reign in the drum song. In place of a trite sentence making fun of the enduring principle that wives were to be feared by their husbands, the drum song had the following to say:

> Committing manslaughter,
> Committing arson,
> Could possibly be taken care of by a hundred thousand taels of silver.
> When the bribe is presented to the governor, the handcuffs might be immediately unlocked.
> But when the lady is on fire
> There is no hiding,
> There is no refuge.
> This prison will be my end.

This departure from convention led him to see the humorous and ludicrous even in the sacred books of Confucianism and to bypass eventually the imposition of the orthodox upon literary taste by culminating his creative activities in the rural vernacular of his native district, which made him the leading figure in creative literature of his age. It is sometimes difficult for us to realize what courage it took to move away from the ruts of literary convention. Most of P'u contemporaries were interested in one ultimate objective in the cultivation of literary talent, namely, the winning of high honors in the competitive literary examination, which honors were directly conducive to wide recognition and, what was more important, the assurance of a comfortable livelihood resulting from immediate appointment to an official position. To attain this end the typical scholar of that age had to submit himself to a long process of technical training in the mastery of the set formulas for the composition of the Eight-Legged Essay and the official form of versification of five-syllable-line poetry with a chosen rhyme specified. In addition it was also one of the requirements to submit a *fu* based on parallel structure and adopting a rhyming scheme that would respond to a given line of poetry. This set of literary gymnastics consumed the major portion of a literary man's life, leaving him only rare moments in which to attempt relatively free composition. Even these, aside from a small number of occasional lyrical poems, were in the main short prose compositions based on well-known models.

This peculiar literary vogue imposed by the imperial government from 1400 to 1900 and humbly accepted by the vast majority of China's literati did prove irksome to a small number of the intellectuals. The rise of scientific classical scholarship, which started in the mid-seventeenth century and reached its high tide a hundred years later, is known in Chinese intellectual history as Han Hsüeh or learning of the Han school. This name is actually a misnomer, for that intellectual ferment was much more than a mere revival of the classical scholarship of the Han dynasties. In Han classical learning the keynote had been the faithful transmission and perpetuation of the theories of a master in the interpretation of the Confucian texts. It was characterized by a profound respect for and almost unconditional submission to the lore of one's acknowledged master. Any deviation from the transmitted teachings of the founder of the school was intellectual tabu. The net result of such an intellectual trend was a slavish acceptance of scholastic commentaries, so much so that sometimes those Han masters were held in greater respect than Confucius and Mencius themselves. This is the general characteristic of Han scholarship which was preserved through the period of the political disunion till the end of the T'ang Dynasty. Since originality was something to be deplored, as it was interpreted as violation of authority, it is easily understandable that medieval thinkers of the Confucian school in China were at best thinkers of only secondary importance.

It was against this tyranny of authoritarianism and this enslavement by the letter of the Confucian classics that Neo-Confucianism was developed in the eleventh and twelfth centuries as a protest. Within the framework of the Confucian classics the Neo-Confucianists sought and found a new meaning and a new message. To them an understanding of the contents of a Confucian classical text, while important and highly desirable in itself, was only a steppingstone to the ordering of life in accordance with the basic teachings of the ancient sages. Hence it was more essential for the scholar to discover the basic reasons in the universe on which the Confucian teachings had been based. Utilizing the teachings of Buddhism and philosophical Taoism for purposes of comparison and incorporation, the Sung philosophers stimulated original thinking. This freedom in speculation was to reach its maximal point in the sixteenth century when, under the influence of Wang Yang-ming, scholars went so far as to discredit book learning altogether and to insist upon the basic importance of introspection. One extremist said that the Confucian classics were no more than "commentaries to what I am and what I say."

Despite the brilliance of some of the revolutionists in this Neo-Confucian school there was a complete neglect of the importance of evidence. Speculation had become completely unharnessed and indulgence in introspection often took the form of intellectual indigence. This lack of emphasis on verifiable knowledge and systematic learning which had bothered the serious searcher after objectivity made him especially susceptible to the influx of scientific learning introduced into China from Europe by Western missionaries, especially the Jesuits.

The preoccupation with evidence and the search for basic rules arrived at from inductive logic became the cornerstone of the "Han learning" of the seventeenth and eighteenth centuries. Instead of worshiping old authorities of the Han and T'ang Dynasties and instead of speculating without discipline and objectives, the scholars of the Han Hsüeh school paved the way to the building up of a scientific and historical method both in their linguistic and philosophical studies. Thus equipped, they were able to reconstruct the pronunciation of words in ancient times, to rediscover the original meanings of ancient philosophical terms, and also to reconstruct deranged texts and to detect forgeries in purportedly ancient writings. The great intellects of the seventeenth and eighteenth centuries were all profoundly affected by this new intellectual creed and methodology. These, however, constituted only an extreme minority of the educated elements of the empire. Monopolizing the attention and energies of the Chinese intellectuals, the examination technique with all its gymnastics and acrobatics was still reigning supreme.

The harmful effect and the sheer wastage of time involved in the mastery of this highly complex but obviously useless technique must have been apparent to many and yet protests were few—although a few sarcastic observations were registered lightly though unmistakably in occasional anecdotal literature. Any formal criticism and castigation of the prevailing literary vogue would be tantamount to a denunciation of established dynastic policy. It is easily understandable that the most eloquent piece of covert indictment should have been carefully cloaked in the form of a novel of satire. This novel was the *Ju-lin Wai-shih* or *The Informal History of the Forest of Scholars*.

The author, Wu Ching-tzŭ (1701-1754) of Anhui Province, a member of an extremely well-to-do family, had made the acquaintance of many brilliant scholars of his time but failing to learn the technique of the conservation of wealth, he became impoverished in his middle life. Later on, his poverty was so badly aggravated that, according to his own confession, he sometimes would fail to get a proper meal in a whole week. On the other hand he had not developed a respect for high honors in the examination system and so he declined the recommendation of the governor of his province to take part in one of the prearranged special-favor imperial examinations. Thus "refusing to take part in the examinations on any level and doing the things that pleased him especially," he spent the rest of his life in poverty but with leisure, dying eventually in the populous city of Yangchow. His collected works, consisting of seven volumes of poetry and five volumes of essays, were soon lost to posterity. From quotations preserved in the writings of other people his attainments in these two fields seem to be highly respectable. Fortunately for us, his epoch-making novel has come down to us intact.

In structure the *Forest of Scholars* consists of fifty-five chapters lightly strung together by the narrator in the style of a picaresque romance. In other words, the fifty-five chapters were actually so many short stories strung together by the central personality of the narrator. These were realistic tableaux of the different classes of

Chinese society all touching on the general theme of the lives of scholars. Many of the characters depicted were actually based on real personalities known to the author. The general theme was the ridiculing of the typical Chinese scholar of the age whose mind was totally preoccupied with the winning of honors and rising in the official hierarchy.

In the first chapter the main theme of the novel is summarized by the fictitious character of Wang Ming who subtly criticized the Ming system of competitive examination as a yardstick in the measurement of the ability and character of men: "when scholars had this avenue opened to them for the glorification of themselves, naturally they would belittle both moral character and technical training." All readers were aware, of course, that the same system was prevailing during the Ch'ing Dynasty and yet in appearance only the fallen Ming Dynasty was criticized.

Again, in the words of another character, Mr. Ma Erh, the inherent value of the competitive system was highly eulogized:

Attention to elevation to honors is something that should be cultivated by everyone from antiquity to the present age. Let us take Confucius as an example. He was living in the Spring and Autumn Period. At that time the basis for elevation consisted in correct speech and honorable conduct and so Confucius said: "When one is not faulty in his speech and breeds no regret in his conduct, therein he would find official rewards." This then is what Confucius was occupied with in elevation. When it came to the Warring States period the short cut to official position was political traveling-salesmanship and so Mencius traveled to Ch'i and Liang trying to sell his political philosophy. This is Mencius' preoccupation with elevation. . . . In the T'ang Dynasty scholars were elevated for their poetry and their fu. If they, the scholars, should speak the words of Confucius and Mencius then they would have no official sinecures, so all T'ang people could write a few lines of poetry. This is the preoccupation of the T'ang people with elevation. In the Sung Dynasty the situation was better. Those who held official positions were philosophers of the Neo-Confucian School and so Chu Hsi and the Ch'êng brothers all talked Neo-Confucian philosophy. This is the way the Sung people were occupied with elevation. In the current dynasty [that is, the Ming] the standard of selection is the Eight-Legged Essay. This is the supremely good yardstick. Even if Confucius were alive today he would have to recite essays and write Eight-Legged Essays and would never think of insisting on eliminating our faults in speech and conduct. Why not? Because even though he cultivated the elimination of faults in speech and conduct every day, who would make him an official? And the way of Confucius would never prevail.

Wu's exposure of the stupidities and shamelessness of his contemporaries indicated a new social philosophy which he meant to uphold: that there was nothing inherently honorable about official elevation; being a real man was more valuable than being a high official; solid learning was more to be prized than ability to write an

Eight-Legged Essay; and a good personality was to be cherished more than riches and honors.

In accordance, he presented characters to illustrate how despicable some of the successful scholars were, how mean and miserly some of them had become, and how a mere actor could be highly respectable as a person and how a mere military officer could be inherently lovable. It is to be noted that all his criticism of his characters were concretely clothed in details which made them real living people. Accusing a Confucian scholar, Fan Chin, of hypocrisy, for example, the author represented him as making a call on Magistrate T'ang in anticipation of a gift from the latter, taking advantage of the recent death of his mother. The magistrate urged him to stay for supper. As the wine cups and chopsticks were silver-inlaid, Fan Chin would not touch them because he was still in mourning. The magistrate ordered porcelain cups and ivory chopsticks instead, but the scholar in mourning still declined to touch them and asked for inferior wares.

Magistrate T'ang, seeing he was so thorough in the observation of mourning rites, became perplexed and felt embarrassed in case the guest should decline to eat meat, for he had not ordered a vegetarian dinner. It was not until he had seen the mourning scholar selecting a huge lump of shrimp from the bird's-nest soup to pop into his mouth that the magistrate felt relaxed.

He was equally vehement in attacking the by-products of an artificially formalized society such as the cherished practice of encouraging a widow to follow her deceased husband to the grave. The character concerned was Third Miss, daughter of the scholar Wang Yü-huei:

When Mr. Wang arrived in the home of his son-in-law, he found the latter seriously ill. . . . A few days later the son-in-law was no more. . . . The Third Daughter said, "Now I want to take leave of my parents-in-law and my father to seek a way of death so as to follow my husband to where he is. . . ." Wang Yü-huei said to her, "My child, if you mean to do this, something that will make you immortal in history, how can I stop you? You can do as you please. I shall go home today to ask your mother to come and say farewell to you." The parents-in-law repeatedly refused to give in. Wang Yü-huei, however, would not change his mind. He rushed home and reported to his old wife. The old lady said, "How is it that the older you get the more stupid you are? When a daughter wants to die you should dissuade her. How can you encourage her to die? What nonsense is this?" Wang Yü-huei answered, "This sort of thing people like yourself would not understand." The old lady, as soon as she heard this, burst out crying and immediately ordered a sedan chair to go to visit her daughter. Wang Yü-huei stayed home continuing his reading and penmanship quietly waiting for news from his daughter. The old lady did her best to dissuade her daughter, all to no avail. The daughter would wash her face and

comb her hair and keep her mother company, declining to eat and drink. . . .
When she had starved herself for six days she could not get up from her bed.
Her mother, seeing this, was stricken in her heart and felt extreme pain in her
internal organs. She also felt ill, returned home in the sedan chair, and lay in
her bed. Three days later, at about the second watch in the evening there
came several people holding torches and knocking at the door, saying, "The
Third Miss, after starving herself for eight full days, passed away today at
noon." The Old Lady, on hearing this, wept and swooned and when she came
to, she wailed unceasingly. Wang Yü-huei walked to her bedside and said,
"You, old woman, are really stupid. Our Third Daughter has now become an
immortal; why should you cry about her? She has died well, this way; I am
only afraid I may not have as good a pretext to die for in the future." Then
he lifted up his head to heaven and laughed, saying, "Well dedicated. Well
dedicated." With this, roaring with laughter, he walked out of her room.

Wang Yü-huei, however, was not beyond redemption. Two months
later when the memorial tablet of his deceased daughter was to be
enshrined in the ancestral temple with a new memorial arch erected
in her honor and after a memorial feast had been arranged near the
Confucian temple to be participated in by all the leading Confucian scholars of the area, he declined the honor. While traveling in
scenic areas of the West Lake, he would see images of his daughter
in the colors of the mountains and reflections in the lake. When he
was resting in a teahouse by the roadside he saw a young woman
wearing white in mourning which reminded him of his daughter and
he was unable to keep hot tears from bursting from his eyes.

It was probably no coincidence that the author had a tailor bringing up the rear of the parade of strange scholars. This tailor, Ching
Yüan, was probably what the novelist wanted to see the real scholar
be. After his professional work, the tailor would spend his day in
playing the ancient lute, in practicing calligraphy, and in writing
poetry. He was often asked by his friends, "Since you have decided
to be an elegant man, why do you want to stick to your profession?
Why don't you seek the company of scholars from the colleges?"
Nonchalantly he answered:

I have not deliberately made up my mind to be an elegant man. I learned
to do calligraphy and so forth simply because I like it. As regards my humble
profession, it is something I inherited from my grandfather. I cannot imagine
that a man who has learned to read and write will be lowering his status by
being a tailor. Moreover, those learned friends from colleges have creeds of
their own. How would they like to be associated with me? Now that I am able
to earn six or seven tenths of an ounce of silver and am able to feed myself,
I enjoy perfect freedom whether I want to play the lute or practice calligraphy.
I neither covet the riches and honors of other people, nor wait upon the countenance of other people. I will not be disciplined by heaven nor controlled by
earth. Don't you think I am happy?

The *Forest of Scholars* was at first circulated only in manuscript but it soon attracted so much attention that various editions soon appeared in print around 1800, thus accounting not only for divergent readings but also for additional chapters that had been interpolated. These interpolations are so clearly discernible that the restoration of the original basic text has been rendered easy.

This novel, epoch-making in its own way, is especially noticeable for several features. In the first place, it was the first outstanding piece of creative fiction written by one hand and entirely independent of the historical cycles which had been either the bases of prose narratives or the scaffoldings of fictional literature into which new characterizations and the enlargements of subplots had been interjected. All the incidents and characters of the *Forest of Scholars* were presented for the first time. In fact, a good many of the outstanding characters in this series of tableaux were embellishments of contemporary scholars and writers of note, some of whom were easily identified. In the second place, the language used was no longer the dialect of a province or the jargon of a limited segment of society but an early specimen of China's national language, later on described as *kuo yü*—a general medium of everyday conversation which was easily understood by the great majority of the Chinese people. This purity of the linguistic medium accounts at least partly for the great popularity of the work. In the third place, the *Forest of Scholars* is distinguished by its high quality of realism and humor and its complete freedom from the use of indecorous descriptions and characterizations which have made Chinese works of fiction in general objectionable to the sensitive Western reader. It is a work that can be safely read by the young and uninitiated without any need of expurgation.

Most important of all, the author of the *Forest of Scholars* was so unbiased and open-minded in his use of satire against the stupidities and corruptions of the scholarly world and of Chinese society at large that his eagerness for reform was apparent and inoffensive. He had no personal axes to grind, no personal vengeance in mind, and he did not preach. Nor did he at any time appear to be using himself as the yardstick of moral perfection, looking down upon the characters of his own creation as so many incorrigibles. His criticism was always tempered with a touch of warm sympathy and his presentation of human foibles was always accompanied by a profound understanding of the conflict of wills in man and by a underlying assurance of his ultimate perfectibility.

When the *Forest of Scholars* was attracting increased attention, Chinese society was undergoing a peculiar change. The vigor of the

Manchu regime was already beginning to decline, although externally the splendor of the empire was more dazzling than ever during the reign of Emperor Ch'ien Lung (1736-1795). Especially among the leading families of the empire, luxury was breeding indolence and corruption and the final disintegration and impoverishment of the classical family system.

Clearly reflecting this trend was a novel which appeared about 1754 in manuscript form in Peking. It was first entitled *Shih-t'ou Chi* or *The Tale of the Rock*. Composed of eighty chapters, the work soon attracted so much attention that in the course of five or six years copies in manuscript were sold at temple markets for forty or fifty taels of silver per set. The meaning of the title was made plain in the opening chapter in which it was stated that in high antiquity when the legendary imperial lady, Nü Wo, attempted to repair the cracks of the firmament with pieces of rock, one such rock was left unused. It lamented its fate and when it saw a Buddhist monk and a Taoist priest it asked to be inscribed upon so that people might know it was no ordinary stone. Many ages later, after it had gone through many trials, it was discovered by a recluse representing the embodiment of Buddhist and Taoist truths who was impressed by the inscriptions and, with the consent of the rock itself, copied them for circulation in the human world.

The main theme of the narrative is as follows: In the city of the rock there was a prominent family—the Chia family—divided into two collateral houses. In one of these houses in which complex genealogical tables were preserved and presented in the novel, there was a boy who had been born with a piece of jade in his mouth. Thus came the personal name of Pao-yü, namely, Precious Jade, the main character of the novel. When he was seven or eight years old, he had exhibited unusual intelligence which was tarnished by one outstanding weakness—an excessive love for girls. Thus he frequently made the statement that girls were made of water whereas boys were made of mud. For this reason his father, Chia Chêng, decided to correct him with strict discipline.

The company in which Pao-yü moved with the greatest satisfaction was an assemblage of beautiful girls known as the twelve beauties. One of these was his cousin, Tai-yü (Black Jade), who, on account of the loss of her mother and her own frail health, had been sent to the Chia family. This girl from the Lin family had a close rival in another cousin from the Hsüeh family named Pao-ch'ai (Precious Hairpin), beautiful and innocent. Besides these there were also numerous young ladies and maiden servants who claimed the attention of Pao-yü. Meanwhile the Chia family, on account of excessive expenditures and growing number of mouths to feed, found it impossible to practice thrift and also maintain its impressive front. Various tragedies began to occur: early deaths, family discord, and the suicide of some of the beauties. The story than rapidly developed to present the acceleration of decline and the accumulation of family tragedies. At the end of the eightieth chapter the catastrophe of the final ruin of this prosperous family in both of its houses was only faintly suggested; no details were given or even predicted of the denouement.

In 1792, however, a printed edition consisting of 120 chapters suddenly made its appearance with the title of the story changed to *Hung Lou Mêng* or *Dream of the Red Chamber*. In this, there were not only forty chapters added to the original but also variations in the text. Thus the composite story of the *Red Chamber* was presented in full. In these last forty chapters the ruination of the house was told step by step. Pao-yü, after losing his piece of mystical jade, seemed to have lost his soul. His father, faced with the trial of an official appointment in a distant province, decided to postpone the journey until the marriage of his son. The dilemma was a choice between the two beautiful cousins, Tai-yü (Black Jade) and Pao-ch'ai (Precious Hairpin). Since marriages in classical China were arranged by the parents of the two individuals, a good deal of family intrigue entered into the deliberations and negotiations. On account of Tai-yü's poor health, it was secretly agreed that Pao-ch'ai should be the choice.

Before the secret was published, Tai-yü learned of the fateful decision and grew increasingly ill, finally dying of hemorrhage on the day of the wedding. On Pao-yü's part, he had taken for granted that his bride was to be Tai-yü, but when at the wedding he had discovered to his great surprise that he was being married to Pao-ch'ai, he could not control his grief and was immediately taken ill. From this point on the tragedy resolved itself rapidly. The political corruption of one of the hero's uncles resulted in the stripping of official privileges and the confiscation of the family wealth of both houses of the clan. All those who had been dear to Pao-yü, old and young, disappeared from the scene by various forms of tragic death and kidnapping by highwaymen.

After enduring numerous ordeals, Pao-yü was on the verge of death himself when he was called upon by a Buddhist monk with the missing jade. This revived him and gave rise to a long dream. When he woke up he decided to begin a new page in life. He not only succeeded in winning high honors in a competitive literary examination but was also greeted by the possibility of the arrival of a son by Pao-ch'ai. When the tide of the family fortune was thus about to take a turn for the better, Pao-yü was nowhere to be found. When his father was on his way back to the capital and when his boat was mooring at the riverbank on a snowy night, he saw a person wearing neither hat nor shoes but wrapped in a crimson cape kneeling in front of him. It was Pao-yü. When he was about to speak to his son there came a Buddhist monk and a Taoist priest who kidnapped Pao-yü to the accompaniment of a mysterious voice singing "Return to the Great Void." Pao-yü's father took pursuit but lost sight of all three, seeing in front of him "merely a stretch of pale and boundless wilderness."

The real meaning and background of this story have suggested various theories: that it was the fictionization of the biography of the gifted Manchu writer and knight, Nara Singde; that it was a record in story form of the devotion of Emperor Shun Chih to his imperial consort who died young; or that it was a political novel of the reign of K'ang Hsi in which the fall of the Ming Dynasty was lamented and the failings of the Ch'ing Dynasty were subtly magnified in allegory. These hypotheses, although painstakingly built up, have little to offer toward an understanding of the composition of this unique novel. The most authentic interpretation is a simple and natural one: the novel was nothing more than a biography, presented in fictional form, of the author himself.

The author, Ts'ao Chan—better known by his courtesy name of Ts'ao Hsüeh-ch'in (1719-1763)—was the scion of a powerful bannerman family—that is, a family which had early surrendered to the Manchus prior to the conquest of China in 1644, hence known in Ch'ing institutional history as Han Chün, usually enjoying special privileges in officialdom. It should be pointed out in this connection that the bannerman families enjoyed the double advantage of firsthand knowledge and inheritance of China's classical culture and of a special social and political status of the newly established aristocracy by way of reward for their participation in the military campaigns of conquest, often serving as vanguards.

It was the military organization to which these early Chinese defectionists were subjected that gave them the nomenclature of bannerman, for they were all members of one army banner or another designated by special colors. Ts'ao's affiliation was with the so-called Pure White banner, a banner of white without any border. The special official position with which the family was awarded was the directorate of silk textiles in the important city of Nanking.

When Emperor K'ang Hsi made his five separate trips of "inspection" to southeast China, the official building of the directorate was designated as the temporary palace of his traveling majesty—a fact indicating the pre-eminence of the office and the luxurious environment of the official building. Ts'ao Chan's grandfather, Ts'ao Yin, was first appointed to this office and, utilizing his enormous income derived from the appointment, financed the republication of numerous literary works of the past which had become rare. Besides this, Ts'ao Yin was a poet of some accomplishment and an author of two plays. As was the custom among bannerman families, many of the official positions held were passed on from father to son until signs of incompetence or corruption were detected.

Consequently, Ts'ao Chan's father, Ts'ao T'iao, inherited the directorship and Ts'ao Chan, the great novelist was, therefore, born in Nanking where he stayed until 1728. After that time, for reasons now difficult to ascertain, the Ts'ao family seemed to decline rapidly after their return to Peking. When the novelist was middle-aged he had become so impoverished that he had to seek temporary lodging in the western suburb of the imperial city and had to sustain himself on rice porridge instead of the customary boiled rice. Still undaunted and proud, he would abandon himself to drinking and poetry writing whenever he could afford it and it was probably at this time that he wrote his novel. In 1762 he lost his only son, and he died on Chinese New Year's Eve of the same year, or February 13, 1763.

This author, who had lived through a fairly long period of political influence and financial prosperity, who had grown up in a family environment replete with the advantages of a huge family library and a notable art collection, and who, toward the end of his life, had to taste the bitter fruit of the fall of a powerful house, was not only well equipped as author of the novel but also bore unmistakable evidence that he himself was the original of the picture he drew of the hero. It was the author's intimacy with the details of how a powerful family was reduced to penury that made the novel touchingly realistic. The cause of the ruination of the Ts'ao family was a simple one—forthright extravagance and inability to budget. In this light, we must conclude that the *Dream of the Red Chamber* was nothing more than the realistic presentation of a chain of complicated but related events describing the rise and fall of an aristocratic clan.

By some scholars, including Hu Shih, the last forty chapters of the 120-chapter edition of the book have been attributed to Kao O, a member of another bannerman clan who was born about the middle of the eighteenth century. This attribution, according to Lin Yutang, may be erroneous in that most likely, Kao was only the editor rather than the author of the last forty chapters, so that problem is still unsettled. At any rate these supplementary chapters, which successfully brought the narration to a completion, were not without their own merits. In keeping with the spirit of the original, the author was unconventional enough to prescribe the premature death of T'ai Yü on her sweetheart's wedding day and the ultimate severance of relations with the world by the hero, Pao-yü, in seeking refuge in Buddhist monkhood. This refusal to conform to the Chinese convention in fiction of an almost invariably happy ending, apparently based on his knowledge of the author's tragic late years in life, and his willingness and eagerness to carry out what he had considered to be the original design of the uncompleted version of the novel, distinguished him from all other writers who attempted other "continuations" and "supplements" to the *Dream of the Red Chamber*. These latter all itched to resurrect one or another of the twelve beauties by some miraculous means and marry her off to Pao-yü so as to make the dream a really happy one for all concerned.

Thanks to the author's genius, his version furnished Chinese literature with the only outstanding novel with a truly tragic ending. The following may be cited as an example among numerous other quotable passages of the realistic technique employed by Ts'ao: an elderly lady from the countryside, old Mrs. Liu, was touring alone the gorgeous garden of the Chia family—the well-known Grand View Garden.

She felt dizzy and, as her eyesight seemed to be growing dim, she could not see her way clearly. She simply followed the raised pebbled pathway, and made two turns before she saw a door. After entering the door she saw a girl coming toward her, and greeting her with a face full of smiles. Old Mrs. Liu immediately smiled, too, in response and said, "The young ladies have left me behind to grope around and here I am!" To this, the girl did not say a word and Mrs. Liu rushed forward to grasp her hand but bang! She was hitting a wall. She took a good look and found that it was only a painting she had seen. "How is it a picture is three-dimensional?" she mused to herself. Thus, thinking hard and looking carefully, she felt it with her hand and found that it was flat. She nodded and heaved a few sighs.

Just then she found a door behind the painted screen, and saw an elderly woman greeting her from the other side of the door. Feeling puzzled and not a little confused, Mrs. Liu thought to herself, "Could this be my son's mother-in-law?" Suddenly she said aloud, "Have you come for me because I have not returned home these few days? Which young lady has shown you the way here?" Then she noticed the elderly lady had flowers all over her hair and she laughed saying, "You simpleton, just because the flowers in this garden are beautiful, should you have loaded your whole head with them, dead or alive?" Seeing that the old woman was only smiling but not answering a word, she suddenly recalled: "I have often been told that people of high class have a kind

of full-length dressing mirror. Can it be that I am now inside such a mirror?"
She decided to stretch out her hand to feel it and then to take an intense look.
Was it anything at all but a huge mirror set in a frame?

(Chapter 41)

One of the characteristics of the *Dream of the Red Chamber*
which seems especially offensive to the translator is the endless
studding of the narrative with bits of poetry—sometimes as interjections by the author but more frequently as the handiwork of the
characters. At times the procedure of a poetry contest will be presented in great detail with practically nothing to contribute to the
development of the plot. Since the readers of fiction in the
eighteenth century were people with considerable literary apprenticeship, who would not readily admit their lack of such apprenticeship, the parading of pedantry and the brandishing of literary gems
soon became integral parts of the business of a novel writer. In
fact, there were novels written as vehicles for the purposeful display
of such articles of book learning.

All through the eighteenth century there seemed to be a clear
parting of the ways between scholarship and creative writing. In
the realm of scholarship there was a tendency to steer away from
history so as to avoid involvement in political persecution. The
Ch'ing rulers were particularly sensitive to scholars dealing with
the history of relations between the Chinese people and the border
tribes. Even harmless references to the so-called Northern Dynasties
of the fourth and fifth centuries might be misconstrued as veiled
attacks upon the reigning alien dynasty. A mere glance at the numerous instances making up the so-called literary inquisition of Ch'ien
Lung, in which many innocent writers were mercilessly incriminated
and punished with death penalties imposed upon themselves and
their whole clans, will impress the modern reader with the wisdom
of choice made by the great majority of scholars of those days in
seeking refuge in philological and exegetical commentaries on the
Confucian classics and in the bypaths of ancient semantics and
phonology. In these fields hardly any heads were cut off. As a result,
the cherished standard in scholarship was evidence based on facts.
With the growth of this new ideal of erudition and emphasis on verifiable knowledge it was only natural that the learned would belittle
what was avowedly fictional.

A great exception to the rule was a scholar who excelled in many
specialties and who had distinguished himself especially in phonological researches, but whose luck in the competitive examination
halls varied inversely with the growth of his erudition. Toward the
end of his life, spending his days listlessly at the seaport county of

Haichow, he devoted more than ten years to the writing of a peculiar novel. Li Ju-chên (1763?-1830), a native of Tahsing, near Peking, rebelled early against the Eight-Legged Essay. At about twenty he was brought to Haichow by his elder brother, who had been appointed a magistrate there. He was immediately attracted by the profound learning of the great scholar Ling T'ing-k'an (1757-1809), with whom he studied the classics, linguistics, and phonology. With an almost endless appetite for content subjects, he also became an expert in astronomy and astrology, calligraphy and fortunetelling, music and chess playing.

Before Li Ju-chên tried his hand at a novel, he had won recognition as a scholar with a treatise on phonology entitled *Yin Chien* or the *Mirror of Phonology,* a work in which he contrasted ancient pronunciation with current speech, a daring innovation in the field. It was probably his refusal to become circumscribed by the technique of the Eight-Legged Essay that made him bold enough to become a novelist, but his acquaintance with many fields of solid training in classical studies burdened his novel with long-winded discourses on scholarship.

His one novel, *Ching Hua Yuan* or the *Tale of the Mirrored Flower,* consisting of a hundred chapters, tells a story of how the Empress Wu of the T'ang Dynasty wanted to enjoy blooming flowers in high winter. She had decreed that the hundred kinds of flowers must bloom together and a garden of flowers, obeying her orders, fulfilled her desire. But since she had violated the ways of nature, she was later on exiled to the world of men by the supreme deity to take the divergent forms of a hundred women.

Meanwhile a young scholar, T'ang Ao, had succeeded in earning the third highest honor in the competitive examination; on account of his purported associations with a rebel, however, he was deprived of his prospective rewards. Thereupon he decided to quit the world and all that pertained to it. His wife's younger brother, Lin Chih-yang, was an international merchant owning various seaworthy ships. On board one of these, Lin undertook extensive travels in overseas areas, meeting numerous unusual personalities and visiting strange lands with unusual customs and rare produce. It was on one of these trips that he had tasted an immortal herb which elevated him above the rank of common mortals. He entered one of the mountains with no intention of returning home. His devoted daughter, Hsiaoshan, went in search of her father but after going through various strange countries and surviving numerous hardships, she failed to recover him. Through a woodcutter, however, she received a letter from her father in which it was suggested that their meeting would be possible only if she won the title of Talented Woman. As she walked farther on she saw an old grave with a tombstone reading "Grave of the Mirrored Flower." Then she entered the village of Water Moon. Still farther on, she found a pavilion called the Pavilion of Weeping Red. Inside there was a tablet on which a hundred names were inscribed, among which her own was number eleven.

Upon her return there was a competitive examination decreed by Empress Wu for the selection of talented women. She took part in it and succeeded in winning the eleventh honor as had been predicted. At the post-examination festivities she met various gifted ladies, including the human personifications of Aunt Breeze and Elder Sister Moon. At last there were insurrections against the usurpation of Empress Wu in which some of the talented women served in both armies and died in action. After the defeat of the troops of Empress Wu, her son, Emperor Chung Tsung, was restored. Nonetheless, Empress Wu continued to be honored by her son as Tsê-t'ien, the Great Holy Emperor (not "empress"). Soon afterward, Empress Wu issued another decree inaugurating another competitive examination for talented women and summoning all successful candidates of the first examination for a great reunion dinner.

At this point, apparently, the end of the first part of the whole narrative was concluded with the author promising at the end of the chapter, "If my readers are interested in the whole image within the mirror, let us wait for a later appropriate occasion." However, the promised continuation was never written.

According to Hu Shih, this novel was one in which the problems of women were discussed. The author's answer to the questions raised was a bold one: that men and women should be accorded equality in treatment in education and in opportunities for selection for civil service. Comparing it to Swift's *Gulliver's Travels,* Hu Shih points out that this novel made use of wonders beyond the seas to highlight inequalities of social practice in China. In Chapters 11 and 12, for example, in which the Country of Gentlemen was described, twelve different social problems were raised. Despite some platitudinous observations on ethical practices in business and the futility of lawsuits, there were problems of magnitude which had been neglected by Chinese society for long centuries. For example, the problem of foot-binding was raised:

I have heard that in your honored country there has been developed the theory of foot-binding among women. At the time of the initiation of the practice of foot-binding the maidens suffer a hundred kinds of pain, grievously wailing as they touch their bound feet. In extreme cases there is rotting of skin and spoiling of muscles resulting in the flowing of blood. At this stage the victim will fail to sleep at night and lose all appetite at table. Numerous types of ailment are said to have emerged from this. I humbly have thought that such a girl might have certain shortcomings and that her mother, refraining for pity from killing her, might have chosen to punish her in this manner. I never imagined that it was invented for beauty and that any deviation from the practice could be considered ugly. Let me ask you this: when we chop a big nose to make it small and plane off a high forehead to make it flat, people invariably say that the victims are deformed. How could it follow, then, that when both feet are crippled and when walking is thus made painful, we could call that person beautiful? Moreover, Hsi-tzŭ and Wang Hsiang were famous beauties of a superlative degree [in the warring states period and the Han Dynasty respectively] and yet in those days they were never subjected to the cruelty of having their feet reduced to half size. After carefully tracing its origin we must conclude that it is a practice to arouse the lustfulness of men. This, then, is something that the sages would unconditionally condemn and all virtuous people will have no use for.

Revolutionary as this discourse is, it is slightly reminiscent of sermonizing by a preacher with a long and unimpassioned face. If the author had adhered to this method of direct presentation and preachment, his writing would not be highly rated as literature. Fortunately such examples are extremely few in the novel. The same problem with related issues was raised, for example, in the chapters describing the land of Maidens—a kind of Utopia invented by the author to criticize all the injustices inflicted upon women:

In this country there have always been menfolk, just as we have, and also marriages between men and women. What makes it distinctive is that there the men wear blouses and skirts, are labeled "women" to take care of the affairs of the home; and girls, on the contrary, wear hats and boots, and are called "men" to deal with the external affairs of state and society.

T'ang Ao, the traveler, having taken a look at those "menfolk," observed to his travel companion,

"Grandpa Nine, don't you see, they are actually nice women, but somehow they purposely want to dress as men. What great artificiality should we call this?"

"Smilingly," Grandpa Nine said in answer, "Elder Brother T'ang, say this as you may. I only fear that when they look upon us, they may also say that we have abandoned our good role as women and artificially usurped the role of men." T'ang Ao nodded his head and said, "How true are your words, Grandpa Nine. As the adage goes, 'Habit makes nature.' Although we may feel that they are strange and abnormal, they have always been like this ever since the beginning of time. When they look upon us, they naturally would consider us abnormal."

Even this method of presentation savors slightly of the voicing of abstract opinion despite the liveliness breathed into it by the use of dialogue. The author strove to go further. In Chapter 33 T'ang Ao's brother-in-law, Lin Chih-yang, the owner of the merchant fleet, was himself to go through the peculiar experience of being selected to become one of the imperial ladies in waiting in the nation of girls. One morning Lin happily observed to himself, "Luckily we were born in the Middle Kingdom. If we were natives of this country we would have been forced into foot-binding. That would be really ruinous." That very afternoon, however, what he had feared was to happen to him. The "king" of the Land of Maidens had been charmed by him and had ordered him to be brought into the palace to receive the honorific title of imperial concubine.

Early in the morning the royal maidservants had prepared an aromatic bath for him. In place of his trousers he now had to wear a blouse and a skirt and on his huge feet he had to wear silk stockings. His hair was now braided and oiled. On his braided hair he wore a phoenix hairpin and on his face he wore scented powder. His lips were tinted a brilliant red. On his finger was put a jeweled ring and around his wrist was placed a golden bracelet.

Then he had to go through the experience of having his ears pierced.

Whereupon Lin Chih-yang cried aloud: "I'm dying of pain." He fell backwards but fortunately was supported by the palace maids. Again his left ear was tweaked several times and then pierced with a pin. Lin felt so much pain that he cried again. After the two ears had been pierced, some lead powder was applied on them to be followed with a few more tweakings. Then he was given a pair of golden earrings studded with precious stones to wear.

Then Lin was subjected to the third degree of discipline, namely, foot-binding. After much struggling and suffering he cried out wildly like a hog being slaughtered.

From this point on he could only endure all pain, following all other men without hedging or disobedience. The various palace maidens knew he was completely frightened but when the hour came for tightening the foot binding they were only interested in efficiency and in pleasing the king. Disregardful of whether he was alive or dead, they would use all energy in tightening the binding. On numerous occasions he wanted to end his own life but on account of the watchfulness of the palace guards he found that he could seek neither death nor life. Without his realizing it, what had been his blood and flesh on his feet had all become water and flowed out. Only the bones were now left and his feet seemed to be thin and tiny.

Thus the ten years of suffering sustained by the average Chinese girl was graphically telescoped into the agony of about ten days.

It is to be underscored, at this point, that all the long pieces of fiction from the fourteenth century onward were written in a style very close to the vernacular of the common people or *pai hua*. Some authors that we have noted even went so far as to use the dialect of an out-of-the-way county of a province, the reason being mainly that they felt much more at home in what might be regarded as their mother tongue. Other authors, who were slightly more conservative, would adopt a medium halfway between literary and somewhat bookish Chinese and the speech of the common people. This was regarded as wise and desirable partly because of the traditional respect for the classical style and partly because of the discipline to which writers of all schools had been subjected. Nonetheless, the target set was intelligibility and liveliness. The occasional insertion of quotations in classical prose or highly ornate poems constituted only exceptions which did not break the rule. The significance of the adoption of a literary medium close to the living speech of the changing ages was the awareness that the traditional classical prose style, despite its dignity and elegance, was not suitable to the telling of a long and complicated story.

The only glaring breakage of this rule was attempted by a peculiar writer in Chekiang Province, Ch'ên Ch'iu, author of *Yen Shan Wai Shih* or *The Informal History of Yen Shan* (about 1810). Trained in the writing of balanced parallelistic prose—*p'ien wên*—and indifferent to literary convention because he was writing for satisfaction, since he could support himself by the sale of his watercolor paintings, he boldly announced, "In historical writing the style of balanced structure utilizing pairs of columns consisting of four and six character units has never been utilized. I fully realize my own foolhardiness and excesses in setting up a new practice against the conventions established since antiquity.... When this new deviation is applied to fiction, however, I shall hope for a reduction of the penalty for my guilt." Despite his proud and bold claims, however, he was actually not the first one to utilize that stilted and highly artificial prose style in fiction because, as we have seen, over a thousand years before him, Chang Chu had already conducted that unprecedented experiment in the telling of a love story in *Yu Hsien K'u* or *Travels to the Lodgings of Immortals* in the eighth century. That he was not an imitator of Chang was obvious from the fact that the eighth-century romance, although it had been well preserved and won many admirers in Japan, was not made available to Chinese readers until the twentieth century. Thus Ch'ên Ch'iu was at least innocent in making his nonauthentic claims.

In Ch'ên's narrative the main plot was taken from an old Ming story and elaborated into a narrative of over 30,000 words. The hero of this tale is Tou Ch'êng-tsu, a native of Peking who had traveled to Chekiang Province for advanced training and fallen in love with a girl from a poor family, Li Ai-ku. Tou was forced by his father to leave Li, as a marriage alliance had been arranged for the young man with a prominent official family. Meanwhile, Li Ai-ku was sold into a house of disrepute as a result of the villainous machinations of a Nanking merchant. Through the generosity of a friend, she was bailed out to be reunited to Tou as his concubine. Unable to endure the jealousies and cruelties of the legal wife, Tou and Li fled from their home but were dispersed on the highway in the midst of great commotion caused by a rebellion. When Tou returned home, he discovered that his family property had been completely squandered by his wife, who now demanded and got a divorce.

While Tou was lamenting his fate and solitude, Li Ai-ku appeared suddenly to tell him that she had been cared for in a nunnery. Thus inspired by the turn in his fortune, Tou succeeded in winning high honors in a competitive examination and in rising steadily in the official hierarchy until he was made governor of Shantung Province. Soon a boy was born and a wet nurse was advertised for. The woman who responded was none other than his divorced wife, who had been widowed after her second marriage. She was employed and well treated, but with her jealousy again aroused, she plotted against Ma Lin, the generous man who had redeemed Ai-ku from the house of prostitution, a criminal case in which Tou himself was also involved. After the clearance of the case, Tou had all his honors and position restored, but disillusioned with the ways of the world, he decided to seek refuge in Tao and became an immortal in the company of Ai-ku.

Thus a conventional story that had little to distinguish it was artificially given turns and surprises, mainly to show the dexterity commanded by the writer in giving color to the narrative. As *p'ien wên*, the piece was inferior not only to the lyrical pieces of the Six Dynasties period but even to the unwarranted deviation by Chang Chu of a thousand years before his time. Though loved for his uniqueness and privately cherished at times by readers of adolescent age, the failure of the experiment was so obvious that no similar attempts were made again until the twentieth century, by writers who had even less success.

When this foolhardy experiment was published in 1810, the Chinese Empire had already lost its vigor and even Chinese civilization was soon to feel less certain of itself. The relative seclusion that the country had enjoyed and the freedom which the imperial court had exercised in the admission of foreigners were both challenged.

CHAPTER 31

The Impact of the West

THE European nations, in their search for regular and legalized commercial relations with China, were knocking at her doors with greater eagerness. Great Britain and the Netherlands had sent official diplomatic agents to seek formal negotiations at the imperial court. Although these early diplomatic missions ended in failure as a result of the refusal of the envoys to perform the kowtow ceremony to the Chinese Emperor, Western attempts to regularize their relations with the Chinese Empire were not relaxed. Even the United States of America had already taken an active part in opening up direct trade with China with the arrival of its first vessel at Canton in 1784. The train of events was to lead up to the first Anglo-Chinese war of 1839, culminating in the defeat of China and the signing of the Treaty of Nanking in 1842.

In the domestic scene within the Chinese Empire itself, changes were also rapid and drastic. In the first place the vigor of the Manchus as a group seemed depleted. They still retained their suspicion of the Han Chinese, whom they had held in subjugation yet tried hard to win over as loyal servants of the reigning house. Manchu soldiers were no longer the well-organized and able fighters which they had been before. All able-bodied adult bannermen were given privileged positions and had become victims of easy life. In addition, members of the Manchu race had been completely softened by their wholesale absorption of Han Chinese culture. As a result, all Manchu detachments sent against the various local revolts were disastrously routed. In their place there grew up a new army system known as *lü ying*, literally, "green encampments," which were composed exclusively of Han Chinese. In the second place, political leadership among Manchus had also undergone a shocking decline both in internal administration and in the handling of diplomatic and military pressure from Western nations. Despite the presence at the Manchu court all through the nineteenth century of a few capable policy-makers for the Empire, they were clearly outnumbered by the non-Manchus. In the third place, Manchu rule was weakened by the depletion of the imperial coffers after the death of Emperor Ch'ien Lung. The expensive activities of that emperor in the form of frequent travels, the continual granting of largess to his ministers, and above all, the so-called Ten Perfect Campaigns against the various border tribes in Central Asia and the Tibetan fringe had drained the resources of the Empire. Moreover, the rapid population increase during the long peaceful period in China proper from 1665 to 1800 had also presented new challenges to economic resources.

The intellectual scene, in keeping with the political and economic deterioration, had also undergone stages of transformation. Within the realm of the so-called Han Hsüeh learning in classical studies, the undivided attention of scholars to objective inquiries in philology and textual and higher criticism began to be replaced by a new tendency inaugurated by the so-called Chin Wên or Modern Script school. According to this new school the Confucian canon still occupied the center of the intellectual stage but the point of emphasis was gradually shifting to a new quest for meaning which might have a contemporary bearing on the solution of urgent problems, both political and ethical. Confucius the historian was now repainted as Confucius the prophet. To implement these new exegetical studies of the Confucian classics, increasing attention was paid to the study of history and geography, fields which had been piously avoided at an earlier age for fear of involvements in the so-called literary inquisitions. As a natural consequence beginnings were made for the first time by native scholars to place China on the world map. The writings of the early Jesuits, especially those of a nonreligious nature, were reissued under native auspices for circulation among a larger number of readers.

Although China's first treaty signed with a Western power was the Treaty of Nerchinsk, concluded with Czarist Russia in 1689, its importance was superseded by the Treaty of Nanking. China had been completely humiliated in the eyes of the world and compelled to sign the so-called First Unequal Treaty. Five principal seaports were opened to foreign trade, as well as to missionary activities. The sale of opium, to which the Chinese government and the Chinese people at large had so strenuously objected, was now made legal. The rights of permanent residence by members of the Western nations in the specified cities was now an accomplished fact.

Protestant missionary activities, which had penetrated China in a surreptitious manner in 1807, were now conducted with guaranteed Chinese government protection. Similarly, the ban placed in 1774 on Catholic proselytizing was also lifted. Mission schools were established for both boys and girls in the port cities—a phenomenon which had disappeared from China after the closing of the Arch-Episcopal Seminary in Peking around 1330.

Under mission auspices, periodicals of general as well as strictly religious interest were inaugurated, soon to be followed by the launching of the first Chinese daily newpapers of the modern type, to open the eyes and ears of the Chinese people. With the setting up of new presses in which Western machinery was utilized, a minor revolution also took place. Printing by movable type, begun in China about 1041 to 1049, had fallen into desuetude in general, although the art was cultivated with continual attention and improved technique in Korea. Printing by movable type in China, despite its occasional revivals in the sixteenth, seventeenth, and eighteenth centuries, had faded out of the publishing scene because clay types were breakable, wooden types were so easily worn out, and bronze types so conducive to conversion into cash. With the importation of Western technique not only were smaller movable types of a strong and inexpensive alloy made available but also the accompanying paraphernalia of the Western power press. In addition, the heavy capital layout involved in the setting up of modern presses was obviated by another Western art—that of book reproduction. Lithography was introduced and facilitated not only the printing of maps, charts, and illustrations, but also the reproduction of Chinese texts in which complicated and out-of-the-way graphs were used. Lithography, therefore, was received with greater enthusiasm in China than it ever was in the Western world. As a result, not only were creative literary activities stimulated but even the reprinting of unavailable old literature was made possible. With the introduction of photolithography, antiquarian as well as literary interests were served by the easy facsimile reproduction of rare and fine printing of bygone periods.

Confining ourselves for the moment to the field of literary creation in fiction, we are greeted by a number of new trends. The facilities of the daily and periodical presses provided new opportunities for serializing of publications and, therefore, a mode of writing not entirely unknown to the Chinese but rarely tried. This trend, which rose to great popularity after the Sino-Japanese War of 1894 to 1895, not only elicited a large number of novels constructed on the model of the picaresque romance, but also left an impressive number of unfinished would-be novels. Second, the availability of world news and extensive background information concerning foreign nations, and especially nations of the Western world, made all writers of fiction sensitive to problems with which China was peculiarly faced and opened their eyes to the prevalence of China's national foibles, especially in economic backwardness and political corruption. In the third place, the presence of foreign missionaries, among whom more than a few were well-meaning and educated, made possible the gradual introduction of Western literature in translation to large numbers of Chinese readers. Besides exerting an immense influence upon the thought and content embodied in Chinese novels of the new school, Western novels also furnished Chinese writers with new patterns and techniques of narration. Despite the insistence of a small number of cultural conservatives on China's unshakable superiority in the fields of the humanities, Chinese literature was already beginning to transform itself into a waterway flowing into the ocean of world literature.

Before we discuss the novels of satire which reflect the increase of foreign influences in China, we should review a number of more or less traditional novels written in the tradition of the *Water Margin* and in apposition to the popularity of the *Dream of the Red Chamber*. Even at the height of the popularity of the *Dream of the Red Chamber*, the common people of China were still absorbingly fascinated by the *Romance of the Three Kingdoms* and the *Water Margin*. Nonetheless, new notes were demanded even in popular literature.

The first herald of a new idealism was the *Erh-nü Ying Hsiung Chuan*, or the *Tale of Heroic Men and Women*, originally in fifty-three chapters, of which only four chapters have been preserved. It was written by a sinicized Manchu, Wen K'ang, who wrote under the nom de plume of Yen-pei Hsien-jên (Loafer from Northern Chihli). A member of the Bordered Red Banner and a grandchild of the Manchu Prime Minister Lipao, he had a checkered career in Chinese politics. Like the author of the *Red Chamber*, he was an eyewitness of a great family in rapid decline. Living in reduced circumstance in a simple bedroom with hardly any more personal belongings than writing brush, ink-slab, papers, and books, he spent the last part of his life writing this novel for amusement. Whereas the author of the *Red Chamber* wrote autobiographically and realistically, Wen K'ang was objective and idealistic. According to the introductory chapter, "this novel was originally entitled 'Chin Yü Yuan' or 'The Tale of the Coming Together by Coincidence of Gold and Jade'; because what is narrated is a major case which happened in the imperial capital. It was also once entitled 'Jih-hsia Hsin Hsu' or 'A New Book Under the Sun.'" This multiplicity of names so carefully recorded seems to indicate that the influence of the *Red Chamber* was not entirely absent.

What was described as a major law case in the imperial capital is as follows: An unconventional girl descended from an outstand-ing family, Ho Yü-fêng (Jade Phoenix), was known for her wisdom and courage. Her father having been murdered by an enemy, she sought refuge with her mother in a deep forest awaiting her chance to seek vengeance. The enemy of the family, Chi Hsien-t'ang, was a wielder of immense political influence in the country on account of his distinguished services with the state. Warranted by circum-stances and her own eagerness for action, the heroine assumed the name of Shih-san Mei (Thirteenth Younger Sister) and made fre-quent sorties into the marketplace, where she completely disre-garded social conventions and derived what funds she could out of the world. At a small inn she made the acquaintance of a filial young man by the name of An Chi who happened to be in great distress and who, after receiving considerable help from the heroine, counted upon the latter as a devoted friend. In due course, before she could lay her hands on the throat of her enemy, Chi Hsien-t'ang was already punished with the death penalty by the imperial court.

With her father thus avenged, Ho Yü-fêng decided to leave the world to become either a Buddhist or Taoist. She was finally dis-suaded from her decision and agreed to be married to An Chi. The young man, however, had already been married and his wife, Chang Chin-fêng (Golden Phoenix), had also been lifted out of distress by the heroine. To solve a legal difficulty by conformity to the Chi-nese spirit of compromise, arrangements were made for An's second wedding to the heroine as his co-wife but not as concubine. Since the result of this bit of polygamy was perfect harmony among the three, the title was justified as the happy coming together of gold and jade, that is, of the Golden and Jade Phoenixes.

The plot of the story contains very few real surprises and the idealism exhibited is definitely of a strained kind. Efforts were made to present a woman character entirely different from the extremely feminine patterns set in the *Dream of the Red Chamber*—a girl in whom the virtues of lover and warrior are combined, resulting in a synthetic and often schizophrenic character. Nonetheless, the new note struck seemed to contemporaries to be so unique as to call for a continuation by an extremely mediocre writer sponsored by the book trade in Peking around 1890.

A superior novel of the same type but stressing the combination of romantic heroism with political loyalty, instead of glorifying out-laws in the tradition of the *Water Margin,* was *San Hsieh Wu Yi* or *Three Heroic Knights and Five Righters of Social Wrongs,* which appeared in 1879. Like other compositions of this nature, the work was pseudonymously published—"originally preserved by the querist of bamboos and edited by the Taoist who had fallen into a maze"—neither of which can be identified.

This novel, in telling of the heroic deeds of latter-day knights for the maintenance of social justice and service to the state, emphasized their subordination to a well-known grand official as their leader. Such a leader in the novel under review was a historic character of the Sung Dynasty who rose to great distinction both as statesman and as moral leader—Pao Ch'êng (999-1062), of whom an official biography is found in the *Sung Dynastic History*. Known in his own days as a sage judge, at once enlightened and incorruptible, Pao, even during his own life span, had received so much popular acclaim in his administration of justice that many legends and myths had already been widely circulated, many of which were worked into the dramas of the Yüan Dynasty, in which numerous supernatural elements had been emphasized. In the Ming Dynasty anonymous writers with limited literary gifts had written various versions of the miraculous cases handled by the reputed judge. These popular tales of the sage decisions of Pao constituted the background and foundations of the 1879 novel.

As is to be expected, the plot is somewhat complicated. Emperor Chên Tsung of the Sung Dynasty had reached an agreement with his two imperial consorts, Lady Liu and Lady Li, that whichever gave birth to the first son would be made empress. As Lady Li was soon pregnant, Lady Liu plotted with a eunuch and other court intriguers to have the newborn baby, if a male, stealthily replaced by a skinned cat; to declare to the palace that a monstrous beast had been born; and to deliver the prospective crown prince to a court maiden, K'ou Chu, who was to strangle the infant and throw the body into a creek.

When all these details of the plot had materialized, the maiden K'ou Chu found herself unable to go through with her role. In secret she entrusted the baby to the eunuch, Ch'ên Lin, who in turn hid it in the mansion of the eighth imperial prince, brother of the emperor. The baby grew up as the third son of the eighth prince. Meanwhile Lady Liu had brought about the degradation of Lady Li by lies and intrigue in which many loyal eunuchs were given the death sentence unjustly. Emperor Chên died without male children and the third son of the eighth prince was adopted into the main imperial line and crowned as Emperor Jên Tsung. At this point the birth of the miraculous judge, Pao Ch'êng, was brought out and the details of numerous cases brought to his court elaborated. Many detective stories were strung together in the style of the picaresque romance, having little to do with the main thread of the narrative but interesting in themselves. When Pao Ch'êng was appointed magistrate of the Sung imperial capital at K'aifeng, he discovered Lady Li still living among commoners. Exposing the case of the substituted crown prince, he made the emperor realize that she was the real empress dowager. Corrective steps were immediately taken.

Even now the eight knightly characters who give the title to the book had not made their appearance. It was not until the unexampled loyalty and honesty of Pao Ch'êng was widely felt that the eight Robin Hoods of Sung China, who had been roving in different parts of the empire as knights errant, all surrendered to him accepting appointments from the imperial government. Soon afterwards, the feudal prince of Hsiangyang fomented a rebellion and hid the roster of his clique in a tall building. Five of the reformed robber barons, after having received instructions from the imperial inspector, were on active duty trying to locate the key document. A sixth, trying to distinguish himself by deviating from the accepted standards of knighthood, scaled the tall building alone but lost his life after he had fallen into a trap made of copper wire netting. This shocking episode concludes the novel.

After the formal opening of China to the West in 1842, the influx of Western influence in all fields of national and cultural activities was steadily increased as a major historical trend. Cultural isolationism, in the following decades of further onslaughts of Western military power, had to yield ground steadily. In 1860 the Anglo-French expedition invaded Tientsin, captured Peking, looted and burned the summer palace. Meanwhile, inspired by a distorted version of Protestant Christianity and secretly aided by Western sympathy in various forms, the internal revolution headed by the southerner, Hung Hsiu-ch'üan, generally known as the T'aip'ing rebellion, had become a major military and cultural threat to the reigning dynasty.

Realizing the increasing importance of the role played by Western powers, the Manchu government had decided in 1861 to establish a new office to supplement, if not to replace, the traditional bureau in charge of the affairs of tributary states—the beginnings of a full-fledged foreign office. In 1867 an advanced foreign language school, the T'ung Wên Kuan, was established for the training of experts in European languages. Shortly afterwards plans were also made for the sending of Chinese students abroad on government fellowships. The conservative social forces, despite the repeated military and diplomatic defeats which China had sustained, were still adamantly opposed to these unprecedented policies. As a result, the foreign language school attracted only mediocre applicants and the students sent abroad were even more questionable opportunists, until a new policy was set up in 1882 by Yung Wing, a Yale graduate of the class of 1854. In spite of these temporary set-backs, the tide of the times could not be permanently retarded.

In the literary field stimulation was provided by the increased volume of translations from Western languages. The first full-fledged daily newspaper with feature columns supplementary to the carrying of international and domestic news, the *Shên Pao,* was established in Shanghai in 1872. Thanks to the extraordinary nature of the foreign settlements in Shanghai and despite the many evils and injustices which they harbored and exemplified under the unfortunate name of extraterritoriality, freedom of the press was safeguarded in a suc-cessful if unwise manner, as the *Shên Pao,* because of its location in the French concession in Shanghai, was beyond the reach of the Chinese government.

Among the Western translators writing in Chinese and co-operat-ing with Chinese colleagues were people like Timothy Richard and Young J. Allen, who were the first Westerners to master the intri-cate Chinese language since the day of the early Jesuits. After the collapse of the T'ai'ping regime, its foremost literary man and scholar, Wang T'ao (1828-1890), who co-operated with Timothy Richard during his political hiding in the Shanghai foreign settle-ment, collaborated with James Legge in the translation of Confucian classical texts during his sojourn in Hongkong, and gave assistance to Edouard Chavannes after his arrival in Europe.

In connection with his attempts to assist James Legge in the translation of the Confucian classics he wrote extensive commen-taries upon the *Book of Songs,* the *Book of Changes,* and the *Book of Rites.* Under the influence of an American Baptist missionary, John Chalmers (1825-1899), he also compiled three works on chro-nology and calendrical compilations to throw light on the *Spring and Autumn Annals.*

Instead of being an accurate translator of important books from the Western world, he preferred to write books of his own based on Western sources. An example was his *P'u-Fa Chan Chi* or *A Record of the Franco-Prussian War,* published in 1872. As the work caught the attention of the Japanese War Department, which re-printed it in 1878, he expanded it to twenty books from the original fourteen and had it printed under the same title in 1886. This brought him immediate fame as one who understood foreign affairs.

The scope of endeavors in translation was for a time rather limited. Of greater importance was the rendering of religious items, including a perfecting of translations into Chinese of the Old and

New Testaments which had been started by Robert Morrison even prior to his arrival in China in 1807. The various versions of the Bible in Chinese, some adopting classical Chinese as a translation medium and others boldly utilizing the vernacular in its divergent dialects, are not quite comparable to the English Bible of the King James version, but the dignity and the readability of the New Testament in the Chinese vernacular has been praised by no less an authority than Hu Shih.

Second to religious books, scientific works claimed the attention of the translators. Next in importance were Western books on Western history and in the social sciences, of which the most important items were digests and summaries of European and American history and the essentials of international law.

The order in which these different categories of works for translation were mapped out was not only natural but also in keeping with the aspirations of the translators and the needs of their prospective readers. Books on religion demanded attention as constituting the core of missionary work among the would-be converts. The physical sciences and the social sciences were fields in which the Chinese intelligentsia were most eager to seek firsthand and authentic information. Western books on philosophy and in literature claimed only an incidental and limited attention, for it was still the belief of the Chinese people that although the West was superior in armament, industrialization, and social and military organization, China was unsurpassed in the higher spheres of the humanities.

This trend was effectively combated and this shortcoming successfully corrected by two outstanding figures in late-nineteenth-century Chinese literature. Yen Fu was the first to introduce Western philosophy into China and Lin Shu was the first to make available to Chinese readers Western literature through translation.

Yen Fu (1853-1921), a native of Foochow in Fukien Province, was sent to Great Britain to pursue what were then called "Western studies" at the age of fifteen. He made the sea voyage, interestingly enough, in the company of a man who was to become the principal builder of the imperial Japanese navy. Both young people underwent naval training in Britain, where they also went into such related fields as shipbuilding. Faced with the choice between modernization of Chinese armament, especially of the naval branch, and modernization of the Chinese mind, Yen Fu was haunted endlessly by the ghosts of China's cultural lineage and decided to dedicate himself to the latter. After his return from Britain he joined the secretarial staff of the modernist viceroy, Chang Chih-tung (1837-

1907), author of the influential cultural tract, *Ch-üan-hsüeh p'ien* or *Exhortation to Learning*, at Wuchang.

Meanwhile, China had gone through a great national humiliation, the defeat by Japan in 1894-95, a nation which had looked up to China for cultural and institutional inspiration for ages but had surpassed China in military power. Eagerness for Western learning was universally whetted. It was significant that in response to the clamor for more and better books on and from the Occident, Yen Fu should present to his compatriots in 1896 a Chinese translation of Huxley's *Evolution and Ethics* which had appeared only three years before in 1893. In his prefatory note he wrote:

> The atmosphere has now become more liberal and scholars have come to realize that lack of information is something to be ashamed of. The number of inquirers seeking information in Western learning has daily increased. On the other hand, there are still a small number of intellectual leaders who brazenly claim that what the Occident excels in is limited to the category of shapes, forms and numbers; that what the Occident has cultivated and is concerned with does not go beyond the field of utility and profit, basing their eloquent talk on sheer imagination without the foundation of facts. Discussions of national issues and international problems with a view to knowing our enemies and assessing ourselves should determinately steer away from such procedures.

After the publication of this epoch-making translation in 1898, Huxley immediately became an eye-opener to the thoughtful elements of the Chinese population, making them realize that aside from battleships and heavy artillery, the West had also a good deal in store for thinking Chinese. Upon this point, we shall not elaborate unduly because the translation was even more vital as a landmark in the fairly complex history of modern China and might have made a subtle contribution to the "hundred days of reform" of 1898.

What demands more immediate attention is the technique which Yen Fu utilized in surmounting the hurdle of linguistic differences between Chinese and English. His guiding principles in translation were clearly set forth in his introductory notes to readers with regard to translation. He called the attention of his readers to what he called the three stumbling blocks to be avoided in translation or, to put them in positive terms, the three yardsticks of success: namely, faithfulness to the original, readability, and elegance. To elaborate on this, he wrote:

> Now what is propounded in this book is the new learning of Westerners in the last fifty years and the volume we propose to translate is a recent writing by the original author. The translated text has been formulated with a view to

making understandable the deep meanings of the original, hence considerable rearrangement and occasional interjections have been introduced without reference to the original word by word and sentence by sentence. My foremost objective is the avoidance of deviation from the original. In consequence I have claimed on the title page only to have "made clear the meaning of" and not "translated," since I am interested in expounding the original, realizing I have deviated from the authentic and orthodox ways of translation. . . . All these endeavors were made to ensure intelligibility, and intelligibility is essential to faithfulness to the original. . . . Besides faithfulness and intelligibility I also seek elegance in style. I envisage this last not only to anticipate wide diffusion but also because it is my belief that the quintessence of reason and the hidden meanings of philosophical observations can be more effectively carried over into Chinese by using pre-Han syntax and vocabulary than by using the popular style of more recent ages, in which one would have to cripple the original to fit the mold of the second language, leading to wide deviations in meaning. My choice between these two vehicles has been inevitable.

This peculiar choice of pre-Han syntax, although not an absolute necessity, was made in consideration of the literary taste of his contemporaries. If he had chosen the vernacular as his medium for translation, he would have found no readers whatsoever. The unhappy choice was rendered happy, however, because the use of pre-Han prose style not only suited the appetite of his elegant readers but also added considerable respectability to Huxley. Perhaps it was in view of the peculiar circumstance with which he was faced that he deemed his choice "inevitable." The tremendous popularity of the translated work was borne out by the words of the leading writer of the classical style in that age, Wu Ju-lun (1840-1903), who said in a special preface requested by Yen Fu:

Although there are many books available on western modern learning, they have been translated by our scholars in the style of Eight-Legged Essays, of official documents, and of novels, which fail to attract the attention of the educated. How can we, under these circumstances, enrich the wisdom of the people? The failure is a simple one: insufficiency of literary attainment [on the part of translators]. With the literary equipment of Yen Fu, one can talk about translation. Now, with the Tao of Huxley and the literary adornment of Yen Fu, the book has become a rival of the late Chou philosophers. How can we say that the literary phase of a translation is unimportant?

Obviously this reference to the late Chou philosophers by Yen Fu's tutor in classical and literary studies was not made as a trite compliment. After the abandonment of his naval career by choice, Yen Fu had assiduously studied the great prose masters of ancient and medieval China. When he reread Huxley seriously for a translation, it is extremely likely that he drew comparisons between nineteenth-century British scientific and social philosophy and the original thinking of the ancient philosophers in China. He must have deemed it appropriate to present Huxley in the garb of Chuang-tzu and Mo Ti. Even with the inevitable loss of flavor of the original after the sieving process of translation, the following passage from the first chapter of Huxley when translated back into English from Yen Fu's Chinese should show inevitable evidence of Yen Fu's attempts to project Huxley back into the cultural and literary milieu of ancient China in the third and fourth centuries before Christ:

As I stretch my eyes gazing eastward I see an expanse of green uninterrupted by fog or smoke. I stand alone near a lagoon extendedly admiring the beauty of moon and water and I see from under that moon to where I am standing a great vista of light and brilliance flittering and flickering. When I examine it intensively at close range it consists of tiny waves rolling endlessly refracting the light they have received from the moon. I pace around for a few steps. This sight seems as though it were following me. Enlightened scholars there are who say this sight is a real entity and so it can follow people who sometimes find themselves surprised. They do not realize that what is seen exists because of people; and that if there were no seers there would be no light and no scenery made possible by light which scenery can follow the movement of men. As the whole surface of the lagoon received light of the moon all parts of it are equally lighted; but as man's eyesight bears a dissimilar relationship to the different parts of the water, light and darkness are subsequently differentiated. It is unjustifiable, therefore, to consider what is not seen as nonextant.

Therefore, although what is seen as a lane of light which does not seem to exist elsewhere, and although as man's eyesight changes its position, what has appeared before as dark is now illuminated—all these appearances are nothing more than illusions. The truth is that the man's eyesight and the moon form two lines to strike the surface of the water. When the angles thus formed with the surface of the water are equal, the person should see light; if the angles are unequal everything will be darkness. [Yen's own note: The equality and inequality of the above-mentioned angles may be subjected to criticism and the statement in the original text is not exactly the above terms.]

When man examines into the affairs of multitudes a similar rule holds: What is seen and observed is regarded as extant and what is not seen and observed as nonextant. Using this limit of observation as a standard to determine the existence and nonexistence of fact, multiple will be the facts uncomprehended in the subsequent philosophical considerations.

The translator was more aware than anyone else that he was being extremely unconventional as compared with the Buddhist translators of early medieval China, for he himself had quoted Kumârajiva in his introductory notes: "Kumârajiva once said, 'Those who imitate me will have many ailments.' My many followers will please avoid using this book as an excuse." Despite his readiness to deviate from the original so as to benefit the original, he did not abuse his profound knowledge of English and Chinese by being halfhearted and careless. In fact, he was so painstaking in his undertaking that he would ponder at length on alternatives in the translation of the book title itself, with the advantage of consultations with some of his most learned friends. It was not until he had weighed and balanced the many suggestions made that he selected the term *tao yen*, meaning "leading words," to translate the English term "introduction." In another note he said, "For the establishment of a term hesitation and deliberation for weeks and months has often been involved. Whether I will be blamed or appreciated will be left to the judgment of my enlightened and sage readers."

Besides *Ethics and Evolution*, Yen Fu also translated Spencer's *Principles of Sociology* and John Stuart Mill's *System of Logic*, all well done. What he had done for Huxley he did also for Spencer and Mill, presenting them in the colorful garb of ancient Chinese classical prose of the late Chou philosophers. In content, the translated works were, of course, much more substantial than the hollow propagandistic writings by a great majority of the ardent advocates of modernization in China. It was, therefore, no coincidence that Yen's influence on his contemporaries was great.

What Yen Fu had done with Western nonfiction, Lin Shu (1882-1924) did even more extensively with European, English, and American narrative prose literature. Like Yen, Lin was a native of Fuchow and, like Yen, Lin held onto the classical prose style as a vehicle of translation. But unlike Yen, Lin had neither traveled abroad nor acquired even the rudiments of any Western language. Depending mainly on his assistants—a practice not wholly unknown in the days of the Buddhist translators—Lin should not be held responsible for some of the errors. In a way, Lin's experiment in using classical prose for lengthy narration was an unprecedented one. His translation of the novel (not the drama) of *The Lady of the Camellias* by Dumas exceeded in length all previous prose fiction in Chinese literature. His other translations, of course, served effectively to confirm the innovation and make it permanent.

According to an imperfect list of his devoted labors, he translated, through oral interpreters, the following number of prose fiction works from different countries: Great Britain, 99; United States, 20; France, 33; Russia, 7; Switzerland, 2; and Belgium, Spain, Norway, Greece, and Japan, 1 each. Besides these there were translations of five titles of which the origin is uncertain. These 171 titles, bound in 270 volumes in the original edition, besides fifteen short stories which we have not counted, make a worthy record of the part-time literary career of any single individual.

On account of his inability to read any foreign language with ease, Japanese included, Lin's selection of materials was naturally far from perfect; he was almost completely at the mercy of his oral interpreters. Again, fairly many of the translations were done through Japanese, that is, they were nothing more than translations of translations. Nonetheless, Lin succeeded not only in making available for Chinese readers a wide range of literature from the Western world heretofore almost entirely neglected, but also in inaugurating a huge movement, participated in by many other younger writers who had been trained in the various foreign languages, to translate directly from the original. It was this movement that furnished Chinese writers with many excellent models and suggested to them many new themes.

The changing trend in types of novels translated into Chinese at the turn of the century and in the early decades of the twentieth century is also worthy of notice. At first, Western novels were prized for their propaganda value in urging political and social reform. These were not only the most numerous but also frequently elicited comments by the translators which would make the purpose of translation absolutely plain. Coming next in popularity and in volume were novels which might be described generally as scientific fiction, closely rivaled by educational fiction, mainly as pleas for reform of the educational system in China, to cultivate the development of a new type of citizenship, and to build up new ideas of loyalty and patriotism.

It was not until after the Chinese taste for Western fiction had been firmly built up by these three types of novels that the readers were eager for the reading of literary masterpieces in Western fiction for pure enjoyment. This, curiously enough, led off on a tangent soon after reaching high tide. People seeking entertainment in Western prose fiction soon made the discovery of and were immediately submerged in detective stories which, fascinating in themselves, reminded their Chinese readers of traditional stories of the *kung-an* or legal-case type. The only difference between modern detective and mystery stories translated from the Western world and the traditional legal-case stories, which were detective stories in themselves, was that the former were presented by the translators in classical Chinese prose in keeping with the standard set by Yen Fu and Lin Shu, whereas the latter, told and written largely for the benefit of the less educated, had been written in the vernacular. This difference spelled an immense disadvantage for the former, since it was difficult to describe the intricacies and to actuate the narrative stunts in a detective story in a highly ornate and semi-petrified language. The fad of the translated detective story was thus short lived, and narrative writers naturally tried new ventures in creative fiction.

Writers of creative fiction did not lose much time in discovering that their age was one saturated with materials for satire. During the latter part of the nineteenth century China's humiliation and growing realization of her own weakness in the family of nations was being universally felt. As modernization at a rapid speed was on the minds of the people it was natural that the southern half of China, especially the coastal regions, should be the herald of a new age on account of its easy accessibility to Western governments and nationals. For centuries China's center of cultural gravity had been shifting steadily southward. As the majority of the leaders for political reform were southerners, so the majority of the leaders for literary innovations were, likewise, southerners. We have just noted that both Yen Fu and Lin Shu were natives of Fuchow on the southeast China coast. Their co-workers in translation, though of more diverse geographical origin, were principally southerners.

The new novels of satire, though nearly all imitations of the *Forest of Scholars,* written by a native of Shantung Province, were mostly the handiwork of southerners. They were all acquainted with the eighteenth-century classic of satire and its effective use of the vernacular for creative narration. They were probably aware, also, of its limitations: complete lack of the elements of mystery and of tender love and the limited range of characterization resulting from its preoccupation with scholars and competitors. As a result, despite many reissues of the *Forest of Scholars* after the collapse of the T'ai'p'ing Rebellion, during which numerous private libraries in the East China area had been completely destroyed, this classic had enjoyed the smallest popularity and circulation among first-rate novels of the eighteenth century. In the eyes of writers, however, its magnetism had persisted. In the first place, it was a newly created style suited to the purpose of social criticism. Second, the language used was the general vernacular of the Yangtze River Delta, easily understood by readers both north and south of the delta, or, in other words, that vernacular which was intelligible to the largest number of Chinese readers. In the third place, the picaresque structure of the story involved almost no special literary architectonics, being, as it was, a number of short stories strung together. With each chapter complete in itself and with endless accretions a possibility, this type of narrative composition was not only easy to learn but also convenient to use. Hence, this pattern was almost universally adopted by the writers of the new novels of satire.

Among these new novelists the most notable was Li Po-yuan (1867-1906), a native of Nanking who had failed in the literary examinations after repeated attempts and decided to go into journalism in Shanghai. After starting numerous dailies and weeklies, he settled down to editing an epoch-making journal entitled *Hsiu-hsiang Hsiao-Shuo* or *Illustrated Stories*. Among the novels he wrote the best known are *Kuan-ch'ang Hsien-Hsing Chi* or *Panorama of Officialdom*, in sixty chapters; *Wên-ming Hsiao-shih* or *A Short History of Civilization*, in sixty chapters; *Huo Ti-yü* or *Living Hell*, in forty-two chapters; *Hai-T'ien Hung-hsüeh Chi* or *Traces of a Swan on Sea and in Sky*, in twenty chapters, besides a long ballad in forty-four cantos entitled "Kêng-tzŭ Kuo-pien T'ien Tz'ŭ" or "The Ballad of the National Crisis of 1900." His other writings in prose fiction were numerous but are now hard to identify on account of his erratic use of numerous pseudonyms.

The *Panorama* is a collection of short stories deriding the various phases of the life of officialdom in rapid succession. Whereas the *Forest of Scholars* presented a number of respectable characters as though for relief besides showing a number of true scholars who had responded to nonliterary vocations for livelihood, the *Panorama* is unremitting in its satire of officialdom in which there was not a single good man. The author himself admitted in Chapter 60 the purport of his novel, suggesting it was nothing less than a guide-book for officials.

The first half of the book is devoted to highlighting the shortcomings of their public service so that they could make adequate amends. The latter half of the book is to show them what they should do as officials. Now that the latter half of the book has been burned beyond recovery, only the first half is left. With this half left it no longer resembles a textbook or manual. It is rather like the *Feng Shen Pang (Deification of the Deities) and Hsi Yu Chi (Records of Westward Travels)* in which devils and spirits, ogres and vampires abound.

Besides presenting some sixty animated cartoons of the corruptions of current officialdom, this novel performed a creditable service to the history of Chinese institutions by preserving a large number of superb real data. Writing under the nom de plume of Nan-t'ing T'ing-chang or Custodian of the Southern Pavilion, the author could afford to draw extremely accurate pictures of the lives of corrupt officials under the Manchus. In the first edition of this novel, published in 1903, there was an interesting preface written by a friend of the author who had likewise adopted a nom de plume:

With the elevation of the system of competitive examinations the avenues to officialdom became complex. Scholars stopped their studies, peasants left their farms, artisans abandoned their crafts and merchants left their firms, all concentrating on the one word "official." Hence, an official is one who enjoys the benefits provided him by the scholars, the peasants, the artisans, and the merchants, without performing the toilsome work of these groups. . . . These officials are insufficient in assisting the Son of Heaven but more than enough in oppressing the common people. . . . Those who talk behind their backs are penalized and those who make fun of them by their side are arrested. . . . The airs of officials are thus expanded and the flames of officials become more burning. The trickeries of wolves avoided by others are adopted by officials. The conduct reminiscent of flies and dogs to which others would not descend, is practiced by officials. . . . As the country grows weak, officials grow strong and as the country grows poor, officials grow rich. The old ideals of filiality, brotherliness, loyalty, and honesty are spoiled by the person of an official and the legacy of courtesy and justice, incorruptibility and self respect, is wrecked by the hand of the official. It is not the result of one morning and one evening but the fruit of a gradual decline that officials have been complained about by men and universally despised.

This contempt is repeated many times throughout the novel, usually expressed by a nonofficial. Thus an underling of an official, a doorman, after his employer had been relieved from public office, makes the following observation in scorn:

I have already packed my bedding waiting for departure. Now that I think of it, one who follows officialdom as a profession is really subject to calamities brought upon himself by way of retribution. You see when he was promoted he wore one face; now that he is dismissed he is wearing another face, not quite like us domestic servants. When we have resigned from a family in the east we still have families in the west where we may eat our meals as usual. Officials have only one emperor, from whom they cannot run away as they please.

Equally devastating is the observation made of an official by a singing girl in a barge in the county of Chiangshan, who compares herself in vicissitudes to that of an official:

In the eighth moon of last year the honorable Mr. Ch'ên, Magistrate of the County of Chiangshan, hired our boat at the bank of the river to travel to the place of his new appointment. People said this honorable Mr. Ch'ên had waited in Hangchow for over twenty years for a vacant position and had been reduced to unsurpassed poverty, having sent everything in his possession to the pawnshops. It was after the endurance of considerable hardship that he had now found a post. Altogether he had a wife, two sons, and nine daughters. His elder son was already over thirty and not yet married. When he started from Hangchow, the baggage of the whole family did not quite make five full coolie loads and the boxes and trunks were all light. When the eighth moon arrived this year he had written us in advance instructing us to fetch him back to Hangchow. When he came on board the boat, of red leather trunks alone there were more than fifty not counting other articles. When he was on his way to the official post his wife wore gold plated hairpins but when he left the post even the wet nurse of his younger son was wearing earrings made of solid gold. On the day of the departure of honorable Mr. Ch'ên, there were even presented to him several ceremonial parasols—the so-called ten-thousand-people parasols—to express the gratitude of the citizenry. Those who saw him off said in one voice that he had been an incorruptible official, never deigning to take money so that people would willingly present him with these gifts. I felt tempted to laugh within my belly and thought to myself if the venerable magistrate did not want money, where had these trunks come from? How can I be deceived? Professional officials, after they become rich, insist upon saying they have been incorruptible. Are they any better than professional sing-song girls?

Equally representative of the trend of public opinion and reflecting the temper of the age is his satiric novel with the somewhat pedantic title of *A Brief History of Civilization*. Civilization, in this novel, of course, has a purposefully slanted meaning—the modernization of China, which had boastfully claimed a civilization of five thousand years. In this novel all groups of political persuasion, from ultramodernists to extreme conservatives, from high officials to the petty people, are evenly represented. Its equal attention to the various parts of the country is also unique: from seaports to interior hamlets, from North China to the extreme south, from coastal areas to the hinterland parts, and even following the principal advocates of modernization to Hongkong, Japan, and the United States of America.

The enormousness of the scope and variety of the characters as well as the multiplicity of urgent issues had forced the author to make a slight change in the organization of the story. Instead of utilizing one unifying narrator or observer, the author entrusts the narrative burden to a rotation of characters. Despite this complete change of characters every so often, the continuity of the narrative is guaranteed by the relatedness of the episodes and the problems. Especially creditable are the chapters describing the local political conditions in Honan Province in which the representatives of corrupt officialdom, impatient modernism, and uncontrollable foreign imperialism are given minute and realistic delineation. Moreover, the sharp edges of lampooning and ridicule are dexterously rounded off with the timely interruption of humorous episodes.

Having made its appearance serially in the *Illustrated Stories,* this novel of satire of almost half a million words was published in book form without the author's name and without illustrations in 1906, five years before the overthrow not only of the Manchu Dynasty but also of monarchic institutions of over three thousand years' standing, in an age of the turbulent currents and countercurrents of convention and revolt, oppression and revolution. The attitude of the author himself was expressed by a transitory figure who made only one fleeting appearance in the narrative, the learned old Mr. Yao, who said, "In all our undertakings of the new and our elimination of the old, we should first of all use our efforts in what has been called the labor of water-grinding so that people will be transformed unawares and change gradually. We should avoid rashness and impetuosity, otherwise we would 'beat the grass and startle the snake' and spoil the whole thing." As an ameliorationist, he believed in gradual change, but he was firm in insisting upon modernization. It is natural that he was opposed to revolution against the Manchus on a racial basis. Like so many of his contemporaries, he was an advocate of nonviolent and gradual reform in politics as well as in other spheres of human activity.

Another journalist who distinguished himself in novel writing was a Cantonese, Wu Yü-yao (1867-1910), better known by his nom de plume, Wo-fo Shan-jên or Native of Fatshan—Fatshan being a suburban town about fifteen miles from Canton. While he was working on a Shanghai daily, he came under the literary inspiration of Liang Ch'i-ch'ao, who had established a new periodical in Japan during his political exile after the collapse of the "hundred days reform" in 1898, a periodical devoted to the publication of new fiction.

Using fiction as a vehicle for the dissemination of new thought and for the delineation of social and political corruption in China, Wu wrote twenty-seven chapters of a story entitled *T'ung Shih* or *Sad Story,* which he did not complete. In addition he tried the experiment of rewriting in thirty-six chapters a detective story which had been in wide circulation for a long time and had become a part of the folklore of the Cantonese people. This was the *Chiu Ming Ch'i Yüan* or *The Strange Injustice of Nine Murders.* In about 1905 he traveled to Hangkow to become the editor of *Ch'u Pao,* a Chinese-language newspaper published by an American firm.

Soon afterward, as a result of anti-Chinese legislation in the United States which had aroused a good deal of anti-American feeling in China, he resigned the editorship "as a matter of conscience." Returning to Hongkong he lent his support to the popular protest against American injustice with regard to Chinese immigration and started a literary journal devoted primarily to fiction known as the *Yüeh-yüeh Hsiao-hsuo* or *Monthly Stories.* Working for his own journal and contributing to the well-established periodical *Illustrated Stories,* he wrote many novels which were nearly all published serially.

The range of subject matter and presentation covered by these was wide: scientific fiction as well as mysteries, love stories and sociological novels, continuations of old classics such as *The New Dream of the Red Chamber,* and historical romances like the *Liang-tsin Yen-yi* or the *Popular History of the Two Tsin Dynasties.* More popular and successful than all these was his great novel of social and political satire, *Ehr-shih Nien Mu-tu Chih Kuai Hsien-hsiang* or *Strange Sights Seen in Two Decades*. First appearing serially in 1902, it was published in full in a definitive edition in 1909.

Adopting the structure of the picaresque romance, the author used the narrator as the main thread to connect the rapidly varying tableaus depicting a wide range of events. Serving as an employee of a powerful bureaucratic family to manage its commercial firm distributed all over the Chinese Empire, the narrator traveled extensively and became intimately acquainted with the lives of the privileged classes and the exploited masses, which he retold with great relish. The great denouement was built up by the continual dwindling of the great family fortune culminating in its complete ruination necessitating the resignation of the narrator. We can easily see that the mechanics of the structure was much more plausible than similar picaresque novels of the time. The narrator's name, Chiu-ssu Yi-shêng, which might be loosely translated as "A Survivor of Nine Deaths," was explained as having adopted the alias for the following reason in his own words:

Ever since I came out to face the world twenty years ago I have met only three kinds of creatures on recollection. The first kind consists of serpents, worms, rats, and ants. The second kind consists of jackals, wolves, tigers, and leopards. The third kind consists of devils of all descriptions. Moving among these for as long as twenty years, I have not been gnawed away by the first, nor gobbled up by the second, nor even seized by the third. Unexpectedly I have escaped from all of them. Isn't my life one pitting against nine possible deaths?

The shortcomings of the novel are many. Its overemotionalism gave rise to a pessimism which was almost unrelieved. His tendencies to exaggerate the evils of the world defeated his avowed hope for reform. As a novel, however, it clearly showed the influence of Western fiction. Not only were the isolated short stories well strung together by the narrator, who was a participant or an eyewitness of them all, but even the presentation of the narrative elements also showed more careful planning. Nonetheless, this, his first novel, was still diffuse in its central points of interest, as many of the episodes, though interesting short stories in themselves, were woven into the pattern in a rather artificial and strained manner.

Dissatisfied with the picaresque romance type of structure as a vehicle, Wu attempted to benefit from the models of the new Westernized fiction in a coherently knitted story, *Hên Hai* or *The Ocean of Sorrow*. This was a problem novel concerned with family life and marriage. A Cantonese official, Ch'ên Chi-lin, was serving his tenure in Peking. His two sons, Po-ho and Chung-ai, had both been engaged; the former to Chang Ti-hua and the latter to Wang Chüan-chüan. The family was scattered by the Boxers in 1899 and both Ch'ên and his wife were mercilessly slaughtered. The two sons, however, both succeeded in surviving the atrocities. Po-ho, the elder son, had escorted the Chang girl and her mother in fleeing Peking but soon lost trace of the party under his care in the turbulent commotion of the multitudes of refugees. Chung-ai, the younger son, barely escaped the atrocities in Peking with his own life. Po-ho capitalized on being alone, and succeeded in amassing a small fortune, which he squandered immediately on reckless living, including gambling and opium smoking. After he had become a regular beggar, he was discovered by the Chang family, who not only literally provided for his livelihood but cheerfully gave him a chance to mend his ways.

Refusing to give up his opium habits, Po-ho rebelliously left the Chang family and finally died in a dingy opium den. His fiancée, who had waited patiently through the years for their reunion, finally sought refuge in a Buddhist nunnery. Meanwhile Chung-ai, the younger son of the family, had arrived in South China after various vicissitudes, but contrary to his expectations he failed to locate the Wang family. Undaunted by his misfortunes, he decided resolutely to postpone marriage, contrary to Chinese tradition, in anticipation of a possible reunion with Wang Chüan-chüan. Finally they met at a banquet in a restaurant. But his fiancée had already become a professional singing girl.

Such a story ending in a double tragedy was a rare exception in Chinese fiction. Nonetheless, possibly on account of the haste in which the novel was written, the narrative elements were too direct and the characterization left much to be desired.

Much more successful was the *Nine Murders*. The core of the narrative was an actual eighteenth-century story of a real murder case in Kwangtung Province which was faithfully adhered to. Although the novel gave due attention to the delineation of popular superstitions, bureaucratic corruption, and social injustices, these elements were dexterously subordinated to the main narrative and had become organic parts of the whole. In the case of the numerous other novels of satire of the age including the author's own compositions of that type, the ridicule meted out was usually too obvious, too superficial, and too exclusively concerned with vituperation. In extreme cases the satiric elements would evoke only faint smiles from readers instead of moral indignation because the indictments were overshadowed by the humorous nature of the ridicule.

The influence of Western fiction on the *Nine Murders* was obvious. The opening episodes described how the Ling clan, a group of thieves and robbers, attacked and looted the Liang family, committing murder and arson. In strict accordance with traditional narrative technique, this episode should belong to the sixteenth chapter. The tragedy of eight lives lost was purposely brought forward to engage the readers' attention and followed by retroactive narration, definitely a non-Chinese technique. Moreover, the author's indebtedness to Western technique was shown clearly in the coherence and unity of the plot.

As we have noticed, Chinese novels were evolved in the main from popular fictionization of history with the scaffolding of dynastic history as their framework. These historical romances begin and end simultaneously with the span of dynastic history. Later on, when fiction writers had realized the undesirable limitations of these conditions, they consciously refused to submit to such regulations and sought refuge in drawing upon history, which was actually no more than the forging of historical incidents and personages against a loosely historical background. The most outstanding case in point is *Shui Hu* or *The Romance of the Water Margin*. Even with these liberties taken in the magnifying of and tampering with a historical episode, romances like the *Water Margin* lacked a closely knit plot, allowing the interjection of various subplots which, though colorful and exciting in themselves, do not contribute to the organic unfolding of the story. In other words, these subplots could be completely deleted without making the novel less intelligible and could be infinitely multiplied without abetting the organic effectiveness of the novel. Even the appearance of the novels of the picaresque romance type was no great contribution to Chinese narrative art. In these, as in the historical romances, characters appear and disappear rather freely.

It can be said comprehensively of the thousand years of Chinese story writing that nearly all the compositions were without a coherent and unified plot. Even such outstanding works as the *Chin P'ing Mei* and the *Dream of the Red Chamber,* which had attained a certain degree of coherence and unity in their plots by adhering closely to the rise and fall of specific families, are loosely knit when measured by the yardstick of later Western fiction. Even in these, loose ornamental episodes were freely introduced—one amorous adventure after another, one literary game after another celebrating chrysanthemums or peonies, as the case might be. While the description of one birthday party with literary games might seem entertaining, its repetition is apt to be irksome. This is precisely why, to most Western readers, even the so-called great classics in Chinese fiction seem vague and unnecessarily repetitious, adding to the confusion caused by the multiplicity of characters. In order to keep the narrative straight, genealogical tables and charts of literary and other coteries would have to be drawn up.

Distinctly different from all its predecessors, the *Nine Murders* inaugurated a new pattern as well as a new technique. Around its close-knit and coherent plot it eliminated all irrelevant subplots and digressions. Moreover, it utilized the satirical technique of Chinese novels to deal with family life and the problems of officialdom and the technique of northern Chinese novels to delineate robber barons and their associates, and adopted the technique of Western detective stories to ensure a well-unified main plot. Thus it was capable of sustaining the rapt attention of its readers from beginning to end.

Another excellent fiction writer was Liu O (also Liu Ê, 1857-1909), a native of Tant'u, not far away from Shanghai. A mathematician and an expert in water conservation, Liu had had practical experience in drawing up and executing plans for the control of "China's Sorrow," the Yellow River. Later, on the recommendation of the governor of Shantung, he was given an official rank and in that capacity memorialized the throne on many public issues. On account of his frequent contacts with foreigners, he was accused by his enemies of being a traitor. During the siege of Peking by the allied forces in 1900 following the Boxer Rebellion many Peking residents were starving owing to food shortage. He proceeded to Peking with sizable funds and plans for relief work. It happened that the rice granary area was occupied by Russian troops, and as European troops were not interested in the consumption of rice, he succeeded in negotiating with the Russians for the purchase of the rice in storage at reduced price for general relief in Peking. A few years later he was accused of having sold granary rice without permission and was exiled to Sinkiang, where he died.

Besides being an early collector and student of the Anyang oracle bones and shells, Liu was also an outstanding novelist. The one novel which made him famous was an autobiographical piece of picaresque fiction originally published in *Illustrated Stories*. Entitled *Lao-ch'an Yu-chi* or *The Travel Records of Lao-ch'an*, it was a realistic account of the experiences of the author and his contemporaries behind the smoke screen of fictitious names. The derivation of the pseudonym Lao Ch'an was explained in the preface by the author: "The chess game is now badly broken up and we are growing old. How can we refrain from weeping and wailing?" The game of chess refers, of course, to the Ch'ing Dynasty, which was rapidly declining toward its end and he, as a devoted subject of the dynasty, could not avoid his feelings of loyalty by weeping over its sad fate.

It is easily understandable that in its original serialized form there was a long discourse in which the revolutionaries were elaborately denounced. On the other hand he did not share the view of the ultraconservatives and so he advocated two main avenues to salvation for China, namely, scientific education and industrialization. These views were often reflected in the novel itself. Aside from the occasional insertion of subplots that made no particular sense— a shortcoming from which the author's contemporaries were rarely free—the novel was a successful one.

Like so many authors of problem novels and novels of satire of the age, he had directed his attention to various social, political, and economic problems with which China was faced. If Liu's formulas for the solution of the urgent problems were little better than those advocated by his contemporary novelists, his technique of delineation was frequently superior. A good example of this technique of his is the following excerpt from Chapter Twelve in which the narrator, Lao Ch'an, was looking at the breaking of ice on the bank of the Yellow River:

As he raised his head he saw on the hilltops to the south a sprig of white light which was unusually attractive in the midst of the moonlit landscape. The tiers of mountains were hardly discernible and the floating of a few white clouds in their midst made it almost impossible to tell which was which. It was not until one had taken a fixed and attentive look that one could discern which was cloud and which was mountain. Although both clouds and mountains were white and although both were illuminated, the moon was above the clouds and the clouds were below the moon, and the illumination of the clouds came from the rear. It was not so, however, with the mountains. The illumination of the mountains was a reflection of the moonlight by the snow, making a different kind of light. This is true, however, only of a close-range view. If one should cast one's gaze eastward from that mountain on, the farther one looked the farther one's eyesight would reach. Then the sky was white, the mountains were white, the clouds were also white, and they were indistinguishable one from the other.

Before we close this section, mention must be made of another novel, one written by a novelist who was equipped to read extensively in European and especially French fiction. Tseng P'o, writing under the name of Tung-ya-Ping-fu, or "The Sick Man of East Asia," published in installments in 1905 and 1906 the novel entitled *Nieh Hai Hua* or *A Flower on the Sea of Agony*. Despite his repeated efforts at revising and adding to the twenty chapters completed in 1906, his cherished scheme of sixty chapters was never fulfilled.

According to the original edition, the novel was "originated by A Lover of Freedom and narrated and edited by the Sick Man of East Asia." For a long time these were supposed by readers to be nothing more than two names for the same person. The riddle was solved in 1927 in the preface to the revised version. Actually the early chapters represented a collaboration between the author and his intimate friend, Chin T'ien-yi, who had proposed that fiction might be more effective in modernizing China's mind than formal essays. After the fifth chapter was completed, however, Chin left the project entirely to his friend. The assignment proved to be in gifted hands, for the influence that the uncompleted novel exerted was great and its wide popularity warranted fifteen printings in two years, totaling fifty thousand copies—a record for fiction at that time.

The popularity that this novel enjoyed was more than coincidental. In the first place it was a clear deviation from the lukewarm progressivism advocated by all previous problem novels. Instead of advocating a compromise between the royalists and the revolutionists, it vehemently attacked such age-old institutions as the competitive literary examination, calling them shackles imposed on the Chinese people by historic despotism, causing "the citizens in general to have brains but no souls, to have blood but no vitality, causing the vast empire extended by Emperor Yü to become the private property of monarchs, and the descendants of the Yellow Emperor to become bonded slaves of despots." Besides attacking institutional monarchy negatively, it also advocated an anti-Manchu revolution as a positive measure. Thus, under fictitious names, all the early leaders of the revolutionary movement and their endeavors were feelingly presented. Besides this, nearly all the important figures in the intellectual and political life of the empire on the eve of the revolution were not only drawn into the orbit of the novel but carefully presented as live figures. It is regrettable that this lively picturization of the last three decades of the Manchu Empire was abruptly ended with the reform movement of 1898. But, thanks to the loose structure of the picaresque romance type, even the uncompleted fragments were able to stand on their own merit. This reveals both the advantages and the limitations not only of the picaresque romance as a universal type but also of Chinese novels at the turn of the nineteenth and twentieth centuries.

CHAPTER 32

The Literary Revolution

THE real impact of Western civilization on Chinese literature was not felt until the last years of the nineteenth century, those few years which were both depressing and stimulating after China's defeat by Japan in the fateful year of 1894. The fermentation process, as we have suggested before, did not begin then but went back to the middle of the nineteenth century when the so-called Sleeping Lion was roused from its slumber by military defeat at the hands of Great Britain in 1841. With the opening of treaty ports both along the coast of China and in the interior along the main waterways, the whole country began to be exposed to the wonders of Western industrialization and militarization.

This awakening process, strangely enough, was long drawn out and divided itself neatly into several discernible though overlapping stages. At the beginning the most obvious aspects of Western civilization impressed themselves upon the Chinese mind, namely, the superiority of Western armaments and industrial progress. The Chinese people, confronted with the latest developments in Western machinery and armament, realized that Western technological progress had been tremendous since the days of the earliest Jesuits in China. Even the most conservative minds admitted that in the building of seaworthy ships and the making of heavy artillery, China had no choice but to acknowledge the superiority of the Occident. For purposes of national defense and survival and to avoid the repetition of another ignominious defeat, the hoary empire had to catch up by learning its rudimentary lessons from the "Western barbarians."

While action was being considered regarding program and procedure the so-called Second Foreign War was already on the horizon. The joint Anglo-French expedition against Peking in 1859 resulted in the capture and occupation of the imperial capital and the flight of the court to the northwest, as well as the signing of an even more crippling treaty in 1860. Meanwhile, capitalizing on the dynastic weakness and interacting with the progress of foreign aggression, a revolution had broken out in South China which, at its high tide, had overrun eleven of the eighteen provinces and gave promise of the possibility of a dynastic overthrow. These T'aip'ing revolutionaries had derived their strength partly from the accumulated grievances and resentment of the Chinese people against alien rule by the Manchus and partly from their acquaintance with the wider world, a distorted version of Christianity included.

When the revolution was finally suppressed at great cost to the tottering empire, destruction in the wealthiest provinces of the empire in the southeast had become so widespread that slow recuperation was bound to give rise to many philosophical inquiries leading directly to a new phase of national self-awakening. In launching isolated but widespread programs of modernization such as were called for in the setting up of new arsenals, shipbuilding dockyards, steamship and railway lines, telegraph and telephone networks, and above all, new programs for the training of modern and Westernized army and naval units, political and social leaders were forced to the realization that new wine called for new bottles. Western methods of organization, administration, and training of personnel became an integral part of the modernization program. Thus the Western world was admitted by Chinese leaders of thought now to excel not only in material advancement but also in organizational efficiency. But in political and social philosophy the celestial empire was still supreme in the universe.

The great slogan of this period was "Chinese learning as the basic substance and Western learning for practical application." The attempt was apparently to bring about a seamless cementing of the Chinese philosophy of life and the Western standard of precision and efficiency. This sounded extremely good as far as it went. When it came to actual application of the formula, however, it was discovered, to no one's great surprise, that the flowing gown of the Confucian scholar did not go too well with the rapidity of action called for by a modern factory, any more than would the adherence to principles laid down in ancient military classics conduce to the efficient command of a modern navy. Moreover, to insure the success of such national reforms as the building up of interprovincial highways and railways, the whole populace must be re-educated. Loose localism had to be supplanted by an intelligent interest in national problems before an old, decentralized empire could be converted into a modern state. By slow degrees people came to realize that even in such spheres as social and political organization, the West had many lessons of value to offer the Chinese people.

The old guards of traditional culture found in this attitude explosive forces which might wreck the entire superstructure of historic Chinese civilization. On the other hand, they could not but admit that heretical as they sounded, Western political theories and organization were not entirely nonsensical. While the controversy was going on and hesitancy marked the stagnation of the period, the crushing blow administered by insurgent Japan cut short all procrastination and hesitation. The small Oriental neighbor had fought as a unit beside which the huge population of China, unorganized and unfocused, seemed like a helpless "pan of loose sand." What procrastination had delayed now was jelled by the shock of pain. Thanks to the many-sided contents of China's historical literature face-saving ways of escape were always available. Rapid modernization was mandatory, but rapid modernization could be advocated in the name of a speedy return to the golden days of high antiquity.

Parliamentarianism in this light was nothing new, nothing inherently Western, for were not the basic principles and features of a parliament fully described in the *Book of Chou-li*? Were not the first lessons in Western science already emphatically taught by Mo Ti over two thousand years ago? Was not the neatly organized educational system of the modern West only an imitation of the ideal classical system laid down in the three dynasties of Hsia, Shang, and Chou? Was not the cross of Christianity only a borrowing from the carpenter's square, the symbol of succession among the ancient followers of Mo Ti? Was not even the weird-looking swallow-tailed coat only the occidental adaptation of something Confucius himself had worn and fully described in the *Analects*? In short, were not all the excellences of Western civilization, which China should lose no time in emulating, parts of China's own cultural legacy? In these terms, Westernization meant neither innovation nor importation of alien cultural assets but mere repossession.

Although the real discovery and full appreciation of Western literature were not to come until several decades later, the deck was now clear for a re-examination of the manner and matter of traditional Chinese literature. Many questions which had not existed were now asked, if not for the first time, at least with new emphasis. Was it enough for writers to cast their looks backward into history to discover an ideal master to follow? Was it necessary, in order to produce first-class literature, to look for perfect models for reduplication? Was the Eight-Legged Essay, which had been adopted for five hundred years as the sole yardstick for the measurement of literary excellence in preparation for civil service, a standard eternally adequate? Would such a yardstick be conducive to real literary progress? Was the classical language an immutable medium for literary expression? Should it and could it be modified for both prose and poetry? Was the function of literature merely the entertainment of a small and highly privileged class? These and other questions began to occupy the attention of Chinese writers, except for a few extreme conservatives.

The Sino-Japanese War of 1894–95 brought about several new trends in Chinese literature. In the first place, in keeping with the historic trend of the southward movement of Chinese culture, the reading public was greeted by an increasing number of writers of southern origin. This is easy to understand, as China's front door, which had for millennia faced the exciting crossroads in Central Asia, had by now been moved to face the South China Sea, the main artery of traffic in commodities as well as ideas resulting from Europe's "discovery" of the sea route. With the establishment of European colonies from Goa eastward through the Strait of Malacca to Hongkong, living samples of Western communities transplanted to Eastern soil became concrete object lessons for Eastern peoples.

It was in the British crown colony of Hongkong itself, established in 1842, that the first modern printing presses were established and the first daily newspapers were printed for popular circulation. These latter so far outstripped their early Chinese prototypes issued in the eighth and ninth centuries for the first time (as daily reports from the imperial court concerning official promotions, demotions, and transfers) that they were hardly recognizable as members of the same class. Though it is difficult to gauge the relative importance to readers of feature items as contrasted with news reports, the fact that fiction was serialized had a definite share, as we have seen, in stimulating unprecedented interest in fiction writing.

This dissemination in Hongkong and later on also in Shanghai, after it had become a conglomeration of foreign concessions, of Western ideals and ideas, not only altered the Chinese outlook upon a living and floating literature but also widened the Chinese horizon of intellectual and political outlook in general. It was no mere coincidence that the two leaders in political reform dedicated to almost diametrically opposed political persuasions were both Cantonese heavily indebted to the impact of Western civilization through the above-mentioned channels: Sun Yat-sen (Sun Wên, 1866-1925), of the Revolutionary Party, and K'ang Yu-wei (1858-1927), of the constitutional monarchy movement.

To return from the exciting scenes of political movements and agitations to the burgeoning of new literary ventures and aspirations, we must note that late-nineteenth-century writers in China had not forthrightly admitted that even in the fields of literature and philosophy China's position of superiority was subject to question. There was no conscientious effort made to westernize Chinese literature as there had been in Japan at this time. Nonetheless, Chinese intellectual leaders were not totally blind to the fact that thenceforth as China was to become a member of the comity of nations, Chinese literature was destined to become a major tributary —possibly an imposing Yellow River—into the ocean of world literature.

In poetry the impact of the new age was felt only slowly, but even in poetry, where conservatism held its own most powerfully, changes were felt. Partly because poets are usually most gifted in creating universes of their own and partly because Chinese poets as a class have always been the most docile pupils of past masters, the kaleidoscopic changes of the age were least noticeable in the writings of the poets. Nonetheless, as an indication of an inevitable fluctuation in taste, nineteenth-century poets in general had semiconsciously drifted away from the company of the T'ang masters of the golden period to seek new inspiration in matter and form from the Sung masters. To be sure, imitative versification was still the order of the day and the prescribed discipline for the prospective poet.

In this respect, however, even imitation had taken a healthier path, for the characteristics of Sung poetry of the *shih* type had always emphasized naturalness in the construction of lines. The result was that imitation had become less self-conscious and less slavish, the ideal being to cherish the company of the established masters for a time and then to part company from them in order to develop a style of one's own. As one poet-critic had put it, in estimating the poetic attainment of a friend, "All the characters [words] are ones commonly recognized and all the lines are ones commonly constructible. But when characters are accumulated to form lines and lines are accumulated to form verses and verses accumulated to form poems, the net result is the absence of any ideas conceived by previous writers or scenes described by previous writers."

The great figure of this main school who swam against the stream was an adherent to the T'ang tradition, Wang K'ai-yün (1833-1916), a native of Hunan province. Having disciplined himself in the company of the great poets of the Southern and T'ang Dynasties, he left to posterity a voluminous amount of poetry in which he had distinguished himself in recreating the works of the great masters. In him we find a superb example of what might be described as pseudoclassicism because, according to one established critic of the old school, "his poems could be inserted into the works of the different masters, each according to his target of imitation, and could not be distinguished from the authentic contents of the original collections. And as they were indistinguishable in this regard, they were not necessarily Wang's own poems." Saying the same thing in fewer words, Hu Shih has called them "counterfeits." Even Wang himself was aware of the peculiar nature of his attainments. He advised a younger poet to read extensively in the poetry of the great masters but not in that of contemporary poets and especially not his own, for, he said, the more one read of Wang's poetry for models, the more confused the seeker would be.

Among the poets who had been nurtured in the ancient tradition but who had been brought in contact with the disquieting currents of the new world, a movement soon generated itself to revolutionize Chinese poetry. The vanguards of this movement who first hoisted the banner of revolution were two young men, both from the south, T'an Ssǔ-t'ung (1865-1898) of Hunan, and Hsia Tsêng-yu (1865-1924) of Chekiang. Their first attempts were mediocre, though novel. One outstanding novelty was the transliteration of non-Chinese words for use in Chinese poetry, such as "caste," "parliament," "Satan," "Babel." This newness in vocabulary was actually an indication that while they were convinced that new territory should be explored, they did not quite know where to find the territory or how to explore it. They had turned away from something but they had turned to nothing in particular. As one of their number, Liang Ch'i-chao (1873-1929), reminisced decades later:

At that time we were of the opinion that Chinese learning since Han was completely worthless and that all learning from abroad was good. As we had downgraded the post-Han we concentrated our readings in Chinese on the Confucian classics and the pre-Han philosophers. As we regarded everything from abroad to be excellent, but as we were all unprepared in foreign languages and, therefore, unable to read Western books in the original, we had to satisfy ourselves with a few translations made available by missionaries, and cherished them as treasures. In addition to this sentiment we had our personal idealism—something like religion and yet not religion, like philosophy and yet not philosophy, like science and yet not science, like literature and yet not literature—something odd and childlike: this we called the New Learning.

Rewarded with much greater success was a senior contemporary of theirs, Huang Tsun-hsien (1848-1905), who had learned to find new inspiration from folk songs. Born in Chiaying, now renamed Meihsien, in the northeastern part of Kuangtung Province, Huang had been impressed ever since his early boyhood with the simple charm of the many so-called "mountain songs" sung responsively by young unmarried men and women as they were working out of doors on hilltops. These folk songs, which were generally distinguished by four doleful interjectional syllables toward the end, furnished the young poet with models for his own compositions.

When he was in his middle twenties, he not only wrote his own "mountain songs" in which he freely and boldly employed the everyday idioms of the common people but also justified the use of vernacular expressions in a poem of the so-called ancient style (*ku shih*). In this poem he ridiculed the pedants of his time who worshipped antiquity to such an extent that in poetry writing they dared not use words which were not found in the Confucian Classics, and who would therefore rather sin against earlier poets by plagiarizing them. From these pedants, he declared he would part company.

> I write as I speak
> How can antiquity bind me?
> Even today's common speech
> If I write it in a book
> In five thousand years
> Will dazzle readers as an ancient gem

This deep interest of his in the Hakka folk songs and this conviction of his that "it is not at all necessary for us to look exactly like the ancients" were not ephemeral, for he continued to write quatrains in the style and language of the folk songs and to experiment with new verse forms throughout his life.

His travels abroad to Japan, England, the United States, and Malaya to fill consular and diplomatic posts broadened his knowledge of the outside world and supplied him with new themes and new ideas, many of which were incorporated in his poems as well as in his prose writings. In order further to free himself from the shackles of convention he boldly adopted the pattern of prose syntax into his poetry by lengthening and shortening the lines as he pleased. In a narrative poem eulogizing the Forty-seven Rōnin of Japan, for example, he wrote lines like the following:

> The forty-seven knights took their lives on the same day.
> Those who marveled at them burst out in praises and songs.
> Those who looked, who knelt (in admiration), who extended condolences and congratulations circled the tomb with myriads of flowers over which the smoke of fragrant incense hovered day after day.
> A spirit, a clog, a chia (armor), a helmet, a sword, a spear, a cane, a hat, a picture—any relic (from them) was treasured like a heavenly sphere!

Although his language was not always that of the everyday speech of the common people in China, he had certainly cleared the fog of artificial rhetoric and obscure allusions which had besmudged Chinese poetry for many generations.

The spirit of experimentation in poetry demonstrated by Huang Tsun-hsien was carried on in prose even more fearlessly by Liang Ch'i-ch'ao.

Liang Ch'i-ch'ao (1873-1929), a native of Hsinhui in Kwangtung Province, was one of the most dynamic figures in recent Chinese political and intellectual history. He played a central role in the dramatic but ill-fated Hundred Days' Reform Movement of 1898 led by his teacher K'ang Yu-wei, and in the campaign against the Restoration plot of Yuan Shih-k'ai in 1916. He took an active part in propagating the Confucianist utopianism of the revived New Script School, and in the evening of his life, he renewed his scholarly contributions to historical studies. His influence on modern China was so extensive and multifarious that we can do no more than note very briefly his contributions to literature.

He won considerable local reputation before he was twenty and trained himself to write in the traditional manner by following diverse models, especially those set up by the T'ungch'êng School. He suddenly freed himself from the old conventions after he had come in contact with what was then known as the "new" learning in his nineteenth year in 1891. His travels to Shanghai and Peking brought to his attention many new publications and translations on Western history and politics as well as on contemporary world affairs. While in Shanghai, he founded a journal devoted to reporting and discussion of current events. After the failure of the Hundred Days' Reform Movement in 1898, he sought refuge in Japan where he founded and edited two other journals. Especially popular was the *Hsin-min Ts'ung-pao* or *New Citizen's Journal,* which not only exerted an immense influence on journalistic writing back in the mother country itself but also inaugurated a new prose style generally among the younger writers.

Liang's new prose style was different from the *p'ien wên* of the Han and Six Dynasties, the Ku wên of T'ang and Sung times, the Eight-legged Essays of the Ming and Ch'ing dynasties, and the relatively new T'ungch'êng and Yanghu styles, but was a sort of new compound in which elements from all of these had been infused. Such a new style, as he himself pointed out had a number of advantages. First, it was so flexible that new terms, transliterations of foreign words and even colloquial expressions could be easily accommodated. Secondly, it was lively and conducive to easy intelligibility, as the sentences are varied and occasionally even rhymed for special effect. Thirdly, it is frequently imbued with a peculiar touch of emotionalism which often produces an enchanting effect on the readers. The following is an excerpt from a long essay of his on "The New Citizen":

What then is the way to avert (our national) disaster and to assure progress? The answer is: it is absolutely necessary to destroy and pulverize the oppressive and turbid form of government of the last several thousand years so that the thousands and myriads of officials who are variously like tigers, like wolves, like locusts, like unfledged locusts, like toads, and like maggots will lose their support just as foxes are driven out of the city wall and rats from the open altars. After which (the nation's) internal organs may be thoroughly cleansed and placed on the road to progress! It is absolutely necessary to purge and eradicate the corruptive, spineless, and effeminate philosophies of the last several thousand years so that the millions of students who are variously like silver fish, like parrots, like sponges, like pet dogs will never again wave their writing brushes and wag their tongues to support the public enemies of the people, after which (the nation's) eyes and ears will be refreshed to materialize progress as a fact!

And the ways to attain these objectives are two: one is destruction (revolution) without bloodshed and the other is destruction with bloodshed. The former is typified by Japan and the latter by France. If it is possible for China to accomplish destruction without bloodshed, I shall bless it with fervent prayers! If it is inevitable that China undertake destructive action (revolution) with bloodshed, I shall lament it in full mourning attire!

Lamentation though there may be, it is impossible for me to seek a way of national salvation apart from these two. Alas! If our China could follow the first alternative; it should be following it, but it is not! Then what I have called the second alternative would eventually be unavoidable. Oh, how can I bear to say this? And how can I bear not to say this?

Although Liang as a new stylist in prose won a huge following in and outside China among young Chinese writers, he was vehemently attacked by the old guardians of literary orthodoxy. Chang Ping-lin (1868-1936), the classical scholar and phonologist who advocated a return to Wei and Tsin standards of elegance, deplored Liang's "low taste." Viceroy Chang Chih-tung (1837-1906) condemned him indirectly by prohibiting the use of new terms imported from Japan. Even Liang's own teacher K'ang Yu-wei, himself a poet and prose writer of no mean repute, denounced the pupil obliquely when he lamented the degradation of literary standards as a result of excessive admiration of foreign models.

In his middle age, when he returned to China in full support of the republican form of government, he gradually corrected some of the excesses and eccentricities of his earlier writing and developed a prose style characterized by lucidity and simplicity; but his contribution to literature was already less notable than his contributions to politics and historical research.

The founding of the Republic of China in 1911 was not only an epoch-making event in the annals of China but also a major milestone in world history. It ended the monarchical system of political control of over three thousand years' standing and it marked the establishment of the first republic by a non-Caucasian people. On the other hand, as the revolution had succeeded without extensive fighting and bloodshed and as the last Manchu emperor had abdicated voluntarily in favor of the Republic to become a state guest of the Chinese people, it was obvious that the superstructure of the Republic rested on fairly unstable foundations. Both politically and economically, the Republic was to suffer a continual disadvantage. The temptations of monarchism continued to be alive among the remnants of the old regime. Not only were there new and old aspirants to the throne of monarchy but also many theoreticians and demagogues writing and speaking in favor of a constitutional monarchy as the surest and shortest way to national revitalization. When the restoration movements had subsided in failure, the forces that fought them from different quarters of the land paved the way, unfortunately, to local autonomies and regional war-lordism. In brief, general chaos in politics prevailed over China for sixteen years after the foundation of the Republic.

Not only were the political achievements of this period far from being impressive or even commendable, but also the international status of China began deteriorating with the mounting of Japan's imperialist aspirations and demands on China, coupled with the failure of the Western powers to check them in China's behalf on account of the eruption of the First World War. Thus no drastic changes marked the line of demarcation separating the Chinese Republic from the Empire. This is true in the intellectual phase of China's national life as well as in politics and foreign relations. Nonetheless, in the minds of the younger generation there was a changing attitude that was present but indescribable. Although what they saw around them was a continuation of the old scene, they eagerly looked forward to a new age.

The impact of the symbolic change was felt most keenly in the field of literature, especially popular literature—that branch of literature which touched the lives of the common people. The culmination of the impact was to break out in the literary revolution of 1916. Before we discuss the literary revolution itself, we should point out that although it was an accompaniment to the political revolution, it was not a direct product of the latter.

We have seen that for over a thousand years the traditional literature produced by scholars for scholars in what purported to be the classical language had been steadily yielding ground to the literature of the common people written in the vernacular used by all and understood by all. For a thousand years novels, metrical romances, ballads, and plays written in the vernacular had competed with the Confucian classics and their commentaries for the attention of the common people. The area in which these masterpieces written in the vernacular were appreciated kept expanding to cover nearly the whole of China proper despite the persistence of local dialects in everyday speech.

Owing to two great drawbacks, a new national literature written in the living language of the people, comparable to Italian literature since Dante and Boccaccio and English literature since Chaucer and Wycliffe, had not won national recognition. These two drawbacks were continuations of the competitive literary examination system and the lack of a conscious advocation of elevating the vernacular to the dignity of the standard literary vehicle.

The stage was partly cleared in 1905 with the formal termination of the old examination system. Since that time different attempts had been continually made to emphasize the usefulness and usability of the vernacular as a communication medium. Occasionally, books were written and newspapers were edited in the vernacular. Programs were even advocated for the invention of an alphabet for the vernacular, to replace the complicated written graphs. These gestures, radical as they were, were insufficient to inaugurate a literary revolution, for the advocates were still halfhearted in that while they were convinced that a simpler medium of expression would benefit the teeming millions, they were not bold enough to uphold the vernacular as a universal standard. In other words, they believed in the substitution of the vernacular for the classical only for the less literate elements of the Chinese population.

It was not until 1916 that a young Chinese scholar studying in the United States, an agriculturalist turned philosopher, insisted that the vernacular was the only instrument for the creation of a new literature for China. To Hu Shih (b. 1891), the vernacular was not merely a bone to be thrown to the dogs but a national treasure to be cherished by all. Furthermore, he frankly announced that the classical language in which the old literature had been written was already a dead language. In fact he boldly proclaimed that *ku wên*, the ancient classical language, had ceased to be alive two thousand years before.

Discussion along this line was first started in a small coterie and it was not until early in 1917 that Hu Shih's ideas were embodied in a proposal written in extremely peaceful and moderate tone. Following the guide of historical evolution, this article, which curiously enough was written in what was considered the easy or watered-down classical style, contained the following basic points:

Literature is something which undergoes changes with the lapse of time. Each age has its own literature . . . evolving with the lapse of time in spite of itself. People in the T'ang Dynasty should not write poetry of the Shang and Chou dynasties. People of the Sung Dynasty should not write the *fu* which had been written by Ssu-ma Hsiang-ju and Yang Hsiung. Even if they should attempt it, they could not possibly excel. To go against the course of nature and to act in reverse to the trend of the age in violation of the principle of evolution can not lead to success. . . . It could be safely assumed in accordance with the point of view of modern historical evolution that vernacular literature should be the orthodox literature of China.

Later on in another article, still written in the simple classical style, his views were further elaborated:

To discuss literary reforms today one should emphasize the historical view of literature. In a word, each age has its own literature. One age may have a relation of continuity with another age but could never be its duplication and what is duplicated can never be true literature. I am deeply convinced of this principle and so I am of the opinion that the ancients have already created ancient literature and that modern people should create literature of their own age. If we review the trends of literature of the different ages [we shall find that] vernacular literature since Sung times has continually developed until now despite its being discarded by the advocates of the ancient style. . . . Isn't this so because of the natural trend in our literature which was insuppressible and ever expanding? We attack the classical writers simply because they do not understand literary trends and wish, on the contrary, to write the prose style current one thousand or two thousand years ago. If this superstition is not demolished, vernacular literature will never see the day in which it can claim orthodoxy. Meanwhile, the literary men of China will continue to belittle it, regarding it as a bypath not to be built up with undivided attention and full vigor. . . . If we do not create literature with undivided attention and full vigor and yet hope for the rise of literature, it is comparable to expecting a harvest without farming and to expect full satisfaction without eating. It is an end unattainable.

According to his own estimation, Hu Shih was too preoccupied with the moderation of the historian to be successful in revolutionary activities. What was needed most urgently in the literary revolution was an impatient vanguard, which role was filled by his friend, Ch'ên Tu-hsiu (1879-1942). After the publication of Hu's article in the January, 1917, number of the popular monthly *Hsin Ch'ing-nien*, with the French title *La Jeunesse*, Ch'ên threw the first bomb in February and hoisted the banner of a literary revolution. He proclaimed forthrightly:

I willingly face the enmity of pedants all over the country and hoist a great banner of the literary revolutionary army in support of my friend. On the banner

I write in bold strokes the three basic principles of our literary revolutionary army:

Down with ornate toadying aristocratic literature, to build a simple and lyrical national literature.

Down with outdated elaborative classical literature to build up a fresh and sincere realistic literature.

Down with obscure and obdurate reclusive literature of mountains and forests to build up a clear, popular social literature.

Ch'ên's principal trait was his unswerving forthrightness. Hu Shih, who was then still in the United States, communicated his own views in a letter to Ch'ên:

The right and wrong of this matter cannot be determined in one morning or one evening, nor by one person or two. I sincerely hope that people in our country can study this problem with us with equanimity and open-mindedness. When our discussions are right, the right and wrong of the issue will be automatically evident. Now that we have hoisted our banner of revolution, although we should not retreat on one hand, we should not advocate on the other that our views are indubitably right and would admit of no assistance or correction by others.

(Letter dated April 9, 1916)

From this it can be seen that Hu Shih admitted that the literary revolution was yet in a discussion stage. At that time he was experimenting with the vernacular as a language for poetry, calling his collection of poems *Ch'ang-shih Chi* or *A Collection of Experimental Verse.* If this attitude of his of leisurely deliberation and peaceful discussion had prevailed, the literary revolution would have been delayed, according to his own estimate, for at least ten years. Hu's moderation was effectively counterbalanced by Ch'ên's impatience:

It is my humble opinion that the toleration of diverse opinion and the freedom of discussion should, in general, be held as basic principles for intellectual progress. When it comes to the point of advocating the vernacular as the orthodox medium of expression for the reform of Chinese literature, its rightness is so crystal-clear that we need not leave room for discussion by our opponents. We should regard our advocacy as absolutely right, admitting no correction by others.

This cocksure and self-righteous attitude naturally provoked considerable general opposition. If it had not been for this extremist position maintained, the movement would not have attracted such enormous attention, for opposition meant intense attention.

In 1918 new grounds were gained by the revolution. The official organ, *Hsin Ch'ing-nien,* was edited at Peking, where both Ch'ên and Hu had joined the faculty of the National Peking University. In place of the so-called easy classical style which even Ch'ên had tenuously adhered to, the vernacular had been adopted as the official medium of the monthly. In April, Hu Shih published an article on constructive theories for the literary revolution. In this article the main point he made was summarized in ten Chinese words as "literature written in a national language and a national language with literary capabilities."

> If we want to create a national language we must create a literature written in the national language. When we have the latter, we shall automatically have the former. . . . A truly effective and influential textbook for the national language is none other than a literature consisting of novels, poems, essays, and dramas written in the national language.

The progress attained during this signal year lay in two directions. In the first place, further experiments were made by Hu Shih and his friends in using the vernacular in poetry. The models of classical poems were abandoned in place of a new prosody consisting of irregular meters commensurate with the living language of the people. In the second place, new translations in the Chinese vernacular were made of European literature. For peculiar reasons special attention was directed to the neglected areas in contemporary European literature, underscoring such authors as Ibsen, Strindberg, Dostoevski, Ephtaliotis, and Sienkiewicz. This faithful and direct translation was to produce a peculiar effect in the Europeanization of Chinese syntax in the vernacular. Many of the finished products of the average translator were at times unreadable as a result of their blindly following the technique advocated by this school of thought, and at other times would impress the reader as positively un-Chinese, often requiring transpositions of words and phrases in a sentence before it could be understood. However, the net result was probably not an entirely unhealthy one on account of the shock that this outlandish technique provided for the conservative readers who needed, above all, to be bounced out of their ruts.

After the first year the literary revolution was effectively buttressed by the appearance of other periodicals with articles written almost completely in the vernacular. At this stage some writers continued using the classical medium, not because they doubted the soundness of the theoretical foundations of the new literature movement but because they still felt more at home in the old vehicle in which they had been brought up. A few writers might even have been tempted to believe that in order to stand themselves in better stead as literary revolutionists they had to give evidence that they were past masters of the old classical style and that their advocacy of a reform had been a well-considered and voluntary choice rather than an immature innovation.

Of the periodicals of this type established in Peking in 1919, two were especially deserving of notice. One was a monthly entitled *Hsin Ch'ao*, which literally means *The New Tide*, edited by a brilliant student of the National Peking University, Fu Ssŭ-nien (1896-1950). Besides this Chinese title, it carried in boldface type on the cover the English official title, *The Renaissance*. The other periodical was the weekly edited in the vernacular by Ch'ên Tu-hsiu, entitled *Mei-chou P'ing-lun* or *The Weekly Critic*. Although the *Critic* was slenderer in contents, consisting generally of only four pages in fine print, it succeeded in exerting considerable influence all over the country because of its frequent appearance. Under the influence of this forceful impact, articles written in the vernacular were gradually accepted for publication in some of the daily newspapers in the big cities.

As the movement was given increasingly hearty support it also aroused mounting opposition by the conservatives. Within the Peking National University itself there had arisen two monthlies dedicated to the continuation of classical literature with numerous propagandistic articles condemnatory of the new movement. Outside of the university the opposition was even more vehement. Not a few had even thought of enlisting the politicians and militarists of the political clique then dominating Peking government and solidly organized under the leadership of the Anfu Club to suppress this new movement by violent means. In the spring of 1919 rumors were heard widely to the effect that the Ministry of Education had decided to intervene and that Ch'ên Tu-hsiu and Hu Shih had been driven out of Peking. Though these rumors were ill founded, they bespoke the wishful thinking of the ultraconservatives.

Among the opponents of the literary reform the most outstanding and colorful was the classical writer Lin Shu, a veteran translator, landscape painter, and poet. In several of his short stories published in the *Hsin Shên Pao*, or the *New Shanghai Times*, Lin stooped to the low level of personal attacks against the principal supporters of the literary revolution under the cover of fictitious names. In one of these entitled "Ching Shêng" or "Mr. Ching," written in conventional classical style, three principal characters of the revolution were represented as engaged in a lively conversation in the well-known teahouse, T'ao-jan T'ing, in the western suburb of Peking. Characters representing Hu Shih and Ch'ên Tu-hsiu were baring their views without reservation to their friend, Professor Ch'ien Hsüan-t'ung, distinguished authority on Chinese phonology and medieval intellectual history. T'ien (purportedly a surname adopted by a collateral branch of the Ch'en clan in 403 B.C.) was fiercely heaping calumny on the good name of Confucius and Ti (etymologically meaning "Northern Barbarian," synonymous to Hu, which means, etymologically, "The Bearded") was enthusiastically glorifying the supremacy of the vernacular language. Suddenly a gigantic man from the adjoining house appeared.

Jumping over the ruins of a low wall he pointed his finger at the three people and said, "What have you just said? . . . How dare you defile my clean ears with words befitting only fowls and beasts!" T'ien still wanted to argue, but the giant pushed his head with two fingers and he felt pain as though his head had been pierced by an awl. In addition, the giant kicked and trampled Ti with his foot and Ti felt a severe pain at his waist as though he had been severed in two. Mr. Chin [meaning gold to suggest the cognate word Ch'ien] was short-sighted. As soon as the giant had grabbed his eyeglasses and thrown them away, he was as scared of death as a hedgehog, touching his forehead to the ground unceasingly. At this point the giant laughingly said, "You are senseless and made like Li Chih. Just a freak in the human world. Today I should wash my hands and feet with fragrant water. I should not have touched the bodies of you beastly people who have rebelled against heaven and violated the cardinal virtues of men. You can now seek your refuge down the hill like rats without sullying my paper. . . . I shall spare you so that you can await your punishments by the devils."

While the discourse of the giant revealed the psychology of people who had appointed themselves as the defenders of conventional ways or Tao, the short comment attached to the story by Lin Shu indicated the desperation of the conservative camp of literary opinion:

In a turbid and confused world like the current one there are only people like T'ien [Ch'en] and Ti [Hu] who are proud of themselves. Where can we find a Ch'ing [the giant]?

The search for the giant continued only for a short while. Attempts were made to induce the National Assembly, then dominated by the Anfu Club, to impeach the Minister of Education and Ts'ai Yüan-p'ei (1868-1940), Chancellor of the Peking National University, but the impeachment was stillborn.

It was extremely fortunate that the National University then was headed by a far-sighted educator well trained in the best traditions of the competitive examination system under the empire. The University also benefited by his long years of residence in Japan and Europe. In his long reply to a letter addressed to him by Lin Shu he made the following points: that the National University should adopt the basic principle of academic freedom and tolerance; that for members of the faculty, the only guiding principle was scholarly attainment with no interference by the university authorities in their opinions advocated as private citizens of the Chinese Republic.

While the Chancellor sounded somewhat noncommital in his letter to Lin, interested as he was only in defending the university against involvement in a national movement and absolving it from responsibilities for the divergent theories advocated by its staff, he, in his own opinion, favored the adoption of the vernacular language, although he also pointed up some of its limitations. Thus in one of his public addresses to various university and college audiences in Peking, he said:

Our Chinese literary language is, therefore, very much like Latin. For this reason, we cannot help changing our ways by using the vernacular, or *pei hua*. . . . Although the syntactical organization of *pei hua* is not perfect at present, we should not miss the significance of this trend.

I can predict with certainty that the vernacular school will emerge victorious. . . . In practical writings of the future the vernacular or *pei hua* will be exclusively used. In artistic writing, however, the classical, or *wên-yen*, may possibly be retained in part.

While this heated discussion between Lin and Ts'ai was going on in March, 1919, the course of the literary revolution was to be accelerated by a major explosion which was to come in less than two months. This was the so-called May Fourth Student Movement. Touched off by the arrival of reports from Paris of China's diplomatic failures at the peace conference, huge demonstrations were organized in Peking demanding the dismissal of three key members of the government regarded as responsible for China's total diplomatic defeat. These demonstrations spread to other major cities in practically all the provinces of the Chinese Republic. Nourished by this spirit of revolt, there sprang up virtually overnight an enormous number of tiny local papers written and edited by student organizations exclusively in the vernacular, with format unmistakably reminiscent of the *Weekly Critic*.

In addition to these numerous sporadic news sheets enlivened by short critical essays, there also arose an impressive array of more dignified semimonthlies and monthlies conducted in the vernacular. According to one estimate, in the year 1929 alone at least four hundred publications of varying types made their first appearance. Some of these, it is true, enjoyed only relatively short spans. Their discontinuation, however, was more than counterbalanced by new births in the journalistic field. By and large, their influence upon journalism was immense. Not only was the vernacular gradually replacing the traditional journalistic style which had been geared to the classical, but also the contents of news reports changed radically with comments, translations, and poems written in the vernacular replacing write-ups dealing with the private lives in the theatrical and singing-girl world.

Most influential in championing the cause of the literary revolution were the weekly literary supplements introduced by the leading newspapers in metropolitan centers. From 1920 on, the oldest and most highly esteemed journals of the nation such as the *Eastern Miscellany* (*Tung-fang Tsa-chih*) adopted the vernacular as their prevailing medium.

The merging of the student movement and the literary revolution in 1919 strengthened the philosophical purport of the literary reform which now had come to mean more than the mere substitution of a new medium for literary expression for an old one. The articulate elements of the Chinese citizenry were quickened in their appreciation of the urgent need for renovation in Chinese thought. Even the conservatism of the defenders of traditional Chinese culture was made moderate by a willingness to re-examine the standing issues. With the ebbing of the forces of opposition, a bold step was officially taken by the Ministry of Education in 1920 requiring language work in the first two years of all elementary schools to be taught exclusively in the vernacular.

According to this official announcement, the Ministry of Education did not mean to be hesitant or halfhearted nor to confine the adoption of vernacular to the first and second grades in the national school system. On the contrary, it made plain to school administrators that its intention in planning a scheduled program was to make the reform well grounded and sound. The difficulty of introducing a forthright change of medium was one of acquiring adequately prepared textbooks on short notice. Hence the ministry in its long-range program accomplished the substitution of vernacular texts for classical texts in 1922.

It should be realized that the reform even at its first stage as confined to the first and second grades throughout the vast country immediately affected the curricular attitudes and educational philosophy in all teacher-training institutions and colleges and universities with education departments. The most interesting repercussion in response to the ministry announcement was the voluntary adoption of texts written in the vernacular among secondary schools and colleges. The dignity of the vernacular language and its usability as a medium for the writing of highly specialized, scholarly books on the collegiate level had been successfully demonstrated by Hu Shih himself in the writing of his first volume of the *History of Chinese Philosophy*.

Another movement not entirely unrelated to the literary revolution was the unification and standardization in the pronunciation of Chinese graphs in accordance with what was regarded as standard usage; that is, a kind of syncretic pronunciation system that would be easily understood by the greatest number over the largest geographical area. The divergence of dialects in China, especially along the coastal areas in the east and southeast where dialect differences had been prominent and numerous, had been a major challenge to reformers who were eager to see the Chinese people attain a greater degree of unity and solidarity. Many proposed devices, such as phonetic alphabets, had been worked out (though never universally adopted) since the last decades of the nineteenth century. Progress had been slow partly because according to the Chinese system intelligibility of the written language had virtually nothing to do with divergence in pronunciation, and partly because the use of the so-called *kuan hua* or official language, based on the spoken tongue of the six provinces of the North China plains and eight provinces of the Yangtze River Delta, could be acquired by inhabitants of the remaining four provinces who had to travel for business or political reasons.

Moreover, in the presentation of plays of the nonlocal type, a kind of standardized pronunciation had been used by actors for many generations, and their audiences, for obvious reasons, had learned to understand if not actually to use this stage language. With the groundwork thus accomplished, the officially proclaimed national phonetic system to aid in the pronunciation of graphs in accordance with national usage was accepted by the nation at large without complaint or protest in 1919 when the new dictionary of Chinese in which the phonetic script to indicate pronunciation was published. Two years later the vernacular language, or *pei hua,* which means nothing more than "plain language," was universally given the new appellation of *kuo yü* or national language. There is no question that the battle of language reform had been securely won.

The progress made by the vernacular literature was slow but steady. In poetry the vernacular language had come to stay although the so-called new poetry was not entirely free from immaturity and therefore could not replace the poetry which continued to be written in imitation of past models and in accordance with traditional rules and regulations of prosody. The reason for this relative lack of success in poetry was not difficult to ascertain, for despite the ample amount of folk poetry, including popular ballads in which the language of the common people was the common medium, its artistic potential had not been completely mastered by the new poets. Despite this, new experiments were bold and uncompromising, ranging from attempts to merge the meters and cadences of the poetry of widely separated past centuries on the one hand to the imitation of the free verse of the Western world on the other.

In the field of prose fiction, especially the short story, progress was more noticeable. The greatest name among new fiction writers was Chou Yü-ts'ai (1881-1936) who wrote under a score of pseudonyms, the best known of which was Lu Hsin (sometimes romanized as Lu Hsün). Awakened by China's defeat in the Sino-Japanese war of 1894-95, he went to study in Japan, a country to which large numbers of Chinese young men migrated to learn the secrets of accelerated and successful modernization. Deploring racial and physical weakness as the main force of China's backwardness and stagnation, he went to study Western medicine in a medical college in Sendai. It was there, in a documentary film of battles fought in Manchuria between Japan and Russia in 1904-05, that he saw Chinese men and women arrested by Japanese soldiers and forced to do manual labor.

From that experience the young student from China began to develop a new diagnosis of the ills of his mother country. What China needed most urgently was a renovation of minds rather than a strengthening of the citizens' bodies. Abruptly he left the study of medicine, greatly impressed though he was with the personal kindnesses and scholarly inspiration of his professor of anatomy. He prolonged his stay in Japan, effectively taking advantage of the high tide of the translation fever then prevailing in the newly victorious island empire, and read omnivorously in Western literature.

In collaboration with his younger brother, Chou Tso-jen, he undertook to translate a number of short stories from diverse Western countries for the various fiction periodicals published in China and Japan. The stories were later collected under the general title of *Yü-wai Hsiao-shuo Chi* or *An Anthology of Foreign Stories*. The medium in translation was the traditional classical style, used by both brothers with a remarkable degree of elegance and dexterity, keeping in step with the best usages, on one hand, and retaining the flavor and even humor of the Western or Japanese originals, on the other. In spite of this, and possibly on account of this, the *Anthology* failed to meet the approval or even to attract the attention of the reading public. Hardly more than a score of copies were sold.

Now partly modernized and wholly cueless, he returned to China in 1909, where he was to go through various vicissitudes on the eve of the Chinese revolution, which included the rounding up by Manchu agents of revolutionary suspects, most of whom had cut off their cumbersome cues in defiance of an early Manchu ordinance issued to the subject race. He narrowly escaped arrest but continually had to face the suspicion and ridicule of his friends and fellow villagers.

When the literary revolution broke out in 1917, Lu Hsin, then a lecturer in the National Peking University, quickly joined forces with the editors of the magazine *Hsin Ch'ingnien* (*La Jeunesse*) and became a frequent contributor and later a member of the editorial committee. His contributions took the form of short stories and critical essays. Among his stories written in the 1920's the most widely enjoyed was probably the "True Story of Ah Q," now translated into various languages, including several versions in English.

As in nearly all his stories, the theme was the ridicule and exposure of China's social and cultural foibles. The hero of this story was christened by the author with a written name which neither looked nor sounded Chinese (the letter Q was used in the Chinese original throughout the story). Whether this singular letter had been inspired by Cervantes is hard to determine. At any rate, like Don Quixote, Ah Q is the epitome of the old forces which had made up the conservative camp, much as Don Quixote is a representative of the last vestiges of a feudal Spain which was rapidly going out of existence. In this piece satire is so successfully softened with pathos that the hero, repugnant and obsolete though he is, tends to win sympathy from the reader rather than censure. Yet, on the other hand, he is so obviously a cultural misfit that he would neither stir the fire of the conservatives nor invite imitation by the young.

Equally illustrative of and imbued with the influence of Western literature is another story by the same author entitled "K'uang-jên Jih-chi" or "The Diary of a Madman." Faintly suggesting the trend of psychological fiction, the hero is a madman by common consent of his physicians and yet he obviously has not entirely lost his mind. During his sober moments, in fact, when he feels inspired to commit his thoughts to writing, he suspects that the world is mad and that he alone is sober and sane. His reflections on political and social issues were all unconventional and his diagnoses of the social evils were surprisingly stimulating if not universally accurate. In course of time as his "insanity" grew from bad to worse, his opinions and his actions became increasingly shocking to his companions. Finally, he was suspected of imminent violence and violent measures were therefore first imposed on him. Manacled and threatened with an isolated cell, he became more confused and abruptly the recording ended. This tragic conclusion was obviously intended by the author to deepen the reader's impression.

In his short stories biographical and even autobiographical elements crept in from time to time. A representative piece of this type is "Tsai Chiu-lou Shang" or "Aloft in a Storied Wine Shop," written in 1924, recounting and fictionalizing a personal episode in which he met an old, old friend who, as an educational worker, had found it increasingly difficult to solve the problem of livelihood. Told in the first person singular, the piece is charmingly nostalgic:

"Could it be that what you are teaching consists of the 'Master said' or the *Book of Poetry* records?" I felt surprised, so I asked.
"Naturally so, can you imagine that I am still teaching A, B, C, and D? I at first had two students, one studying the *Shih Ching* and the other the *Book of Mencius*. Recently there has come a third, a girl, who studies the *Classic for Young Women*. I am not even teaching arithmetic. Not because I don't want to teach it, but because they don't want me to teach it."
"I really could not imagine you have come to do this type of teaching. . . ."
"Their old men wanted them to study these. I am an unconcerned party with no "yes" or "no." Why should we bother with all these listless affairs. Let's take things as they come. . . ."
"With this can you maintain a living?" I asked as I was preparing to leave.
"Yes—I have twenty dollars a month and can barely make ends meet."
"Then what are you planning to do in the future?"
"In the future? I don't know. Which would you say among the many things we then anticipated has turned out to our satisfaction? Now I don't seem to know a thing. Not even what tomorrow will be like. Not even the last minute . . ."
The waiter handed over the bill to me. He was entirely unlike the way he had been. He had stood on ceremony when we first arrived at the restaurant. Now he just looked at me once, went on smoking, and let me pay the bill.
Together we walked out of the store. As his hotel was situated in the direction opposite to mine, we parted company at the door. I walked alone to my own hotel. The chill wind and the snowflakes brushed my face and made me feel pleasant and fresh. The sky was already dusky and was woven together with the houses and streets into a pure white and fluctuating net under heavy snow.

Besides excelling in the writing of short stories, Lu Hsin was also one of the leading masters in the essay field. Purposely leaving the writing of long and formal essays to other hands, he seemed to favor the familiar essay type, although he himself was a man of erudition. He could do first-class jobs in the scholarly field such as his *Outline History of Chinese Fiction,* which he chose to write, strangely enough, in the classical style, and his various dissertations on Chinese cultural history. Nevertheless, he was most at home with himself when he vented his invectives against his opponents, or when he subjected certain of China's national traits to revaluation, or when he was reminiscing on and magnifying small fragments of his personal experiences. For many of the essays of this category he would not even bother to think of a title, using such noncommital captions as "Pu-pai," meaning "filler." Many of the essays he would present purposely in fragments connected only tenuously. The following paragraphs might illustrate his style:

The difference now between strength and weakness lies naturally in the possession or nonpossession of armaments but particularly in the people handling armaments. If the nationals were mean and timid even though they might have guns and cannon they could only slaughter those who had no guns and cannon. If their opponents had these also, victory and defeat would be unpredictable. It would be under this circumstance that real strength and weakness would be evident.

Our bows and arrows are what we can manufacture ourselves, but we have been defeated by the Chin, by the Yüan, and by the Ch'ing. I happen to remember that in a book of miscellaneous entries by a Sung author, there is recorded a humorous incident in the market place in which comparisons were made between the Chin people and the Sung people. To the question, what the Sung people had comparable to the arrows of the Chin people, the answer was: lockshaft arrow . . . and to the question what the Sung people had comparable to the four princes of the Chin, the answer was: Yüeh Fei [a brilliant military leader who was recalled when he was scoring signal victories over the Chin invaders], and finally, to the question what the Sung people had comparable to the wolf-toothed club, a club used to crush the skulls of the enemy, the answer was: a blessing firmament.

From Sung times down we have finally had only a blessing firmament. Now we have discovered a kind of "spirit of the people," something even more mystical and ethereal. . . .

But I don't mean to say at all that the Chinese are conservative because I truly believe opium and poker will never be among the things violently opposed. Moreover, haven't the patriots told us mahjong is already very popular in the Western world, fulfilling our vengeance. . . .

Patriots have also said the Chinese love peace. But I don't understand at all why, as we love peace, we should for years wage internecine war in the country. Perhaps we should revise that saying to read: the Chinese love peace in relation to foreigners.

We should scrutinize ourselves carefully. The time should come for us not to tell any more lies. Once the moment has arrived when we no longer deceive ourselves and others, we shall see seedlings of hope.

I don't consider it more ignominious to admit one's own helplessness than to brag about the love of peace.

Lu Hsin's eagerness to see China modernize herself culturally as well as politically in the shortest possible time and his acquaintance with the different forms and guises of corruption in Chinese history made him increasingly rebellious and increasingly suspicious of those advocates of reform who preferred piecemeal and gradual amelioration to sudden and wholesale revolution.

The Chinese Communist Party, which had been organized in 1921 as a direct result of Russian propaganda and machinations, had made its influence felt in literature in 1925 and by 1930 had already formulated a systematic program for the fostering in China of a proletarian literature. Many attempts were made in the late twenties to "capture" prominent writers for the service of the Communist Party and Lu Hsin was foremost among their targets. Having depended on the Japanese and German languages exclusively for his access to contemporary world literature, his attention was soon drawn to the numerous Communist writings in Japanese or German translation. He alienated himself from his former associates in the literary revolution, whom now he considered as having turned conservative and reactionary. With the formation of the League of Leftist Writers in Shanghai in 1930 (?) he was hailed by the leftists as the grand old man of revolutionary literature, and with the growth of rumors that he was to be assassinated by secret Nationalist Party agents he went underground in the international concession in Shanghai and poured out vituperations under endlessly changing pseudonyms against the Nationalist government.

Rallying around him was a sizable cordon of young writers of prominence with varying degrees of indoctrination in Marxism and Leninism. For theoretical inspiration and contacts of the Chinese Communist Party he depended primarily on two young writers— the vanguards of Communist literature, Hsiao Chün and Hu Fêng. Although never himself a party member, Lu Hsin continually received instructions and directives from the Chinese Communist Party cadre. While leftism was fascinating for a time its novelty soon wore off and its regimentation was something that a man like Lu Hsin could not tolerate, especially not toward the end of his life. Thus, on September 12, 1935, he said in a letter to Hu Fêng:

> In recent years I have felt that it was only among outsiders that there have sprung up a few new writers with some fresh records. Once a person goes inside [the Communist Party (?)] he would be bogged down in meaningless complications and quarrels which would make him unproductive and completely silent. Speaking of myself, I only feel that I am fettered by an iron chain, that there is a foreman standing back of me and whipping me, whipping me no matter how strenuously and vigorously I work. But when I turn around to ask him about my errors he bows politely and says I have done well indeed and that he and I are the best of friends.
>
> These ideas of mine, in the eyes of the commander-in-chief, are bound to be criminal—though he and I are surely good friends as usual—but I sincerely believe that I am right.

Lu Hsin did not live long enough to see the Chinese Communist Party rise to power. His two young friends, who had so much in common with Lu Hsin, did. Hsiao Chün was liquidated in 1950 and Hu Fêng was purged in 1954.

Index